EXPERIENCING GOD

EXPERIENCING GOD

Theology as Spirituality

KENNETH LEECH

1817

HARPER & ROW, PUBLISHERS, SAN FRANCISCO
Cambridge, Hagerstown, New York, Philadelphia
London, Mexico City, São Paulo, Singapore, Sydney

FIRST U.S. EDITION

Library of Congress Cataloging in Publication Data

Leech, Kenneth.
  Experiencing God.

  Includes index.
  1. God.   2. Spirituality.   I. Title.
BT102.L437   1985   248   84-48237
ISBN 0-06-065226-8

85 86 87 88 89 10 9 8 7 6 5 4 3 2 1

Contents

Preface   vii

 1   What Has Happened to God?   1
 2   God of Abraham, Isaac and Jacob   27
 3   God of Jesus   73
 4   God, Christ and the Church   96
 5   God of the Desert   127
 6   God of Cloud and Darkness   162
 7   God of Water and Fire   199
 8   God in the Flesh   236
 9   The Eucharistic God   265
10   The Crucified God   299
11   God of the Abyss   323
12   God the Mother   350
13   God of Justice   379

Postscript
Towards a renewed spirituality: a manifesto   421
References   423
Acknowledgements   482
Index   487

Preface

This book is the third of a series, and, as far as I can see, brings the series to an end. In *Soul Friend* (1977) I attempted to describe the tradition of spiritual direction, and to relate that tradition to the needs of the contemporary Church. *Soul Friend* arose out of a series of seminars over a three-year period with people preparing for the priesthood of the Anglican Church. It was addressed primarily to those people, and to priests who were seeking nourishment for their own ministries of personal guidance. I was taken by surprise when the book sold to thousands of people outside these categories. *True Prayer* (1980) followed, and sought to provide a more general introduction to the life of prayer which had been discussed in two of the chapters of *Soul Friend*. It was addressed more generally, and in the course of that book I tried to introduce people to a range of writers within the spiritual tradition.

The present work takes up and develops this concern. What I have tried to do is to describe something of the experience of God by drawing upon some of the key symbols which have been used about that experience. This is not a work addressed to academics who will find much to criticize in its summary treatment of many complex issues. I have addressed myself to the 'ordinary Christian', and have assumed little knowledge of the tradition: but I have assumed a thirst for knowledge, and I have tried to provide such references as will help the reader to pursue particular paths more thoroughly. My concern throughout this book, as in the earlier ones, is primarily pastoral. I write as a pastor who has been concerned throughout his ministry both with the inner needs of the soul, and with the pursuit of Christian discipleship in an unjust world. Linked with this concern has been the desire to unite theological work with the spiritual quest. It is therefore an exploration in spiritual theology, that is, in the search for a transforming knowledge of God, a knowledge in which the seeker is deeply changed. All true theology is about transformation, about changing human beings and changing the world, in and through the encounter with the true God. It is as a small contribution to that process that I offer this work to my fellow pilgrims.

Kenneth Leech, 1985

I

What Has Happened to God?

There is no point in being too theological
Editorial (on incomes policy) in *The Guardian*,
(London). 22 May 1972.

'Dr Soper, do you believe that God is dead?'
'I didn't know he'd been ill.'
Conversation between an American journalist and Dr
Donald Soper.

That we live, in the West, in an atmosphere of spiritual deprivation and impoverishment is abundantly clear. For whatever reasons, conventional western religion does not provide adequate nourishment for the souls of men and women. So, as the wastes of the decayed inner city districts tell their gloomy story of desolation and despair, there is a wasteland of the spirit which speaks a similar language. We seem to have entered what Koestler has termed 'the spiritual ice age', an age in which 'the established churches can no longer provide more than Eskimo huts where their shivering flocks huddle'.[1] The imagery of ice and cold has not only been applied to the *loss* of God, but also to the *concepts* of God which, by their very lack of warmth and life, have contributed to the present climate. Thus A. N. Whitehead wrote in the 1930s that 'God made his appearance in religion under the frigid title of the First Cause, and was appropriately worshipped in whitewashed churches'.[2] This god, the god of much conventional theism, was seen as the 'Great Architect of the universe', the 'Great Original' of Addison's hymn, and the 'Watchmaker' of Archdeacon Paley. But God remained remote from the lives and concerns of living people. 'God had been thrust into the frigid altitudes of infinite space. There was a limited monarchy in heaven as well as on earth.'[3]

The loss of any sense of a living experience of God was leading many, by the 1930s, to speak of a 'post-Christian age', that is, an age in which Christianity was no longer taken for granted, and no longer provided a set of shared values and frame of reference. In 1924 Leon Trotsky could write of Britain:[4]

There is no country in Europe where church influence in political, social and family life is so great as in Great Britain. Over there, for a man to say that he does not belong to a church, does not go to church, and, even more, that he does not believe in God, requires quite exceptional personal courage.

Whether Trotsky had accurately understood the British situation is open to doubt, but the fact that it was possible for a perceptive and intelligent observer to write that is itself significant. Today, however, it is clear that there has been a collapse of the Christian basis of culture in the West. T. S. Eliot argued that it was wrong to deny that our culture was still in some sense Christian since it had not been replaced by any alternative framework.[5] Nevertheless, what remains is a residual and vague religiousness, 'a kind of believing'.[6]

A series of surveys since the early 1970s have produced broadly similar results. In 1973 a national study of the religious attitudes of British people showed that, of some 1,026 people, only 12 per cent claimed to be complete unbelievers, though 64 per cent adhered to no form of regular religious observance. Only 5 per cent were atheists.[7] In a study in 1976, one-third of all women and just under one-third of all men questioned claimed some religious experience.[8] In 1978 a study of young people's beliefs showed that half of those interviewed claimed to be Christian. Reporting this survey, *The* (London) *Times* announced 'School-age faith in rapid decline', while *The Guardian* assured us that 'Teenagers reveal belief in God'.[9]

Recent studies have reinforced the view that a vague belief in God is still common, but does not manifest itself in any specific act of commitment.[10] Where there is unbelief, it is rarely atheism. Indeed atheism has remained a largely middle-class pursuit, deriving its adherents from the ranks of the churches rather than from the majority of unbelievers. Certainly organized Christianity in general is losing support, though there are significant exceptions. The decline in mainstream churchgoing has been noted in most surveys.[11] In 1980 it was estimated that around 11 per cent of the British population were regular church attenders, though there were striking variations from one part of the country to another.[12] Nor is the decline of organized religion a peculiarly British phenomenon. Data from the United States suggest that churchgoing is more embedded in the American culture, but that the process of decline is in operation there also. In 1979–80 it was reported that 94 per cent of Americans believed in God and 78 per cent claimed some religious affiliation.[13] However, while new cults continue to attract support, and the present conservative backlash movement has strengthened those churches for whom it is congenial, there is evidence of a drift away from mainstream denominations in many places. In Britain the influence of Christian ideas on political life seems to be declining. The situation in the United States is more complex. On the surface, religion and belief in God seem to be very much alive. Religious book sales represent one-third of all sales, and a book such as Billy Graham's *Angels* could become a best-seller. In one study, 94 per cent of all Americans claimed to believe in God, 89 per cent saying that they prayed, and 78 per cent having some church affiliation. But 48 per cent believed that religion was losing its influence on American life.[14] An earlier survey of American Roman Catholic adolescents had shown that only 68 per cent of them believed in God.[15] Support for mainstream churches is no guarantee of belief in God or in basic Christian doctrines. The increased interest in 'fringe religions' inside and outside the Christian tradition has worried the mainstream churches, though most of these churches continued to grow between 1952 and 1971.[16]

However, writers have questioned how deep this American religion goes. The influential evangelical Jim Wallis has claimed that all that remains of Jesus in much American Christianity is his name.[17] The growth of the new fundamentalist Right, associated with groups such as the Moral Majority and Christian Voice, has helped to provide a religious underpinning for the Reagan government and its ideology.[18] Belief in God is often invoked by those who oppose communism, abortion, homosexuality, and so on: some of those involved in recent bombings of abortion clinics claimed that God had told them to behave in this way. In most sections of the fundamentalist Right there is a close link made between belief in God and the American way of life. Some would claim that only Christians can be loyal and faithful Americans. 'If a person is not a Christian', claims the television preacher Jerry Falwell, 'he is inherently a failure.'[19]

There is no precise equivalent of these movements in Britain. Many Conservatives in the Thatcher period have recognized a growing gulf between the churches and the Conservative Party.[20] The Christian influence on the labour Party has certainly declined. However, the sense of Britain as a 'Christian nation' is still present, and one recent criticism of the Queen reflected the tendency to identify Christianity with 'Britishness'.[21] In the United States, the identification of Christianity with the 'American way of life' has led many American Christians into a position of opposition and resistance to the dominant culture.[22] In Britain, on the other hand, the alienation of the majority of the population, particularly the urban population, from organized religion of any kind has been well-documented for many years. What is new, it is argued, in the present situation is that the entire religious frame of reference, the sense of the sacred and even the idea of God in any meaningful sense have been eroded. God is dead. Hegel had referred to the sense that God was dead in 1802, but it was Nietzsche who publicly celebrated his death. 'God is dead! God remains dead!' was the cry of the madman in his *Joyful Wisdom*. Nietzsche himself held that the Christian concept of God was one of the most corrupt concepts, and possibly even the low-water mark of divine types. For this God contradicted life and did not transfigure it. This God was opposed to the human will to life, and so the death of the Christian God was a genuine cause for celebration.[23] However, Nietzsche is asserting more than the desirability of God's death, he is asserting that death as a cultural fact. Quite simply, belief in God is no longer an option. The recognition of this cultural fact, that 'the Christian God has become unworthy of belief', is experienced as a liberation of humanity, and is a cause for cheerfulness, not mourning. So he writes:[24]

> In fact, we philosophers and 'free spirits' feel ourselves irradiated as by a new dawn by the report that the 'old God is dead'; our hearts overflow with gratitude, astonishment, presentiment and expectation. At last the horizon seems open once more, granting even that it is not bright; our ships can at last put out to sea in face of every danger; every hazard is again permitted to the discerner; the sea, *our* sea, again lies open before us; perhaps never before did such an 'open sea' exist.

Thus for Nietzsche the death of God is the sign of human liberation. Only through the experience of God's death in fact can human beings experience their own boundless possibilities and escape from their captivity. After the initial confusion and anxiety which follows the death of God, its positive and liberating character is seen. Man has taken the place of God.

> Before God! – Now however this God has died! You higher men, this God was your greatest danger. Only since he lay in the grave have you again risen. Now only comes the great noontide, now only does the higher man become – master! Have you understood this word, O my brethren? You are frightened: do your hearts turn giddy? Does the abyss here yawn for you? Does the hell-hound yelp at you? Well! Take heart, you higher men! Now only travails the mountain of the human future. God has died: now do *we* desire – the Superman to live.[25]

Nietzsche died in 1900. But it was in the 1960s that the theme of the 'death of God' was taken up by the American theologians William

Hamilton[26] and Thomas Altizer.[27] *Time* magazine announced God's death in its Easter issue of 1966. In fact, while Hamilton and Altizer were the names most commonly linked with the death of God movement, Gabriel Vahanian had published a book entitled *The Death of God* in 1961.[28] As the subtitle, 'The Culture of our Post-Christian Era', indicated, Vahanian's concern was with the characteristics of the society in which Christian theism had ceased to be a possibility. Looking back on the movement in 1978, Vahanian emphasized that 'by the death of God I meant – and continue to mean – the cultural phenomenon which, so to speak, accounts for that cleavage', that is, the cleavage between the generations of Christian and post-Christian.[29] Clearly Hamilton and Altizer were saying more than this. The death of God was not only a cultural fact: it was a theological fact. Altizer held that the death of God inaugurated a new era for Christian belief. Christians alone could speak of God for our time, and their message was precisely the good news of the death of God, itself a redemptive act. Christian theology must confront the fact of the death of God. Altizer held that a new kind of atheistic theologian was emerging who could speak of the death of God as a Christian confession of faith. For God had not simply died: he had died in Jesus. God had negated himself in the process of incarnation and redemption. Altizer adopted Blake's term 'self-annihilation' to describe the death of God.[30]

The word 'death' was therefore used differently by various writers, sometimes to denote a cultural change, sometimes to express a theological approach. Other writers preferred the language of 'eclipse'. Thus Ronald Gregor Smith wrote:[31]

> The vast body of Christian people are suffering from an eclipse: they do not see the sun, they walk in shadows, and have almost forgotten what it is like to live in the full splendour of light. To say that they are suffering from an eclipse means that between God and them something has been interposed. It is really God who is in eclipse.

The same theme had been used earlier by Martin Buber.[32] The hour through which the world was currently passing was one of an eclipse of light and of God. Such an experience, far from being the liberating experience celebrated by Nietzsche and later by Altizer, was rather one of spiritual deprivation and impoverishment. Jacques Ellul similarly spoke of our age as one of abandonment, an age in which God has turned away from us and no longer utters his word. The problem is not the death of God but his silence.[33]

It was in the context of some kind of eclipse of God that John Robinson released his best-selling work *Honest to God* upon the 'post-Christian' west in 1963.[34] The *Observer* had anticipated the publication of the book with an extract headlined 'Our image of God must go'. Robinson's book led to a violent controversy, many aspects of which must appear, some twenty years later, to be somewhat bizarre.[35] While it can be argued that his understanding of what constituted traditional Christian orthodoxy was seriously deficient,[36] there is no doubt that Robinson's critique was valid in relation to a good deal of conventional religion. Several years later Robinson returned to the theme of 'the displacement effect of theism' and to the question 'God – dead or alive?'[37] Though Robinson used the word 'theism', it is clear that much of what he was criticizing was not far removed from 'deism' in which God became the 'Great first Cause', a transcendent object. (Indeed, when Robert Boyle established his Boyle Lectures in the late seventeenth century, he ruled that they were to defend the Christian religion against 'theists' as well as atheists, pagans, Jews and Muslims – an indication of how debased the word had become.[38]) The 'god' whose image must go might well have been a caricature of the Christian God, but it was a caricature which corresponded with a widely held view, a view which effectively prevented any real engagement with God as a living reality. Robinson did not create this situation: he merely laid bare the reality of existing confusion and unbelief. It was not, as David Jenkins observed, simply that the god of theism *could not* be believed in, but that, as a matter of fact, he *had not* been believed in.[39]

Nevertheless, while there was a questioning of images of God, and widespread reports of his death, silence or impotence, there was no shortage of books about, or lack of interest in, God during the 1960s. Among many books in this period were J. C. Murray's *The Problem of God*, Gollwitzer's *The Existence of God as Confessed by Faith*, Robert Gleason's *The Search for God*, Paul Weiss's *The God We Seek*, Alfred Starratt's *The Real God*. Schubert Ogden's *The Reality of God*, and Frederick Herzog's *Understanding God*, while Langdon Gilkey wrote on 'the renewal of God-language'.[40]

The critique of conventional theism which is often associated chronologically with the *Honest to God* period in fact goes back a number of years. In 1956 Alasdair MacIntyre, answering the question 'What is this theological revolution?', had written: 'It is the recognition that God is not a super-object behind phenomena, and that if he were, the atheists would be right.'[41] It is this rejection of the super-object which is the central element in the critique of the type of theism which has been called the attempt to understand and express God's relation to the world by a literalization of this-worldly categories ... The result is a God who *exists* as *a* being, *above* the world ... Thus God is described as an entity within the subject–object structures of the spatio-temporal world.[42]

However, the evidence for the 'death of God' has not been entirely convincing. For, while it is clear that both conventional religion and conventional theism are suffering major sicknesses in various places, it is equally clear that atheism remains a minority belief, and that the widespread unbelief is more often than not marked by a sense of confusion and bafflement. There is indeed considerable evidence not of God's death but rather of his absence and of the continued, and at times frenzied, quest for his presence by many people. There is 'an immense body of testimony in philosophy and theology and imaginative literature of the last fifty years whose purpose it is to suggest that behind the deep sense of loss in the twentieth century – of cultural order, even of what our psychologists call identity – is a sense of the loss of God'.[43] Certainly it is this sense of bafflement and loss which comes over in the novels of Camus, Hemingway, Beckett, Hesse and Bellow.[44] As Bellow himself has written:[45]

> But what is the philosophy of this generation? Not God is dead, that period was passed long ago. Perhaps it should be stated death is God. This generation thinks – and this is its thought of thoughts – that nothing faithful, vulnerable, fragile, can be durable or have any true power. Death waits for these things as a cement floor waits for a dropping light bulb.

If there has been a 'death of god' therefore, we need to ask: which god died? It would seem to be the god of conventional western theism, the supreme being whose existence was demonstrated by various kinds of proofs. But this god, in whom the nineteenth and twentieth centuries have chosen to disbelieve, is itself a product of the seventeenth century. Moreover, this god of theism has been so closely identified with the Christian God that many people have assumed that the rejection of the one is synonymous with the rejection of the other. Yet clearly this is not so. The super-object god was the product of a particular cultural epoch which is now past: as part of the framework of that epoch, he has disappeared with it. The God of Christian belief is a God in whom one *chooses* to believe, indeed a God who chooses his believers. MacIntyre has rightly pointed to the crucial importance of Pascal in this connection. For Pascal's view that belief in God was a matter of *choice* was a major innovation in the history of theism. In this he was the precursor of Kierkegaard and of Karl Barth, but he himself had no predecessors. In witnessing to the possibility of both belief and of unbelief as chosen paths, Pascal witnessed to the death of the god of conventional theism in whom belief was rather a matter of cultural baggage.[46]

To hold to a false and inadequate view of God is more serious an obstacle to faith than atheism, and so the abandonment of false views is a necessary purifying element. If it is true that 'in most secular writing, and certainly in the mainstream of philosophy since Descartes, by and large only one concept of God has been under review',[47] then it would seem that some kind of atheism is a necessary prelude to the discovery of faith and to a more wholesome theology. Yet for the Christian, the atheism which purifies is the rejection of false gods. This must be sharply distinguished from the view that there can be a form of Christian faith which abandons belief in God altogether. To the extent that theologians may be saying this, it must be rejected as nonsensical. As John Macquarrie has said, 'theology without God would indeed be like *Hamlet* without the Prince of Denmark . . . the whole theological vocabulary is tied in with the word "God" '.[48]

> Let us be quite clear at the outset that if anyone wants to construct a theology without God, he is pursuing a self-contradictory notion, and is confusing both himself and other people. He may construct a philosophy of religion . . . or he may construct a doctrine of man (anthropology) or a doctrine of Jesus (Jesusology) or an ethic or a mixture of all of them, but whatever results from his endeavours it will not be a theology.[49]

Schubert Ogden agrees with this assessment. 'However absurd talking about God might be, it could never be so obviously absurd as talking of Christian faith without God.'[50]

While absurdity in itself has never prevented people from committing it, undoubtedly many people have been hindered in their search for faith by the belief that to speak about God is to fly in the face of scientific objectivity or of philosophical precision. God, the astronomer Laplace told Napoleon, was a hypothesis of which the scientist had no need. But science has moved a long way since then, even though, in the minds of many people, the idea remains that science and faith are incompatible. While the controversy between representatives of organized Christianity and Darwinism, culminating in the debate between T. H. Huxley and Bishop Samuel Wilberforce, led many to identify religion with obscurantism, by 1981 we can find the distinguished anthropologist Sir Edmund Leach telling the British

Association that the best scientists would accept much of Wilber-force's critique.[51] The contrast between objective, rational science, and mysterious, irrational theology is no longer so clear as it once seemed. Writers such as Kuhn and Polanyi have cast doubt on the equation of science with rationality,[52] and it can no longer be said that science involves the expulsion of mystery.[53]

This is not, of course, to say that the 'conflict' between science and religion can now be forgotten. The notion that the relationship between the two disciplines involves conflict has been assumed since the late nineteenth century.[54] But this has not prevented many scientists from believing in God. 'God' is not a scientific word at all, nor is belief in God a question on which scientific research can help to demonstrate the existence of God.[55] But today it is more common to find scientists emphasizing the need for a sense of mystery and openness in both science and theology. Schilling, for example, has argued that the radical changes within the natural sciences during the twentieth century have led many to accept the truth that mystery is discernible through the eyes of science.[56] Today, he suggests, the scientific community is more aware of its own limitations as well as of the genuine mystery in nature. So post-modern science has contributed to our awareness of the ineffability of nature and perhaps prepared the way for faith in God.

Similarly we have moved a long way beyond the days when a crude form of logical positivism (the 'Ayerian heresy') felt able to dispose of God-language as *a priori* meaningless. The question of meaning and of the status of religious utterances has been discussed for many years by philosophers and theologians.[57] Writing in the late 1950s I. M. Crombie summarized the position well:[58]

> If you are to understand theological statements in the sense which their users intend, it is essential to do equal justice to each of three propositions. First, that the theist believes in God as a transcendent being, and therefore intends what he says about him to be referred directly to God and not obliquely to this world; second, that the theist genuinely believes God to be *transcendent* and therefore beyond our comprehension; and third, that since on the one hand God is a mystery and since, on the other hand, if a man is to talk at all, he must talk intelligently, therefore he only talks about God in images.

While we might regard the description of God as '*a* . . . being' to be confusing, Crombie's central point is that in using God-language we are not merely talking about human relationships in an indirect or symbolic way. We *are*, however inadequately, talking about God, and yet we are doing so by the use of images and by stretching ordinary language. It has been said that 'God is a new language'.[59] Certainly to place the infinite God as the subject of a finite verb is to use language in an odd way, more akin to the language of poetry than of science. The discussion of God-language and of religious language in general raises the question of whether it is not that 'God is dead' so much as that much God-language has gone dead on us. It no longer vibrates, no longer articulates a living and lived experience, no longer communicates life and vigour. Clearly while God-language is odd, it is not so odd that it is totally incomprehensible. The language of religious faith, expressed most powerfully and most significantly in worship, has close affinities with ordinary everyday language. It could therefore be criticized as irrelevant, dead, ridiculous in content, but not meaningless. The question is whether the reality to which it purports to refer and point *is* real or whether it is illusory. The most powerful critiques of God-language in the modern world therefore are not those which focus on alleged linguistic defects, but those which radically question the reality to which it refers. The two most important such critiques have, of course, been those of Marx and Freud.

God and the Marxists

In 1967 a series of articles appeared in *Literarni noviny* in Prague by Vitezslav Gardavsky, and they were later published as a book entitled *God Is Not Yet Dead*.[60] Gardavsky's book was seen by some as a Marxist equivalent of *Honest to God*.[61] But the context was very different. Since then we have seen a number of studies of Christian faith and of belief in God by Marxists, and there is a growing sense that the battle for atheism has not been won. The situation is in sharp contrast to that of twenty years ago and indeed to the claims frequently made by Marxist propagandists that atheism is essential to the health of a Marxist society. In the preface to the 1955 Moscow edition of Marx and Engels *On Religion*, for example, the Institute of Marxism-Leninism of the Soviet Communist Party's Central Committee commented on Marx's 'opium of the people' reference, stressing that it was 'the cornerstone of the whole Marxist outlook on religion'. It went on optimistically to say that the social and ideological roots of religion had now been torn out in Soviet society, although there were 'still remnants of religious outlooks in some Soviet people'.[62] Today, however, there is clear evidence not merely of survival but of revival of faith in God in a number of Marxist societies. God is not yet dead, indeed appears to be very much alive. However, the question remains, is this resurgence of religion evidence of the

spiritual inadequacy of Marxism as a world-view, or is it simply a form
of regression, indicating the need for more intensive education and
the removal of the causes of religion? To move towards an answer, it is
necessary to look at the roots of Marxist atheism and of the Marxist
critique of religion.

Marx had come to reject Christianity and all forms of theism on
philosophical grounds when he was a student in Berlin in 1836, and he
later developed a critique of religion on the grounds of the harmful
uses made of it by states. To understand Marx it is necessary to go
behind him to Hegel and to Feuerbach. The transition from Hegel via
Feuerbach's *The Essence of Christianity* (1841) to Marx's critique of
religion has often been described.[63] Hegel held that God was to be
identified with our true and essential self, and that Christianity had
encouraged belief in an alien god. The self *is* absolute being, yet
Christianity has objectified the divine, set it over against man and
society, and introduced a false transcendence from which man is
alienated. Feuerbach developed Hegel's position and then rejected it
and moved beyond it, and in so doing prepared the way for Marx's
materialism.

In the 1840s Marx came to believe that the philosophical criticism
of religion was complete. His principal concern was more with the
uses to which religion was being put. Protestant Christianity seemed
to have been particularly well suited for use by capitalist states, a fact
which was to figure prominently in the work of later Marxist
historians. The central concern of Marx was not therefore with the
irrationalism of belief in God, which he took for granted, but rather
with the harmful results of such belief. He held that the criticism of
religion was the premise of all criticism because the struggle against
religion was in fact the struggle against the world of which religion was
the 'spiritual aroma'.[64] Religion offered an illusory happiness. The
essential task was to demand real happiness. Thus 'the criticism of
religion is . . . in embryo the criticism of the vale of tears the halo of
which is religion'.[65] Marx's concern then is to seek a more adequate
and complete answer to the questions which religion purports to
answer.

The oft-quoted (and oft-misquoted) statement by Marx that
religion is the opium of the people is not original. Comparisons of
religion with opium and with other drugs were common at the time.[66]
However, the point of Marx's words is not that religion offered a way
of escape but that it killed pain without removing the underlying
causes of the pain. Belief in God would therefore not be eroded by a
theoretical attack alone but by removing the conditions which made
such a belief necessary. If God was the product of objective social and

cultural conditions, then the modification of these conditions should modify the belief in God, and the suppression of the conditions should lead to its disappearance. However, as Segundo has pointed out,[67] there is in Marx, and even more in later 'Marxist' states, another view, that is, that religion should itself be suppressed as a part of the revolutionary process. The intensity and ferocity with which this suppression has taken place has varied enormously from time to time and from place to place, but the attempt to suppress religious belief and to promote 'scientific atheism' has been a feature of most 'Marxist' states. It is this promotion which, on the evidence of recent research, would seem to have failed.

So we have the paradoxical situation that Christian faith now flourishes in societies which are nominally Marxist, and indeed it could be argued that there are more Christians in Marxist societies than there are in the western capitalist states where organized Christianity is in decline in many places. A good deal of documentary evidence now exists that religious faith is increasing in the Soviet Union, and that it is no longer restricted to the intelligentsia but is growing among working people too.[68] A Leningrad school leaver explained that 'religion gives the believer some hope in life. He believes in something, mythical though it may be, for a person cannot live without faith.'[69] Of course, claims are still made that atheistic propaganda has been successful. In 1966 the Department of Scientific Atheism of Herzen Pedagogical Institute in Leningrad undertook a survey of Leningrad schools to assess the effectiveness of atheistic education there. They concluded that 97 per cent of pupils were free of religious ideas. But this is highly questionable, and reports in *Komsomol Truth* in 1973 were suggesting that the programmes were not working very well.[70] In recent years we have seen the growth of both Orthodox and Baptist Churches in the Soviet Union as well as of the Roman Catholic Church in other parts of Eastern Europe.

Even more remarkable to many western observers has been the revival of faith in China. In the early years of Mao's rule, religion was strongly attacked as perpetuating the attitudes of the old order, and Christianity was particularly associated with dependence on the missionary West. By 1952 the foreign missionaries had gone or were in prison. Public worship declined during the 'great leap forward' in the late 1950s, and by 1962 there was only one theological seminary with about one hundred students. However, since Mao's death in 1976, religious worship has been resumed and churches have been restored. Today the numbers of worshipping Christians are greater than they were before 1956, and there is a revived interest in the place of religion in a socialist society. Alongside these developments must be set the growth of movements of creative theology within both Marxist states and traditions of Marxist analysis. As a Marxist thinker said at Marienbad in 1967, 'our Christian friends have awakened in us the taste for transcendence'.[71] It has been said that Mao was 'the only modern Marxist to harness the spiritual dimension to a socialist society',[72] but today there are many Marxists who are re-examining the place of religious faith. It is too early to know the direction in which such a movement might lead. Some writers, such as Roger Garaudy, have referred to the vision of the future as one of 'Christian Marxism',[73] while MacIntyre who is sceptical of both Christianity and Marxism insists that one cannot entirely discard either without discarding truths not otherwise available.[74] Certainly many Marxists are recognizing the inadequacy of a world-view which totally excludes the transcendent. As long ago as 1927 Trotsky had quoted approvingly a letter to him from Adolph Joffe which pointed out that human life only had meaning if lived 'in the service of something infinite'.[75] He took that 'something' to be humanity: today many are questioning so narrow a position.

It is not possible to examine here the question of how necessary atheism might be to the Marxist world-view.[76] What is clear is that in practice it has not been found possible to do away with faith in God: on the contrary, it has grown and flourished. Recent developments within world Marxism raise important questions for the traditional Marxist view of religion. Historically, Marxists have been particularly critical of Christian belief, for Marxism is itself a growth out of the Judaeo-Christian tradition. It is both 'the more important of the two major attempts in our post-Christian era to create an entirely secular view of the world' and yet 'a secularism and an atheism such as only a Christian culture can produce'.[77] Today both Marxists and Christians are undergoing necessary processes of self-criticism, mutual criticism and purification. Garaudy has suggested that a central role of religion is to go on raising questions indefinitely, and that Marxist atheism is being enriched by the need to answer the objections of faith.[78] Certainly Christian faith in the true and living God must emerge purified and strengthened by the Marxist critique of false religion. Yet if we are not to be seduced by a dangerous form of spiritual self-sufficiency and complacency, the relationship between Christian faith and Marxist faith needs to remain one of unceasing interrogation and criticism.

God after Freud

Like Marx, Freud was suspicious of the *reasons* which believers were accustomed to offer in support of their beliefs. Both thinkers held that an adequate account of belief could not exclude the area of the non-rational. While Marx focused on the economic and social factors which provided the context of belief, it was the pathology of belief which was the concern of Freud. In each, the issue of atheism was seen to be inseparable from the wider contexts, that of phenomena external to the person, and that of the personal psyche. So Marx wrote, in the Preface to the 1867 English edition of *Capital*:[79]

> The English Established Church will more readily pardon an attack on thirty-eight of its Thirty-Nine Articles than on one thirty-ninth of its income. Nowadays atheism itself is *culpa levis* as compared with criticisms of existing property relations.

Marx would have had interesting comments on the current scene in the Church of England where those who sit lightly to credal orthodoxy often take up entrenched positions on social and political matters.

Freud, on the other hand, was concerned throughout his life with the study of the pathological, with neurotic forms of behaviour, and with the effect of the unconscious on human personality and human society. It was within this framework of thought and activity that he saw religious belief, and as a result of his work he became strongly opposed to religion. By 1907 when he published *Totem and Taboo* he had come to see religion as intrinsically pathological, a disturbed condition, the universal obsessional neurosis of humanity. This basic outlook never changed, though in the years after 1907 his anti-religious position was strengthened. In 1926 he produced *The Future of an Illusion*, and this was followed by *Moses and Monotheism* in 1939. Whether or not religion was obsessional, it seems clear that Freud himself was obsessed with it. He saw God as modelled on the human father. The relationship of the child to the father was projected on to the universe. Belief in God therefore represented a form of immaturity, a failure to transform the sexual desires of early childhood into mature adult attitudes.

However, it is clear that, in his critique of the pathological factors in belief, Freud moves over into an assumption of the *untruth* of the belief. Chapter 5 of *The Future of an Illusion* is concerned not simply with the psychological causes of belief in God but with the falsity of such belief. Yet clearly this is a matter on which psychology as such can have nothing to say. To demonstrate the neurotic origins and character of some belief in God is to say nothing about the truth or untruth of the belief itself. And in fact, in his assumption of the untruth of religion, Freud is dependent not on his psychological work but on conventional Victorian rationalism. Atheism is therefore something which is assumed in Freud.

Thus, while many people have held that Freud had undermined belief in God, by the nature of his work this could not have been so. What he was able to show was that a good deal of religious belief and practice exhibits neurotic and disturbed characteristics. His work is thus a valuable, if inadequate and now increasingly dated, critique of unreal, immature faith, a critique for which religious believers should be grateful. Thoughtful Christianity after Freud cannot evade the responsibility for developing its own critique of illusion and falsehood within religious life. However, many Christians have combined faith in God with Freudian insights,[80] while others have shown that Freudian understandings can be applied equally to the critique of atheism and unbelief. Rumke, for example, has argued that unbelief shows more neurotic features than does real belief, and can equally be shown to manifest pathological features.[81] As with belief, the critique of unbelief is essentially negative: it can uncover harmful and untruthful features. As Eric Fromm has written, 'the legitimate goal of psychology is negative: the purging of mistakes and illusions not the full and total knowledge of the being of man'.[82]

It was, of course, Jung who turned the Freudian critique on its head, holding that the identification of neurotic forms of religion testified not to the essential untruth of religion but to the need to discriminate true from false. Jung ridiculed the notion of religious belief as a deranged condition. On the contrary:

> Failure to adapt to this inner world is a negligence entailing just as serious consequences as ignorance and ineptitude in the outer world. It is after all only a tiny fraction of humanity, living mainly in that thickly populated peninsula of Asia which juts out into the Atlantic Ocean and calling themselves 'cultured' who, because they lack all contact with nature, have hit upon the idea that religion is a peculiar kind of mental disturbance of undiscoverable purport. Viewed from a safe distance, say from Central Africa or Tibet, it would certainly look as if this fraction had projected its own unconscious mental derangement upon nations still possessed of healthy instincts.[83]

In Jung's view, knowledge of God was possible, and, in a famous interview, he claimed that he himself possessed such knowledge. God, he exclaimed, was 'one of the most certain and immediate experiences . . . I do not believe: I know, I know.'[84]

However, there has been considerable dispute about the sense in which Jung used the term 'God'. Is it true to say that Jung had 'turned theologian'?[85] Certainly he wrote that there was no knowledge of what lay behind the phenomenal world,[86] and that God was simply a projected complex of representation of energy.[87] 'The concept of God is simply a necessary psychological function of an irrational character which has nothing to do with the question of the existence of God.'[88] It would seem from statements such as these that Jung was not concerned with the metaphysical questions about the existence of God, and that he believed that the mind was exceeding its limits if it moved into this area of speculation.[89] The objective reality of Christ as a divine person too does not seem to have been his concern, and there is some evidence that he rejected such a view.[90] On the other hand, there are statements in Jung's writings which suggest that, while he is careful not to overstep the bounds of psychological inquiry, he does at least raise questions which belong to the realm of theology, and some writers insist that he does make explicitly theological claims.[91] Certainly, he sees religious faith and life as therapeutically respectable and indeed necessary for the integration of the personality and the health of society, and, as one of his disciples has written, it may be that analytical psychology itself as a discipline may be seen as 'a new kind of way of understanding God himself'.[92]

What is abundantly clear is that psychology and psychotherapy have moved way beyond the limitations of Freudian concepts. Today there is a vast area of exploration of the inner world which is open to the insights of spiritual disciplines. More and more psychotherapy has moved from the excavation of neurosis to the 'transpersonal' area, the opening up of the higher, latent areas of consciousness. Some have suggested that psychotherapy is taking over the role once filled by organized religion and is being transformed into a 'syncretic, salvational discipline'.[93] The theme of psychotherapy and the experience of 'madness' as a pilgrimage of exploration is a common one.[94] The changes in consciousness which have brought about this situation make many earlier assumptions of irreconcilable conflict between psychotherapy and spirituality obsolete. Much current therapy is in strong reaction to the long tradition of physically based psychiatry with its mechanistic assumptions about the nature of illness and its treatment by centrally-acting drugs. Paradoxically, it was the explosion of the drug culture of the 1960s which was, for many young people, the beginning of a rediscovery of the inner world.

The Psychedelic Route – to God?

The association between mind-altering chemicals and the quest for God was not an invention of the 1960s but is of great antiquity. Cannabis was mentioned in the Zend-Avesta in the sixth century BC, while one-tenth of the Rig Veda refers to the drug *soma*, sometimes identified with the 'sacred mushroom' *amanita muscaria*, though others say that this was cannabis.[95] Certainly cannabis was used by mendicants and sadhus from an early date as an aid to meditation, and the concept of the magic food providing inner nourishment for the spiritual journey is one which appears in much ancient religious literature. Even the modern interest in the spiritual significance of drugs long antedates the psychedelic movement: all the important questions about the nature of mind and of consciousness were raised by William James in 1901 in relation to his work with nitrous oxide and the 'metaphysical significance' which he ascribed to his experiences.[96] It is therefore a serious error to assume that the connection between drugs and the search for God is a recent idea. Indeed, as the 1960s reached its close, one writer argued that the origins of Christianity itself lay in a psychedelic cult linked with the mind-altering mushroom!

However, it was the mass interest in the drug LSD-25 after 1967 which led to the revival of concern with what Aldous Huxley, twenty years earlier, had termed the 'chemical conditions of transcendence'.[97] The history of the psychedelic culture which grew out of the early movement in Haight-Ashbury, San Francisco, has been documented in much detail.[98] But LSD did not come out of the San Francisco culture: it had been introduced at Powick Hospital in Worcestershire in 1954, and had been hailed in some psychiatric circles in the 1950s as 'the royal road to the unconscious'. It was Timothy Leary who, in 1964, directly linked the use of LSD and other psychedelic chemicals with the quest for God. It was Leary who set the use of LSD firmly within the framework of a religious movement.[99] The use of LSD was a religious pilgrimage and a sacrament. All religions, claimed Leary, were 'founded on the basis of some flipped-out visionary trip'.[100] LSD was simply the latest of a series of chemicals which, at every turning-point in history, God had provided for illumination and liberation. 'The LSD trip is the classic visionary-mystic voyage.' 'The levels that you get into with LSD are exactly those which men have called the confrontation of God.'[101] It is this confrontation which is vital to human life. 'The real trip is the God trip.' 'I can teach you to find God.'[102]

The psychedelic cult did not lead to a mass popular movement until the Haight-Ashbury experience of 1966–7. What happened then was that a large body of alienated youth, very dissatisfied with the materialistic values of America, suddenly became aware of the vast possibilities of psychedelic drugs, became aware of new vistas of experience. LSD enabled them to break out of limited and restricting perceptual positions and to consider alternative approaches to reality.

As in the earlier movement around Leary at Harvard, young people were taking LSD not to forget what they had been, but to discover and attain what they had not.[103] For years, conventional, physical-based psychiatry had used chlorpromazine (Largactil) as a means of 'treating' psychotic experiences, and one of the drug's principal protagonists had commented that 'under chlorpromazine a patient should be more immune to the spell of the witch doctor and probably to the religious revivalist as well'.[104] According to the pharmacology textbooks, the antidote to LSD was chlorpromazine. So, to the post-Leary generation, LSD was the way to experience, not avoid, the realms from which mainstream medicine and mainstream society wished to protect them. Of course, there were risks involved, but if the result was the experience of God, the risks were worth it. So a psychologist, writing on psychedelic drugs in 1973, observed that 'at the centre of both Christian religion and serious psychedelic drug use lies the search for spiritual growth'.[105]

However, the psychedelic path to God was not without its critics. That the experiences under LSD were comparable to those of the mystics was, in principle, not in doubt.[106] The central issue was whether external, chemical change was a secure basis for spiritual progress. The point was put crudely and directly by Leary's former disciple, Allan Cohen. In a paper delivered in London at St Anne's, Soho, in 1969, Cohen conceded that 'the experience under these materials was sufficiently dramatic that, with the proper set and setting, you could be 100 per cent sure that you had experienced God. But the question which had to be faced was: *did* you experience God?'[107] Cohen did not question the ability of LSD to bring about a religious experience. 'If I stick you in a church and give you 500 microgrammes of LSD, I will guarantee you a religious experience.' But did the reliance on chemicals aid the growth of spiritual life? Cohen was dubious:

> You can't carry over even the profound experiences you have. You can feel very loving under LSD, but can you exert that love to someone whom previously you didn't like? The long-range answer is No. It is almost beyond controversy. The controversy has now shifted into: Maybe it can get you started, but something else has to end it – one's own effort. But when you see the psychedelic leaders of the world, after a gorgeously mystical brotherhood love session, as they are coming down, having a bitter argument about who should wash the dishes, a sense passes through one that somehow sainthood has been missed.[108]

Roszak was similarly critical:

The gadget-happy American has always been a figure of fun because of his facile assumption that there exists a technological solution to every human problem. It only took the great psychedelic crusade to perfect the absurdity by proclaiming that personal salvation and the social revolution can be packed into a capsule.[109]

Nevertheless, while it is true that 'the search for God through drugs must end in disillusionment',[110] there is no doubt that it was the psychedelic drug movement which provided for many people the occasion for a radical questioning of prevailing materialism. It was not a simple cause–effect relationship, but rather a spiritual movement of great complexity. For a time it became sidetracked within the chemical approaches of the West. But out of the drug culture there has grown up a massive spiritual movement which has moved beyond the drug experience. This movement has, for the most part, remained outside the mainstream churches. So we have entered an era of private religion, in which the search for God itself has become privatized.

From Nihilism to Cultism: the House Swept and Garnished

In 1956 the philosopher Alasdair MacIntyre gave a remarkable lecture entitled 'A society without a metaphysics'.[111] Both the society and the metaphysical scene have undergone striking changes over the thirty years since he spoke, and yet his thesis is even stronger now than it was then. Indeed the lecture impressed me when I first heard it as a correct analysis of our situation, and the more I reread it, the more prophetic it seems. MacIntyre began by recalling the words of Bukharin, the Soviet leader, just before he was put to death during the Stalinist purges of the 1930s. Bukharin made the point that no longer in Russia was there the possibility of a 'Dostoevskian existence'. Dostoevsky's characters, tortured by hate and doubt and love, saw themselves and their fate against the background not only of Russia but of the universe. What destroyed Dostoevskian Russia, MacIntyre claimed, was a revolution with a clear metaphysical perspective, bringing a metaphysical certainty.

But, he went on, our western society has also made such a Dostoevskian existence impossible, but for different reasons. For

.. whereas the Russians have exchanged one metaphysics for another, we have become a society without a metaphysics... This lack of beliefs is fundamental to our situation, characteristic of our mode of life, and until this is appreciated, most argument about metaphysical beliefs – about religion, for instance – must proceed in an unreal way.

Our lack of any over-all belief structure, any world view, is thus not an accident. Indeed, some would see it as desirable, a victory for realism, for pragmatism, for piecemeal reformist methods:

> But there is another perspective from which the landscape looks very different. For the loss of a general framework of belief engenders a loss of any overall sense of significance.[112]

MacIntyre concludes that 'the curious flavour that a combination of liberal morality and metaphysical meaninglessness gives to social life is the characteristic flavour of our time'. However, he warns that this may not be the end of the matter. For the lack of religion leaves a symbolic gap, a loss of imaginative power. So society becomes like the man in the Gospel from whom a devil was cast out:

> To have got rid of our metaphysical beliefs is to have swept the house and garnished it with science and morality: that there are evil spirits that may come and dwell in the house we learned in the fate of Nazi Germany. Those for whom life is emotionally empty may be at first content with limited perspectives; but later they may become cynical and disillusioned; and later still they may be the prey of any passing evangelist of unreason who will promise a coherent view of the world and a coherent programme for changing it.[113]

In fact, this is precisely what has happened to many people all over the post-Christian West.

In discussing the emergence of the quest for spirituality through drugs, it was clear that many people felt deprived of inner experiences of the spiritual realm. So much conventional religion seemed second-hand. It did not apparently offer any real experience. So in the years since the 1960s we have seen 'the popular unfolding of an authentically spiritual quest, which has been driven into a variety of unorthodox channels by the rigidity of conventional religion in the western world'.[114] Yet linked with this search for authentic experiential knowledge of God and of 'inner space' there has been a narrowing of vision, a desire for instant ecstasy, instant salvation. The idea of 'God in a Pill'[115] is not very far removed from that of salvation by technique. It is the quest for the correct method, the right mantra, the short cut which brings insight, which has marked so much of the recent spiritual undergrowth.

It is therefore more correct to see our society as an idolatrous society than simply as a secular one. For idolatry is in essence a failure of vision, a diminished level of consciousness. Idols can be seen, touched, confined. Idolatry may take the form of packaged religion in which, for a fee, God-consciousness can be acquired. So, as the 'charisma hunger' follows the twilight of conventional religion, people seek for God in a variety of more or less idolatrous channels. The first is the quest for secular messiahs, false gods. The post-war world is littered with messianic movements and totalitarian god-figures. Undoubtedly Hitler was viewed by many of his supporters not simply as a political saviour and a moral crusader but also as the personalization of the spirit of Germany. Even Christian churches proclaimed the virtues of Hitler as the new light, and Yuletide sermons were preached with no reference to Christ but with celebrations of the Führer. Nazism was far more than a political ideology: it was a religious movement on a vast scale. Hitler was seen in transcendent terms and many young Germans died invoking his name.

Throughout the Nazi period and in the subsequent history of fascist groups, including those in Britain today, one sees the persistent fascination with pagan gods, with 'nature's eternal religion'. Thus the Odinist movement has been attractive to British Nazis who find in it a doctrine of the supreme power manifest in nature, loyalty to the family, nation and kin, and so on. They see this as the indigenous religious faith of the British from which they were led away by Christianity. In the pagan nature religions, there is a hostility to strangers, a commitment to inequality and to the rule of the strong, and to the 'blood brotherhood'.

Secular messianism may take a different form as was seen in the cult of Stalin, or, in a more extreme form, in Maoism. 'We must study the works of President Mao each day', said Min Ho. 'If we miss only one day the problems pile up. If we miss two days we fall back. If we miss three days we can no longer live.'[116] Or consider this account of a rally in Peking in 1966:[117]

> The great mass of Red Guards and revolutionary teachers and students, militant and alert and with red flags and portraits of Chairman Mao held high, began converging from all directions... They recited over and over again passages of Chairman Mao's writings... Countless hands waved dazzling copies of *Quotations from Chairman Mao*, and countless pairs of eyes turned towards the direction of the reddest red sun... When Chairman Mao drove past the ranks, many students quickly opened their copies of *Quotations from Chairman Mao* and wrote the same words on the fly leaf: 'At 1.10 p.m. on 18 October, the most happy and the most unforgettable moment in my life, I saw Chairman Mao, the never setting sun.'

In the cult of Mao, hymns and litanies were a common feature. The proclamation of the Great Covenant would be read with all eyes turned towards the portrait of Chairman Mao. Then the portrait would be saluted, and heads would be bowed very low towards the ground. At the end of the 1960s this ceremony took place twice daily in the factories. There were also prayers to Mao, and sometimes the burning of incense sticks before his portrait. It is beyond dispute that this was a deeply religious phenomenon.

Of course, it is said that Stalin and Mao were parasitic, abnormal growths upon modern Marxism, which has now purified itself of them. But it is extremely difficult to disentangle the religious, visionary and messianic elements from Marxism. For where the worship of God is suppressed, the world-view which takes over is held to with a zeal and a devotion which can only be understood in religious terms. The appearance of messianic figures is not simply a phenomenon of post-revolutionary, atheistic societies. Lanternari[118] has shown the persistence of messianic ideas over a wide area of the world, while Cohn[119] has suggested that both Nazism and Communism are inheritors of the millenarian traditions of medieval Europe. It seems that idolatry is very much alive, not least in societies which claim to have outgrown religion.

Secondly, we have seen a massive revival of false spiritualities. Since the 1960s an epidemic of 'private religion' has gripped parts of North America and Europe. The private religions offer a range of techniques and methodologies by which salvation and enlightenment can be acquired. Many of these religions have become wealthy and flourishing corporations. The sale of enlightenment has become highly profitable. Indeed, businessmen in the Unted States have supported some meditation schools on the grounds that they contribute to profits by increasing wakefulness, efficiency and compliance in the workforce. Such private religions are invariably non-prophetic. They do not disturb the economic and political order, and so they fit easily and comfortably into the culture of capitalism. The god they offer is a private god, a wholly inward god. In the context of public enterprise and private religion, spirituality can quickly degenerate into a search for better, perhaps more thrilling and unusual, experiences. So much of the current interest in 'the god within' has moved in the direction of a narrow and limited understanding of God and of the nature of religion.

Thirdly, there has been a continued popularity of some older fundamentalist and adventist groups, and the appearance of new ones. Fundamentalism of a simple, uncritical, unquestioning type seems particularly likely to flourish in periods of social upheaval and confusion. Many of the groups have been around for a long time. It is surprising, for example, that no theologians have given serious, if any, attention to the persistent appeal of Jehovah's Witnesses to working-class people. More recently, we have seen the spread of such groups as the Children of God, now re-named the Family of Love. Among black Christians, the revivalist tradition has flourished in the 'black churches', mainly of Pentecostalist ethos, while fundamentalist Christianity continues to attract the young, white, middle-class in the suburban churches. Finally, we have seen in recent years an explosion of the irrational. Jacques Ellul has claimed that it is the recourse to magic which is central to our condition, and rational conduct which is peripheral. For many people in our society the void of emptiness has been filled by magic and the occult. 'The void may not be empty', predicted R. D. Laing in 1967.[120] 'It may be peopled by visions and voices, ghosts, magic shapes and apparitions.' Since then, there has been a revival of interest in the occult. By 1972 Pan Am was offering a 'psychic tour' of Britain,[121] while studies of various towns have indicated a significant growth of superstition.[122] It has been claimed that more young people believe in UFOs and in life on other planets than believe in God.[123] Jeremy Seabrook has written:[124]

> Talking to young people about their interest in the occult and science fiction, and the success of films like *Alien* and *The Omen*, it appears that a whole generation has been delivered to private enterprise for their most exalted spiritual experiences. The material obsessions of the world in which they have grown failed to extinguish their spiritual needs: these are being met not by religion but by the artefacts of the same world, the film and junk fiction industries.

Of course, this upsurge of the occult is wide open to exaggeration.[125] Yet it would be utterly irresponsible to ignore it. One of the most disturbing aspects of it has been the trivialization of the sacred. Roszak cites Uri Geller and his kitchen spoons as an example of this trivialization process. Here we see 'the lumpen-occult version of Abbott and Costello meet Jehovah'.[126] Geller and his imitators appeal to the crude materialism and power lust of the age, cashing in on the impoverished spiritual experience which drives people to the paranormal and the bizarre. Thus 'the impoverishment of the inner life leads the twentieth century towards drugs, crime, and a compulsive grabbing for consumer goods and transient external experience'.[127]

Of the upsurge in interest in spirituality there can be little doubt. The urgent need is for spiritual discrimination and discernment between the phoney and the authentic, between the false gods and the true God. What is certainly clear is that the uncritical espousal of the total secularization of the West, widely held in the 1960s, is wrong. Yet so many assumptions about the strategy of the Church were based on this view. As Terwilliger wrote:[128]

> We came increasingly to believe that all this was true. Even our religious establishments, our various Vaticans, came to believe that it was true. They have been operating, more or less, on this assumption ever since. The assumption is not true; it has been discredited, not by theologians, but by events. In fact, we were entering – not a secularized age, as we thought – we were entering then an age of incredible religiosity.

By the 1970s it was being realized, as the Chicago sociologist Andrew Greeley noted, that secular man, man come of age, technological man, even modern man, if he existed at all, only existed on university campuses, and increasingly only among the white, middle-aged and senior faculty members. Meanwhile the students indulged in astrology, witchcraft and other bizarre religious practices.[129] Never has there been a time when people have believed so much. Whatever we may think of it, 'the modern world is above all else a religious world ... not really secularized at all... This is essentially a world of the sacred.'[130] What is different is that the sacred is now the private.

Thus, while we are in the midst of a 'startling shift of the sensibilities towards deep subjectivity' and even a 'religious renaissance',[131] public, as opposed to private, life is marked by effective nihilism. In MacIntyre's term, we remain a society without a metaphysics, without any fundamental beliefs. And it is this combination of private religion and effective nihilism which most of all marks our age. Camus wished to transcend nihilism, holding that a literature of despair is a contradiction. But more and more existentialism has moved away from being an intellectual cult to being a dreary atmosphere of emptiness. And it is precisely this emptiness which can quickly be filled by any number of devils. For, as Viktor Frankl observed, 'the gas chambers of Auschwitz ... were ultimately prepared not in some ministry or other in Berlin, but rather at the desks and in the lecture halls of nihilistic scientists and philosophers'.[132]

Are idolatry and nihilism then the only alternatives which face us? Must one move from unquestioning and irrational belief to total meaninglessness, from believing everything to believing nothing, and back again? G. K. Chesterton's comment that, when people cease to believe in God, they do not believe in nothing but in anything, is true, though the two styles of belief are significantly close. For a belief structure which excludes doubt and purports to offer total certainty can only be preserved from collapse by constant reinforcements and new protective measures. To recognize the possibility of doubt is to risk total disintegration. Hence the tragic, but all too common, phenomenon of the Christian believer, whether of catholic or evangelical variety, who protects himself or herself from any real critique or threat by an acquired jargon. Certainties and pious clichés are repeated parrot-fashion, real dialogue becomes impossible, and conflict and questioning are systematically repressed. The fate of such believers can be really terrible, for the slightest doubt can lead to total collapse and loss of faith. For they have become like an iron bridge with no 'give' in it, and, from apparently believing everything without question, they cease to believe anything.

The essential difference between orthodox Christianity and the various heretical systems is that orthodoxy is rooted in paradox. Heretics, as Irenaeus saw, reject paradox in favour of a false clarity and precision.[133] But true faith can only grow and mature if it includes the elements of paradox and creative doubt. Hence the insistence of orthodoxy that God cannot be known by the mind, but is known in the obscurity of faith, in the way of ignorance, in the darkness. Such doubt is not the enemy of faith but an essential element within it. For faith in God does not bring the false peace of answered questions and resolved paradoxes. Rather, it can be seen as a process of 'unceasing interrogation'. Alan Ecclestone has expressed its character well.[134] The spirit enters into our lives and puts disturbing questions. Without such creative doubt, religion becomes hard and cruel, degenerating into the spurious security which breeds intolerance and persecution. Without doubt, there is a loss of inner reality and of inspirational power to religious language. The whole of spiritual life must suffer from, and be seriously harmed by, the repression of doubt.

But to the eyes of conventional religion, this mingling of faith and doubt appears as atheism. This is not a new reaction: the early Christians were called atheists. Justin Martyr even welcomed the title as it implied the rejection of self-styled gods.[135] Today's atheism may be a purification, and where the true God is not preached, atheism may well be the one surviving fruit of the Gospel. Yet the reality of the God beyond atheism continues to haunt and trouble us. Try as we may, we cannot explain that reality away by the methods of reductionism, nor can we reduce that reality to the size of our conceptual scale. The reality of God is a continually experienced reality, the God not of the philosophers but of Abraham, Isaac and Jacob, and of many thousands since their day. The God of biblical faith is a God who is known only in the context of a shared and lived experience. Without that experience, God remains an intellectual abstraction. As Bultmann has written:[136]

> If a man must say that he cannot find God in the reality of his own present life, and if he would compensate for this by the thought that God is nevertheless the final cause of all that happens, then his belief in God will be a theoretical speculation of a dogma; and however great the force with which he clings to this belief, it will not be true faith, for faith can only be the recognition of the activity of God in his own life.

2

God of Abraham, Isaac and Jacob

I appeared to Abraham, Isaac and Jacob as God Almighty,
but by my name Yahweh I did not make myself known to
them.
Exod. 6.2

I am who I am.
Exod. 3.14

God of the Desert

Testimony to the fact that the 'desert period' was the time of
Israel's encounter with Yahweh runs through so many writings
that exist quite independently of one another, which shows that
this was something so deeply rooted in the settled and basic
tradition about the origin of Israel's religion in the Old Testament.[1]

The God of the Old Testament is the God of the wilderness. The
wilderness (*midhbār* in the Old Testament, *erēmos* in the New)
denoted a region in which pasture and water was scarce, and where, as
a result, flocks had to be driven from place to place. It was therefore a
region populated by semi-nomads.[2] Though often described as
uninhabited by humans – 'a land where no man is ... the desert in
which there is no man' (Job 38.26) – there were in fact some towns in
the wilderness (Josh. 15.61). The Old Testament often refers to
specific areas of wilderness – the wilderness of Shur, Paran, Judea,
and so on.

It was in these regions that the early Jewish experience of God
occurred. The early Israelites were small livestock nomads who lived
in these semi-desert and steppe regions with four to twelve inches of
annual rainfall. Their desert experience is of the most fundamental
importance in understanding their knowledge of God, for 'we can
only understand the originality and the coherence of their speculations if we relate them to their experience in the desert'.[3] Desert lay to
the south and east of Palestine, and it was in the desert that God
revealed himself to Moses. Yet it was as the God of Abraham, Isaac
and Jacob (Exod. 3.6,15) that he was revealed. The God of the

Mosaic revelation was identified as the God also of the early patriarchs. Abraham is of particular importance, for his appearance marks the first clear evidence of a personal relationship between God and one individual. One writer has referred to 'the loneliness of the biblical figures'. For here, in the Old Testament writings, 'we find single men in terrible isolation facing a transcendent God'.[4]

The movement of Terah from Ur to Haran in North Mesopotamia, and of Abram (later known as Abraham) from Haran southward to Canaan, was part of a general migration. At Haran, Abraham was urged to forsake his country and kindred for an unknown land (Gen. 12.1). Hebrews 11.8 claims that 'he went out not knowing where he was to go', living in tents, and looking towards the City of God. He became the key figure in a tradition of wandering, a tradition in which individual pilgrims came to know and experience God in the course of travel. In stark contrast to the resident gods of paganism, territorial and static, the God of Abraham was a *deus mobilis*, a moving God, a God who called people out into uncertain paths, and whose presence went before them. Abraham is described as belonging to a class of Amorite breeders of sheep and cattle. From Haran he moved to the sanctuary at Shechem where God revealed to him that the land was to be given to his descendants. At Shechem, Abraham built an altar to the Lord who had appeared to him (Gen. 12.7). From here he moved on, building another altar between Bethel and Ai, where he 'invoked the Lord by name' (12.8; 13.4). After God had confirmed that the land would indeed belong to his descendants, Abraham moved to Hebron where he built another altar (14.18). Later he was blessed by Melchisedek, king of Salem, in the name of 'God Most High' (14.19–20), and afterwards God revealed himself in a vision as his shield (15.1). God is seen too as the originator of his migrations. 'I am the Lord who brought you out of Ur of the Chaldees' (15.7). His descendants were to be 'sojourners' (15.3). So Abraham became the founder of a pilgrim people, a people whose knowledge of God would come through wandering and through movement, a wilderness people. A contemporary hermit has said of him:

> His disestablishment – his desert experience – is the original revolution: the creation of a distinct community with its own deviant set of values and its coherent way of incarnating them.[5]

The relationship of God to Abraham is thus established within the context of pilgrimage. It is in the course of his journeying that revelation takes place and covenant is established. The relationship is deeply personal. God calls him out (Gen. 12.1), speaks with him on the way (13.14f; 15.1f), makes a covenant with him (15.18; 17.2–21), speaks with his maid (16.8), gives him a new name (17.5), visits him in the form of strangers (18.2), and tests him (22.2f). And this personal relationship is continued with Isaac his son, and with Jacob and their descendants. Future generations were to express in almost credal form their relationship to Abraham as father (Josh. 24.2f), while later Israelites, reciting the origins of their nation, would proclaim 'My father was a homeless Aramean' (Deut. 26.5). We know that the original Arameans were nomads of mixed origin who began settling on the fringes of the Syrian desert in the third quarter of the second millennium.

Thus it was in the process of wandering that Abraham and his children encountered the true and living God. However, it is likely that in the early period several gods were worshipped. Genesis preserves a series of names – El Elyon (14.18), the God of Abraham (15.1; 28.13; 31.42, 53), Yahweh (15.7), the fear, or kinsman, of Isaac (31.42, 53), the strong one, or bull, of Jacob (49.24), El Shaddai or God Almighty (49.24). But what is central to the patriarchal experience of God is that the God they follow is not the god of a specific location, a territorial god. Rather he is associated with movement from place to place, and with a people on the move.

One of the important side-effects of Abraham's nomadic existence was the abandonment of statues of God. Sir Leonard Woolley, who excavated Ur and its environs, concluded that 'it is difficult to escape the view that the prohibition of statues does go back to patriarchal times'.[6] This is not because Abraham had made a decisive break with anthropomorphic ideas; it was simply a consequence of nomadic life. Statues were made for temples, and were hardly practicable for tents. However, there was a theological aspect to the abandonment of statues. For as Abraham's God came to be seen as *the* God, so his portrayal became more difficult. Thus, while we cannot see monotheism in this period, we can see the beginnings of a purified religion, a religion in which there is a stress on peace (13.8f), generosity (14.21f), hospitality (18.1f), intercession for sinners (18.23f) and the pursuit of justice (18.19).

Again, it is in the stories of Abraham that the theme of *covenant* (berit) comes to the fore, although it is stressed that God had also established covenant relationships with Adam (1.29) and with Noah (9.3). God's covenant with Abraham is sealed with circumcision, a kind of tribal mark and convenantal guarantee (17.9–14). There is also an earlier covenant ceremony (15.7–21) in which God is revealed in a 'dread and great darkness' (15.12) and assures Abraham of his future inheritance.

Another characteristic and essential feature of these early stories is the stress on the personal encounter. While individuals sometimes stand as representative figures for entire communities, as in the blessings of Jacob and Esau (Gen. 27.27-40), there is an intensely personal character which 'remains an obstinate feature of Old Testament religion throughout its entire development',[7] and which emerges first in a clear form in the patriarchal narratives. One writer speaks of the 'easy familiarity' with which Abraham relates to God,[8] and later biblical writers refer to him as the 'friend of God' (Isa. 41.8; 2 Chron. 20.7; Jas. 2.23). Here in the story of Abraham, we see most clearly the solitary human being confronting God. Thus in the account of the sin of Sodom, Abraham 'stood before the Lord' questioning him and bargaining with him (Gen. 18.22).

It was as the 'God of Abraham' (31.42) that his descendants came to know God, and Israel itself was described as 'the people of the God of Abraham' (Ps. 47.9), the people of God who made covenant with Abraham and his children (Ps. 105.9f). God was Abraham's redeemer (Isa. 29.22) and the future of Israel was seen in terms of God's 'steadfast love to Abraham' (Mic. 7.20). Throughout Scripture, Abraham is seen as 'Father' (Josh. 24.3; Isa. 51.2; Luke 1.73; 16.24; John 8.39, etc.). Through Abraham blessings came to the people of God (Gal. 3.14). Moreover these Abrahamic blessings were to be experienced on earth. One rabbinic text claims that before Abraham, God was King in heaven, but Abraham made him also King on earth. So while it is true to see the call of Abraham as the call of an individual, it is equally necessary to see that 'Abraham's story widens to become the story of Israel'.[9] In the small community of Abraham, Sarah, Lot and their friends (Gen. 12.5) we see the nucleus of the family of God.

The Christian community too as a 'called-out' minority stands within the tradition of Abraham and the wandering Arameans. Christ was the greatest of Abraham's sons (Matt. 1.1–17), the one who could assert 'Before Abraham was, I am' (John 8.58). We are Abraham's offspring (Gal. 3.29). It is in the mini-exodus of Abraham's migration that we see the beginnings of a Church, a pilgrim people of God. As Abraham's offspring, Christians are strangers (Heb. 11.3) and wanderers (1 Pet. 2.11). However, it was not in the patriarchal period that we see the origins of monotheism. Abraham was the father of Israel and of the Church. 'But it was in Egypt that the new religious idea sprang forth that was to transform their life and the lives of many nations.'[10]

In the history of Moses and the liberation of Abraham's descendants from Egypt we see the most dramatic symbols of the Jewish experience of God in history. It is in the drama of Moses that we read of the revelation of the name of God as Yahweh (Exod. 3.13–14), of the Passover and the crossing of the Red Sea (12ff), and of the giving of the Law on Mount Sinai (20ff). The Exodus has remained throughout the Christian era the central symbolic framework for the understanding of redemption.

In Exodus 3, Moses leads his flock to 'the west side of the wilderness ... to Horeb, the mountain of God' (3.1). Here an angel appears in a flame of fire out of the midst of a bush. The bush was burning but was not consumed. God calls out of the bush to Moses, and warns him that the place is holy ground. He then announces himself as 'the God of your fathers, the God of Abraham, the God of Isaac, and the God of Jacob' (3.6). Moses hides his face, afraid to 'look at God'. He then asks for the name of God, and he is told 'I am who I am' (3.14). Several times in the account God is identified as the God of Abraham (3.15; 4.5), but he then tells Moses: 'I appeared to Abraham, to Isaac, and to Jacob as God Almighty, but by my name Yahweh I did not make myself known to them' (6.2). So the God of the patriarchs is now identified with Yahweh, and in the Book of Exodus we read of the formal establishment of the worship of Yahweh, focused upon Mount Sinai as the place of revelation.

In the story of God's encounter with Moses, the personal relationship which was so central to the Abraham story is again evident. But now there is an even stronger emphasis on the role of the individual, for 'here, for the first time in history, a prophet is commissioned by a god to redeem men'.[11] Revelation and liberation go together. The revealing of the name of God at Sinai was inextricably bound up with the announcement of liberation from Egyptian bondage. 'Let my people go!' is the persistent refrain which runs through the early chapters of Exodus. The drama reaches its climax in the rite of Passover (Exod. 12), the solemn commemoration of the smiting of the Egyptians and of Israel's liberation. For 'on that very day the Lord brought the people of Israel out of the land of Egypt by their hosts' (12.50). Moreover, the Passover is no mere memory of a past event, unconnected with the present community of God's people. The people are instructed: 'And you shall tell your son on that day, "It is because of what the Lord did for me when I came out of Egypt".' (Exod. 13.8) Similarly Joshua, addressing people whose immediate ancestors, let alone themselves, would have been too young to have known the Exodus, says: 'Your eyes saw what I did to Egypt, and you lived in the wilderness a long time' (Josh. 24.7). Similarly, in the Passover ritual in every generation, it is the duty of every Jew to imagine that he himself has come out of Egypt. These events of deliverance from Egypt are seen as *the* saving events, they are the salvation of the Lord (Exod. 14.13). It is in these events above all others that God is known, and for which he is praised from generation to generation:

> I will sing to the Lord, for he has triumphed gloriously; the horse and his rider he has thrown into the sea.
> The Lord is my strength and my song and he has become my salvation.
> This is my God, and I will praise him, my father's God, and I will exalt him.
> The Lord is a man of war; the Lord is his name. (15.1–3).

After the crossing of the Red Sea, Israel entered the wilderness (15.22f). This wilderness period became normative for Israel's life, for it was in this period that Israel was moulded into the people of the Lord. In the wilderness of Sinai, there was a further revelation of God to Moses in a thick cloud (19.16f). From Mount Sinai the Law was given (20). Yet the actual presence of the Lord was hidden. His glory settled upon Mount Sinai, and was 'like a devouring fire' (24.17). Moses is said to have known the Lord 'face to face' (Deut. 34.10). So the personal relationship with God, established in the Abraham story, is continued and reinforced.

It is difficult to exaggerate the importance of the events of the Exodus in the history of Israel. 'The Exodus is the touchstone and foundation of all biblical thinking about God.'[12] Its importance is therefore a theological importance. The God of the Old Testament *is* the God of the Exodus, the God who is revealed in the process of deliverance from oppression. The prophets place a great deal of attention on the Exodus and the events which followed it (e.g. Amos 2.10; 5.25; 9.7; Hos. 2.15; 9.10; 11.1,5; 12.13). The Psalms also lay stress on this period (e.g. 78, 106, 114, 136). By contrast only slight attention is given to the Abraham period (Ps. 105.6, 9, 42; Isa. 41.8; 51.2; Neh. 9.7). The Exodus is seen as an act of national liberation, but it is much more than that. It is an assertion of God's sovereignty over the earth. The liberation of Israel is a demonstration of this sovereignty to Pharoah: 'that you may know that the earth is Yahweh's' (Exod. 9.29), 'that Egypt may know that I am Yahweh' (14.4). And it was the Exodus which helped to transform Yahwism from the faith of a tiny minority to a world faith. The assertion of God's work of liberation became both a confessional statement and a guarantee. Thus in the early credal formula of Deuteronomy, the Exodus is the central act (26.8) as it is in Joshua where it becomes more explicit (24.5–7). It is in fact the oldest element in Israel's tradition, and has a 'pivotal significance'[13] for its faith. As one writer has put it, 'Exodus is genesis'.[14]

So later Christian thought came to interpret the redeeming work of Christ in terms of the Exodus story. 'In the Exodus, in the death and resurrection of Christ, it is the same redeeming action which is accomplished at different levels of history.'[15] The Christian liturgy celebrates the work of Christ by using the symbol of the Exodus, and the Christian Scriptures use the Exodus as the framework of their teaching. It was 'the manifest intention of the authors of the New Testament to present the mystery of Christ at the time as prolonging and as surpassing the great events of Israel's history at the time of Moses'.[16] This Exodus symbolism comes over in many hymns:

> The Lamb's high banquet we await
> In snow-white robes of royal state;
> And now, the Red Sea's channel past,
> To Christ our Prince we sing at last.

> Where the Paschal blood is poured,
> Death's dark angel sheathes his sword;
> Israel's hosts triumphant go
> Through the wave that drowns the foe.

> Come, ye faithful, raise the strain
>   Of triumphant gladness;
> God hath brought his Israel
>   Into joy from sadness;
> Loosed from Pharoah's bitter yoke
>   Jacob's sons and daughters;
> Led them with unmoistened foot
>   Through the Red Sea waters.

There are many other examples. As in the deliverance from Egypt, so in the Paschal mystery, God's people are set free from slavery. But now, in the words of Hippolytus of Rome, there is a 'cosmic and universal Pasch'.[17]

Not only the deliverance itself, but also the wilderness period holds a key place in Christian spirituality. For it was in the wilderness that the people of Israel experienced the care and guidance of God: 'He found him in a desert land, and in the howling waste of the wilderness; he encircled him, he cared for him, he kept him as the apple of his eye.' (Deut. 32.10) Yahweh is first and foremost the God of the desert. It was in the desert that Israel came to experience its own sense of helplessness and weakness and its dependence on God. Wilderness and desert are not identical, denoting as they do two distinct regions; but they are often found together in Israel's history. In both there is the awareness of conflict with evil. Israel sought help in the wilderness, for it was the dwelling-place of demons, of poisonous serpents, of the hostile forces of darkness. It was the place of trial; it was on the day of Massah in the desert that Israel put the Lord to the test (Ps. 95). It is in the midst of trial and temptation that God is made known as healer, strengthener and faithful shepherd. So the wilderness time was a time of struggle. It is mistaken to see it as a 'home' for Israel, for, as Kaufmann has pointed out, the Israelites 'have none of the love of the desert that is found to this day among true desert nomads. While their most exalted religious memories are associated with wandering, this period is uniformly represented as one of hardship and suffering.'[18] The Israelites were more semi-nomads for whom the desert was the place both of hardship and of revelation. The wilderness stories in Exodus and Numbers combine the elements of danger and grace. 'The wilderness is the place that threatens the very existence of Yahweh's chosen people, but it is also the stage which brightly illumines God's power and readiness to dispel the threat.'[19]

There is a strong sense of threat and of danger. The wilderness is the abode of threatening beasts – fiery serpents (Num. 21.6–9) and scorpions (Deut. 8.15), hawks and porcupines, owls, ravens, jackals and ostriches (Isa. 34.9–15), vultures, hedgehogs (Zeph. 2.14f) and wild beasts in general (Ezek. 34.5, 25). It is the land in which people driven from the community find refuge. 'Through want and hard hunger they gnaw the dry and desolate ground... They are driven out from among men... Among the bushes they bray; under the nettles they huddle together.' (Job 30.3, 5, 7) The wilderness is also a place marred by sin, for sin can turn good land into waste (Jer. 12.4). Ezekiel connects the wilderness with the land of the dead, and with the deep. Together they constitute 'the three non-worlds' (cf. Ezek. 26.19–21).[20] Moreover, in Leviticus 16, Azazel, the spirit to whom the scapegoat who bears the sins of the people is sent, dwells in the wilderness. Inter-testamental writers see Azazel as the leader of the evil angels. He is the 'seducer of the desert' (4 Macc. 18.8; cf. Matt. 12.43: 'When the unclean spirit has gone out of a man, he passes through waterless places seeking rest').

But the view of the wilderness as threatening and dangerous is not the only aspect which appears in the Old Testament, and to study the prophetic writings is to see how danger and grace are mingled in wilderness spirituality. For the wilderness is the *locus* of the formation of Israel as the people of God: 'it can be said that Israel's fundamental belief in her election as God's chosen people is rooted in the wilderness tradition ... the constitutive element of Israel's faith and life are rooted in the wilderness tradition.'[21] As late as the ninth century, the prophet Elijah goes on pilgrimage to Mount Sinai to revive his faith in Yahweh (1 Kings 19.8), and it was there that he heard the 'still small voice' (19.12). David took refuge in the wilderness (1 Sam. 23–26), and Naaman the Syrian was cured of his leprosy by washing in the Jordan, the river which flowed through the wilderness (2 Kings 5). The Rechabites and Nazirites, during the period of the monarchy, pursued a 'back to the wilderness' ideal (Jer. 35.1–19; 2 Kings 10.15–28). By the time of the eighth century prophets, references to the Exodus and the wilderness are part of an accepted tradition. So Amos speaks of the deliverance of Israel from Egypt (9.7) and links it with the forty years wandering (2.10).

There is, however, an emphasis on the future also. Hosea claims that Yahweh will make Israel dwell in tents again as in the wilderness times (12.9). He sees the wilderness as the place of discovery of Israel by God. 'Like grapes in the wilderness, I found Israel' (9.10). Similarly, Ezekiel speaks of Israel as having been 'cast out on the open field' (16.5), a probable reference to the wilderness period, while Jeremiah sees the wilderness as a time of grace. 'The people who survived the sword found grace in the wilderness.' (31.2). But it is Hosea who holds the most exalted view of the wilderness period (11.1–3). Israel had subsequently become disobedient to Yahweh, and so she would become like a wilderness and a parched land (2.3). But God would 'allure her, and bring her into the wilderness, and speak tenderly to her' (2.14). So the wilderness brings both judgement and healing: a return to the wilderness is a return to the life of grace. Hosea speaks of a new covenant initiated in the wilderness when Israel will respond to God as in her youth (2.14–15). To him it is the Exodus experience which provides the framework for the identifying of God: he is 'Yahweh your God from the land of Egypt' (12.9; 13.4).

Elsewhere in the prophetic writings, the wilderness period is seen as a time of purity and as a type of the gathering of Israel into a restored creation. So Jeremiah describes the wilderness period as one of faithful devotion to Yahweh, comparing it to bridal love (2.2). Ezekiel, on the other hand, sees the period only as one of rebellion and infidelity (20.10ff). There are positive and negative understandings of the wilderness running through the Old Testament traditions.[22] So, says Jeremiah, the devotion of Israel in the wilderness was 'the devotion of your youth'. For there 'Israel was holy to the Lord, the first fruits of the harvest' (2.2–3). In Ezekiel, on the other hand, it is the murmuring which dominates. The house of Israel rebelled against God in the wilderness, rejecting his ordinances and profaning the Sabbaths. The wilderness was the scene of God's wrath when Israel came close to destruction (20.13–17). However, Ezekiel goes on to announce a new Exodus into the wilderness. In the first Exodus, Israel was led 'to the wilderness of the land of Egypt' (20.36). But after the exiles are gathered, Yahweh will 'bring you into the wilderness of the peoples' (20.35) where judgement will take place. As on Sinai, Israel will again encounter God face to face, but as an act of purgation. Ezekiel does however end on a note of hope. Israel will finally serve God on the holy mountain (20.40). Moreover there is the suggestion in Ezekiel 34 that the good shepherd ('my servant David') will transform the wilderness into good pasture. Israel will then 'dwell securely in the wilderness' (34.25).

In Second Isaiah, the renewal of Israel is seen as involving a return to and through the wilderness. It is in the wilderness that the way of the Lord is to be prepared (40.3). The harsh and painful aspects of the desert land will be transformed, and water will flow (35.1, 6; 41.17–20; 49.10) and well-prepared paths appear (40.3; 43.19; 49.11). The wild beasts will no longer do harm (35.9; 43.20). There are clear associations with the first Exodus, but the new Exodus will not be marked by fear or haste (52.12). The wilderness will be transformed, for God 'will make the wilderness like Eden, her desert like the garden of the Lord' (51.3). And this transforming of the wilderness is linked with the transforming of the wilderness of the human heart. For it is the heart which constitutes thirsty land and dry ground, and which needs the outpouring of the Spirit (44.3). As with the first Exodus, so with the second, there will be the abiding presence and grace of the Spirit.

The theme of the wilderness God is also celebrated in the Psalter. But the psalms of praise (e.g. 105, 135, 136) pass over the wilderness period if they mention it at all. It is the rebellion which receives emphasis here. Thus Psalm 78 describes 'a stubborn and rebellious generation' (78.8). In spite of the fact that God had led them, cleaving rocks in the wilderness and making streams flow, they sinned more and more, 'rebelling against the Most High in the desert' (78.15–17). The desert is seen as the place of God's wrath (78.21) and yet it is also the place of outpouring of manna, 'the grain of heaven . . . the bread of the angels' (78.24–5). It was a time both of rebellion and also of divine compassion and restraint (78.38). 'How often they rebelled against him in the wilderness, and grieved him in the desert.' (78.40; cf. v. 56) Yet God had led them in safety like a flock (78.52–3), bringing them to his holy mountain. The psalm ends with the assurance of divine guidance (78.72).

Similarly Psalm 106 begins as an act of praise of God's mighty deeds, including his leadership of Israel 'through the deep as through a desert' (106.9). Yet the wilderness was marked by 'wanton craving' and by temptation (106.14), by idolatry and neglect of God (106.19–21), by murmuring (106.25) and by provocation of God's anger (106.29, 32, 40). As a result of their rebellion, they were brought into subjection. But God relented and remembered his covenant (106.45). Psalm 95 sees the wilderness as the time of trial and of hardening of hearts (95.8–9). As a result of this, God loathed that generation for forty years (95.10). In Psalm 68, the wilderness is transformed by the grace of God into fertile land. It is one of the elements of chaos which is defeated by Yahweh. This psalm is one of praise to God who rides on the clouds, the God who leads prisoners to prosperity, while the rebels dwell in a parched land (68.6). It goes on to celebrate God's 'march through the wilderness' (68.7) when the earth and Sinai quaked at his presence. The triumphant march to Sinai is a symbol of God's victory over all hostile forces.

It is not correct therefore to claim, as some writers do, that the wilderness for Israel was simply the land of curse. There is certainly the sense of danger and of terror as well as the symbolism of trial and rebellion, but the wilderness is also the place of grace and revelation. It was in the wilderness that the people of God saw how they were truly carried and guided by God (Deut. 1.31). For the Old Testament church was a pilgrim church, and its faith was 'the faith of a people for ever marching, a people of tents rather than a temple, learning to read God's law in their hearts, a people committed to giving the stranger welcome, facing a new world with a deep trust in God'.[23] Between the Testaments, the desert continues to play a key role, and many Jews sought refuge in the desert during the Maccabean revolt (1 Macc. 2.79; 2 Macc. 5.27; 6.11; 10.6).

As the Old Testament period moved to its close, the wilderness was again the scene of protest and of the quest for devotional purity. The excavations around the Dead Sea have uncovered a vast area of intertestamental and post-Christian material relating to the desert spiritual movements which spanned the period. Attention has been focused mainly on the settlement at Qumran on the edge of the Judean wilderness. Their choice of habitation can be seen clearly as a choice of a desert location. They saw themselves as exiles of the desert and used Isaiah 40.3 as the basis of their settlement. Their role was to clear a way in the wilderness, to make ready a righteous people for the *eschaton* or time of the end. For the wilderness was to them the place of eschatological revelation: it would be there that the waters would divide and the river of life would flow. It has been said that in the cells of Qumran could be found 'evidence of that lofty and spiritual life which was to animate the Christian cloisters, both those of the desert and of the Middle Ages: a rigorous rule, asceticism, divine election to the perfect life, meditation and contemplation, the confident expectation of the final judgement'.[24]

It was out of this desert movement that John the Baptist emerged as a new Elijah figure, linking the world of the Old Testament prophets with the proclamation by Jesus that the Kingdom of God had drawn near. The context of John's ministry was 'the wilderness', and specifically the 'wilderness of Judea' (Matt. 3.1), though he seems to have moved around 'the deserts' (Luke 1.80. Cf. Luke 3.3). He looked back, as did the Qumran sect, to Isaiah 40.3, the preparation of 'the way of the Lord', and it is possible that the term 'the Way', used later as a description of Christianity (Acts 9.2), originated with John. (Cf. 'the way of righteousness', Matt. 21.32.)[25]

We need therefore to see the central place occupied by the wilderness and the desert as the context of divine revelation as well as of human rebellion. But what are the characteristics of the God who was revealed in the wilderness of Sinai? The Old Testament writers stress two characteristics in particular: holiness and justice.

The Holy God

The God of the Old Testament is often described as the Holy One. 'Holy and terrible is his name.' (Ps. 119.9) Holiness is the fundamental characteristic of God, virtually synonymous with divinity itself. It is 'the most intimately divine word of all'. God stood beyond, and in contrast with, all living things. While he might be revealed in close association with such natural phenomena as stormy winds or earthquakes (Isa. 18.7f), he was not to be identified with these forces. Yahweh was always and essentially 'the Holy One of Israel'. Yet he was also 'the Holy One in your midst' (Hos. 11.9), and his glory filled the whole earth (Isa. 6.3). It has been said that 'holiness is not . . . an attribute of God; it is not one divine attribute among others; rather it expresses what is characteristic of God and corresponds to his deity'.[26]

What then is holiness? The adjective *qodesh*, holy, was probably not originally applied to God. It is a word which is not peculiar to the Old Testament, but is part of the common vocabulary of the Semitic world. In origin it means 'cut off', 'separate'. The opposite of 'holy' is common (*chol*). To make something holy is to cut it off from its natural environment and to transfer it into a different environment. Holiness thus involves separation: 'If an object or a place or a day or a man is "sanctified", this means to begin with only that it is separated, assigned to God, for God is the source of all that is holy.'[27] It has also been suggested that 'holy' may derive from an Akkadian root meaning 'shining' or 'gleaming'.

So places may become holy, sacred sites, separated areas. Thus Jacob awakes in fear at Bethel, recognizing its awesome character (Gen. 28.17). Moses is told that the place on which he stands is 'holy ground' (Exod. 3.5), and therefore must not be tainted by the elements of the profane which cling to shoes. The regulations about keeping holy and common places separate arose partly from the need to protect the holy places from contamination, and partly from a fear of the unpredictable effects of holiness. So Aaron is ordered to 'distinguish between the holy and the common' (Lev. 10.10), and Ezekiel, in one of his visions, is ordered to measure the temple area and to 'make a separation between the holy and the common' (42.20). Holy places inspire awe and dread. 'Terribilis est locus iste!' 'How dreadful is this place!' These words, uttered by Jacob and later applied by Jesus to himself (John 1.51), later entered the liturgical vocabulary of the western Church in the rite for the dedication of a church.

The setting aside of consecrated places, 'sacred space', within the land must, however, be seen in the context of the view that the land itself is holy. And within the holy land, certain places were seen by the Jews as places where holiness was concentrated. Jerusalem was the holy city. Mount Sinai was holy and could not be touched without peril to life (Exod. 19.12ff). The temple was holy (Hab. 2.20), the place where God's glory dwelt (Ps. 26.8), the courts of the Lord (Ps. 84.2), the house of prayer for all the peoples (Isa. 56.7). It was seen as an earthly copy of the heavenly palace. Yahweh's name would dwell there (Deut. 12.5). Other sites were also holy – Gilgal, Bethel, Shiloh, Mizpah. And within the holy places, objects were seen as particularly holy. So special garments were made for Aaron when he ministered in the holy place: they are called 'holy garments' (Exod. 39.1). Altar bowls, cups, and other vessels were holy (Num. 3.31; 1 Kings 8.4) as were the materials used in divine worship – oil, water, the people's offerings, and so on (Exod. 28.1–4, 38; Lev. 22.14–16).

With the sense of holiness of places and objects goes a sense of danger, of the destructive potential of the holy. So Uzzah was struck dead when he tried to touch the holy ark with unconsecrated hands (2 Sam. 6.6f). The altar was holy and could not be touched (Exod. 29.37) while holy objects were not even to be looked at. 'They shall not go in to look upon the holy things even for a moment lest they die.' (Num. 4.20) Holiness could also be transferred. So whoever touched the flesh of the sin offering became holy, and when any of the blood was sprinkled on a garment, it had to be washed in a holy place (Lev. 6.27).

It is important not to neglect the *material* dimensions of holiness by concentration upon the human soul. For the emphasis on the holiness of places and of material things is a fundamental aspect of Jewish faith and of the Christian sacramental theology which developed from it: 'Israel at all times believed that Jahweh did not reveal his holiness only to men, but that he also sanctified things or places or times, and this meant that he claimed them as his own.'[28] Indeed Zechariah looked forward to the day when even the household pots and pans will be as holy as the sacred vessels in the temple (14.20f). Holiness was also applied to time. The Sabbath day was holy (Gen. 2.2–3; Exod. 20.8), and so were certain feasts (Lev. 23.4). So in the instructions for Passover it was laid down that a 'holy assembly' should be held on the first day and on the seventh day (Exod. 12.16). In fact all the 'appointed feasts of the Lord' were 'holy convocations' (Lev. 23) through which God's name was to be hallowed, and through which he would sanctify the people (Lev. 22.32). And within each day there were times which were set aside, made holy, for prayer.

Finally, holiness could be applied to people. Priests and Levites were holy, and so they alone were allowed to enter the house of the Lord (2 Chron. 23.6). Higher standards were demanded of them by virtue of their holiness (Lev. 21), and they were contrasted with 'the common people' (Lev. 4.27). Kings too were holy, for they were anointed by the Lord (1 Sam. 24.7, etc.) and with holy oil (Ps. 89.20). There was also the holy war, for which a trumpet would sound (Judg. 3.27; 6.34) and for which men were made holy. So Joshua says: 'Sanctify yourselves: for tomorrow the Lord will do wonders among you.' (Josh. 3.5) David and his men were allowed to eat the 'holy bread' on condition that their own vessels were holy (1 Sam. 21.4–5). And when a war was completed, all the booty was destroyed, apparently because it also was regarded as holy. Achan was condemned for not doing so (Josh. 7.18f). It is also significant that the cultic prostitutes who were attached to shrines were holy. The Hebrew term for a cultic prostitute was *qedesha* while the male prostitute was a *qadesh* (Deut. 23.17).

So in its origin holiness is a metaphysical rather than a moral notion. That which is holy is that which is set apart for God, and therefore shares something of the mystery and power of the divine. It is 'a relationship more than a quality'.[29] Places, objects, times of the year, and people were only capable of partaking of holiness in so far as they were related to God, for he was holiness itself.

To apply the notion of holiness to God therefore did not originally involve an ascription of goodness but rather of separateness, remoteness, otherness, and danger. The association of the holy with terror comes out clearly in 1 Samuel 6 where some of the men of Bethshemesh were killed because they looked into the ark of the Lord. For 'who is able to stand before the Lord, this holy God?' (6.20) Here holiness is ascribed not to the ark but to God himself, and it is associated with power.

The holiness of God is linked also with jealousy, a link which is made very clear in Joshua 24.19: 'You cannot serve the Lord; for he is a holy God; he is a jealous God'. To speak of God as holy is thus to speak of power and transcendence, of glory and terror. It is this mingling of glory and terror which is the central theme of Rudolf Otto's great work *The Idea of the Holy*.[30] Otto has been rightly criticized for his superficial treatment of the Old Testament and for ignoring much of its teaching on holiness. Yet his stress on the *mysterium tremendum et fascinans* is of the greatest importance for religious life in all periods, and it points to an inescapable element in all religious experience and life. Some years before Otto published his book in 1917, he had been on a Mediterranean trip, in the course of which he wrote:

> I have heard the *Sanctus Sanctus Sanctus* of the cardinals in St Peter's, the *Swiat Swiat Swiat* in the Kreml Cathedral, and the *Hagios Hagios Hagios* of the patriarch in Jerusalem. In whatever language they resound, these most sublime words that have ever come from human lips always grip one in the depths of the soul, with a mighty shudder, exciting and calling into play the mystery of the otherworldly latent therein.[31]

It is this sense of the otherness, the mystery, the transcendence of God to which the idea of holiness testifies. There is none like God, magnificent in holiness (Exod. 15.11), none holy as Yahweh is holy, and no other beside him (1 Sam. 2.2). In comparison with him, no one is holy, not even the 'holy ones' (Job 15.15).

The idea of the holy not only points to transcendence, it is itself a transcendent idea, beyond adequate conceptualizing. The Japanese theologian Kosuke Koyama speaks of holiness as 'deep, pervading and focusing', a depth reality rather than a surface reality, always more than we can conceive.[32] It is a holistic and unifying idea:

> More than any other term, 'holiness' gives expression to the essential nature of the 'sacred'. It is therefore to be understood not as one attribute among other attributes, but as the innermost reality to which all others are related. Even the sum of all the attributes and activities of 'the holy' is insufficient to exhaust its meaning, for to the one who has experienced its presence there is

always a plus, a 'something more' which resists formulation or definition.[33]

Holiness then is a massive theme to such a degree that one writer has suggested that it is 'even more essential than the notion of God'.[34] Yet holiness and divinity are so close that in the Old Testament Yahweh swears by his own holiness (Amos 4.2).

As we pointed out above, in its origin holiness was 'not directly linked with morality or ethics'.[35] Speaking of the Levitical rules, Snaith observed: 'None of this had any ethical associations whatever in early days, and it is hard to see what ethical content there ever was or is.'[36] However, in later Jewish thought, holiness does come to be seen as supreme goodness. The clearest evidence for this development is in Isaiah who often spoke of Yahweh as the Holy One. So rejection of the Holy One is linked with iniquity, evildoing, and corrupt dealing (Isa. 1.4). Similarly we see that the response to the vision of the holy God is a sense of personal sinfulness:

> In the year that King Uzziah died I saw the Lord sitting upon a throne, high and lifted up; and his train filled the temple. Above him stood the seraphim; each had six wings: with two he covered his face, and with two he covered his feet, and with two he flew. And one called to another and said:
> 'Holy, holy, holy is the Lord of hosts;
> the whole earth is full of his glory.'
> And the foundations of the threshold shook at the voice of him who called, and the house was filled with smoke. And I said: 'Woe is me! For I am lost; for I am a man of unclean lips, and I dwell in the midst of a people of unclean lips; for my eyes have seen the King, the Lord of hosts!' Then flew one of the seraphim to me, having in his hand a burning coal which he had taken with tongs from the altar: 'Behold, this has touched your lips; your guilt is taken away, and your sin forgiven.' (Isa. 6.1–7)

Again, there is a link made between holiness and ethics in Isaiah 30 where the prophet responds to those who despise the word of the Holy One and trust in oppression and perverseness, the false prophets who prophesy illusion (30.9–14). The connection between holiness and justice is made explicit in Psalm 15 where, in answer to the question 'who shall dwell upon thy holy hill?', the psalmist answers that it is those who walk uprightly and do justice. Similarly, Habakkuk unites holiness and ethical purity in his ascription of praise to Yahweh, the Holy One whose pure eyes cannot look upon evil (Hab. 1.12–13).

However, it would be a mistake to see the holiness of God to involve a denial of his closeness. So the Deuteronomic writer asks: 'What great nation is there that has a god so near to it as the Lord our God is to us?' (Deut. 4.7) Jewish faith stressed the glory and awesome vocation of humanity, made in God's image. A human being is 'little less than God' (Ps. 8.5). The God to whom belong heaven and the heaven of heavens, as well as the earth and all its contents, has yet set his heart in love on particular people, and has chosen them and their descendants. And so we find in Old Testament religion a mingling of the 'unapproachableness'[37] of God with a sense of intimacy. God communicates with people as in the stories of Abraham and Moses. We find examples of personal communication in the accounts of Enoch (Gen. 5.24), Hannah (1 Sam. 1.10f), Samuel (1 Sam. 3.4ff), and Amos (7.15). There was a kinship between God and the people of God, and this was sometimes manifested in the gift of *ruach*, spirit, by which individuals were inspired to speak in God's name.

So the holiness and closeness of God focus the paradox of transcendence and immanence which lies at the heart of the Judaeo-Christian tradition. God who is Spirit (Isa. 31.3) and cannot be seen by human beings (Exod. 33.20), for they cannot endure the sight of him (Judg. 13.22), yet communicates with them at a deeply personal level. The Old Testament spoke of God walking in a garden and conversing with people (Gen. 3), shutting doors (7.16), inspecting building work (11.5) and making visits (18). Closely linked with the theme of Yahweh's communication with people is that of a range of ancillary divine beings, messengers, holy ones, angels; beings which had no independent significance, so that 'angel of Yahweh' became a euphemism for Yahweh himself. Again, the presence of Yahweh in the midst of his people is often referred to as his 'word', and this word is not far off but very near (Deut. 30.11, 14). Most important of all is the stress on *knowing* God, and knowledge for the Old Testament indicated a very intimate relationship indeed. 'So when the men of ancient Israel spoke of the "knowledge of God", they were not talking merely of *information concerning* God, but of an intimate personal attachment to him'.[38] The sense of God's intimacy is brought out in the anthropomorphic ways in which he is described: he speaks (Gen. 1.3), hears (Exod. 16.12), sees (Gen. 6.12) and smells (1 Sam. 26.19). He laughs (Ps. 2.4; 59.9) and even whistles (Isa. 7.18). He has eyes (Amos 9.4), hands (Ps. 139.5), arms (Isa. 51.9; 52.10), ears (22.14) and even feet (63.3).

And yet there remains a tension between the demands of the Holy God and those of everyday life. For in the Old Testament, close acquaintance with God, and the pursuit of holiness, involved a degree of separation. Holiness therefore was 'not consistent with the claims of everyday life'.[39] People were given holiness for periods but then discarded it. However, in the Holiness Code (Lev. 17–26) we see a call to holiness for the whole people. 'You shall be holy, for I, the Lord your God, am holy.' (Lev. 19.2) Israel had already come to be seen as a holy nation (Exod. 19.6), as 'holy to the Lord' (Jer. 2.3). But in the Holiness Code there is a new emphasis. Holiness seems now to be not simply an objective description of a state of separation, but rather a call to achieve an ideal. The call to holiness in Leviticus 19.2 is followed by instructions relating to reverence for parents and for the Sabbath, to respect for the poor and the stranger, to social justice, and to the demands of love. Israel is called, in obedience to the Holy God, to reject the pagan notions of 'sacralization' in the quest for true holiness and true freedom. This demands the uprooting of men and women from the sacral structures, and a willingness to live within the insecurity of being human. So Yahweh undermines the stable pagan order with his demand for total allegiance and his establishment of a unique relationship with Israel. Israel becomes the peculiar possession of Yahweh – *my* people (Amos 7.8, 15; 8.2; Isa. 1.3; 5.25; Hos. 2.25), the vineyard of the Lord (Isa. 5.1f), the first-born son (Exod. 4.22; Jer. 31.20), the people holy to the Lord and for his own possession (Deut. 7.6). The vocation of the holy people is subversive of the pagan notion of the secure, sacral order with its predictable rhythms and cycles, and its predictable gods. The holiness of Yahweh is unpredictable.

So divine holiness is demanding and dangerous. The demands of holiness were embodied in the Old Testament in a series of codes relating to sexual purity (Lev. 18.7ff), general social ethics (Exod. 20.3–17), cultic observances (Exod. 34.14–26) and so on. The rite of the covenant at Mount Sinai emphasized strongly the connection between holiness and obedience. After sprinkling one half of the blood of the victims over the altar, Moses read the Book of the Covenant to the people who responded with a commitment to obedience. Moses then sprinkled the remainder of the blood over the people. So the choice of Israel as a holy people had its necessary consequence in the call to obedience to the commandments.

> You have declared this day concerning the Lord that he is your God, and that you will walk in his ways, and keep his statutes, and his commandments, and his ordinances, and will obey his voice; and the Lord has declared this day concerning you that you are a people for his own possession as he has promised you, and that you are to keep all his commandments . . . and that you shall be a people

holy to the Lord your God as he has spoken. (Deut. 26.17–19) Holiness also carried its dangers. Holiness was contrasted with uncleanness, but both were contagious. Unclean things were also seen as dangerous, and whoever came into contact with something unclean became unclean (Lev. 5.2; 15.21–4, etc.). Holiness too was contagious and could be shown forth in destruction. Thus Nadab and Abihu offered 'unholy fire', that is, fire not made up according to the holy prescription. It was 'lay fire', not 'priest fire'. As a result of this act, the holy fire blazed out from the presence of the Lord and devoured them. The Lord then announced through Moses: 'I will show myself holy among those who are near me.' (Lev. 10.3) Holiness could take the form of destruction, and people were warned to keep their distance. For God is a devouring fire (Deut. 4.24).

God of Justice

The God of Israel was not only the holy God: he was also the God of justice. Holiness and justice were closely related in Old Testament thought. 'The connection between holiness and righteousness is unmistakable.'[40] God is a just God and a Saviour (Isa. 45.21), in him alone are justice and strength (45.24). Justice and salvation are interlocked (46.12–13). To seek justice and to seek Yahweh are virtually identified (51.1), and those who do so are called oaks of justice, the planting of Yahweh (61.3). What is this justice of which the Bible speaks?

There are two key words in Hebrew which relate to justice issues: *tsedeq* and *mispat*. *Tsedeq*, which, with its associated words, occurs over five hundred and twenty times in the Old Testament, is usually translated 'righteousness' in our English versions. But because of the modern tendency to see righteousness in terms of interior, personal qualities, 'justice' renders its biblical meaning more accurately. In origin, the word refers to that which is the norm, the standard. To be righteous or just is to conform to a social norm, to be 'in the right'. It is in essence a legal term rather than a moral one.[41] The associated word *mispat*, usually translated 'justice', refers more specifically to the actual process of judgement through the exercise of law. It is the term used for a legal decision, but it can be used also to refer to 'the done thing', the accepted way of life of a community. In the prophetic writings, *tsedeq* is understood in ethical terms and is increasingly related to the theme of salvation. Justice involves equal rights for all people, and there is a strong and persistent emphasis on God as the vindicator of the poor and helpless: 'He has distributed freely, he has given to the poor; his justice endures for ever.' (Ps. 112.9) Those

who follow the just God must themselves practise justice. So Daniel
advises Nebuchadnezzar to practise justice and show mercy to the
oppressed (Dan. 4.27).

But human beings can only 'do justice' because God *is* just.
Conversely, it is in the actual process of doing justice that we come to
know the God of justice. There is a two-way relationship. The rooting
of justice in theology does not mean that justice is first conceptualized
and later applied: it is rather that in struggling to achieve justice we
come closer to understanding the character of God. That character is
accurately described in the Old Testament as justice: God's throne
stands on justice and on judgement (Ps. 89.14; 97.2), he acts in justice
to rule the world (96.13). So the Psalmist prays that God would judge
him 'according to your justice', and his tongue talks of that justice all
day long (35.24ff). And God's justice is seen in the Old Testament as
manifested particularly in his concern for the poor and the rejects.
Snaith refers to 'the bias of righteousness in favour of the helpless'.

> Inasmuch, therefore, as it is God's concern to establish *tsedeq*
> (righteousness) in the land, he must perforce pay particular
> attention to the case of the poor and outcast, the widow and the
> orphan. The result is that, even as early as the eighth century,
> *tsedeq* is more than a barely ethical word. Already it is invading the
> salvation vocabulary. *Tsedeq* certainly stands for the establishment
> of justice in the land... It means not only the establishment of
> righteousness on equal terms for all, but also the vindication by
> God of those who cannot themselves secure their own rights.[42]

God is just, and he is known to us through our pursuit of justice. That
is the clear teaching of the Old Testament. It is expressed most
forcibly in Jeremiah 22. Here the man who builds his house by 'non-
justice' and completes its upstairs rooms by 'non-right' is condemned.
In contrast to such behaviour, the prophet asks:

> Did not your father eat and drink
> and do justice and righteousness?
> Then it was well with him.
> He judged the cause of the poor and needy;
> then it was well.
> Is not this to know me?
> says the Lord. (Jer. 22.15–16)

The knowledge of God is thus a practical knowledge. Such an
understanding is not a novel idea, the invention of left-wing radicals in
the twentieth century. It is deeply rooted in the biblical record. For
the Bible, to know the Lord does not refer to some separate

department of life called 'religion'. The way of justice was manifested in very earthy and material ways. For instance, the Old Testament writers often speak of 'almsgiving' as 'justice'.[43] The fundamental point to grasp is the closeness, amounting to virtual identification, between the pursuit of justice and the knowledge of God. The theme of Jeremiah's question comes out with equal force in Hosea, where the prophet complains that 'there is no faithfulness or kindness, and no knowledge of God in the land' (4.1). After a recitation of the crimes of the people – swearing, lying, killing, stealing, adultery – he says that the people are 'destroyed for lack of knowledge' (4.6). Justice and knowledge go together. In a later passage in Hosea, compassion and the knowledge of God are found in parallel (6.6), and it is to this association that Jesus appeals (Matt. 9.13; 12.7). Compassion, justice and right are often found together in the Old Testament (e.g. Jer. 9.23; Isa. 16.5; Mic. 6.8; Hos. 2.21–2; 6.6; 10.12; 12.7; Zech. 7.9; Ps. 25.9–10; 33.5; 36.6–7; 36.11; 40.11; 85.11; 88.12–13; 89.15; 98.2–3; 103.17; 119.62–4). To do that which is right is more pleasing to the Lord than sacrifice (Prov. 21.3). The contrast between justice and sacrifice (Hos. 6.6) is one which is repeated on many occasions in the prophets. Later in Hosea, there is a further identification of justice with Yahweh, while contrasted with this is the world of oppression and falsehood.

> Sow for yourselves justice,
> reap the fruits of steadfast love;
> break up your fallow ground,
> for it is time to seek the Lord
> that he may come and rain salvation upon you.
> You have ploughed iniquity,
> you have reaped injustice,
> you have eaten the fruit of lies. (Hos. 10.12–13)

Thus Yahweh and justice stand against oppression and falsehood. Miranda, after an exhaustive study of all the references to justice and the knowledge of God in the Old Testament, concludes:[44]

> The God who does not allow himself to be objectified, because only in the immediate command of conscience is he God, clearly specifies that he is knowable exclusively in the cry of the poor and the weak who seek justice... The knowledge of Yahweh and the realization of justice are understood to be the same thing... 'knowledge of Yahweh' absolutely cannot be understood if we do not realize that it is a strict synonym for the realization of justice.

The Old Testament prophets in particular were obsessed with the question of social justice, and their obsession was rooted in their understanding of God. We see this concern in Nathan's visit to David when he rebuked him for his lack of pity, and for his theft of Bathsheba from Uriah (2 Sam. 12.1–15), and in Elijah's condemnation of Ahab's theft of Naboth's vineyard (1 Kings 21.1–4). We see it in Samuel's attack on the monarchy when the old desert tradition of equality had collapsed and massive confiscation of property had become the norm. So the prophet warned of the evils of monarchy:

> He [the king] will take the best of your fields and vineyards and olive orchards and give them to his servants. He will take the tenth of your grain and of your vineyards and give it to his officers and to his servants. He will take your manservants and maidservants and the best of your cattle and your asses and put them to his work. He will take the tenth of your flocks, and you shall be his slaves. And in that day you will cry out because of your king whom you have chosen for yourselves; but the Lord will not answer you in that day. (1 Sam. 8.14–18)

On the other hand, it is written that David as king executed judgement and justice to all the people (2 Sam. 8.15) and that this is the ideal of true kingship (Ps. 45.4–8; 72.1–3).

The writing of the prophet Micah contains fierce condemnation of the 'free enterprise society'[45] which flourished in his day. He attacks those who covet and seize fields (2.2), who divide fields (2.4) and strip the robe from the peaceful (2.8). The call to 'know justice' is a call from Yahweh to those who 'tear the skin from off my people' (3.2–3). Such people will not be heard by the Lord when they cry (2.4). They identify peace with their own self-satisfaction (3.5). Israel's leaders are accused of rejecting justice and building Zion with blood and wrongdoing (3.10). Their injustice, moreover, is located in specific acts – 'wicked scales', 'deceitful weights' (6.11), and bribes (7.3). The prophet, on the other hand, filled with the Spirit and with justice (3.8), looks towards a time of justice and peace when Yahweh will teach his ways (4.1–5). These ways are ways of justice and compassion.

> He has shown you, O man, what is good:
> and what does the Lord require of you
> but to do justice and to love kindness
> and to walk humbly with your God? (6.8)

In Amos, we find condemnations not only of Israel but of surrounding countries, for their cruelty in war, their slave traffic, and so on (1.3—2.16). But the prophet's fiercest attack is on Israel itself, and specifically on those who have sold the righteous for silver and the poor for a pair of sandals, trampling the poor in the dust, and turning aside the way of the afflicted (2.6ff), those who store up robbery and violence (3.10), and those who oppress the poor and crush the needy (4.1; 8.6). Drunkenness also comes under fire (4.1). Again, very specific forms of injustice are mentioned – exactions of wheat from the poor (5.11; 8.4), bribery, rejection of the needy (5.12), complacency and false security (6.1), excessive wealth (6.4–6), and the use of false balances (8.5). God's anger is especially aroused by the perversion of justice.

> Seek the Lord and live,
> lest he breaks out like fire in the house of Joseph
> and it devour with none to quench it for Bethel.
> O you who turn judgement to wormwood
> and cast down justice to the earth! (5.6–7)

And later Amos speaks of those who 'have turned judgement into poison, and the fruit of justice into wormwood' (6.12). He calls for the establishment of justice in the gate (5.12) and cries:

> ... let judgement roll down like waters
> and justice like an overflowing steam! (5.24)

Hosea's identification of injustice with lack of knowledge has already been mentioned. For him the lack of knowledge of God was manifested in injustice (4.1–2). The people, he complains, 'have ploughed iniquity ... reaped injustice ... eaten the fruit of lies', and this injustice is specifically associated with military aggression (10.13). Again, 'false balances' are cited as signs of oppression (12.7). On the other hand, the covenant relationship with Yahweh, involving a state of harmony with nature and the rejection of war, is described as a betrothal in justice and compassion, and is identified with 'knowing the Lord' (2.19–20). So Hosea exhorts the people to 'hold fast to love and justice, and wait continually for our God' (12.6).

Isaiah begins his prophecies with a condemnation of worship which ignores justice, and of worshippers whose 'hands are full of blood' (1.15). They are urged to seek justice and to correct oppression (1.17). Injustice is again associated with bribery, desire for riches, and neglect of the fatherless and the widow (1.23), with 'grinding the face of the poor' (3.15), with personal luxury (3.18–24), with violence and bloodshed (5.7), with the accumulation of property (5.8), with drunkenness (5.11), and with neglect of the hungry (3.26). And, again, such injustice is identified with a 'want of knowledge' (5.13). Because of this the divine 'woes' are uttered against those who subvert God's justice in the specifics of legislation.

> Woe to those who decree iniquitous decrees,
> and the writers who keep writing oppression,
> to turn aside the needy from justice,
> and to rob the poor of my people of their right. (10.1)

There can be no redemption without the recovery of justice. It is by justice that Zion will be redeemed (1.27) as it is in justice that God is exalted (5.16; 28.5). The Spirit of God is a 'spirit of justice' (28.6). And, as we have seen elsewhere in the prophets, God's justice is shown particularly in the defence of the poor and underprivileged: 'with justice shall he judge the poor, and decide with equity for the meek of the earth' (11.4). The yearning for the Messiah is for one who 'judges and seeks right, and is swift to do justice' (16.5), for a time when judgement will be the line and justice the plummet (28.15). Peace cannot exist if there is no justice for peace is the fruit of justice (32.17).

The zeal for the divine justice is continued in Second Isaiah (40–66). Israel, the servant of Yahweh, is called to bring forth justice for the nations, to establish justice on earth (42.1, 4). Through obedience to God's law, peace and justice will issue forth (48.18), but there can be no peace for the unjust (48.22). The discipline of fasting is particularly associated with the liberation of the oppressed and the feeding of the hungry (58.6–7). Injustice, however, leads to separation from God and to darkness and untruth (59.1–15). Yahweh loves justice and will cause it to flourish (61.8–11).

The prophet Jeremiah also laments the lack of justice in Jerusalem.

> Run to and fro through the streets of Jerusalem.
> Look and take note!
> Search her squares to see
> if you can find a man,
> one who does justice
> and seeks truth. (5.1)

The search is fruitless for the people 'judge not with justice the cause of the fatherless to make it prosper, and they do not defend the rights of the needy' (5.28). There is nothing but oppression in the city (6.6). Jeremiah condemns those who seek easy solutions: 'they have healed the wound of my people lightly, saying "Peace, peace" when there is no peace' (6.14). Trusting in sacred sites, even in the temple itself, he warns, is useless without the execution of justice. Justice once again is linked with care of the alien, the fatherless and the widow, and with avoidance of violence against the innocent (7.5–6). 'Unjust gain' (8.10) and 'heaping oppression upon oppression' (9.6) are attacked.

The wise and the rich are warned not to glory in their wisdom and wealth, but only in their knowledge of the Lord who practises kindness and justice (9.23–4). The call to do justice is well summed up in one line:

> Thus says the Lord: Do judgement and justice, and deliver from the hand of the oppressor him who has been robbed. And do no wrong or violence to the alien, the fatherless, and the widow, nor shed innocent blood in this place. (22.3)

Jeremiah attacks those who build their houses by unjustice and who make their neighbours work for no wages, and he contrasts with this behaviour the behaviour of his ancestors for whom justice and concern for the poor constituted knowledge of God (22.13–16). He predicts the coming of a 'just branch', a king who will 'execute judgement and justice in the land' and whose name will be 'the Lord our Justice' (23.5–6).

Concern for justice is an essential feature of the rest of the prophetic writings. In Ezekiel there is a lengthy passage dealing with the characteristics of the just person, including avoidance of idolatry, sexual purity, avoidance of robbery and of violence, care for the hungry and the naked, avoidance of usury, and obedience to divine statutes (18.5–9). Ezekiel pronounces doom upon injustice (7.10). Jerusalem is described as 'the bloody city' (22.2), a city in which parents are despised, in which the sojourner suffers extortion, and in which bribery, violence, and dishonest gain flourish (22.6–13). Nahum's short prophecy is a cry of triumph over the fall of Nineveh, the Assyrian capital, to the Babylonians and Medes, but his words are applicable to oppressive imperialism everywhere:

> Woe to the bloody city,
> all full of lies and booty –
> no end to the plunder! (3.1)

The prophet rejoices at Nineveh's desolation, and indeed 'all who hear the news of you clap their hands over you, for upon whom has not come your unceasing evil?' (3.19)

The prophet Habakkuk is also concerned with destruction and violence, with a situation in which 'the law is slacked and justice never goes forth' but rather 'goes forth perverted' (1.4). Habakkuk probably wrote at the time of the rise of the Chaldeans. He attacks drunkenness, arrogance, and greed (2.5), laying particular stress on the evil of accumulation of wealth. 'Woe to him who heaps up what is not his own' (2.6). The Chaldeans have plundered many nations, and so they themselves will be plundered 'for the blood of men, and violence to the earth' (2.8). Again, the establishment of towns by violence is condemned. 'Woe to him who builds a town with blood, and founds a city on iniquity' (2.12). The 'day of the Lord' will bring judgement on violence and fraud, according to Zephaniah (1.7). Wealth will be useless on that day (1.18) though the pursuit of justice may result in deliverance (2.3). For God is just, and he will show forth his justice (3.5). Obadiah develops the notion of injustice to include inaction. He condemns Edom for its failure to help Jerusalem at the time of the Babylonian captivity. The prophecy is a massive indictment of the sin of omission, of complacency, of complicity in oppression through one's inaction.

> On the day you stood aloof,
> On the day that strangers carried off his wealth,
> and foreigners entered his gates
> and cast lots for Jerusalem,
> you were like one of them. (11)

Injustice can be committed and reinforced by doing nothing. The call to do justice is repeated by Zechariah:

> Thus says the Lord of hosts: Render true judgements, show kindness and mercy each to his brother, do not oppress the widow, the fatherless, the sojourner or the poor; and let none of you devise evil against his brother in your hearts. (7.9)

Again, justice and peace are seen as inseparable (8.16). Finally, as the Old Testament ends, the prophet Malachi speaks of 'the God of justice' (2.17) who draws near in judgement against those who practise injustice and oppression (3.5). But to those who fear the Lord's name, the 'Sun of justice' will rise with healing in his wings (4.2).

If the prophets are a major source for the concern for the divine justice in human life, it is in the Mosaic Law that we find that concern embodied in the pattern of a society. In the law we see most clearly the biblical idea of a just social order which approximates to the divine order. The role of the judge is to justify the righteous and to condemn the wicked (Deut. 25.1). In the process of judgement there was to be no partiality either towards the poor or towards the mighty. Nevertheless, there is the emphasis which we saw in the prophets on responsibility towards the disadvantaged. The stranger is singled out for attention, and this is rooted in God's own care for the children of Israel when they were strangers in foreign territory. Indeed, the entire edifice of Jewish social ethics is based on God's action: because God has behaved in this way, so must God's people. As in God, so in human society, justice and mercy go together. So we find in the Deuteronomic code 'a humane tendency that distinguishes it favourably from other legal codes of the ancient Near East'.[46] The fundamental assumption of the law was that the land belonged to God. In other words, there was no private property, for all creation belongs to God (Gen. 1.1; Ps. 24.1; Deut. 10.14). The land has been entrusted by God to his people, not simply to a privileged few among them. It was therefore divided among tribes and families on an egalitarian basis. Abuse of the land will lead to serious consequences: the land may vomit out its people (Lev. 20.22). Fertility will not come through sacrifice but through justice. So there is a covenant relationship between Creator and creation, including the land. Yet, because of human sin, there is a need for safeguards, and the law included a series of checks so that sin might not undermine the just basis of society. Firstly, there was the landmark. The law of the landmark prohibited the ploughing up or alteration of the division between one man's property and his neighbour's. 'You shall not remove your neighbour's landmark' (Deut. 19.14. Cf. Hos. 5.10; Prov. 22.28; 23.10). Secondly, there was the prohibition of usury. If a man borrowed from his neighbour and demanded interest, that interest might cripple his neighbour, and make his work impossible, or even make him sell his land. So usury was banned in Israel. 'You shall not lend upon interest to your brother, interest on money, interest on victuals, interest on anything that is lent for interest' (Deut. 23.19. Cf. Exod. 22.25; Lev. 25.36). Thirdly, there was the Year of Release. The idea of 'release' originally referred to release from oppression in Egypt. However, it later came to be applied to oppression by Israelites of one another, with the growth of economic inequality, commerce, and landlordism. The Year of Release was an extension of the Sabbath principle. Thus the ordinances in Exodus 21 begin with an instruction that Hebrew slaves shall serve six years, and that in the seventh year they shall go free (21.2). At first the release referred to the practice of allowing land to lie fallow every seventh year (Lev. 25.3f). Later it was extended to apply to the accumulation of debt. Within certain limits, debts were to be cancelled in the Year of Release (Deut. 15.1–3). Again, the basis of this law was a concern for the elimination of poverty, and this is clearly stated. 'There will be no poor among you.' (Deut. 15.4)

Finally, there was the Year of Jubilee. The Year of Jubilee was introduced after the destruction of the monarchy. It went further than the earlier Sabbatical year which was meant to apply to the private contracts of individuals. Under the Jubilee legislation, the entire community was to observe a collective year of release:

You shall hallow the Fiftieth Year, and proclaim liberty through-out the land to all its inhabitants; it shall be a Jubilee for you, when each of you shall return to his property, and each of you shall return to his family... The houses of the villages which have no wall around them shall be reckoned with the fields of the country; they may be redeemed, and they shall be released in the Jubilee... And if (a slave) is not redeemed ... then he shall be released in the Year of Jubilee, he and his children with him. (Lev. 25.10, 31, 54)

The principle behind the Year of Release and the Year of Jubilee was that of liberation from oppression by the activity of God's justice. As God set free the people of Israel from *external* bondage in the Exodus, so he sets them free from *internal* bondage in the Jubilee. The Jubilee is therefore 'Exodus spelled out in terms of social salvation'.[47] The nineteenth-century writer Frederick Verrinder summarized the Mosaic Law's view of land:

The principle which underlies the Mosaic agrarian legislation is absolutely fatal to what we know as landlordism. Jehovah is the only landlord; the land is his, because he and none other created it: all men are his tenants.[48]

Other laws stressed the need for just weights and measures (Deut. 25.13–16). The death penalty was exacted for murder, for offences against parents, and for selling a man into slavery (Exodus 21.11–17), but cities of refuge were appointed where a man could escape punishment (Num. 35.9–15). The treatment of slaves by their owners was a matter of community concern (Exod. 21.20, 26), and there was provision for asylum for runaway slaves, a provision which stands in sharp contrast with all other codes of the period in which harbouring of runaways was a serious offence with heavy penalties. Yet Deuteronomy is explicit:

You shall not give up to his master a slave who has escaped from his master to you; he shall dwell with you, in your midst, in the place which he shall choose within one of your towns where it pleases him best; you shall not oppress him (Deut. 23.15–16).

Throughout the law there is a stress on responsibility for the land, yet persons are seen as of more value than property. Thus no property offence carried the death penalty, whereas kidnapping was a capital offence (Exod. 21.16). In Deuteronomy 27 there is a series of cursings, all of them concerned with responsibility to God and to people – removing one's neighbour's landmark, misleading the blind, perverting the justice due to the sojourner, and so on (Deut. 27.15–

26). Subject to certain limitations, one might satisfy one's hunger with another person's grapes or grain (Deut. 23.24–5). Labourers must be paid on the same day for their work (Deut. 24.15). Animals too were to be protected (Deut. 22.1–4; 25.4). We have therefore in the Law a remarkable collection of statutes based upon a high view of man as made in the divine image, and a high view of the created order. In relation to both people and to the creation, the divine justice was to be sought and expressed.

It is however in the later prophets, and particularly in Second Isaiah, that the link between justice and salvation was 'invading the salvation vocabulary' by the eighth century.[49] In Second Isaiah this invasion has become a settled position:

> Listen to me, my people,
> and give ear to me, my nation;
> for the law will go forth from me,
> and my justice for a light to the peoples.
> My deliverance draws near speedily,
> my salvation has gone forth. (Isa. 51.4–5)

In the process of deliverance, or redemption, the poor and needy will be nourished (41.14–18). The servant of Yahweh will bring forth justice to the nations, and establish justice on earth (42.1, 4). God himself is described as a just God and a Saviour (45.21). And the work of salvation is seen in terms of the gathering in of the outcasts. Thus Yahweh, the Creator, the Redeemer, the Holy One and Saviour, announces that he will gather in peoples from east, west, north, and south, including the blind and the deaf (43.1–8). Justice and deliverance are inseparable from salvation (46.13) while the absence of justice is equated with the absence of salvation:

> Therefore judgement is far from us
> and justice does not overtake us...
> We look for justice but there is none,
> for salvation but it is far from us. (59.9, 11)

There is no justice, and none can intervene. So Yahweh himself puts on justice as a breastplate and salvation as a helmet (59.17).

In Isaiah 61, attention is turned back to the Jubilee Year:

> The Spirit of the Lord God is upon me,
> because the Lord has anointed me
> to bring good tidings to the afflicted;
> he has sent me to bind up the broken-hearted,
> to proclaim liberty to the captives,

and the opening of the prison to those who are bound;
to proclaim the Year of the Lord's Favour. (61.1–2)

God, says the prophet, has clothed himself with the garments of
salvation and with the robe of justice, and he will cause justice to
spring forth before all nations (61.10–11). By this time the word
justice had become so integral a part of salvation language that it could
be said that 'in Second Isaiah the word ... has come to mean
salvation'.[50]

Finally, it must be emphasized that in the Old Testament justice is
related closely to love. The just God is the God whose nature and
name is love. In the past some theologians have made a rigid
separation between justice and love.[51] Love comes to be limited to
personal, face-to-face relationships, while justice is applied to social
relations. Others, under the influence of Luther, have associated
justice with God's wrath, and with law, while love belongs to the
Gospel and to the order of redemption. Such divisions are unsatisfac-
tory. But it is equally inadequate to say that 'love and justice are the
same for justice is love distributed'.[52] Love is not the same as justice,
but it should both seek justice and be a transforming influence upon
justice. For love goes beyond justice, an emphasis which comes
through strongly in the prophets, but which is fully developed in the
New Testament teaching about the character of God. Yet there are
not two Gods, one of the Old, and the other of the New Testaments;
and the God of Israel is the God of love as well as of justice. 'Justice
alone cannot and must not rule; justice and love together must
determine and shape the life men live together.'[53] God betrothes
Israel to himself in justice and in love (Hos. 2.19–20). It is also
because Israel is *known*, that is, loved and cherished, by God, that
judgement will come (Amos 3.2). The unique relationship of Israel to
Yahweh and to his justice is in stark contrast to the world of the pagan
deities with their ritually reinforced societies. The justice of Yahweh
is demanding and disturbing, and it presents his disciples through the
centuries with baffling dilemmas and challenges to end established
forms of oppression and inequality. On the other hand, 'all poly-
theisms tend to be religions of the *status quo* and ... none of them has
ever produced a thorough-going social revolution based upon a high
concept of social justice'.[54]

The Name of God

The holiness and justice of God, his unique relationship with Israel
and his exclusive demand for allegiance, receive their most powerful
symbolic expression in the name of God: Yahweh, the great I Am. In

Hebrew thought, power resides in the name. To give a name is to possess power over the named one. To know a name is to enter in some way into the mystery of the person's being. The greatest significance therefore must be attached to the name of God as revealed, first, to Moses. The name is a mark of identity to such an extent that to be without a name is virtually to be without existence. Names were essential to the being of gods as well as humans. Thus the Babylonian creation epic began:

> When on high the heaven had not been named,
> Firm ground below had not been called by name,
> . . .
> When no gods whatever had been brought into being,
> Uncalled by name, their destinies undetermined –
> then it was the gods were formed within them [i.e. the primeval waters]
> Lahmu and Lahamu were brought forth, by name they were called.[55]

Genesis too associates creation with naming (1.5, 8, 10; 2.19). To know someone's name is to have power over them, and so to withhold one's name is to prevent the acquiring of such power. However, nowhere does the Old Testament give the name of Abraham's God. He himself did not know it, nor did Jacob discover it (Gen. 32.29). He is therefore identified simply as 'the God of Abraham', for a relationship with a nameless God raised problems. (On one occasion, Abraham's God speaks of himself as 'the God of Bethel' (Gen. 31.13), but this was to connect himself with an earlier revelation. Bethel never became a permanent seat.) The possession of a name was thus of great importance, and when Moses was to return to Egypt he knew that the first question he would be asked about his encounter with God was 'What is his name?' (Exod. 3.13). In fact, the question 'What is his name?' became a form of denial of existence (cf. Prov. 30.4).

In the Book of Exodus we are told that it was only in the time of Moses that God revealed himself by the name Yahweh. The Lord who appeared to Abraham, Isaac, and Jacob as God Almighty had not been known in those days by his name Yahweh (Exod. 6.2). There are several passages in Genesis where the name Yahweh is used, and one tradition assumes that its use goes back to the beginning of history. Thus, in relation to the time of Adam, we are told that it was then that people began to invoke Yahweh by name (Gen. 4.26). But in other passages the name is avoided in the pre-Mosaic period. In its place we find the name El, the name of one of the two principal deities of Canaan.

Originally El designated any god, but it also occurs as a proper name for specific deities. Some hold the view that El was a high god who was worshipped all over the West Semitic world under a variety of names.[56] In the Old Testament, El occurs some 217 times, usually in conjunction with another name. Thus Abraham worships El Elyon (God Most High) at Salem (Gen. 14.17–21), El Shaddai (God Almighty) at Hebron (17.1) and El Olam (God Everlasting) at Beersheba (21.33). Isaac worships El Roi (God of Seeing) at Beer-lahai-roi (16.14; 24.62). Jacob worships El Bethel (God of Bethel; 35.6–7) and erects an altar to El at Shechem (33.20). It seems that El was a common name for the senior deity of the Canaanite divine hierarchy. In the patriarchal period there is a merging of the worship of ancestral gods with the worship of the Canaanite god El. The Ras Shamra texts show a society of gods with no clear antecedent for the later monotheistic world-view of Yahwism.

However, while the Elohim (plural of El) were absorbed into the faith of Yahweh, the same was not true of the Baal cult, an equally important part of Canaanite religion. There is some slight evidence of attempts to identify Yahweh with Baal (2 Sam. 5.20; 2.10; 9.6). In the early days of the monarchy, Yahweh may have been addressed as Baal; but its association with the Canaanite cults led to the banning of the name. So Hosea insists that God will no longer be referred to as 'my Baal' and that the very names of the Baalim will be wiped out (2.16).

Yahweh is the name under which Israel's God is to be known. The name of Yahweh occurs over 6,000 times in the Old Testament. According to Exodus 3–4, it was to Moses that God revealed himself first under this name. But this God was not a different God from the God of the patriarchs. Yahweh is the God of all the earth (Isa. 54.5). While the name was unknown to the patriarchs (Exod. 3.13f; 6.2), it would seem that various earlier gods were merged into Yahwism.[57] Abraham is said to have instructed his descendants to observe the ways of Yahweh (Gen. 18.19), but the revelation at Sinai initiated a new era in the history of Israel:

> The theophany takes place in the desert, at a site without cultic significance before or after. . . Moses comes to the place ignorant of its holiness. He beholds something for which he was totally unprepared. He was not informed by Jethro either of the sanctity of the place, or of the name of the God who revealed himself there. The theophany of the bush has no roots in any existent cult, Kenite or Midianite, nor does the Hebrew people know of the sanctity of

the place or the name of the God who manifested himself there. Moses is the first to discover both.[58]

So Yahweh became Israel's banner (Exod. 17.15) and individuals were called by names based on Yahweh (1 Kings 11.29; 14.1). The name was to be revered and not blasphemed, hence the prohibition of its use in curses and in magic (Exod. 20.7).

The use of the plural form Elohim as a name for God was common in Israel, but it had the disadvantage that it was also applied to the false gods of Canaan. Thus 'Thou shalt have no other *elohim* but me' (Exod. 20.3). So, from the time of Amos and Hosea, the alternative usage of *Yahweh Tsebaoth* (Lord of Hosts) enters the vocabulary, and is adopted by Jeremiah and the post-exilic prophets. Yahweh and Elohim were not mutually exclusive. Yahweh Tsebaoth was the Elohim of the armies of Israel (1 Sam. 17.45). The 'hosts' were not only Israel's armies, for Yahweh was Lord of the stars and of the angels. So the visitor who met Joshua at Gilgal announced himself as captain of the hosts of Yahweh (Josh. 5.14). In Isaiah 6 the hosts appear, distinct from Yahweh, yet giving glory to him, and praise is seen as their central role (Ps. 148.2).

What then is the meaning of the revelation to Moses of the name of Yahweh? The name is usually rendered into English as 'I am that I am', though the RSV margin reads 'I will be what I will be'. To say simply that Yahweh means the self-existent nature of God, being itself, is to reduce Jewish theology to static notions of essence. Yahweh is not the god of the philosophers. The Hebrew denotes not so much a static idea (being) as a dynamic process (becoming). 'I become what I become', or 'I will be what I will be', are closer to the underlying sense of the moving, living God. Yahweh is revealed as the God who *will* bring Israel out of Egypt, and who *will* be with Moses (Exod. 3.7–10): he is the God of the future, the God of creative history.

The revelation of the name of God is a kind of self-emptying, an act by which Yahweh surrenders himself into the hands of men. The true name of Pharaoh was kept secret, yet Yahweh, the God of all the earth, reveals his identity to Moses. Before Moses the goodness of God passes, and in his hearing the name of Yahweh is pronounced (Exod. 33.19). At the same time, the inner essence of Yahweh remains unknowable, for he is a God who hides himself (Isa. 45.15; Job 11.7; Ps. 97.2; Exod. 33.10). God cannot be described directly, but only in his relationships and in action. The recognition of this fact, that God cannot be portrayed or directly seen, is a fundamental principle of Yahwism, and of the Christian mystical tradition which grew from its roots. Jewish theology came to be wary even of uttering the name of Yahweh, and substituted Adonai, the Lord, in public use of the divine name. In Greek versions of the Old Testament, *kurios* translates both Adonai and Yahweh. In the period of the second Temple, the name Yahweh was pronounced once a year, by the High Priest on the Day of Atonement; but after the destruction of the Temple in 70 AD, the priests forgot the form of the name, and it ceased to be used.

Yahweh is God of nature and of the historical processes, and yet is superior to them and beyond them. Unlike the pagan deities, Yahweh is not identified with the forces of nature, but is in control of them. Thus earthquakes and volcanoes are the fingers of Yahweh, he appears in clouds and stars, and he speaks through the thunder. The wind is his breath. But these natural phenomena are all his creatures, essentially distinct from him. Yahweh is no storm god or volcanic deity, nor does he have his permanent home within the mountain. He descends upon it, but speaks from heaven. He is distinct too from the gods, for there are many *elohim*, but Yahweh is one. There can be no rival. Thus to sacrifice to the *elohim* is a capital offence (Exod. 22.20).

So in the Old Testament the name of Yahweh is the expression of his character, his holiness, his power and majesty. Holy and terrible is his name (Ps. 111.9). Yet this name, the revelation of transcendence, dwells upon the earth, in a specific place (Deut. 12.5, etc.), in Jerusalem (1 Kings 8.27–9), and among his people who are called by his name.

Spirit and Word

In Hebrew thought, the spirit is 'the motive power of the soul . . . the strength emanating from it'.[59] Like the wind, from which the word *ruach* is derived, God's breath is powerful and mysterious. *Ruach* means both wind and breath, and in the Old Testament the wind is seen as the breath of God (Ps. 18.15; cf. Ezek. 14.21; 15.8), the breath which gives life to men and women and to the creation (Gen. 6.17; 7.15; Num. 16.22; Judg. 15.19; Ps. 104.29; Eccles. 3.21; 9.21; 12.7; Isa. 37.6, 8; Zech. 12.1). The Spirit of God, his power and life, was present at the creation of the world, transforming chaos into cosmos as it hovered over the primeval waters (Gen. 1.2).

Genesis tells us that God 'breathed' the breath of life into man (2.7). A clear distinction is made between men and women, and the animals. Only into human beings did God transfer his own life force, his breath, *neshamah*. *Neshamah* and *ruach* are sometimes used interchangeably (cf. Isa. 30.33; Ezek. 37.1–10). There is thus within human beings a divine spark, the Spirit, which is not of this world but formed by God (Zech. 12.1). God himself is *ruach* (Isa. 31.3). The Spirit therefore is 'at all times plainly superior to Man, a divine power within his mortal body, subject to the rule of God alone'.[60] It is contrasted with the flesh which stands for the natural world (Isa. 31.3). And, like the holiness of God, *ruach* is explosive and unpredictable. Early Old Testament writers use *ruach* to describe abnormal occurrences or qualities. So Gideon's courage is due to possession by the Spirit of the Lord (Judg. 6.34), while Samson's strength is ascribed to the fact that 'the Spirit of the Lord began to stir him' (Judg. 13.25) and 'came mightily upon him' (14.6, 19; 15.14). Saul and his messengers were possessed by the Spirit and prophesied (1 Sam. 19.23–4). Balaam's oracular utterance is due to the fact that 'the Spirit of God came upon him' (Num. 24.2). Spirit is thus linked with power. It is through the Spirit that men tear lions in pieces (Judg. 14.6), kill thousands of people (15.14), and execute beautiful works of craftsmanship (Exod. 31.3–5).

Such possession was relatively rare, but it was regarded, at least by some writers, as desirable that the Lord's people as a whole should become prophets, and that he 'would put his Spirit upon them' (Num. 11.29). At the same time, possession by the Spirit could have harmful effects and still be attributed to Yahweh. Thus we are told that 'the Spirit of the Lord departed from Saul and an evil spirit from the Lord tormented him' (1 Sam. 16.14). For even evil forces were seen as being subject to God and incapable of independent activity.

To speak then of God's *ruach* is to speak of the mystery of life itself. But the combination of the sense of the universal breath of life with the Israelite belief in Yahweh as personal led to a stress on the work of the Spirit as intensely personal rather than as some pantheistic life force. In many accounts the Spirit seems to assume personal characteristics, speaking (1 Kings 22.21), capable of movement (2 Kings 2.16), able to depart (1 Sam. 16.14). The Spirit was outside man's control and could rush upon him and overpower him. Its operation, like that of the wind, was essentially erratic and unpredictable. It could not normally be bequeathed or transferred, and its power passed on, although there are hints of an association of Spirit with office (Num. 11.14ff).

For the prophetic movement of the ninth century BC, 'the presence of "the spirit of Yahweh" was absolutely constitutive'.[61] The early prophetic scene was dominated by an experience of God as Spirit. However, the word *ruach* fell into decline in the period before the Exile. The pre-Exilic prophets wrote little about the Spirit. So we have 'the astonishing fact that in the line of divine messengers from

Amos onwards, there is absolutely no mention of the *ruach* as the power that equips and legitimates the prophet'.[62] The decay of the idea of *ruach* was probably due to a reaction against false prophets, and the consequent growth of a process of reinterpretation in prophetic spirituality. Later the term was to be readmitted to the prophets' vocabulary. But the early writing prophets rarely attribute their inspiration to *ruach*. Amos, Zephaniah, Nahum, and Jeremiah never mention the Spirit of Yahweh or link their work with it. Isaiah does not associate the Spirit with his prophetic ministry. Where spirit-inspired speech is alleged, there is the suspicion of false spirituality or of Canaanite influence. Amos denies that he is a *nabi* (7.14), the term used to describe the earlier ecstatic prophets, and this suspicion of the *nebiim* (plural of *nabi*) extends to all the writing prophets. Only in Hosea, Micah, and possibly Habakkuk are there hints of *ruach* (cf. Mic. 2.7; 3.8; Hos. 9.7). There is no use of *ruach* in Deuteronomy, while the account of Elijah's experience of Yahweh in Mount Carmel is very explicit that Yahweh was not in the *ruach* (wind) or in the earthquake or in the fire, but rather in the still, small voice (1 Kings 19.11f). There are some references to *ruach* in Isaiah where the Spirit of Yahweh is seen, not as an occasional and extraordinary manifestation, but as a permanent presence in the person of the Messiah (11.2). Elsewhere *ruach* is seen as the imperishable life of God as contrasted with the perishable life of the Egyptians (31.3). The 'spirit of justice' is identified with the glory, beauty and strength of Yahweh (28.5), preparing Israel for Yahweh's visible presence in her midst (4.4).

However, *ruach* reappears in Ezekiel and Second Isaiah as a major idea, the power of the coming new age. In Ezekiel, the Spirit is not so much evidence of the authenticity of his message as an explanation of his experience. It is as a result of listening to the Word of the Lord that *ruach* becomes the power of resurrection. In Ezekiel, the Spirit assumes a place which is unknown elsewhere in the prophetic writings, and it is closely linked with his awareness that 'that hand of Yahweh' is upon him. But while *ruach* occurs over fifty times in the book, the 'Spirit of Yahweh' is only mentioned twice (11.5; 37.1) and the 'Spirit of God' once (11.24).

In Ezekiel, the Spirit enters into the prophet and sets him on his feet so that he may hear the words from one identified as 'the likeness of the glory of the Lord' (1.28—2.2). It lifts him up alongside the glory of the Lord (3.12), carries him away in bitterness of spirit with the hand of the Lord upon him, to the place of exile (3.14–15), where later it again enters him and sets him on his feet (3.24). Later, the hand of the Lord comes upon him, and the Spirit lifts him up between earth and heaven (8.1–3). The liftings up are repeated (11.1, 24, etc.). Spirit is associated with movement, but also with inner renewal. So the Lord tells him:

> And I will give them one heart, and put a new spirit within them; I will take the stony heart out of their flesh and give them a heart of flesh, that they may walk in my statutes and keep my ordinances and obey them; and they shall be my people, and I will be their God. (11.19–20).

The promise is later repeated and is linked with purifications and cleansing of heart (36.25–7). In Chapter 37, the Spirit is the power which raises the dead, the dry bones. The Lord tells the bones that he will cause *ruach* to enter them so that they may live (37.5). By this act, they will know that he is Yahweh. The passage continues:

> Then he said to me, 'Prophesy to the breath, son of man, and say to the breath, Thus says the Lord God: Come from the four winds, O breath, and breathe upon these slain, that they may live.' So I prophesied as he commanded me, and the breath came into them, and they lived, and stood upon their feet, an exceedingly great host. (37.9–10)

In Second Isaiah, Yahweh is he who 'gives breath to the people upon [the earth] and spirit to those who walk in it' (42.5). The abiding presence of the Spirit is the sign of Yahweh's covenant (59.21). In particular, the Spirit is seen as the power which guided Israel in the past, preserves her in the present, and will be her future hope of renewal. A passage in Isaiah 63 makes this clear:

> But they rebelled
>   and grieved his holy Spirit;
> therefore he turned to be their enemy,
>   and himself fought against them.
> Then he remembered the days of old,
>   of Moses his servant.
> Where is he who brought up out of the sea
>   the shepherds of his flock?
> Where is he who put in the midst of them
>   his holy Spirit,
> who caused his glorious arm
>   to go at the right hand of Moses,
> who divided the waters before them
>   to make for himself an everlasting name,
>   who led them through the depths?

> Like a horse in the desert,
>   they did not stumble.
> Like cattle that go down into the valley,
>   the Spirit of the Lord gave them rest.
> So thou didst lead thy people,
>   to make for thyself a glorious name. (63.10–14)

Similar ideas appear elsewhere in the prophets. The Spirit is seen both as the force which inspired the prophets (Zech. 7.12) and as an abiding presence with the people of God (Hag. 2.5). Joel writes of a new outpouring of the Spirit before the Day of the Lord:

> And it shall come to pass afterward,
>   that I will pour out my spirit on all flesh;
> your sons and your daughters shall prophesy,
>   your old men shall dream dreams,
>   and your young men shall see visions.
> Even upon the menservants and maidservants
>   in those days, I will pour out my spirit. (2.28–9)

Closely connected with the theme of God's Spirit is that of God's Word, *dabhar*. The Word of God goes forth and prospers (Isa. 55.10–11), it goes forth in righteousness (45.23). Like *ruach*, the Word comes forth from the mouth of God (1.20, etc.). It is endued with God's life, and communicates his character. As the Spirit of God is the breath of life, so the Word of God is the breath of his mouth (Isa. 11.4; Ps. 33.6). Often in the Old Testament it would seem almost as if the Word had acquired a separate identity. Yet the Word remains God. Moreover, Word and Spirit are inseparable. 'The man of the spirit' (Hos. 9.7) is also the man who proclaims the Word; the Word and the Spirit are the evidence of the covenant which links men with God (Isa. 59.21). Like the Spirit, the Word is close, within mouth and heart (Deut. 30.14).

Zechariah links Word and Spirit together. So the angel announces: 'This is the word of the Lord... Not by might, nor by power, but by my Spirit, says the Lord of hosts' (4.6). He describes the delivery of both Law and Word as the work of the Spirit through the prophets (7.12). In Nehemiah, an association is made between the indwelling Spirit and the heavenly food of manna (9.20). Again, like the Spirit, the Word is powerful. Jeremiah writes: 'Is not my word like fire, says the Lord, and like a hammer which breaks the rock in pieces?' (23.29). It is like 'a burning fire shut up in my bones' (20.9). The Psalmist sees the Word as the agent of creation (Ps. 33.6) and of its renewal (147.15–18). The Word brings healing (Ps. 107.20). For the prophet, the Word was a compelling presence which could not be ignored. 'The Lord God has spoken; who can but prophesy?' (Amos 3.8). In fact, it was the Word, rather than the Spirit, of God which was seen as the primary source of the prophetic ministry and message. It was a dynamic force, an extension of Yahweh's own being, which was communicated to the prophets. It was the conscious, inner possession of the Word which distinguished the true prophet from the false. A passage from Jeremiah is important in this connection:

> Am I a God at hand, says the Lord, and not a God afar off? Can a man hide himself in secret places so that I cannot see him? says the Lord. I have heard what the prophets have said who prophesy lies in my name, saying, 'I have dreamed, I have dreamed!' How long shall there be lies in the heart of the prophets who prophesy lies, and who prophesy the deceit of their own heart, who think to make my people forget my name by their dreams which they tell one another, even as their fathers forgot my name for Baal? Let the prophet who has a dream tell the dream, but let him who has my Word speak my Word faithfully. (Jer. 23.23–8)

To the prophets, the Word of God was both external proclamation and internal presence, received into the mouth, inwardly digested and sweet as honey (Jer. 1.9; Ezek. 2.9—3.3). It was 'no mere thing' but rather 'the living, personal and free God'.[63]

God of the Jews

The history of Israel is in a sense the history of God. That is the crude and startling fact of Old Testament revelation. In the progress from Haran to Babylon and beyond is to be found the earthly progress of God himself, a progress which culminates in the incarnation of the Word, and the raising of humanity to share the divine life. In the Old Testament, God enters into human history through a covenantal relationship with a particular people, the Jews. And, so Jesus tells us, it is from this people that salvation comes (John 4.22). It was to the Hebrew people that God said 'You only have I known of all the families of the earth' (Amos 3.2); upon Israel God had 'set his heart in love' (Deut. 10.15; cf. 23.5).

Jewish experience of God, from Abraham to the present, has been the experience of people in solidarity with each other, responsible for each other. 'Where is your brother?' (Gen. 4.9) has remained, across the centuries, a fundamental test of discipleship. 'Unless your . . . brother comes down with you, you shall see my face no more' (Gen. 44.23) might be seen as God's own words to his people. For it is in community that God makes his presence known. The experience and vision of God is inseperable from the experience and vision of the brother/sister: to see our brothers and sisters in true perspective is to see something of the divine. In their desert experience of struggle, and in their attempt to embody both holiness and justice in the Law, the Jewish people came to know God not on the fringes, but in the midst of human society. Jewish theology can therefore be seen as a 'theology of recital', a proclamation of the acts of God. For the Jews, Word is inseparable from Act. It is in social history that God is revealed and that redemption occurs.

It is vital that we see the Christian understanding of God against the Old Testament background. The neglect of the Old Testament and of the essential 'Jewishness' of Christian theology and spirituality has led to the most appalling distortions of the gospel. The contempt for the material world and relapse into pagan approaches to matter, nature, and history; the 'privatizing' of God and the false interiority which reduces spiritual life to an inner experience of the individual; the loss of the link which joins social justice to spiritual insight: these and many other evils are connected with the neglect of the Old Testament roots of Christian faith. The Christian God is first of all a Jewish God.

The contrast with pagan notions of God's relationship with the world is striking. This is why 'one of the functions of the Old Testament in the church has always been its role as a bulwark against paganism'. For 'Israelite faith as represented in the earliest as well as in the latest literature was an utterly unique and radical departure from all contemporary pagan religions'.[64] This departure is seen particularly in relation to the powers of the natural world. In pagan religion, the life of the individual was an integral part of the sacred, rhythmical pattern of nature, a divine state of order and harmony, in which both humans and non-humans had their appointed place. Paganism was essentially a religion of hierarchy, order, and preservation of the *status quo*. However, the biblical God was revealed as Lord of nature, transcending the natural order. While his revelation is associated with thunder and lightning, wind and sea, the stress is on his use of these natural forces. Yet he remains beyond them all, and the unique relationship with Israel, involving an absolute demand and even jealousy, undermined and destroyed the whole basis of pagan religion. The doctrine of Yahweh's jealousy is of particular importance, for it introduces a tension at the heart of the spurious harmony of the pagan order, destroying man's integration into the structure of nature.

Biblical faith, therefore, could never be a religion of the *status quo* for its faithful adherents. Dynamic change and revolution are to be expected because God is a dynamic being, external to the processes of life, engaged in the active direction of history to his own goals. The tension which he places at the heart of existence excludes a peace of integration in the rhythmic cycle of nature.[65]

God's jealousy, it has been argued, was the source of the passion and vitality of Israel's faith.[66] Undoubtedly it was deeply subversive of the static character of paganism. The Jewish God therefore enjoyed a unique relationship with matter. He was also the Lord of history. Again, the contrast with paganism is very clear, for pagan religion had no doctrine of God in history, no doctrine of election, no covenant relation. Jewish theology sees knowledge of God as historical knowledge, but history means not simply general history, but salvation history, the history of God's dealings with Israel in specific acts and events. It has been said that history is the lengthened shadow of a man, and Israel, before it denoted a people, was an actual person, Jacob, the cheat (Gen. 27.36), who deceived his father, robbed his brother, and wrestled with God in a conflict from which he emerged wounded. The community of Israel, the community of salvation, received its name from this rather dubious character. And in a sense one can portray the entire history of the people as the lengthened shadow of Jacob, a prolonged wrestling with God until the light dawns, a process of perpetual interrogation and struggle. It is this history of persons and communities in conflict which provides the content of revelation. To neglect the Old Testament and the historical revelation is thus to fall prey to an idealist notion of God as pure spirit, a reversal to paganism. Today's 'Christian paganism', abandoning its Jewish insights of materialism and historicity, offers religion as an integrating process, a civic cement, a protection against disturbance. In so doing, it protects itself against the disruptive, disturbing God of Jewish and Christian history. The sense of disturbance and conflict is central to Jewish spirituality. Jewish religion could therefore never be merely the private spiritual experience of those who fit, uncritically and complacently, into secular society. It is perhaps this sense of wrestling with God and of struggling for the divine justice on earth which has made the Jews a stumbling block to those who seek a religion which sanctifies the *status quo* in the classic pagan mode. Such a religion offers no threat to the powers of evil. 'The Prince of Darkness is a gentleman to those who know their place. He has no objection to religion. He has not, save in the case of the Jews, found it a serious source of disquiet'.[67] In fidelity to their understanding of God, Jewish people today are deeply involved in the affairs of the material world and in the political sphere in a way which can be deeply shocking to those with a 'purely spiritual' idea of religion.[68]

The God of the Jews is Lord of creation and of history. But his relationship with the people of Israel finds its central focus in the idea of the covenant (*berith*). Walther Eichrodt[69] has shown the central role of the covenant in Old Testament theology, although he tends to limit the covenant relationship to that between God and Israel, neglecting the wider understanding of a covenant with humanity and with the natural world. However, it is the theme of covenant which is the key to the unity of the Old Testament and to the uniqueness of the faith of Israel. There was a disagreement about the nature of the covenant which is reflected in the Old Testament, between those who saw the covenant as established between God and the entire people of Israel (Exod. 19.3–6), and those who saw it as a covenant with Moses (34.27) and later with the royal house of David (2 Sam. 23.5). In Numbers 16 there is a record of conflict in the wilderness period about the authority of Moses and Aaron. Here the people complained to them, 'You have gone too far! For all the congregation are holy, every one of them, and the Lord is among them; why then do you exalt yourselves above the assembly of the Lord?' (Num. 16.3). The details of the differing understandings are not our concern here.[70]

In Old Testament times, covenants were established between individuals, between husbands and wives, between tribes, between monarchs, or between a ruler and his people. When such a covenant was established, there were rights and duties on both sides, and covenants were sealed by gifts, by a kiss or a handshake, or by the sharing of a common meal. The origins of the covenant between Yahweh and Israel are not clear. It is possible that there is a link with the Shechem deity Baal-berith ('Baal of the covenant') whose sanctuary was taken over for the worship of Yahweh (Judg. 8.33; 9.4; 36; cf. Josh. 24).[71] But it was the covenant at Sinai which was the central event in placing Israel in a relationship with God. This relationship depended upon the earlier redemptive work of God in the Exodus, and it was the combination of these events of deliverance and covenant which led to Israel's existence as the people of Yahweh. 'The redemption from Egypt received its *definitive interpretation* at the covenant-making on Sinai – and thus became the foundation and the orientation of all the mutual relations of Yahweh and his people.'[72] Exodus and covenant belong together, for the covenant was introduced by the proclamation of the Exodus event (Exod. 20.1–2). Like the Exodus, the covenant was an actual historical occurrence, not simply an idea. The biblical view of the relationship between God and

Israel is rooted in the specificity of time and place: at Sinai in the thirteenth century BC the relationship was established in covenant form. Moreover, the covenant was initiated by God himself, who called for obedience and fidelity as a response to the Exodus (Exod. 19.4–5). And yet the covenant also looked forward to the mighty acts of Yahweh in the future.

> And he said, 'Behold, I make a covenant. Before all your people I will do marvels, such as have not been wrought in all the earth or in any nation; and all the people among whom you are shall see the work of the Lord; for it is a terrible thing that I will do with you.' (Exod. 34.10)

Yet it was the present reality of Yahweh's presence on Mount Sinai which gave to the covenant the character of revelation as well as response to past events. The Exodus account makes it clear that God was really present, and that his presence was manifested to the people (Exod. 19.16–20) and, more intimately and uniquely, to Moses (20.18–21; 33.18–23; 34.5–6). Finally, the covenant was not between equals, for Yahweh was the Lord of the covenant. So there was a call for obedience (19.5–6). In the covenant relationship, Israel was to be a kingdom of priests and a holy nation.

It was to the Sinai covenant that the prophets looked back. Thus in Ezekiel, Yahweh addresses Jerusalem, using explicitly sexual language:

> Your origin and your birth are of the land of the Canaanites; your father was an Amorite and your mother a Hittite. And as for your birth, on the day you were born, your navel string was not cut, nor were you washed with water to cleanse you, nor rubbed with salt, nor swathed with bands. No eye pitied you, to do any of these things to you out of compassion; but you were cast out on the open field, for you were abhorred, on the day that you were born. And when I passed by you, and saw you weltering in your blood, I said to you in your blood, 'Live, and grow up like a plant of the field.' And you grew up and became tall and arrived at full maidenhood; your breasts were formed, and your hair had grown; yet you were naked and bare. When I passed by you again and looked upon you, behold you were at the age for love; and I spread my skirt over you and covered your nakedness; yea, I plighted my troth to you, and entered into a covenant with you, says the Lord God, and you became mine. (Ezek. 16.33–8)

However, there is also the hope of the new covenant, a hope which is expressed most clearly in Jeremiah:

> Behold, the days are coming, says the Lord, when I will make a
> new covenant with the house of Israel and the house of Judah, not
> like the covenant which I made with their fathers when I took them
> by the hand to bring them out of the land of Egypt, my covenant
> which they broke, though I was their husband, says the Lord. But
> this is the covenant which I will make with the house of Israel after
> those days, says the Lord: I will put my law within them, and I will
> write it upon their hearts; and I will be their God, and they shall be
> my people. And no longer shall each man teach his neighbour and
> each his brother, saying 'Know the Lord', for they shall all know
> me, from the least of them to the greatest, says the Lord; for I will
> forgive their iniquity, and I will remember their sin no more. (Jer.
> 31.31–4)

Only Jeremiah, and he only in this one passage, speaks so explicitly of
Yahweh's future relationship as a *new* covenant. However, Ezekiel
also speaks of a future 'covenant of peace' and he also echoes
Jeremiah's theme of a new age of the Spirit (Ezek. 37.26; 36.26f).

The Jews then are the covenant people: 'to them belong . . . the
covenants' (Rom. 9.4). Yet throughout the 'Christian' centuries, it
has been the Jews, the heirs of God's promises, recipients of the
revelation, who have been of all people the most despised and
rejected, often deprived even of human dignity. Christian believers
cannot escape the fact that anti-Semitism finds much of its theological
support within the Christian tradition itself. Viewing the Jews as the
murderers of the Son of God, and therefore as a people rejected by
God, Christian spirituality prepared the ground for the Nazi
atrocities. Even during the Nazi period, most German Christians
failed to see any theological problem in the attack on the Jews, a failure
which Karl Barth attributed in part to the neglect of the Old
Testament prophetic tradition.[73]

We need them to face the question: is Christian spirituality possible
after the holocaust? Or dare we even think that 'the furnaces of
Auschwitz . . . may be the fires in which the heart of mankind must be
purged anew'.[74] Ecclestone has suggested that Auschwitz and all that
it symbolizes represents the last chance for European Christians to
pray responsibly for mankind. It is essential that Christian spirituality
should recover from its false Gentile consciousness and rediscover the
Jewish roots of its faith in, and following of, God. Much Christian
theology, including much biblical study, has helped to sever the links
between the Old and New Testaments, thus disconnecting the history
of Israel from that of the Christian Church. This severance has
formed the basis for a whole pathology in which materialism and

spirituality, politics and prayer, are seen as opposites. To turn from such a deranged spiritual tradition to the faith of Israel, the faith of *our* fathers, is to begin the painful process of unlearning, and relearning what religion is about. 'To enter the inner world of the Jewish religion requires therefore an initial stripping, a deliberate unlearning of what religion is about, and a new definition of words.'[75] We need to rediscover the Old Testament as *Christian* Scripture, and the Christian God as a *Jewish* God. And this rediscovery is of the greatest urgency. In Ecclestone's words:[76]

Today, when the nations lurch in uncertain fashion towards the one world that their many achievements make possible, we must turn to the basic suggestion of Israel's faith with new force. It is the faith of a people for ever marching, a people of tents rather than a Temple, a people learning to read God's law in their hearts, a people committed to giving the stranger welcome, facing a new world with a deep trust in God. Our task today is the recovery of what is essentially a Jewish concept of man's destiny.

3

God of Jesus

No one has ever seen God; the only Son, who is in the bosom
of the Father, he has made him known.
John 1.18

Christians hold that, in the person and life of Jesus, a unique and supreme revelation of God has taken place. The God who has been revealed is identified with Yahweh, the God of Israel. Early heresies spoke of two gods, one of the Old Testament, one of the new; but Christian orthodoxy has insisted on *one* God, Creator, Redeemer, Sanctifier. In the Jesus event, so Christians insist, the God of the wilderness, the holy and just one, the God who revealed himself at Sinai, and who, through his Spirit, empowered and guided Israel, took flesh and tabernacled among us. In the Gospels, Jesus is referred to as the Son of Man, he announces the Kingdom of God, he addresses God as 'Father', and he promises eternal life to those who follow him.

The Man at His Right Hand

Christians believe that God is supremely revealed in the person of Jesus, that Jesus is in fact God made flesh, true God from true God. But how did Jesus see himself? In the Synoptic Gospels (Matthew, Mark and Luke), the most common title is that of 'Son of Man'. It occurs in the singular eighty-four times in the New Testament – thirty-one times in Matthew, fourteen in Mark, twenty-six in Luke, and twelve in John. But, while this title is so common in the Synoptics and in John, it occurs only three times in the rest of the New Testament (Acts 7.56; Rev. 1.13; 14.14) and not at all in St Paul. Again, it is noticeable that 'Son of Man' is described as Jesus' own expression, yet it is not used in the Gospels *about* Jesus, only *by* him. In fact, the early Church never addresses or invokes Jesus as Son of Man. It would seem, therefore, that in the term 'Son of Man' we are encountering a title which conveys and expresses the consciousness of Jesus himself about his identity and mission. Moreover, while the development of Christology occupied hundreds of years – indeed the process still goes on – there was, none the less, 'a direct line of continuity between Jesus' self-understanding and the Church's

Christological interpretation of him'.[1] In considering, first, the title of 'Son of Man', we are probably in touch with 'the oldest Christological traditions'.[2]

That Jesus used the expression 'Son of Man' is not in doubt. But did he use it about himself, or about some other, future, apocalyptic figure? Some have argued for the latter view. Our purpose here is not to enter into that ongoing debate, but rather to examine the uses of the term in the Gospels, the understandings of it to which Christian reflection over the centuries has led, and the relevance of it to the Christian understanding of the nature of the God who was revealed in Jesus. In Jesus' own use of the term, it is almost always '*the* Son of Man', in contrast to earlier Jewish usage, and there are good grounds for believing that Jesus originated this usage. However, the Son of Man sayings in the Gospels are of various types.

In the Synoptic Gospels, there are three main groups of sayings.[3] First, those which refer to the *apocalyptic Son of Man*. In these, the Son of Man is a future figure who comes from heaven. He is referred to in the third person, and the speaker is always Jesus. Thus whoever is ashamed of Jesus and his words, of him will the Son of Man be ashamed when he comes in glory (Mark 8.38). (In Matthew's version of this saying, 'Son of Man' is dropped, and Jesus speaks explicitly of himself in the first person. See Matt. 10.32-3.) The Son of Man sows good seed in the world and will send his angels at the close of the age to gather the chaff (Matt. 13.37-41). In the 'little apocalypse' in Mark 13, after the appearance of false prophets and of cosmic tribulation, it is said that the Son of Man will come with clouds, and with great power and glory (13.26). His coming will be like lightning flashing from east to west (Matt. 24.27; Luke 17.24), it will be sudden and unexpected (Matt. 24.37-9). The most famous of these future Son of Man sayings is that in Mark 14.62 where, in response to the High Priest's question, Jesus announces that the Son of Man will sit at the right hand of power and will come with the clouds of heaven.

Secondly, there are sayings which refer to *the suffering and death of Jesus*. The Son of Man, Jesus tells his disciples, must suffer many things, be killed, and after three days rise again (Mark 8.31; cf. 9.31; 10.33; Luke 9.22). His three-days' sojourn in the heart of the earth is compared to Jonah's period inside the whale (Matt. 12.40). Whether these sayings are original or not, undoubtedly the early Church identified the Son of Man with Jesus.

The third group of sayings is *more general*. The Son of Man is said to have authority to forgive sins (Mark 2.10), to be Lord of the Sabbath (2.28), to have come eating and drinking and to be the friend of tax collectors and sinners (Matt. 11.19), to be homeless with nowhere to lay his head (8.20). Here the identification between the Son of Man and Jesus is the obvious sense of these passages.

In the Gospel of John there are important differences. In the first Son of Man reference, Nathanael is told that he will see heaven opened, and the angels of God ascending and descending upon the Son of Man (1.51), a clear reference to Jacob's dream (Gen. 28.10–17). There is considerable emphasis on the future exaltation and glory of the Son of Man (3.14; 6.62; 12.23, 34; 13.31). However that glory is to be manifested on earth, the scene of judgement is brought into the present and is associated with Jesus' own presence (3.19). So Bultmann comments that 'Jesus is the Son of Man, not, as understood by Jewish and early Christian apocalyptic, as he who one day will come on the clouds of heaven, but in his earthly presence: for in this earthly presence, in which he enjoys continual communion with the Father, he shows to faith the miracle of his glory.'[4]

Again, in the dialogue with Nicodemus, Jesus explains that no one has ascended to heaven except the Son of Man who also descended from heaven (3.13). And this Son of Man must be lifted up, as Moses lifted up the serpent in the wilderness so that those who believe in him may have eternal life (3.14). Like the Servant in Second Isaiah who is to be lifted up and glorified (Isa. 52.13), the Son of Man is to experience his exaltation through death. Later, in the 'eucharistic chapter' of John 6, the Son of Man gives the food of eternal life, his own flesh and blood (6.27, 53), and will ascend to where he was before (6.62).

A most important reference is John 8.28: 'When you have lifted up the Son of Man, then you will know that I am he.' By lifting up Jesus in crucifixion, they will come to recognize him in his heavenly glory. More than that, they will recognize in Jesus the presence of the great 'I am'. For, in the exaltation of the Son of Man, the identity of him who said 'Before Abraham was, I am' (8.58) will be revealed. The Son of Man must be lifted up, Jesus insists (12.34), clearly referring to himself (12.32), and in the lifting up is the glory of the Son of Man (12.23f).

Jesus then spoke of himself as the Son of Man, at least in some of the sayings. But how would his hearers have understood this term? And what were the sources which he might have used? The Hebrew term *ben' adam* simply denoted a member of the human race. To be a son of man was to share full humanity (Num. 23.19; Ps. 8.4). It is in this sense that we find the term used in Ezekiel, where it occurs eighty-seven times. In Ezekiel it is a form of address and it seems unlikely that this has in any way influenced its usage in the Gospels. In fact, the only explicit reference to the Son of Man sayings in the Old

Testament by Jesus is to Daniel 7.13. Thus in Mark 14.62 we read: 'And Jesus said, "I am; and you will see the Son of Man sitting at the right hand of power, and coming with the clouds of heaven."' There is dispute about the identity of Daniel's Son of Man. While some argue that the reference is to 'the saints of the Most High' (7.18), the persecuted, loyal Israelites, others claim that hosts of angels and heavenly beings are the subject. But the central point of the passage concerns the vindication of man by God and the need for faithfulness to divine vocation. In Rabbinic literature, the text in Daniel 7.13 is invariably interpreted with reference to the Messiah. It seems probable that it is Daniel which provides the context for Jesus' use of 'Son of Man'. However, in Daniel, the Son of Man does not sit at God's right hand. This phrase comes from Psalm 110.1, and in Psalm 80.17 the Son of Man is identified with 'the man of thy right hand'. In Mark 14.62 these different scriptures are fused together.

Another important source, it is alleged, for the 'Son of Man' sayings is the apocalyptic Jewish work known as 1 Enoch, a product of the first century BC. Here the Son of Man is a supernatural figure who exists from the beginning of creation, and is given power and judgement over all things (48.2; 62.6; 69.27). In language similar to that of the New Testament, the Son of Man is described as 'a staff to the righteous whereon to stay themselves . . . the light of the Gentiles and the hope of those that are troubled at heart' (48.4).

There are other uses of 'Son of Man' in the Old Testament (e.g. Num. 23.9; Ps. 8.4) where the point is one of contrast between the frailty and weakness of men, and the transcendent glory of God. There are references also to the 'Son of Man' in gnostic writings, and some have related the Gospel sayings to the gnostic myth of the Primal Man.[5] However, there is virtually no evidence for the use of the definite article before 'Son of Man' in biblical or post-biblical writing apart from the use by Jesus himself, and it has therefore been argued that what appeared in the teaching of Jesus was the use of the *title* 'Son of Man', a Galilean Aramaic usage, as a circumlocution for 'the self'.[6]

The debate about the origins of the Son of Man language shows no signs of abating, but it is not our concern here. The crucial point is that the term 'Son of Man' represents a major element in the Gospel teaching about God, his relationship to Jesus and his relationships with men and women who come to him through Jesus. Subsequent Christian reflection on the theme can be summarized briefly as follows.

First, the term 'Son of Man' expresses Jesus' *essential unity with mankind* and above all with the weak and humble'.[7] There are strong corporate aspects to the title. The Son of Man is destined to suffer and to give himself in service to the world. But, beyond this servant role, he is 'the true self of the human race'[8] which others may share. Through this man, all humankind may share a new relationship with God. The Son of Man is thus both a personal and a social symbol, the symbol of the solidarity of God with the lowliness and anguish of humanity.

Secondly, the title expresses Jesus' vocation as *the representative of Israel*. The term 'Son of Man' is a representative term. T. W. Manson has claimed that it is the final term of a series of concepts – Remnant, Servant of the Lord, and the 'I' of the Psalms – which stress the Remnant theme. The Son of Man then stands for the manifestation of God's Kingdom in the corporate personality of a dedicated people, the saints of the Most High.[9]

Thirdly, the title contains the element of *glory and of future judgement*. Whether there is direct influence on the New Testament from Daniel or from Enoch, there is no doubt that subsequent Christian reflection came to see the exalted and glorified Christ in terms of the heavenly Son of Man and expected his return.

Fourthly, in John in particular, the Son of Man is himself the place of *revelation of the glory of God*. There are, because of this very fact, real difficulties in accepting some of the Johannine sayings as the actual historical words of Jesus. For instance, how could one who was truly man utter the words in John 8.58. 'Before Abraham was, I am'? Or speak of the glory which he had with the Father before creation (17.5)? Can such sayings, if they were uttered by Jesus himself, be reconciled with a doctrine of incarnation? On the other hand, it is obvious that the author of the Gospel wrote with the stated intention of defending the truth of Jesus' divine origin and nature (1.1–14; 5.18; 10.33), and so there are more explicit claims to divine status placed into the mouth of Jesus than figure in the Synoptic writers. Most scholars hold that the Fourth Gospel ought not to be read simply as historical reporting but rather as a statement and defence of the claims of faith.

Thus in the Gospel symbol of the Son of Man we see the identification of God with a suffering man, a man in whom the vocation of Israel is fulfilled, a man who sits at God's right hand and shares his glory. The association of suffering with the Son of Man and with Christ has led some to make a link with the 'Suffering Servant' of Second Isaiah. T. W. Manson has spoken of a 'servant Messiah',[10] while other writers have seen in the Gospels a fusion of Son of Man, Messiah, and Servant themes in the person of Jesus.[11] Again, like the Son of Man theme itself, this is a complex debate. However, the Servant figure in Isaiah 52.13—53.12 is not a servant of humanity, but rather a *slave* of God. In the Greek of the New Testament, slave is the correct translation of the word *doulos*, while the word *diakonos* means a servant, one who serves, a minister. The words are quite different but are often confused in the English versions. Whatever may have been the use made of Second Isaiah, the theme of Jesus as the *diakonos*, the one who comes to serve and to wash the feet of his disciples is clearly present in the Gospels. So Jesus addresses his followers:

> The kings of the Gentiles exercise lordship over them; and those in authority over them are called benefactors. But not so with you; rather let the greatest among you become as the youngest, and the leader as one who serves. For which is the greater, one who sits at table, or one who serves? Is it not the one who sits at table? But I am among you as one who serves (*ho diakonon*). (Luke 22.25–7)

Service is emphasized as a central mark of discipleship. Those who would be great must be servants (Matt. 20.25), those who are last will be first (Mark 10.31). It is in the passage in Mark 10 that we see the link between service, suffering, and sacrifice. Here Jesus tells the disciples:

> You know that those who are supposed to rule over the Gentiles lord it over them, and their great men exercise authority over them. But it shall not be so among you; but whoever would be great among you must be your servant, and whoever would be first among you must be slave of all. For the Son of Man also came not to be served but to serve, and to give his life as a ransom for many. (Mark 10.42–5)

This saying, linking the servanthood of Jesus with his sacrificial death as Son of Man, comes as the climax of a passage about baptism. Jesus here speaks of the baptism with which he *is* being baptized and the cup which he *is* drinking (the tenses are present), and goes on to relate baptism to death. He sees his baptism as 'his whole existence in the form of a servant'.[12]

Thus the death of the Son of Man is the culmination of a life of lowly service in which God's presence is manifested in the humility of Jesus and his identification with the poor and the outcast. This identification with the poor and the outcast is an important factor of the revelation of God's character, for the God of Israel is the God of the *anawim*, the little people. So early in the ministry of Jesus he is attacked for eating with tax collectors and sinners (Mark 2.16). He proclaims that tax collectors and prostitutes will go into the Kingdom before the devout (Matt. 21.31) and that it is sinners, not the righteous, whom he has come to call (Matt. 11.19). He is accused of being a glutton and a drunk as well as a friend of sinners (Matt. 11.16–19; Luke 7.31–5). He allows his disciples to break the Sabbath regulations (Mark 2.23–4) and does so himself by acts of healing (Mark 3.1–6). In John, he even justifies his Sabbath healing by asserting that God his Father also works on the Sabbath, thus 'making himself equal with God' (John 5.15–18). His friendships with women would certainly have been seen as scandalous (Mark 15.40–41; Luke 8.1–3; 10.38–42; 11.27–8). The hero of his most famous parable, the Good Samaritan, was a member of a despised half-breed, sectarian group, and Jesus himself was called a Samaritan (John 8.49), that is, a heretic, as well as a blasphemer (Mark 2.7), devil-possessed (3.22) and a subversive (Luke 23.2). So, like the Suffering Servant (Isa. 53.3, 12), Jesus was despised and rejected, to be numbered finally with the transgressors. Like the Good Samaritan, Jesus goes out of his way to accept as his neighbours, his brothers and sisters, the broken and rejected members of the human family, and so becomes one with the homeless and rootless of all times and places. It is to such as these that the Kingdom of God belongs.

God and His Kingdom

That the theme of the good news of the Kingdom of God is the heart of the message of Jesus is not in doubt today, and there is an encouraging and highly significant recovery of the centrality of the Kingdom in much Christian thought, both catholic and evangelical. In 1922 Canon Percy Widdrington predicted that the recovery of the centrality of the Kingdom as the 'regulative principle of theology' would bring about a new Reformation.[13] Certainly the theme dominates the thinking of the new radical evangelical movement which is among the most important of the renewal movements in the contemporary church. As one of its leading spokesmen has written:[14]

> The proclamation of the New Testament is the gospel of the kingdom, a gospel of a 'new order', a 'new creation', a 'new world', a 'new age', as it is variously referred to by the biblical writers. Jesus proclaims that a new age has come and calls us to be free of former allegiances, attachments, securities and assumptions in the present age, to break from our bondage to the standards of the world that are passing away. Clearly, the New Testament evangel is something much more than a gospel of individual salvation and personal fulfilment. The evangel is something much more than a gospel of social action. It is even more than an attempted synthesis which combines a personal gospel with social reform. In fact, the

meaning of the gospel that dominates the New Testament is not usually the same as the meaning of the various gospels that dominate the evangelism and preaching of our churches. The gospel of the kingdom is the central message of the New Testament. The inauguration of a whole new order in Jesus Christ and the establishing of a new peoplehood whose common life bears witness to that new order in history is what the New Testament message seems to be all about. The proclamation is not a personal gospel, not a social gospel, not even a gospel of 'both', but rather the gospel of a new order and a new people. The evangel is not merely a set of principles, ethics, and moral teachings. It is about a Person and the meaning of his coming.

In order to make sense of this Kingdom theme we need to return briefly to the Old Testament.

Whatever disagreements there have been, and still are, among biblical scholars, it is agreed that the origins of the symbol of the Kingdom of God lie in the Jewish theology of the Old Testament. 'The roots of the symbol Kingdom of God lie in the ancient Near Eastern myth of the Kingship of God.'[15] In the Old Testament we read of the concrete activity of God the ruler (Exod. 25.11–13; Pss. 93; 97; 145.11). It has been said that 'elsewhere the king was a god, in Israel it was God who was King'.[16] The prophetic tradition in particular rejected the idea of sacral kingship, for the eschatological King undermined the claims of present earthly rulers. 'God's kingship in most of the ancient Near East was an ideological support for earthly states. In Israel exactly the opposite conclusion was drawn from Yahweh's kingship.'[17] The contrast between the freedom of God's rule and the slavery of earthly monarchy is brought out in a remarkable anarchist parable'[18] in the Book of Judges (Judg. 8.22–3; 9.7–15). According to this parable, the olive, the fig and the vine rejected the application that they should abandon their natural lives in order to rule over the trees. Only the idle bramble accepted the lure of monarchy. The hostility to monarchy is further illustrated in Samuel's attempt to dissuade the people of Israel from following pagan ways and choosing a king. In doing so, they were rejecting Yahweh as King over them (1 Sam. 8.7).

It is in the writings of the prophets that the idea of the Kingdom of God as a future eschatological reality first appears (Mic. 2.12; 4.1–7; Isa. 24.21–3; 33.22; 52.7–10; Zeph. 3.14–20; Obad. 21, etc.). However, the normal Jewish term was not 'Kingdom of God' but rather 'Age to Come'. It was the theme of a new age, a 'good time coming', which was central to prophetic yearning. There is not much evidence that the theme of kingship was given specifically theological connotations before the Book of Daniel. But the theme of the 'Kingdom of God' was from the start theological. *Malkuth Shamayim* is in fact a late Jewish euphemism for 'God'. It was 'from the start a purely theological conception formed in late Judaism, not a transference of the secular term *malkuth* to the religious sphere'.[19] The Kaddish prayer used in the synagogue – and used there in the time of Jesus – is so close to the opening clauses of the Lord's Prayer that some have suggested conscious adaptation.

Magnified and sanctified be his great name in the world which he has created according to his will. May he establish his Kingdom in your lifetime and in your days and in the lifetime of all the house of Israel even speedily and at a near time.[20]

The actual term 'Kingdom of God', however, remains rare in Judaism before the time of Jesus.[21] But the reality behind the symbol was very clearly present. Yahweh is Lord of heaven and of earth, and his power and glory are to be manifested within a transformed and glory-filled creation.

There has been a debate for many years about the sources of the Kingdom and Son of Man themes in the teaching of Jesus. Schweitzer encouraged the belief in a sharp contrast between the prophets who, he argued, hoped for an earthly messiah and an earthly kingdom, and the apocalyptic writers who pushed both the messiah and the kingdom into a transcendent and otherworldly realm. Bultmann and his followers maintained this position. On the other hand, T. F. Glasson has fiercely attacked the dependence on Schweitzer's ideas as a 'colossal blunder'.[22] The term 'Kingdom of God', he rightly says, does not occur in any of the apocalyptic writers, nor is there any reference to any of these writers in the Gospels or in Paul – indeed there is only one reference in the whole of the New Testament (Jude 14–15, citing Enoch 1.9). Nevertheless, since Schweitzer's day, the view that Jesus based his teaching on the Kingdom on late Jewish apocalyptic has become widespread. Jesus 'accepts the late Jewish view', Schweitzer wrote,[23] and, shortly before his death, he claimed that Jesus had 'spiritualized' the doctrine of the Kingdom.[24]

Whatever may be the facts about the sources of Jesus' teaching, it is important to stress that the apocalyptic tradition did not lose sight of the earthly context of redemption. So the late Norman Perrin wrote

It is universally acknowledged that Jewish apocalyptic in general envisages the earth as the stage for the final act of the eschatological drama... The earth may be described as purged, transformed renewed, even recreated, but it is nonetheless the earth, not a transcendent realm beyond it.

Against this 'there is not to be found in Palestinian Judaism at the time of Christ any real evidence for a belief in a state of salvation to be experienced in a transcendent realm beyond time and space'.[25] Thus, while late Jewish apocalyptic is of crucial importance in understanding the background to Jesus' teaching, it needs to be set against the context of the prophetic tradition and its vision of a new and transformed world order. The violent contrast between prophecy and apocalyptic has been overdrawn. If apocalyptic vision provides the framework for the teaching of Jesus, it is to the prophetic hope of a new and transformed world that we must look for its source.

However we should not write off the apocalyptic movement, as many do, as the deluded fantasies of disillusioned escapists. Robert Carroll, in a recent study, has described apocalyptic as 'the triumph of imagination over reality',[26] but he goes on to point out that it did keep the vision of a new world alive. In apocalyptic vision there is a mingling of heavenly and earthly. Their yearning for a new world is not necessarily a negation of this world so much as a renunciation of a fallen world order. 'Whether this conception of history is to be understood as a necessary counterbalance and a breakthrough to a new theological perspective or whether it is a fatal distortion of Yahwistic faith is a question which is still far from finding an answer.'[27] In apocalyptic it is the radical discontinuity between the old age and the new which is stressed, and at times this sense of conflict becomes a withdrawal into a religious ghetto. At other times it takes the form of revolutionary militancy. In New Testament times we see the conflicting options of Essene purity and Zealot revolt. The contrast between Jesus and the Essenes is very marked, while the Gospels themselves make a distinction between the way of Jesus and that of the Zealots. How then are we to understand the teaching of Jesus about the Kingdom of God?

However Jesus may have viewed the Kingdom, there can be no doubt whatever that it was the heart of his preaching and message. Today both conservative and liberal scholars agree on this fact. 'The central aspect of the teaching of Jesus was that concerning the Kingdom of God. Of this there can be no doubt, and today no scholar does in fact doubt it.'[28] 'The whole message of Jesus focuses upon the Kingdom of God.'[29] 'New Testament scholars generally agree that the burden of Jesus' message was the Kingdom of God.'[30] Jeremias adds the comment that 'Jesus not only made the term the central theme of his proclamation but in addition filled it with a new content which is without analogy.'[31] But the critical question is: what did Jesus mean? What kind of kingdom did he proclaim? The facts can best be summarized by a series of negations.

Firstly, the Kingdom of God in the New Testament is not an otherworldly hope. 'That this Kingdom is not just an invisible spiritual abstraction peopled with ethereal redeemed souls is very clear in the New Testament.'[32] The saying 'My kingdom is not of this world' (John 18.36) is the text most often cited in support of the view that the Kingdom of God has nothing to do with this earth, that it is in fact unearthly. Yet clearly this cannot be the meaning: in fact, it is precisely because the Kingdom does not originate in this world-order that its impact upon the world takes the form of conflict and collision. The Kingdom is otherworldly only in the sense that its origin and values lie in the divine order, and because of this its earthly appearance is marked by struggle. Yet that struggle is the struggle for a new world, for the Kingdom is to come 'on earth as in heaven' (Matt. 6.10). The meek shall inherit the earth (Matt. 5.5). The parables of the Kingdom use earthly images and are to do with relationships on earth. In this concern for the transforming of earth and of matter, the New Testament continues the prophetic emphasis, 'for the prophets do not have much to say about the Kingdom except in its earthly manifestation'.[33]

Secondly, the Kingdom of God is not seen as a gradual evolutionary movement. However dear that gradualist model is to Christian people, both liberal and conservative, it does not find its basis in the Gospels. The parable of the leaven is frequently invoked to support this view, and the mustard seed is also cited. But the point of the parable of the mustard seed is not gradual growth, but the contrast between the hidden Kingdom and the coming Kingdom which will cover the earth. The parables as a whole emphasize suddenness and surprise rather than gradual growth. As for the leaven,

> the truth is not that of the gradual permeation of the world by the kingdom. Scripture nowhere else teaches this. The truth is the same as that of the mustard seed. In its present manifestation, the Kingdom of God is like a handful of leaven in a big bowl of dough. The dough swallows up the leaven so that one is hardly aware of its presence. . . But one should not be deceived thereby: some day the whole earth will be filled with God's Kingdom even as the leavened dough fills the entire bowl. The means by which this end is accomplished is no element in the parable.[34]

The 'concept of gradualness and slow development is a modern and not a biblical idea'.[35] A. M. Hunter has suggested that those who associate leaven with gradualness and gentle progress have not seen leaven at work. The Kingdom, he reminds us,

> is being compared not to leaven, but to what happens when you put leaven into a batch of meal – a heaving, panting mass, swelling and bursting with bubbles, and all the commotion indicating something alive and at work below: in one phrase, a ferment, pervasive, dynamic, resistless. Even so, when God's rule enters the world there must arise a disturbing process which ultimately nothing in the world can escape.[36]

Thirdly, in the New Testament the Kingdom is not an individual, inner experience. The interior view of the Kingdom was held by Harnack,[37] and became a popular view among Christians of widely differing theological traditions. *Entos humōn* (Luke 17.21) has often been cited in support of this view that the Kingdom is *within* us, an interior disposition. Certaintly the meaning 'within you' is possible. However, nowhere else, either in the Old Testament or in Judaism or elsewhere in the New Testament, do we find the idea that the Kingdom is an inner experience. 'Such a spiritualizing understanding' says Jeremias,[38] 'is ruled out both for Jesus and for the early Christian tradition'. Men shall come from the east and west and sit down with Abraham, Isaac, and Jacob (Matt. 8.11) – in what? In the quiet reign of God within the individual heart? The idea reduces the text to nonsense.

Fourthly, the Kingdom of God is not wholly future. The late C. H. Dodd may have over-emphasized the present reality of the Kingdom to the neglect of the future.[39] Today, however, 'there is a growing consensus in New Testament scholarship that the Kingdom of God is in some sense both present and future'.[40] 'Simply to call the coming Kingdom, spoken of in the Bible, a future Kingdom is to impoverish its meaning almost to the point of destroying it.'[41] In the preaching and ministry of Jesus, the Kingdom has come near, the future is drawn into the present, and we taste the powers of the Age to Come. The theme of the 'two ages' is sometimes used to distinguish the Kingdom of God from the kingdoms of this age in a chronological way. But this is not the contrast which the Bible makes, and to do so is 'a betrayal of biblical theology'.[42] The point is rather that the new age, the Kingdom, eternal life, is already present. 'If I by the finger of God cast out demons, then has the Kingdom of God come upon you' (Luke 11.20). Now is the *krisis* of the world (John 12.31), it is now that Satan falls like lightning from heaven (Luke 10.18). The Kingdom is a present reality, not simply a future hope.

Finally, it must be emphasized that the Kingdom of God is not the same as the Church. The parables in particular indicate the distinction between the visible Church of this age and the Kingdom of God. Many who prophesied and cast out demons in the name of Christ will be rejected from the Kingdom (Matt. 7.22f) while those who served Christ in the persons of the oppressed will often have done so unawares (Matt. 25.44). The Church stands in relation to the Kingdom as herald and foretaste, a distinction which comes out clearly in the prayer in the Didache: 'Remember, Lord, thy church ... gather it together ... to thy Kingdom which thou hast prepared for it' (Didache 10.5). But it is the Kingdom, not the Church, which is the end of creation, and in the redeemed, renewed creation there is no temple (Rev. 21.22). The Church looks beyond itself to the Kingdom of God as a kind of 'eschatological sign erected in the world'.[43] But membership of the Church is no guarantee of sharing in the Kingdom, for, as Conrad Noel wrote, 'many who assist at Mass will most assuredly be damned'.[44]

In the proclamation by Jesus of the Kingdom of God we have the living heart of his message, and the Church is only true to itself when it points beyond itself to that Kingdom. 'The Church, if we rightly understand it, lives always from the proclamation of her own provisional character and her progressive historical surrender to the coming Kingdom of God towards which she moves like a pilgrim.'[45] Thus, like Abraham and the wilderness people, the Church is always on the move towards a God of the future, who draws history towards himself, and whose character is already manifested in the present reality of his Kingdom. For that manifestation, the period during which the Son of God was revealed in human flesh is of crucial importance.

The Christ, the Son of the Living God

The creeds of the Christian Church speak of Jesus as the Son of God. 'We believe in one God, the Father almighty... We believe in one Lord, Jesus Christ, the only Son of God.' However, the term 'Son of God' was not original to Jesus, but a later development from reflection on the Son of Man in his relationship to God. In itself, it was a title with no major transcendental significance. In the Old Testament it was used to describe angelic beings (Dan. 3.25; Job 38.7; Ps. 82.6) though it was also a Messianic term (Pss. 2; 80; 89.26f). In the Gospels, the identity of Jesus as Son of God is proclaimed by devils (Mark 3.11; 5.7) and by the heavenly voice (Mark 1.11; 9.7) as well as by Peter at Caesarea Philippi (Matt. 16.16). Indeed it is only by the devils that he is addressed as such in the Synoptic Gospels. But does Jesus see himself in this way?

Certainly it is clear that the Synoptic writers saw Jesus as God's Son, recognized as such at Jordan, manifesting his power as such throughout his ministry and in his trial, and vindicated as such in his death and resurrection. At the baptism he is addressed, 'Thou art my beloved Son' (Mark 1.11; Luke 3.22; cf. Matt. 3.17: 'This is my beloved Son...'). The words are reminiscent of various Old Testament texts (Ps. 2.7; Isa. 42.1; 44.2) in which there is the notion of messianic status and of servanthood. But it is possible that the words 'beloved Son' also recall the descriptions of Isaac, son of Abraham (Gen. 22.2, 12, 16) and that there is therefore the idea of personal relationship. If this is so 'the saying probably contains more than a messianic element, and it leads beyond messiahship to that personal relationship to God which is basic for the self-understanding of Jesus'.[46] The same words are repeated at the transfiguration (Mark 9.7; Matt. 17.5; Luke 9.35). Here the face of Jesus shines like the sun, and he is accompanied by Moses and Elijah, the messianic witnesses. The scene is reminiscent of the revelation of God's glory at Sinai. Here, however, Jesus shares that glory.

It is clear from the Gospel evidence that Jesus, in his prayers, addressed God as *Abba*, Father. Jeremias points out that he did so in *all* his prayers.[47] From the prayers of Jesus, 'Abba' entered the liturgical vocabulary of the apostolic Church (Rom. 8.15; Gal. 4.6). This use of 'Abba' is actually remarkable. It is an Aramaic usage and is without parallel in contemporary Judaism. It represents a relationship of intense intimacy, an exclusive relationship with God. When Jesus addresses God as 'Abba', it is as '*my* Father', expressing a relationship essentially different from that of others. And in this usage we may justifiably assume that Jesus was expressing his own experience of God. From its central place in the prayer of Jesus, the *Abba* formula entered the liturgical vocabulary of the apostolic Church (Rom. 8.15; Gal. 4.6). But Christians can only address God as 'Abba' in so far as they are incorporated into Christ; their relationship is derived from his. And that relationship, as we see it expressed in the Gospel narratives, was unique: the whole life of Jesus was lived *in* the Father. Abba then is the term which most powerfully expresses the consciousness of the divine sonship of Jesus. It is, according to Jean Galot, the key to the significance of the great 'I am' sayings. 'The name *Abba* thus has a primordial force which illuminates all the expressions of the consciousness of Jesus.'[48]

However it is wrong to see Jesus' use of the idea of God's fatherhood as being in itself a new idea. Nor does he restrict the fatherhood of God to the devout or to some inner circle of disciples. God is the Father of the evil and the good, the just and the unjust (Matt. 5.45;

21.28–32). But it is in the pursuit of the commandment of love and in prayer for one's enemies that we become worthy of the status of sonship. Indeed, perfection is the goal of sonship since our Father is himself perfect (Matt. 5.44ff). On the other hand, Jesus nowhere speaks of God as 'our Father' except in his instructions to his disciples (Matt. 6.9). It is always as 'my Father and your Father', the latter relationship depending upon the former. It is through Jesus that we have access to the Father, and it is his relationship with the Father which is central to his understanding of his life and ministry. While some modern writers have laid emphasis on the role of Jesus as a 'free man', it is simply not possible to separate that freedom from his dependence upon God.

> We have no evidence of Jesus' freedom apart from evidence that his freedom was based upon his life for God the Father. The freedom of Jesus was a God-oriented freedom. He was not just free, he was free for a reason, and that reason structured his life. Jesus was showing through his freedom that there is a source of life beyond the world, obedience to which makes one free in the world. His freedom *is* reference to a source beyond the world, to the Father.[49]

It is only through his acceptance and assertion of the dependence on and attachment to God alone that he is able to be free from temptations to seek worldly power and free from the ultimate oppression of death. Alan Richardson claimed that 'there is little in the Synoptic Gospels which bears directly on the theme of man's knowledge of God', but he went on to point to one Gospel saying which is so important that 'everything else in the New Testament that deals with this subject might be regarded as commentary upon it'.[50] The saying is contained in Matthew 11.27. Luke 10.22:

> All things have been delivered to me by my Father; and no one knows the Son except the Father, and no one knows the Father except the Son and any one to whom the Son chooses to reveal him.

There is no comparable passage elsewhere in the Synoptics, and some have therefore seen it as a fragment of gnostic origin.[51] But it is entirely consistent with the rest of Jesus' teaching. So, while it is probably not original, its presence here is an accurate précis of how Jesus saw his relation to God the Father.

From apostolic times, Jesus has been spoken of, and proclaimed, as the Christ, the anointed One. While such usage is common in the earliest Christian preaching, it is not common in the Gospel accounts, although Peter proclaims Jesus as the Christ at Caesarea Philippi (Mark 8.29; Matt. 16.16; Luke 9.20). However, Mark tells us that

Jesus forbade his disciples to speak of this (Mark 8.30), and he himself does not speak of himself as the Christ (apart from the two references in Matt. 23.10 and Mark 9.41 which are from secondary sources). Christ, Messiah, was not at this time a divine or even supernatural title, but was associated with an act of earthly liberation, with the restoration of Israel. Whether Jesus ever specifically accepted the title is not clear. When asked by the High Priest about the claim to messianic status, he seems to have accepted it (Mark 14.61; Matt. 26.63) though this may simply reflect the early Church's view. Yet within a generation of the crucifixion the name 'Christian' was being used in Antioch (Acts 11.26), and King Agrippa II knows and understands this usage (26.28). In view of the clear centrality of the identification of Jesus with the Christ/Messiah in the early Church's preaching, it is significant that there is so little evidence in the Synoptics, or even in John, for an explicit claim from the lips of Jesus himself. Had there been more evidence to produce, the early Church would surely have produced it in support of their belief. In the Synoptics, however, there is a rejection of the title 'Son of David' (Mark 12.35–7) and a suggestion that the Messiah might still be awaited in the final days (Mark 13.6; Matt. 24.5). Even in John, while there is an identification of the Christ with Jesus (4.25; 17.3) there is still no public claim by Jesus to this identity. It was out of the experience of what Jesus had achieved, in his ministry, death, and resurrection, and out of reflection on this achievement in the light of the Jewish hope, that the early Christians came quickly to see Jesus as the Messiah.

How then did Jesus see his ministry? His first sermon at Nazareth is of central importance (Luke 4.16–30). Here Jesus cites a key passage in Isaiah (61.1–2). He

> ... found the place where it was written,
> 'The Spirit of the Lord is upon me,
> because he has anointed me to preach good news to the poor.
> He has sent me to proclaim release to the captives
> and recovering of sight to the blind,
> to set at liberty those who are oppressed,
> to proclaim the acceptable year of the Lord.'
> And he closed the book, and gave it back to the attendant, and sat down; and the eyes of all in the synagogue were fixed on him. And he began to say to them, 'Today this scripture has been fulfilled in your hearing.' (Luke 4.18–21)

Now Jewish thought placed far more importance upon the messianic *functions* than it did upon the person or title of the Messiah himself:

The literature of Judaism, both biblical and post-biblical, evidences a much greater interest in the Messianic Age itself and in the activity of God during the Age than in the person or persons whom God would use to bring it about and to accomplish his purposes. The semitic mind thinks more in terms of ultimates than secondary agency and of functions than persons, resulting in an emphasis upon the fact and character of the coming Age more than in the nature or personality of God's anointed instrument to bring it about.[52]

This is not to say that the title of a personal Messiah, associated with the coming of the messianic age, is absent from Judaism. Indeed it was becoming more important in the period immediately prior to the ministry of Jesus.[53] Nevertheless if we are to understand the role of Jesus as the One whom God has anointed, that is, as the Christ, it is to his work, rather than to his claims to title, that we should look.

Now the sermon in Luke 4 has at its background not only the eschatological hope of Isaiah 61, but also the Year of Jubilee of Leviticus 25. Jesus is clearly setting his ministry in an eschatological perspective and himself as the agent of the New Age. It can be said therefore that this fact 'clearly demands the analysis of this passage along christological lines'.[54] Luke is presenting Jesus as the Messiah, and the Nazareth sermon as 'the messianic programme'.[55] God has *anointed* (*enchrisen*, christened) Jesus to be the bearer of the Spirit, for the result of anointing was the coming of the Spirit. The messianic age was an age of the Spirit's outpouring. Thus Jesus in his sermon initiates the messianic age in which the Kingdom of God was to be manifested and the Holy Spirit was to be poured out.

Again, just as 'Christ' becomes the key title of Jesus in the preaching of the apostolic Church, so 'Jesus is Lord' (Rom. 10.8) becomes the central pre-baptismal formula. Yet in the Gospels, the title *kyrios* is not of major importance. Thus in Matthew it is rare, and where it occurs, usually refers to God. Jesus was probably not called 'Lord' to a significant extent before the resurrection. He is addressed as *kyrie* but so is Pontius Pilate (Matt. 27.63). But only the disciples call him Lord. Judas, for example, calls Jesus 'Rabbi' (26.25) while the Scribes and Pharisees call him 'Teacher'. So Matthew probably sees *kyrios* as a major title. Yet, as with the messianic formula, it is the function and the achievement of Jesus which is central. Through reflection of what Jesus *did*, the disciples came to assert more precisely who he *was* and *is*.

The ministry of Jesus is therefore of fundamental importance for Christian teaching about the character of God and our relationship with him. Jesus' experience of God is crucial to our faith for it is through Jesus that we have access to the Father. In the Gospels, we see both Jesus' sense of intimacy with the dependence upon his Father, a relationship expressed prayerfully in the formula 'Abba', and also his manifestation of the powers of the messianic age, the age of the Spirit, through his preaching of the Kingdom, his teaching, his healings and his exorcisms. While it is possible to *describe* Jesus by use of the traditional titles of prophet, rabbi, or exorcist, there remains an element of 'otherness' which eludes labelling. Certainly, Jesus was a prophet, and recent study has shown how important was the theme of the Spirit-filled prophet in the growth of Christology.[56] Yet Jesus nowhere appeals to the classical prophetic formulae. Again, Jesus is undoubtedly a supremely able teacher, and yet he confronts the literal texts of the Law with his own sense of God's presence, even asserting his freedom over the Law. And his exorcisms are of central importance in the Galilean ministry. But there are none of the characteristics of the traditional exorcist about Jesus. The exorcisms point beyond themselves to the coming of the Kingdom (Matt. 12.28; Luke 11.20). But it was above all in the death and resurrection of Jesus, and in the subsequent experience of his abiding life in the midst of the Christian community, that the early Christians saw the 'otherness' of Jesus which, without reducing the importance of these roles, yet moved beyond them. As Moule has written:[57]

> A person who had recently been crucified, but is found to be alive, with 'absolute' life, the life of the age to come, and is found, moreover, to be an inclusive, all-embracing presence – such a person is beginning to be described in terms appropriate to nothing less than God himself.

The Word of Eternal Life

The Gospel of John has been seen as different from the Synoptics from the time of Clement's description of it as a 'spiritual gospel' and Origen's claim that the conveying of spiritual truth involves an abandonment of strict historical accuracy.[58] Many have seen in it gnostic and Greek influences, alien to the Jewish roots of the Gospel. Yet this Gospel is steeped in Jewish history and theology and in a deeply Jewish view of the relationship of God and the world. The Prologue, and in particular the first five verses of the Gospel, is a kind of microcosm of the theme of the entire work:

> In the beginning was the Word, and the Word was with God, and the Word was God. He was in the beginning with God; all things

were made through him, and without him was not anything made
that was made. In him was life, and the life was the light of men.
The light shines in the darkness, and the darkness has not
overcome it. (John 1.1–5)

The Prologue has been called 'a philosophical rationale of the main
thesis of the Gospel'.[59] At the centre of this thesis is the struggle of
light and darkness. Thus in the first five verses

> ... the Word, Life and Light are set in the widest possible context
> of the cosmic struggle, for the light in the darkness corresponds to
> the taming of the primeval chaos in Genesis 1.2. Thus in these first
> five verses we can already see a summary of the plot of the whole
> book, the struggle of the Incarnate Word with the powers of
> darkness.[60]

The Prologue is, in fact, a bare outline of the world-view which is
filled in in the rest of the Gospel.[61] The Word, *Logos*, was in the
beginning with God, and was God. 'What God was, the Word was'
(1.1 NEB). Everything came into being through the Word, and he
was the source of life and of light (1.4–5), the true light who
enlightens every person (1.9). Through the Word, people received
power to become children of God, 'born, not of blood nor of the will of
the flesh nor of the will of man, but of God' (1.13). This Word is then
explicitly identified with the historical Jesus: the Word became flesh,
and his glory was revealed. Grace and truth came through him (1.14–
17). 'No one has ever seen God; the only Son, who is in the bosom of
the Father, he has made him known.' (1.15)

The purpose of John's Gospel is to enable its readers to recognize
and hold fast to the truth about God's gift of eternal life in Jesus
Christ: '... these are written that you may believe that Jesus is the
Christ, the Son of God, and that believing you may have life in his
name.' (20.31) Only in John is this gospel purpose so explicitly
defined. Jesus is the Messiah, the Christ of God, but he has only
revealed himself in his true nature to his disciples, not to the whole
world (14.22). However, the time will come when every eye will see
him (Rev. 1.7). About half of the Gospel consists of discourses of
Jesus which are unparalleled in the Synoptic writers. The style and
the Christology are markedly different. There is, for instance, no
concept of the human ignorance of Jesus, of his desolation or his self-
emptying. Rather, the stress is on his *glory*. Because of this, some have
seen the Jesus of the Fourth Gospel to be inhuman, and have spoken
of John's 'naive docetism', or failure to take Jesus' humanity
seriously.[62] Yet it is the human Jesus who enjoys a state of unbroken

communion with the Father. It is the earthly Jesus who is called the
Son of Man. It is through the human personality that divine
revelation occurs. So the human, historical Jesus stands at the mid-
point of world history. In the words of T. W. Manson:[63]

> The Jesus of the Fourth Gospel is the middle term between the
> *logos* and the *paraklētos*. The *logos* is the term that covers all divine
> revelation up to and including Jesus himself: the *paraklētos* is the
> term that covers all the Christian era from Jesus himself to the
> Church.

However, the coming of the Word of God into the world brings about
a collision with the power of darkness (1.5). The world does not know
him (1.10). Jesus speaks of his alienation from the world: neither he
nor his disciples are 'of the world' (17.14). So there is a judgement
upon the world, and the casting out of its ruler (12.31).

It is correct then to see in John a dualism. But it is not the dualism of
the gnostics for whom evil resided in matter. The conflict which John,
and the Qumran community, sees is between the old order and the
new; it is an eschatological, and not a physical, dualism. There are
marked similarities between the theology of John and that of Qumran.
But in the Qumran theology, there is a created spirit of light, and one
of darkness, and a struggle of light with darkness. However, in John,
the Word is himself the light (1.4, 9; 3.19; 9.5; 12.46). Again, in
Qumran theology, men and women are aligned, apparently with little
or no choice, under the banners of light or of darkness. In John, they
choose freely (3.19); it is faith in the light which makes one a child of
light (12.36, 46).[64]

We see then in the Gospel of John a contrast both with the
determinism and future-orientation of the cosmic conflict described
by the Qumran sect, and with the anti-materialism of the gnostics.
John certainly uses language similar to that used by the gnostics, but,
as Bultmann has shown, he does so with a different theology and a
different aim:

> In his gnostic form a pointed anti-gnosticism is expressed. John
> knows no gnostic dualism. Therefore in John, man is not seen
> dualistically. Flesh and Spirit do not stand opposed as substances
> of the demonic and divine realms. Rather it is stressed, with all
> sharpness, that the Redeemer has become *flesh* and shows his glory
> precisely as the one made flesh. Man's lostness in the world is not
> the lost condition of a heavenly substance in the power of darkness,
> but the sinful turning away of the creature from the Creator. In
> place of cosmic dualism steps a dualism of decision; life and death

are not determined for all time on natural grounds, but depend on the decision of faith and of unbelief.[65]

This dualism of decision is related to the perception and practice of the truth. So the conflict of light with darkness is also that of truth with error.

In John's thought, to be in darkness is to be alienated from the truth, that is, from the reality of God. The Word of God *is* the truth (14.6), he is full of grace and truth (1.14). In the beginning of creation the Word was with God and shared his nature. There is therefore 'a *Jesus principle* built into the universe'.[66] Through his coming into the world, the blind are enabled to see, while those with sight become unable to see the truth (9.39). As the source of grace and truth, Jesus needed no one to bear witness of man but was able to see into the heart of man (2.25). At the same time, he speaks on the basis of his knowledge of heavenly realities (3.11–12) and utters the words of God who is true (3.33–4; 7.28; 8.26). His teaching is not his own but God's (7.16). Thus knowledge of God and practice of truth are identified. To do the truth is to come into the light of God (3.21). To worship truly is to do so in spirit and truth (4.23–4). True testimony is that which the Father bears of the Son (5.32). Jesus, according to John's account, lays emphasis on what modern theological thinkers would term *praxis*, on 'doing the truth'. Those who continue in his word will be true disciples; they will come to know the truth which will make them free (8.31–2). They will walk in the light and become children of light (12.35).

In John's Gospel, a variety of terms are used to describe Jesus, his role and his relationship with God. The use of the Son of Man symbol in John has already been mentioned.[67] The Gospel was written in order that people would come to recognize Jesus as the Christ, the Son of God, and through that recognition and belief would come to share in eternal life (20.31). It is as the Christ that Andrew identifies Jesus to his brother Peter (1.41). Nathanael tells Jesus that he is both Son of God and King of Israel (1.49), while Jesus himself, in conversation with a woman from Samaria, explicitly identifies himself as the Christ (4.25–6). Martha proclaims him as Christ and Son of God (11.27). In Chapter 6, towards the end of a long discourse about heavenly bread, Peter assures Jesus that he and his fellow disciples will not leave him: 'Lord, to whom shall we go? You have the words of eternal life; and we have believed, and have come to know, that you are the Holy One of God.' (6.68–9) This title does not occur elsewhere in John, and only appears once in any other part of the New Testament (Mark 1.24). It is unknown in Judaism. In Mark it is a demon which addresses Jesus in this way, as indeed it is demons who hail him as Son of God (Mark 3.11; 5.7). Luke, in describing the announcement of the birth of Jesus, uses the term 'holy thing' and 'Son of God' together (1.35). It is possible therefore that 'the Holy One of God' and 'Son of God' were parallel titles.

In John, Jesus not only claims messianic status but also goes on to assert that this involves a relationship of equality with God:

> So the Jews gathered round him, and said to him, 'How long will you keep us in suspense? If you are Christ, tell us plainly.' Jesus answered them, 'I told you, and you do not believe...' (10.24–5)

He then continues:

> 'I and the Father are one.' The Jews took up stones again to stone him. Jesus answered them, 'I have shown you many good works from the Father: for which of these do you stone me?' The Jews answered him, 'We stone you for no good work, but for blasphemy; because you, being a man, make yourself God.' (10.31–3)

However, in order to establish a capital offence for blasphemy, it had to be shown that the offender had uttered the name of God. This was based on an interpretation on the prohibition in the Mosaic Law of cursing God and blaspheming his name (Lev. 24 15–16). In John, the Jews insist that Jesus ought to die because he claimed to be the Son of God (19.7).

Unique to John's account, and of great importance, are a series of 'I am' sayings. These fall into three categories. In the first category, Jesus uses the 'I am' formula absolutely without any predicate. Thus 'you will die in your sins unless you believe that I am' (8.24). 'When you have lifted up the Son of Man, then you will know that I am.' (8.28) 'Truly, truly, I say to you, before Abraham was, I am.' (8.58) 'I tell you this now, before it takes place, that when it does take place you may believe that I am he.' (13.19) In each of these references except the third, the Revised Standard Version translates 'I am he', and the New English Bible 'I am what I am'. But the Greek says simply 'I am', and there is a probable link with the Old Testament form of the divine name.

Secondly, there are two sayings where there is a predicate implied (6.20; 18.5). But it is the third group which is particularly distinctive of John's account of Jesus' discourses. Here there is a series of symbols in which Jesus identifies himself by the use of an 'I am' saying.

> I am the bread of life; he who comes to me shall not hunger, and he who believes in me shall never thirst. (6.35; cf. 6.51)

I am the light of the world; he who follows me will not walk in darkness, but will have the light of life. (8.12; cf. 9.5)

... I am the door of the sheep ... I am the door. (10.7, 9)

I am the good shepherd. (10.11, 14)

I am the resurrection and the life; he who believes in me, though he die, yet shall he live, and whoever lives and believes in me shall never die. (11.25–6)

I am the way, and the truth, and the life; no one comes to the Father, but by me. (14.6)

I am the true vine, and my Father is the vinedresser ... I am the vine, you are the branches. He who abides in me, and I in him, he it is that bears much fruit, for apart from me you can do nothing. (15.1, 5)

In all these sayings, major claims are made both about the relationship of Jesus with his followers, and about the relationship with God on which it depends. He is the living bread through which comes resurrection and eternal life; the light of those who follow him; the door through which entrance to life is gained; the shepherd of the flock; the source of risen life; the way to the Father; and the source of communion in and with the Father. Everything that Jesus does in and for the world is based on his relationship with the Father.

This relationship is one of equality and mutual indwelling. He and the Father are one (10.30). Through his works he seeks to show this: 'that you may know and understand that the Father is in me and I am in the Father'. (10.38) The person who believes in Jesus believes not only in him but also in the Father who sent him (12.44). The Father has given all things into Jesus' hands, for 'he had come from God and was going to God' (13.3). Christians are thus called to be one in God as the Father and the Son are one (17.21f). This sense of mutual indwelling and communion with God is central to Johannine mysticism. While there is not very much use of the language of 'Spirit' in John, there is the sense of the Spirit's power completing the ministry of Jesus and perpetuating his presence within the community of love. It is the communion with the Father which is dominant in John: the word 'Father' occurs 107 times in the Gospel, and twelve times in the First Epistle. It is this communion and mutual indwelling which constitutes the true Christian knowledge (*gnōsis*). For the Christian, as C. H. Dodd stressed, *gnōsis* is to be understood as an 'awareness of a relation of mutual indwelling of God and man'.[68] Through Christ, men and women are brought to share in his relationship. We become children of God (1.12; 11.52; 1 John 3.1, 2, 10; 5.2).[69]

Two words which are crucial to John's teaching about the relationship of humanity to God are *life* and *love*. The Word is seen as the source of life (1.4). As the Father has life in himself, so he has given life to the Son (5.26). Through the Son, life is to come to the world (6.33, 51; 8.12; 11.25; 20.31, etc.). The word *zoē* life, occurs thirty-six times in John, while *zēn*, 'to live', occurs seventeen times. The life which Christ gives is described as *eternal* life. It is because God loved the world so much that he gave his Son so that those who believe in him might have eternal life (3.16). Those who eat the flesh and drink the blood of the Son of Man have eternal life (6.54). Eternal life is equated with the knowledge of the true God and of Jesus Christ whom he has sent (17.3).

But the living, life-giving Word is also the source of love. Love is the test of discipleship (13.35). There is no greater love than that which leads Jesus to lay down his life for his friends (15.13). But the source of his love is God. It is the love with which the Father has loved Jesus which is to be given to his followers (17.26). So the 'new commandment' which Jesus gives us is that his followers should love one another as he has loved them (15.12, 17).

In the Fourth Gospel we are brought to the very core of Christian theology and spirituality, to the source of life and of love, to the God in whom light and life and love are one. We love him because he first loved us (1 John 4.19).

4

God, Christ and the Church

*No one has ever seen God; if we love one another, God
abides in us and his love is perfected in us.*
1 John 4.12

The roots of a specifically Christian spirituality lie in the worship and
reflection of the earliest Christian communities. In the letters and
other writings of the apostolic period, we find an abundance of
material which shows how these early Christians thought and spoke
about God and their relationship with God. Certain key themes are of
great importance. God is the source of the unity of humankind, and in
the achievement of Jesus has restored the human race to communion
with God and to its own fundamental unity. God in Christ has
wrought salvation, reconciliation, deliverance. Through our unity
with Christ, we share in a solidarity in God which is one of light and of
love. We share too in the experience of the Holy Spirit, the Spirit of
power and of freedom. We are built into a new people, a holy
priesthood, the Body of Christ. The new age, God's future, has
dawned upon us, but there is more to come. In this chapter we can
only begin to draw out some of the central teachings in these areas of
Christian experience.

God the Unity of Humanity

There is one God, and the unity of the human race is rooted and
grounded in the being of God. It is from the divine unity that human
unity derives. The idea of human unity is a central one in early
Christianity, for the gospel is 'obsessed with the idea of the unity of
human society'.[1] It is a theme which is stressed particularly in the
Pauline letters. While we were alienated from God, he reconciled us
by the death of Christ (Rom. 5.10). We have been united with Christ
in his dying and rising (6.5) and so there is nothing that can separate
us from his love (8.38). Christians achieve their unity in Christ
(12.5f). The unity of the body is stressed also in the Corinthian
correspondence (1.10ff; 10.17; 12.12). In Christ there is already a
new Creation (5.17).

The theme of the new creation is contained also in the Letter to the Galatians (6.15). Earlier in this letter, Paul has stressed that those who have been baptized into Christ have 'put on Christ'. So 'there is neither Jew nor Greek, there is neither slave nor free, there is neither male nor female; for you are all one in Christ Jesus'. (3.27–8) It is, however, in the Letter to the Ephesians that the theme of human unity, and indeed of the entire creation, is placed in a theological framework. God has made known the mystery of his will 'as a plan for the fullness of time, to unite all things in him, things in heaven and things on earth' (1.10). Christ, the focal point of this destined unity of the created order, is also the head of his body, the Church, which is described as 'the fullness of him who fills all in all' (1.23).

Paul goes on to explain that those who were previously alienated from the commonwealth of Israel have now been brought near through the blood of Christ:

But now in Christ Jesus, you who once were far off have been brought near in the blood of Christ. For he is our peace who has made us both one, and has broken down the dividing wall of hostility, by abolishing in his flesh the law of commandments and ordinances, that he might create in himself one new man in place of the two, so making peace, and might reconcile us both to God in one body through the cross thereby bringing the hostility to an end. (2.13–16)

It is possible that the reference to the breaking down of the wall is to the wall of Jerusalem, and that 'the great historical catastrophe of Jerusalem's fall is here adorned with christological meaning'.[2]

The letter sees Christian life as a movement towards maturity and fullness. Its aim is 'that you may be filled with all the fullness of God' (3.19). To this end, Christians are urged to keep the unity of the Spirit (4.3). The unity of the Body is closely associated with the unity of God and with the unity into which Christians are grafted in the baptismal liturgy (4.4ff). Again, the unity of the Body is not static, but dynamic. For the purpose of Christ's ascension was that he might 'fill all things' (4.10). So we are all in process of attaining that fullness in the building up of Christ's Body: '. . . until we all attain to the unity of the faith and of the knowledge of the Son of God, to mature manhood, to the measure of the stature of the fullness of Christ.' (4.13) The Body is knit together by Christ (4.16f). Through their following of Christ, Christians are being renewed, and become sharers in a 'new nature' which is created after the likeness of God (literally, 'after God', 4.24).

The theology of unity and of Christ's reintegration of the universe is further developed in the Letter to the Colossians, which has been called 'the gospel of the cosmic Christ'.[3] Here Christ is seen as the 'future corporate consciousness of the race'.[4] At first sight the Christ of Colossians might seem an inhuman and unreal Christ, a far cry from the human Jesus of the gospel record. One's initial reaction might be to see this Christ as representing 'a separation of the person of Jesus of Nazareth from true human experience. He seems a remote figure, cast in a transcendental mould, and far removed from the prophet of Galilee.'[5] In fact, the letter is opposed to those who would remove Jesus from the human realm, and insists that he has come in a body of flesh (1.22; 2.11), has made peace by his blood (1.20), and has suffered affliction (1.24). In him the fullness of God dwells bodily (2.9).

The first chapter of the letter contains a magnificent description of Christ, his relation to God and to the universe, and his work of salvation:

> He is the image of the invisible God, the first-born of all creation; for in him all things were created, in heaven and on earth, visible and invisible, whether thrones or dominions or principalities or authorities – all things were created through him and for him. He is before all things, and in him all things hold together. He is the head of the body, the church; he is the beginning, the first-born from the dead, that in everything he might be pre-eminent. For in all the fullness of God was pleased to dwell, and through him to reconcile to himself all things, whether on earth or in heaven, making peace by the blood of his cross. (1.15–20)

Those who had been estranged have now been reconciled (1.21). As in Ephesians, the progress towards maturity is stressed. The aim is to 'present every man mature in Christ' (1.28).

In him the *fullness* of deity dwells bodily, and we come to *fullness* of life only in him (2.9). The Body of Christ is not a static entity but grows 'with a growth that is from God' (2.19). Again there is the stress which we saw in Ephesians on the 'new nature'. Christians

> have put on the new nature, which is being renewed in knowledge after the image of its creator. Here there cannot be Greek and Jew, circumcised and uncircumcised, barbarian, Scythian, slave, free man, but Christ is all, and in all. (3.10–11)

Thus, in these three letters to Galatia, Ephesus, and Colossae, we find the clear teaching that humanity is being renewed after the likeness of God. A new creation, a new order of reality, has come into being through the dying and rising of Christ, and Christians have been incorporated into that new creation. God has delivered them from the dominion of darkness and transferred them into his Kingdom (Col. 1.13). Christ is himself in them (1.27); they have died, and their lives are hidden with him in God (3.3). This theme of unity and communion in God recurs in other letters. For the Christian, to live is Christ (Phil. 1.21), it is to share his mind (2.5) and to shine as a light in the world (2.15). God is actually working in the Christian person (2.13), and he shares the suffering and death of Christ in his own body (3.10).

It is in the Letter to the Romans that Paul speaks most frequently of his understanding of God. The word 'God' occurs more frequently in Romans than in any other New Testament book except the Acts of the Apostles, and more than in any other Pauline letter except the very short First Letter to the Thessalonians. In the Letter to the Romans, there are 153 references to God, an average of 4·5 references per page.[6] In his letter there is a particular stress on God's righteousness. Salvation itself is, as we shall consider later, seen as the result of the righteousness of God (1.16–17). But there is also a good deal of teaching about the unity of God, and his revelation of himself to humanity. God's eternal power and deity are, Paul says, revealed through the created order (1.20). Yet 'all have sinned and fall short of the glory of God' (3.23). It is through faith in Christ that we find peace with God (5.1) and the hope of sharing his glory (5.2). God's love has been poured into our hearts through the gift of the Holy Spirit (5.5), and we now live 'the new life of the Spirit' (7.6). Christ is in us, and we are in the Spirit (8.9–10). Paul speaks of the movement of the whole creation towards its liberation in the Holy Spirit:

> For the creation waits with eager longing for the revealing of the sons of God; for the creation was subjected to futility, not of its own will but by the will of him who subjected it in hope; because the creation itself will be set free from its bondage to decay and obtain the glorious liberty of the children of God. We know that the whole creation has been groaning in travail together until now; and not only the creation, but we ourselves, who have the first fruits of the Spirit, groan inwardly as we wait for adoption as sons, the redemption of our bodies. (8.19–23)

There is thus an essential unity between the hope for the inward liberation of the children of God, and the liberation of the entire physical creation from its bondage and oppression.

A central theme of the Letter to the Romans is that of the unity of God. Is God the God of the Jews only, Paul asks, or also of the Gentiles? He answers: 'Yes, of Gentiles also, since God is one' (3.30).

God is one: this theological assertion is crucial to the entire argument of Chapter 3. So there is an essential unity between Jews and Greeks. The phrase 'Jew and Greek' is often used by Paul (see 1.16–17; 2.9–10; 3.9; 3.29–30; 4.11–12. 16; 9.24; 10.11–13; 11.25–6; 15.8–9). The truth that 'God is one' (3.30; cf. Gal. 3.20) is, in fact, the 'decisive argument'[7] in asserting the unity of Jew and Greek. As in Ephesians and Colossians, a vital relationship is made between the unity of God, the remaking of humanity in the image of its Creator, and the unity within the human family (see Eph. 2.11–22; Col. 3.10–11). The emergence of the new social structure of Christ's body, reflecting the unity and communion within God, subverts the division of the world. 'The image of the body of Christ thus served as a way of describing a social revolution.'[8]

In Galatians, to be one in Christ is linked with the status of being Abraham's offspring:

> For as many of you as were baptized into Christ have put on Christ. There is neither Jew nor Greek, there is neither slave nor free, there is neither male nor female; for you are all one in Christ Jesus. And if you are Christ's, then you are Abraham's offspring, heirs according to promise. (Gal. 3.27–9)

In Romans, Paul takes up this theme, relating the unity of God to the new Christian community, in which membership and inheritance of the promises is based not on physical descent but on spiritual renewal. The true Jew is the inward Jew, circumcised in the heart (2.29). Abraham is the father of us all (4.16). For not all are children of Abraham simply because they are his physical descendants (9.7). Paul distinguishes between 'the children of the flesh' and 'the children of the promise' (9.8): it is those born not after the flesh but after the Spirit (cf. John 1.13) who are the seed of Abraham.

The continuity between the promises of God to Israel and the events of Christ and the Church is central to the preaching of the early Christians recorded in the Acts of the Apostles. In no sense is the Jewish heritage repudiated, for it is the essential foundation of the new revelation in Christ. But there is an emphasis on progress and fullness. So, in their meeting with the Jew Apollos who was 'well versed in the scriptures', 'instructed in the way of the Lord' and even 'spoke and taught accurately the things concerning Jesus, though he knew only the baptism of John', Priscilla and Aquila 'expounded to him the way of God more accurately' (Acts 18.24–6). Paul similarly says that his concern was to declare 'the whole counsel of God' (20.27).

At the heart of the preaching of the apostolic Church was the great work which God had accomplished in Jesus, the mighty works of God in him (2.11, 22). For it was God who had raised him from the dead (2.24, 32; 3.26; 4.10; 5.30; 10.40; 13.30). It was God who had made him Lord and Christ (2.36). Moreover, the God who had done these great works in Jesus was the God of Abraham, Isaac and Jacob (3.13). Jesus is God's holy servant (4.30), the author of life (3.15), through whom salvation comes (4.12). One text identifies Jesus with God himself (20.28). The continuity with God's revelation to Israel is particularly stressed in the speech of the martyr Stephen (7.1ff). He begins by praising the God of the patriarchs, the God revealed in Israel's history. But that history had been marked by resistance to the Holy Spirit (7.51). Stephen therefore points both to the faithfulness of God and to the faithlessness of Israel, and he is accused of speaking against God (6.11). Luke, however, describes him, just before his death, as 'full of the Holy Spirit' (7.55). The unity between old and new covenants is emphasized elsewhere in Acts. God is the Creator and God of the Old Testament (4.24ff), the God of *our* fathers (24.14; 26.6), the God of all nations and races (10.28, 35). His glory is not to be shared with lesser gods, whether false claimants to deity such as Herod (12.27f) or idols (14.15). The conflict with idolatry is brought out in the important passage in Acts 17 where Paul visits Athens and finds a city full of idols. Here he proclaims the knowability of the allegedly unknown God, pointing out that the true God is not limited to shrines but is the source of life in whom 'we live and move and have our being' (17.28). We are, moreover, God's offspring (17.28–9).

The conquest over false deities and spiritual forces in the cosmic order is the central theme of the Pauline language about 'principalities and powers'. It was the 'rulers of this age' who crucified the Lord of glory (1 Cor. 2.8), and the end of all things is seen in terms of the destruction of these illegitimate powers: 'Then comes the end, when he delivers the kingdom of God the Father, after destroying every rule and every authority and power.' (15.24) In the Letters to the Galatians, Ephesians, and Colossians in particular, salvation is described in terms of liberation from the powers. Christians, who once were enslaved to the 'elemental spirits of the universe' (Gal. 4.3), are now redeemed from slavery and recipients of the Holy Spirit. As a result, they are no longer in bondage to beings who are in fact no gods, the 'weak and beggarly elemental spirits' (4.9). Again, Paul proclaims that Christ has been exalted far above all rule and authority and power and dominion (Eph. 1.21). Thus Christians no longer follow 'the prince of the power of the air' (2.2). On the contrary, through the Church, the truth of God is revealed to the principalities and powers themselves (3.10). Paul goes on to stress the cosmic nature of the Christian's warfare:

> For we are not contending against flesh and blood, but against the principalities, against the powers, against the world rulers of this present darkness, against the spiritual hosts of wickedness in the heavenly places. (Eph. 6.12)

In Colossians too the conflict with the powers is central to the understanding of Christ's saving work. He has delivered us from the dominion of darkness (1.13). No longer are Christians to live according to the 'elemental spirits of the universe' (2.8) but according to Christ who, in his death, has disarmed the principalities and powers and triumphed over them (2.15). In Christ, we have died to the elemental spirits (2.20).

The language of principalities and powers is of really central importance in understanding the Pauline doctrine of salvation and of the unity of the human race and of the creation which is the end of God's saving work.[9] It figures in the most ancient Christian confessions (cf. 1 Cor. 15.24–5; 1 Pet. 3.22). Paul took over the symbolism of the powers from apocalyptic writing, but whereas they are portrayed there as heavenly angels, in Paul they are 'structures of earthly existence':[10]

> In the light of God's action, Paul perceived that mankind is not composed of loose individuals, but that structures, orders, forms of existence, or whatever they be called, are given us as a part of creaturely life, and that these are involved, as much as men themselves, in the history of creation, fall, preservation, reconciliation and consummation. This insight he expressed in the terms and concepts of his time.[11]

Thus the salvation which Paul describes is not only personal but cosmic: 'just as these demonic spirits are essentially cosmic powers, so is the redemption which Christ wins a cosmic redemption'.[12] The entire creation is affected by the redemptive events, for in Christ all things have been reconciled. The word *ktisis* (creation, Rom. 8.19) means not only men and women, but all created things, perhaps including the demonic powers themselves.

Thus, in Pauline theology, God in Christ is bringing about the unity of the human race, bringing an end to the disintegration and disunity brought about by the Fall. The rulers of this world are being put out of action, being progressively neutralized(1 Cor. 2.6). So the victory of the cross begins the process of restoration of the original cosmic order, an order which the hostility of the powers had deranged and dislocated. Jesus is the focus of a new world in which the powers themselves will be remade according to the purpose of creation, for they also 'subsist' or 'hold together' in him (Col. 1.17).

Salvation and Reconciliation in Christ

That God has destined men and women for salvation is assumed in the New Testament (1 Thess. 5.9). He wills all people to be saved, and to come to knowledge of the truth (1 Tim. 2.4). And this salvation is the work of divine grace (Titus 2.11), it is 'the gospel of God' (Rom. 1.1), the 'power of God for salvation' in which 'the righteousness of God' is revealed (Rom. 1.16–17; 3.21–5). And this righteousness, like salvation itself, is not primarily a personal but a social reality. The Pauline letters are saturated with the language of social salvation:

> Justification in Christ is thus not an individual miracle happening to this person or that person, which each may seek or possess for himself. Rather justification by grace is a joining together of this person and that person, of the near and far . . . it is a social event.[13]

It is important to stress this social understanding of salvation, for it has been eroded by centuries of western individualism which has reduced the common salvation to a purely personal experience.

The letters speak of God's salvation as a past event: he saved us (2 Tim. 1.9; Titus 3.5; etc.) 'The death he died he died to sin, once for all . . .' (Rom. 6.10). Yet it is also seen as present and continuing: we are 'being saved' (1 Cor. 1.18). And there is a future aspect: 'we shall be saved' (Rom. 5.9 cf. 13.11; 1 Thess. 5.9). In the history of salvation, the death of Christ is of central significance. The events of his passion and death dominate the Gospels – one third of Mark's account is devoted to the final week of the life of Jesus – while Paul shows little interest in Jesus' earthly life, but only in his death, resurrection, and presence in the Church.

Salvation according to the Pauline letters comes through Christ. He came into the world to save sinners (1 Tim. 1.15). He is the one mediator between God and men (2.5). He was put to death for our transgressions and raised for our justification (Rom. 4.25). We have been justified by his blood (5.9). It is in the writings of Paul that the saving work of God in Christ is described and explained most clearly, and therefore these writings are of central importance for understanding the Christian teaching about salvation.[14] In the letters, the work of Christ is described by a variety of terms. It is *justification*: we are justified by the faith of Christ (Gal. 2.16; Rom. 3.26–8; 4.25; 5.18). It is *salvation* (2 Cor. 7.10; Rom. 1.16; 10.10; 13.11). It is *expiation* by the blood of Christ (Rom. 3.25). It is *redemption*: in Christ we have been ransomed, bought back (1 Cor. 1.30; Rom. 3.24; 8.32). It is *sanctification*, a word closely associated with redemption, cleansing, and justification (1 Cor. 1.2, 30; 6.11). It is *freedom*: in Christ we have been set free from bondage (Gal. 5.1, 13; Rom. 8.1–2, 21; 2 Cor. 3.17). It is *transformation*: we are being changed from glory to glory, being renewed in our whole beings (2 Cor. 3.18; Rom. 12.2). It is *new creation* (Gal. 6.15; 2 Cor. 5.17; Rom. 6.4; 1 Cor. 15.45). And it is *reconciliation* (2 Cor. 5.18–20; Rom. 5.10–11; 11.15).

Paul sees the relationship of human beings to God as having been radically changed by the work of Christ. Having been previously enemies, we have now been reconciled to God by the death of Christ, and we will be saved by the life of Christ (Rom. 5.10–11). Through the cross, peace has come to the disordered world (Col. 1.19–22), and those who were afar off have been brought near to God (Eph. 2.13). The fundamental idea in Paul's understanding of Christ's saving work is that of participation. Through Christ's dying and rising, a new system of relationships has been brought about. We have been changed as a result of what has happened to Christ. Christ is the first-fruits, the foretaste of the harvest of the dead (1 Cor. 15.20–23). Paul explains: If the dough offered as first fruits is holy, so is the whole lump; and if the root is holy, so are the branches.' (Rom. 11.16) Thus the purpose of Christ's death was to bring about life in us (1 Thess. 5.10).

In describing the saving work of Christ, Paul draws on the sacrificial language of Israel. In 1 Corinthians 10, the Exodus drama is recounted. But, says Paul, these events were described for the Christian era: 'Now these things happened to them as a warning, but they were written down for our instruction, upon whom the end of the ages has come.' (1 Cor. 10.11) Christians are living in 'end-time', in the time of fulfilment of the ancient hopes of Israel, the fulfilment of the sacrificial symbols of the past, the time of the new Passover.

> For Christ, our paschal lamb, has been sacrificed. Let us therefore celebrate the festival, not with the old leaven, the leaven of malice and evil, but with the unleavened bread of sincerity and truth. (1 Cor. 5.7–8)

Christ is the *pascha*, the new Passover Lamb, the 'lamb without blemish or spot' (1 Pet. 1.19). Elsewhere, other sacrificial terms are used of Christ. He is described as a sin offering, who 'has appeared once and for all at the end of the age to put away sin by the sacrifice of himself' (Heb. 9.26). He is compared to the scapegoat of Leviticus who bears the iniquities of the people (Lev. 16.22). So Peter writes of Christ: 'He himself bore our sins in his body on the tree that we might

die to sin and live to righteousness. By his wounds you have been
healed' (Pet. 2.24; cf. Isa. 53.5). Similarly, Paul says that God 'made
him to be sin who knew no sin, so that in him we might become the
righteousness of God' (2 Cor. 5.21).
    In Paul's theology, salvation and righteousness are inseparable.[15]
Salvation is the work of the righteous God. Through his saving acts
we are delivered from slavery (Rom. 6.20; 8.15, 21), from un-
righteousness (6.13), from condemnation (5.18; 8.1) and from
hostility (Eph. 2.15). We are restored to freedom (Rom. 6.7; 8.21;
Gal. 5.1), and reconciled to God (Rom. 5.10; 2 Cor. 5.18–19). God's
righteousness is manifested (Rom. 1.17; 3.26), and Paul even asserts
that we *become* the righteousness of God (2 Cor. 5.21). And this
salvation is a social and cosmic event: it is the world, the *kosmos*,
which is reconciled to God in Christ (2 Cor. 5.19).
    A key idea in the Christian doctrine of salvation is that of
reconciliation. Through Christ, Paul says, we have received reconciliation (Rom. 5.11). The group of reconciliation words have as their
basic meaning the changing of a relationship. To reconcile is to make
otherwise, to alter a state of affairs. In secular language, the words
were used of social and political change. Reconciliation is similar in
meaning to the English word 'atonement', a word with no equivalent
in other modern European languages. There is, however, no
connection with the themes of expiation or propitiation.
    It has been suggested that the theme of reconciliation is a minor one
in the New Testament.[16] But this view can hardly be sustained. It is
true that the actual words 'reconcile' and 'reconciliation' do not occur
frequently in the New Testament as a whole. Apart from Matthew
5.24, most of the references are in Paul (see Rom. 3.24–6; 2 Cor.
5.18–21; Col. 1.15–20; Eph. 2.11–27).[17] But the idea is a much
wider one and pervades a good deal of New Testament teaching. In
Paul, it is always God who reconciles and human beings who are
reconciled. As a famous evangelical scholar of the past wrote:[18]

> Where reconciliation is spoken of in Paul, the subject is always
> God, and the object is always man. The work of reconciling is one
> in which the initiative is taken by God, and the cost is borne by
> him; men are reconciled in the passive, or allow themselves to be
> reconciled, or receive the reconciliation. We never read that God
> has been reconciled.

The good news of the reconciliation which has been accomplished in
Christ, and the 'ministry of reconciliation' (2 Cor. 5.18) which is a
continuing work, are central to the work of the Church. On one level,
the work of reconciliation has been done: God was in Christ

reconciling the world to himself. And yet, as Moule has reminded us, 'there can never be an end absolutely to this reconciliation, for it is the living God at work, and it is part and parcel of the fellowship which issues from his work and in which it is perpetuated'.[19]

Much Christian preaching, however, has emphasized only the finished work of Christ, and has done so in a 'substitutionary' way. Christ took my place, he died instead of me. It would be wrong to claim that there was no basis for substitutionary ideas of atonement in the New Testament, but the support is very slight.[20] In Paul, the stress is rather on the restoration of relationship: because we are justified by the blood of Christ, we will be saved from the wrath of God. For in Christ we are reconciled (Rom. 5.9–10). There are in fact only three passages in Paul which can be cited in support of a substitutionary view. First, in Romans 8, Paul writes that God sent his Son 'in the likeness of sinful flesh' (8.3) to fulfil the just requirement of the law. Christ was sent, moreover, 'for sin'. This usage 'for sin' indicates *purpose* (cf. Lev. 4.3). Christ comes to deal with sin.

There is a second passage in 2 Corinthians 5.21 in which Christ is said to have been made to 'be sin' for us. The point which is being made is that Christ became fully human: he who knew no sin shared in human nature, became human.

Thirdly, Christ is said to have become 'a curse for us' (Gal. 3.13). But the context makes it clear that the reference is to the legal curse upon a hanged man (Deut. 21.23). There is no real support in any of these passages for the doctrine of substitutionary atonement.

At the centre of the discussion of the nature of Christ's work is the theme of redemption. Originally the word *lutron* meant the price paid for one's freedom. But the verb *lutrousthai* came to be used, with God as its subject, to mean the securing of release by the power of God. Often in the New Testament the language of redemption is used without any reference to price. Thus God has redeemed his people (Luke 1.68). Anna spoke to those who awaited the redemption of Jerusalem (2.38). Christ secured an eternal redemption (Heb. 9.12). Christians have been redeemed by the precious blood of Christ (1 Pet. 1.18). In all these cases the words used are redemption (*lutrōsis*) or the verb, to redeem (*lutrousthai*). The word *lutron*, which originally conveyed the notion of price, occurs only once in the New Testament, in Mark 10.45 and its parallel verse Matthew 20.28. (A similar word *antilutron* occurs in 1 Timothy 2.6.) It is not a Pauline word at all. In Paul's writings, there are only four references to purchase: two uses of the phrase 'You were bought with a price' (1 Cor. 6.20 and 7.23), and two references to redemption in Galatians (3.13 and 4.5). In none of these cases is there any reference to the person to whom the price is being paid. It seems reasonable to conclude that the terms are being used to describe the achievement of liberation and release, not a literal activity of payment of a ransom.

In Romans 3.25 Christ is described as an 'expiation' (*hilastērion*).[21] It is possible that this means a propitiation, though it is unlikely. Certainly it cannot be seen as a kind of bribery, for 'the notion of a process of celestial bribery is entirely absent from the New Testament'.[22] It is more likely that *hilastērion* refers to the place of cleansing. Through Christ, we have been cleansed from sin. This has been accomplished, not by a legalistic payment, but by 'an absorption by the very God himself of the fatal disease so as to neutralize it effectively'.[23]

The very God himself: that is the heart of the gospel proclamation, the astonishing truth that God is himself the Saviour. It is in the later New Testament writings, particularly in the Letters to Timothy and Titus, that the notion of 'God the Saviour' is explicitly stated.[24] The word 'Saviour' itself is rare in the New Testament, apart from the Pastoral Epistles and 2 Peter. However, on two occasions, we find the expression 'God and Saviour' (Titus 2.13; 2 Pet. 1.1) with the clear sense that the two are the same. On five occasions we find 'God our Saviour' (1 Tim. 1.1; 2.3; Titus 1.3; 2.10; 3.4). So, it is asserted, God is directly involved in the work of salvation. Jesus is also described as the Saviour in these writings (2 Tim. 1.10; Titus 1.4; 3.6), while the expression 'Lord and Saviour' is used of Jesus in 2 Peter (1.11; 2.20; 3.2; 3.18). While these terms are almost unique in the New Testament, they state in a precise and clear form the fundamental truth of Christian faith, that God was in Christ reconciling the world to himself. In the suffering of Jesus, we see the suffering of God. God suffered and was crucified, and in these saving acts his glory was revealed. Thus the gospel of reconciliation is the 'centre of all Christian knowledge',[25] the revealing of the God who became human. In Barth's words:[26]

> So dark is our situation that God himself must enter and occupy it in order that it may be light. We cannot fully understand the Christian 'God with us' without the greatest astonishment at the glory of the divine grace, and the greatest horror at our own plight.

God of Light and Love

The revelation of God, in both the Old and New Testaments, is a revelation of light in the midst of darkness. In the account of the creation, God said 'Let there be light!' (Gen. 1.3). He led the pilgrim people of Israel by a pillar of fiery light (Exod. 13.21; Ps. 78.14). He was proclaimed by the Psalmist as light and salvation (Ps. 27.1), as one who covers himself with light as with a garment (104.2), whose word is light for guidance (119.105). He is everlasting light and glory to his people (Isa. 60.19). The glory of God is frequently described in terms of light and brilliance. Thus Habakkuk:

> God came from Teman,
>   and the Holy One from Mount Paran.
> His glory covered the heavens,
>   and the earth was full of his praise.
> His brightness was like the light,
>   rays flashed from his hand;
>   and there he veiled his power. (Hab. 3.3–4)

In the Gospels, Christ is proclaimed as the light of the nations (Luke 2.32), the light of men, the true light (John 1.4, 9). At the transfiguration, his raiment and his countenance shone as white as light (Mark 9.2; Matt. 17.2; Luke 9.29). His disciples also are told that they are to be lights of the world (Matt. 5.14), deriving their light from Christ himself, the true light of the world (John 8.12; 9.5; 12.46). The theme of God as light and the source of light is also present in the letters. The God who said 'Let there be light!' has also shone in our hearts to give 'the light of the knowledge of the glory of God in the face of Christ' (2 Cor. 4.6). This light, on which God dwells, is associated with immortality. God, who alone possesses immortality, dwells in unapproachable light (1 Tim. 6.16), marvellous light (1 Peter 2.9). He not only dwells in light: he is light itself (1 John 1.5) and the Father of lights in whom there is no variation or shadow due to change (Jas. 1.17).

This God, who is light, has shone upon us, and his light is within us. Our relationship to the light is therefore not simply one of perception but one of abiding within, standing in, the light. The New Testament sees Christian people as 'children of light', 'children of the day ... not of the night or of darkness' (1 Thess. 5.5). They are to wear the armour of light (Rom. 13.12), to walk as children of light (Eph. 5.8):

> This is the message we have heard from him and proclaim to you, that God is light and in him is no darkness at all. If we say we have fellowship with him while we walk in the darkness, we lie and do not live according to the truth; but if we walk in the light, as he is in the light, we have fellowship with one another, and the blood of Jesus his Son cleanses us from all sin. (1 John 1.5–7)

According to John then we are sharers in the light of God. We are therefore to 'walk in the light' of fellowship and truth. The test of being 'in the light' is a practical one: the person who says that he is in the light, and yet hates his brother or sister, is in the darkness still. For to dwell in the light means to love our brothers and sisters. The person who does not love is blinded, and 'does not know where he is going' (2.9–11).

The practical and ethical character of sharing in the divine light is brought out in the Letter of James which deals with the practice of Christian living. Yet James insists that to live in the light is inseparable from faith in God. God is the source of light, he is 'the Father of lights' (1.17), as Christ is 'the Lord of glory' (2.1). However, belief in this God is not enough, for even the demons believe in the unity of God (2.19). We are called to be 'doers of the word'.

> But be doers of the word, and not hearers only, deceiving yourselves. For if any one is a hearer of the word and not a doer, he is like a man who observes his natural face in a mirror; for he observes himself and goes away and at once forgets what he was like. But he who looks into the perfect law, the law of liberty, and perseveres, being no hearer that forgets but a doer that acts, he shall be blessed in his doing. (1.22–5)

Only in James, in English versions, do we find the word 'religion'. It is identified with visiting orphans and widows in their affliction, and with maintaining oneself unstained from the world (1.27). So purity of heart and practical caring are placed together.

God is light, but he is also love, and the sources of love, a theme which dominates the First Letter of John. In the Old Testament, Hosea in particular spoke of the love of God for his people (Hos. 3.1; 11.4). Paul in Romans explains that nothing in the universe can separate us from the love of Christ (8.35f), and claims that love is the fulfilment of the Law (13.10). God is 'the God of love and peace' (2 Cor. 13.11). The love of Christ is said to surpass knowledge, and is linked with the 'fullness of God' (Eph. 3.19). But it is in 1 John that we find most clearly stated the identity of God as love:

> Beloved, let us love one another; for love is God, and he who loves is born of God and knows God. He who does not love does not know God; for God is love. In this the love of God was made manifest among us, that God sent his only Son into the world, so that we might live through him. In this is love, not that we loved God, but that he loved us and sent his Son to be the expiation for

our sins. Beloved, if God so loved us, we also ought to love one another. No man has ever seen God; if we love one another, God abides in us and his love is perfected in us. (1 John 4.7–12)

This is the heart of Johannine theology. John does not say that love is God, but that God is love: in other words, it is in love of one another that we see most perfectly shown forth the character of the Godhead, and it is in love shown forth among human beings that we come closest to the imitation of the divine life.

The loving character of God has already beeen manifested in the Word made flesh. We know what love is because he laid down his life for us (3.16). The truth that Jesus Christ has come in the flesh is of the greatest importance: failure to recognize this truth, according to John, means that one is not 'of God' (4.2–3). God's love, manifested in Jesus, is the basis of human love: 'we love, because he first loved us' (4.19). And it is from the Word made flesh that we receive the commandment to love as he loved. John stresses that the commandment is not new, but rather is one that 'we have had from the beginning' (2 John 5), that is, from the beginning of the Christian era. So, as a result of the taking flesh of the Word ('that which was from the beginning ... which we have looked upon and touched with our hands', 1 John 1.1), the loving community of God is to be reflected and in some sense reproduced in the new community of the Church, the community of those who practise the new commandment:

> The life of God is a life in which love is common to the Persons who share it. Of this common life of love we partake through the gift of the Spirit. Thus the whole of the divine *koinonia* is present in each disciple and in the community to which he belongs. The Church is the community in which the interchanges of love belonging to the divine life are reproduced in human form.[27]

The Christian community is therefore not simply a community which practises a commandment of love, a community of imitators of Christ, but a community whose very being is rooted in the being of God. This is central to John's teaching. We dwell in God, we have fellowship (*koinōnia*) with him (1 John 1.3). Human participation in the divine life is emphasized by the frequent use of the verbs *einai en* (to be in) and *menein en* (to remain in, to abide in). The verb *einai* is the most frequently used verb in both the Gospel and Epistles, occurring ninety-nine times in the First Epistle.[28] We share God's life, and we are his children:

> See what love the Father has given to us, that we should be called children of God; and so we are. . . . Beloved, we are God's children

now; it does not yet appear what we shall be, but we know that when he appears we shall be like him, for we shall see him as he is. ... No one born of God commits sin; for God's nature (literally 'seed') abides in him, and he cannot sin because he is born of God. By this it may be seen who are the children of God, and who are the children of the devil: whoever does not do right is not of God, nor he who does not love his brother. (3.1–2, 9–10)

Several key themes stand out in this most important passage. We are already God's children, but we are in process of becoming something even greater, more closely conformed to the likeness of Christ. We share the nature of God: his seed is in us. And the evidence of our sharing the divine nature is the practice of justice (3.10) and love.[29]

Because of God's love which has been planted within us, we are to exhibit love, to be 'lovers of God' (2 Tim. 3.4). Our love for God is itself derived from God who first loved us (1 John 4.10). There is therefore an orientation to love within the human community. St Augustine claimed that God is loved, knowingly or unknowingly, by all things capable of loving.[30] But Christian love is also love of one another, following the pattern of Christ:

A new commandment I give to you, that you love one another; even as I have loved you, that you also love one another. By this all men will know that you are my disciples, if you have love for one another. (John 13.34–5)

The Epistles of John look back to this new commandment:

Beloved, I am writing you no new commandment, but an old commandment which you had from the beginning; the old commandment is the word which you have heard. Yet I am writing you a new commandment, which is true in him and in you, because the darkness is passing away and the true light is already shining. (1 John 2.7–8)

That which the community heard in the beginning is to abide in them and in this way they too will abide within God (2.24). And what is the message, the word, which has been heard from the beginning? It is the commandment of love (3.11). Through mutual love, we know that we have passed from death to life (3.14). Belief and love are inseparable: And this is his commandment, that we should believe in the name of his Son Jesus Christ, and love one another just as he has commanded us.' (3.23)

The practice of love within the community of children of light was also a central theme of the Qumran community. But there is a sharp distinction between the love which is to be shown within the community, and the hatred of the children of darkness. The community is ordered 'to love all the sons of light, each according to his lot in God's design, and to hate all the sons of darkness, each according to his guilty place in God's vengeance'.[31] In the Old Testament, love of one's fellow Israelite as oneself was enjoined (Lev. 19.18), and to this was added the injunction to love the foreigner in the same way (19.34): 'but there is no clear evidence in the Old Testament that these commands received special attention'.[32] In the gospel, however, love of enemies is strictly enjoined (Matt. 5.43–4; Luke 6.27–8), and Tertullian claimed that this love of enemies was peculiar to the Christian community.[33] Certainly there is no support for hatred under any circumstances in the New Testament.[34] Rather, through Christlike love of enemies and the manifesting of Christlike love within the Christian community itself, we are to show forth to the world the mutual love within God. For love 'is something quite literally divine. It is a sharing by the creature in the mutual love of the Father and the Son.'[35]

God the Spirit

God is Spirit (John 4.24). God is holy. And at the heart of Christian experience and doctrine is the 'Holy Spirit'. We shall have more to say later about the ways in which the Holy Spirit has been experienced and described in Christian history, and here our concern is simply with the New Testament material. The word *hagios*, holy, occurs 227 times in the New Testament, in 93 of which it is joined with *pneuma*, spirit. Most of the New Testament references, however, occur in the Acts, the Epistles, and Revelation, while there are relatively few references in the Gospels. Most references to the Holy Spirit in the Synoptic Gospels occur in the early chapters. Thus we are told that Mary was pregnant 'of the Holy Spirit' (Matt 1.19, 20), while in Luke, Mary herself is told that the Holy Spirit will come upon her (Luke 1.34). It is predicted that John the Baptist will be 'filled with the Holy Spirit' (1.15), and Elizabeth, rejoicing in her pregnancy, was also filled with the Holy Spirit (1.41), as later was Zechariah (1.67). John the Baptist grew and became strong in spirit (1.80). The Holy Spirit came upon Simeon (2.35–7). John announces that Jesus will baptize with the Holy Spirit (Mark 1.8) and with fire (Matt. 3.11; Luke 3.16). At his baptism, the Spirit descends like a dove, a possible reference to the creation and to the subsequent deliverance from the flood. (Matt. 3.16; Mark 1.10; Luke 3.22).[36] Jesus is led into the wilderness by the Spirit (Matt. 4.1; Luke 4.1), Mark saying that the Spirit 'drove him' there (1.12). Luke tells us that, as he had returned from his baptism 'full of the Spirit' (4.1), so he returned 'in the power of the Spirit' from the wilderness to Galilee (4.14). There, citing Isaiah 61, he announces that the Spirit was indeed upon him (4.18). But after the Nazareth sermon, there is little specifically about the Holy Spirit in the Gospels. The Spirit is said to be the power by which demons are expelled (Matt. 12.28). In fact, the largest single group of uses of *pneuma* in Mark consists of references to unclean spirits. Of Luke's thirty-seven uses of the word, ten are in the first two chapters, and the remaining twenty-seven include fourteen references to unclean spirits. Only two refer directly to the Holy Spirit: 10.21 where Jesus rejoices in the Holy Spirit, and 11.13 where the disciples are told that the Father will give the Holy Spirit to those who ask him.

It has been suggested that one reason for the scarcity of references to the Spirit may be the reserve which Jesus shows about his own messianic role. Certainly the contrast between the 53 uses of *Christos*, Christ or Messiah, in the Gospels, with the 280 or so references in the rest of the New Testament might be seen as comparable with the situation *vis-à-vis* the Spirit.[37] On the other hand, while the Spirit is not referred to directly, clearly the entire ministry of Jesus is a Spirit-filled ministry. He operates in the power of the Spirit, exercising the charismatic gifts of discernment, wisdom, prophecy, and so on. Not only is Jesus himself a prophet, but he treats his hearers as prophets (Matt. 5.12), as those to whom the secrets of the Kingdom have been revealed (13.11), as people through whom the Holy Spirit is at work. In the hour of trial, the Holy Spirit will speak through them (Mark 13.11; Matt. 10.20; Luke 12.12).

In the Gospel of John, there is no sense of the sporadic possession of a wandering prophet by the Spirit, but rather of an abiding relationship of the Son with the Father in the communion of the Spirit. John's spirituality has been called a 'prophetic mysticism'.[38] Not only is this relationship of union experienced by Jesus, but it is to be shared by believers. Of the twenty-two uses of *pneuma* in John, most are general references to God. But in four places John introduces the term 'Paraclete' (14.15–17 and 25–6; 15.16–17; 16.7–14). The 'Spirit of truth' is described as 'another *paraklētos*' (14.16), implying that Jesus was the first Paraclete. He will be with the disciples for ever: they know him already, for he dwells *with* them and will be *in* them (14.17). He will teach all things (14.26), will bear witness to Jesus (15.26), and will guide into all truth (16.13). Outside the New Testament, the usual meaning of the word *paraklētos* is one called to help, an advocate or pleader. In the New Testament, *parakalein* and *paraklēsis* are used about Christian preaching (Acts 2.40). The Greek versions of the Old Testament use the terms about the divine consolations in the messianic age, hence the English term 'comforter'.[39]

In the Acts of the Apostles, the stress is on the present work of the Holy Spirit in the Church. The book begins with the promise of power when the Holy Spirit comes upon the community (1.5, 8), a promise which is fulfilled in Chapter 2. All those who were gathered together were filled with the Holy Spirit and spoke with the prophecy of Joel that there would be a mighty outpouring of the Spirit in the 'last days' (2.15ff). The pouring out of the Spirit is seen as the result of the exaltation of Jesus to the right hand of God (2.33), and it is assumed that subsequently those who repent and are baptized will also receive the gift (2.38). The rest of the book in fact is an account of the Spirit's work and continued presence within the Christian community.

There are some 140 uses of *pneuma* in Paul's letters (excluding the Pastorals). Romans and 1 Corinthians are of particular importance. The Spirit is described as 'the Spirit of holiness' (Rom. 1.4), and Christians are to live 'the new life of the Spirit' (7.6). The law of the Spirit of life in Christ has set Christians free from the law of sin and death (8.2). They now live according to the Spirit, setting their minds on the things of the Spirit (8.4–5). In fact, they are 'in the Spirit' and the Spirit dwells in them. This abiding presence is closely linked with the presence of Christ, and the Spirit is seen as the same Spirit who raised Christ from the dead (8.9–11). This presence of the Spirit leads to freedom and the experience of being children of God. As John links the experience of being begotten of God with love, so Paul relates it to the Spirit and to freedom. 'For all who are led by the Spirit of God are sons of God' and have received 'the spirit of sonship'. As a result, they are able to pray as Jesus prayed, 'Abba, Father' (8.14–16). In the prayer of Christians, it is the Spirit who prays within them 'with sighs too deep for words' (8.26). They are urged to 'be aglow with the Spirit' (12.11). The Spirit is closely related to the Kingdom. 'For the Kingdom of God is not food and drink but righteousness and peace and joy in the Holy Spirit.' (14.17)

In 1 Corinthians, the writer is said to be taught by the Spirit and to be interpreting spiritual truths to others who possess the Spirit (2.13). The passage continues:

> The unspiritual man (*psychikos anthrōpos*) does not receive the gifts of the Spirit of God, for they are folly to him, and he is not able to understand them because they are spiritually discerned. The spiritual man (*pneumatikos*) judges all things, but is himself judged by no one. For who has known the mind of the Lord so as to

instruct him? But we have the mind of Christ. (2.14–16)

The bodies of Christians are temples of the Holy Spirit (6.19) and the
Spirit dwells in them (3.16). It is the Holy Spirit who enables them to
say 'Jesus is Lord' (12.3) and who distributes a variety of spiritual gifts
(12.4ff). The resurrection is related to the Spirit (15.44f).
The Spirit is the lifegiver (2 Cor. 3.6) and the source of freedom
(3.17). The Spirit is the guarantee or first instalment (1.22; 5.5) of
glory. Indeed, 'the Lord is the Spirit' (3.17–18), and Paul ends this
Second Epistle with a prayer that 'the grace of the Lord Jesus Christ
and the love of God and the fellowship of the Holy Spirit be with you
all' (13.14). The language used about Christ and the Spirit might
almost suggest an identification. Thornton describes the relationship
in this way:[40]

> Christ and the Spirit dwell in the Christian soul, but act in the same
> way. Christ is the indwelling content of the Christian life. He is
> being 'formed' in us . . . we are to be 'conformed to his image' . . .
> and we are to 'grow up into him'. Spirit is the quickening cause, the
> indwelling of Christ is the effect of that cause.

Every Christian has received his or her gifts of the Spirit and has the
privilege and responsibility of using them for the building up of the
community (1 Cor. 12.11). To recognize the workings of the Spirit in
prophetic word and testimony is to recognize the presence of God
(14.25). The Spirit must not be quenched (1 Thess. 5.19). Individuals need to 'rekindle' the gift (2 Tim. 1.6) and to remember that
the Spirit dwells within them (1.14).

The personal work of the Spirit in sanctifying and empowering the
saints of God is a central concern of the New Testament teaching. In
fact, of the 227 uses of *hagios* in the New Testament, 61 apply to
Christians. Christians are called into a new peoplehood, a new
community, the body of Christ. To be a Christian is identical with
membership of this body.

God and His People
Union with God is seen in the New Testament as a social reality. It is
within a community that God is known, and it is through that
community that men and women are sanctified. God 'has chosen you',
Paul tells the Christians at Thessalonica (1 Thess. 1.4), and this act of
choosing by God is linked with a call to share in his Kingdom and
glory (2.12). Throughout the pages of the New Testament runs the
theme of the high calling of God's people, a calling which is an integral
part of the whole work of redemption. For Jesus Christ gave himself

to redeem us and also to purify for himself a people of his own (Titus 2.14).

The achievement of Christ is seen throughout as a social act. If anyone is in Christ, there is a new creation (2 Cor. 5.17). The new age has already begun. Being a Christian cannot be seen in isolation from this essentially corporate reality, indeed it is the corporate reality which defines what being a Christian means: 'Becoming a Christian means being recreated by being incorporated into the glorified manhood of the ascended Christ.'[41] The process of being a Christian begins with baptism. In Paul's writings, baptism is associated with sharing Christ's burial and his resurrection, and with the putting on of Christ. All those who have been baptized into Christ have been baptized into his death (Rom. 6.4). But they have not only been buried but also raised (Col. 2.12). They have 'put on Christ' (Gal. 3.27), been 'Christened'. The phrase 'in Christ', is crucial to Pauline theology and Christology. The Christian person is incorporated into Christ so that he or she possesses a new identity, a new nature. In a study of Pauline mysticism published over fifty years ago, Albert Schweitzer expressed it very powerfully:

Grafted into the corporeity of Christ, he (the believer) loses his creaturely individual existence and his natural personality. Henceforth he is only a form of manifestation of the personality of Jesus Christ which dominates the corporeity.[42]

One might quarrel at the implication of the language that in some way the human personality is reduced to an aspect of Christ. Schweitzer's 'only' is unfortunate if it suggests any kind of reduction. Rather is there a transcendence, a transformation and glorifying of the personality as it is transfigured and renewed in that of Christ himself. The essential point is that, for Paul and the early Christian community, to be a Christian is far more than an experience of personal salvation. It is a social experience of being 'in Christ'.[43]

And so the Christian experience is the experience of a society, a communion. The Church is an integral part of the gospel, not an optional extra, not a subsequent addition, not a logical result of becoming a Christian, but the context within which the Christian experience occurs, and the place where it is recalled and renewed. The New Testament has a very 'high' doctrine of the Church. It is 'the household of God ... the Church of the living God, the pillar and grounds of the truth' (1 Tim. 3.15). It is the community of God (1 Thess. 2.14; 1 Cor. 1.2; 10.32; 11.16, 22; 15.9; 1 Thess. 1.4; Acts 20.28), the community of Christ (Rom. 16.16; 1 Thess. 1.1), the temple of the Holy Spirit (1 Cor. 3.16; 6.19). It is a holy priesthood (1 Pet. 2.5), a chosen race, a royal priesthood, a holy nation, God's own people (2.9). It is God's people (2.10), God's flock (5.2). While it is not to be identified with the Kingdom of God, it is the new people to which the Kingdom is to be given (Matt. 21.43). To this New Testament teaching, the early Christian fathers added even greater emphasis on the centrality of the Church in revelation. The Church is a 'son of God',[44] it is 'the tribe of Christians . . . the race of those who honour God'.[45] The Church is therefore a new people, owing its origins to the gospel.

In the Pauline writings the solidarity of the Christian in Christ is expressed in the concept of the *sōma tou Christou*, the Body of Christ. The Church is addressed, and described, as the Body of Christ (1 Cor. 12.27; Eph. 1.23). But to speak of the Body of Christ is to speak of Christ himself.[46] The new community therefore constitutes one new person in Christ. It has been truly said that 'the concept of the body forms the keystone of Pauline theology',[47] and that we can identify a threefold pattern in the way in which the term 'body' is used in the letters. First, there is the *body of flesh*. Flesh, *sarx*, stands for the unredeemed nature, the unredeemed world. Christians, Paul insists, have renounced this lower nature, and live not according to the flesh, *kata sarkos*, but according to the spirit, *kata pneuma* (Rom. 8.4). 'While *sarx* stands for man in the solidarity of creation in his distance from God, *sōma* stands for man in the solidarity of creation as made for God.'[48] Christ, however, has come 'in the likeness of sinful flesh' (Rom. 8.4), has died in the flesh and crucified the flesh. So we can speak, secondly, of the *body of the cross*. According to Paul, Christians share in the death of Christ. 'The body nailed to the Cross was therefore, in this sense, the new organism of the One Man in whom we all die.'[49] Then, thirdly, there is the *body of the resurrection*. The risen body is not seen as a purely future prospect, for the risen life begins at baptism, not at death. The person who has been united to the Lord has become one spirit with him (1 Cor. 6.17), the person who is baptized into Christ has put on Christ (Gal. 3.27).

The relationship between Christ and the Church is thus one of intimate solidarity. As his Body, we shared in his death. In baptism we were 'grafted into the organism of the Crucified Man'.[50] The Christian man or woman is thus a person in whom a mighty act of renewal and re-creation has occurred. In speaking of the Church, we are thus not speaking of a collection of individuals, or of an organization, but of a living organism, an extension of the personality of Christ. The Church is, according to Pope Pius XII, 'another Christ' (*altera Christi persona*).[51] The Church is the social expression of the

Christ/Christian experience. In Thornton's words:

> ... what happened to Christ happened to us. We died, when he
> died upon the Cross. We rose with him. Because he ascended, we
> are 'seated with him in the heavenly places'. Thus, as sharer in the
> messianic Kingdom, the church is already co-partner with her
> Lord in that dominion of Adam which he has restored.[52]

Baptism is therefore of the greatest social importance in the theology
and spirituality of the early Church. It 'begins the substitution of the
solidarity of one body by that of another'.[53] It is not an individualistic
experience, but the act by which a person is made a sharer in the social
reality of redemption. The social reality of redemption: that is the
reality of the Church, however obscured it may be by the distortions
and betrayals of history. Within the broken world of flesh and
fallenness, the Church is the 'stamp, footprint and sign of God', 'an
eschatological sign erected in the world'. It is 'God's plantation in the
world, the new man created by God of former enemies, the
construction lot of God on earth'.[54] The Church is the organism of
Christ.

> We are members of that body which was nailed to the Cross, laid in
> the tomb, and raised to life on the third day. There is only one
> organism of the new creation; and we are members of that one
> organism which is Christ.[55]

Within the Church which is Christ's Body, the Word of God is
proclaimed, and sacraments are celebrated. The word 'sacrament'
does not occur in the New Testament, but there is a strong emphasis
of the place of baptism and of the Eucharist in the Church's life.
Christians are those who have been reborn of water and the Spirit,
those who have been incorporated, through the liturgy of baptism,
into the mystery of Christ's dying and rising. Christians are those who
constitute the Body of Christ, and their continued communion in that
Body, is both the manifestation of this reality, and also its repeated re-
enactment. More will be said later (in Chapter 9) of the Eucharist in
relation to our understanding of God. But the New Testament lays
equal stress on the Word of God. Christ is himself the Word (John
1.1–14; 1 John 1.1ff). And this Word is at work within believers (1
Thess. 2.13). Through him Christians have been born anew (1 Pet.
1.23). The Word is said to be sharper than a two-edged sword,
piercing to the division of soul and spirit, joints and marrow,
discerning the thoughts and intentions of the heart (Heb. 4.12; cf.
Eph. 6.17; Rev. 19.5). Spirit, Word and power are united in Hebrews

6.4 where Christians are described as those who have 'become partakers of the Holy Spirit, and have tasted the goodness of the Word of God and the powers of the age to come'. There is a sense in which the Word stands over against the Church in proclamation and judgement. It is a Word of contradiction as well as of nourishment. It is a Word to be received with meekness, for it is a soul-saving Word (Jas. 1.21). It is the Word of life (Phil.2.16; 1 John 1.1), the sure Word (Titus 1.9), the Word of God which is not fettered (2 Tim. 2.9) but free. It is the Word of freedom from which there is a constant tendency and temptation to retreat into the pre-baptismal bondage of laws and forms.

Being a Christian, in the New Testament understanding, is thus not a purely personal, but a social, reality. At the same time, within the body of Christ, there is an encounter with God, and a continuing and developing relationship with God, at the personal level. The individual Christian is addressed as 'man of God' (1 Tim. 6.11; 2 Tim. 3.17), and shares a new nature made after God's likeness (Eph. 4.24). the theme of the 'imitation of God' or 'imitation of Christ' certainly cannot be excluded from the New Testament. Paul reminds the Thessalonians that they 'became imitators of the Lord' (1 Thess. 1.6). Elsewhere he speaks of Christians as 'imitators of God' (Eph. 5.1). Christ's patience is specifically cited as an example to be followed (1 Tim. 1.16) as are kindness and forgiveness (Eph. 4.32) and love (5.2). But the Christian life is more than imitation. Paul speaks of becoming like Christ in his death (Phil. 3.10). The verb used here, *summorphizesthai*, takes up the *morphē* (form) of Philippians 2.5–7 ('form of God . . . form of a servant'). The idea is far greater than that of imitation, the copying of a model. Rather does it denote a *conformity* to Christ, involving change, and rooted in the fact of his indwelling. We are to be 'conformed to the image' of Christ (Rom. 8.29). And this *form* of Christ is related to his *glory*. To make someone conformable is to give him or her a share in glory by allowing a share in the Son's image. Among those who are conformed to Christ, there is a daily renewal, moving towards an eternal and incomparable glory (2 Cor. 4.16–17). Imitation is thus a very inadequate way of describing our union with Christ.[56] And there are in fact only a few passages which do speak of imitation (see 1 Thess. 1.6; 2.14; 2 Thess. 3.7–9; Phil. 3.17; 1 Cor. 4.16; 11.1; Eph. 5.1; and, possibly, Phil. 4.9 and Gal. 4.12). Rather the key themes are those of conformity, union, and communion in Christ.

The life of the Spirit is thus a social life, a corporate life. Without the Church there never was any Christianity. The entire Christian experience of deliverance and of transformation occurs within the context of the living body, the new social reality. God living and working in and through his people.

God and the Future

The New Testament ends with the enigmatic and perplexing Book of Revelation, a book which has for centuries been a happy hunting ground for speculators, doomwatchers, and those for whom prediction of the future lies at the heart of theology. Yet it is a most important work, in which the crises of an oppressed Church in a pagan state are related to the vision of God's future and the coming Kingdom. The Church, as we saw above, is itself an eschatological community, a community looking to the future, experiencing already the powers of the new age.[57] The Book of Revelation looks beyond the Church to the City in which there will be no temple (2.22) but where God will be all and in all. The God of past history and of present revelation is seen here as the God in whose hand is the future. Christ had finished his work on earth (John 17.4), but there are greater realities yet to be unveiled. So it is with an 'apocalypse', an unveiling, that the New Testament closes.

It is often said that the early Christians believed that the end of the world was near, and there is certainly some basis for this (see 1 Pet. 4.7; Jas. 5.8; 1 John 2.18). Yet it is not so clear as many have assumed that Jesus himself believed this.[58] The term 'Second Coming' does not occur in the New Testament (though Hebrews 9.28 comes close to it). Not until the mid-second century do we read of two comings of Christ. Justin Martyr speaks of 'two Parousias'[59] and of a 'first and second Parousia'.[60] However, the New Testament certainly contains the hope that Christ will, in some sense, 'come again', that he will appear, be manifested, be revealed. There will be an apocalypse, an unveiling of the reality of the Son of Man as the End of history and its Lord. It is wrong therefore to regard apocalyptic writing as *per se* pessimistic. The Book of Revelation is full of hope for this world, for the kingdoms of the world are to become the Kingdom of God (11.15). Nor is it clear that the 'delay of the Parousia' was a serious problem for the early Church. The earliest credal confessions stress the *present* Lordship of Christ, while the eucharistic liturgies contain no explicit reference to a return of Christ until the fourth century. There are many problematic areas in this field, but certain things are clear.

The early Christians believed that the 'time of the End' had begun in Jesus, but that there was more to come. There was to be a culmination of the saving process. Jeremias stresses how central to early Christian belief was the theme that Satan had already fallen from

heaven (Luke 10.18), and that the conquest of the dominion of evil
had already begun:

> The casting of Satan out of the heavenly world presupposes an
> earlier battle in heaven, like that described in Revelation 12.7–9.
> Jesus' visionary cry of joy leaps over the interval of time before the
> final crisis, and sees in the exorcisms performed by the disciples the
> dawn of the annihilation of Satan. This stage has already been
> reached: the evil spirits are powerless, Satan is being destroyed
> (Luke 10.18), paradise is opening up (v. 19), the names of the
> redeemed stand in the book of life (v. 20). There is no analogy to
> these statements in contemporary Judaism: neither the synagogue
> nor Qumran knows anything of a vanquishing of Satan that is
> already beginning in the present.[61]

The future, God's future, has been drawn into the present, but there
is still the climax to come.

Because of this emphasis on the present manifestation of the
eschatological Kingdom, it has been claimed that 'apocalyptic was the
mother of all Christian theology'.[62] Christian theology, it is argued,
cannot survive without the theme of the manifestation of the Son of
Man. It is wrong to see apocalyptic simply as fantasy, the otherworldly dreamings of those who have lost hope in this world's future.
Nor does it imply the negation of history, or the idolatry of the details
of prediction. Rather

> Apocalypse means not only the revealing of details ... but the
> disclosure of possible participation in the final and unique, all
> encompassing coming of God among men. An apocalypse is
> therefore designed to be 'the revelation of the divine revelation' as
> this takes place in the individual acts of a coherent historical
> pattern.[63]

There is a continuity of ideas between the theme of the Day of the
Lord in the Old Testament and the apocalyptic theme of the signs of
the End. Rather than seeing a sharp contrast and conflict between
prophecy and apocalyptic, most modern scholars would hold that
apocalyptic took up elements in the prophetic tradition and teaching,
and developed them.[64]

It is against the background of Jewish and Christian apocalyptic
writings that we should see the Book of Revelation. It is a book which
is concerned with interpreting present and future history, with 'what
is and what will be' (1.19), but not in the sense of a predetermined
divine plan as we find in some Jewish apocalyptic writings. John's
view of history is rooted in the redemptive work of Christ and his

coming again. His victory has already been accomplished: the Lion of the Tribe of Judah has conquered (5.5). The Lamb has been slain and has ransomed people for God from all nations (5.6–12). There is no prediction of specific events, but rather an interpretation of the meaning and nature of history. It is a prophetic interpretation, based upon the two divine interventions, Christ's incarnation and awaited return in glory. The past event in some sense shapes the course of the future. Thus John 'presents the materialization of salvation as a consequence of events whose unfolding lies grounded in the nature of salvation history'.[65] In many respects the book is closer to prophecy than to the fantastic visions and images of some apocalyptic writing. 'It is not a book of fantastic speculations about a distant future age; it is the authentic voice of prophecy pronouncing God's judgement upon the corrupting influence of power.'[66] It is possible that its context is the paschal liturgy.[67]

While it is the Book of Revelation which most dramatically relates the saving work of God in Christ to the future of the world, it is not only here that there is teaching about a future coming. The theme of a coming of Christ in the future is present, if not central, in most New Testament books. The first reference to a *parousia* occurs in 1 Thessalonians 1.10: 'to wait for his Son from heaven, whom he raised from the dead, Jesus who delivers us from the wrath to come'. Paul ends the First Letter to the Corinthians with the prayer 'Our Lord, come' (16.22). But the future coming is not included in the list of foundation beliefs in Hebrews 6.1f. However, only in Galatians, Ephesians, Philippians, and 2 and 3 John is it entirely absent.

The term *parousia*, on the other hand, is only used of a future coming of Christ in four places (1 Cor. 15.23; Jas. 5.7f; 2 Pet. 3.4; and 1 John 2.28), apart form its uses in Thessalonians and in Matthew 24. By the third century the term had entered popular usage, though Clement of Alexandria uses it about the incarnation itself.[68] Earlier, Ignatius (Philad. 9.2) had used '*parousia* of the Saviour' about the whole ministry of Jesus. Other terms used are *apokalypsis* (unveiling, 1 Cor. 1.7; 2 Thess. 1.7; 1 Pet. 1.7, 13; 4.13), *epiphaneia* (appearing, 2 Thess. 2.8; 1 Tim. 6.14; 2 Tim. 4.1, 8; Titus 2.13), and Day of the Lord/Son of Man (Matt. 24.42; Luke 17.22–31; 1 Cor. 1.8; 5.5; 2 Cor. 1.14; Phil. 1.6, 10; 2.16; 1 Thess. 5.2–4; 2 Thess. 2.2). Jesus is also said to be manifested (Col. 3.4; 1 Pet. 5.4; 1 John 2.28; 3.2), seen (Heb. 9.28), and revealed (Luke 17.30). There is reference to the ingathering of the elect in Mark 13.26f/Matt. 24.30f and in Paul (e.g. 1 Thess. 4.17; 2 Thess. 1.10; 2.1, etc.); to the end of all things (1 Pet. 4.7), the last hour

(1 John 2.18; 1 Pet. 1.5), the close of the age (Matt. 24.3) and the last day (John 6.39–54; 11.24; 12.48); and, in Acts, to the times of refreshing, that is, the messianic age (3.13–26).

Let us now return to the Book of Revelation and consider how God is seen and described there. Chapters 4–5 are central to the book. The visions there of the worship of God and the Lamb precede all the other visions. A door is opened in heaven, revealing God seated on his throne (4.1–2). The description is one marked by awe and majesty: jewels, a rainbow, twenty-four crowned elders, flashes of lightning, peals of thunder, torches of fire, and a sea of glass (4.3–6). A ceaseless Sanctus is sung to the God 'who was and is and is to come' (4.8). Then in the next chapter comes the vision of the Lamb before whom a 'new song' is sung.

The God who is revealed is the God who was revealed in past history and in creation itself: he is 'the Alpha and the Omega . . . who is and who was and who is to come' (1.8). He is 'the living God' (7.2) who reveals both grace and wrath (1.4; 16.1): the rainbow and the lightning are symbols of mercy and wrath (4.3, 5).

This God also is the Father of Jesus Christ (1.6; 2.28; 3.5, 21; 14.1). Christ is his Word (19.13), and it is through him that he acts (6.1ff). The Book of Revelation has no hesitation in giving divine epithets to Christ. When John saw him, he fell at his feet as if dead (1.17). He is described as 'the Amen, the faithful and true witness, the beginning of God's creation' (3.14). He is 'the Alpha and the Omega, the first and the last, the beginning and the end' (22.13). Because of his conquest, he sits with the Father on his throne (3.21). His shape and description are taken from Daniel's description of the Ancient of Days, God himself (1.14; cf. Dan. 7.9). He receives worship: 'to him who sits upon the throne and to the Lamb be blessing and honour and glory and might for ever and ever' (5.13). 'Salvation belongs to our God who sits upon the throne and to the Lamb' (7.10). 'Now the salvation and the power and the kingdom of our God and the authority of his Christ have come' (12.10). He has won the victory, and because of this he is able to open the book (5.5). He *has* conquered. The word used is *enikēsen*, a word which, according to one writer, 'marks the centre of the Revelation's Christology'.[69] The victory has already been achieved, a once-for-all event in history has taken place. So Jesus appears as a Lamb bearing still the marks of slaughter upon him. His death has delivered us from bondage to the powers (5.9; 14.4); he has conquered so that we can conquer (12.10). Thus in the victory proclamation in 5.5 we can feel 'the heartbeat of the whole Christology of John'.[70] The passage continues with the song of the living creatures and the elders:

Worthy art thou to take the scroll and to open its seals,
for thou wast slain and by thy blood didst ransom men for God
from every tribe and tongue and people and nation,
and hast made them a kingdom and priests to our God,
and they shall reign on earth. (5.9–10)

The vision in Chapter 5 is therefore central to the whole work. One writer points to the words in 5.9, commenting:

We must not neglect this clue to the meaning of the whole vision. It is a description of the operation of forces which were released by the single event of suffering and victory. . . . The prophet is seeking to describe the repercussions, the echoes, the continuing effects of the Passion story.[71]

Specifically the Book of Revelation describes a threefold pattern of events through which the redemptive work of Christ reaches its climax and consummation: the harvest, the vintage, and the great white throne.

The truth that Christ will gather his own to himself is an important aspect of the gospel (John 14.3), symbolized by the separation of wheat and tares, the drag net and so on. In Revelation, there is the picture of the Son of man as reaper:

Then I looked, and lo, a white cloud, and seated on the cloud one like a son of man, with a golden crown on his head, and a sharp sickle in his hand. And another angel came out of the temple, calling with a loud voice to him who sat upon the cloud, 'Put in your sickle, and reap, for the hour to reap has come, for the harvest of the earth is fully ripe.' So he who sat upon the cloud swung his sickle on the earth, and the earth was reaped. (14.14–16)

The harvest theme looks back to the celebration of the firstfruits of the earth (Exod. 23.16; Lev. 23.9ff), and it is the firstfruits which is the concern of Revelation 14.

But, secondly, there is the vintage of the earth, the vengence of God upon evil. Another angel with a sharp sickle appears, and is ordered: 'Put in your sickle and gather the clusters of the vine of the earth.' Having done so, he 'threw it into the great wine press of the wrath of God', which was then trodden outside the city. (14.18–20)

Finally, there is the scene before the 'great white throne' (20.11). Upon the throne sat one from whose presence earth and sky fled away.

In this threefold pattern the work of God is seen in terms of the gathering in of the faithful believers, the destruction of the forces of evil, and the final judgement and triumph of God and the Lamb. The book ends with a magnificent vision of the City of God:

> Then I saw a new heaven and a new earth; for the first heaven and
> the first earth had passed away, and the sea was no more. And I saw
> the holy city, new Jerusalem, coming down out of heaven from
> God, prepared as a bride adorned for her husband. (21.1–2)

God's dwelling is now with the human race who will be his people
(21.3). All things are to be made new (21.5), and the City of God is to
reflect his presence and glory:

> And I saw no temple in the city, for its temple is the Lord God, the
> Almighty and the Lamb. And the city has no need of sun or moon
> to shine upon it, for the glory of God is its light, and its lamp is the
> Lamb. By its light shall the nations walk; and the kings of the earth
> shall bring their glory into it, and its gates shall never be shut by
> day – and there shall be no night there; they shall bring into it the
> glory and the honour of the nations. (21.22–6)

Through the City flows the 'river of the water of life' (22.1), while the
tree of life stands on either side of the river: 'the leaves of the trees
were for the healing of the nations'. (22.2) So the Bible ends with the
prospect of the renewal of heaven and earth, of a social life
characterized by equality and sharing in the divine light and the divine
name. For 'they shall see his face, and his name shall be on their
foreheads. And night shall be no more; they need no light of lamp or
sun, for the Lord God will be their light, and they shall reign for ever
and ever.' (22.4–5)

Some have seen in the future orientation a form of passive
acquiescence in suffering and oppression. Eschatology becomes a
narcotic, a way of diminishing action, of clouding consciousness, of
transferring all hope to a distant and remote future. Undoubtedly that
is both possible and common in Christian history. Yet eschatology
need not lead to quietism, nor should the hope of God's future action
lead to reduced action in the present. The German theologian
Christoph Blumhardt, from whom Karl Barth learnt a great deal, saw
the openness to the future as a call to vigilance and dynamic action.
'We cannot be swallowed up by the present age because we are bound
to the future and because we experience the future in the present.'[72]
Blumhardt saw that the early Church 'understood in the future of
Jesus Christ the prospect of an alteration in heaven and earth',[73] and
in this he was followed by Barth with his insistence on 'the confidence
and unsettlement of the expectation of the Kingdom of God which
will rectify the whole world and all life even to its deepest recesses'.[74]
Far from leading to an otherworldly escapism, eschatology was the

basis of Christian resistance: 'Just because I set such emphasis Sunday by Sunday on the last things, it was no longer possible for me personally to remain suspended in the clouds above the present evil world.'[75]

It is the God who is always beyond us, always future, always moving onwards, who prevents us from being enslaved to passing trends and to the present age.

5
God of the Desert

It is no whim of history that the birth of the first monotheistic faith took place in a desert ...
Michael Evenari, Leslie Shanan and Naphtali Tadmor,
The Negev: the challenge of a desert.[1]

We have seen earlier in this study how central was the desert in the emergence of Israel as a people and of Israelite faith in Yahweh. It was in the desert, barren, unpredictable, surprising, that the people of God were to learn the lesson and privilege of dependence upon Yahweh in the simplicity of naked faith. It was in the desert that Israel was found, receiving her identity in the howling wastes of the wilderness (Deut. 32.10). It would be in the desert that renewal would take place, there that the wastes would rejoice and blossom like the rose, there that waters would flow again (Isa. 35.1–6). Throughout human history, religious and secular, the desert has played a crucial role:

> It is no whim of history that the birth of the first monotheistic faith
> took place in a desert, or that it was followed there by the other two
> great religions, Christianity and Islam. The prophets of Israel
> repeatedly sought and found inspiration in the desert. Christian
> hermits fled to it to escape the pollution of the world and to
> commune with God, and in modern times the secular literature of
> the desert in the works of Doughty, Lawrence, Philby, Thomas,
> and many other famous travellers reveals the powerful influence it
> exerts on the minds and spirits of all who seek its mysteries.[2]

We may see the beginnings of the experience of God in the context of the desert in Abraham's journey into the unknown. Abraham, set free of the false gods of his past history (cf. Josh. 24.2), moved out in the darkness of faith. As the sun went down, we are told that 'a dread and great darkness fell upon him' (Gen. 15.12). But it was in the period of Moses and the Exodus from Egypt that the desert as a place of revelation and of spiritual struggle comes into its own. After the crossing of the Red Sea, Moses led Israel into the Wilderness of Shur where they tasted the bitter waters of Marah (Exod. 15.22–3). There was bitterness, murmuring, and crying to the Lord. The waters of

Marah were followed by the springs and palm trees of Elim, the place of refreshment (15.27). Again, the movement into the Wilderness of Sin was marked by murmuring and by complaints that it would have been better to have died in Egypt amid plenty than in the desert amid hunger (16.3). This was itself followed by the appearance of Yahweh in glory in the cloud (16.10) and by the provision of quails and of manna (16.13–15, 31). There was further murmuring at Rephidim, to be followed by the striking of the rock and the appearance of water at Massa and Meribah, places to be enshrined for ever in the morning office of the Church as symbols of wilderness infidelity (17.7; Ps. 95.8–9). But they are symbols also of God's holiness (Num. 20.13). The arrival at the Wilderness of Sinai was marked by the assurance from Yahweh that, through the experience of wandering, he had borne them on eagle's wings and had brought them to himself to be his own possession, a kingdom of priests and a holy nation (19.4–6). The desert experience of Israel reaches its climax in the cloud and the thick darkness of Mount Sinai, the place of the divine revelation. At Sinai, the people cried out, 'You speak to us, and we will hear; but let not God speak to us lest we die' (Exod. 20.19). The picture throughout is one in which murmuring and groaning are mingled with refreshment and revelation. It is in the process of such troubled interrogation of God that the revelation occurs.

The desert regions of south and east Palestine, regions character-ized by waste, darkness, and struggle, formed the scene for the experience of the wasteland of the spirit, the darkness of the divine withdrawal, and the struggle for the divine encounter and for human identity. Never was location so suited to the spiritual exploration and crisis which occurred within it:

From this quarter came the locusts, before which 'the land is as the garden of Eden and behind them a desolate wilderness' (Joel 2.3). From there the Sirocco blew as a blast from a fiery furnace, the ordeal of fire, of which Amos speaks, which dried up even the subterranean waters (Amos 7.4) – the whirlwind or dust storm also came from the great empty quarter (Amos 1.14). The 'darkness' or obscuration associated with both Sirocco and dust storm, owing to the fact that the atmosphere is heavily charged with fine particles of dust, is also connected with the desert. Such a darkness obscures the heavenly bodies, and both sun and moon appear 'blood-red'. A prolonged visitation of the Sirocco, called in Palestine the Hamsim (literally 'fifty') with drought and famine, causes plague. All these are common manifestations of the presence of Yahweh in the Hebrew prophets ... They are not rare, supernatural phenomena, but are all too common in the experience of dwellers in Palestine in all ages, and to ancient Israel (e.g. Amos) they signified the dreaded presence of Yahweh their desert God.[3]

So the desert witnesses to the confrontation with God in terrible simplicity, it is the 'primal scriptural symbol of the absence of all human aid and comfort'.[4] Here, in the experience of waste and emptiness, of liberation through and from oppression, Christians have seen the foreshadowing of the redeeming work of God in Christ. The Exodus thus holds a central place in Christian luturgy and spirituality as we celebrate and experience inwardly our own deliverance from bondage. So St Gregory of Nyssa told his hearers:[5]

> Cross the Jordan, hasten towards the new life in Christ, to the land that bears fruit in happiness, flowing with milk and honey, according to the promise. Overthrow Jericho, your former way of life! . . . All these things are figures of the reality which is now made manifest.

It has, however, not been merely to the Exodus event that later spiritual explorers have looked, but also to the solitaries and prophets who found nourishment and stimulus in the desert. Elijah, who journeyed into the desert for forty days and forty nights, and, arriving at Horeb, lodged in a cave (1 Kings 19.3–9), has been seen as a key figure for those seeking God in solitude and stillness. Thomas Merton, in his poem 'Elias', portrays him as the type of all contemplatives:

> Under the blunt pine
> Elias becomes his own geography
> (Supposing geography to be necessary at all).
> Elias becomes his own wild bird, with God in the center,
> His own wide field which nobody owns.
> His own pattern, surrounding the spirit
> By which he is himself surrounded:
> For the free man's road has neither beginning nor end.[6]

The Carmelites look to Elijah as their spiritual founder, for he lived for periods as a hermit on Mount Carmel, while some modern Carmelites speak of the need to recover the spirit of Elijah who combined solitude with such a profound impact on the heart of the prevailing culture.[7]

In the New Testament, the Judaean wilderness was the context for the preaching of John the Baptist, identified as a 'voice crying in the wilderness' (Matt. 3.3 citing Isa. 40). Jesus too was led by the Spirit into the wilderness where he experienced temptations (Matt. 4.1; Mark 1.12; Luke 4.1), and throughout his ministry he is described as having sought solitude in deserts and lonely places, instructing his disciples to follow his example (Mark 6.30). The desert experience was one with which the early Christians too were familiar, for they saw themselves as a pilgrim people, seeking a better country (Heb. 11.16). On their path to the City of God they 'went about in skins of sheep and goats . . . wandering over deserts and mountains, and in dens and caves of the earth' (11.37–8). The sense of belonging nowhere, of having no continuing city, is one which comes across powerfully in the literature of the early Christian centuries. Thus the Shepherd of Hermas tells its readers: 'You servants of God should know that you are living in a land which is not your own. Your own city is a long way from this one.'[8] However, as the centuries moved on, a movement began which saw the desert as itself a city, a place of perpetual solitude and struggle for the purity of the faith:

> In the fourth century AD the deserts of Egypt, Palestine, Arabia and Persia were peopled by a race of men who have left behind them a strange reputation. They were the first Christian hermits who abandoned the cities of the pagan world to live in solitude. Why did they do this? The reasons were many and various, but they can all be summed up in one word as the quest for 'salvation'.[9]

It is to this movement, the movement of the 'Desert Fathers', that we must now turn our attention.

The Desert Fathers and Their Quest for God

The deserts of Egypt and Syria provided the setting for the movement of purity and protest which we associate with those groups of holy men who are now called the Desert Fathers. Their quest was for purity, authenticity, in a period of compromise, and their retreat into the desert was a form of protest against a compromised Church. It was this protest which paved the way for the monastic movement, itself 'a highly responsible and effective protest and opposition to the world, and not least to a worldly Church, a new and specific way of combating it, and therefore a direct address to it'.[10] The impetus of the movement was a desire to live the baptismal life in its perfection. Deprived of the stimulus of persecution, the Church was only too vulnerable to the path of compromise. The external profession of the Christian religion had become easy, and a modified, compromised form of Christian life was growing. It was the sensitivity to this real danger of compromise and loss of pure discipleship which led to the desert movement. As early as the end of the second century, it was related that Narcissus, Bishop of Jerusalem, 'fled from the whole body of the Church, hid himself in the deserts and secret places, and remained there for many years'.[11] If it was persecution which began the shift to the desert, it was the fear of compromise which strengthened it. So the Desert Fathers lived in silence and solitude, conscious of the severe temptations which the desert environment itself held. For these waste regions were the abode of the demons and the forces of evil, and so they saw their life as one of ascetical conflict, the life of Christian athletes. In the deserts, at the margins of human society, they sought God, and their own inner identity.

The solitary life has continued to puzzle the Christian believers of later generations. Phyllis McGinley, in her poem about St Simeon Stylites (390–459), caught something of the puzzlement:[12]

> On top of a pillar Simeon sat.
> He wore no mantle,
> He had no hat,
> But bare as a bird
> Sat night and day,
> And hardly a word
> Did Simeon say.

> Under the sun of a desert sky,
> He sat on a pillar
> Nine feet high.
> When Fool and his brother
> Came round to admire
> He raised it another
> Nine feet higher.

> The seasons circled about his head.
> He lived on water
> And crusts of bread
> (Or so one hears)
> From pilgrims' store
> For thirty years
> And a little more.

> And why did Simeon sit like that,
> Without a mantle,
> Without a hat,
> In a holy rage
> For the world to see?
> It puzzles me.
> It puzzled many

A desert Father,
And I think it puzzled the
Good Lord rather.

Admittedly, Simeon, the greatest of the pillar ascetics, was not in the mainstream of the desert tradition. As Evagrius wrote of him, 'abandoning the beaten path which the saints had trodden, he was pursuing another, altogether unknown'.[13] Yet in a sense he simply presented in an extreme form the problem of the life of desert spirituality as a whole. What was its rationale? Was it a rational lifestyle at all? The Syrian hermit Philoxenos, who wrote in the sixth century, explained that the life of the solitary had no rational explanation, but was a life without law. Commenting on his claim, Thomas Merton observed that 'to be a contemplative is therefore to be an outlaw'.[14] At the core of the spiritual quest of the Desert Fathers was a rejection of convention, but there was much more:

> The flight of these men to the desert was neither purely negative nor purely individualistic. They were not rebels against society. True, they were, in a certain sense, 'anarchists', and it will do no harm to think of them in that light. These were men who did not believe in letting themselves be passively guided and ruled by a decadent state and who believed that there was a way of getting along without slavish dependence on accepted conventional values.[15]

While the majority of Christians did not follow the exodus to the desert, that exodus and the theological movement which inspired it and flourished within it, was to nourish the faith of Europe for centuries.

St Paul of Thebes (died 340) has been given the title of 'the first hermit', but it was St Antony of Egypt (251–356) who is rightly seen as the pioneer of the desert movement. He is alleged to have observed that 'a time is coming when men will go mad, and when they see someone who is not mad, they will attack him, saying "You are mad, you are not like us"'.[16] Many people journeyed into the desert to seek counsel from Antony, and to learn from his silence. In the life and spiritual experience of Antony, we see the centrality of spiritual warfare and of spiritual discernment in the search for God. Asceticism without discernment, he saw, was dangerous. 'Some have afflicted their bodies by asceticism', he complained, 'but they lack discernment, and so they are far from God.'[17] It is from the early desert tradition that the theme of discernment, spiritual discrimination, enters the literature of Christian spirituality and spiritual guidance.

Antony himself sought spiritual direction before he moved into the desert at all,[18] and when, fifteen years later, he went further into the desert regions alone, he tried to persuade his elderly spiritual director to accompany him.[19] Throughout the literature of the desert there is a continuing stress on the need for direction in the life of the spirit.[20]

It was said that, wherever God was, Antony would be there too, and many people would journey into the desert simply in order to see him. He was believed to be 'Spirit-born' and carried along by the Holy Spirit.[21] However, there is little stress in the accounts of his life and sayings on any special experience of God. In Athanasius's *Life of Antony* we find no mention of his own experience of God, and such accounts are also absent in the descriptions of Pachomius and of Basil. Yet the impact of Antony on future generations of those who sought holiness and purity of heart was tremendous. When Antony emerged from his desert cave after twenty years, it was written of him:

> After that many longed and sought to copy his holy life and some of his friends came and forcibly broke down the door and removed it: and Antony came forth as from a holy of holies ... This was the first time he showed himself from the fort to those who came to him. When they saw him, they marvelled to see that his body kept his former state, being neither grown heavy for want of exercise, nor shrunken with fastings and strivings against demons. For he was such as they had known him before his retirement. The light of his soul too was absolutely pure. It was not shrunken with grieving, nor dissipated by pleasures; it had no touch of levity nor of gloom. He was not bashful at seeing the crowd, nor elated at being welcomed by such large numbers, but was unvaryingly tranquil, a man ruled by reason, whose whole character had grown firm-set in the way that nature had meant it to grow.

From Antony's original movement there grew a variety of forms of monastic life. Egypt was the centre of the movement. In Lower Egypt were the hermits, while the organized monastic movement of Pachomius (290–347) developed in Tabennisi in Upper Egypt. At Nitria and Scetis there grew up another form of monastic life in which several monks lived together as disciples with a spiritual father (*pneumatikos pater*). Mount Sinai itself began to attract solitaries during the persecutions of the third century, and the first monastery was built there in the fourth century.

At the heart of the spirituality of the desert was the emphasis on purity of heart, on freedom from passion and disturbance, and the acquiring of unified vision and purpose. But such authentic purity could only be attained through conflict and struggle, a theme which is brought out in the writings of Evagrius (345–99). Evagrius lived as a hermit for sixteen years at the high point of the desert movement. He believed that the life of the solitary was particularly vulnerable to demonic attack:

> The demons fight hand to hand with the hermits, but in their battle against those who live a life of virtue in a monastery or a community they fight only indirectly – through the more negligent brethren. The latter battle is a much slighter affair than the former since never will you find on earth men as spiteful as the demons, or able to work all wickedness so quickly.[23]

The demons, says Evagrius, attack the areas of the imagination but God knows the heart. In a sense, the entire solitary tradition can be seen as a battle for the heart. Abba John the Dwarf is said to have prayed for deliverance from passions, and his prayer was answered. But a senior brother advised him to ask God to give him his passions back! This was essential, said the old man, 'so that you may regain the afflictions and humility that you used to have, for it is by spiritual warfare that the soul makes progress'.[24] The stress on spiritual warfare comes out also with great clarity in the writings of Cassian (360–435) who entered a monastery at Bethlehem towards the end of the fourth century, and, after some years there, moved into Egypt. Cassian saw the desert as the abode of the spiritually mature, and saw very grave dangers there for those with unresolved problems:

> It is the perfect men, purged of every fault, who ought to go into the desert. And when their faults are annihilated in their cenobitic life, they should enter solitude; not because they are cowards, running away from their sins, but because they are pursuing the contemplation of God, and desire a more sublime vision which cannot be found except in solitude, and then only by perfect men. For every fault we bring not purged into the desert will still be felt hidden and undestroyed inside us. To a life that has been cured of sin, solitude can unlock the purest contemplation and unfold the knowledge of spiritual mysteries to its clear gaze. But in the same way it usually preserves and even worsens the faults of those who have not been cured of them.[25]

To enter the desert then is to enter the arena of spiritual conflict.

Equally strong is the emphasis in desert spirituality on solidarity, on the common life. 'The monk', wrote Evagrius,[26] 'is separated from all and united to all. The monk is one who regards himself as one with all because he sees himself appearing continually in each person'. Antony had insisted that 'our life and death is with our neighbour'.[27]

His letters describe heaven as a state where we see each other face to face. On the other hand, in hell 'it is not possible to see anyone face to face, but the face of one is fixed to the back of another. Yet when you pray for us, each of us can see the other's face a little.'[28] In similar vein, Abba Lucius emphasized the need for true communion before true solitude could be enjoyed, for 'if you have not first of all lived rightly with men, you will not be able to live rightly in solitude'.[29] 'God the Creator arranged things,' wrote St Basil,[30] 'so that we need each other.' Basil in fact was hesitant about the solitary life. The life of society was the natural life.[31] For, in the solitary life, he asked: 'Whose feet will you wash, whom will you look after, how can you be last of all, if you live by yourself?'[32] At the end of the day, he saw the life of solitude as a valid form of Christian discipleship, but a rare form calling for great inner strength and centredness. It was those who were, in common understanding, most mature and most socially aware who might receive the call to the life of inner solitude, to the quest for the inner heart. For, as the Macarian Homilies of the late fourth century expressed it, 'the chief task of the athlete is to enter into his heart'.[33]

Most of the desert monks were peasants. Some, such as Arsenius, were aristocrats, others, such as Evagrius, were scholars. Antony was the son of peasant farmers, while it was said of Apollo that 'he had been a shepherd and was very uncouth'.[34] Out of this social mix came a new religious counter-culture. Peter Brown has described the ascetical movement as 'a long drawn out ritual of dissociation – of becoming the total stranger'.[35] Conformity to society was seen as dangerous, for 'society . . . was regarded as a shipwreck from which each single individual man had to swim for his life . . . These were men who believed that to let oneself drift along, passively accepting the tenets and values of what they knew as society, was purely and simply a disaster.'[36] In the monastic society which grew up in the desert, there was a great concern with agriculture and cultivation. Concern for the poor was also evident, and it was common knowledge that there were no poor in the vicinity of the monasteries. So the desert monks created an alternative culture amid the desert wastes:

> While one of the themes for the monks themselves was a radical withdrawal from society and its concerns, they inevitably created a new focus of order. In a visible as well as a spiritual way, the monks made the desert blossom.[37]

Throughout the literature of the desert movement there is a concern to create the conditions for gospel living, the environment in which spiritual progress is made easier. Here, deprived of human resources, the monks and hermits threw their powerlessness before God. At the same time, the spiritual discipline of the desert was not a purely negative one, and there is considerable emphasis on the cultivation of virtues. Humility in particular is seen as a prerequisite of the approach to God, and with humility goes penitence and a sense of one's weaknesses. Spiritual poverty and meekness are also stressed, and Athanasius speaks of the desert as 'the land of the meek'.[38] Grief and weeping over sin figure prominently with much emphasis on the place of tears in prayer. The desert has been compared to a university, and it certainly was a centre of intensive spiritual education.[39]

At the centre of this educational process was the spiritual father, the *pneumatikos pater*. 'Where are the great and wise men,' Jung once asked,[40] 'who do not merely talk about the meaning of life and the world but really possess it?' The holy men of the desert were seen as more than tutors. They were bearers of the spirit, charismatic figures, and between them and their disciples there was a relationship comparable to that of apprenticeship. Thoughts and feelings, the innermost motions of the heart, were exposed to the spiritual father, as a necessary part of coming to know oneself, to be free of dishonesty, and to mature. 'Give me a word, father' is a recurring demand of the desert disciple. Often the response would be a short gospel word to be brooded upon in silence and solitude.

Peter Brown, in a study of the holy man in the ancient world, has pointed out that 'in studying both the most admired and the most detested figures in any society, we can see, as seldom through other evidence, the nature of the average man's expectations and hopes for himself'.[41] The desert holy men were figures of great importance, consulted by bishops, magistrates, and public figures as well as by the unemployed, the blind, and the poor. The name which was given to the spiritual father was *abba*, and it was not given lightly. They were old men, but length of years was not enough. Cassian warned:

> Abba Moses told me: It is good not to hide the thoughts but to disclose them to discreet and devout old men; but not to men who are old merely in years, for many have found final despair instead of comfort by confessing to men whom they saw to be aged, but who in fact were inexperienced.[42]

What was being sought was a human relationship through which the reality of God might be both recognized and also applied to the concrete life situation of the disciple. It was from this search for guidance that the tradition of spiritual direction arose, a tradition which depends upon the doctrine of the incarnation. As God became flesh in Christ, so he continues to heal and nourish through the fleshly relationship, through human friendship, warmth, and sensitivity. Through the intimate relationship with the spiritual father, the divine revelation is personalized. In Brown's words:[43]

> The holy man carried the burden of making such a distant God relevant to the particularity of human needs. In his person the acute ambivalence of a Christian God was summed up in a manageable and approachable form . . . The values of the Christian man of the world were, as it were, rendered safe and efficacious by being drained into him.

The abba then was sought 'for his mysterious life-giving power to nourish the seeds of holiness'. While the Holy Spirit was seen as the source of all spiritual life and progress, the abba was seen as a channel of grace which enabled the Spirit to flourish and to transform the life of the monk. More than all else, it was holiness which was looked for in the abba:

> The title 'Abba' was not lightly bestowed by the monks of the desert. The primary criterion was knowledge of the secrets of the desert life, attained through experience and solitude. The Abbas are unfailingly old men, although a man could strive for years without coming to the required wisdom. More than experience, evidence of transformation, of holiness, was basic. This holiness endowed the Abba with the charismatic gift of discernment, enabling him to detect and dispel the illusions that inevitably afflict the beginning monk, or any monk not yet confirmed in the vision sustained by purity of heart, the vision of depth into the veiled motivations of man.[44]

Through the spiritual disciplines of the desert, the seekers after God hoped to achieve discernment, *diakrisis*, 'a right judgement in all things'. They would travel miles to hear a brief word which would speak directly to their condition and illuminate it. The goal was not survival or a minimal level of efficiency, but perfection, a 'Godlike state of fulfilment'; they wished to become 'true citizens of heaven'.[45] Their path was not smooth or untroubled, for only the experience of inner confusion, turmoil, and pain can enable one to be of service to others in their deepest need. The desert road was therefore littered with casualties. Discernment involved the recognition of limits, the humility to see that one is not God, and that God does not seek one's spiritual destruction.[46]

One of the old men used to say, 'If thou seest a man who hath fallen into the water, and thou canst help him, stretch out thy staff to him, and draw him out, lest if thou stretch out thy hand to him and thou art not able to bring him up, he drag thee down and both of you perish.' Now he spake this for the sake of those who thrust themselves forward to help other people who are being tempted, and who, through wishing to help (others) beyond their power (themselves) fall. It is right for a man to help his brother according to the power he hath, for God demandeth not from a man beyond his strength.[47]

A serious danger to the spiritual life then is the danger of over-activity, of stretching oneself beyond one's powers, and so leading to spiritual exhaustion and restlessness. External silence, say the Desert Fathers, is useless if the heart is still babbling.[48] Inner peace is the fruit of wrestling, but also of the practice of the presence of God in stillness. While the desert writers make no virtue of conflict in itself, they recognize the transforming power of pain and struggle. 'It is meet for a monk to have pain within himself.'[49] So in much of the writing there is a harsh and aggressive tone, as in St John Climacus's *Ladder of Divine Ascent*. Climacus (570–649) entered the monastic community on Mount Sinai but later became a solitary. It has been said that his book presents 'a spirituality as severe, as inflexible, as rugged, as the landscape in which it was born'.[50] At the centre of his approach is the invocation of the Name of Jesus, the uniting of that Name with one's breath, as both a weapon against the demons and as the way to inner silence, to *hēsychia*.

The concept of *hēsychia* is undoubtedly 'the central consideration in the prayer of the desert fathers'.[51] Silence and continual prayer are seen to be the roots of sinlessness,[52] and we find throughout the literature a stress on the importance of silence in the approach to God. God has chosen silence above all other virtues, he dwells within it, and it is through the cultivation of the inner spirit of *hēsychia* that union with God is attained. In its early uses the term *hesychast* referred to a solitary or hermit. But *hēsychia* is used not only of physical solitude and quiet, but also of interior vigilance and spiritual sobriety. 'Go and sit in your cell, and your cell will teach you all things' was the advice of Abba Moses.[53] The cell, to the monks of the desert tradition, was the 'workshop of unceasing prayer',[54] the place of continual recollection of God. It is the environmental space in which the disciple becomes acclimatized to the presence of the divine, and in which God can reveal himself without the obstacles created by noise and fragmentation of the spirit. This stress on the cell, the small house, is among the central features of the teaching of the desert, and it testifies to a permanent truth in the quest for God: the need to withdraw, close the door, and find God in that physical seclusion and peace which enables inner, spiritual seclusion and peace to grow. So the hermit John of Gaza, speaking of one of his fellow-solitaries writes:

> The cell in which he is enclosed alive as in a tomb, for the sake of the Name of Jesus, is his place of repose; no demon enters there, not even the prince of demons, the devil. It is a sanctuary for it contains the dwelling place of God.[55]

Hēsychia, in its external sense, refers to the practice of the solitary life. But there is a deeper, more inward, sense in which it points to the reality of inner prayerfulness, inner quietude. So eastern Christian writers come to speak of the 'binding of the mind', the unifying of the thoughts through the practice of silence, and the movement towards unceasing prayer, the continual recollection of the presence of God. It is in fact to this spirit of *hēsychia* that the entire desert testifies. One could say that the desert is one great cell, one great centre of stillness, one huge silence: *silentium ingens, quies magna.* 'This is the utter desert, where each monk remains alone in his cell . . . there is a huge silence and a great quiet there.'[56] Many have testified to the healing power of this spirit of silence.[57] But the aim of the solitary life was more than therapeutic; it was nothing less than the attainment of the vision of God. Thus there is a story of two monks, one who practised a ministry of healing, and one whose pastorate focused around reconciliation. Together they visited another monk, a desert solitary, and related to him the tribulations and conflicts which had befallen them in the world. They asked him to relate something of his life in the desert. After a time of silence, he spoke to them:

> 'Come, let us each go and fill a vessel of water'; and after they had filled the vessel, he said unto them, 'Pour out some of the water into a basin, and look down to the bottom through it', and they did so: And he said unto them, 'What do you see?' and they said, 'We see nothing'. And after the water in the basin had ceased to move, he said to them a second time, 'Look into the water', and they looked, and he said unto them, 'Whom do you see?' And they said unto him, 'We see our own faces distinctly'; and he said unto them, 'Thus it is with the man who dwelleth with men, for by reason of the disturbance caused by the affairs of the world, he cannot see his sins; but if he live the peace and quietness of the desert, he is able to see God clearly.'[58]

The protest of the solitary is not against human companionship as such, but against the evasion of self which can easily occur when involvement with people obscures and prevents any real encounter with one's own identity. Only in stillness can the truth be seen.

Yet alongside the stress on solitude and interiority runs the equally important insistence on the common life of prayer and sacrament. Cassian claims that the solitaries, like all Christians, seek the life of the Kingdom of God: 'The ultimate end of our profession is the Kingdom of God ... The proximate end, to which we direct our immediate strivings, is purity of heart.'[59] Those desert pilgrims who went 'off the rails' did not do so through a deficiency of ascetical practices or visionary experience, but rather because they neglected the common life and the sacraments. The liturgy and the divine office were at the centre of desert spirituality, and emphasized the fact that the solitaries and the desert monks saw themselves as essentially one with the entire Body of Christ. The desert movement was saturated in the Scriptures, learning whole books by heart. The Desert Fathers held, with Epiphanius of Cyprus, that 'ignorance of the Scriptures is a precipice and a deep abyss'.[60] They used the Psalms constantly. Their prayer was utterly and profoundly biblical. The contemplation of God was inseparable from the response to God's word in revelation, and the deep, inner struggle with the heart involved the interiorizing and digesting of the Scriptures.

Similarly, desert prayer was rooted in the Eucharist. Apollo advised frequent communion for the desert monks, and in his monastery the Eucharist was celebrated daily:

> Monks if possible should communicate daily in the mysteries of Christ. ... It is therefore useful for monks ... to be ready every day and to prepare themselves in such a way as to be worthy to receive the heavenly mysteries at any time, because it is thus that we are also granted the forgiveness of sins.[61]

This practice was, however, unusual, and the usual pattern, which we find in Cassian, was the extended Saturday night vigil reaching its climax in the Eucharist of Sunday.[62]

Again, the desert tradition laid an emphasis on sound doctrine. It is a serious error to see the desert movement as an esoteric, semi-heretical growth which sat light to Christian orthodoxy. On the contrary, it was from the desert that Athanasius received the strongest support in the conflict with Arianism. Athanasius was the first of the Greek fathers to preach in Coptic, and had a close link with the monastic movement there. The stress on sound doctrine comes out in an amusing form in the story of Abba Agathon:

It was said concerning Abba Agathon that some monks came to

find him, having heard tell of his great discernment. Wanting to see if he would lose his temper, they said to him, 'Aren't you that Agathon who is said to be a fornicator and a proud man?' 'Yes, it is very true', he answered. They resumed, 'Aren't you that Agathon who is always talking nonsense?' 'I am.' Again they said, 'Aren't you Agathon the heretic?' But at that he replied, 'I am not a heretic.' So they asked him, 'Tell us why you accepted everything we cast at you, but repudiated this last insult.' He replied, 'The first accusations I take to myself, for that is good for my soul. But heresy is separation from God. Now I have no wish to be separated from God.'[63]

The people of the desert were not concerned simply with a private quest for inner peace and holiness, but with truth, with the integrity of the faith, and they made a close connection between the ascent to truth and union with God.

It has often been claimed that the desert movement was a form of derangement, of spiritual pathology, a movement of dubious value. Gibbon wrote scathingly of 'hideous, distorted and emaciated maniacs, without knowledge, without patriotism, without affection, spending their lives in a long routine of useless and atrocious tortures and quailing before the ghostly phantoms of their delerious brains'.[64] They have been seen as madmen, as world-denying gnostics, as escapists who retreated from the world of matter and of human relations. But this is to misunderstand the movement to a profound degree. It was 'no mere flight, nor a rejection of matter as evil. . . . It was rooted in a stark realism of faith in God.'[65] It was a search for authenticity, for realism, for clarity of vision, and purity of discipleship. Far from being an escape, the desert quest was rooted in a sense of solidarity, in the need to preserve the Christian organism through the dark centuries of compromise and accommodation to the world. The Desert Fathers saw that solitude and solidarity hang together, and that the deepening of the inner life and the purification of the heart are vital if human society is to be healed and made whole. It was said of them that 'it is clear to all who dwell there that through them the world is kept in being, and that through them too human life is preserved and honoured by God'.[66]

The Monastic Route to God

The influence of the desert was extensive. The history of Irish monasticism, for example, shows many signs of the desert influence, and many Irish place-names suggest the idea of desert. The eastern monastic movement, centred in the desert, provided the underlying inspiration for the spread of monasticism to the West. Like the desert communities, the monastic movement, in its western and its eastern forms, can be seen as 'an effort after social righteousness'.[67] There is no greater lesson that modern Christian disciples can learn from monasticism than this: our life and death are with our neighbour. There can be no private way to God, and only those who have learned the way of community can safely move towards that of solitude. The monastic life sought to offer in a concentrated form the life of the Christian Church, itself seen as a foretaste of the life of the Kingdom of God. Throughout the writings of the early Fathers, there is a repeated insistence that community and the life of sharing (*koinōnia*) is the life of God and of the new age, while individualism represents a regression to the unredeemed order.[68] It was this common life which early monasticism sought to express.

Paradoxically, the word *monachos*, which arose in Egypt, derived from *monos*, alone, or solitary. 'They were called monks,' wrote Cassian, 'from the strictness of their lonely and solitary life.'[69] Later, however, the word was given a wider connotation. By the time of Eusebius (260–340) the monk was described as *monotropos*, one-directional.[70] No longer was physical solitude stressed so much as singleness of focus and purpose. The term *monastērion* was also changing. Originally referring to the dwelling of a solitary, by about 390 it had come to mean a community.

Monasticism was a direct growth out of the desert movement, and through the centuries it has retained the signs of its wilderness origin. Thomas Merton expressed it well:

> The monastic church is the church of the wilderness, the woman who has fled into the desert from the dragon that seeks to devour the infant Word. She is the church who, by her silence, nourishes and protects the seed of the Gospel that is sown by the Apostles in the hearts of the faithful. She is the church who by her prayer gains strength from the Apostles themselves, so often harassed by the monster. The monastic church is the one who flees to a special place prepared for her by God in the wilderness, and hides her face in the mystery of the divine silence, and prays while the great battle is being fought between earth and heaven. Her flight is not an evasion. If the monk were able to understand what goes on inside him, he would be able to say how well he knows that the battle is being fought in his own heart.[71]

Merton here draws on the imagery in the Book of Revelation for his theme of the monastic movement as being an integral part of the

Church's conflict with an oppressive world system. In the midst of conflict and threats to the Church's life, the wilderness Church keeps the faith and protects the seed for future generations. In obscurity and inwardness, she prays and waits – and watches.

The theme of watching is a central one in monastic spirituality. The monk is a watchman, a person of vision. The monastic orders have been called the eyes of the Church. 'The monk should be all eye, like the cherubim and seraphim.'[72] For the purpose of the movement into desert solitude is not simply survival and protection, but also the enriching of vision. Similarly, the Christian in any generation who seeks the life of the desert is seeking not only spiritual survival, but also the deepening of spiritual awareness, the intensified perception of the will of God. To see with new eyes, with purified eyes, with the eyes of the Dove, is the aim of monastic and of all Christian contemplation.

The spread of the movement has often been described. The Rule of Pachomius, which has served as a model for St Basil, was translated into Latin by St Jerome around 404. Through Jerome's work, the ascetic movement spread into Italy, and by the late fourth century, monasteries were established in Italy and the Mediterranean, and from here they spread through Gaul. But it was Benedict of Nursia (480–550) who shaped the Latin monastic movement. His Rule, of seventy-three chapters, provided the basis for the growth and development of the Benedictine life of the Middle Ages. It was a 'common rule' and throughout there is a stress on the common life. Thus there is to be a 'common meal'; the term *congregatio* is used twenty-five times; and there is a call for fraternal charity.[73] On no less than ninety-three occasions the monk is referred to as *frater*, brother. The Rule in fact was an attempt to fuse two streams, those of the cenobitic (community-based) type of monasticism, and of the semi-cenobitic, in which solitaries co-existed with the monks in the community. The Rule was a social document, the word of the father to the children. It began with the words, 'Listen, my son'. Throughout its pages we find a threefold emphasis: on the value of the person; on the dignity of work; and on the contemplation of God. The Rule is very practical, and seeks to create the practical conditions in which it becomes possible to open our eyes to the divine light (*deificum lumen*, literally the 'divinizing' light). So Gregory the Great (540–604), writing of Benedict, could say:

> If anyone would like to get the true picture of this man of God,
> let him go to the Rule he has written,
> for the holy man could not have taught anything

but what he had first lived.[74]

Around the Rule of St Benedict there grew up a distinctive
monastic theology of the spiritual life, a theology which was nourished
by the liturgy, by a concern with personal spiritual guidance, and by
the life and culture of the monastery. Benedict had set out to 'establish
a school for the service of the Lord' (Prologue to the Rule). Within
this school, manual work was obligatory, and learning was assumed.
The principal concern of the monk is to seek God (*quaerere Deum*).
So Benedict was concerned to identify those spiritual disciplines
which would aid that quest. He recommended that monks should read
the Bible, Cassian, and St Basil. *Lectio divina* was vital, and it
denoted an actual reading with the lips. *Meditari* similarly was not
simply interior reflection, but was originally used of the reciting of
Scripture, murmuring it, learning it by rote, and thus imprinting the
text upon the heart. Contemplative prayer in fact is defined as praying
with the heart in a state of inward simplicity.[75] In order to attain to the
spirit of interior prayerfulness, it was recognized that certain very
practical external acts were required.

Hence manual work receives in monasticism an emphasis without
parallel elsewhere. It is seen as an essential part of the quest for God.
The notion that manual work and contemplation could go together at
all was a startling one for many of Benedict's contemporaries. In
contrast to much of the conventional wisdom of his day, Benedict held
that manual work was actually conducive to holiness, and he therefore
made it compulsory for all his monks. For the holy and the common
were a unity. The sanctification of the common life was of the essence
of the monastic movement. In the Old Testament, there is a prophecy
that 'the pots in the house of the Lord shall be as the bowls before the
altar; and every pot in Jerusalem and Judah shall be sacred to the Lord
of hosts' (Zech. 14.20–21). In similar vein, Benedict instructs the
cellarer of the monastery; 'Let him regard all the utensils of the
monastery and its whole property as if they were the sacred vessels of
the altar.'[76] So we find in this monastic spirituality the seeds of a
rejection of the false division between sacred and secular. As, through
the constant recitation of the divine Office, all the hours of the week
were sanctified, so, through the liturgical consecration, all matter
became sacred to the Lord.

The common is holy, the holy is common: this truth is basic to
monastic theology. It is through experience of common things that
holiness is achieved. But it is also through the common life, the life in
community, that saints are made. Monasticism stands therefore for
oneness, not in the sense of isolation, but in the sense of comm-*unity*,

unity within and through the common. As Augustine put it:[77]

> *Monos* means 'one'. Not one in any sense, for a man in a crowd is one: but though he can be called one along with others, he cannot be *monos*, that is, alone: for *monos* means 'one alone'. They who thus live together to make one person so that they really possess what is called in Scripture 'one mind and one heart', many bodies but not many souls, many bodies but not many hearts, can rightly be called *monos*, one alone.

The ideal of unity in community was the motivation behind the work of St Romuald (950–1027) who founded the Camaldolese Order at Camaldoli near Arezzo. St Peter Damian (1007–72), who wrote the life of Romuald and praised the solitary life, was also responsible for a work entitled *The Book of The Lord be with You*. Here he raises the question, can a person reciting the office alone, say the words 'The Lord be with you?' He answers in the affirmative, for, he says, every individual is a 'little church'.[78]

This combination of the personal and the social runs through the history of monasticism. It has been said that 'the history of piety is the history of monasticism',[79] and there is a good deal of truth in this in relation to the Middle Ages. It reached a peak in the growth of the Cistercian Order under the influence of St Bernard of Clairvaux (1090–1153). The spirit of that order, with its profound sense of the spirituality of the desert tradition, is expressed in some words by the twelfth-century Cistercian Guerric of Igny. He wrote:[80]

> By a wonderful grace it is given to us to enjoy in our deserts the calm of solitude, without being deprived of the consolation of holy society. Each one can be at peace, solitary, in silence, for no one addresses him. And yet he does not draw upon himself the curse pronounced against the man who is alone and has no one to support him. He has no fear of being alone, deprived of the friendship that would cheer him, or the hand that would lift him up if he were to fall. We are here in the company of men, and yet away from the crowd. In our wilderness we combine the calm of solitude with the comfort of holy society. We live as in a town, and yet no clamour prevents us from hearing the voice of him who cries in the wilderness, only provided that our inner silence corresponds to this outward silence.

Later came the movements of friars, led by the Dominican and Franciscan Orders, while the Counter-Reformation gave new impetus to a reform of monastic life and the growth of new orders.

While the monastic movements were spreading in these varied

forms in the West, the eastern pattern remained essentially as it had been shaped by St Basil and the hermits of the desert, though later ages built upon it. The hesychast movement, the spiritual core of eastern monasticism, in fact had three phases. First came the early Sinaite movement associated with Nilus, John Climacus, and Hesychius of Sinai. Then, in the eleventh century, there was the period of St Symeon the New Theologian (949–1022). Symeon, the most remarkable and foremost of the Byzantine medieval mystics, continued and developed the spiritual tradition of the earlier period. Finaliy, there was the period in the fourteenth century when the movement was consolidated on Mount Athos. St Gregory Palamas (1296–1359) was the crucial figure of this phase. More will be said of these figures at other points in this study. Their lives and spirituality were rooted in the Jesus Prayer, the continual invocation of the divine Name, linked with the breathing and the cultivation of uninterrupted prayerfulness of heart.

Yet throughout the eastern monastic tradition there remains the awareness that, without adequate physical and spiritual preparation, without ascetical discipline, the life of solitude, and even the use of the Jesus Prayer itself, can be dangerous. 'Solitude,' warned the fifteenth-century Russian St Nil Sorsky, 'demands the fortitude of an angel',[81] while it was written of St Seraphim of Sarov:[82]

> He was reluctant to advise others to live in the desert. One who lives in the desert, he warned, must be like a man nailed to the cross, and he added that if, in the struggle against the enemy, monks in a monastery fought as though they contended with doves, the man in the desert had to fight as one contending with lions and tigers.

Today there is a crisis in many of the older religious orders; at the same time there is an upsurge of interest in new community lifestyles with new experiments in community living taking place in many parts of the world. The future issue for monasticism, as Thomas Merton pointed out so often, is not survival but prophecy.[83] It is in fact in the writings of Merton, the Cistercian monk who died in India in 1968, that we see some of the most penetrating and valuable approaches to the role of the monk in the contemporary world. His thinking and conclusions have relevance beyond the limited confines of the monastic orders. Indeed, if we place Merton alongside a number of other recent writers and thinkers, we find a number of themes which are important in assessing the contemporary place of monasticism: while some are new emphases, others are more reinforcements of older ideas.

A central idea in Merton's writings towards the end of his life was the theme of *marginality*. He saw the monk as 'a very strange kind of person, a marginal person'.[84] The monk is one who deliberately withdraws to the margins of human society, and, in so doing, finds a certain solidarity with other marginal people, some of whom have been effectively marginalized by social and political forces. There are signs that Merton had been reflecting on this marginal, social critical role for the monk as early as the late 1950s. In 1957 he had written that 'in the night of our technological barbarism, monks must be as trees which exist silently in the dark, and by their vital presence purify the air'.[85] He linked monks closely with poets, artists, and others whose life was a contradiction of, and a puzzle to, a functional, materialistic culture. Later, in the 1960s, he came to see the monk as a social critic, existing at the fringes of society. This view seems very close to the early desert tradition with its rejection of compromise and convention. In terms of the Christian presence in the secularized West, marginality may be of increasing social importance.

Closely associated with the idea of the monk as a marginal person is that of monasticism as a form of *protest*, a theme stressed by a former monk, Adrian Hastings.[86] Certainly there was a strong element of protest in the early desert movement. However, there is a constant danger that the established communities simply absorb and reflect the prevailing values of the surrounding culture, and cease to question them in any radical, critical way. A major question for monasticism today is whether it can retain, or recover, that spirit of protest, of resistance, of 'creative subversion',[87] which should be one of the principal signs of its witness to the reality of God.

A third important theme is that of *freedom*. The monastic movement is a witness to Christian freedom, to a refusal to be bound by current conventions and trends. There is an element of utopia about the monastic life: a dissatisfaction with social life as it is, a refusal to accept that this is all that can be, and an assertion that freedom in Christ is not limited to the individual in isolation. In theory, monastic life has held to the concept of the community as a 'counter-culture', a liberated zone, however much in practice it has become enslaved to the spirit of the age.

Again, running throughout the entire monastic movement, whether in desert wastes or in cultivated mini-cities, is the theme of *solidarity*, of the vision of God as a common vision. No more powerful witness against a purely private spiritual quest has ever been made. And today, as many recognize the futility of seeking spiritual satisfaction in the private realm, it is striking that there is a revived interest in tapping the wisdom of the monastic orders.

Fifthly, there is the abiding sense of *conflict*, of struggle, of spiritual warfare, which was so central in the spirituality of the Desert Fathers. It is ironical that Milton has often been quoted in criticism of the monastic vocation. He wrote:[88]

> I cannot praise a fugitive and cloistered virtue, unexercised and unbreathed, that never sallies out and seeks her adversary, but shrinks out of the race where that immortal garland is to be run for, not without dust and heat. Assuredly we bring not innocence into the world, we bring impurity much rather; that which purifies us is trial, and trial is by what is contrary.

This, as we have seen, is precisely what the monastic and solitary vocations are about. Nothing could be more misleading than to suggest that those who pursue these paths escape trial; on the contrary, the evidence suggests that the trial becomes more violent and more fundamental. But the monastic trial merely expresses in concentrated and specific form that which must take place in the heart of all Christians, the trial from which we run away when we evade the disturbing and frightening experience of solitude. Against such evasion, the monastic movement stands as a protest and a warning.

Finally, there is the element of *vision*. Again, it is in Merton that we find the visionary, perceptive, role of the monk most strongly emphasized. In his poem 'The Quickening of St John the Baptist', Merton speaks of the place of attention, the place of the sentinel.[89]

> Night is our diocese, and silence is our ministry,
> Poverty our charity, and helplessness our tongue-tied sermon.
> Beyond the scope of sight or sound we dwell upon the air,
> Seeking the world's gain in an unthinkable experience.
> We are exiles in the far end of solitude, living as listeners,
> With hearts attending to the skies we cannot understand,
> Waiting upon the first far drums of Christ the Conqueror,
> Planted like sentinels upon the world's frontier.

For this vocation of watching, waiting, listening to what Merton called the neglected voices which proceed from the inner depths of the world, there is no escape from, no substitute for, solitude and silence. Whether in the early centuries or today, it is the role of the monk 'to be so well rooted in the transcendent that he does not fear to be *monachos*, alone'.[90] For through that aloneness, that wrestling with the forces of darkness and fragmentation, comes a deeper sense of reality, a purer vision, itself issuing forth in renewed struggle. So a writer on St John the Baptist, gazing across the centuries of desert influence, points to the abiding role of the monastic movement:

As long as the battle against Satan continues on earth, Chistian monasticism will continue to establish at the very heart of Christianity those solitary places, the monasteries, where, in the silence of the cells, apocalyptic struggles against the forces of evil may be resumed.[91]

Solitude and Contemplation

It is thus the stress on solitude as an inescapable element in the encounter with God which is perhaps the central feature of desert spirituality, and which presents us today with its contemporary and abiding value. It is in solitude that we begin to discover our true self, and this begins with an awakening to the unreality of our false self. The desert is initially a negative encounter; it is the place where illusions are smashed, the place of stripping, of unmasking, of purgation. It is therefore inevitably a place of great pain and upheaval. It is also the place of discovery of that central solitude which exists at the core of each of us. The desert symbol is therefore of the greatest significance to Christians in all ages for it witnesses to a principle in Christian life and growth which goes beyond the experience of the literal desert. In the encounter with God, the dimension of physical solitude must never be abandoned. Of course, it is possible to emphasize the solitary path in such a way that it becomes an alternative to the social experience of God (though this is virtually never done by solitaries). Yet the cost of ignoring the solitary dimension as an element within Christian life is a certain superficiality and loss of depth.

In all generations there will be some Christians who are called to follow a path of physical solitude, as hermits or solitaries. As we have seen, the experience of the desert tradition is that such a life is fraught with great danger unless there is rigorous and disciplined preparation in the common life. The life of solitude can come dangerously close to madness; it is possible to lose one's bearings, to become off-centre (eccentric), lost in one's own inner space. And yet, in spite of the clearly documented risks, the desert tradition insists that in solitude there grows a consciousness of God, of truth, and of oneself which cannot be obtained in any other way. A Caribou Eskimo solitary, Igjugarjuk, wrote of his thirty days of fasting in the Arctic:[92]

True wisdom is only to be found far away from people, out in the great solitude, and is not found in play, but through suffering. Solitude and suffering open the human mind, and therefore a shaman must seek his wisdom there.

The desert, the mountain top, the frozen regions, the wild woods: all testify to the same experience of solitude and space. Spiritual maturity, like physical maturity, demands space, vastness, wildness. Wildness is a vital part of the desert reality; indeed, it is the wildness of God who reveals himself in this insecure and unpredictable environment.

Of course, it is possible to stress only the negative aspects of solitude, the conflict rather than the joy. But, as Cassian stresses, while we seek through solitude 'to keep our heart invulnerable to all wicked passions', the final purpose is that we might ascend to 'the perfection of charity'.[93] Again, St John of the Cross (1542-91) in *The Dark Night of the Soul*, a work often wrongly seen as gloomy and morbid, speaks of the desert as a place of delight and beauty:

> Besides its usual effect, this mystical wisdom will occasionally so engulf a person in its secret abyss that he will have the keen awareness of being brought into a place far removed from every living creature. He will accordingly feel that he has been led into a remarkably deep and vast wilderness, unattainable by any human creature, into an immense, unbounded desert, the more delightful, savorous and loving, the deeper, vaster and more solitary it is.[94]

If we enter into the solitude, loving it, letting ourselves relax into it, we will discover that there is the warmth and peace of God.

At the same time, in an over-active world, in which illusions are fostered and reinforced, rather than rejected, the resistance to silence and solitude is considerable. Henri Nouwen has written of the necessity for the desert experience in both its facets, of conflict with illusion, and of encounter with God:[95]

> Solitude is the place of the great struggle and the great encounter – the struggle against the compulsions of the false self, and the encounter with the loving God who offers himself as the substance of the new self.

Yet it is an expression from which even pastors run in fright. Jung recounts a story of a clergyman who had been working fourteen hours a day and was suffering from emotional exhaustion. Jung's advice was that he should work eight hours a day, then go home and spend the evening alone in his study. The clergyman agreed to follow Jung's advice precisely. He worked eight hours, and then went home and to his study, where he played some Chopin and read a novel by Hesse. The following day he read Thomas Mann and played Mozart. On the third day he went to see Jung and complained that he was no better 'But you didn't understand,' Jung replied, on hearing his account. '

didn't want you with Hermann Hesse or Thomas Mann or even
Mozart or Chopin. I wanted you to be all alone with yourself.' 'Oh,
but I can't think of any worse company,' answered the clergyman.
Jung replied, 'And yet this is the self you inflict on other people
fourteen hours a day.'[96]
Solitude is not selfishness. No person who is obsessed with,
enclosed within, the false self can be a true solitary, for the experience
of solitude will be terrifying and disintegrating. It will provoke a
confrontation with the false self which must issue in transcendence of
that self, or in breakdown. In fact, there is a close link between the
experience of solitude and that of communion, for 'the solitary, far
from enclosing himself in himself, becomes every man'.[97] But a
society which has no room for solitaries and fears solitude is a society
which has become inhuman. The great spiritual guides have always
stressed the point made in *The Cloud of Unknowing* in the fourteenth
century: 'A soul that is wholly given to contemplation ... does
everything it can to make all men as whole as itself.'[98] Certainly they
do not hold the notion of a double standard in which the solitary is
seen as superior to other Christians. Solitude is rather a specific form
of servanthood to which the solitary is privileged to be called:

> For him, solitude is the milieu for his growth in a mature
> relationship with God, and in the knowledge of God's will for the
> world. For him, withdrawal emphasizes the fact of his relationship
> with man, because through the deepening of his prayer in solitude,
> he comes to a deeper realization of his coinherence in mankind.[99]

His cutting off from physical contact is intended to purify the
awareness that the solitary has of the needs of the world and of
individuals. Never can he doubt the truth of Antony's words: our life
and our death is with our neighbour.[100] The solitary goes inward,
grows downward, and through this process becomes more, and not
less, sensitive to the needs, pains, confusions, and concerns of
humanity:

> Solitude is opposed to insularity which is a form of bombast, a real
> cancer. The humble hermit has a gay, smiling, relaxed face. He is
> pleased at the arrival of a brother, even if the visit prevents him
> fulfilling his daily programme of prayer and austerity. He is
> forbearing, peaceful, always full of good cheer. He does not
> irritate, he does not know what malice is; he radiates peace,
> concord ... The solitary is not an isolated man: animals live
> isolated lives; but the Christian life is a communion with all the
> members of the meek and humble Christ: but is filled with Jesus

Christ only by means of those two virtues. Those who go to the hermit to find Christ will find him there if the hermit possesses the virtues, and if Christ truly abides and presides in his soul.[101]

Solitude and communion are inseparable. Without solitude and inwardness there can be no true communion, for 'togetherness without solitude is merely side-by-sidedness'.[102] Thomas Merton often pointed back to Gandhi as the great figure of the twentieth century who saw the interconnection between personal solitude and social health:

> This is his lesson and his legacy to the world. The evils we suffer cannot be eliminated by a violent attack in which one sector of humanity flies at another in destructive fury. Our evils are common, and the solution of them can only be common. But we are not ready to undertake this common task because we are not ourselves. Consequently the first duty of every man is to return to his own right mind in order that society itself may be sane.[103]

If this is true, then the presence of solitaries, and the practice of solitude, are factors of political, as well as personal, significance. Repressive political regimes, governments which seek uncritical devotion to their policies and programmes, value religion only when it fulfils the role of blessing and reinforcing the *status quo*. A superficial, vaguely reformist, but non-prophetic style of religion suits them well: the growth of the reflective, contemplative, critical, questioning spirit is not to their liking. For the contemplative who looks deep into reality will be far more disturbing and threatening to structures of injustice than will the social reformer who acts pragmatically, tinkers about here and there, but does not see through the world of political illusion. Hence the truth of Berrigan's words that the pursuit of contemplation becomes a subversive activity.[104]

Yet even religious people find the perpetual solitary difficult to justify or explain. Merton wrote a magnificent essay on the philosophy of solitude in which he said:[105]

> In the eyes of our conformist society, the hermit is nothing but a failure. He has to be a failure – we have absolutely no use for him, no place for him. He is outside all our projects, plans, assemblies, movements. We can countenance him as long as he remains only fiction, or a dream. As soon as he becomes real, we are revolted by his insignificance, his poverty, his shabbiness, his total lack of status. Even those who consider themselves contemplatives often cherish a secret contempt for the solitary. For in the contemplative life of the hermit, there is none of that noble security, that

intelligent depth, that artistic finesse, which the more academic contemplative seeks in his sedate respectability.

A year later he wrote:[106]

There must therefore be hermits. Nor is this only because there will always be men who desire solitude. The Christian hermit is one who is led into the desert by the Spirit, not by the flesh, even though he may well have a normal inclination to live alone . . . The true reason for the persistence of hermits even in ages which are most hostile to the solitary ideal is that the exigencies of Christian life *demand* that there be hermits. The Kingdom of God would be incomplete without them, for they are the men who seek God alone with the most absolute and undaunted and uncompromising singleness of heart.

But it is not enough to see the place of the hermit in the Christian scheme. We need also to identify the hermit dimension in ourselves. The solitary points to the place of solitude in every person, to the interior desert in every heart, to the need for a desert spirituality which is appropriate for every age.

Desert Spirituality Today

The Constantinian phase in Christian history is coming to an end . . . The flight into the desert was a revolutionary innovation, dating from the fourth century when St Antony inaugurated the age of monks, the withdrawal of the contemplatives from a world in which Christianity was compromised, into the solitudes where they might keep alive the faith of the martyrs. That age is passing – St Anthony is coming back from his desert.[107]

Those words were written towards the end of the 1950s by the Jesuit Father (later Cardinal) Jean Daniélou. Today, a quarter of a century later, we can see the prophetic insight of his words. The Constantinian era is indeed slowly coming to its end – in some places much more slowly than in others! We are seeing, it is true, a last-ditch resurgence of the Constantinian view of the Church as those who see the Church as no more than the religious arm of the state make a final, desperate defence of their position. But the days of a Church/state alliance are clearly at an end, and increasingly the Church in most countries is revealed as a minority group. It is in this context that 'St Antony is coming back from his desert'; the contemplatives are moving to the cities, and the desert life is being sought in the midst of the secular city.

So it is not surprising to find considerable attention being devoted in modern writing on the spiritual life to the theme of desert. Thus Susan Muto, in a widely-used guide to spiritual reading, devotes an entire section to 'Living in the desert experience',[108] while one volume of the *Studies in Formative Spirituality* is devoted to 'Spirituality and the Desert Experience'.[109] Clearly these writers are not urging a return to the literal desert, or even a rediscovery of places of physical solitude, however important both may be. Rather does the desert symbol stand for something of permanent importance in the encounter with God.

> The physical desert, with its appearance of unlimited Godforsaken emptiness, is a symbol of the human experience of the absence of God in our life, and the feeling of being abandoned by him and left to our own empty resources ... In the spiritual life, a desert experience is the feeling of inner emptiness that comes from being somehow cut off from the divine presence that is our deepest satisfaction and fulfilment.[110]

If today we contemplate the reality of the desert, we see it as a place of marginal life, marked by sparseness, by hunger and thirst, by heat and cold, a place where the extremes of nature are most fiercely experienced. In the desert we face our own weaknesses and the perils which they involve. Comradeship becomes a matter of the shadow of death. The desert is supremely the place of trial, and, because of this, the place of holiness and of transformation. Yet all these are realities which we encounter in day-to-day existence: the sense of being 'marginalized', pushed to the edge; the experience of hunger, of oppression, of our own weakness; the desperate need of support in our journey; the reality of danger; the terrifying possibility of our own sanctification. In our daily search for God, what can we learn from the desert tradition which will nourish us?

We can learn, first, the importance of *simplicity*. A main theme of the desert tradition is that of detachment. We need to detach ourselves from dependence on created things and on other people, as well as from false ideas of self, in order to stand before God in nakedness and simplicity. The desert is a place of stripping and purifying, a place where there are no luxuries. We confront God in utter helplessness. In the words of Père Voillaume:[111]

> The desert – the real desert – bears in its physical reality the sign of isolation not only from people and human life but from any semblance of man's presence and activity. Being something that man cannot put to use, it likewise bears the sign of aridity, and consequently of the subduing of all the senses, including both sight

and hearing. It also bears the sign of poverty and austerity, and of the most extreme simplicity. In short, it bears the sign of man's complete helplessness, as he can do nothing to subsist alone and by himself in the desert, and he thus discovers his weakness and the necessity of seeking help and strength in God.

The simplicity which is sought in the desert experience is the simplicity of faith, the condition of utter reliance on God. It is in the desert that we are brought to see that religion and its paraphernalia can obscure the vision of God, that even prayer can be a barrier between a person and God. This is why pure faith can often seem dangerously close to atheism, for faith rejects false piety. To enter the desert is to leave behind the false trappings of religion in so far as these keep us from facing reality. And that separation can be very painful, for the trappings will be associated with people, whose friendship and support we have come to value, but who, often without knowing it, are helping to preserve us in immaturity and prevent our progress. The path into the desert is a lonely path, requiring courage and the willingness to trust the obscurity and uncertainty of the road – and the obscure God who calls us forward.

In fact, detachment is seen in negative terms as long as we see the process from the human side. If we were able to see it from the perspective of God, it might be possible to see the process rather as a clothing, a process of divinization, of the taking of our humanity into God. The purpose of detachment is freedom, to respond to God, to be clothed with the divine nature. In Van Zeller's words:[112]

> As they develop, the detachments are more and more a putting on of Christ. The process, from the point of view of its effect upon the soul, is rather one of inflowing than of emptying. But because the body and mind see so much more of the human than of the divine, the operation is regarded primarily as a stripping. Detachment, whichever way you look at it, is the condition of the Christ-life. It is always an effect. It is not, seen simply as a stripping, the End. The End is the Christ-life. The End is love.

To progress in the grace of Christ towards the freedom of love, we need to undergo that radical purification of the heart which the classical mystics call the Way of Purgation, and which is represented by the symbol of the desert. It involves the willingness to become childlike, to become as receptive as a child, with the simplicity which is the vital condition of entry into the Kingdom (Mark 10.15).

But to rid oneself of complexity is to risk the terror of loneliness, of separation from those people and things which seem to hold us together, to risk disintegration and collapse. To go straight from a world of ceaseless activism into total, uninterrupted solitude can be frightening, and we need to be prepared for panic. At such a point the 'soul friend', the spiritual companion or guide, is of crucial importance, for we will need to be held, warmly, firmly, and with the reassurance that we are still whole, still travelling, still safe. This frenzied time of ours, which is so hostile to the silent dimension, desperately needs people who can guide others into, and through, their initial, nervous, trembling, experiments with silence, and so enable them to continue and deepen that movement towards the ultimate silence of God.

An extreme form of isolation, involving acute loneliness, was experienced and later described by the French scientist Michel Siffre who spent two hundred and five days in total isolation in a cave, one hundred feet below ground, with no supports except food and reading materials. He describes how his early experience was of great loneliness, which, by the eighty-sixth day, had moved towards thoughts of suicide: he speaks of a 'long loneliness . . . beyond all bearing'. But by the hundred and fifty-sixth day, he had come to see the value of solitude:

> When you find yourself alone, isolated in a world totally without time, face to face with yourself, all the masks that you hid behind – those to preserve your own illusions, those that project them before others – finally fall, sometimes brutally.[113]

But the experience of solitude can help free us not only from our own falsehoods and facades, but also from our dependence on frameworks, on structures, on places. We come, slowly and often tearfully, to see the transient character of our possessions and securities, and to say, with Luther:

> And though they take our life,
> Goods, honour, children, wife,
> Yet is their profit small.
> These things shall vanish all.
> The City of God remaineth.

To enable us to become rootless, without firm base in this world, seeking the City which is to come: that is the aim of the desert experience. We need, in Simone Weil's words, 'to be rooted in the absence of a place'.[114] Each foreign land must become a fatherland, every fatherland a foreign land.

So, stripped of the alleged but unsure securities, we are able to move towards the one secure foundation, the living God. The desert experience is inseparably linked with the deliverance from idols, from false gods, and the liberation of the soul, through darkness, by and into the light of the God beyond all forms:

> That is the desert – darkness: all the lights go out, fashions fizzle, idols topple, structures crumble, attachments are sundered, ordinary supports are withdrawn. There is nothing but a veiled God and a promise – what we now call the Hebrew Covenant.[115]

In this way, the desert offers 'the clearest and most merciless light in this world for seeing things as they really are'.[116]

The desert calls us to simplicity. It is not grand, dramatic, flamboyant. It is very ordinary, humdrum, hidden. In fact, it is in the very lowly, obscure and apparently trivial events that we are most likely to grow in simplicity of spirit. As Merton wrote:[117]

> We need to be emptied. Otherwise prayer is only a game. And yet it is pride to want to be stripped and humbled in the grand manner with thunder and lightning. The simplest and most effective way to sanctity is to disappear into the background of ordinary everyday routine.

In the midst of daily work, play, love, pain, we need to find our desert, our interior aloneness. In so doing we will begin to encounter the desert in others, for in moving inwards to the centre, we must also and inevitably move outwards: our life and our death is with our neighbour. We need to heed T. S. Eliot's warning against those who 'neglect and belittle the desert':

> The desert is not remote in southern tropics,
> The desert is not only around the corner,
> The desert is squeezed in the tube train next to you,
> The desert is in the heart of your brother.[118]

Then if the desert is about simplicity, it is also about *waiting*. A desert spirituality is a spirituality of waiting upon God, and this will be a vital part of our prayer. And never has the need for such waiting upon God been so urgent as today:

> This waiting is decisive, since we should know that nothing will come to pass without it – nothing. There is no return, no Kingdom, if we fail to live in this fervour of eyes lifted up to the hills awaiting our help, the fervour of the watchman, trembling with fear, awaiting the dawn . . . Let us be fully aware that nothing comes except through him who waits. Take all the other directions, and nothing will come. It is the *word*, spoken and spoken again by

tireless hope, striking the empty sky throughout the years, which suddenly one fine morning of flame is taken up by God, is assumed by him, and bears truly a Word of God.[119]

Our desert times then will be marked by the prayer of simple waiting, empty-handed, open to the moving of the Spirit. But this means that we must cultivate a silent, reflective spirit, uncluttered by distractions, calm, trustful, prepared for darkness and the wasteland. Our prayer will be very largely wordless, a vigilant state of abiding, of seeking, in peace and dark faith, to discern the signs of God's activity, yet prepared to wait without sign. That is of the essence of true prayer, as the eastern bishop Theophan the Recluse (1815–54) recognized, and expressed in classic and memorable terms: 'The principle thing is to stand before God with the mind in the heart, and to go on standing before him unceasingly day and night until the end of life.'[120]

Thirdly, desert spirituality is marked by *adoration*. In the twentieth century the rediscovery of the place of the desert in the Christian life owes a tremendous debt to the ministry of Charles de Foucauld (1858–1916), the 'hermit of the Sahara'. Brother Charles lived in a hut in Nazareth, later in a hermitage at Beni-Abbes in Algeria, and finally among the Hoggar Mountains. From his life of prayer has developed the communities of Little Sisters and Little Brothers of Jesus, as well as a secular fraternity, seeking to live out the life of the desert in the midst of the city. At the centre of their life is adoration of Jesus, sacramentally present in the Eucharist. His disciple, Père Voillaume, writes:[121]

> Contemplation of this kind finds both its natural expression and its food in adoration of the Eucharist because we of today have need of a prayer reduced to essentials and made simple; we can no longer do with complicated methods whose effectiveness is out of keeping with our tiring, overburdened day. We also need a place where we may meet the divine Object of our love. And it is for these reasons that we see in adoration of the Eucharist, as I say, both the essential food of contemplation and the place where we will meet, not an impersonal God, nor a remote one, but a living Person, the Person of Jesus Christ, Son of God.

Like the manna in the desert of the Old Testament, the eucharistic food is given by God to nourish us and build us up to eternal life. The primary purpose of the Eucharist is communion, but we should not cast aside the profound tradition which also points to the sacrament reserved as *par excellence* the place of prayer and worship. Through the lowly form of bread, Jesus has graced certain places with his sacramental presence. We need not get into tangled debates about how his presence in the sacrament differs from his presence elsewhere; the essential point is to recognize, with gratitude, the gift of his presence, and the strength and help it gives us in both praying and living. To pray before the eucharistic Christ is to accept gratefully the help he offers, the initiative he takes. Often our prayer before him will be a weary, helpless, silent abandonment; often that is the best form of prayer, for it is when we are empty, receptive, weak, that we are often most open to God's grace. The movement deriving from Charles de Foucauld has rightly stressed the need for such a simple way of adoration, and has rightly placed it at the centre of its life.

The Charles de Foucauld movement has also helped us to see, and has inspired many other individuals and groups to rediscover, the need for a movement of desert spirituality in the urban context. As Daniélou predicted, St Antony is returning from his desert; the contemplatives are moving back into the city, into the back-streets, into the centres of urban decay and urban conflict. As one of them has written:[122]

> The noisy streets of the inner city are our cloister, the wilderness of human hearts is our desert, and our hermit's cell is the deep centre of our heart where we seek to foster an interior life of union with the Holy Trinity. We live in prayerful solidarity with the poor and the outcast, and assume the simple circumstances of our neighbours. Our vocation is to enflesh the spirit of the desert fathers in our times and in the city.

It is significant that this writer – and he speaks for many – has found in the use of the Jesus Prayer, as used by the hesychasts of the east, the ideal form of prayer for the busy streets of the city. As a monk, he has also found himself drawn closer to other marginal people in his new environment. St Antony indeed is coming back from the desert and finding the desert conditions and consequent struggles in the midst of the city.

For, finally, desert spirituality, today as in the early centuries, is a spirituality of *struggle*. Indeed, there is an element of dying which is inescapable in the desert journey. We are being called to die to safe, conventional, protective piety; to dependencies; to spiritual immaturity; to the cult of safety first. Much in our religious life is geared to safety, not to sanctity, for sanctity involves danger, involves launching out into the deep, facing the wilderness, the dark night and the perils of Babylon. As the early Desert Fathers stressed so often, salvation is impossible without temptation and trial: 'it is by warfare that the soul makes progress'.[123]

Frequently the movement into the desert is linked with a turning-point in life, often in middle age. The consciousness of one's loneliness, the threat of meaninglessness and emptiness in life, the intensifying of doubt – these may propel a person towards a desert experience which may change the direction of his life. The raising of fundamental doubts and questions is a vitally important aspect of the work of the Holy Spirit, and the desert tradition reinforces the need both to face such doubts and questions, and to live with them, rejecting the bogus security of more refined surroundings. Alan Ecclestone has powerfully expressed the centrality of doubt and questioning in the spiritual life:[124]

> It is a function of the Spirit as Jews and Christians have known it to enter searchingly into man's house, and there to put questions, now like a breath, and now like a wind, to try all things that it finds there, to question their fitness to endure. The process in our own night-sky is one of near gale-force winds. It is a delusion to suppose that the disturbing questions will, if ignored, go away, if suppressed, be forgotten, or that by hiding ourselves like naked Adam we can escape them. It is no less delusive to expect that we shall get comforting answers to our questionings. To live with our uncertainties is not simply a necessary part of our education at all levels: it is the very truth of faith. To endure the sifting process of interrogation is the hall-mark of discipleship.

Such creative questioning, wrestling in the darkness of faith and doubt, is of the essence of discipleship; far from being the enemy of the life of faith, such questioning is vital to a living, growing faith.

Again, not only is there a revival of the contemplative life, and the appearance of new forms of contemplative living, but there is also a revival in recent years of the solitary life. In a period which has witnessed evil and destruction on a massive scale, witnessed the atrocities at Auschwitz and Belsen, at Hiroshima and Nagasaki, and the continuing evils of nuclear build-up and institutional violence, the return of solitaries to the Church must be seen, not as a form of spiritual escapism, a quest for neutrality, but as a major contribution to the conquest of evil. The solitary life exists 'at the point where the forces of evil, and the redemptive power of God meet'.[125] Yet that encounter with evil calls forth from all of us the resources which only the desert can give: the resources of spiritual renewal, the fruit of purification, of wrestling, of confronting ourselves against the stark reality of God. The life of the hermit points to a permanent need in the Church if it is to be a pilgrim Church, a wilderness people.

The hermit is simply a pioneer . . . in the way of the desert which the whole of humanity must follow of necessity one day, each one according to his measure and his desire. This eremitical vocation, at least embryonically, is to be found in every Christian vocation, but in some it must be allowed to come to its full flowering in the wind of the Spirit. It is not enough to affirm that the thing is good in itself, it is necessary too that the Church and society do something, so that this life may be realizable, so that each may at least touch it, be it only with the tip of his little finger.[126]

6

God of Cloud and Darkness

Reconcile yourself to wait in this darkness as long as is
necessary, but still go on longing after him whom you love.
For if you are to feel him or to see him in this life, it must
always be in this cloud and in this darkness.
The Cloud of Unknowing[1]

We have seen, in considering the Old Testament experience, that the Jewish understanding of God was rooted in the sense of mystery, of awe, and of the essential unknowability of the true God. The human person could not see God and live. So Manoah exclaimed, 'We are doomed to die, we have seen God' (Judg. 13.22). Paradoxically, the Sinai revelation was one in which God was said to have been encountered face to face. Here indeed is the central paradox of Jewish theology: that God is seen and yet not seen, known and yet unknowable, revealed but always in hiddenness and obscurity. The knowledge of God is a dark knowledge, a knowledge which involves the encounter with the unutterable. For not only is the encounter itself clothed in mystery; there is a sense in which the mystery must be preserved by the discretion of human speech. Hence the restraint shown in Jewish spirituality on uttering the divine name. It has been said that 'talking about God is one of the things which the Bible hardly permits us to do'.[2] And the symbol which is at the heart of this tradition of divine unknowability is the cloud. It is in the obscurity and the hiddenness of the cloud that something of the divine brilliance is perceived. Moses sees God by partial vision (Exod. 33.20).

Here too, as was shown above, is the great and startling contrast with the idols. For the idols can be seen directly, their form delineated, their nature conceptualized, their territory and limits defined. On the other hand, 'the God of the Bible is not knowable directly. The idols are. And the mental idols are more important than the material ones.'[3] So the obscure vision of the true and living God is in sharp contrast to the clear vision of the false and dead idols.

God is known in the midst of darkness. This must not, of course, be taken to mean that all darkness is an experience of the divine. In the Bible, darkness often conveys the experience of hostile forces of chaos and meaninglessness, of the formless void and waste of the primeval deep (Gen. 1.1ff). Darkness may be an experience of despair, desolation, and confusion (Job 30.26; Ps. 88.18; Isa. 59.9). Darkness may stand for loss of vision and of the prophetic spirit (Mic. 3.6). And there is the darkness of the Day of the Lord (Joel 2.31; Zeph. 1.15). Yet the Bible also speaks of 'the thick darkness where God was' (Exod. 20.21):

> And you came near and stood at the foot of the mountain, while the mountain burned with fire to the heart of heaven, wrapped in darkness, cloud, and gloom. The the Lord spoke to you out of the midst of the fire; you heard the sound of words, but saw no form; there was only a voice. (Deut. 4.11–12)

God's voice was heard 'out of the midst of the darkness' (Deut. 5.23). Darkness was his covering (Ps. 18.11), his canopy (2 Sam. 22.12), his dwelling (1 Kings 8.12).

From Scripture to the Eastern Fathers

To move from the Bible to the world of the early Eastern spiritual tradition is to encounter the influence of Plato and the Neoplatonic tradition. That the Platonic influence on Christianity, eastern and western, was considerable is beyond dispute. It is also undisputable that, at the end of the day, there is an irreconcilable gulf between Platonism and Christian belief.[4] Nevertheless, the Platonic influence spread in Alexandrian Christianity, particularly through the work of Philo, who, while he learnt much from Plato's thought, remained essentially Jewish. God, Philo insisted, was unknowable *in himself*, but knowable through his works. It is because of this contrast between the essential unknowability of God and the knowledge that we can acquire through the works and manifestations of the divine in human life that Philo has been called 'the father of negative theology'.[5] Negative theology, a theology rooted in the rejection of concepts and the acceptance of darkness, is central to the development of the spiritual tradition of Eastern Orthodoxy.

Philo interpreted the ecstasy of the Jewish prophets to be the result of what he termed 'the setting of reason, and the darkness which surrounds it'.[6] In his *De Specialibus Legibus* Philo spoke of the gulf between human knowledge and the divine reality:

> I freely bestow what is in accordance with the recipient; for not all that I can give with ease is within man's power to take, and therefore to him that is worthy of my grace I extend all the boons which he is capable of receiving. But the apprehension of me is something more than human nature, yes, even the whole heaven and universe will be able to contain. Know thyself, then, and do

not be led away by impulses and desires beyond thy capacity, nor
let yearning for the unattainable uplift and carry thee off thy feet,
for of the obtainable nothing shall be denied thee.[7]

God, says Philo, allows himself to be known, while at the same time
remaining 'beyond form and beyond sight ... apprehensible by no
one.'[8]

The Platonic influence is equally evident in the writing of Plotinus
(205–70), two centuries after Philo. Here we see an emphasis on an
original conformity of humanity to the divine image. However, this
original simplicity has been lost, and so humankind has come to be
'dwellers in the Place of Unlikeness, where, fallen from all resemb-
lance to the Divine, we lie in gloom and mud'.[9] This phrase, 'the Place
of Unlikeness', originates with Plato,[10] and was later used by
Augustine, after which it entered medieval theology as *regio dissimili-
tudinis*, land of unlikeness. The essential point made by Plotinus is
that, by loss of original likeness to the divine image, the human soul
has lost its centre; it has, literally, become ec-centric.[11]

It was through Origen (185–254) that Platonism assumed a
Christian form, and it is in Origen's writing that we find some of the
earliest Christian references to darkness in spiritual theology. There is
no hint of any 'dark night' or of any 'cloud of unknowing' in Origen's
thought, for his is a mysticism of light and joy. When darkness occurs,
it is only as a passing phase, perhaps due to lack of effort. However,
there are occasional references to a deeper darkness, the darkness of
the divine unknowability:

> God is enveloped in darkness, for no one can formulate any
> conception rich enough to do him justice. It is then in darkness that
> he has made his hiding place; he has made it thus because no one
> can know all concerning him who is infinite.

But Origen continues:

> In a manner more paradoxical I would say also of the darkness
> taken in a good sense that it hastens towards light, seizing it and
> becoming light, because, not being known, darkness changes its
> value for him who now does not see, in such a way that, after
> instruction, he declares that the darkness which was in him has
> become light once it has become known.[12]

Thus, while in Philo, and later in Gregory of Nyssa, God *is*
unknowable, Origen speaks both of 'knowing God' and of 'seeing
God'. He 'seems reluctant to entertain the notion of the ultimate
unknowability of God'. Rather, for him, 'there is no ultimate darkness

in God'.[13] According to Lossky, in Origen's theology 'the terminology of night in relation to the knowledge of God is entirely absent'.[14] Similarly, in the writings of Clement of Alexandria (150–215), Origen's contemporary, we find the symbol of the Abyss (*bathos*) and hints of the negative tradition of knowledge of God through 'unknowing'.

> We fling ourselves upon the majesty of Christ. If we then advance through holiness towards the Abyss, we shall have a kind of knowledge of God who contains everything, knowing not what he is, but what he is not.[15]

Yet there is no real parallel here to the radical unknowing which occurs in later writers.

It is in the theological writers of the fourth century that we find the most detailed discussion of the divine incomprehensibility and the divine darkness. Thus St John Chrysostom (347–407), who had studied under Diodorus of Tarsus, the leader of the Antiochene school, wrote of *The Incomprehensibility of God*:

> Let us invoke him as the inexpressible God, incomprehensible, invisible and unknowable; let us avow that he surpasses all power of human speech, that he eludes the grasp of every mortal intelligence, that the angels cannot penetrate him, nor the seraphim see him in full clarity, nor the cherubim fully understand him, for he is invisible to the principalities and powers, the virtues and all creatures without exception; only the Son and the Holy Spirit know him.[16]

Chrysostom was Bishop of Constantinople, but at the beginning of the fifth century was deposed and banished to Pontus where he died. From Pontus, born around the same time as Chrysotom, came Evagrius (346–99), one of the greatest figures in the spiritual succession of Origen. Like Origen, Evagrius holds no doctrine of the radical unknowability of God, but he does lay stress on the place of 'ignorance' in spiritual awareness, and on the laying aside of thought. 'Blessed is he who has reached the ignorance that is inexhaustible', he writes.[17] Spiritual knowledge comes through a process of stripping and nakedness of the mind. For Evagrius too there is paradox at the heart of spirituality. 'The beginning of salvation', he says, 'is to contradict yourself.'[18] The life of prayer involves the rejection of concepts, the exclusion from the mind of all knowledge except that of God.[19] Moreover, because prayer involves a confrontation with the God who is beyond mind and conceptualizing, prayer must be accompanied by ascetical discipline and purification of the heart.

Without such purification, prayer can be dangerous:

> As it serves nothing except to injure the eyes to look on the sun intently and without a veil at high noon when it is hottest, so for an impure mind, still bound to the passions, to counterfeit the awesome and transcendent prayer which is in spirit and in truth, avails absolutely nothing, but rather the opposite, for it arouses the divine vexation.[20]

While Evagrius does not develop the theme of the divine darkness, he does emphasize that God cannot be grasped by the intellect, and that if he could be so grasped, he would not be God.[21]

From the same period as Evagrius come the Macarian Homilies, compiled in Syria towards the end of the fourth century. Here we find an emphasis on the experience of light and the importance of the 'inward eye'. 'There is a thing which everyone ought to know, that there are eyes that are more inward than these eyes, and hearing more inward than this hearing.'[22] While the symbolism here is centred on light rather than on darkness, the essential point is the same: the divine glory, which transforms the human person, and which remains ineffable and beyond the power of mind and of concept:

> The soul who has been perfectly illuminated by the ineffable beauty of the glory of the light of the face of Christ, and has perfect participation in the Holy Spirit, and become worthy to be a dwelling place and throne of God, becomes wholly eye, and wholly light, and wholly face, and wholly spirit, being so made by Christ who drives and guides and carries and tears her about, and graces and adorns her with spiritual beauty.[23]

This process of illumination is linked with the mystery of Christ's transfiguration. Through the transfiguration, the bodies of those who are made holy also shine.[24]

In fact, the language of light and of darkness in the life of the spirit contains a dialectic in which, at different times, God may be spoken of in terms of illumination, or of the darkness of faith. But the language used of both light and darkness is so close since the reality of which the writers speak is the same. The basis of the tradition of divine darkness in the theology of the Eastern Church is the recognition that it is impossible to know God directly in his essential being. It is impossible, as St Cyril of Jerusalem (315–86) stressed, to gaze directly at the face of God.[25] In the same period, St Basil of Caesarea (330–79), by his distinction between God's essence and his activities, had laid the foundations of a theological tradition which was to become central to Eastern thought, and of a deep-rooted suspicion of theological systems which seek to limit and contain God. One cannot gaze into the face of the sun. The words of Evagrius find echoes in Jewish rabbinic accounts. An emperor who visited Rabbi Joshua ben Hanahiah asking to see God was taken by the rabbi to look at the sun. 'I cannot', he complained to the emperor. 'The sun,' replied the rabbbi, 'is only one of God's servants; and you ought to admit that, as you cannot look into it, much less can you behold his glory.'[26]

It is this recognition which lies at the basis of the Eastern tradition of apophatic theology, a tradition which only speaks of God by negation, by what cannot be said. The tradition is summed up well by the late Vladimir Lossky:

> It is prostration before the living God, radically ungraspable, unobjectifiable and unknowable, because he is personal, because he is the free plenitude of personal existence. *Apophasis is the inscription in human language, in theological language, of the mystery of faith.*[27]

As Lossky says elsewhere, apophaticism is 'the fundamental characteristic of the whole theological tradition of the Eastern Church'. In Eastern Orthodox thought, 'all true theology is fundamentally apophatic'.[28] Against those who sought to reduce theological work to the assertion of simple philosophical concepts, the defenders of orthodoxy asserted the mystery of the divine darkness. The apophatic tradition is not therefore simply a way of negating and contradicting positive statements, it is 'the basis or springboard for a leap beyond all language and discursive theology'.[29]

Of central importance in any examination of the spirituality of the Eastern Church is the figure of St Gregory of Nyssa (330–95). The rediscovery of Gregory among Western Christians might help to reverse the harmful emphasis on human fallenness which has distorted much Western thought since Augustine. Gregory lays great emphasis on the divine likeness on the human person:

> For he who made you did at the same time endow your nature with this wonderful quality. For God imprinted on it the likeness of the glories of his own nature as if moulding the form of a carving into wax.[30]

At the same time God remains utterly transcendent, and his essence unknowable. No human concept is adequate to describe his being, and the human understanding cannot approach him except through a process of purification. It must be purified by *negation, by saying what God is not.* Thus Gregory speaks of the journey of the soul in search of God as a process of elimination:

... it passes through the assembly of celestial beings, looking to see if its Beloved is among them. In its quest it passes through the whole angelic world, and when it does not find the One it seeks among the blessed ones it encounters, it says to itself: 'Can any of these at least comprehend the One whom I love?' But they hold their tongues at this question, and by their silence make him realize that the One whom he seeks is inaccessible even to them. Then, having, by the action of the Spirit, passed through the whole of the hypercosmic city, having failed to recognize the One he desires among intelligible and incorporeal beings, and abandoning all that he finds, he recognizes the One he is seeking as the only One he does not comprehend.[31]

This process of elimination, however, in Eastern theology, is not only an intellectual process, but a spiritual purification, a *katharsis*, which discards all idolatry.[32] Moreover, it should be noted that Gregory of Nyssa does not associate the incomprehensibility of God with the fallen nature of humanity, or (as the Neoplatonists did) with the material body. Incomprehensibility and unknowability are of the very essence of God, so that even the angels cannot comprehend him. Because of this essential unknowability, there is an important place in Gregory's teaching for what we might call a 'theology of silence'. Commenting on Ecclesiastes 3.7 ('a time to keep silence and a time to speak'), Gregory says:

In speaking of God, when there is a question of his essence, then is the time to keep silence. When, however, it is a question of his operation, a knowledge which can come down even to us, that is the time to speak of his omnipotence by telling of his works and explaining his deeds, and to use words to this extent. In matters which go beyond this, however, the creature must not exceed the bounds of its nature, but must be content to know itself. For indeed, in my view, if the creature never comes to know itself, never understands the essence of the soul or the nature of the body, the cause of being ... if the creature does not know itself, how can it ever explain things which are beyond it? Of such things, it is the time to keep silence; here silence is surely better. There is, however, a time to speak of those things by which we can in our lives make progress in virtue.[33]

What is said of silence can also be said of darkness. In the spiritual journey, there is a movement from speech to silence, from light to darkness. Gregory speaks of the latter in connection with Moses: 'Moses' vision of God began with light; afterwards God spoke to him in a cloud. But when Moses rose higher and became more perfect, he saw God in the darkness.'[34] Spiritual knowledge thus involves progress from light to obscurity and darkness. In the first stage, the stage of light, there is a purifying of some of the alien elements, and the restoration of the image of God. It is a stage characterized by struggle, and corresponds to what later became known as the Way of Purgation. Through the experience of *apatheia* (detachment) and of *parrēsia* (confidence in God), the soul becomes more akin to God. So the enlightened soul moves into the second stage, symbolized by the cloud:

> Next comes a closer awareness of hidden things, and by this the soul is guided through sense phenomena to the world of the invisible. And this awareness is a kind of cloud, which overshadows all appearances, and slowly guides and accustoms the soul to look towards what is hidden.[35]

Gregory stresses that there is a true knowledge of, and indeed presence of, God within the soul, a true divinization. He speaks of it as a looking at the Sun with the self as in a mirror.[36] But it is when the soul goes on to progress in the knowledge of God that it recognizes his utter transcendence. And it is this discovery which leads it into the third stage, the stage of darkness. For the true knowledge of God is the knowledge that 'our goal transcends all knowledge, and is everywhere cut off from us by the darkness of incomprehensibility'.[37] The soul now becomes 'surrounded by the divine darkness, searching for him who is hidden in the dark cloud'. By the abandonment of all finite modes of comprehension, God is found in the obscurity of faith.[38]

In Gregory's *Life of Moses* the same three stages appear: light, cloud, and darkness. The dark cloud symbolizes God's invisible and incomprehensible nature. The progress of the soul towards the divine darkness leads to a deeper knowledge and a true vision. The passage which contains the words cited above is worth quoting in full.

> It thus leaves all surface appearances, not only those that can be grasped by the senses, but also those which the mind itself seems to see, and it keeps on going deeper, until by the operation of the spirit, it penetrates the invisible and the incomprehensible, and it is there that it sees God. The true vision and the true knowledge of what we seek consists in not seeing, in an awareness that our goal transcends all knowledge, and is everywhere cut off from us by the darkness of incomprehensibility.[39]

Moreover, the progress towards deeper and deeper knowledge is neverending. 'This is the real meaning of seeing God: never to have this desire satisfied.' For there is no limit to the progress towards and in God.[45]

Through darkness comes closeness. It has been said that there are two ways of seeing God in the thought of Gregory, and they are represented by the two symbols of the cloud and the mirror, the mirror standing for the positive side of the experience.[41] Like St John of the Cross many centuries later, Gregory speaks of the soul as being 'encompassed by a divine night' in which God 'gives the soul some sense of his presence even while he eludes her clear apprehension, concealed as he is by the invisibility of his nature'.[42] Thus Gregory of Nyssa represents a landmark in the development of spiritual theology, for he 'develops a mysticism that knows God beyond knowledge, that feels the presence of God in the darkness of unknowing. This mysticism of feeling radically transcends what we have found so far in the history of mystical thought.'[43]

His contemporary and namesake, St Gregory of Nazianzus (329–89) also bears witness to the centrality of light and darkness in the experience of God. One of his theological poems in particular brings out the identity of light and darkness. It is the very illumination of the divine which is experienced by the human recipient as obscurity:

> From the day whereupon I renounced the things of the world and consecrated my soul to luminous and heavenly contemplation, when the supreme intelligence carried me hence to set me down far from all that pertains to the flesh, to hide me in the secret places of the heavenly tabernacle; from that day my eyes have been blinded by the light of the Trinity, whose brightness surpasses all that the mind can conceive: for from a throne high exalted the Trinity pours upon all the ineffable radiance common to the Three.[44]

Gregory goes on to speak of the Trinity and of 'the gathered brightness of its splendour ... Trinity, whose dim shadows exalt me'.[45] The Trinity for him is the 'one torch', the 'undivided light'.[46] Darkness and light are thus two sides of the experience of God who is light, and whose splendour strikes the finite soul with blindness and plunges it into the night of faith.

It is in the writing of Dionysius the Areopagite, often known as Pseudo-Dionysius, that we find further development of the tradition of apophatic theology and spirituality, and of the theme of the divine darkness. Dionysius lived at the beginning of the sixth century. Dionysius speaks of apophatic theology (*theologia apophatikē*) as a necessary corrective and complement to positive or cataphatic theology (*theologia kataphatikē*). The latter proceeds by positive statements, the former by negations pointing to the unutterable. He speaks also of two ways in which human beings can attain some knowledge of God, through reason (*logos*), and through mystical contemplation. The superior knowledge is mystical knowledge for it is ineffable and intuitive in character. Since the transcendent God cannot be known through reason alone, the mystical path is one of ignorance. It cannot be learnt from books, but is a gift from God for which people can prepare themselves by prayer and inner purification of the heart. Thus Dionysius introduces the term *mystical* into the vocabulary of mainstream Christianity, and rescues it from its earlier associations with the mystery cults and their initiation rites and essentially secret knowledge. In Dionysius also we find the description of a threefold path of purgation (*katharsis*), illumination (*phōtismos*), and perfection (*teleiōsis*).

In the first stage, the stage of purgation, there needs to be a radical stripping, in order that we can move towards an 'unveiled knowledge', *agnōsia*, unknowing.[47] Dionysius develops the theme of knowing through unknowing in his book *The Divine Names*:

> On no account therefore is it true to say that we know God, not indeed in his nature (for that is unknowable and is beyond any reason and understanding), but by the order of all things that he has established and which bears certain images and likenesses of his divine paradigms, we ascend step by step, so far as we can follow the way, to the Transcendent, by negating and transcending everything, and by seeking the cause of all. Therefore God is known in all, and apart from all . . . For these things we can rightly say of God, and he is praised in due proportion by everything among all those things of which he is the source. And this is, moreover, the most divine knowledge of God, that he is known through unknowing, according to the union which transcends all understanding, when the understanding withdraws from all and abandons itself, and is united with the dazzling rays, and in them and from them is enlightened by the unsearchable depths of his wisdom.[48]

In his best-known work *The Mystical Theology*, Dionysius expounds the apophatic way. The mysteries of heavenly truth, he says, are hidden in 'the dazzling obscurity of the secret silence'. So he advises his disciple, Timothy:

> . . . and thee, dear Timothy, I counsel that, in the earnest exercise of mystic contemplation, thou leave the senses and the activities of the intellect, and all things that the senses or the intellect can

perceive, and all things in this world of nothingness or in that world of being, and that, thine understanding being laid to rest, thou strain (so far as thou mayest) towards an union with him whom neither being nor understanding can contain.[49]

In this way the disciple can move towards 'the divine gloom', 'the Darkness of Unknowing'. The author goes on to stress that God transcends 'all positive and negative distinctions' and is 'beyond all things'. Even Moses, he points out, did not meet with God himself but rather with the place of his dwelling. He explains:[50]

And this I take to signify that the divinest and the highest of all things perceived by the eyes of the body or the mind are but the symbolic language of things subordinate to him who himself transcendeth them all.

Through the renunciation of the understanding, through the attainment of 'the passive stillness of all his reasoning powers', the disciple comes to possess a knowledge which is beyond understanding.

Thus the divine darkness is 'beyond light' and is known through 'a loss of sight and knowledge'. By ceasing to see and know, by an 'emptying of our faculties', we can come to know that which is beyond perception and understanding. This process of emptying and of denial constitutes the *via negativa*, the way of ignorance. Its aim is

That we may attain a naked knowledge of that Unknowing which in all existing things is enwrapped by all objects of knowledge, and that we may begin to see that super-essential Darkness which is hidden by all the light that is in existent things.[51]

For, as we soar upwards, our language becomes more restricted to 'the compasss of purely intellectual conceptions'. And, because such conceptions are inadequate, we are led towards a theology of silence. So 'plunging into the Darkness which is above the intellect, we shall find ourselves reduced not merely to brevity of speech but even to absolute dumbness both of speech and thought'.[52] *The Mystical Theology* ends with a classic account of the inapplicability of descriptions of God. God cannot be grasped by the understanding, and so all purported descriptions must be subjected to the purifying process of unknowing. Even the concept of existence is rejected:

. . . nor does it belong to the category of non-existence, or to that of existence; nor do existent beings know it as it actually is, nor does it know them as they actually are; nor can the reason attain to it to name it or to know it; nor is it darkness, nor is it light, or error, or truth, nor can any affirmation or negation apply to it.[53]

The importance of Dionysius for Christian spiritual theology 'cannot be exaggerated'.[54] William Johnston has written of him:[55]

> The insight of Dionysius is one of the greatest importance for anyone who wishes to grasp the meaning of mysticism. For mysticism is non-discursive. It is not a question of thinking and reasoning and logic, but of transcending all thinking, and entering into what modern people might call an altered state of consciousness. Here one is in darkness, in emptiness, in the cloud of unknowing, precisely because one does not know through clear images and thoughts, nor with the eyes of the body. There is a great inner silence, but it is rich silence – and that is why we call it silent music. There is conceptual darkness: but the inner eye is filled with light.

Such a sense of inner silence and openness to the light beyond understanding is vital if we are to make progress in the knowledge of God.

The theme of the divine darkness in the theology of the Eastern Church is related to that of the transcendence of God. Some have argued that this is quite different from the role of purification which darkness plays in much Western, particularly Carmelite, spirituality, where the stress is rather on the interior, personal experience of darkness of soul. The 'divine darkness', it is argued, is not the same as the 'dark night of the soul', for the one is concerned with a dogmatic theological reality, the other with a personal affective experience.[56] Lossky claims that the 'dark night' is unknown in Eastern spirituality:

> States of dryness, of the dark night of the soul, do not have the same meaning in the spirituality of the Eastern Church as they have in the West . . . Dryness is a state of illness which must not last; it is never thought of by the mystical and ascetical writers of the Eastern tradition as a necessary and normal stage in the way of union.[57]

Andrew Louth, however, has suggested that the difference is chiefly one of perspective.[58] As we shall see, it is a mistake to identify the dark night of the soul with states of dryness, and Eastern writers certainly teach the same understanding of 'dark faith' and 'unknowing' which for St John of the Cross are crucial marks of the Illuminative Way. The spiritual tradition of the East is more prone to lay stress on the illumination by God than on the darkness into which the soul may be plunged by its excessive brilliance. Thus the writings of St Symeon the New Theologian (949–1022) are filled with the symbolism of God the brilliant and transforming Light. The transfiguration is a central icon of Orthodox worship. Light is emphasized more than darkness, but the experience remains unutterable, beyond conception. The reality is the same. For 'the realities of the world to come have no proper and direct nomenclature. One can only have a certain simple knowledge, above all words, elements, images, colours, pictures or names of whatever sort.'[59] In these words, St Isaac the Syrian sums up the essence of the apophatic tradition.

The importance of the apophatic dimension for Christian spiritual theology can be summarized under four heads. Firstly, this tradition refuses to separate the study of theology from the personal transformation of the theologian. Lossky has emphasized the essentially mystical character of *all* theology.[60] The idea of a detached cerebral theology, unconnected with the encounter with one's own personal darkness and with personal sanctity, would be inconceivable to the Eastern Fathers.[61] Apophaticism goes beyond the language of the intellect to the inner language of the soul in pilgrimage.

Secondly, the apophatic tradition emphasizes the spiritual and ethical character of the quest for God. The desire to conceptualize and to 'capture' God within the mind is not simply mistaken, but sinful, the product of an unredeemed mind. Growth in theological knowledge must go hand in hand with moral and spiritual growth. This is put well by Didymus the Blind (313–98), one of the earliest of the Eastern Fathers to write of theology as a spiritual discipline: 'Man needs to have a pure heart in order to be able to glorify God with hymns and theologies. The knowledge of God exists only where there is satisfaction and peace.'[62]

Thirdly, the apophatic tradition insists on the utter transcendence of God, refusing to reduce God to the status of an object, or even of an existing being. Like Dionysius, St John of Damascus rejects the concept of existence as inapplicable to God's being:

> God does not belong to the class of existing things: not that he has no existence, but that he is above all existing things, nay even above existence itself. But if all forms of knowledge have to do with that which exists, assuredly that which is above knowledge must certainly be also above essence; and conversely that which is above essence will also be above knowledge.[63]

God does not exist, for only beings exist. But God, as Dionysius said, is 'non-being'.[64] He is known not in his essence but in his energies, that is, in the ways in which he opens up himself to human knowledge and voluntarily reveals himself to humankind.

The distinction between God's essence and energies was developed particularly by St Gregory Palamas (1296–1359). Eastern theologians insist that the distinction goes back further, to Athanasius, the

Cappadocians, Dionysius, Maximus the Confessor, and others. But it is Palamas who expresses it in the most clear and detailed way. His aim was to affirm the possibility of mystical union between God and human beings without falling into pantheism or reducing God to human scale. The question of whether 'Palamism' can rightly claim to be *the* spiritual theology of Orthodoxy does not concern us here.[65] But the entire apophatic tradition reaches its climax in Palamas who sums up the teaching of knowledge of God through participation in the divine energy, a transforming relationship of sharing in the light of God:

> He who participates in the divine energy becomes himself, to some extent, light; he is united to the light, and by that light he sees in full awareness all that remains hidden to those who have not this grace: thus he transcends not only the bodily senses but also all that can be known by the intellect. For the pure in heart see God ... who, being Light, dwells in them, and reveals himself to those who love him, to his beloved.[66]

Finally, the apophatic tradition, while avoiding an anti-intellectual stance, rejects the primacy of thought, and asserts a necessary unity of mind and heart in the quest for God. It is this unity, of the mind within the heart, which is so central to the Eastern understanding of all spiritual theology, which, after the twelfth century, was being lost in Western Christianity, and which is still in urgent need of reaffirmation today.

'The Cloud of Unknowing' and the Western Tradition

In some respects St Augustine of Hippo (354–430) is closer to the Eastern Fathers than is often thought. He too saw the limitations of mind and concept, speaking of 'light ineffable and uncreated ... above the intellect',[67] and calling for a recognition of the inexpressible character of experience of God: 'Before experiencing God you thought you could talk about him; when you begin to experience him you realized that what you are experiencing you cannot put into words.'[68] Augustine's vision of the City of God was one in which both experience and intellectual work had their place, in which heart and head together were involved in the transforming work of God. But from about the time of St Bernard (1090–1153) onwards, this unified understanding began to break down in the West, with 'a wedge being driven between heart and head'.[69] Academic theology and spiritual experience came to be seen as two separate zones, a disastrous split from which the Western Christian world has not yet recovered. Formal theology came to be more and more concerned with positive assertions and affirmations, although it is important to recall that St Thomas Aquinas (1225–74) witnessed to the importance of the apophatic, negative dimension in the knowledge of God. 'We cannot know what God is, but only what he is not',[70] he stressed. Recalling that Dionysius had rejected the concept of existence as applied to God, Aquinas argued that God was beyond understanding and transcends existence.[71] Elsewhere he wrote:[72]

> The final attainment of man's knowledge of God consists in knowing that we do not know him, in so far as we realize that he transcends everything that we understand concerning him. Having arrived at the term of our knowledge, we know God as unknown.

In spite of such testimony as this, the gulf between theology and spirituality, between head and heart, grew in the West, so that the essentially mystical character of all theology came to be lost.

However the fourteenth century saw a flowering of mysticism, and the themes of the divine darkness and of 'unknowing' received a new attention. The anonymous work known as *The Cloud of Unknowing* is of the greatest importance in relating the apophatic tradition to the West. But there were other spiritual writers in this period who focused upon the experience of darkness and light in the knowledge of God. The theme of a 'dark night' occurs in the work of Walter Hilton, an Augustinian canon who died at the end of the century. Hilton, like the author of *Cloud*, is critical of the attachment to sensible devotion based on 'heat, sweetness and song', a tradition associated particularly with Richard Rolle and his disciples.[73] Both Hilton and the *Cloud* anticipate much of the teaching of St John of the Cross on the dark night.[74] Yet Hilton's thought seems not to have been influenced by the Dionysian tradition, and, while he speaks of 'lightsome darkness', his use of the term 'has no apophatic overtones at all'.[75] The darkness of which he speaks is the darkness, not of God, but of fallen humanity. It is a necessary darkness in which the soul must abide for a time, and indeed Hilton speaks of the dark night as bringing with it a closeness to God which cannot be found in the false light of the world.

> It is much better to be cut off from the view of the world in this dark night, however painful this may be, than to dwell outside occupied by the world's false pleasures ... For when you are in this darkness, you are much closer to Jerusalem than when you are in the false light. Open your heart then to the movement of grace and accustom yourself to dwell in this darkness, strive to become familiar with it, and you will quickly find peace, and the true light

of spiritual understanding will flood your soul.[76]

According to Hilton, there are two days or lights: the false light, love of the world, and the true light, perfect love of Jesus. But it is impossible to move directly from one light to the other except by way of the darkness of night. While the night is thus a transitional phase, it is used in a very wide sense. 'For Hilton the night is the whole spiritual life of a man after he has turned seriously from the love of the world and set his heart on the love of God.'[77] The night may be painful, but it is often restful. Moreover, Hilton stresses, that Jesus is present within it. 'For Jesus who is both love and light is in the darkness whether it is distressing or peaceful.'[78]

There is a concern with the experience of darkness also in the work of the Flemish mystic Jan van Ruysbroeck (1293–1381). Ruysbroeck was certainly influenced by Dionysius. He speaks of the presence of God within the soul as involving the experience of both darkness and light.

> The interior man enters into himself in a simple manner, above all activity and all values, to apply himself to a simple gaze in fruitive love. There he encounters God without intermediary. And from the unity of God there shines into him a simple light. This simple light shows itself to be darkness, nakedness and nothingness. In this darkness, the man is enveloped, and he plunges in a state without modes, in which he is lost. In nakedness, all consideration and distraction of things escape him, and he is informed and penetrated by a simple light. In nothingness he sees all his work come to nothing, for he is overwhelmed by the activity of God's immense love, and by the fruitive inclination of his spirit he . . . becomes one spirit with God.[79]

Similarly, the German Dominican Johann Tauler (1300–61), describing mystical knowledge of God, says that it

> is ineffable darkness and yet it is essential light. It is called an incomprehensible and solitary desert. This it certainly is; no one can find his way through it, or see any landmarks, for it has no marks which men can recognize. By 'darkness' here you must understand a light which will never illuminate a created intelligence, a light which can ever be naturally understood; and it is called 'desolate' because there is no road which leads to it. To come there the soul must be led above itself, beyond itself, beyond all its comprehension and understanding. Then it can drink from the stream at its very sources, from those true and essential waters. Here the water is sweet and fresh and pure, as every stream is sweet

at its source, before it has lost its cool freshness and purity.[80]

It was in the fourteenth century also that the symbol of the cloud came to the centre of Christian prayer through *The Cloud of Unknowing*, one of the classics of the spiritual tradition. It is the work of an unknown author who also wrote a later, and less well-known, book *The Book of Privy Counsel*. It was probably the same author too who had popularized the thought of Dionysius through a translation of the *Mystical Theology* entitled *Denis Hid Divinity*. Certainly the debt to Dionysius in the *Cloud* itself is clear and explicitly recognized towards the end of the book. Here the author stresses that

> Our spiritual faculties ... are equally limited in relation to the knowledge of God as he is in himself. For however much a man may know about every created spiritual thing, his intellect will never be able to comprehend the uncreated spiritual truth which is God. But there is a negative knowledge which does understand God. It proceeds by asserting everything it knows: this is not God – until finally it comes to a point where knowledge is exhausted. This is the approach of St Denys who said: 'The most divine knowledge of God is that which is known by not knowing.'[81]

The author goes on to say that anyone who reads Dionysius will find that he endorses everything that is in his own work. Indeed, it has been said that 'it is Dionysius, translated and modified indeed within the Augustinian tradition, who holds the key to the *Cloud*'s distinctive theology'.[82]

The *Cloud* is directed towards those who seek God himself, that is, 'himself and none of his goods'. And it is precisely at this point of seeking the divine reality that the seeker comes face to face with the darkness:

> For in the beginning it is usual to feel nothing but a kind of darkness about your mind, or, as it were, a *cloud of unknowing*. You will seem to know nothing and to feel nothing except a naked intent toward God in the depths of your being. Try as you might, this darkness and this cloud will remain between you and your God. You will feel frustrated, for your mind will be unable to grasp him, and your heart will not relish the delight of his love. But learn to be at home in this darkness. Return to it as often as you can, letting your spirit cry out to him whom you love. For if in this life you hope to feel and see God as he is in himself, it must be within this darkness and this cloud.[83]

The author goes on to distinguish between 'knowing power' and 'loving power' (ch. 4). It is by the latter that God is known. The whole idea of darkness is identified with a 'lacking of knowing'. Paradoxically, it is through unknowing that one draws closer to God. By the abandonment of thought, God comes to be known by love. Chapter 6 is crucial, and is worth quoting in its entirety:

> But now thou askest me, and sayest: 'How shall I think on himself, and what is he?' Unto this I cannot answer thee, except to say: 'I know not'. For thou hast brought me with thy question into that same darkness, and into that same cloud of unknowing, that I would thou wert in thyself. For of all other creatures and their works – yea, and of the works of God himself – may a man through grace have fulness of knowing, and well can he think of them; but of God himself can no man think. And therefore I would leave all that thing that I can think, and choose to my love that thing that I cannot think. For why, he may well be loved, but not thought. By love may he be gotten and holden; but by thought neither. And therefore, although it be good sometime to think on the kindness and the worthiness of God in special, and although it be a light and a part of contemplation: nevertheless in this work it shall be cast down and covered with a cloud of forgetting. And thou shalt step above it stalwartly but listily with a devout and a pleasing stirring of love, and try to pierce that darkness above thee. And smite upon that thick cloud of unknowing with a sharp dart of longing love; and go not thence for aught that befalleth.[84]

The author stresses the importance of the 'naked intent directed unto God' (ch. 7), the 'loving stirring and a blind beholding unto the naked being of God' (ch. 8). And in all there must be perseverance: 'And therefore, if thou wilt stand and not fall, cease never in thine intent, but beat evermore on this cloud of unknowing that is betwixt thee and thy God with a sharp dart of longing love.'[85] The central conviction of the *Cloud* then is that God is known through love, and not through conceptual reasoning which must be buried beneath the cloud of forgetting. In this process, the mind has to be emptied of all images, for only through such emptiness can the 'blind stirring of love', the 'naked intent towards God', arise. Through such love there develops a kind of knowledge which is beyond concepts and essentially dark. From time to time God may pierce the cloud with a 'beam of ghostly light'. But for the most part, the spiritual life of the cloud is a 'blind groping for the naked being of God' (ch.8). For God himself is 'shrouded in the cloud of unknowing' (ch. 32).

The *Cloud* has often been seen as an anti-rational work, and certainly it sees conceptual reasoning as an obstacle to the knowledge of God. Even knowledge of holy things is included. However, it is essential to recognize that the book is addressed to those who have already made some progress in spiritual life, and have already been drawn into some degree of solitude. It seeks to lead such people towards perfection. The entire process is one of longing, and the author makes it clear that this longing for God includes thought. So he tells his readers to 'hate to think of anything but God himself, so that nothing occupies your mind or will but only God' (ch. 3). It is in the context of describing the longing for God that the term 'cloud of unknowing' is first introduced in Chapter 3. However, the author goes on to say that God adapts his Godhead to human power to comprehend, and this is not difficult since we are made in his image and likeness, and so have an affinity to him already:

> The soul, when it is restored by grace, is made wholly sufficient to comprehend him fully by love. He cannot be comprehended by our intellect or any man's – or any angel's for that matter ... But only to our intellect is he incomprehensible: not to our love.[86]

Both angels and humans possess the dual powers of *knowing* and *loving*. But to the intellect God is 'forever unknowable'. By love he is 'completely knowable'. Thus 'whoever hears or reads about all this, and thinks that it is fundamentally an activity of the mind, and proceeds then to work it all out along these lines, is on quite the wrong track.'[87] Attempts to know God in this way are likely to lead to madness or more serious damage. The author's language here is remarkably strong: to seek 'to achieve this experience intellectually', he says, can lead to eternal loss.

By darkness then is meant a 'lack of knowing'. The disciple places a cloud of forgetting between himself and the created world. This is not because the created world is sinful or contaminated, indeed even holy things and holy thought are seen as obstacles to contemplative knowing. In fact, everything has to be put beneath the cloud of forgetting. The author stresses that he is speaking here specifically of contemplation, and that in other areas of life and activity it is helpful to think of creatures. But in this work it is virtually useless since it deflects from attention to God. Even to think about God's works is to deflect. 'It is far better to think about him as he is.'[88] But this cannot be done, the author says, for 'of God himself can no man think'. Only love is able to pierce this darkness, and so even thoughts of God's kindness and God's works must be put down, as the disciple seeks to penetrate the darkness with the sharp dart of longing love. Of course, there is no rejection of thinking as such. The author emphasizes that no person can hope to achieve contemplation without the foundation of many thoughts. He stresses that 'reason is a godlike thing' (ch. 8). But in the work of contemplation, the naked intention is what is needed. If accumulated learning and knowledge undermines this simple attention to God, it becomes the enemy of the spiritual life. Similarly, the vigorous working of the imagination must be suppressed in favour of a blind outreaching love (ch. 9). Such a love is not merely passive and quietist but dynamic. We are to beat away at the cloud with our love: 'hammer away at this high cloud of unknowing – and take your rest later.' (ch. 26)

So the *via amoris*, the way of love, has to be preceded by a *via negativa*, a way of ignorance, the negative dimension which makes possible the blind stirring of love which is the purpose of all prayer. There is no exception to this rule, and 'no one in this life, however pure, and however enraptured with contemplating and loving God, is ever without this intervening, high and wonderful cloud' (ch. 17). It can be pierced by urgent and short prayer, for 'short prayer pierces heaven' (ch. 37). The author recommends one-word prayers, contemplative cries, comparable to agonized cries of 'Help!' or 'Fire!' Indeed, it is in the context of such urgent, short prayer, that he recommends the use of the name of God. 'In the same way too you should use this little word "God". Fill your spirit with its inner meaning . . . and mean God wholeheartedly, and the whole of him.' (ch. 40) On the other hand, the author of the *Cloud*, like Walter Hilton, is very wary of attempts to 'feel' the fire of God's love, and warns of self-induced sensations of heat in the breast. The devil too has his contemplatives, he warns. Contemplative seekers need to be on their guard against false lights and false heat:

> They imagine it to be the fire of love, lighted and fanned by the grace and goodness of the Holy Spirit. In truth, from this falsehood, many evils spring: much hypocrisy and heresy and error. For hot on the heels of false experience comes false knowledge in the school of the fiend, just as true experience is followed by true knowledge in the school of God. For I tell you truly that the devil has his contemplatives as God has his![89]

Instead of relying on feelings of intense passion, the contemplative soul needs to remain in stillness and simplicity, rejoicing in the dramatic and wondrous experiences of warmth when they come, but being content for the most part to abide in quietness and stillness. In such quietness and confidence will be their strength.

However, intensity of love remains a key element in the teaching of the *Cloud* on knowing God. It is in its stress on the place of love that this work moves beyond the theology of Dionysius on which it depends so much. Forgetting and unknowing are placed within the context of the growth of knowledge through love. The 'blind stirring of love' is the crucial development. In *The Book of Privy Counsel*, a later work by the same author, we find further emphasis on the blind stirring of love and the naked intent towards God. The practice of unknowing is always a preparation for this stirring of love which is the most important reality in life.[90] This emphasis on the primacy of love entirely alters the perspective of Dionysian theology. In translating Dionysius, the author of the *Cloud* stressed that Moses was drawn on towards God by great love. In *The Book of Privy Counsel*, he goes on to speak of love as the key to the piercing of the cloud:

> Moreover, in this time of suffering, your love becomes both chaste and perfect. It is then that you will see your God and your love, and, being made spiritually one with his love, nakedly experience him at the sovereign point of your spirit. Here, utterly despoiled of self, and clothed in nothing but him, you will experience him as he really is, stripped of all but the trappings of sensible delights, though these be the sweetest and most sublime pleasures possible on earth. This experience will be blind as it must be in this life: yet with the purity of an undivided heart, far removed from all the illusion and error liable to mortal man, you will perceive and feel that it is unmistakenly he, as he really is.[91]

The entire spiritual life is here described as an abiding within a 'quiet darkness', within the security and love of the divine presence, nourished always by that 'simple awareness' which is the goal of all contemplative prayer:

> Let that quiet darkness be your whole mind and like a mirror to you. For I want your thought of self to be as naked and simple as your thought of God, so that you may be spiritually united to him without any fragmentation and scattering of your mind. He is your being, and in him you are what you are, not only because he is the cause and being of all that exists, but because he is *your* cause, and the deep centre of *your* being. Therefore, in this contemplative work, think of yourself and of him in the same way: that is, with the simple awareness that he is as he is, and that you are as you are. In this way, your thought will not be fragmented or scattered, but unified in him who is all.[92]

In its stress on the necessity of ignorance and the primacy of love in the knowledge of God, the influence of the *Cloud* is of the greatest importance for spiritual theology. Many writers have shown their debt to its teaching. In the fifteenth century, the emphasis on unknowing and 'learned ignorance' comes through particularly in the thought of Nicholas of Cusa (1400–64). Drawing on the Dionysian tradition, Nicholas argues that it is through *ignorantia* that the soul moves towards divine perfection. In his *De Docta Ignorantia* (1440), he twice cites Dionysius in support of his view of the way of purgation as a necessary part of learned ignorance. Nicholas seems to identify this way with the Dionysian theme of *agnōsia*:

Sacred ignorance has taught us that God is ineffable, because he is infinitely greater than anything that words can express. So true is this that it is by the process of removal and the use of negative propositions that we come nearer to truth about him.[93]

God himself is the 'most sacred ignorance', beyond all understanding:

As far as negative theology is conerned, we must conclude that God cannot be known in this life, or in the life to come. God alone knows himself; he is as incomprehensible to creatures as infinite light is to darkness.[94]

Moreover, it is not *through* ignorance but *in* ignorance that we behold God, a view which Nicholas shares with Gregory of Nyssa.[95]

The tradition of knowing through unknowing, while it has been obscured in the West, has never totally disappeared. It recovery is vital if Western Christianity is to recover that essential unity between theology and the life of prayer. The tradition of the *Cloud* recalls us to the fact that the central element in this unity is the fact of loving. As Eric Fromm wrote, echoing the language of the *Cloud*, 'only loving can lead to the full knowledge that exceeds thought and words'.[96]

St John of the Cross and the Dark Night

In the apophatic tradition of spiritual theology, there is a close link made between the negative experience of darkness and unknowing, and the positive inflowing of love. Darkness and love are closely oned in the knowledge of God. It is in the thought of the sixteenth-century Spanish Carmelite, St John of the Cross (1542–91) that we find the most extensive discussion of these themes in their effect on the progress of the individual soul. The titles of two of his major works symbolize the fundamental theological unity: *The Living Flame of Love* and *The Dark Night of the Soul*. For in fact the living flame and the darkness are the same reality of God, and all that changes is the perspective of the person who experiences it.

St John of the Cross is often 'regarded as a life-denying and world-hating ascetic when in reality his mysticism superabounds in love, vitality and joy'.[97] In his writing there is a remarkable and vital unifying of the traditions of unknowing and of warmth. The influence of Dionysius and of Gregory of Nyssa is clear.[98] But equally important is his stress on the transformation of the affections and on the work of the Holy Spirit in creative love. John is of particular relevance in our own day when many Christians, through the movements of charismatic renewal, are finding that they are encountering levels of spiritual experience for which their theological traditions have left them unprepared. He remains a wise guide to the movement of the spiritual life, and his importance is increasingly recognized, sometimes in surprising places. Thus the Cambridge theologian Don Cupitt recommends *The Ascent of Mount Carmel* to his philosophy students as the best guidebook to the knowledge of God.[99]

The spiritual theology of St John of the Cross begins with the belief that all human beings are rooted in God's love. To live in awareness of this reality is a sign of what he terms 'the great awakening'.[100] To live, on the other hand, with oneself as central, is a sign of illusion. The Dark Night of which St John writes at length is essentially a process of *dis-illusionment*, of ridding oneself of illusions. But this deliverance from illusion is merely a prelude to glory. Detachment is necessary if we are to follow Jesus, to be disciples of the Kingdom which can have no rivals. According to St John, the Dark Night of sense involves the detachment from the quest for pleasure, detachment from one's own concern for self-satisfaction. It is natural that such detachment should be seen as a mainly negative phenomenon. Yet, as Van Zeller has written, it depends on one's point of vision. Detachment is always a condition of the life in Christ, it stands for the negative way in the total experience of transforming love.[101]

However, there is a deeper and more radical detachment, the detachment from the conscious ego. This is manifested most dramatically in the shift in prayer life, a shift which is often mistaken for collapse. Conscious, self-aware methods of praying seem to cease, cease to work. What has happened is that spirituality has moved from the head to the deeper regions of the personality:

> Prayer that once seemed centred in the ego has moved into deeper unknown areas of the person, and as we, with God's grace, learn to trust this, we gradually come to a very new and different sense of who we are.[102]

There is thus a radical shift in perspective. Prayer becomes less *my* work and more God's prayer within me. In a further movement of stripping, this progress inwards towards God brings a new sense of peace, but it is combined with a deeper awareness of sin. This is a

healing process. Our self-importance, our prestige, our ego-centred-
ness, collapse, and, through the integration of conscious and
unconscious, of light and dark, of head and heart, we come to know
ourselves for the first time at a mysterious, wonderful and awesome
level. We see ourselves as we really are, sinners who are loved.
The movement which St John describes is a weaning process from
sweetness and pleasure towards pure aridity and inward darkness.
This darkness certainly contains painful and terrifying aspects. Not
only is there the pain involved in the loss of material pleasure. There is
a deeper and more terrible conflict with illusion, in which God himself
vanishes, and chaos overwhelms us. In this conflict, symbols fall
away, meanings crack, all is void and emptiness. And yet, in the midst
of chaos and of breakdown, we come to see more clearly, though more
painfully, into the roots of reality. Everything here depends on the
deliverance from illusion. In his concern with the question of illusion,
St John has been compared with Martin Luther (1483–1546):

> He and Luther are, among the great writers of the Christian past,
> the most poignantly aware of the ways in which spirituality can be
> an escape from Christ. For both of them, as for so many others, the
> test of honesty is whether a man or woman has looked into the
> darkness in which Christianity has its roots, the darkness of God
> being killed by his creatures, of God himself breaking and
> reshaping all religious language by manifesting his activity in
> vulnerability, failure and contradiction.[103]

St John of the Cross stands firmly within the tradition of negative
and apophatic theology. He speaks of the way of negation, the way of
unknowing. The soul which seeks to approach God must proceed 'by
way of negation, and by admitting as little as possible its own
concepts, natural as well as supernatural'.[104] Again, 'in order to come
to union with the wisdom of God, the soul has to proceed rather by
unknowing than by knowing'.[105] He continues:[106]

In order to arrive at having pleasure in everything,
    Desire to have pleasure in nothing.
In order to arrive at possessing everything,
    Desire to possess nothing.
In order to arrive at being everything,
    Desire to be nothing.
In order to arrive at that wherein thou hast no pleasure,
    Thou must go by a way wherein thou hast no pleasure.
In order to arrive at that which thou knowest not,
    Thou must go by a way that thou knowest not.

> In order to arrive at that which thou possessest not,
> Thou must go by a way that thou possessest not.
> In order to arrive at that which thou art not.
> Thou must go through that which thou art not.

It is this fundamental detachment from self, from the whole way of seeing reality in which the ego is at the centre, which is so essential a preliminary to any authentic growth in the spirit. Thomas Merton saw this emphasis in the teaching of St John of the Cross to be close to the teaching of the Zen masters.

> It becomes overwhelmingly important for us to become detached from our everyday conception of ourselves as potential subjects for special and unique experiences, or as candidates for realization, attainment and fulfilment. In other words, this means that a spiritual guide worth his salt will conduct a ruthless campaign against all forms of delusion arising out of spiritual ambition and self-complacency which aim to establish the ego in spiritual glory. That is why St John of the Cross is so hostile to visions and ecstasies and all forms of 'special experience'. That is why the Zen Masters say, 'If you meet Buddha, kill him.'[107]

So if we are to reach God, we need to proceed by not understanding, by a process of blinding, by placing ourselves in darkness.[108] Obscurity is of the essence of faith. And yet, beneath that obscurity, the intellect is united to God, and God is hidden beneath it. For, according to St John, darkness is essential until the divine light can be perceived directly.[109]

However, St John teaches that the darkness *is* in reality the light of God as received by finite human persons. This truth, that darkness and light are in effect the same reality, is of the greatest importance in understanding the teaching about the Dark Night. It is expressed well in *The Ascent of Mount Carmel*:[110]

> Hence the excessive light that is given in faith is thick darkness for the soul, because the greater overwhelms and eclipses the lesser. The light of the sun overwhelms all other lights so that they do not seem to be lights at all when it shines and overwhelms our power of vision. It blinds the eyes and deprives them of sight because its light is excessive and beyond all proportion to the faculty of vision. In like manner, the light of faith, by reason of the excessive intensity, oppresses and overwhelms the light of the intellect, which of its own power extends only to natural knowledge, although it has a capacity for the supernatural, whenever Our Lord

wishes to actuate it supernaturally.

So faith blinds the soul, negates the natural light, and *is* dark night for the soul. And, according to St John, it is precisely in this way that it gives light. So 'the more darkness it causes, the greater light it gives'.[111]

The symbol of night is a central one in St John of the Cross.[112] The night changes its nature, manifests itself in a variety of ways, yet the whole life of the Christian is an abiding within this night of faith. The teaching of St John on this theme begins with an assertion of the goodness and essential loveliness of darkness:

> Oh night that guided me, Oh night, more lovely than the dawn,
> Oh night that joined Beloved with lover, transformed in the
>   Beloved![113]

The experience of darkness stands at the centre of all Christian spirituality, for 'God will lead the soul by a most lofty path of dark contemplation and aridity wherein it seems to be lost'.[114] Faith itself is compared to midnight darkness, the 'abyss of faith'.[115] St John gives three reasons why the progress towards God is called night. Firstly, the seeker must strip himself of desire for worldly possessions in a 'night of sense'. Secondly, the road by which the seeker treads is the road of faith, and this is like a dark night to the intellect. Thirdly, God himself is the goal and end of the process, and he is darkness to human sight. St John speaks also of three phases of the night:[116]

> These three parts of the night are all one night; but like night itself, it has three parts. For the first part, which is that of sense, is comparable to the beginning of night, the point at which things begin to fade from sight. And the second part, which is faith, is comparable to midnight, which is total darkness. And the third part is like the close of night, which is God, the which part is now near to the light of day.

So it is that God, who is ultimate light, is known by the soul in profound darkness. God's light is so clear, so pure, that it is invisible, like a ray of sunlight which is only shown up by the dust in its path. The movement of illumination is a movement beyond the limitations of thought and of concept. As Rowan Williams describes it: 'Illumination is the running out of language and thought, the compulsion exercised by a reality drastically and totally beyond the reach of our conceptual apparatus.'[117]

According to St John then, the Illuminative Way is a way which must be taken as 'progressives and proficients' in the Christian life move from dependence on the passions towards dependence on God:

> This house of sensuality being now set at rest, that is, mortified, its passions extinguished, and its desires set at rest and put to sleep by means of this more fortunate night of sensible purgation, the soul went forth to set out upon the road and way of the spirit, which is that of progressives and proficients, otherwise called the Illuminative Way or the way of infused contemplation.[118]

But why is an entry into darkness called 'illumination'? St John explains it thus: 'The clearer the light, the more it blinds and darkens the eye of the soul; and the more directly one looks at the sun, the greater the darkness and privation it causes to the visual faculty.'[119] In his book *The Living Flame of Love*, St John stresses that the fire which glorifies the soul is the same fire which once purged it. The darkness and the light are one: 'to sight that is weak and not clear, infinite light is total darkness'.[120] Thomas Merton develops the theme:[121]

> The darkening is therefore at the same time an enlightenment. God darkens the mind only in order to give a more perfect light. The reason that the light of faith is darkness to the soul is, says St John, that this is in reality an *excessive light*. Direct exposure to supernatural light darkens the mind and heart, and it is precisely in this way that, being led into the 'dark night of faith', one passes from meditation, in the sense of active 'mental prayer', to contemplation, or a deeper and simpler intuitive form of receptivity in which, if one can be said to 'meditate' at all, one does so only by receiving the light with passive and loving attention.

Like the author of the *Cloud*, St John of the Cross acknowledges his debt to Dionysius. In *The Living Flame of Love*, he speaks of the obscurity of divine knowledge:[122]

> But in the contemplation we are discussing (by which God infuses himself into the soul) particular knowledge as well as acts made by the soul are unnecessary, because God in one act is communicating light and love together, which is loving and supernatural knowledge. We can assert that this knowledge is like light which transmits heat for that light also enkindles love. This knowledge is general and dark to the intellect because it is contemplative knowledge which is a ray of darkness for the intellect as St Dionysius teaches.

It seems then that the symbol of the Dark Night of the Soul is a way of expressing a major theological reality, one which is basic to apophatic theology, the reality of the divine darkness:

The dark night is a negative way of experiencing God. It is the counterpart of negative or apophatic (dark) theology. Negative theology proceeds by denying to God all the limitations of created reality; in a true sense, it is non-knowledge. The dark night is the experience of void, of emptiness, of no-thinking and non-being: it is the condition of *kenosis* and poverty of spirit.[123]

According to St John of the Cross, there are three signs by which a person may know that he is being led towards contemplative prayer, and as a result of which he may safely leave aside the techniques of formal meditation. Such a transition is of central importance, but it may not take place until the person is ready – 'neither sooner nor later than when the Spirit bids him'. The three signs are as follows:

1 His realization that he can no longer meditate or reason with the imagination, neither can take pleasure therein as he was wont to do aforetime.

2 A realization that he has no desire to fix his meditation or his sense upon other particular objects, exterior or interior.

3 That the soul takes pleasure in being alone, or waits with loving attentiveness upon God without making any particular meditation . . . and without any particular understanding.

St John adds that 'these three signs, at least, the spiritual person must observe in himself, all together, before he can venture safely to abandon the state of meditation and sense and to enter that of contemplation and spirit.'[124]

As a result of entering the Dark Night, 'the soul must be led in a way entirely contrary to the way wherein it was led at first'. St John is very hard on spiritual directors who, by their ignorance and incompetence, may maintain people in unsuitable forms of prayer for years. He calls them spiritual blacksmiths.[125] The fact is that the soul has reached a point of spiritual crisis, the point which Dom John Chapman (1865–1933) called the 'ligature', a point at which the soul seems to be bound and cannot move easily. One of the greatest mistakes in the current pastoral scene is the assumption that only a tiny minority of Christians attain to this state. In fact, as Trueman Dicken has stressed, this is not at all the case:[126]

It may be confidently said that many many souls in this country at the present time reach this stage of the ligature. Because few directors are able to recognize the state or have sufficient knowledge of the principles involved at this point, only a very small proportion of such souls is adequately directed.

St John of the Cross is of the utmost importance today when so many Christians are finding themselves led towards contemplative prayer, and towards the quest for God in darkness. In our situation, we need to recover the centrality of dark knowledge and of the way of ignorance.

The Darkness and Contemplation Today

> The first step into the hiddenness of God is a hard one: it is a deliberate act of unlearning. We think we know who we are; we have some idea of what it is to be a human being, even to be a Christian. These ideas for the most part have to be abandoned.[127]

Thus Alan Jones describes the early stages of the 'journey into Christ', and he goes on to point to the central place in this journey of the experience described in the spiritual tradition in the language of darkness and negativity:

> The formlessness, the emptiness, the void – these are unavoidable, and are the various words used to denote that which lies at the heart of human consciousness. The great mystics have struggled to describe it. Depth psychology has helped us to enter it creatively. It is the place of the Spirit, the arena in which the self emerges. The infinite emptiness of the human heart is first experienced as terror. When we are content to wait, it is transformed into an eager emptiness waiting to be filled.[128]

His words are an urgent call to us to recover the apophatic dimension in Christian theology and spirituality, a dimension which has been eliminated and virtually lost in the West since the seventeenth century.[129]

Recent theological writing has included a concern for this dimension. Indeed, earlier theologians such as Barth and Tillich laid great emphasis on the transcendence and hiddenness of God. Barth is well known for the stress he placed on the 'otherness' of God.[130] This otherness he associated with the theme of negation: 'God is pure negation . . . He is negation of the negation in which the other world contradicts this world, and this world the other world.'[131] The God whom Christians adore is revealed as a hidden God. In a famous passage on revelation and hiddenness, Barth wrote:[132]

> Thus God's revelation is precisely his revelation as the *hidden God*. And therefore faith in God's revelation can only give a very *humble* answer to the question 'Who is God?', and it is faith which will confess God as the God of majesty, and therefore as the God unknown to us. It is faith in God's revelation, which is deadly fear

of God's mystery, because it sees how God himself veils himself in mystery. Scepticism, which thinks it also knows that God is hidden, has not reached the point of being such fear unto death. Scepticism has not been taught by God himself that he is hidden, but is a human answer to a human question. One must know the darkness of Sinai and of Calvary, and must have faith to know the God who is *above* us, and his hidden nature.

From his very different perspective, Paul Tillich spoke of 'the God above God', rejecting the idea of divine existence.[133] Tillich's ideas about God as 'depth' and as the 'ground of being' were picked up and developed by a number of theologians in the 1960s.[134]

More recently, Thomas Altizer has spoken of a new kind of unknowability. Altizer sees the language of eclipse, cloud, and darkness to be difficult to use today, because there is running through it the possibility of some opposite state of affairs. Today, however, there is a breakdown of the transcendent centre. Altizer moves from the recognition of this breakdown to the belief in what he terms a 'total presence' of what was once termed God.[135] In another recent study, Richard Rubenstein has claimed that the experience of the holocaust has been fatal to the theology. The God of traditional Christianity died at Auschwitz. Now we live in a silent, godless world. Yet Rubenstein argues:[136]

The time of the death of God does not mean the end of all gods. It means the demise of the God who was the ultimate actor in history. I believe in God the Holy Nothingness, known to mystics of all ages, out of which we have come, and to which we shall ultimately return.

We are certainly seeing a rejection by many Christians of the God who is reached at the end of a process of reason, indeed the rejection of the God of reason altogether. Much earlier Christian writing stressed the 'reasonableness' of belief in God, drawing on arguments from human reason to demonstrate the existence of such a being. So the influential evangelical writer Fred Catherwood writes of the 'God of reason', stressing that God spoke to Moses in 'reasonable language'.[137] It is difficult to escape the conclusion that the mysterious and unknowable God of the Sinai and apophatic traditions has been lost in such writing. It is important therefore that we recall the central truth of mystical theology that God is beyond reason and concept, and that 'when we speak of God we have to use language which is, taken at its face value, contradictory'.[138]

But this central apophatic insight has to be grasped not only by the intellect as it struggles with the paradoxes of theological work; it has to become a disturbing and troubling force working within the personalities of people. Perhaps this time, marked by great disillusionment and confusion, is one in which it might be easier to wrestle with this central truth than a period of peace and calm. Today, on many sides, there is the sense of collapse of established positions with its accompanying insecurity and bafflement. Alan Ecclestone has called this time 'the night sky of the Lord', and has suggested that there are some positive aspects of this time in terms of vision and perception. For 'there are things that can only be seen in darkened skies, questions only heard in the silence of utter dismay. Such a time is ours.'[139] Yet the heart of the theological dilemma remains the same as it was in ancient time. How can we speak of a God who is both other and near, beyond understanding and yet closer to us than we are to ourselves? No one has ever seen God (1 John 4.12): how then can we see him as he is (3.2)? He whom no one can see has been manifested in his Son (John 1.18). He dwells in unapproachable light, and cannot be seen (1 Tim. 6.16): will he then be seen and known by humankind (1 Cor. 13.12)?

The question calls for a profound questioning of all our assumptions about truth and about our own identity, a profound shaking of the foundations of our being. It calls for a kind of inner scepticism at the heart of the life of prayer. Scepticism need not be the enemy of faith; indeed, a faith which cannot include the radical questioning of the sceptic is unsure and incapable of growth. Don Cupitt, in a recent study, has related the need for a sceptical dimension to the mystical tradition:

> The Christian gospel declares that if we avail ourselves of the disciplines and practices of religion, and are willing to pass through the fire of nihilism, it will burn out our natural egoism, and bring us through on the far side to a new kind of human reality and a basis for social life.[140]

Cupitt sees such a process as a contemporary form of the way of *agnōsia* claiming that 'in our cultural situation the stringent intellectual purity of the Negative Way is the best way to maintain a truly religious spirit'.[141] While one might have doubts as to the way in which Cupitt interprets the relationship between negation and dogma, his claim is undoubtedly correct in its general tenor: that the way of negation and of ignorance is of vital importance in the nourishment of a healthy spiritual life today.

Thus we need at the centre of our lives in Christ a spirit of questioning, and this involves cultivating such qualities as silence, listening, and entering into the meaninglessness and helplessness of others as well as our own. It calls for an ascetical practice of silence in darkness. It was this practice which Thomas Merton came to see as essential to the monastic struggle and witness, and in his later writings he grappled with the issues of the monastic encounter with darkness:

> The monk who is truly a man of prayer and who seriously faces the challenge of his vocation in all its depth is by that very fact exposed to existential dread. He experiences in himself the emptiness, the lack of authenticity, the quest for fidelity, the 'lostness' of modern man, but he experiences all this in an altogether different and deeper way than does man in the modern world, to whom this disconcerting awareness of himself and of his world comes rather as an experience of boredom and spiritual disorientation. The monk confronts his own humanity and that of the world at the deepest and most central point where the void seems to open out into black despair.[141]

The monk, Merton says, confronts such despair and rejects it. Through his life of prayer and contemplation, it is transformed into hope.

The encounter with despair and with the absence of God is an integral part of dark faith. No spirituality can be of lasting value or provide adequate nourishment which has not faced the realities of despair and dereliction. Such a confrontation is an essential aspect of relationship with God. It involves not only the facing of the divine absence, the apparent loss of God, but also the acceptance that we ourselves will seek to run from the encounter. Relationship with the God of the cloud and of the darkness is not comfortable and cosy, and it should not surprise us that there are times when we are terrified by it. In Paul Tillich's words:[142]

> A man who has never tried to flee God has never experienced the God who is really God . . . For there is no reason to flee a God who is the perfect picture of everything that is good in man . . . who is simply the universe, or the laws of nature, or the course of history . . . who is nothing more than a benevolent father, a father who guarantees our immortality and final happiness. Why try to escape from someone who serves us so well? No, those are not pictures of God, but rather of man trying to make God in his own image and for his own comfort.

Similarly, Kierkegaard stressed the positive spiritual value of despair. Only terror to the point of despair, he claimed, develops a person to the utmost, though many succumb and fall by the way.[143] However, the rejection of God may be the result not of despair but rather of a cool, recollected yet passionate, decision against the inadequacy of theism. To the extent that atheism points to the limited and potentially misleading character of all assertions about the divine, it can act as a necessary purification, the painful and disturbing friend of true faith.[144] As a protest against the claim to a clear, conceptual awareness of God, atheism is more true than are the many forms of idolatry which parade under Christian labels. On the other hand, if there can be *no* knowledge of God of any kind, theology is reduced to nonsense. 'If God is in principle unknowable, then theology must either change its character, as Schleiermacher taught, or disappear, as it seems about to do in some areas of the discipline.'[145] To recover a way of knowing which does not rely solely on the intellect but demands a total shaking and re-shaping of the knowing person, a radical *metanoia*, is the purpose of all contemplative theology.

In the recovery of the contemplative nature of all theology, the monk Thomas Merton has been of the utmost importance. Merton was one of the greatest exponents of the apophatic tradition and of the centrality of contemplative prayer. It has been said of Merton that 'symbols of darkness and night appear more frequently in his works than symbols of light ... His enthusiasm for eastern religions was in part sparked by elements in these traditions that correspond to Christian apophaticism.'[146] Merton sees the experience of the Dark Night as a crucial time of anxiety and hazard, a time too of difficult options, a time of decision, a turning-point in the spiritual journey. Confronted by the darkness, we are being invited to move out of ourselves, beyond our limits, away from safety and defences. And this can be terrifying:

> If we set out into this darkness, we have to meet these inexorable forces. We will have to face fears and doubts. We will have to call into question the whole structure of our spiritual life ... We are entering the night in which he is present without any image, invisible, inscrutable, and beyond any satisfactory mental representation. At such a time as this, one who is not seriously grounded in genuine theological faith may lose everything he ever had.[147]

Elsewhere Merton speaks of the 'curtain of darkness', the 'cloud of darkness', the 'night of aridity and faith', the 'night of faith', the 'power of an obscure love', and the 'ray of darkness'.[148] The symbolism of night is at the centre of his entire approach to spiritual theology. For, as he explained in an early work:[149]

The way of faith is necessarily obscure ... We drive by night. Nevertheless, our reason penetrates the darkness enough to show us a little of the road ahead. It is by the light of reason that we interpret the signposts and make out the landmarks along our way.

Writing ten years later, he developed the theme in a memorable passage:[150]

> The very obscurity of faith is an argument of its perfection. It is darkness to our minds because it so far transcends their weakness. The more perfect faith is, the darker it becomes. The closer we get to God, the less is our faith diluted with the half-light of created images and concepts. Our certainty increases with this obscurity, yet not without anguish and even material doubt, because we do not find it easy to subsist in a void in which our natural powers have nothing of their own to rely on. And it is in the deepest darkness that we most fully possess God because it is then that our minds are more truly liberated from the weak, created lights, and are filled with his infinite light which seems pure darkness to our reason.

Nothing could be further from the truth than the view that, in the tradition of apophatic mysticism, we are confronted by an anti-dogmatic tendency working against the mainstream of Catholic theology. This is, of course, a popular view of the mystical way. Aldous Huxley, for example, contrasted the mysticism of the 'Dionysian tradition' with those whom he regarded as more truly Catholic. The mysticism of the *Cloud*, on Huxley's view, belongs to the world of free, undogmatic mysticism, a phenomenon which exists uncomfortably on the margins of the Catholic world, but whose spirit and ethos are essentially alien to it.[151] But this is a mistaken view. Catholic mysticism and Catholic dogma go together. It is certainly true that many Catholic Christians receive, and seek to defend, dogmatic propositions in a way which is utterly immature and insensitive to the inner meaning of dogma. And without the spiritual integration which is the goal of mystical theology all dogmatic systems are likely to become sterile and repressive. But this is not to say that the mystic seeks a path which is without guidelines, or that the stress on darkness and obscure faith involves the abandonment of theological truth. In fact, the very assertion of the hiddenness of God is a basic dogmatic truth, as Karl Barth often stressed. God is a *Deus absconditus* because of his perfection. It is because of the holiness and transcendence of God, because knowledge of him comes through his own initiative, that we must speak of him as a hidden God.[152] This God cannot be domesticated and brought down to size. This God is a consuming fire.

The centrality of struggle and conflict in the life of the spirit is therefore a consequence of the theological reality on which the mystical writers lay such great emphasis. To neglect or reject this is to choose a comforting idol in place of theological faith. In Merton's words:[153]

> We too often forget that Christian faith is a principle of questioning and struggle before it becomes a principle of certitude and of peace. One has to doubt and reject everything in order to believe firmly in Christ, and after one has begun to believe, one's faith itself must be tested and purified. Christianity is not merely a set of foregone conclusions. The Christian mind is a mind that risks intolerable purifications, and sometimes, indeed very often, the risk turns out to be too great to be tolerated. Faith tends to be defeated by the burning presence of God in mystery, and seeks refuge from him, flying to comfortable social forms and safe conventions in which purification is no longer an inner battle, but a matter of outward gesture.

Faith in God thus involves struggle and an encounter with our own inner darkness. The late Carl Jung wrote a great deal about the dark side of the personality, and warned of the danger of using religion as a way of avoiding this necessary encounter:

> Woe to them who use religion as a substitute for another side of the life of the soul. They are in error, and will be accursed. Religion is no substitute, but is to be added to the other activity of the soul as a completion. Out of the fullness of life shall you bring forth your religion. Only then will you be blessed.[154]

It follows from what has been said that the personal life of the spirit will be characterized by much struggle, much pain and anguish. There has to be a breaking process on the road to union with God, and it is self-delusion to think that this road can be pleasant and gentle throughout. It will involve a fierce battle with the hidden and terrifying regions within oneself. Harry Williams has described the process of self-knowledge as a journey through uncomfortable regions:[155]

> To arrive at my truest self where God dwells, it is necessary for me to pass through some pretty rough and decidedly ugly country. To find God within me I have on the way to encounter aspects of myself from which I tend to run away and hide . . . I have not only to encounter all those ugly aspects of what I am. Indeed, I have to

learn to love them as I would love a naughty and wayward child. And that can't be done without considerable turmoil and perhaps agony. I shall find God within me all right. I shall find the love, joy and peace which is my truest self. But the discovery will for a long time be mixed up with the pain and the discomfort of the journey.

If we are able to trust the discomfort, to trust the darkness, we shall find not only that we come to know our own darkness along with our light, but that in the midst of the darkness we can grope towards the reality of God. For God reveals himself in the midst of the dark cloud. That truth is best grasped in prayerful waiting, and expressed in the language of poetry. Thus Sebastian Moore and Kevin Maguire write of their experience of dark prayer:[156]

In the time of the year's darkness,
At the Winter Solstice,
We embraced the darkness
And we chose the madness
Of chaos and oblivion;
Because we chose to shut our eyes
To the darkness that was there,
And saw in the fantastic lights
That swam in our fevered eyes
A glimmer of daylight in the distance;
And this we chose, and called it Light;
Called it Light and the Will of God,
Because we had learned, living in the dark,
To identify God with the unseen light;
And in extremity we comforted ourselves
With the hope of a light we did not see.
We hoped for a light and called it God;
And so, with screwed-up eyes and heated mind,
We said we saw a glimmer and we called it God.
Yet we were in the darkness all the time,
And our fevered crazy choosing
Chose the one thing that it would not see:
That which strikes terror to the marrow of the heart;
The dark, the dark, the awful total night.
And so, for all our crazy games and blundering,
Wrapped in the darkness, we have stumbled on
The one thing that we feared and fled so long.
In the darkness we have found the centre of the darkness,
And we are overwhelmed by a strange, dark, power.
This is a knowledge we have lived in constantly,

And yet had kept it hidden from our minds.
But this is now the ending of our day.
That regal splendour of our lighted world.
Now can our eyes spring free to see the night,
, And the darkness that is vibrant with our God.

7

God of Water and Fire

God has a terrible double aspect, a sea of grace is met by a seething lake of fire, and the light of love glows with a fierce dark heat of which it is said, 'ardet non lucet' – it burns but gives no light.

C. G. Jung, *Answer to Job*[1]

Recovering the Fire of God's Spirit

In 1968 the Metropolitan Ignatios of Latakia addressed the World Council of Churches Assembly in Uppsala. He pointed to the terrible consequences of the neglect of the doctrine and experience of Holy Spirit:

Without the Holy Spirit, God is far away,
Christ stays in the past,
the Gospel is a dead letter,
the Church is simply an organization,
authority is a matter of domination,
mission a matter of propaganda,
the liturgy is no more than an evocation,
Christian living a slave morality.

But in the Holy Spirit:
the cosmos is resurrected and groans with the birth pangs of the Kingdom,
the risen Christ is there,
the Gospel is the power of life,
the Church shows forth the life of the Trinity,
authority is a liberating service,
mission is a Pentecost,
the liturgy is both memorial and anticipation, and
human action is deified.[2]

We are in the midst today of a long-overdue renewal of belief in, and stress upon, the role of the Spirit of God in the Christian community. Much earlier reflection on the doctrine of the Holy Spirit (pneumatology) in both Catholic and Protestant traditions was heavily dominated by interest in personal piety. But in order to make sense of the place of the Holy Spirit in the Christian understanding of God, we need to widen the perspective. It is necessary to place our doctrine of the Spirit within the context of the history of salvation and of the struggles of the world, and specifically within the context of the empowering of the Christian community. For in the New Testament 'Holy Spirit' is the name given to the experienced presence of the living God in the Christian community. The subsequent history of Christian thought has seen a deterioration in understanding of the Spirit so that the Spirit has come to be seen as an impersonal force, an 'it', a power or presence, but not the personal power and presence of God.

Of course, the category of power (*dunamis*) was an important one in the New Testament description of the work of the Holy Spirit. Moreover, there is no direct ascription of personality to the Holy Spirit in the New Testament itself. Both in the New Testament and in the writings of the early church, we are confronted with attempts to express an overwhelming, shattering experience. So unspeakable is this experience that the early Christian writers 'lack the power to clothe it in precise language'.[3] For the Holy Spirit is the very atmosphere within which prayer and theological reflection are possible at all. And the early Church was marked by an overpowering sense of the Spirit's presence. As a community, it was 'essentially charismatic and enthusiastic in nature, in every aspect of its common life and worship, its development and mission'.[4] The experience of the charismatic gifts was seen as due to an act of God, its purpose being the building up and nourishing of the common life of Christ's body in the world.

The results of the neglect of the Holy Spirit by many sections of the Church have been utterly disastrous. Deprived of the sense of power and of the experience of God's life, religion deteriorates into a lifeless and dreary system of rules and ceremonies. It becomes content with a 'diminished mode of consciousness'.[5] So religion ceases to mediate the world of the Spirit, and becomes a second-hand account of what was once experienced by people long since dead. And this, as R. D. Laing saw in 1967, produces a condition of spiritual famine:

> We live in a secular world. To adapt to this world, the child abdicates its ecstasy ... Having lost our experience of the Spirit, we are expected to have faith. But this faith comes to be a belief in a reality which is not evident. There is a prophecy in Amos that there will be a time when there will be a famine in the land, not a famine for bread, nor a thirst for water, but of *hearing* the words of the Lord. The time has now come to pass. It is the present age.[6]

Laing wrote those words during a time of spiritual confusion, a time when many young people were seeking spiritual experience by discovering the disciplines of the eastern non-Christian traditions, as

well as in a variety of other ways. But during the same years, there was
a remarkable renewal developing within the Western Christian world,
both Catholic and Protestant, a renewal associated with the recovery
of the centrality of the experience of the Holy Spirit.

As the Second Vatican Council opened Pope John XXIII prayed
that the Church might relive the experience of the apostolic age,
might experience a new Pentecost. He prayed: 'Renew your wonders
in our day, as by a new Pentecost.' The documents of the Council lay a
new stress on the Spirit as the source and instrument of perpetual
renewal in the Church.[7] In the Church 'Christ, through his very flesh,
made vital and vitalizing by the Holy Spirit, offers life to men.'[8]
Later, Pope Paul VI emphasized that the recovery of the study of, and
devotion to, the Holy Spirit was 'the indispensable complement of the
teaching of the Council',[9] and, in announcing the Holy Year of 1975,
he stressed the need for a 'truly spiritual (pneumatic), that is,
charismatic movement' among Christian people.[10] This sense of the
continuing, empowering and renewing activity of the Spirit has been
expressed in the renewal of the liturgy, one of the most striking
examples being the collect used at Pentecost in the Roman Communion in Canada:

> Father of light, from whom every good gift comes,
> send your Spirit into our lives
> with the power of an irresistible wind,
> and by the flame of your wisdom
> open the horizon of our minds.
> Loosen our tongues to sing your praise
> in words beyond the power of speech.
> For without your Spirit it is not given to man
> to raise his voice in words of peace
> or announce the truth that Jesus is Lord.[11]

At the same time, the charismatic renewal has been affecting many
thousands of people all over the Christian world.

At the centre of the renewal has been the recovery of the sense of
power. In the Old Testament, the spirit is not so much the centre of a
human personality as the strength which emanates from it.[12] Sharing
a common origin with 'word' and 'breath', the spirit is described in
terms of power and mystery. The ruach (breath, word, spirit) of God
is strong and life-giving (Gen. 6.17; 7.15; Num. 16.22, etc.).
Equally, the prophets of the Old Testament, people possessed and
driven by the spirit, were powerful and violent figures. The early
word for an ecstatic prophet, nabi, literally signifies a 'bubbling
forth'.[13] However, ecstasy was always somewhat suspect in the

prophetic tradition. The prophets never appealed to inner experience to prove their authenticity. On the contrary, the ecstatics were likely to be seen as belonging to the category of false prophets.

At the same time, while it is probably a mistake to see ecstasy as the fundamental experience behind all types of prophecy,[14] the historical accounts of prophecy in the Old Testament do contain strong evidence of personal, inner upheaval, disturbed patterns of behaviour, and uncontrollable passion. Thus the experience of Saul:

> On his way there the spirit of God came upon him too, and he went on, in a rapture as he went, till he came to Naioth in Ramah. There he too stripped off his clothes, and, like the rest, fell into a rapture before Samuel, and lay down naked all that day and all that night. That is why men say, 'Is Saul also among the prophets?' (1 Sam. 19.23–4).

Sometimes similar behaviour is seen as originating in an evil spiritual force. Thus an evil spirit seized Saul, and he fell into a frenzy, or as the New English Bible translates, into a 'prophetic rapture' (1 Sam. 18.10). The prophets were regarded sometimes as being mad (Hos. 9.7; Mic. 2.11; Jer. 5.13; Zech. 13.3). But *ruach* was associated also with great strength, as in the case of Samson (Judg. 14.6), with leadership, as in the case of Joshua (Num. 12.18), and with wisdom (Prov. 1.23). Moreover, the power of *ruach* can bring about social, not only personal, change. So Ezekiel speaks of the renewal of the community of Israel:

> And I will give them one heart, and put a new spirit within them; I will take the stony heart out of their flesh, and give them a heart of flesh, that they may walk in my statutes and keep my ordinances and obey them; and they shall be my people, and I will be their God. (Ezek. 11.19–20)

> Again he said to me, 'Prophesy to these bones, and say to them, O dry bones, hear the word of the Lord. Thus says the Lord God to these bones: Behold I will cause breath to enter you, and you shall live. And I will lay sinews upon you, and will cause flesh to come upon you, and cover you with skin, and put breath in you, and you shall live; and you shall know that I am the Lord.' (37.4–6)

The result of the activity of the Spirit of God was thus seen as involving a revolutionary change, nothing less than resurrection from death to life.

The prophets, those extraordinary individuals who were set on fire by the Spirit of God, were people of tremendous power. They were 'some of the most disturbing people who have ever lived'.[15]

They suggest a disquietude sometimes amounting to agony. Yet there are interludes when one perceives an eternity of love hovering over moments of anguish; at the bottom there is light, fascination, but above the whole soar thunder and lightning.[16]

The prophetic temperament is very far removed from Wordsworth's 'emotion recollected in tranquillity'. It is marked more by agitation, protest, lack of poise, and a sense of alarm. The prophet's language is charged with fire, it is explosive. 'His images,' says Heschel, 'must not shine, they must burn.'[17] We are in the presence of fire.

The later Old Testament prophets looked forward to a new age of the Spirit. This would be a time when the Spirit would be poured out, the wilderness would become fruitful, and justice would dwell there (Isa. 32.15ff). The pouring out of the Spirit was seen as the manifestation of God's face (Ezek. 39.29). In the prophecy of Joel, it is associated with visions and dreams:

And it shall come to pass afterwards, that I will pour out my spirit on all flesh; your sons and your daughters shall prophesy, your old men shall dream dreams, and your young men shall see visions. Even upon the menservants and maidservants in those days I will pour out my spirit. (Joel 2.28–9)

It is this prophecy which is taken up in the Acts of the Apostles when the Holy Spirit equips the Church for proclamation and for fullness of gospel living. The day of Pentecost is of central importance for the early Church's awareness of the presence and power of God in their midst, and later there is a second Pentecostal empowering of the Gentiles (Acts 10.44ff). So the coming of the Holy Spirit was seen as time of newness, a renewal and re-formation.

In the accounts of the experience of the Spirit of God, a number of elements appear. There is the sense of power. There is the sense of intoxication. The apostles were accused of being 'filled with new wine' (Acts 2.13), and the association of spirituality with drunkenness is evident in the language of 'sober intoxication' which entered the spiritual vocabulary with Gregory of Nyssa, and is evident in the hymn of St Ambrose:

Laeti bibamus sobriam
Ebrietatem spiritus.[18]

'Let us joyfully drink of the sober drunkenness of the spirit'. There is also the sense of hope, something which is brought out very powerfully in a letter from Cardinal Suenens in which he links hope with the experience of the Holy Spirit. Why, he is asked, is he a man of hope? His answer embodies a whole theology of the Holy Spirit:

> Because I believe that God is born anew each morning, because I believe that he is creating the world at this very moment. He did not create it at a distant and long-forgotten moment in time.
> It is happening now: we must therefore be ready to expect the unexpected from God.
> The ways of Providence are by nature surprising.
> We are not prisoners of determinism, nor of the sombre prognostications of sociologists.
> God is here, near us, unforeseeable and loving.
> I am a man of hope, not for human reasons, nor from any natural optimism.
> But because I believe the Holy Spirit is at work in the Church and in the world, even where his name remains unheard.
> I am an optimist because I believe the Holy Spirit is the spirit of creation.
> To those who welcome him, he gives each day a fresh liberty and renewed joy and trust.
> The long history of the Church is filled with the wonders of the Holy Spirit.
> Think only of the prophets and saints who, in times of darkness, have discovered a spring of grace and shed beams of light on our path.
> I believe in the surprises of the Holy Spirit.
> John XXIII came as a surprise, and the Council too.
> They were the last things we expected.
> Who would dare to say that the love and imagination of God were exhausted?
> To hope is a duty, not a luxury.
> To hope is not a dream, but to turn dream into reality.
> Happy are those who dream dreams, and are ready to pay the price to make them come true.[19]

There is too the stress on freedom in the Spirit. Where the Spirit of the Lord is, there is freedom (2 Cor. 3.17). Scholastic writers claim that only God can move people from within, while at the same time preserving their freedom. Thus St Thomas speaks of the freedom of the Spirit:[20]

> When a man is inwardly disposed by the gifts of the Holy Spirit – and this is, in fact, a way of telling whether a man is spiritual or not – he feels himself remarkably free in all he does, unconstrained and

unimpeded, without confusion, obstacles or inhibitions, for 'where the Spirit of the Lord is, there is freedom'. . . . In case we might make the mistake of thinking that people born of the Spirit are being driven by some kind of raving mad urge, like those whom some evil spirit has got hold of, the first thing the Lord requires on the way of the Spirit is that he should 'blow where he wills', to show that birth from the Spirit enhances rather than destroys freedom of choice.

Similarly, Pope Paul VI, in an address in 1969, spoke of the freedom of the Spirit in the future Church:[21]

We shall have, therefore, a period of greater freedom in the life of the Church and of her individual members. It will be a period of fewer legal obligations and fewer interior restraints. Formal discipline will be reduced; all arbitrary intolerance and all absolutism will be abolished. Positive law will be simplified, and the exercise of authority will be moderated. There will be promoted the sense of that Christian freedom which pervaded the first generation of Christians.

The coming of the Holy Spirit is thus experienced as profound personal liberation.

There is the sense of great love. It is through the Holy Spirit that the love of God is inflamed within us. God's love has been poured into our hearts through the Holy Spirit (Rom. 5.5). Love is seen as the greatest of the spiritual gifts (1 Cor. 13). To know the love of Christ is to be filled with God's fullness (Eph. 3.19). St John, in the First Epistle, writes of love as the nature of God. Mutual love is the sign of the resurrection (3.14), the person who loves is born of God and knows God (4.7). Moreover, the gift of the Spirit is the proof that God dwells within us (3.24).

The experience of the Holy Spirit is thus described in terms of power, of intoxication, of hope, of freedom, of love. Throughout the literature of spirituality from biblical times onwards, a recurring symbol for the divine activity is the symbol of fire. The fire is one of the earliest symbols of divine presence and action. In the covenant with Abraham, a smoking fire pot and a flaming torch were the signs given (Gen. 15.7). In the account of the sin of Nadab and Abihu, the fire of the Lord came forth and devoured them (Lev. 10.2). Similarly, in Elijah's struggle against false religion, the fire of the Lord fell both on the altar of Baal (1 Kings 18.38) and on the messengers of Ahaziah (2 Kings 1.10, 12). Elijah was particularly seen in later Jewish thought as a prophet of fire (Ecclus. 48.1) who would appear before the great and terrible Day of the Lord, the day burning like an oven

(Mal. 4.1, 5).

The fire symbolizes the power of God, but it also is used of his glory. The angel of the Lord appeared to Moses in a flame of fire (Exod. 3.2). The Lord descended upon Mount Sinai in fire, and the people were warned not to 'break through to come up to the Lord, lest he break out against them' (19.18, 24). We are told that 'the appearance of the glory of the Lord was like a devouring fire' (24.17). After the encounter with the divine glory, Moses' own face shone with glory (34.35). In the writing of Ezekiel, fire is again used as a symbol of God's glory and splendour. Having described his vision of four living creatures, he goes on:

> In the midst of the living creatures there was something that looked like burning coals of fire, like torches moving to an fro among the living creatures; and the fire was bright, and out of the fire went forth lightning. And the living creatures darted to and fro, like a flash of lightning. (Ezek.1.13–14)

He then looked and saw a throne upon which was seated 'a likeness as it were of a human form'.

> And upward from what had the appearance of his loins I saw as it were gleaming bronze, like the appearance of fire enclosed round about: and downward from what had the appearance of his loins I saw as it were the appearance of fire, and there was brightness round about him. Like the appearance of the bow that is in the cloud on the day of rain, so was the appearance of the brightness round about. Such was the appearance of the likeness of the glory of the Lord. (1.27–8)

In the similar vision in Revelation, there are flashes of lightning, and seven torches of fire burn before the throne of God (Rev. 4.5). God, the Scriptures assert, is a devouring fire (Deut. 4.24; Heb. 12.29). And when, on the Day of Pentecost, the Spirit of God fell upon the apostolic community, it was in tongues of fire (Acts 2.3). Fire symbolism is also used in relationship to the last time, the Day of the Lord, the day of judgement, and the experience of hell. In the Old Testament, there are twenty-four occasions on which fire language is used in connection with God's wrath, though there is only one instance where it is used directly of hell (Deut. 32.22). In the Synoptic Gospels, however, *pur* is used twenty-two times, of which fourteen are with reference to eschatological judgement. In these cases, the fire represents the wrath of God, the converse of his glory. In the mystical writers, fire comes to be used of the intensity and burning love of God, while the Pentecostal movements have laid great stress on the power and inexpressible joy brought about through the 'baptism of fire'.

At the heart of the language of fire in relation to God is the sense that any encounter with the divine is marked by terror, awe, and the possibility of being consumed. For no one can see God and live (Exod. 33.20). And yet, in a strange and terrifying way, Moses saw the face of the Lord (Num. 12.8), spoke mouth to mouth and face to face with him (Deut. 34.10) as one speaks with a friend (Exod. 33.11). In all experience of God there is this mingled sense of terror and intimacy, as we encounter the fire which warms and heals while it holds out the possibility of danger and death. We find the mingling of death and birth, tomb and womb, in the Christian liturgy of Baptism.

Baptism by Water and Fire

In the Christian liturgy of Baptism there is a complex symbolic structure, involving water, fire, light, and the strengthening power mediated through anointing and the laying on of hands. Throughout the entire rite, the underlying theme is that of renewal in the Holy Spirit. Baptism occurs once for all just as Christ's death occurred once for all: *ephapax* (Rom. 6.10). It is unrepeatable, yet its results are continually manifested in Christian lives. All prayer in fact is a manifestation of baptismal grace, and this grace is daily renewed. So the liturgy of Baptism is a microcosm of the entire spiritual path with its threefold process of purgation, illumination, and final union.

The first constituent element in the liturgy is the renunciation of the forces of evil. In the early rites, the candidate faced west, the region associated with darkness, and publicly renounced Satan, his works and pomps. S/he was then anointed with the oil of catechumens, sealed against the powers of evil, and, thus strengthened, s/he made a profession of faith in Christ. Stripped naked, the candidate was then ready for the baptismal death, the plunging beneath the waters of renewal.

And so, secondly, the candidate was baptized in water, and anointed with the oil of chrism. In the early rites, these two elements, later distinguished as Baptism and Confirmation, were parts of a unified whole. The positive aspect of baptism, the aspect of purification and strengthening by and in the Spirit, is often termed 'illumination' by the Fathers. The verb *phōtizein*, to enlighten, was used in the mystery religions about saving knowledge, whereas the Fathers used it in relation to baptism. (There may be a hint of such use in the reference, in Hebrews 6.4, to those 'who have once been enlightened, who have tasted the heavenly gift, and have become partakers of the Holy Spirit, and have tasted the goodness of the word of God and the powers of the age to come'.)

Finally, the baptismal liturgy reaches its climax in Holy Communion, in union with God through the sacrament of Christ's body and blood.

Baptism was seen from the beginning as being particularly linked with the activity of the Spirit. In the New Testament there are six references to baptism with the Holy Spirit (Matt. 3.11; Mark 1.8; Luke 3.16; John 1.33; Acts 1.5; 11.16). The first four are associated with the preaching of John the Baptist. According to him, Jesus will baptize with the Holy Spirit, and Matthew and Luke add the words 'and with fire'. The accounts of Jesus' own baptism are reminiscent of the creation of heaven and earth from chaos as well as of the renewal of the earth after the flood. The dove reappears as a symbol of the hovering and restoring Spirit.[22]

In the use of the phrase 'baptize with the Holy Spirit' by John the Baptist, the context is one of judgement and mercy, as well as of the messianic woes and of the eschatological river of fire and spirit. The association of fire with the final judgement is probably based on Numbers 31.23: 'everything that can stand the fire, you shall pass through the fire, and it shall be clean. Nevertheless it shall also be purified with the water of impurity; and whatever cannot stand the fire, you shall pass through the water.' This, linked with Malachi 3.3 ('he is like a refiner's fire') probably provided the source for the symbolism of 'baptism of fire' as it occurs in John's preaching. Behind this may lie the Persian eschatology in which the mountains, made of metal, melt at the end of the world, and the molten metal pours over the earth, forming a river of fire. All the people pass into this river, and are either purified or destroyed by it. This may well be the source of the river of fire in Daniel 7.10, as well as of the idea of the fiery breath of the Messiah.[23] The baptism of fire was the symbol of entry into a new order:

> It was an initiatory metaphor – that is, it denoted the means by which the new age would come to birth ('the travail of the Messiah') and the means by which the penitent would enter into the new age and be fitted for the new age, refined and cleansed.[24]

The term 'baptism *in* the Holy Spirit', though popular today, does not occur in the New Testament at all. The references to being baptized *with* the Spirit, apart from those relating to John the Baptist, refer to crisis initiations of Jews and Gentiles into the Church. After Caesarea, the phrase disappears from the New Testament vocabulary altogether. To speak, as some do, of 'baptism in the Holy Spirit' as an experience distinct from the one baptism in water and the Holy Spirit is not scriptural. While the detailed ritual and ceremonial acts varied, baptism was seen by the early Christian community as the complete rite of initiation which involved of necessity the imparting of the Spirit. Thus in the Acts, water and the filling with the Spirit are inseparably linked as parts of the process of initiation. The Holy Spirit does not belong to some subsequent stage in the Christian life. We know little about the details of the earliest baptismal liturgy. There are references to laying on of hands (Acts 8.17; 19.6; Heb. 6.2), to anointing (2 Cor. 1.21; 1 John 2.20, 27) and to sealing (2 Cor. 1.22; Eph. 1.13; 4.30), but these are not easy to interpret. It is possible that 1 Peter is a baptismal homily. However, we know from early non-biblical sources that the Easter liturgy of the early Church was a baptismal liturgy, and the accounts of the crossing of the Red Sea, of the three children in the fiery furnace, and of Jonah in the womb of the whale, all became part of baptismal symbolism from an early stage. At the centre of this symbolic frame is the theme of water as representing both destruction and life:

It is the mysterious depth which kills and annihilates, the dark habitation of the demonic powers, the very image of the irrational, uncontrollable elements in the world. The principle of life, and life-giving power, and the principle of death, the power of destruction: such is the essentially ambiguous intuition of water in man's religious world-view.[25]

At the end of the second century we begin to find detailed accounts of baptismal liturgies, as in Tertullian's *De Baptismo* and *The Apostolic Tradition* of Hippolytus. There are other references. Both Clement of Rome and Barnabas refer to the pouring out of the Spirit, while 2 Clement speaks of those who have not kept the seal (2 Clem. 7.6). However, it is not at all clear what the seal is. In Hermas (Sim. 9.16, 2ff) it means water, but it can mean the sign of the cross (cf. Rev. 7). None of the early accounts of baptism is complete. But we can gain some important insights into the way in which the sacrament was being interpreted. Tertullian, for example, speaks clearly of the descent of the Holy Spirit upon the water:[26]

Therefore in consequence of that ancient original privilege do waters when God is invoked acquire the sacred significance of conveying sanctity: for at once the Holy Spirit comes down from heaven and stays upon the waters, sanctifying them from within himself, and when thus sanctified they absorb the power of sanctifying.

Through baptism, Tertullian claims, humanity is restored to the likeness of the image of God.

The Fathers also associate the baptismal waters with the waters of creation. Baptism is seen as effecting a new creation, and there are many references to the waters of life, to the tree of life, and to the drowning of demons in the water.[27] The Holy Spirit is not seen as being given in the water, rather the water is 'made ready for the Holy Spirit'. Tertullian goes on to speak of the laying on of hands and invocation of the Holy Spirit, but he calls the whole rite *baptismus* or *aqua*. We are called Christians, he says, from the chrism. After the anointing with consecrated oil, there occurs the laying on of hands, 'the imposition of the hand in benediction, inviting and welcoming the Holy Spirit'.[28] Like Tertullian, Hippolytus also stresses the unity of the rite. The association of the name of 'Christian' with anointing is common throughout the Fathers. Thus Theophilus of Antioch (c. 180) says that we 'are called Christians on this account because we are anointed with the oil of God'.[29] The gnostic sects, who tried to appropriate the gifts of the Spirit to themselves, often saw the gift of the Spirit in anointing as superior to baptism in water. Thus the Gospel of Philip:[30] 'The chrism is superior to baptism, for from the chrism we are called Christians.' And a number of the ideas which are found in the gnostic writings also occur in writers of impeccable orthodoxy.[31] St Ambrose certainly held that 'after the font, the fulfilment is still to be accomplished', yet he saw the 'water bath in the Spirit' and the 'seal of the Spirit' as together forming one act of illumination.[32] St Cyprian wrote of a twofold rite:

> Moreover, a man is not reborn through the laying on of the hand when he receives the Holy Spirit, but in Baptism, so that he is born first, and then receives the Spirit, as happened in the case of the first man Adam. God created him first, and then breathed into his nostrils the breath of life.[33]

A theme which occurs in a number of early writers is that of living in the waters like a fish. Some writers call Christ the heavenly Fish while baptized Christians are seen as little fish. 'We are the small fish, taking our name from our *Ichthus* (fish),' says Tertullian.[34] The big fish is seen sometimes as a dolphin, a lover of humans and protector of sailors. Also there is a theme of spiritual life within water. 'We are born in water and can only be saved by staying in the water.'[35] (This is an idea which appears in the songs of Leonard Cohen in the late 1960s. In his song 'Suzanne' he speaks of Jesus as a sailor, and of how only drowning men can see him. So all must become sailors.) Christians, according to these early writers, are born in and live in the waters. Thus the funeral inscription of Pectorius of Autun says that within the 'divine waters' which renew the soul 'the divine race of heavenly fish receives immortal life'. In the act of communion we eat of the *Ichthus* 'which you hold in the palm of your hand'.[36]

So the early celebration of baptism included a number of elements. The use of water was certainly not the only element. Tertullian certainly sees the giving of the Holy Spirit as subsequent to the use of water, for he says: 'not that the Holy Spirit is given in the water, but that in the water we are made clean by the action of the angel, and made ready for the Holy Spirit'.[37] He describes, in addition to water baptism, an anointing with oil and an imposition of the hand, which is directly linked with the giving of the Spirit, for 'after that the hand is laid upon us, in benediction, invoking and inviting the Holy Spirit'.[38]

There is no reference to what we now call confirmation until the fourth century in the East, and the fifth in the West, and no indication of confirmation as a separate rite until the twelfth century. By the twentieth century it has been rightly said that 'we are still without a satisfying theology of the sacrament'.[39] Much recent Anglican discussion has made the subject more confused by its assumption that confirmation is essentially an act of commitment and adult re-affirmation of baptismal vows. Such an act is highly desirable, to be encouraged, and ought to happen at least annually, but it is not confirmation. It is essential to stress that

... confirmation is not and never has been a sacrament of commitment: it is the sacrament of the mystery of Pentecost in the life of one who in conversion and baptism has committed himself to Christ and is reborn to a new existence.[40]

So, in the prayer for the consecration of the chrism on Maundy Thursday, the bishop prays for those who are to be reborn in the waters of baptism: 'By this sacrament (i.e. chrism) give them the fullness of royal, priestly, and prophetic honour, and clothe them with the robe of unending life.' The clothing, however, takes place in baptism, and the gift of unending life is mentioned *after* the share in Christ's threefold dignity. Thus the gift of the Holy Spirit and participation in the life of Christ are two facets of the same divine action.

By this fundamental act of baptism, grace is conferred. 'Everyone who has been validly baptized has received all grace hiddenly.'[41] The rest of the life of Christian discipleship consists of a revealing, a manifestation of baptism. The experience of *metanoia*, of awakening and repentance, can be seen as a showing forth of the grace given in baptism. Thus St Symeon the New Theologian writes of the Christian who is enslaved to sin and helpless, and who then meets with a trusted friend of God:

> And if he bids you stay in quietness, saying, 'Sit here without going
> out, until you are clothed with power from on high', obey him with
> firm hope and insatiable joy. Such a teacher is true and no deceiver.
> There will come down upon you too, even in this age, the same
> power of the all-holy Spirit, not visibly in the form of fire, but you
> will see it spiritually in the form of spiritual light, with all
> tranquillity and enjoyment.[42]

In this experience, he goes on, there is healing of passions and of
bodily sickness. The 'eyes of the heart' are cleansed, and the soul is
filled with joy and amazement which may be expressed in tears. As a
result of this experience, 'a man is totally changed and knows God as
he is first known by him'.[43] Elsewhere Symeon tells us that those who
thus experience the Holy Spirit will cry out 'We've got the treasure of
the Spirit in us, we have! We've got eternal life in our hearts!'

This account is actually very close to the experiences described in
the charismatic renewal. In fact we can probably say with confidence
that we are dealing with the same experience. Graces given in baptism
come to the surface later. It is therefore better to speak of the
'discovery' or 'manifestation' of the Holy Spirit rather than, by using
the term 'baptism in the Holy Spirit', to suggest that somehow the
original act of baptism was deficient or inadequate. Kilian McDonnell, while he continues to use the term, stresses that 'baptism in the
Holy Spirit manifests itself in an adult when, by either a crisis act of a
growth process, he says Yes to what objectively took place during the
rite of initiation'.[44] We are not then speaking of a new action of God
but rather of the manifesting of the grace given in the baptismal act.
Simon Tugwell summarizes it well:[45]

> So, all told, the Pentecostal doctrine of 'baptism in the Holy Spirit'
> does not survive critical examination at all well. It is not validated
> by Scripture or tradition, and in fact tradition gives us very cogent
> reasons for regarding it with great suspicion. However, the
> tradition in different terms is as adamant as the Pentecostals on the
> need for spiritual experience and on the possibility of there being a
> decisive initial experience.

God is revealed in the intensity of fire and in the mysteriousness of
water. St Symeon compares the knowledge of God to the sea:[46]

> God can be known to us in the same way as a man can see an endless
> ocean by standing at the shore of night with a dimly lit candle. Do
> you think he can see much? He knows that there is an ocean in front

of him, that this ocean is huge, and that he cannot see it all at once. The same is true of our knowledge of God.

It is this knowledge of God in mystery with which the mystics are absorbed.

Fire and the Mystical Tradition

From Cassian to Symeon, from Ruysbroeck to Catherine of Genoa, from William Law to St John of the Cross, fire has been a symbol of divine nature and of divine love. The fire delights and deifies human beings, wounding the soul with the tenderness of the life of God. Fire is often associated, as we have seen earlier, with intoxication. Thus Philo, writing of the colours associated with spiritual experience, says that mystical union bears the colour of ruby and sapphire, for

> to him who makes the confession of praise, the hue of the ruby belongs, for he is permeated by fire in giving thanks to God, and is drunk with a sober drunkenness. But, to him who is still labouring, the hue of the green stone is proper, if men in exercise and training are pale.[47]

In mystical prayer, the light and fire of God is seen not as a simple experience but as something which is 'a light and a fire that can grow indefinitely in power, and take possession of all the faculties of a man'.[48] All prayer contains the elements of wildness and terror, the recognition that it is terrible to fall into the hands of the living God. Prayer is thus not a gentle activity but an entry into a state of danger:

> The Christian at prayer, therefore, does not always sit in a serene and tranquil posture of stillness and receptivity. Sometimes he pounds his fists on the wall or paces the floor: sometimes, like Job, he argues with God, or, like Jacob, wrestles with him and comes out maimed for life; sometimes he dances joyfully like David in the Lord's presence. In general, whenever the Christian enters into prayer, he assumes he may not come out alive! God is not nice; he is not a buddy, an uncle, or a mascot; he is an earthquake. When we pray we enter the cave of a tiger, and jeopardize our safety in a life-or-death situation.[49]

One of the earliest accounts of the prayer of fire is contained in the writings of the fourth-century monk John Cassian (360–435). In his Ninth Conference on Prayer, Cassian speaks of the contemplative kind of prayer to which we are led as grace works like a flame in the soul. He calls such prayer 'the prayer of fire' (oratio ignita). Cassian held that, while such prayer was known only to a few, it ought to be seen as the ordinary fruit of a life of personal prayer. He wrote:[50]

> Soaring above every human sense, it is uttered not by the sound of the voice nor by the movement of the tongue nor by any formation of words. Filled and illumined with light from heaven, the mind does not utter this prayer in limited and human expression, but with all its powers gathered together in unity it pours forth this prayer abundantly as from a copius fountain, and offers it up to God in a way beyond expression, telling him so much in that brief moment of time that when we return to ourselves afterwards we are not able easily to state or even to go over in our minds all that took place.

Like the prayer of tongues, the prayer of fire involves the Spirit of God speaking through the human person in words which are beyond comprehension. The mind leaps upwards like a flame. Yet such fiery prayer is simply the normal fruition which bursts forth, by God's grace, when vocal prayer is well made. Cassian says that the use of the Lord's Prayer leads all those who practise it well into fiery prayer.

Other writers in the early centuries speak of fiery prayer as an interior condition of the heart. Thus Macarius of Egypt writes of 'the fire which lives inside in the heart', the great spiritual force working towards transformation and which will, in time accomplish the resurrection. Like Macarius, Diadochus, writing towards the end of the fifth century, speaks of the work of grace in the heart:[51]

> Grace hides its presence in the baptized, waiting for the initiative of the soul; but when the whole man turns towards the Lord, then grace reveals its presence to the heart through an ineffable experience ... And if man begins his progress by keeping the commandments and ceaselessly invoking the Lord Jesus, then the fire of holy grace penetrates even the external senses of the heart.

Earlier, St Ephraim the Syrian had linked the fire of the Spirit to the reception of the Eucharist, for, he wrote, 'he who eats this bread with faith eats at the same time the fire of the Holy Spirit'.[52]

The Eastern writer who, more than anyone, expresses the sense of the presence and power of the Spirit in the language of fire is St Symeon the New Theologian (949–1022). He has been called 'the singer of fire and light',[53] and certainly for him the experience of God was an 'intoxiation of light', a 'movement of fire', and a 'swirling of flame within me'. The fire which comes forth from God's glory is identified with the Holy Spirit. And this grace from the Holy Spirit kindles the souls of men and women so that all may come close to the fire and be kindled by it, and so may shine like gods. The 'sun-like' experiences described by St Symeon have attracted much attention, including that of Jung.[54] Like Ephraim, Symeon also wrote of the effects of the Eucharist in terms of the inflaming of an interior fire:

> Thy whole body, pure and divine, blazes with the fire of thy divinity ineffably united to it. Thou hast granted, Lord, that this corruptible temple – my human flesh – be united to thy holy flesh, that my blood mingle with thine: from henceforth I am a transparent and translucid member of thy body.[55]

In his hymns of divine love, Symeon sees the Spirit of God as a brilliant and transforming light:

> As I was meditating, Master, on these things
> suddenly you appeared from above, much greater than the sun
> and you shone brilliantly from the heavens down into my heart . . .
> O what intoxication of light, O what movements of fire.
> O what swirlings of the flame in me, miserable one that I am
> coming from you and your glory.
> Thy glory I know it and say it is your Holy Spirit . . .
> but while I was there surrounded by darkness
> you appeared as light, illuminating me completely from your total light
> and I became light in the night.[56]

In his invocation of the Holy Spirit, Symeon addresses the Spirit as 'ineffable reality', 'inconceivable person', 'non-setting sun'.[57] The Spirit is fire in the heart. Symeon speaks of God as 'all vivid with the fire of your divinity' and as 'the source of fire'.[58] Seized by the fiery light and divinized by it, the human person becomes 'completely like a fire . . . in the centre of my heart'.[59] Sharing in the light of God, s/he participates in the glory, so that her face shines and all her members become bearers of light.[60] Symeon speaks often of the experience of being interiorly 'consumed as by fire',[61] and in one hymn he addresses God thus:[62]

> It is the effervescence of love which makes me fire and ray.
> Indeed, when the coal of tenderness has enkindled in you
> then I also, seeing the desire of your heart
> find myself united to this desire and I bring light,
> and I show myself as fire, I who created fire by my word.

The action of God in the Eucharist is also compared to the action of fire in a hymn which speaks of transformation:

> I was enflamed, I burned,

my whole being was on fire.

Symeon goes on to speak of the vision of God:

> He was suddenly completely there,
> united with me in an ineffable manner,
> joined to me in an unspeakable way,
> and immersed in me without mixing,
> as the fire melds one with the iron,
> and the light with the crystal.
> And he made me as though I were all fire.[63]

A preoccupation with the symbolism of fire has remained a central mark of Eastern, and particularly Russian, spirituality. A writer on Russian culture has observed:[64]

> Even stronger ... in the forest was the fear of, and fascination with, fire ... Russians often mention Christ's statement that 'I have come to send fire on the earth', and the fact that the Holy Spirit first came down to man through 'tongues of fire' ... A basic metaphor for explaining the perfect combination of God and man in Christ had long been that of fire infusing itself with iron ... Heat not light, warmth rather than enlightenment, was the way to God ... Small wonder that fire was the dominant symbol of the Last Judgement in Russian iconography.

Western Christian writers in the Middle Ages also used the fire symbol. In a famous sentence, St Augustine wrote that 'love grown cold is the heart's silence: love on fire is the heart's clamour'.[65] Later St Bernard speaks of the rapture and delight which overwhelm the soul, so that 'the soul, drunk with the divine love, forgetful of self, and seeming to itself a broken vessel, goes out completely into God, and cleaving to God becomes one spirit with him'. He goes on to say that 'to feel thus is to be deified' (sic affici, deificari est).[66] Bernard however lays great stress on the soothing and gentle nature of God rather than on his terrible aspect, and he speaks again of the effect of God on the soul, using the language of fire:

> As a bar of iron, heated red-hot, becomes like fire itself, forgetting its own nature, or as the air radiant with sunbeams, seems not so much to be illuminated as to be light itself; so, in the saints, all human affections melt away, by some unspeakable transmutation, into the will of God.[67]

In the fourteenth century, Richard Rolle, the Yorkshire hermit (1300–49), gave to fire symbolism a permanent place in the Western mystical tradition. So inflamed with divine love was Rolle that he ran his hand across his chest to see if he were actually on fire!

I cannot tell you how surprised I was the first time I felt my heart begin to warm. It was real warmth too, not imaginary, and it felt as if it were actually on fire. I was astonished at the way the heat surged up, and how this new sensation brought great and unexpected comfort. I had to keep feeling my breast to make sure there was no physical reason for it.

He then realized that the fire was interior and was a gift from God, a 'spiritual flame', 'a honeyed flame'. 'It set my heart aglow as if a real fire was burning there.'[68] Rolle goes on to describe the experience of being on fire with love for Christ. That love, he says, at the peak of its heat, is indescribable, the awareness of inner fire bringing security to the whole of one's being.

Rolle emphasizes that, before the flame of love can be experienced, there must be a conversion to God and a rejection of sin. Even so, the experience of inner warmth does not come at once, and cannot come at all unless the individual has severed herself from all forms of vanity. But the fire, when it enters and inflames people's hearts, makes them glow and burn and purges them of sin. They become 'fiery lovers'.[69] Rolle goes on to describe the experience of fiery love as one of personal song:

Flowering through this loving flame into all virtue, they rejoice in their Maker. Their mind is changed and passes into lasting melody. From now on their meditations become song. Melancholy has been driven out of the mansion of their spirit, and it now resounds with wondrous melody. The one-time torment of their soul has vanished, and now in glowing health they dwell in the heights of harmony, in the wonderful rhythm of sweet and melodious meditation.[70]

Rolle later speaks of the peace which lovers of Christ know, 'a peace that sings and loves and burns and contemplates'. 'Very sweet indeed is the quiet which the spirit experiences. Music, divine and delectable, comes to rejoice it; the mind is rapt in sublime and gay melody and sings the delights of everlasting love.' The heart of the singer is 'altogether ablaze with heavenly fire. And he is transformed into the likeness of him in whom is all melody and song... A man overflows with inner joy, and his very thought sings as he rejoices in the warmth of his love.' Moreover, once the experience of fire has occurred, 'there always remains a sort of glow'.[71]

He speaks also of solitaries who are 'straining every nerve to burn with the fire of the Holy Spirit'. The true solitary, according to Rolle, possesses an inner blaze of love, for 'his heart is shaped by the divine fire'.[72] In the account of his own experience of 'the warmth of eternal love', Rolle says:[73]

> I was sitting in a certain chapel, delighting in the sweetness of prayer or meditation, when suddenly I felt within myself an unusually pleasant heat. At first I wondered where it came from, but it was not long before I realized that it was from none of his creatures but from the Creator himself. It was, I found, more fervent and pleasant than I had ever known. But it was just over nine months before a conscious and incredibly great warmth kindled me, and I knew the infusion and understanding of heavenly and spiritual sounds. Sounds which pertain to the song of eternal praise and to the sweetness of unheard melody; sounds which cannot be known or heard save by him who has received it; and who himself must be clean and separate from the things of earth.

He speaks of a 'symphony of song' and of an inward singing, and bursts out in a prayer of thanksgiving to the Lord Jesus.

> So, Jesus, I want to be praising you always, such is my joy.
> When I was down and out you stooped to me,
>   and associated me with those sweet ministers
>   who through the Spirit give out those lovely and heavenly
>   melodies.
> I will express my joy and gratitude
>   because you have made me like one of those
>   whose superb song springs from a clear conscience.
> Their soul burns with their unending love.
> And your servant too, when he sits in prayer,
>   glows and loves in his fervour.
> His mind is transformed; he burns with fire;
>   indeed he expands in the vehemence of his longing.[74]

The heat is such that only those who have experienced it can even imagine it. Their hearts burst with song. In all truly loving minds, says Rolle, 'there is always a song of glory and an inner flame of love'. And this flame brings about an actual likeness to God.

> Love has also the power of transforming, for it transforms the lover into his Beloved, and makes him dwell in him. Thus it happens that when the fire of the Holy Spirit really gets hold of the heart, it sets it wholly on fire, and, so to speak, turns it into flame, leading it

into that state in which it is most like God.[75]

He goes on to say that this fire of love cleans out vice and sin from the heart:

> Yet this perfect love does not make a man incapable of sinning, but no sin can persist in him because it is at once purged by the fire of love. Again, one who loves Jesus Christ like this does not say his prayers the same way as other men, however righteous they may be, because his mind is raised to great exaltation, and is rapt with love for Christ. He is taken out of himself into indescribable delight, and the divinest music floods into him.[76]

Of lovers such as these, Rolle observes:[77]

> They are alight with the flame of the heavenly vision, and know themselves free from the burden of sin, and now no longer sin in their wills. The heart that has turned to fire embraces nothing of the world but strives always to pierce heaven.

So 'the deep recesses of his soul' are filled with joy, and yet there is at the centre an inner stillness and silence.

> His inner being is ablaze with the fire of love; his very heart is alight and burning; ... He praises God in song – but his song is in silence. His lays are not meant for the ears of men, but in the sight of God he utters his praise in unspeakable sweetness.[78]

Of such a person it can be said that his whole being has become a hymn. But throughout Rolle is emphatic that the experience he is describing is due to 'the love of the Godhead that gets right into a man and inflames him with the fire of the Holy Spirit'.[79]

The use of this kind of language recurs in other medieval writers. *The Cloud of Unknowing* speaks of enabling the affections to 'flame with the fire of his love'.[80] while Ruysbroeck speaks of the way in which 'the naked will is tranformed by the eternal Lord as fire by fire'.[81] 'We are like coals,' he says,[82] 'burned at the hearth of infinite love.' St Catherine of Siena (1347–80) speaks of souls thrown into the furnace of the divine charity. They are inflamed in God, she says, and are like brands which are not wholly consumed in a furnace. No one can take hold of them or extinguish the flame: they have become wholly fire. She advises the soul, 'Labour therefore to increase the fire of thy desire',[83] and speaks of it as a 'holy and amorous fire', the 'force and heat of love'.[84] God, in her visions, speaks of a baptism of fire which is available for all who desire it with the affection of love.[85] The fire of which she writes is identified with illumination, and she cites

Augustine, Jerome, and Aquinas as examples of illuminated people. From the heart of the divine fire comes light and truth: 'And I, Fire, accepter of sacrifices, ravishing them away from their darkness, give the light; not a natural light, but a supernatural, so that, through the darkness, they know the truth.'[86] The fire continues, after death, to transform the soul:

> When the soul leaves the body, the tears remain behind, but the affection of love has drawn to itself the fruit of the tears, and consumed it, as happens in the case of the water in your furnace. The water has not really been taken out of the furnace, but the heat of the fire has consumed it and drawn it into itself. Thus the soul, having arrived at tasting the fire of my divine charity, and having passed from this life in a state of love towards me and her neighbour, having further possessed that unitive love which caused her tears to fall, does not cease to offer me her blessed desires, tearful indeed, though without pain or physical weeping, for physical tears have evaporated in the furnace, becoming tears of fire of the Holy Spirit.[87]

A century later, St Catherine of Genoa developed the theme of the transforming fire in her *Treatise on Purgatory*, part of a much longer manuscript. Here she writes of the experience of purgatory as one of contentment:

> The hindrance is the rust of sin, and the fire keeps on consuming the rust, and so the soul is increasingly uncovered to the divine inflowing. An object that is covered cannot respond to the rays of the sun which beat upon it, not through any fault of the sun's – for the sun does not cease to shine – but because the covering is in the way. If the covering is destroyed, the object will be exposed to the sun, and will respond to its rays in proportion to the rate at which the destruction of the covering goes on. In the same way, sin is the soul's covering, and this covering is gradually consumed away in Purgatory by means of the fire. The more it is consumed, the sooner does the soul respond to the true Sun, God, and uncover itself to the divine ray.[88]

When the soul sees any impediment between God and itself, she says, 'an extreme fire . . . similar to that of hell', springs up in it.[89] She goes on to speak of the purifying process, comparing it to the action of fire on gold.

> Gold, when once purified, can be no further consumed by the action of fire, however great this may be, since fire does not, strictly

speaking, consume gold, but only the dross which gold may chance to contain. So also it is with regard to the soul. God holds it so long in the furnace until every imperfection is consumed away. When it is thus purified, it becomes impassable, so that if, thus purified, it were to be kept in the fire, it would feel no pain. Such a fire would be to it rather a fire of Divine Love, burning without opposition, like the fire of life eternal.[90]

Mystical writers through the centuries have continued to use the symbol of fire in their accounts of the divine love and of its activity within the human person. In the twentieth century, one of the most interesting meditations on the divine fire occurs in Teilhard de Chardin's *Hymn of the Universe*. In his reflections on the 'Mass on the World', Teilhard writes of fire as the source of being. 'In the beginning, there were not coldness and darkness: there was the Fire.'[91] He prays to God as the 'Blazing Spirit' and calls upon him to transfigure the world. The meditation continues with the theme of the penetration of the earth by the divine fire, the climax being the communion:

If the Fire has come down into the heart of the world, it is, in the last resort, to lay hold on me, and to absorb me. Henceforth I cannot be content simply to contemplate it, or, by my steadfast faith, to intensify its ardency more and more in the world around me. What I must do, when I have taken part with all my energies in the consecration which causes its flames to leap forth, is to consent to the communion which will enable it to find in me the food it has come in the last resort to seek.[92]

With even greater power and persistence, the poet Edith Sitwell made use continuously in her poems of the symbol of fire. In her 'Metamorphosis' (1946) she wrote of the emergence of fire from darkness:

So, out of the dark, see our great Spring begins
– Our Christ, the new Song, breaking out in the fields and
    hedgerows,
The heart of man! O the new temper of Christ, in veins and
    branches!
He comes, our Sun, to melt the eternal ice
Of Death, the crusts of Time round the sunken soul –
Coming again in the spring of the world, clothed with the scarlet-
    coloured
Blood of our martyrdoms – the fire of spring.[93]

Throughout her poetry runs the theme of the divine fire. 'The fires of God go marching on.'[94] The same theme is repeated in 'An Old Woman'.[95] But it is perhaps in 'Eurydice' that the symbolism is most powerful. The poem begins:

> Fires on the hearth! Fires in the heavens! Fires in the hearts of Men!
> I who was welded into bright gold in the earth by Death
> Salute you! All the weight of Death in all the world
> Yet does not equal Love – the great compassion
> For the fallen dust and all fallen creatures, quickening
> As is the Sun in the void firmament.
> It shines like fire. O bright gold of the heat of the Sun
> Of Love across dark fields – burning away rough husks of Death
> Till all is fire, and bringing all to harvest![96]

Finally, in the 'Canticle of the Rose' – the rose is 'the voice of fire' – Sitwell explains that the fire is Christ himself:

> But high upon the wall
> The Rose where the Wounds of Christ are red
> Cries to the Light
> 'See how I rise upon my stem, ineffable bright
> Effluence of bright essence . . . From my little span
> I cry to Christ, Who is the ultimate Fire
> Who will burn away the cold in the heart of Man . . .[97]

The Fire of Holiness

The burning away of the cold within the human heart is what the spiritual writers call sanctity, and, in the spirituality of the Eastern Orthodox tradition in particular, the sanctified heart is often seen as a heart on fire. In the Sayings of the Desert Fathers, we read of a visitor to Abba Arsenius who saw him to be 'entirely like a flame',[98] while in one of the sayings of Joseph of Panephysis we read:

> Abba Lot went to see Abba Joseph and said to him, 'Abba, as far as I can, I say my little office, I fast a little, I pray and meditate, I live in peace, and, as far as I can, I purify my thoughts. What else can I do?' Then the old man stood up, and stretched his hands towards heaven. His fingers became like ten lamps of fire, and he said to him, 'If you will, you can become all flame'.[99]

From these early writers onwards, a close association is made in spiritual theology between the light of the Spirit and the deepening of inward love. Thus the Macarian Homilies, written in Syria in the late fourth century, stress the central place of experience and of feeling in the growth of the inner life:

> There is a thing which everyone ought to know, that there are eyes that are more inward than these eyes, and hearing more inward than this hearing. As the eyes sensibly behold and recognize the face of a friend or beloved one, so the eyes of the worthy and faithful soul, being spiritually enlightened by the light of God, behold and recognize the true friend, the sweetest and greatly longed-for bridegroom, the Lord, while the soul is shone upon by the adorable Spirit; and thus beholding with the mind the desirable and only inexpressible beauty it is smitten with a passionate love of God, and is directed into all virtues of the Spirit, and thus possesses an unbounded, unfailing love for the Lord it longs for.[100]

And it is this inner longing, nourished by the inner divine light and warmth of the Spirit, which issues in the loving heart of which St Isaac the Syrian speaks so eloquently:[101]

> It is a heart, which is burning with charity for the whole of creation, for men, for the birds, for the beasts, for the demons – for all creatures. He who has such a heart cannot see or call to mind a creature without his eyes being filled with tears by reason of the immense compassion which seizes his heart . . . That is why such a man never ceases to pray also for the animals, for the enemies of Truth, and for those who do him evil . . . moved by the infinite pity which reigns in the hearts of those who are becoming united with God.

In the spirituality of the Eastern Christians, the symbolism of fire comes most powerfully in the life of St Seraphim of Sarov. Born in 1759 in Kursk, Russia, Prokhov Mochnin was given the name of Seraphim, the Hebrew word for 'flaming'. Throughout his teaching on the life of prayer, Seraphim stressed the experience of spiritual warmth, seeing the goal of the Christian life to be the acquiring of the Holy Spirit. The best-known incident in the life of Seraphim is his conversation with Nicholas Motovilov which took place in 1831 on the theme of the Holy Spirit. In the discussion, Seraphim points out that the Spirit appears to all those in whom God manifests his actions as an ineffable light. The apostles, he further claims, were sensibly aware of his presence. Then occurs the following dialogue:

> 'My friend, both of us are in the Holy Spirit, you and I. Why won't you look at me?'

'Father, I can't look at you, because your face has become brighter than the sun, and it dazzles my eyes.'
Don't be afraid, friend of God, for you too have now become as bright as I. You yourself are now in the plenitude of the Holy Spirit, although you do not think you can look at me.'[102]

Then Motovilov continues:

> Then I looked at him and was terror struck. Picture for yourself the sun's orb and, in the brightest part of its noonday shining, the face of a man who talks with you. You can see his lips moving, see the expression in his eyes, and hear his voice; you can feel his arm round your shoulders, but can neither see this arm, nor face, but only a blinding light which shines all round you, illumining with its light the layer of snow that is reflecting its brightness, and the fire flakes that are falling like gold dust.

He goes on to speak of his own experience of calm and peace as 'an ineffable warmth'. St Seraphim assures him that this warmth is in fact the plenitude of the Holy Spirit. As Motovilov left him, he wrote that 'the ineffable light that I had seen with my own eyes continued to illumine his whole being.'[103]

The spirituality of warmth and of light which we find in St Seraphim has been compared with that of St Francis of Assisi. Leclerc has commented on the place of the sun in the spirituality of Francis:

> Francis is clothed with the sun ... A great symbol of the Most High, and yet a brother. A sun at once sacred and yet close to us. Francis does not simply see this sun, with his enfeebled eyes, shining over the plain of Assisi. He experiences it with all his being. The great cosmic image rises from the depths of his being. It is the expression of an inner fullness ... In it, Francis' soul recognizes and celebrates symbolically, although unconsciously, his own transfiguration, his own transformation in the Kingdom ... This marvellous substance of the sun, all of light, so brotherly yet marked with the seal of the Most High, is the unconscious but infinitely expressive image of the soul which finds itself in the fullness of its energies and destiny, open to the whole of its mystery, reconciling in itself the lower and hidden powers of life and matter, with the awareness of its highest destiny and the radiant certainty of its divine calling.[104]

However, it is some centuries later in the West, in the writings of St John of the Cross, that we find a detailed treatment of the

transforming, sanctifying power of the Holy Spirit under the symbol
of the 'living flame of love'. St John begins his work by comparing the
intensifying of love within the soul to the activity of fire and its effect
on wood:

> Although the fire has penetrated the wood, transformed it, and
> united it with itself, yet as this fire grows hotter and continues to
> burn, the wood becomes much more incandescent and inflamed,
> even to the point of flaring up and shooting out flames from itself.
> (Prologue)[105]

Thus, inwardly transformed in the fire of love, the human soul itself
produces within itself a living flame. In language which is both deeply
sexual and also in sharp contrast to the language used in *The Dark
Night of the Soul*, St John addresses the flame:

> O living flame of love
> That tenderly wounds my soul
> In its deepest center! Since
> Now you are not oppressive,
> Now consummate! if it be your will:
> Tear through the veil of this sweet encounter. (Stanza 1)

St John, in his commentary on the stanzas, tells us that the flame is the
Holy Spirit (1.1), and that 'the soul feels him within itself not only as a
fire which has consumed and transformed it, but as a fire that burns
and flares within it' (1.3). The more intense the fire of union, the more
vehemently does this fire within the soul burst into flames. Indeed the
soul in St John's account is 'so close to God that it is transformed into a
flame of love' (1.6.) It is clear that the author is describing a state of
great holiness and love. For the soul has actually moved nearer and
nearer to its centre.

> The soul's center is God. When it has reached God with all the
> capacity of its being and the strength of its operation and
> inclination, it will have attained to its final and deepest center in
> God, it will know, love, and enjoy God with all its might ...
> Although it is in its center, it is not yet in its deepest center, for it
> can go deeper in God. (1.12)

The final goal of this process of interiority is deification, for the love of
God will have arrived at 'wounding the soul in its ultimate and deepest
center, which is to transform and clarify it in its whole being, power
and strength, and according to its capacity, until it appears to be God'
(1.13).

However, St John is emphatic that the reality which is experienced as fire is the same reality which was previously encountered as darkness and night. 'The very fire of love which afterwards is united with the soul, glorifying it, is that which previously assails it by purging it.' (1.19) During the Purgative Way, he explains, 'this flame is extremely oppressive'. It strikes the soul as darkness:

> In this preparatory purgation the flame is not bright for a person, but dark. If it does shed some light, the only reason is that the soul may see its miseries and defects. It is not gentle, but afflictive. Even though it sometimes imparts the warmth of love, it does so with torment and pain. And it is not delightful but dry . . . Neither is the flame refreshing and peaceful, but it is consuming and contentious, making a person faint and suffer with self-knowledge. Thus it is not glorious for the soul, but rather makes it feel wretched and distressed in the spiritual light of self-knowledge which it bestows. (ibid.)

So the early experience of the fire is one of pain and affliction, for 'when the flame tenderly and lovingly assails the will, hardness is felt beside the tenderness, and dryness beside the love. The will does not feel the love and tenderness of the flame, for, on account of its contrary hardness and dryness, it is unprepared for this, until the love and tenderness expel the dryness and hardness, and reign within it' (1.23). St John refers readers back to *The Ascent* and *The Dark Night* for accounts of the afflictive phase of the work of the flame, and again stresses:

> Let it suffice to know that the very God who desires to enter within the soul through the union and transformation of love is he who first assails and purges it with the light and heat of his divine flame, just as the fire that penetrates the wood is the same that first prepares it for this, as we said. Hence the very flame that is now gentle, since it has entered within the soul, is that which was formerly oppressive, assailing it from without. (1.25)

However, once the flame has entered the depths of the person, transforming her into a closer likeness to the divine love, the fire becomes so intense as to be almost beyond description. 'When he will to touch somewhat vehemently, the soul's burning reaches such a high degree of love that it seems to surpass that of all the fires of the world; for he is an infinite fire of love.' (2.2)

The work of sanctification involves the burning away of dross prior to the intensity of union with the holy God. It includes times of great pain and terror as the alien contents of the soul are expelled. The love and purity of God are experienced as darkness and affliction. To be made holy, as a community consecrated to God, as individuals transformed by the divine fire, is to enter into the experience of being consumed. As a contemporary writer has said, 'The fire of the Spirit in the heavenly realm, whether in a divinely appointed community on earth or in the life beyond death, is so fierce and consuming of all dross that only the transfigured ones can hope to survive in it.'[106]

Pentecostal Fire

All experiences of the Spirit working as a fire within the Christian community have looked back to the original Pentecost experience. In our day many Christians have felt that they have entered afresh into that initial experience. Modern Pentecostalism was a growth from the Holiness movement which itself looked back to Wesley and his doctrine of entire sanctification. The years preceding the revival were marked by a serious neglect of the Holy Spirit throughout many sections of the Church in the West. So in 1897 Pope Leo XIII had lamented, 'Perhaps even today if we were to ask some Christians whether they have received the Holy Spirit, they would answer, like the disciples St Paul met at Ephesus, "We had not even heard that there was any such thing as the Holy Spirit".'[107] While there had been some isolated figures, such as J. G. Arintero (1860–1920) who warned Roman Catholics not to fight shy of charismatic gifts,[108] the general atmosphere was one of neglect in all the mainstream churches. As late as 1950, the Anglican bishop J. E. Fison noted that there were virtually no creative theologians grappling with the doctrine of the Holy Spirit in recent times apart from Berdyaev, Martin Buber, and some of the works of R. C. Moberly.[109] By the end of the 1950s, however Pope John XXIII was calling for a new Pentecost, and his successor, Paul VI, called for 'a new cult of the Holy Spirit, precisely as the indispensable complement of the teaching of the Council'.[110]

In the earlier Pentecostal revivals at the end of the nineteenth century and the early years of our own, there was a strong emphasis on fire. In the case of Thomas Ball Barratt, it was claimed that flames of fire were actually visible, while the Danish singer Anna Larsen Bjorner spoke of 'waves of fire going through me'.[111] Many Pentecostal hymns prayed in such words as 'Set hearts and tongues afire.'[112] In recent years, the 'charismatic renewal' movements have seen the spread of the Pentecostal experience within many of the traditional churches. In the Roman communion, 1967 was the crucial year. The renewal spread rapidly among students in Duquesne University in Pennsylvania, and then at the University of Notre Dame. Kevin Ranaghan has explained the spiritual background to the renewal. The people involved were already committed and serious-minded Christians:

> In spite of all this they felt there was something lacking in their individual Christian lives. They couldn't quite put their finger on it, but somehow there was an emptiness, a lack of dynamism, a sapping of strength in their lives of prayer and action. It was as if their lives as Christians were too much their own creation, as if they were moving forward under their own power and of their own will. It seemed to them that the Christian life wasn't meant to be a purely human achievement.[113]

Since then there is no doubt that many thousands of Christians from widely differing traditions have found their lives, their ministries, and their entire understanding of the Christian life transformed by the charismatic renewal. Through their experience of the power of the Holy Spirit, they have been led to see in a most vivid and revivifying way the range and the potential which is available within the Body of Christ. They have felt close to the experience of the earliest Christian community which was overwhelmed by the Spirit and manifested spiritual gifts, *charismata*. At the same time, the charismatic renewal has also been very Christ-centred. The experience of the Spirit has pointed people to Christ, and to Christ both as a human Saviour and as transcendent Lord. The clearest evidence of this is the language and atmosphere of the hymns and songs which have emerged from the renewal: 'Jesus is Lord of all the earth', 'Holy, holy, holy is the Lamb that was slain', and so on. It is incorrect to accuse the charismatic renewal of developing a sense of the Holy Spirit in isolation from the presence and work of Christ, although, of course, such deviations have occurred in revival movements, not only those of twentieth-century origin. Tom Smail has stressed that 'fears that a gospel of the baptizer in the Spirit might replace the gospel of the crucified Saviour, and we might escape from repentance into a spurious triumphalism of spiritual experience and gifts, are real fears',[114] while James Dunn has added that 'as soon as charismatic experience becomes an experience only of the exalted Christ, and not also of the crucified Jesus, it loses its distinctively Christian character'.[115]

However, what has attracted popular attention to the renewal, and drawn more and more people to it, has been the obvious sense of enjoyment and exultation. To those accustomed to somewhat dreary, cerebral, and repressive forms of worship, the renewal has led to a tremendous experience of liberation, freedom in the Spirit, and deep joy. It is the experience generated by the Spirit, which comes first, and the enrichment of the life in Christ which follows. So we see in the charismatic experience precisely the sense of warmth and of power which Christians throughout the ages have described by use of the symbol of fire. And closely linked with the experience of warmth and power is the sense of transcendence of words and concepts. The experience is seen as essentially ineffable. There is a feeling of being devoured, consumed, as by fire, or of being drowned by the waves of God's love. There is a sense of release, and, since this release is the fruit of the resurrection, it is manifested in bodies which are set free to praise, and which experience modes of expression beyond their normal range. The resurrection of the body and the charismatic release of the Spirit are inseparable, just as body and spirit are inseparable. For the power which enables this renewal of spiritual life is not simply the power of many Spirit-filled persons; it is the power which revives and renews them by virtue of their incorporation into the risen Christ. This experience of incorporation is, of course, the central truth of Christian baptism, and so it is common for those within the charismatic renewal to speak of their experience of the fullness of the Spirit as a 'baptism in the Holy Spirit'. What is happening is the surfacing and revealing of this fundamental truth in the actual, lived experiences of individuals and communities, the explosion of a *dunamis* (dynamite is derived from *dunamis*!) which has often been latent for years. Now fact and realization are united in one tremendous, exhilarating experience. It has been called a 'baptism of fire'.

It is important to distinguish the experience from the theological interpretations placed upon it. But not surprisingly, many within the charismatic renewals have gone to classical Pentecostalism to find categories of interpretation of their experience. Pentecostal theology has drawn heavily on a number of key texts in the Acts of the Apostles for its doctrine of the baptism in the Holy Spirit.[116] From these texts and from others, the idea is developed of a two-stage process of Christian initiation. This two-stage process is central to all forms of Pentecostal theology. The actual term 'baptism in the Holy Spirit' was taken over from the Holiness churches in the nineteenth century.[117] The Holiness movement, which drew heavily on Wesleyan teachings on entire sanctification, stressed the importance in the Christian life of a second Christian experience, subsequent to baptism. The theme occurs in an early version of the hymn 'Rock of Ages':

> Be of sin the double cure,
> Save from wrath, and make me pure.[118]

Here there is envisaged a double process ('double cure'), marked by salvation from wrath and later by purity of heart through the inflowing of the Holy Spirit, a division which is not far removed from that in St John of the Cross's distinction between the flame which afflicts and the flame which unites. However, unlike later Pentecostalists, the Holiness movement saw the 'Second Blessing' or 'baptism in the Holy Spirit' in terms of sanctification and purity of heart, and did not associate it with the phenomenon of speaking in tongues. R. A. Torrey, President of the Moody Bible Institute in Chicago, was one of the people who began to place this second experience at the centre of a spiritual theology. Torrey wrote:[119]

> The baptism with the Holy Spirit is an operation of the Holy Spirit distinct from and subsequent and additional to his regenerating work. A man may be regenerated by the Holy Spirit, and still not be baptized with the Holy Spirit. In regeneration, there is an importation of life, and the one who receives it is filled for service. Every true believer has the Holy Spirit. But not every believer has the baptism with the holy spirit, though every believer ... may have.

In distinguishing regeneration from sanctification, Torrey stood within the tradition of Wesley's *Plain Account of Christian Perfection* (1741), and it has been claimed that 'Pentecostalism is primitive Methodism's extended Incarnation':[120]

> The theological centre of the holiness movement, true to its name and its Wesleyan heritage, was a second experience, specifically a conversion into Scripture holiness, sanctification, or, as it was often called, perfect love. This centre assured 'the subsequent experience' an importance it was later to assume in Pentecostalism.[121]

Modern Pentecostalists, like their predecessors, tend to associate this second experience with power. It is 'a second encounter with God, in which the Christian begins to receive the supernatural power of the Holy Spirit into his life ... This second experience ... is given for the purpose of equipping the Christian with God's power for service.'[122]

Many, however, would see this subsequent experience of the Spirit in power not so much as a new experience as a release of the already present Spirit, and as a point of spiritual breakthrough in the Christian's life. Traditional Pentecostalist writers have stressed that the purpose of the experience is not the giving of life but rather the imparting of power. Thus Donald Gee wrote that 'its purpose is not to impart life but to impart power. Its characteristic accompaniments are not fruits but gifts.'[123] It is therefore possible to interpret the experience without the theological understanding of a two-stage process of initiation. Indeed, the two-stage view of Christian life, the central point of Pentecostal theology, is also its weakest point. For 'while the Pentecostal's belief in the synamic and experiential nature of Spirit-Baptism is well founded, his separation of it from conversion-initiation is wholy unjustified.'[124] There is no room in Paul's theology for a Christian who is still waiting to receive his "anointing" or "sealing" with the Spirit.'[125] Rather, in Simon Tugwell's words:[126]

> In the New Testament, in the early Church, all that Pentecostals understand by 'baptism in the Spirit' is referred quite strictly and simply to what it means to be a Christian at all. The experience of the Spirit is not subsequent to that of conversion and faith: the experience of Pentecost is identical with the baptismal confession that 'Jesus is Lord' (and how often the New Testament warns us against Pentecostal manifestations divorced from this confession!).

There is one Baptism in which the Spirit is given. The term 'baptism with the Holy Spirit' does not survive in the New Testament beyond the experience at Caesarea, while 'baptism in the Holy Spirit' is not a New Testament term at all. However, to reject a two-stage initiation view does not mean that there are not stages and developments, points of breakthrough, spiritual crisis moments, and so on, in the Christian life itself; and in so far as the charismatic renewal, and earlier movements, have reminded us of this, they are of considerable importance. The Christian life is not monochrome, and is marked by growth and by change; and many of the most significant changes are associated with very disturbing, exhilarating and 'transcendental' experiences.

For the Pentecostal movements, a central feature of the experience of the Holy Spirit is the phenomenon of 'speaking in tongues'. Glossolalia was familiar among both Jewish and Hellenistic Christians in the first century, and it was certainly recognized as a manifestation of the Spirit.[127] It was also common in the early Church.[128] In the New Testament itself, there are five, possibly six, passages which refer to speaking in tongues.[129] The term 'glossolalia' does not appear in the New Testament though glōssai (tongues) is used. Its original meaning is 'language', but the term is also used of particular kinds of language, for instance, tongues of angels (1 Cor. 13.1), unutterable words (2 Cor. 12.4). However, while tongues are seen as a spiritual gift, they are not regarded as of very great importance. Paul places them at the bottom of his list (1 Cor. 12.8–10; 12.28, 29) and even sees them as a sign of immaturity (12.11; cf. 14.20). In the list in Romans (12.6–8) they are not mentioned at all. It is possible that tongues were seen by some Christians as signs of the new age. Thus Mark 16.17 refers to 'new tongues', and some have associated this with the eschatological tongues of the new creation (2 Cor. 5.17), the new song by the redeemed (Rev. 14.3). Later writers were to focus on the idea of a 'new song' for the 'new man'. Thus Augustine:[130]

> You have learnt the new song: forget the ancient one. We are a new humanity, we have a new alliance with God; so let our song be new; a new song is not for the old man. Only the new mankind can learn it, mankind made new out of the ancient stuff; whose new alliance is the kingdom of heaven . . .
>
> This is the way of singing God gives you; do not search for words. You cannot express in words the sentiments which please God: so, praise him with your jubilant singing. This is fine praise of God, when you sing with jubilation.
>
> You ask, what is singing in jubilation? It means to realize that words are not enough to express what we are singing in our hearts. At the harvest, in the vineyard, whenever men must labour hard, they begin with songs whose words express their joy. But when their joy brims over and words are not enough, they abandon even this coherence and give themselves up to the sheer sound of singing.
>
> What is this jubilation, this exultant song? It is the melody that means our hearts are bursting with feelings words cannot express. And to whom does this jubilation most belong? Surely to God who is unutterable. And does not unutterable mean what cannot be uttered? If words will not come and you may not remain silent, what else can you do but let the melody soar? What else, when the rejoicing heart has no words and the immensity of your joys will not be imprisoned in speech? What else but 'sing out in jubilation'?

St Augustine's theme of 'jubilation' is not so far removed from the idea in some modern Pentecostalist writers that tongues are a form of divine speech. Thus one exponent:[131]

> The child of God is privileged to have speech with God and no man understands this secret speech, for the saint is allowed to speak in the language of Divinity – a language unknown to humanity . . . The humblest saint can enjoy supernatural converse with him who made the worlds, in a language not understood by man, or by the devil either.

In this interpretation, tongues is a way of singing the new song of those who have been made new in Christ, a form of speech and of song which moves beyond the utterable, which seeks to express that which strains conventional forms of speech to breaking point. However, almost all Pentecostal groups see tongue-speaking also as the *initial* evidence of the presence of the Spirit, though the evidence in Acts is restricted to three cases.[132] Nowhere in the New Testament are tongues actually sought. Also in the accounts in Acts, tongue-speaking is always a group experience, not a personal one as so often today. Commenting on the manifestations in Acts, Bruner observes:[133]

> Not here, or elsewhere in the New Testament, is tongues-speaking recorded as occurring in a single seeking *individual*, as it is, however, in most Pentecostal instances. In Acts, on the three occasions where tongues occur, they come to an entire group at once, with prophecy, bringing complete Christian initiation, and occur, in all three cases, apart from recorded effort on the part of the recipients. Speaking in tongues in Acts is on all three occasions a corporate, church-founding, group-conversion phenomenon, and never the subsequent Spirit-experience of an individual.

The phenomenon of speaking in tongues, while it should not be dismissed as being of no spiritual importance, must not be exaggerated. This is recognized by many of those within the charismatic renewal. Thus Kilian McDonnell:[134]

> This charism whose existence in the New Testament communities and in early post-apostolic times is well attested, should neither be given undue attention nor despised. Since it is the lowest of the charisms, it should not be a matter of surprise that it is so common.

Simon Tugwell, while he is critical of Pentecostal theology, lays great stress on the charismatic movement's recovery and re-emphasis on the centrality of experience in the spiritual life. And in this recovery, tongues are not incidental but central. Speaking in tongues 'provides a key to everything', it is an experience of God which is of the greatest significance. For, Tugwell says,

> ... there is good evidence in Scripture and in early Christian tradition that it is an essential characteristic of the indwelling Holy Spirit that he opens our mouths to speak words that will truly be in various ways united with the words, with the Word of God.[135]

At its heart, the manifestation of tongues is a physical and emotional expression of a person's experience of the reality of the divine. It is a *felt* experience. 'You will know it,' wrote a friend to Thomas Ball Barratt, 'for he will be in your very flesh.'[136] Pentecostal writers have insisted on the emotional intensity and the physical dimensions of the experience:

> A weak human vessel is being filled with a divine fullness. To tell us, as some wish to tell us, that such an experience can be received without any emotional manifestation is to do violence to all sense of reality. With all due respect, we refuse to be satisfied that so-called 'Pentecostal' experiences without a physical manifestation are valid according to the scriptural pattern or even common sense.[137]

Many have testified that the experience of tongues 'lifted me into a higher realm and gave me a sense of the nearness of God', or that it provided a way of 'speaking to God with feeling rather than with reason'.[138] Again, traditional Pentecostal writers advise their disciples to 'let go' and become passive as they await the divine gift. Barratt's friend wrote to him:[139]

> We are praying the full pentecostal baptism upon you! So that you may be equipped for his service as you never have been! There has to be a complete coming out and leaving all for Jesus ... and just *letting* God have his own precious way with us. After you have fully consecrated and know God has cleansed your heart, then just wait upon God. Keep yourself in a receptive attitude – and no matter what workings go on in your body, continually let and ask God to have his own way with you. You need have no fear while you keep under the blood – 'Perfect love casts out all fear'. Sometimes a wonderful shaking takes place, and sometimes the language comes at first, as a baby learning to talk. But let God have all – tongues, hands, feet – the whole body presented to him as your reasonable service. When the Holy Ghost comes in, you will know it, for he will be in your flesh. Be obedient on every line. *Be nothing* – then he may be all in all.

We are therefore dealing with that necessary dimension in spiritual life which involves total surrender and abandonment of fear and of inhibition. Indeed a vital aspect of the experience of tongues is the sheer folly and irrationality of it all. For, as Tugwell has stressed, 'you cannot pray in tongues unless you are prepared to make a fool of yourself, and let something happen to you over which your mind has none of its usual control'.[140] Tongues cannot be engineered any more than weeping or contemplative stillness. It is a form of Christian experience in which the person opens herself to the liberating activity of the Spirit. Through the act of surrender, the whole person is enabled to respond with greater depth and spontaneity to God in praise and prayer. While it is not by any means the only form, tongues, for many in the West, can represent what has been called 'the inarticulate element in religious experience'.[141] It is this to which Augustine referred in his splendid passage on jubilation. It is this too of which the great contemplatives often speak when they stress the need to move beyond the restrictions of speech and of intellect. As in the activity of fire, we see in the charismatic experience in its various forms, the attack on hardness of heart, the infusion of warmth and light, the setting of the person on fire with the love and power of God. The God who is manifested and felt is the God of fire, of intense heat and fierceness. And, in some sense, this is an experience which must be shared by all God's people. Orthodox spirituality cannot tolerate divisions into first-class and second-class Christians, a danger which has often been pointed to within charismatic movements, but which has an application throughout many sections of the Church. The truth is that 'to be Christian is to be charismatic; one cannot be a member of the body without sharing the charismatic spirit'.[142]

8

God in the Flesh

You say, Christianity, you say
That the Trinity is unchanging from eternity.
But then you say
At the incarnation he took
Our Manhood into the Godhead
That did not have it before
So it must have altered it,
Having it.

Oh what do you mean, what do you mean?
You never answer our questions.
Stevie Smith, 'How do you see?'[1]

The Word Made Flesh
The belief that the Word of God, the eternal self-manifestation of the
Creator of the universe, took to himself human nature is so basic to
orthodox Christianity that without it the entire edifice crumbles and
falls. Without the incarnation, the belief in the Word made Flesh,
there can be no Christianity, no Christian theology, no Christian
spirituality. Yet no belief is more outrageous, more scandalous, more
extraordinary, more incredible than this. So much so that it has been
relegated by many conventional Christians into the world of Christmas legend, where it cannot and does not affect the central framework
of one's life and faith. Yet it is a Christmas carol which presents the
belief in its stark and crudest form:

> The great God of heaven is come down to earth,
> His mother a Virgin, and sinless his birth;
> The Father eternal his Father alone:
> He sleeps in the manger; he reigns on the throne . . .
>
> The Wonderful Counsellor, boundless in might,
> The Father's own image, the beam of his light;
> Behold him now wearing the likeness of man,
> Weak, helpless and speechless, in measure a span.
>
> O wonder of wonders, which none can unfold:
> The ancient of Days is an hour or two old;
> The Maker of all things is made of the earth,

Man is worshipped by angels, and God comes to birth.[2]

Even to contemplate the truth revealed in these words is to open oneself to the experience of utter amazement. While the truth of the incarnation has always faced Christian people with a mystery, caused perplexity and puzzlement, and led many to reject the possibility of its truth, it has generally been assumed that, with all its difficulties, this *is* a central element in being a Christian. In recent years, however, we have seen the emergence of a school – or rather groups of individuals loosely united by their disbelief – within academic theology which wishes not only to deny the truth of the incarnation, but also to deny its necessity to Christian faith. 'It is impossible', wrote the American theologian John Knox, 'that God should become a man'.[3] Such a belief is 'simply incredible'. And in Britain too we have seen attempts by various theologians to create a form of Christianity in which the incarnation is no longer an element, though there remains a vague devotion to Jesus. Thus Don Cupitt views Christianity as a family of monotheistic faiths which sees Jesus as 'a key' (not *the* key, but *a* key) to understanding the relationship of human beings to God.[4] Writers in the symposium *The Myth of God Incarnate*,[5] while they held varying views about the incarnation, united around a devotion to the human figure of Jesus as in some sense a man approved by God. Maurice Wiles, a leading Anglican scholar, believes that the incarnation is not necessary to Christianity, and that the dogmatic definition of the Council of Chalcedon is a mistake. Christianity and incarnation are not synonymous, the incarnation is perhaps not even intelligible today, and an 'incarnational' faith is still possible without belief in an actual incarnation.[6] So, in the ideas of Wiles and others we have a new departure within the Christian movement, and we are offered 'the first form of Christianity in which the deity of Jesus is looked upon as optional'.[7]

In the early centuries of the Church's life, the Arians argued that it was impossible for God to become a man. For, they argued, there was in God an absolute transcendence and otherness, an incomprehensibility and remoteness from the world, which made such an action absurd and out of the question. The Word, they claimed, was a mediator who brought God and humanity together. But God himself was incapable of becoming involved in the crude details of human, material existence. God could not share his nature with humankind, and, because he could not, he did not. The Arian god could not, by his very nature, be directly involved in the work of salvation at all. It was against this view that St Athanasius (296–373) directed his *De Incarnatione*. In contrast to the remoteness of the Arian god,

Athanasius stressed the taking of humanity into the Godhead. The Son of God became man in order that the sons of men might become God: he was *humanized* so that we might be *deified*. But, Athanasius argued, man could not be deified if joined to a creature, or unless the Son were himself true God. Nor could humanity be brought into the Father's presence unless it had been his true and living Word who had put on the body. It has been said that 'Athanasius' case depends upon the capacity of God to involve himself in the historical order'.[8] This was a conflict which raised, in embryo, many of the controversies which were later to divide Christians, and which are still with us today: specifically, the question of the relationship of God to the world of matter and history, and the materialistic and historical dimensions of salvation. There is a continuous thread of incarnational faith which unites Athanasius with the liberation theologians of Latin America, and with those who seek to defend Christian materialism against the false spiritualizers of the twentieth century.

The incarnation is thus far more than a claim about a specific event, though it is at least that. Essentially the dogma asserts that God took to himself human flesh, assumed humanity into the Godhead. He *became* man: that is, he became what he was not. The eternal became temporal.

> He is that he was, and for ever shall be,
> But becomes that he was not, for you and for me.[9]

The dogma is therefore saying more than that Jesus the man was so 'open to God' that divine attributes could be attributed to him. To move from the human Jesus, the man for others, the faithful servant, to God Incarnate, is a dubious move. Jesus may well have possessed a high degree of 'God-consciousness' and yet not *be* God in any unique sense. The recognition of the divinity of Jesus is not something to which one can move simply by logical argument. Flesh and blood has not revealed it. Moreover, if one attempts to make Jesus so 'open to God', there is a danger that he becomes less human in the process, a kind of superman. But, as the Epistle to the Hebrews stresses, Jesus is utterly human and utterly divine. There is no way that we can remove the scandal of the incarnation, and it is likely that a Christology 'from the side of God' may, in the end, offer a more adequate and satisfactory picture than is offered by those who restrict themselves to the human Jesus.[10]

The early Church grappled for centuries with the issues of Christology because they saw that they raised all the central questions of salvation and of spirituality. St Ignatius of Antioch is probably the first Christian writer to describe Jesus as God absolutely. Ignatius also is prepared to attribute suffering to God, while insisting too on the divine impassibility. He speaks of the passion of God and of the blood of God.[11] Later Tertullian points to the absolute centrality of the flesh in the work of salvation. The flesh, he says, is the hinge of salvation. 'If Christ's being flesh is found to be a lie, then everything which was done in it was done falsely ... God's entire work is subverted.'[12] Similarly, Irenaeus emphasizes the importance of the flesh, the material world, and the incarnation in his controversies with the gnostics and those who wished to promote a purely 'spiritual' religion. The glory of God, he stressed, was a living human person.[13] The stress on the fleshly basis of spirituality comes through even more strongly in the writing of St Gregory of Nazianzus (329–89). 'We needed a God made flesh and put to death in order that we might live again,' he says.[14] Gregory speaks also of the 'blood of God' and of the 'crucified God'. But his most memorable phrase, with abiding theological importance for today, is his claim about the taking by Christ of the whole of human nature, and not simply a part of it. For, he says, 'what has not beeen assumed has not been healed'.[15] It was necessary for salvation and for spiritual integrity that the whole of humanity in all its complex make-up should have been assumed and taken into God, and thus saved and healed in its entirety.

In all this discussion, the central truth is that God was in the human story, that there was only one story: so it was God who was born and suffered in the flesh for the salvation of humankind. There were many who wished to keep the divine and the human apart: and so the role of Mary in relation to the incarnate Christ became a vital test of faith. In 431 the Council of Ephesus gave to Mary the title of *Theotokos*, Mother of God: mother, that is, not only of the flesh of the human Jesus but of the flesh of God. And, because of this union of natures, all humanity was called to communion with God in and through the flesh. The human is the gateway to the divine: there is no other way to God. And so, in spite of all his entanglements with the Manichean heresy, St Augustine can still insist: *per hominem Christum tendis ad Deum*. You come to Christ through Christ as a man.[16]

So the incarnation, in Christian theology and spirituality, is not simply an event but a process, 'a dynamic principle of transformation ... an action, an operation ... which continues without ceasing'.[17] Through the incarnation, the Word of God has assumed human nature and united it permanently to the divine. To speak of God 'with us' thus is not only to report on the being of God, but also on our own relationships. As Karl Barth wrote, 'a report about ourselves is included in that report about God.'[18] We see something of the early Church's sense of the 'taking of manhood into God' in the kind of language they used about Christ's ascension. They see the ascension not as a solitary act by which Christ is removed from us, or, as the dreadful modern hymn proclaims:

> And still the holy Church is here
> Although her Lord is gone.

Rather, in these early sermons, the ascension stands for the raising of the human race to divine fellowship. 'It was not merely one man, but the whole world that entered', announced St Ambrose,[19] while St John Chrysostom, in one of the earliest Ascensiontide sermons, says: 'We have scaled the heavens ... The universal nature was brought into heaven through the firstfruits.'[20] This is very much in line with the only theology of the ascension that we find in the New Testament. Here we are told that Christ ascended *beyond* the heavens in order to fill the universe with his presence (Eph. 4.10). But to fill the universe was a sign of deity (Jer. 23.24). The ascension is thus both the vindication of Christ and the 'apotheosis of man'.[21]

A spiritual theology which is rooted in materialism and in the incarnation is inevitably linked with the understanding of the atonement and of the sacraments. In fact, the dogma of the incarnation is right at the heart of all Christian understanding. It is, in the strict sense of the word, crucial. The entire Christian understanding of salvation depends upon the truth that God was in Christ.[22] Without the incarnation, the work of atonement and our participation in Christ's sufferings become meaningless. Moltmann has spoken of our participation in 'the trinitarian process of God's history'.[23] The Eastern Church, which has never separated theology from anthropology, has consistently stressed that human nature is, in its origin, *deiform*. From the origins of humankind, the divine grace flows within us. So the incarnation is both the culmination of a process which goes back to the beginnings of the human race, and the beginning of a new phase of deified humanity. The contemporary Orthodox theologian John Meyendorff puts it thus:[24]

> At a time when Christian theology realizes the insufficiency of the old Western concept of the supernatural for the understanding of man's destiny and salvation, and when the idea of grace as extrinsic to nature is increasingly challenged, it is important, before venturing into the dangerous paths of secularized Christianity, to rediscover the notion upon which the whole Eastern patristic understanding of salvation is based. Man is truly man when he participates in God's life. This participation therefore is not a supernatural gift but the very core of man's nature.

Beyond Chalcedon
In 1882 H. M. Gwatkin, in his *Studies in Arianism*, described the
Arian theology as a mass of presumptuous theorizing, and a lifeless
system of unspiritual pride and hard unlovingness. Gwatkin realized
that christological controversies go deep into the nature and style of
our pastoral praxis, our common life, our care for the poor, our love of
people. In similar vein, the Anglican socialist Thomas Hancock, in a
sermon in 1875, reminded his hearers that 'the battles the believers of
the faith fought against the heretics, they fought not only for the
Church but for humanity'.[25] At the heart of the conflict as Hancock
saw it, was the clash between a view of God and humanity in social
terms, and a view which separated human beings both from God and
from each other in an atomistic type of individualism. The dogma of
the Trinity was an explicit denial of individualism, for it asserted that
the nature of God was social and egalitarian, and that human beings
were called to share this relationship.

The Council of Chalcedon in 451 was concerned with the identity
of Christ. Maurice Wiles has summarized its aim as follows:[26]

> On the one hand was the conviction that a saviour must be fully
> divine; on the other was the conviction that what is not assumed is
> not healed. Or, to put the matter in other words, the source of
> salvation must be God; the locus of salvation must be man. It is
> quite clear that these two principles often pulled in opposite
> directions. The Council of Chalcedon was the Church's attempt to
> resolve, or perhaps rather to agree to live with, that tension. Indeed
> to accept both principles as strongly as did the early Church is
> already to accept the Chalcedonian faith.

The formula of Chalcedon asserts that there is one Lord, one Son. In
other words, in the historical event of Christ, two stories come
together as one single event. And it is wholly the act of God, for Christ
is 'of one substance with the Father'. And yet it is also the life of a man
who is 'of one substance with us according to his humanity'.

Having stressed the two natures of Christ, divine and human, the
formula goes on to state four negatives. The truth of Christ's
incarnation, it says, must be held *without confusion*, *without change*,
without division, *without separation*. *Without confusion*: because the
life of man is also the saving presence of God. *Without change*;
because the story of Jesus is both fully human and fully divine.
Without division: because neither the divine nor the human story can
be omitted. And *without separation*: for there is only one story, the
act of God in Christ. In these assertions, Chalcedon insists that its
truths are not simply historical, concerning events in the past, but

theological, truths concerning a present Christ.

It is common to accuse the Council of Chalcedon of having imprisoned the gospel within the dated philosophical categories of a former age. In reply to this accusation, Jean Galot points out that the Chalcedonian dogmas 'must not be envisaged as a pillory from which one tries, if one can, to get free, but as a foundation on which theology can build up its development in confidence that it is rightly orientated.[27] Admitting that the affirmations of Chalcedon are made from a static perspective of being rather than of happening, Galot argues that we need to build on Chalcedon in terms of a dynamic christology. The Council did not offer ready-made answers: it offers possibilities for further development.

And in fact there were important developments after Chalcedon. But from the seventh century onwards there has been little positive progress in christological thought. In the words of Claude Tresmontant:[28]

> We have made hardly any progress since. This does not mean that in the future the thought of the Church will make no progress in understanding what the incarnation is. But in fact and broadly speaking, christological dogma, as it was formed, at the end of the seventh century, has remained what it was until today.

It is necessary to see Chalcedon as opening up a new era in Christian thought, and to build upon it an incarnational spirituality. This must take as its foundation the materialistic basis of spiritual life.

Incarnation and Christian Materialism

It is the whole person who shares the image of God. This truth is emphasized in the works of a whole range of Eastern spiritual writers, including Irenaeus, Gregory of Nyssa, and Gregory Palamas. According to the last: 'The word Man is not applied to either soul or body separately, but to both together, since together they have been created in the image of God.'[29] In fact Palamas argues that human beings are more in the image of God than are the angels, since human beings possess a life-giving energy by which the bodily nature is quickened and controlled. Angels, as bodyless spirits, lack this facility. Earlier, Gregory Nazianzen stressed that it was the whole of humanity which bore the likeness of the divine.[30]

However, in spite of these emphases, there has been a serious neglect of the body and of matter in most Western spirituality. Matthew Fox has frequently argued that what he calls 'creation-centred spirituality' has been undermined by tendencies within Western theology which have stressed sin and redemption in such a

way as to devalue matter and the creation. 'The fact is,' says Fox, 'that
creation spirituality remains an unwanted step-child in Western
Christianity whose mainstream has invested so heavily and so long in
Augustinian original sin and redemption motifs.'[31] Fox goes on to
outline the marks of such a creation spirituality:[32]

> Christian spirituality, then, is a rootedness of being in the world.
> In history, time, body, matter and society. Spirit is found there (or
> better, here) and not outside of these essential ingredients to
> human living. This means that economics and art, language and
> politics, education and sexuality are equally an integral part of
> creation spirituality. And, not least of all, joy. The joy of ecstasy,
> and shared ecstasy in celebration. This is a non-elitist spirituality.
> A 'folk' spirituality one might call it. Of the folks, by the folks, and
> for the folks. It is spirituality as if people mattered.

But the development of such a creational and incarnational spirituality demands that Western Christianity makes a decisive break with
its Neoplatonist background and assumptions. It means too that we
recognize, in our day and not only in previous centuries, the deadly
danger of all forms of Gnosticism, and the degree to which gnostic
ideas have continued to penetrate and influence mainstream Christian
assumptions.

Gnostic spirituality is in fact a fundamental denial of the Christian
spiritual path, an abandonment of its materialistic and historical
character. In Gnosticism, God and the world are utterly alien to each
other. Matter is the source of sin and impurity. For the spiritual
person, the seeker after salvation, the rejection of the realm of matter,
of the physical, of sexuality, and of historical reality, is of first
importance. So, for the gnostic, the human life of the historical Jesus
becomes irrelevant, since what really matters is not acts but
information. How different is the Christian view of salvation through
historical acts:

> The life of Jesus has sanctified the particular, the 'spare and
> strange', manifesting God in a conditioned human story. Hence-
> forth it is clear that the locus of God's saving action, his will to be
> known, loved, encountered, is the world of historical decision,
> whether individual or corporate. It is not, and cannot be, in a
> 'privileged' dehistoricized ecstasy nor in the mechanisms of the
> gnostics' spiritual science.[33]

We see the beginnings of a distorted spiritual tradition within
Christianity as early as Clement of Alexandria who sees salvation as
concerned with the virtues of the spirit, and not with external

things.[34] In the writings of Clement we can see a shift towards interiorization, spirituality becomes more to do with the inner life of the disciple, and the flesh and its 'fetters' come to be devalued.[35] Similarly, in Origen, the spiritual person is glad to lay aside his body at death, and so to escape the tyranny of the flesh.[36] The account of Jesus in Gethsemane is a distinct embarrassment to Origen in its suggestion of Jesus' 'unspiritual' fear of death. In Origen's understanding of the life of the spirit, Christian maturity must involve the detachment of the spiritual person from the fleshly Jesus. Incarnational faith comes to be merely the first stage of the process of deliverance.[37]

So we can see the early stages of a process of separating flesh and spirit, the material and the spiritual world, which has continued to damage and disfigure Christian spirituality to this day. By contrast, the Jewish tradition had laid great emphasis on the unity of flesh and spirit. The notion that flesh is the principle of sin, so central to gnostic ideology in all ages, is quite alien to the Old Testament, and only appears in Wisdom 9.15 under Greek influence.[38] Rather is the human soul seen as a unified whole, *nephesh chayyah*, not a deposit in a body, but a reality at once both spiritual and physical, a living being. The notion that the body is of less importance than the spirit is quite unbiblical:

> According to the Bible, God not only created souls and spirits but also bodies, and in fact all material creatures. It is true that these have had their nature perverted by the Fall according to the teaching of both Jewish apocalyptic and Paul. The body has become fleshly (the *'soma'* has become *'sarkinos'*). But 'material' is not the equivalent of 'fleshly' (carnal). The body as a material entity has its proper place in creation. This is why it too will enter the Kingdom of Heaven in the form of a body free from corruption, realizing the ideal of a restored material substance such as can be at the service of the Holy Spirit instead of rebelling against God's law in the manner of Romans 7.2–25. Thus every sin against the body is also a sin against the will of God and may involve the risk of losing the inheritance of the Kingdom.[39]

Against those who denied the importance of the flesh, St John asserted that the Word had become flesh, *sarx*. The juxtaposing of Word and flesh in John 1.14 is probably part of an early polemic, aimed against those who rejected the fullness of Christ's humanity.[40] In the First Letter of John, the flesh of Christ again becomes a crucial test of spirituality. The Word, which was from the beginning, is the same Word which we have touched and handled (1.1). So basic is the

truth that Jesus Christ has come *in the flesh* that those who deny this
are not of God (4.2).

The salvation and transfiguration of the body and of matter is a
preoccupation of the Eastern Fathers of the Church. Irenaeus, in his
conflicts with the heretics who devalued the flesh and the material
substance of the world, linked together the incarnation and the reality
of Christ's presence in the Eucharist:

> If the flesh is not saved, then the Lord did not redeem us with his
> blood, the chalice of the Eucharist is not a share in his blood, and
> the bread which we break is not a share in his body. For the blood
> cannot exist apart from veins and flesh and the rest of the human
> substance which the Word of God truly became in order to redeem
> us.[41]

Later St Gregory Palamas pointed to the importance of the participation of the body in the celebration of life and worship. For, he argued,
'if the body is to participate together with the soul in the ineffable good
things [of the new age], it is certain that it ought to participate now, to
the extent possible . . . For the body also has the experience of divine
things when the passionate forces of the soul are not put to death but
transformed and sanctified.'[42] The incarnation then is more than an
assertion about the reality of the flesh and materiality of Christ; it is a
governing principle of the Church's life, of God's relationship with
the world, of the structure of all spiritual life and experience. In the
words of Frederick Hastings Smyth, in his important but neglected
study *Manhood into God*:[43]

> . . . the Catholic Religion, as the Religion of the Incarnation, is, in a
> sense, rooted in a proper and thoroughgoing materialism; for the
> method of the Incarnation demonstrates to us that the necessary
> and prerequisite foundation for all intellectual and spiritual order
> is, so far as this world is concerned, the development of an
> organized material body.

So God begins the restoration of the material world by uniting a
portion of it to himself. And this process must then spread outwards,
so that we can speak of the extension of the incarnation, of an
incarnational principle running through life and human, spiritual
struggle.

A major consequence of taking incarnational faith seriously is that
the spiritual person, far from despising or fearing or withdrawing
from the world, needs to be inflamed by a passionate and intense love
of the world, seeing in the material things of the world that handiwork
of God, and in the people of the world the face of Christ. In the
Eastern

spiritual tradition, St Isaac the Syrian, towards the end of the seventh century, described the marks of the loving heart:[44]

> What is a charitable heart? It is a heart which is burning with love for the whole creation, for men, for the birds, for the beasts, for the demons – for all creatures. He who has such a heart cannot see or call to mind a creature without his eyes being filled with tears by reason of the immense compassion which seizes his heart; a heart which is softened and can no longer bear to see or learn from others of any suffering, even the smallest pain, being inflicted upon a creature. That is why such a man never ceases to pray also for the animals, for the enemies of truth, and for those who do him evil, that they may be preserved and purified. He will pray even for the reptiles, moved by the infinite pity which reigns in the hearts of those who are becoming united with God.

Here then is the overflow of the incarnation in a highly sensitized individual. The heart which Isaac describes is deeply spiritual, but it is a spirituality which radiates fleshly warmth, which issues in material and bodily care, and which is marked by a very powerful sense of com-passion, suffering with and in solidarity with, all created things. Many have made the further point that such a person, filled with the love of the incarnate Christ, is able to see the marks of Christ himself in all creatures. This sense of recognition comes over very powerfully in Gerard Manley Hopkins' poem 'As Kingfishers Catch Fire':[45]

> I say more: the just man justices;
> Keeps grace: that keeps all his goings graces;
> Acts in God's eye what in God's eye he is –
> Christ – for Christ plays in ten thousand places,
> Lovely in limbs, and lovely in eyes not his
> To the Father through the features of men's faces.

It is this awareness of the universal Christ, 'lovely in eyes not his', the hidden Christ manifest in the hearts of his sisters and brothers, which is at the heart of an incarnational spirituality. Nowhere has the incarnational basis of both spirituality and social action been more strongly expressed than in much of the Anglican theology of the late nineteenth and early twentieth centuries. In this tradition the figure of F. D. Maurice (1808–72) is of crucial importance. Maurice held that all human beings were created in God's image and knit together in Christ, and that baptism was the sacramental recognition and assertion of what was already in principle the case. For Christ had 'entered into the state of the lowest beggar, of the poorest, stupidest, wickedest wretch whom that Philosopher or that Pharisee can trample upon', in order that he might 'redeem the humanity which Philosophers, Pharisees, beggars and harlots share together'.[46] Motivated by the rich incarnational and materialistic theology of Maurice, the Anglo-Catholic socialists of the late nineteenth century, such as Thomas Hancock and Stewart Headlam, combined an incarnational and sacramental theology with a deep love of humanity and a commitment to art, music, drama, and human amusement and pleasure.

For Thomas Hancock (1832–1903) the orthodox theology of the incarnation was absolutely central to his approach to the issues of society. To find one's true self in one's childhood of God is to find the eternal Son within us. When a person has achieved this discovery he has 'come to himself'. Yet this discovery depends on the reality of the incarnation itself:

> If there be no absolute Co-eternal Son, there can be no absolute Eternal Father. Unless there be an Only-Begotten Son of God, unless this Only-Begotten Son be the one in whom we all consist, we may have an omnipotent Manufacturer – or rather some omnipotent Manufacturer may have us, as the potter has the vessel, but we men can have no Divine Father.[47]

Hancock goes on to speak of the Godhead as relationship, and of our nature as being rooted and grounded in that divine society.

Similarly, Stewart Headlam (1847–1924) made the closest link between the divine and the human, and saw the incarnation as leading directly to social and political action:

> You are literally, as he himself said, feeding, clothing, housing Jesus Christ when you are feeding, clothing, housing any human being; bad food, ugly clothes, dirty houses, not only injure the body, but injure the soul; nay more, they do great injury unto God himself.[48]

For Headlam human pleasure and amusement was also rooted in the Word who became flesh. Thus he defended the ballet and music hall by appeal to the Athanasian Creed. In a sermon preached on 7 August 1881, Headlam proclaimed:

> The Athanasian Creed teaches that the manhood has been taken into God; that it is necessary to everlasting salvation that we believe rightly the Incarnation of our Lord Jesus Christ; that the Holy Spirit is incomprehensible, immense, boundless in his influence. These are the theological facts on which I base my

vindication of the stage.

For Christ had taken the *whole* of human nature, not just religious nature, into God, and this includes the world which finds expression in the theatre, a place of education in which human nature is enhanced through the tragic and comic dimensions. There, Headlam claimed,

> ... in the pit and gallery, tenanted by those whom, for the most part, we clergy cannot touch, and who have little inclination or opportunity for other education, you will be sure that the Holy Ghost, the educator, is at work.[50]

Moreover, Headlam believed, the theatre had achieved a major work of restoration of dimensions of incarnational theology which churches had lost:

> Having for three centuries worshipped a God of gloom, having had Manicheism and Puritanism established over us by the State, we have learnt to think that there is some contradiction between the love of beauty and the love of God. Counteracting all this, the theatre has been at work with its heavenly mission: there the contemplation of beauty has been made possible for the people; there, in spectacular drama, pantomime, ballet, comic opera, burlesque; there with the art of the scene painter and the musician and the dancers with their poetry of vital motion, their artistic and unconventional dress, and the harmonious blending of beautiful colours; there the people have been educated, i.e. taken a little out of themselves, and received hints of how beautiful this world will be when at last order has overcome chaos and when God is seen in perfect beauty.[51]

Headlam saw also that the incarnation had major social and political consequences, and in 1877 he founded the Guild of St Matthew as a parish guild in Bethnal Green. One of its aims was 'to promote the study of social and political questions in the light of the incarnation', and within a short time it had become the red-hot centre of the Christian Socialist movement in Britain. According to Headlam, 'in the light of the incarnation, the present contrast between rich and poor cannot be justified for a moment. In the light of the incarnation, the social revolution, in the plain meaning of the words, is justified, nay, demanded.'[52]

Headlam and Hancock stood within a developing tradition in the nineteenth century which laid great emphasis on the phrase in the Athanasian Creed: 'one, not by conversion of the Godhead into flesh, but by taking of manhood into God'. One of the earliest and clearest statements of the doctrine of the incarnation as it influenced the Tractarians is Robert Isaac Wilberforce's *The Doctrine of the Incarnation of Our Lord Jesus Christ*, published in 1848. Here Wilberforce argued that the meaning of incarnation was not that God became *a* man, but that God became *the* man, the representative man, and thus established a permanent bond between himself and the human race.[53] Pusey also stressed that God had exalted human nature to union with the divine, and that the hunger of the poor is the hunger of Christ.[54] The theology was developed by Charles Gore (1853–1932) who in 1889 edited the volume *Lux Mundi*, 'a series of studies in the religion of the incarnation'. In this volume, R. C. Moberly wrote of the incarnation as 'the basis of dogma'.[55] Two years later, in 1891, Gore produced his Bampton Lectures *The Incarnation of the Son of God*, of which it has been said that it inaugurated a new type of incarnational theology within the Church of England.[56] Many years later, Temple wrote his important work *Christus Veritas* in which he discussed the doctrines of God and man in the light of the incarnation.[57] Gore's influence continued to be very important, not only in creating a theological framework, but also, particularly through the Community of the Resurrection which he founded, in applying an incarnational approach to the affairs of the social order. One of the members of that community, Lionel Thornton, wrote in *The Return of Christendom*, the volume which led to the League of the Kingdom of God and later to the Christendom Group, of the conflict between the incarnation and the current social order.

> If God Incarnate lived as a poor man and worked in a carpenter's shop, and if the Manhood in which he did these things suffered death for all and is now on the throne of Heaven; then it is a blasphemous insult to that Manhood to treat any man's liberty as an indifferent thing on grounds of class or colour.

Thornton went on to say that if Christ's incarnation has sanctified all humanity

> then the present social order is an open denial of Christ; for it condemns the majority of mankind to be economic slaves ministering to the selfishness of the minority. To acquiesce in it is to crucify Christ afresh.[58]

What is central to this whole tradition is not only the belief that in Christ humanity has been taken into God, but also that this process of taking humanity into God is going on all the time, that reality *is* incarnational, and that therefore to hold an incarnational faith is of the greatest importance if we are to view humanity and the material order in a way that can lead to their sanctification and transformation. The incarnation goes on, as Conrad Noel (1869–1942), the fiery prophet of Thaxted, wrote:[59]

> God is *perpetually* 'intruding' himself into this world, and is himself its very subtance. Every wayside flower is a sacrament of his Body and Blood, and every human heroism a revelation. This is the Catholic Faith which except a man believe faithfully, without doubt he will shrivel into mean and narrow death.

Incarnation and Sexuality

It is through the flesh that salvation comes. And yet so much in Christian spirituality and Christian life is flesh-denying, flesh-despising, flesh-devaluing. It is head-centred, ponderous, life-extinguishing, devoid of passion. It was this life-denying effect of Christian spirituality which led Nietzsche to reject Christianity. He articulated the feelings of many in his call for a dancing God:

> I would believe only in a God who could dance. And when I saw my devil I found him serious, thorough, profound and solemn: it was the spirit of gravity – through him all things fell. Not by wrath does one kill but by laughter. Come, let us kill the spirit of gravity! I have learned to walk: ever since, I let myself run. I have learned to fly: ever since I do not want to be pushed before moving along. Now I am light, now I fly, now I see myself beneath myself, now a god dances through me.[60]

But Nietzsche could not find this dancing God in the cold, frozen Christian world which he saw around him. What he saw was a religion which seemed to dampen passion, was mistrustful of sexuality and of the physical side of human nature, and pointed spiritual men and women away from it towards a higher world of pure spirit. The religion of incarnation and of the taking of manhood into God did not seem to apply its doctrines to human sexuality.

And in fact the Christian tradition has been weak in the whole area of a theology of sexuality: in contrast, interestingly, to Hinduism, in which Shiva, half man, half woman, stands for the wholeness of created existence, the unity of male and female principles in one total experience. Yet the blossoming of human sexuality, and its relationship to the recovery of the divine image in men and women, is, one would have thought, of the greatest theological and practical importance. It is disturbing to see how Christian history and Christian spirituality has been so marred by a highly ambivalent tradition which, while officially rejecting gnostic denials of the goodness of the flesh, has nevertheless been affected to a great extent by those gnostic tendencies within orthodoxy itself:

> There is a paradox here, for the Church has in fact stood firm against Manicheism, Catharism, and Jansenism, and has not denied that sex and the flesh are a human good. But, on the other hand, where theology has so far feared to tread, has been over a principle of the Greek Fathers about the reality of the humanity of Christ. 'What was not assumed (by Christ) was not healed', they held. Later generations never inquired if that was true of human sexuality.[61]

For it was the raising up of the *whole* person, the penetration of the *whole* of human experience by God, which was so central to the theology of the Cappadocian fathers. 'The whole of nature', insisted Gregory of Nyssa, must be raised from death.'[62]

It is not difficult to see how theologies which are suspicious of the flesh tend also to be suspicious of the world of politics and of the natural life of human society. 'Non-bodily theologies are anti-self, anti-neighbour, anti-society, and anti-world.'[63] As we have seen earlier, Hebrew theology was deeply committed to the goodness of flesh and of matter, seeing human nature as a unity. In the Old Testament, the theme of human erotic love as directly comparable to divine love finds its classic statement in the Song of Songs. Indeed, the Hebrew language has only one word for love: *ahava*. Unlike Greek, there is no attempt to divide various kinds of love. And, at its best, the Christian tradition has sought to maintain the unity of love. Even Augustine, for all his suspicion of human sexuality, held strongly to the close connection between spirituality and human emotions. Those who sought to put emotion behind them, Augustine said, 'have lost the fullness of their humanity rather than attaining true peace'. 'Do not try,' he advised, 'to keep your soul free from emotional influences.'[64]

However there is a more negative and depressing side of the story. Much Christian history, particularly in the West, has been marred by a fear of the body. Ashley Montagu, in his study of touch and skin, speaks of 'a fear associated with the Christian tradition in its various denominations, the fear of bodily pleasures'.[65] And this fear goes back to a very early stage in the movement. So Origen saw the soul as stained because it was clothed in the body.[66] Within this body, sex could never occur without stain and was always impure. Because sex derived from the fall of man, all sexual intercourse was an impediment to prayer and spirituality. It was this tradition which St Augustine (354–430) inherited and developed.

In his study *The Freedom of Man*, the Syrian Orthodox theologian Paul Verghese has criticized Augustine's 'incapacity to take the flesh of our Lord sufficiently seriously'. Such a failure is the beginning of a whole range of deviations in Christian understanding. For, says Verghese, once one devalues the flesh, many distortions follow. 'Regard the flesh, the body, matter, as evil, or even inferior, and one has already begun the deviation from Christian truth.'[67] Augustine held that the incarnation belonged to the 'transitory' aspect of the reality of Christ. For, he wrote:[68]

> There is one thing that is transitory in the Lord, another which is enduring. What is transitory is the Virgin birth, the Incarnation of the Word, the gradation of ages, the exhibition of miracles, the endurance of sufferings, death, resurrection, the ascent into heaven – all this is transitory . . .

That which belonged to the realm of the physical and material was, it seems, of a lower order than that which was spiritual, for 'not in the body, but in the mind, was man made in the image of God'.[69]

Augustine's influence was particularly harmful in relation to sexuality. While he did not actually identify concupiscence with sexual desire, his general orientation – and even more, that of his successors – did lead to a devaluing of sex. Sex was in fact basically bad, but tolerable for the purpose of procreation.[70] In Paradise, the bodily (that is, female) side of man would have been subordinate to its (male) head, and so there would have been no lust or libido in procreation, no uncontrolled rush of disordered affection. The male would simply have sown his seed in the female as a farmer sows seed in a field.[71] For, in Augustine's view, the essence of the fall was loss of control of mind over body. On this view, *all* sexual acts have the nature of sin, because they are inherently lustful. The view that original sin was actually transmitted by sexual intercourse was accepted by Thomas Aquinas, and has remained a powerful strain within conventional Western Christianity to this day.[72] Thus Rosemary Ruether can say, with some degree of understatement, that 'Augustine's view of sexuality is the foundation of unfortunate views which have continued to shape Western Catholicism down to recent times'.[73]

The idea that sexuality and spirituality were, if not incompatible, at least mutually hostile remained influential through the Middle Ages. Eckhart, for all his 'creation-centred' approach, held that 'there is no physical or fleshly pleasure without some spiritual harm'.[74] For centuries, the Western Church saw nocturnal pollution as an impure action, and medieval canonists debated the lawfulness or unlawfulness (even to the point of mortal sin) of receiving the sacraments after making love the previous night. St Bernardine of Siena stated that husbands and wives were guilty of mortal sin if they did not abstain from sexual intercourse before receiving Holy Communion.[75] In the sixteenth century, St John of the Cross certainly was suspicious of human affection, and was inclined to see it as hostile to the attainment of illumination. While the anti-sex strain in Christianity can be overstated, it is hard to resist Alex Comfort's claim that 'the fact of having made sex into a "problem" is the major negative achievement of Christendom'.[76]

The origins of the negative tradition and the devaluing of the body have been seen in the ancient association of the male principle with the head and the intellect, and the female with the genitals, passion and the 'lower nature'. In Greek mythology, Zeus gave birth to Athena from his brain! Alan Jones comments:[77]

Here are the seeds of a primal heresy which infected Christianity: namely that spirituality and sexuality are opposed. In this context the older of the two Genesis myths of creation comes off rather well. Eve is not born from Adam's head but from his *side*.

By contrast, incarnational theology involves the acceptance of the goodness and wonder of our physical bodies, and more than acceptance: a joyful, awesome, tender joy in them. Sebastian Moore, in a moving prayer-poem, speaks of the 'accuracy of the flesh', the place of knowledge:

Christ! I'm ready now
ready to get lost in the evangel of people's bodies
accuracy of the flesh
kiss of truth
we cannot say what we are
we can only be to each other
touch each other with truth.

He goes on:

Having known deeply and quietly the goodness of the flesh
I cannot follow the safe self-crucified men who say 'God alone'.[78]

'Accuracy of the flesh', 'touch each other with truth': such themes run counter to the belief, so deeply entrenched in Western Christian circles, that the flesh is an unreliable, unstable area. Only in the purity of intellect and reason can we have trust. Yet the notion of total rational control over the body and the emotions cannot be the ideal of the Christian who holds to an incarnational faith. In the words of

Charles Davis:[79]

> Complete rational control over the body is not an ideal. To make it
> so would be to reject the body and the spirit. A rejection of the body
> would be implied, because it is the very nature of bodily sensitivity
> to respond immediately and spontaneously to the appropriate
> objects. There is no disorder in responding sensuously to what
> meets us in the flow of sense experience. The disorder lies in the
> lust to possess for ourselves all we meet; in other words, in turning
> sensuousness into sensuality by subordinating it to the narrow
> purposes of an egocentric self.

Such sensual spontaneity is necessary to the receptive spirit, and
therefore to an authentic and wholesome spirituality. Those who
believe in the Word made flesh need to learn to trust the body and the
feelings.

And such a trust in the wholeness and goodness of the flesh involves
a break with the one-dimensional view of sex which restricts our
consciousness to the phallic and genital area. We need to recover the
sense of the mystery and glory of the body in all its complex aspects; to
recover the essential goodness and splendour of the erotic. Andrea
Dworkin expresses it well:[80]

> ... there is an erotic passion and intimacy which comes of touch
> and taste, a wild salty tenderness, a wet sweet sweat ... a sensual
> passion as deep and mysterious as the sea, as strong and still as the
> mountain, as insistent and changing as the wind.

If such language, the language of exultation in bodily experience,
seems strange in a study of spirituality, it is only an indication of how
far we have moved from a truly incarnational faith. Without such a
sense of the place of the flesh and of feeling in Christian and human
experience, spirituality must remain a half-life for half-people,
instead of a total response of our whole being. We need to rediscover
that total body response to the created world, that joy in existence,
which Morley Callaghan in his novel *They Shall Inherit the Earth*[81]
describes as characteristic of Anna:

> She went on from day to day, living and loving and exposing the
> fullness and wholeness of herself to the life around her. If to be
> poor in spirit meant to be without false pride, to be humble enough
> to forget oneself, then she was poor in spirit, for she gave herself to
> everything that touched her, she let herself be, she lost herself in
> the fullness of the world, and in losing herself she found the world
> and she possessed her own soul. People like her could have

everything. They could inherit the earth.

Such a delight in creation and in people is one of the marks of sanctity. For to be a saint is, in a sense, to become more intensely ordinary, more deeply human, more passionate, so that love and tenderness flow from every pore. Yet such a degree of love cannot be achieved – or rather received – without the giving and receiving of human affection and human love.

Of course, the ways in which we give and receive love are immensely varied. But all of them involve the discovery and enrichment of our sexuality. This applies equally, and powerfully, to the love of the celibate, as the Carmelite monk William McNamara points out in his study significantly entitled *Mystical Passion*.[82] Lovers, McNamara complains, are not sexual and passionate enough, and that includes celibate lovers who ought to be at least as sexual and passionate as married people. For there is no other way to be a great lover. All of us need an inflow of passion, for without passion, religious and human life decays into lukewarm niceness. And because we are human, our love must be human love: for how can we love God whom we have not seen if we have not learned to love our fellow humans whom we have seen? According to the pattern of the incarnation, the human is the gateway to the divine. The New Testament knows no other road to the knowledge of God but through the human. We need therefore to be wary of theologies which seek to make human love and divine love wholly different. Love is one. And there can be no growth in spirituality without the necessary basis of human loving. Nothing – no technique, no religious training, no ascetical disciplines – can make up for an incapacity to love.[83]

We have then a major task in the Church to seek to reverse the tendencies in Christian theology and spirituality which are suspicious of the flesh and of human passion and erotic love. There have been pointers in Western Christian history to a more whole theology of the body and the passions than the negative Augustinian tradition. St Thomas Aquinas, for example, in opposition to his own Augustinian contemporaries, held that the passions of aggression (*irascibilis*) and desire (*concupiscibilis*) were the subjects of virtues, even in their physiological engagement. He strongly defended the morality of the passions. But his view was not popular and many of his propositions were condemned. In the fourteenth century, Julian of Norwich appealed to an earlier and healthier tradition when she wrote:[84]

For I saw with absolute certainty that our substance is in God, and moreover that he is in our sensuality too. The moment the soul was made sensual, at that moment it was destined from all eternity to be the City of God. And he shall come to that city and never quit it.

Julian goes on to say that 'our substance and our sensuality together are rightly named our soul'.[85] Here is the voice of a whole, incarnational spirituality in which flesh and spirit are seen as a unity in God. But it did not prevail in the West.

One of the most remarkable and impressive statements of the need to recover this dimension in understanding incarnation in recent years was Sam Keen's *To A Dancing God*.[86] Keen speaks of the need to recover a sense of the wonder and the deep goodness of carnality. He complains that education in many of our schools tends to function as if the fact of incarnation was incidental, and so there is little attempt to educate and resensitize the body and the emotional life. Nor does Christian theology offer much help. So Keen asks:

> What has happened to me? How am I to understand this warmth and grace which pervade my body? As I begin to reflect I realize that neither the Christian nor the secular culture, in which I have been jointly nurtured, have given me adequate categories to interpret such an experience. Neither has taught me to discern the sacred in the voice of the body and the language of the senses. In the same measure that Christian theology has failed to help me appreciate the *carnality of grace*, secular ideology has failed to provide me categories for understanding the *grace* of carnality. Before I can understand what I have experienced, I must see where Christian theology and secular ideology have failed me.[87]

Keen goes on to claim that Christianity has not succeeded in escaping from the dualist, gnostic tradition, and that a 'deep-seated suspicion of the carnal' remains a major element in the Christian Church. And yet 'incarnation, if it is anything more than a "once upon a time" story, means grace is carnal, healing comes through the flesh'.[88] It is a life principle:

> The factor governing full incarnation is the willingness to trust that which cannot be controlled. The moment I identify myself with my body and become fully incarnate, I involve the essence of what is me with something over which I have no ultimate control.[89]

Moreover, the recovery of a sense of carnal grace involves identification with the flesh of another, the discovery of grace in others.

> If the Church fails to develop a visceral theology and fails to help modern man rediscover and reverence his flesh and his feelings, it will neglect a source of common grace as well as the seed from which compassion grows. It will thereby turn its back on the

incarnation of the sacred in our history, in our flesh.[90]

Our bodies are our bridge to the world; as we are in our bodies, so will we be in the world. More than that, we will be in eternity, for the road to the sacred runs through the carnal.

If we are to absorb incarnational spirituality at a gut level, and not merely 'believe' it in the head – what could be more opposed to incarnation than a 'head theology'? – we need to recover this close and intimate link between the flesh and the divine. And this involves going behind the distortions of earlier centuries, going back to a more truly biblical understanding of the unity of passion and spirituality, of sex and spirit. As we saw earlier, there is no dualism in the spirituality of the Old Testament. Passions are often ascribed to the soul, thoughts to the regions of the body. In Jacob's words:[91]

> The desire expressed by *nephesh* is in general violent. In character as well as in piety, passion prevails over meditation, and it is with the same ardour that Old Testament man desires to satisfy his hunger, has vengeance upon his enemies, or enters into communion with God.

For the Old Testament, the source of evil was not in passion, but in hardness of heart, callousness and insensitivity. Today, after centuries of gnostic disfiguring of the image of God in the human person, we have to recover that approach to incarnation which relates that which is to be assumed and therefore healed to human sexuality:

> The affirmation of human sexuality is basic to a positive doctrine of the *imago Dei*, the image of God in humankind . . . The insistence upon human bodiliness is also an affirmation of human transcendence. And the move to find sexual identity as incarnational is a move towards radical human equality which itself is inherent in an adequate understanding of and doctrine of the *imago Dei*.[92]

To rejoice in the wonder and joy of sexuality is to experience something of the love that moves the sun and the other stars. Yet Christian spirituality would move *beyond* sexual experience, affirming and yet transcending it, 'for our enjoyment of God in heaven will be more, not less, ecstatic than the most passionate sexual experience on earth'.[93]

'Manhood into God'

Yet even to imagine such a degree of enjoyment is to move to the boundaries of human language. So tremendous and wonderful is the transformation which is envisaged, and partially experienced now, that we should not find it surprising that, in Mascall's words, 'there is a persistent tradition in Christian thought which finds it impossible to do justice to the transformation that a human being undergoes when he is incorporated into Christ except by saying that he is *deified*'.[94] The language of deification is particularly a feature of Eastern Orthodox spiritual writers who, from very early times, have spoken of our participation (*metochē*) in God. Deification is the work of divine grace by which human nature is so transformed that it 'shines forth with a supernatural light and is transported above its own limits by a superabundance of glory'.[95] It is such a transformation which is the purpose and aim of the Jesus Prayer in Orthodox spirituality. As Meyendorff points out:[96]

> The luminous vision that may then be experienced will not be a mere symbol or an effect of imagination, but a theophany as true as that on Mount Tabor since it is a manifestation of the same deified Body of Christ ... The spiritual life of the monks of the desert is so closely bound up with the theology of deification that we find in the Greek Fathers.

So, according to Maximus the Confessor, man 'becomes God by deification'. So central is the theme of deification in Eastern tradition that it is seen as the meaning of theology itself. For according to Orthodox theologians there can be no theology apart from the process of transformation. The work of theology involves a radical re-creation of the human person. In Lossky's memorable words:[97]

> It is an existential attitude which involves the whole man: there is no theology apart from experience; it is necessary to change, to become a new man. To know God one must draw near to him. No one who does not follow the path of union with God can be a theologian. The way of the knowledge of God is necessarily the way of deification.

Deification language first entered the Christian vocabulary with Clement of Alexandria and Origen, though it is possible to see its beginnings in the New Testament itself where we find the reference to our being made 'partakers of the divine nature' (2 Pet. 1.4). Irenaeus speaks of our 'sharing in God', while a little earlier he has introduced into Christian vocabulary a phrase which was to reappear in various forms throughout the Eastern Fathers: 'The Son of God became the Son of Man to the end that man too might become the Son of God.'[98] Nor was such language totally unknown in the West. St Augustine wrote that 'out of sons of man he makes sons of God, because out of the Son of God he made a Son of Man ... and in this is our promise of a share in divinity'.[99] In Anglicanism, Lancelot Andrewes (1555–1626) used the language of *theōsis*.[100] And in the Roman rite of the Mass to this day, the priest prays, at the mingling of wine and water, that he who shared our human nature may make us sharers in his divinity.

But it is to the East that we need to look for the clearest and most persistent statements of this theology. St Athanasius, in his teaching on the incarnation, stressed that the Word became man in order to deify us in himself.[101] He became man so that the sons of man might become the sons of God.[102] He was humanized that we might be deified.[103] Both Athanasius and other Eastern Fathers use the term *Theon genesthai*, to become God. It is, of course, necessary to stress that, by this extravagant language, they did not mean to suggest that human beings shared in the divine substance, but rather that they came to enjoy the divine life of relationship and communion. Like later Orthodox writers, Athanasius stressed that God is *in* everything through his *love*, but *outside* everything by his *nature*.[104] Deification is thus a relationship of love brought about by the incarnation; it is 'the "flip side" of incarnation'.[105]

Eastern writers use various words to describe this transformation, the two commonest ones being *theopoiēsis* (deification) and *theōsis* (divinization). Macarius speaks of our being 'changed into the divine nature' and of our 'participation in the divine nature'.[106] At the same time, he is careful to insist that the creature 'nevertheless remains outside the essence of God'.[107] Similarly, Anastasius of Sinai says that deification does not involve 'an increase or change in nature'.[108] Gregory of Nyssa says that at the incarnation 'God joined himself to our nature that by union with the Divine it might become divine, being freed from death',[109] while Gregory Nazianzen says that 'he is man by reason of thee, that by reason of him thou mayest become God'.[110] And there are many other examples of such language, all combining the insistence on intimate union with an equally important stress on the distinction between man and God. In Florovsky's words:[111]

> But even in this, the immutable unchangeable gap between natures will remain: any 'transubstantiation' of the creature is excluded. It is true that, according to a phrase of St Basil the Great preserved by St Gregory the Theologian, creation 'has been ordered to become God'. But this deification is only communion with God, *participation* (*metousia*) in his life and gifts, and thereby a kind of acquisition of certain similitude to the Divine Reality.

Not surprisingly, as in the West too, the language of transforming love is used most effectively by poets rather than theologians. However, in the East poets and theologians are sometimes the same people, and we find the poetry of deification most of all in the writings of St Symeon the New Theologian (949–1022). The soul, says Symeon, becomes vivid with the fire of divinity:

> Your nature is your essence, and your essence your nature,
> Thus uniting with your body, I participate in your nature,
> and I really take as mine a part of your essence,
> uniting with your divinity, much more becoming
> heir, in my body. I see myself superior
> to incorporeals. I become Son of God as you have said,
> not for the angels, but for us, calling us gods in these terms:
> 'I have said: "You are all gods and sons of the Most High".'
> Glory be to your mercy and to your divine plan,
> because you became man, you who by nature are God,
> without change or confusion, for ever God and man,
> and that you have made me, a mortal by my nature, a god,
> god by adoption, god by your grace, by the power of your Spirit,
> uniting miraculously, God that you are, the two extremes.[112]

Symeon describes the human soul as being seized by the light of the Holy Spirit, so that it becomes 're-created and even divinised'.[113] God, who is beyond comprehension, through the incarnation has 'become seizable'. 'By the flesh you belong to our race, by divinity we belong to your ... And so we are now 'all of the same race'. We are Christ's fingers and feet, for we have 'put on the total Christ'.[114] Human beings, as a result of the incarnation, share the divine glory:

> I share in the light, I participate also in the glory,
> and my face shines like my Beloved's,
> and all my members become bearers of light.[115]

Later Symeon speaks of the deifying effect of Holy Communion in which 'I too become God ... become God by participation',[116] while, in a passage included in the *Philokalia*, he sums up the teaching on deified creature-hood in this way:[117]

> What is the aim of the incarnate dispensation of God's Word, preached in all the Holy Scriptures, but which we, who read them, do not know? The only aim is that, having entered into what is our own, we should participate in what is his. The Son of God has become Son of Man in order to make us men sons of God, raising our race by grace to what he himself is by nature.

The spiritual tradition of deification presents us with one of the central paradoxes of Christian theology: it tries to hold together the realities of divine otherness and divine union. In the daring language of Symeon, the human soul is seen as sharing in the essence of God, at least in part. It was the more precise formative theological minds such as Gregory Palamas who hammered away at the distinction between the essence and the energies of God, stressing that 'the divine and divinizing illumination and grace is not the essence but the energy of God'.[118] 'The divinizing energy by participation of which one is divinized is a divine grace but in no way the essence of God.'[119]

Perhaps the chief reason why Eastern theology has so few inhibitions about speaking of the deification of man is that it starts from a doctrine of nature and grace which avoids the sharp distinctions in much Western thought. For the Orthodox, human nature is already deiform, that is, the divine and the human natures do not belong to wholly distinct realms. Human nature is in its original essence open to God, open to the possibility of transformation, and so, in the joy of spiritual union, humanity is fulfilling its own natural direction. This deeply incarnational theology is expressed very strongly by a modern Orthodox theologian, Paul Evdokimov. Evdokimov stresses that the image of God in humanity is *natural*:

> For Orthodox theology it is at its source that created nature sees grace as involved in the creative act itself . . . It is in his essence that man is struck in the image of God, and it is this ontological deiformity that explains that grace is 'connatural' to nature, in the same way that nature is conformed to grace. They are complementary and compenetrate each other mutually: in participation, each exists in the other . . . Man is created sharing in the nature of God . . . and God, in the incarnation, shares in human nature. To the deiformity of man there corresponds the humanity of God.[120]

Earlier Orthodox theologians such as Soloviev[121] had used the term 'God-manhood' to describe the divine/human relationship. Evdokimov is critical of Western tendencies to see the work of grace as extrinsic to nature, and to see the following of natural instincts to be always contrary to grace. While this is not a fair or accurate representation of all Western theology – for Aquinas, for instance, grace does not take away, but presupposes, nature, and transforms it[122] – he is certainly right to see in much of it a false supernaturalism which drives a wedge between that which is human and natural, and that which is godly and spiritual. By contrast, Evdokimov stresses:[123]

> For the East, 'man in the image of God' defines exactly what man is by nature. To be created in the image of God carries with it the

grace of this image, and this is why, for Eastern asceticism, to follow one's true nature is to work in the direction of grace.

Towards a More Incarnational Devotional Life

If all this is true, then certain consequences follow for Christian devotion. We need to relate our devotion to our humanity, to our bodies, far more than is often the case. Again, the Eastern Christians have always laid great emphasis on the physical aspects of worship, and so the 'sacrament of tears' has been evident in Orthodox spirituality since Isaac of Nineveh. In the West, Augustine laid emphasis on the restlessness of the heart and on the need to discover God in the midst of human emotional turmoil. St Bernard's great contribution to the life of prayer lay in his insistence that 'carnal love' is the first degree of the love of God. In Bernard's theology, the humanity of Christ is the gateway to union with God, and the imagination, the affections, and senses become the instruments of transformation. His devotion to the incarnation and the passion of Christ is deeply affective and rooted in the flesh. 'The secret of his heart lies visible through the clefts of his body: visible too the great mystery of his love, and the bowels of his mercy.[124] For all its crude bizarre, and sentimental aspects, the cult of the Sacred Heart, which took as its biblical origin the saying in John 7.38 that from the heart of the believer would flow rivers of living water, was an attempt to preserve the truths of the humanity of Jesus, and the affective character of devotion.[125]

We can see the combination of affection, human warmth, and joy in the goodness of the physical world in the spirituality of St Francis of Assisi (1181–1226). The sense of celebration of the natural creation is, of course, expressed very movingly in Francis' *Canticle of the Creatures*. Here sun and moon, earth and air, fire and water, life and death, are the vehicles of the divine. Leclerc says of Francis:[126]

> In opening himself to the world, in taking his place among the creatures, in becoming profoundly aware of them as 'brothers' and 'sisters', Francis also opened himself to that obscure part of himself which is rooted in nature; unconsciously he was fraternizing with his own depths.

In Francis we see a joy in all God's works. He saw beauty itself in all things beautiful, for 'he embraced all things with a rapture of unheard of devotion, speaking to them of the Lord, and admonishing them to praise him'.[127] So he exclaims:

> Be thou praised, my Lord, with all thy creatures, especially

Brother Sun, who brings us the day, and through whom thou
givest light; and he is beautiful and radiant with great
splendour. He signifies thee to us, Most High.

Be thou praised, my Lord, for Sister Moon and the stars; thou
hast formed them bright, precious and fair in the sky.

Be thou praised, my Lord, for Brother Wind, and for air and
cloud, calms and all weather thou hast granted us.

Be thou praised, my Lord, for Sister Water, who is humble and
dear and pure.

Be thou praised, my Lord, for Brother Fire, through whom
thou dost illumine the night, he is beautiful, strong and
merry.

Be thou praised, my Lord, for our sister Mother Earth, who
sustains us and holds us to her breast, and produce abundant
fruits, flowers and trees.

However, this passionate and human Franciscan devotion gave way in
the fifteenth century to a type of piety of a more inward, individualistic, and 'spiritual' kind; and, under the influence of Thomas à
Kempis's *Imitation of Christ* and other works, the idea gained ground
that, in order to come close to God, one must withdraw more and
more from creatures. While the *Imitation* continues to be popular
among many Christians, it must be said that, in this major regard, its
influence has been a harmful one. The late Urban Holmes wrote of
it:[128]

The book is misnamed. It is really not devoted to the ascetical
practice of the imitation of Christ, although it is principally a
treatise on instrumental or ascetical images rather than terminal or
mystical images ... The author is sceptical as to the possibility of
the vision of God, particularly in God's essence. He embodies that
curious sharp division between nature and supernature, and
embraces anti-rationalism, both of which are characteristic of
pietism ... The impact of this book on subsequent centuries,
including Martin Luther, has been immense. Since it is not
spiritual writing of particularly high quality, this is to be regretted.

The notion that creatures and material things are a block and a barrier
to experience of God remains widespread in Christian circles, and it is
difficult to see the influence of à Kempis's book as other than
damaging in this regard. The more healthy, more incarnational and
sacramental, approach to devotion reappears in the work of the

metaphysical poet and Anglican divine Thomas Traherne (1636–74). Traherne, like Francis of Assisi, was filled with the beauty and wonder of the natural order, and with the need for bodily and spiritual identification with that order as a necessary foundation for prayerfulness and praise.

> You never enjoy the world aright till the sea itself floweth in your veins, till you are clothed with the heavens and crowned with the stars; and perceive yourself to be the sole heir of the whole world: and more than so, because men are in it who are everyone sole heirs as well as you ... till your spirit filleth the whole world, and the stars are your jewels, till you are familiar with the way of God in all ages as well as with your walk and table ... till you delight in God for being good to all: you never enjoy the world.[129]

Today more and more theologians are recognizing the serious mistake in spiritual and ascetical teaching which encourages withdrawal from the material world and from men and women. So Hans Urs von Balthasar emphasizes that we cannot be satisfied with a tradition of prayer which actually reduces and diminishes our humanity:

> The act of contemplation in which the believer hears the word of God and surrenders himself to it, is an act of the whole man. It cannot therefore assume a form in which man truncates his own being, whether for a short or longer time – for instance, by *systematically* training himself to turn from the outer world and attend wholly to the inner world, or turning from both the outer and inner senses (the imagination) to the pure, 'naked' spirit. That kind of deliberate artificial restriction reduces man to a shadow of himself, and is a misunderstanding of God's demand, namely 'conversion', a turning from the manifold to the essential.[130]

Christian devotion and prayer needs to be more humanized, more sensitized, less concerned with the inner world in isolation from the demands of the poor and the hungry, more concerned with the hallowing of the world and the transfiguring of the flesh. We need to develop the facility for turning simultaneously inwards to God who is at the centre of our beings, and outwards to the children of God, made in his image and shining in the world. Twenty years ago, the late Fr Geoffrey Curtis observed that 'the whole concept of contemplation is still in need of being fully *incarnationalized*'.[131] His words abide; the task remains urgent.

9

The Eucharistic God

*The human race can only become the unity which in
principle it is, if each solemnly takes off his old clothes,
spattered with blood and dirt, and undertakes to go a new
way. And the new way is to sit down and break bread
together, each deferring to his neighbours. So the Church of
Jesus is constituted by those two actions of washing and
eating, with a form of words referring to his example.*

John Pairman Brown[1]

*Just as this Eucharistic action is the pattern of all
Christian action, the sharing of this Bread the sign of the
sharing of all bread, so this Fellowship is the germ of all
society renewed in Christ.*

John A. T. Robinson[2]

From very early times, human beings have shared meals together, and
seen in such an act a symbol of fellowship, common life, common
love. The sharing of food and fellowship, the drinking of wine in the
atmosphere of warmth and joy, such activities are among the most
important in life. It is not surprising therefore that at the heart of the
worship and experience of God in Christian tradition is the activity of
a meal, the Eucharist. Christian spirituality is of a eucharistic type,
that is, it comes to see and know and even digest God within the
framework of the liturgy of eating and drinking. It has thus the marks
of an active and social experience, not those of a passive and private
one. And both the involvement in action, and the social character of
the experience, are of the essence, and not simply incidental aspects,
of the Christian spiritual path. It is an experience of God which takes
place within the context of an action involving movement, responses,
manual acts, greetings of our fellow participants, the offering of gifts,
the receiving of communinion; and this action is the action of a
community in which individuals are caught up. It is not therefore on
the fringes of the common life, but at its centre, that Christian
spirituality, even Christian contemplation, happens. 'Now is the time
for God to act' as the Eastern liturgy says of the eucharistic action. To
come to the sacred meal of the community is to expect a divine
encounter, it is both to consume and be consumed.

The idea of the sacred meal in which the worshippers feed upon the life of their god is, of course, considerably older than Christianity. In primitive sacrificial systems, the meal was central to the communal life. And yet 'the common life which united the worshippers was the divine life; their god became their life within them; they partook of his being'.[3] The fellowship which was enjoyed and shared was a divine fellowship. Indeed we can say that the notion of the sacred meal probably preceded belief in God. In primitive societies, the social organism was seen as a single animal with one corporate life-blood. From time to time the common life was in need of revitalization. The hunters would gather with the meat which they had gathered from their expeditions, and it would be consumed in a common meal. It was in the fusion of the common meal with the theme of the revitalization of the common life that we see the beginnings of sacrifice, though the notion of communion is pre-sacrificial. Some of the earliest rituals of which we have knowledge are connected with the obtaining and consuming of food.[4] However, Bouyer has claimed that in origin sacrifice was a sacred meal,[5] and this view finds considerable support in the earlier important work by Yerkes on the origins of sacrifice. Yerkes saw the beginnings of sacrifice in the common meals of primitive hunters, but the meal was far more than a purely utilitarian activity:

> The word *sacrifice*, which means 'to make a thing sacred' or 'to do a sacred act', was used in Latin to describe various rites which arose from the common meal when that meal was held, not for the ordinary purpose of satisfying hunger, but for the purpose of entering into union with the mysterious Power or powers which men felt within them and about them as life itself, and which they recognized in all their environments as both menacing and strengthening the life which they loved and to which they belonged.[6]

The link between divinity and food was thus one with which early human communities were very familiar.

The Holy Meal in Scripture

When we turn to the Old Testament, we find a meal linked with the covenant in Exodus. The covenant was sealed in blood, 'the blood of the covenant' (Exod. 24.8) which Moses flung upon the people, and this act was immediately followed by a gathering of elders of Israel when they saw the God of Israel and celebrated a common meal: 'they beheld God, and ate and drank' (24.11). Sacred meals were held also at other shrines, as at Mizpah where Jacob offered a sacrifice on the mountain, and the people ate bread and tarried all night (Gen. 31.54), or at the site in the wilderness to which Jethro came and ate bread with Moses and the elders (Exod. 18.12). In Deuteronomy, Israel is instructed to 'eat before the Lord your God' (12.7), and this must be at a specific site:

> You may not eat within your towns the tithe of your grain or of your wine or of your oil, or the firstlings of your herd or of your flock, or any of your votive offerings which you vow, or your freewill offerings, or the offering that you present; but you shall eat them before the Lord your God in the place which the Lord your God will choose ... (12.17–18).

In the celebration before the Lord, at the place where his name dwells, the grain, the wine, and the oil, were consumed in joy and fear (Deut. 14.23, 26; cf. 15.20; 27.7).

Moreover, the prophetic and apocalyptic writings see the coming age of the Messiah in terms of unlimited supplies of food and drink. Then men and women will feed along the ways, and will not hunger or thirst (Isa. 49.9). Ezekiel outlines the 'covenant of peace' in terms of fruitfulness and the removal of hunger:

> I will make with them a covenant of peace and banish wild beasts from the land, so that they may dwell securely in the wilderness and sleep in the woods. And I will make them and the places round about my hill a blessing; and I will send down the showers in their season; they shall be showers of blessing. And the trees of the field shall yield their fruit, and the earth shall yield its increase, and they shall be secure in their land; and they shall know that I am the Lord, when I break the bars of their yoke, and deliver them from the hand of those who enslaved them. They shall no more be a prey to the nations, nor shall the beasts of the land devour them; they shall dwell securely, and none shall make them afraid. And I will provide for them prosperous plantations so that they shall no more be consumed with hunger in the land, and no longer suffer the reproach of the nations. And they shall know that I, the Lord their God, am with them, and that they, the house of Israel, are my people, says the Lord God. (Ezek. 34.25–30)

The servants of the Lord will eat and drink, while the enemies of Israel will experience hunger and thirst (Isa. 65.13). Earlier, Isaiah had described the feast on the mountain of the Lord, a theme which was to reappear in the notion of the messianic banquet. Referring back to an early reference to the mountain of the Lord (2.2–4) as a place of eschatological *shalom*, peace and harmony, Isaiah goes on to describe it in terms of feasting:

> On this mountain the Lord of hosts will make for all peoples a feast of fat things, a feast of wine on the lees, of fat things full of marrow, of wine on the lees well refined. And he will destroy on this mountain the covering that is cast over all peoples, the veil that is spread over all nations. He will swallow up death for ever, and the Lord God will wipe away tears from all faces, and the reproach of his people he will take away from all the earth; for the Lord has spoken. It will be said on that day, 'Lo, this is our God; we have waited for him, that he might save us. This is the Lord; we have waited for him; let us be glad and rejoice in his salvation.' (25.6–9)

So salvation is seen in terms of a feast including vast quantities of food and wine, the removal of death and of weeping, and unending joy. The later apocalyptic writers develop this imagery. The new age, in Ezra, is an age of abundant food (4 Ezra 8.52–4), while there is a marvellous account in Baruch of the age of the Messiah as a time of ever-flowing wine. Every vine will have a thousand branches, every branch will yield a thousand clusters of grapes, every cluster will yield a thousand grapes, and every grape will produce a cor of wine! (2 Baruch 29.5). And later in Baruch is the vision of the manna of Exodus which, it is said, will be restored in the last days:

> And it shall come to pass at that selfsame time that the treasury of manna shall again descend from on high, and they will eat it in those years, because these are they who have come to the consummation of time. (2 Baruch 29.8)

So the new age will be an age of new manna, and this would involve a sharing of the divine life. For manna was directly associated in Jewish thought with the nature of God. It was 'thy sustenance', *hē hypostasis sou*, translated in the Vulgate as *substantia tua* (Wisd. 16.20). To enjoy the new manna was to enjoy the life of God himself.

This imagery of the great feast in the new age was part of the background against which Jesus came with his message of the imminence of the Kingdom of God, a Kingdom which he saw as a time of feasting. For 'many will come from east and west and sit at table with Abraham, Isaac and Jacob in the kingdom of heaven' (Matt. 8.11; cf. Luke 13.29). The new age is presented, as in the prophetic tradition, as a time when hunger will be satisfied (Luke 6.21; Matt. 5.6). Mary celebrates the dawning of salvation as the reversal of the structures of power and the distribution of food:

> He has shown strength with his arm,

he has scattered the proud in the imagination of their hearts,
he has put down the mighty from their thrones,
and exalted those of low degree;
he has filled the hungry with good things,
and the rich he has sent empty away. (Luke. 51–3)

The hungry have a central place in the Kingdom, a fact which is made clear in the parables with their stress on food and the correction of present injustices. The Kingdom is directly compared to a marriage feast to which the poor and the people of the streets were invited (Matt. 22.1–14; Luke 14.15–24). Indeed, the place of the outcasts at the Kingdom feast is of great importance. So Jesus says:

> When you give a dinner or a banquet, do not invite your friends or your brothers or your kinsmen or rich neighbours, lest they also invite you in return, and you be repaid. But when you give a feast, invite the poor, the maimed, the lame, the blind, and you will be blessed, because they cannot repay you. You will be repaid at the resurrection of the just. (Luke 14.12–14)

The centrality of food in the Kingdom and in the achievement on earth of God's will is brought out in the close association between these realities in the Lord's Prayer, where the hallowing of God's name, the coming of the Kingdom, and the provision of daily bread are placed together (Luke 11.3; Matt. 6.11). The word translated 'daily', epiousios, has been a cause of much debate. It was a rare, almost unknown, word at the time. Some have suggested a link with the 'continual bread' of the Levitical cult (Numb. 4.7). By the time of Cyril of Jerusalem the prayer was being applied to the Eucharist.[7] Many of the Fathers interpret epiousios as referring to the future, perhaps as meaning 'bread for the coming day', perhaps even more as 'bread for the coming age'. Origen was the first Christian writer to apply this phrase of the Lord's Prayer directly to the age to come,[8] and Athanasius followed him in this interpretation.[9] St John of Damascus (675–749) spoke of this bread as the 'first fruits of the bread to come'.[10] Whatever the precise meaning of epiousios it seems clear that the petition is not simply that God would provide daily sustenance, but that he would lead us to the Kingdom feast. The whole prayer in fact is a Kingdom prayer, and the prayer for bread has to be set in this framework of thought about the coming Kingdom as banquet. If the petition is seen also as having a direct eucharistic reference, this strengthens the link between the Eucharist and the Kingdom as well as that between the Eucharist and daily life and struggle. Geoffrey Wainwright sums up the point of the prayer:[11]

The bread for which we pray is *at one and the same time* both the earthly bread to meet the hunger and need of the present day, and also the future bread which will satisfy the elect in the eschatological Kingdom and is already given to us in anticipation . . .

There is further use of the symbolism of food in the long Chapter 6 of St John's Gospel, almost certainly a chapter with strong eucharistic undertones. In this chapter, after the feeding of 5,000 people (6.1–14), Jesus introduces the theme of the bread of life (6.25–65). The eating of bread is here placed in the context of eternity and of 'eternal life', John's synonym for the Kingdom of God of the Synoptic writers. The Son of Man will give the food which endures to eternal life (v. 27), the 'true bread from heaven' (v. 32). Jesus identifies this bread with himself (vv. 35, 48), and even claims that those who do not eat his flesh and blood have no life in them at all (v. 53). On the other hand, those who eat this bread will live for ever (v. 58).

Finally, in the Gospel we have the account of the institution by Jesus of the memorial, the *anamnēsis*, at the Last Supper. Whether the Last Supper was a Passover celebration or not, it occurred close to the Passover and contained Passover elements. Messianic expectation was particularly high at Passover time, and so the Last Supper occurred within an atmosphere of yearning for the age to come. In Jesus' actions we see a link both with earlier events in his own ministry, in which publicans and sinners were welcomed to meals and received forgiveness, and with the expectation of the Kingdom. Jesus links the 'blood of the covenant', represented by the outpoured wine, with the Kingdom. 'Truly, I say to you, I shall not drink again of the fruit of the vine until that day when I drink it new in the Kingdom of God' (Mark 14.25). For as the Kingdom will be a time in which new manna will be provided, so also it will be a time in which new wine will be drunk. The *anamnēsis* is therefore both a remembrance of the saving events of Jesus' life and death and also a looking to the fulfilment of the Kingdom.

At the Last Supper Jesus took bread and wine, elements which have remained the basic materials of the Christian Eucharist. It is possible that, following the Old Testament Passover ritual, the bread was unleavened, though all New Testament writers use *artos* and not *azymos*, the term for unleavened bread, in the accounts of the Last Supper.[12] Certainly there is considerable evidence that ordinary bread was used in the early centuries of the Church. Augustine uses the theme of 'one loaf, one body', and it is clear from his account and from other evidence that unleavened bread was not used in the North African church at this time. 'My bread,' says Ambrose,[13] 'is of the usual kind' (*meus panis est usitatus*). Jesus associates the bread with his body, and the wine with the blood of the new covenant, a clear reference to the blood of the covenant in Exodus. There is evidence that in the early Church the use of wine in the Eucharist was at times optional, though later both bread and wine came to be used at every celebration.[14] The linking of wine with blood was a natural symbolic usage, for wine was referred to as the blood of the grape (Gen. 49.11; Deut. 32.14; Ecclus. 39.26), and the wine of Passover was red in order to make the connection with blood and with death. The use of a common cup (Mark 14.23; Matt. 26.27) also looked forward to the messianic feast when all would share the cup of David. The Last Supper thus contains within it the memorial of the past events of Israel's history and the anticipation of the new age.

This sense of anticipation is evident elsewhere in the New Testament as well as the liturgies of the early Christians. Christians are described as those who have *tasted* the powers of the age to come (Heb. 6.5). Yet there is still the sense that all is not fulfilled. The liturgy is celebrated *till he come* (1 Cor 11.26), a theme which received liturgical embodiment in the 'Maranatha' of the early rites. The marriage supper of the Lamb is still in the future (Rev. 19.7–9). However, it has been suggested that the Book of Revelation itself reflects the structure of the Paschal liturgy, and if this is so, the link between the Eucharist, as the climax of that liturgy, and the marriage supper of the Lamb in Chapter 19 is very close.[15] Whether this is so or not, it is clear that, as in Revelation 4–5, the account in Chapter 19 is both a vision of the future and a reflection of the worship of the Church on earth as it shares the life of the age to come.

Continuing Steadfast

It is said in the Acts of the Apostles that the early Christians continued steadfast in the Apostles' teaching and fellowship (*koinōnia*) and in the breaking of the bread and the prayers (2.42). Certainly it is clear that from the earliest times the celebration of the Eucharist was at the centre of the life of the Christian community. It was a eucharistic community, its fundamental experience of union with God being a social eucharistic experience. The Eucharist was the heart of Christian mysticism: not a flight of the alone to the alone, but a real communion with God through the materiality of bread and wine shared together. In the atmosphere of persecution and oppression, there was a sense of mystery and even secrecy about the liturgical celebration. It has been suggested that the description of the holy meal as 'the breaking of the bread', a completely new usage by the early Christians, can only be explained by the assumption that it was a cryptogram, and that the non-Christian was not supposed to understand its meaning.[16] Meeting together on a certain day before it was light, explained Pliny the Younger to the Emperor Trajan, the Christians would bind themselves together by a *sacramentum*.[17] Week by week, day by day, they continued to 'remember' the Lord. As Hippolytus expressed it:[18]

> Doing therefore the anamnesis of his death and resurrection, we offer to thee the bread and the cup, making Eucharist to thee, because thou hast bidden us to stand before thee and minister as priests to thee.

'Holy Communion' accurately sums up the common experience of the holy in early Christian life: celebrated in a liturgy in which the sense of the glory of God was embedded in a materialistic context.

Certainly there was the awareness of the divine glory, the sense of the presence of God in the midst of his people. The threefold Sanctus of Isaiah 6.2 entered into the eucharistic liturgy at an early stage, while the idea of progress from one degree of glory to another (2 Cor. 3.18), used by St Paul with reference to the Christian life as a whole, received its eucharistic application in the Liturgy of St James where, after communion, was sung the hymn 'From glory to glory advancing'. A version of the hymn is preserved in modern English hymnbooks:

> From glory to glory advancing, we praise thee, O Lord;
> Thy name with the Father and Spirit be ever adored.
> From strength unto strength we go forward on Sion's highway,
> To appear before God in the city of infinite day.[19]

However, the perception of the glory of God was not seen among the early Christians as some distant reality, involving a movement away from matter to the world of pure spirit, as the gnostics held. It was in the midst of matter that God was perceived in his glory and in his provision of common grace. Nowhere is the sense of the material basis of sacramental grace more strongly expressed than in the writings of Irenaeus against the gnostic aberrations of his day. For Irenaeus, the Eucharist presupposes the goodness of matter and of the physical world. It is the first-fruits of the creation.[20] But it also presupposes the goodness of matter and of the flesh, and their potential for sanctification. For, he asks the heretics who deny both flesh and Eucharist:[21]

> Since then the cup which is mixed and the bread which is made received the Word of God and become the Eucharist of the body and blood of Christ, and of them the substance of our flesh grows

and subsists: how can they deny that the flesh is capable of the gift of God which is eternal life, that flesh which is fed by the body and blood of the Lord and is a member of him?

At the centre of the eucharistic worship of the early Church was the firm conviction that God was encountered through material things. An equally striking feature of the eucharistic life was its orientation towards the future. The celebrating Church looked forward to the greater life of the Kingdom, as the words in the Didache make clear: 'As this broken bread was scattered on the mountains, and then, being gathered together, became one, so may thy Church be gathered together from the ends of the earth into they Kingdom.' Later in the Didache comes the first clear evidence of the liturgical use of 'Maranatha', the cry of the coming of the Lord.[23] The longing for the coming of Christ in his Kingdom, for his *Parousia*, was linked with the present experience of Christ in the Eucharist. Later, the Maranatha cry was replaced in the liturgical celebration by the *Benedictus qui venit*: Blessed is he who comes in the name of the Lord. Hosanna in the highest! In its origin in the Old Testament, this cry was specifically associated with messianic expectation (Ps. 118.26), and it is right therefore to see its presence in the liturgy as 'the legitimate replacement of *Maranatha*'.[24] The link between present experience and future hope comes out strongly also in the remarkable liturgy of Addai and Mari, the Syriac rite which is still the rite used by the Nestorian Christians, and which is marked by the absence, in the original form of the liturgy, of any words of institution. However, in the invocation of the Spirit over the oblation, there is a prayer that God would 'bless it and hallow it that it may be to us . . . for the great hope of resurrection from the dead and for new life in the Kingdom of Heaven with all those who have been well pleasing in thy sight'.[25] Similarly, in the Armenian liturgy, the prayer at the washing of hands includes the words: 'Let us stand in prayer before the Holy Table of God, and find the grace and mercy in the day of his appearing and at the Second Coming of Our Lord and Saviour Jesus Christ.'[26]

There are other elements in the early liturgies which emphasize the future dimension. The importance of Sunday as the 'Lord's Day', the day of resurrection, has often been stressed. But Sunday was also seen as the 'Eighth Day', the day of the ending of Sabbaths, the anticipation of the eternal Sabbath of the Kingdom. It was the day not only of the resurrection of Christ in time, but also of the new creation, the resurrection and transformation of the creation. Again, the custom of facing east, the region of the sun's rising, was closely linked with the eschatological waiting, for it was in the east that the sign of the Son of Man was to appear. And there was the theme of the new wine of the Kingdom. So St Jerome says that

> from these vines we drink the new wine in the Kingdom of the Father, not in the oldness of the letter, but in the newness of the Spirit, singing the new song which no one can sing except in the Kingdom of the Church which is the Kingdom of the Father.[27]

The Eucharist was seen as the pledge of future glory, as it was, many centuries later, described in the Antiphon for the Magnificat on the feast of Corpus Christi, composed by St Thomas Aquinas. The Nestorian theologian Narsai, who wrote his homilies on the Eucharist in the early sixth century, said of the Christian soul: 'with bread and wine he purposed for it a mark towards the things to come, that it might be aiming at the renovation that is prepared for it',[28] while a prayer in the Mozarabic Office runs: 'Today may he sanctify you perfectly, and may he tomorrow allow you to take your place worthily at his banquet.'[29]

There are other important aspects of the eucharistic liturgy which are stressed in the early Christian rites and writings. There is a considerable use of language about sacrifice from an early period. There is a stress on the kiss of peace, the sign of harmony and reconciliation and of the unity of the community in love. There is, in a number of writings, the idea of the Eucharist as medicine, a theme developed by Gregory of Nyssa who speaks of it as an antidote to the poison of sin,[30] and in Cyril of Alexandria who speaks of it as the seed of eternal life.[31] And, of course, there is the repeated stress on sharing and common life, which comes out not only in the writing about *koinōnia* but also in the apostolic communism and the practice of economic sharing within the community. In explaining the meaning of 'communion', the Eastern writer Isidore of Pelusium, in the middle of the fifth century, says: 'The reception of the divine mysteries is called communion (*koinōnia*) because it unites us with Christ and makes us sharers (*koinōnous*) in his Kingdom.'[32]

The Middle Ages saw the beginnings of the disintegration of the primitive rite, and of the distorted view of sacrifice against which the Reformers revolted and which, to a great extent, has shaped and confused Christian thinking on the Eucharist ever since. Some changes which were to become of crucial importance at a later stage were already under way in the early centuries. The stress on awe and on distance was building up in Syria from the fourth century onwards. Chrysostom's phrases 'the terrible sacrifice' and 'the shuddering hour'[33] give some indication of the shift that was taking place towards a greater stress on the transcendence of God, and the loss of a sense of the holy in the common. Of course, the sense of mystery is important, but the corresponding sense of the common life and the 'ordinariness' of the eucharistic God was in danger. It was in the fifth century that the great hymn 'Let all mortal flesh keep silence' entered the Liturgy of St James, and this too symbolized the move towards the distancing of the sanctuary from the people. The role of the celebrant came to receive greater stress in this period. Theodore of Mopsuestia, in the fifth century, calls the priest the mediator of the sacrament.[34] The secret recitation of the eucharistic Prayer ('the silent canon') probably began in the fourth century with Cyril, Basil, and Chrysostom, and, though it was forbidden as an abuse by the Emperor Justinian in the sixth century, it gradually became the norm in the Roman rite until the 1960s.[35] In the East, veils were introduced to divide the altar from the congregation, and the eastward (backs to the people) position became general in the Eastern Church, though the 'across the altar' position remained general in the West for hundreds of years. However, in the ninth century, the spread of the custom of placing relics on the altar, as well as the tradition of reserving the Blessed Sacrament on the altar, led to the general acceptance of the eastward position in the Western Church also.

This combination of changes created an atmosphere in which the entire framework of eucharistic worship and spirituality was disfigured and severely narrowed. While the Mass in its splendour remained central to the worshipping community, it no longer bore the distinctive marks of the holy meal out of which it grew. The notion of presence became localized, associated with the words of institution, with a 'moment', and the late practice of the elevation assumed a disproportionate place in the rite. Sacrifice came to be associated exclusively with death, while the whole sacramental action came more and more to be seen in terms not of the incorporation of the community into Christ but rather of the descent of Christ into the elements and on to the altar. Today, as we seek, through eucharistic worship, to encounter the living God, we will need particularly to reflect on the two central themes of sacrifice and presence, those essentially interrelated themes which, in spite of all distortions, remain basic to any Christian understanding of worship.

This Our Sacrifice

Biblical thought associates sacrifice with blood rather than with death, death being rather an incident in the action of sacrifice. Blood stands for life rather than for death. Thus, while the cross is at the centre of Christian reflection and Christian preaching, it is not seen, in the apostolic preaching, in isolation from the entire work of Christ in his life, and in his exaltation. The New Testament does not speak of the 'sacrifice of the cross', and the expression 'once for all' is used not of the cross but of the entry into the Holy Place (Heb. 9.21). Sacrifice, however, is closely associated with blood, for 'the life of the flesh is in the blood' (Lev. 17.11) and it was through the blood of Christ that deliverance was wrought (1 Pet. 1.18–19). The role of the priest in the Old Testament was connected not with the slaying of the victim but with the offering of the blood (Lev. 4.13–18). It was because of the association of blood with life that the Jewish law prohibited the consumption of blood (Deut. 12.23). The recognition of the importance of blood was something which Israel shared with most early societies: 'Primitive man felt so strongly about blood that a very rich mysticism centring upon it grew up very early in the story of mankind, and was established as early as history or archaeology can take us back.'[36] However, while in most cultures the blood was consumed, this was not allowable under the Jewish law. For, as the Lord said to Moses:

'Say to Aaron and his sons, and to all the people of Israel, This is the thing which the Lord has commanded. If any man of the house of Israel kills an ox or a lamb or a goat in the camp, or kills it outside the camp, and does not bring it to the door of the tent of meeting, to offer it as a gift to the Lord before the tabernacle of the Lord, bloodguilt shall be imputed to that man; he has shed blood; and that man shall be cut off from among his people.' (Lev. 17.1–4)

To take the life of another person into oneself was a blasphemous act. The blood must therefore be poured out to the Lord:

'If any man of the house of Israel or of the strangers that sojourn among them eats any blood, I will set my face against that person who eats blood, and will cut him off from among his people. For the life of the flesh is in the blood; and I have given it for you upon the altar to make atonement for your souls; for it is the blood that makes atonement, by reason of the life. Therefore I have said to the people of Israel, No person among you shall eat blood, neither shall any stranger who sojourns among you eat blood. Any man also of the people of Israel, or of the strangers that sojourn among them, who takes in hunting any beast or bird that may be eaten shall pour out its blood and cover it with dust. For the life of every creature is the blood of it; therefore I have said to the people of Israel, You shall not eat the blood of any creature, for the life of every creature is its blood; whoever eats it shall be cut off.' (17.10–14)

So the life-blood was offered in sacrifice to make atonement, and to restore the broken relationship between God and the people. This restoration of a broken relationship is fundamental to the early ideas of sacrifice. The purpose of sacrifice in early societies was to re-establish the covenant or harmony between the natural and the supernatural, between the human and the divine societies.[37] The essential element in all sacrifice is the act of giving. Whereas in popular usage today, to sacrifice is often interpreted as meaning 'to give up', this was not its original sense at all. Rather, to sacrifice was to *give*, to give a present to someone. The actual word sacrifice is derived from *facit sacrum*, make holy.[38] In primitive societies, the clan was seen as a single animal which from time to time was in need of revitalization and this was achieved through the sharing of blood. The gods were seen, along with humans and animals, as sharing in this corporate state of anaemia, and therefore as being equally in need of revitalizing. However, as ideas of a transcendent god or gods developed, the sacrifice came to be burnt. It is possible that *theoi*, gods, is derived from *thu*, smoke, and it is certainly from *thu* that the word *thuein*, to sacrifice, comes. Through the process of burning, the god(s) would consume the sacrificial gift.[39]

In the idea of sacrificial gift there were a number of elements which can be simply described by the analogy with the human act of present-giving. In the giving of a birthday present, or some other present, there are a number of processes:

(i) the *remembrance* of the recipient of the proposed gift;
(ii) the *desire to please* this person;
(iii) the *construction*, or *purchase*, of the gift, which should be marked by its
(iv) *appropriateness* in relation to the recipient;
(v) the *packing* and *wrapping* of the gift in an acceptable way; and
(vi) the *presentation* of the gift

This cluster of attitudes and processes can be called the *substance*, that is, the structure of relationships which go into the making and offering of the gift. In the sacrificial action, these attitudes and processes go to make up the *offertory*, and they include the reality of sin which must be seen as a component factor in the structure. As Marx called commodities 'definite masses of congealed labour time', so we can see the offertory as a symbolic representation of these historical and social processes which go into the making of a gift.

Yet all this work is pre-sacrificial. The sacrifice is still in need of the work of *conveyance*, of being transferred from one reality to another. In primitive societies, food and offerings would be left for the god who would simply 'come and get it' – including, at times, from tombs. We can see the practice of burning the gift, and that of pouring the blood upon the earth, as technical refinements of the conveyance process, ways in which the sacrifice could be conveyed to the recipient, to the divine world. The purpose, then, of such sacrifice is to bring about revitalization, renewal, transformation, and the question is how this offering, which has been prepared with such care, can *break through* from the human to the divine. Hence the importance of death: for through death the life of an animal or a human person is transmitted, but it is also, through the process, transformed.

The Jews took great care over the preparatory work of sacrifice. There was, for instance, a stress on the fact that the offering should be unblemished:

> If his offering is a burnt offering from the herd, he shall offer a male without blemish; he shall offer it at the door of the tent of meeting, that he may be accepted before the Lord; he shall lay his hand upon the head of the burnt offering, and it shall be accepted for him to make atonement for him. (Lev. 1.3–4)

Hence Malachi complains of the offering of polluted food:

> You say, 'How have we despised thy name?' By offering polluted food upon my altar. And you say, 'How have we polluted it?' By thinking that the Lord's table may be despised. When you offer blind animals in sacrifice, is that no evil? And when you offer those that are lame or sick, is that no evil?... (1.6–8).

So the sacrificial offering must be pure and spotless.

Moreover, at the centre of the Jewish liturgical life was the *anamnesis*, the remembrance of the past events of saving history, and the making present of those events in the lives of the worshippers. Through the great rituals of Passover week the deliverance from oppression in Egypt was both remembered and recalled, in a sense re-enacted, re-lived. And it is this recalling of dramatic past events in such a way that their power and life become effective now which is the background to the Christian Eucharist. There are thus two basic elements from Jewish history: the spotless victim, and the *anamnesis* of saving events; and in the eucharistic action, Jesus is the Lamb of God who takes away the sin of the world, while those called to his supper are blessed. He is the spotless victim and the host at the festive banquet of God's people.

That the Eucharist is in some sense a sacrificial act is really basic to mainstream Christianity, and was recognized from a very early time in the history of Christian thought. Thus 'there are few points more

incontestable than that, in the ancient Church, the structure upon
which the elements for the Holy Eucharist were placed was designated
an altar, and in the generally accepted and proper sense of the word'.[40]
St Ignatius of Antioch spoke of 'one Eucharist ... one altar',[41] and,
while there is little historical authority for a precise theory of the mode
of the eucharistic sacrifice, there is overwhelming testimony to the
fact of its sacrificial nature.[42] However, sacrifice was not associated, as
it came later to be, exclusively with death; rather there was a
celebration of the whole work of Christ. In the words of St Cyril of
Alexandria:[43]

> We proclaim the death in the flesh of the only-begotten Son of
> God, Jesus Christ, and acknowledge his return to life from the
> dead and his ascension into heaven, and as we do this we perform
> the bloodless sacrifice in the churches: thus we approach the
> consecrated gifts of the sacrament and are sanctified by partaking
> of the holy flesh and the precious blood of Christ the Saviour of all.

Nor was the sacrificial action in the Eucharist seen as something
different from, or additional to, the sacrifice of Christ. Rather in the
words of St John Chrysostom, 'we do not make a different sacrifice ...
but always the same, or rather we celebrate a memorial of a
sacrifice'.[44] The positive and dynamic character of the theme of
'memorial' has been expressed well by Geoffrey Wainwright:[45]

> The Eucharist is a dominically instituted memorial-rite which, not
> only serving to remind men but also being performed before God,
> is sacrificial at least in so far as it recalls before God with
> thanksgiving that one sacrifice, and prays for the continuing
> benefits of that sacrifice to be granted now.

The eucharistic action thus recalls, re-members, the mighty acts of
God in Christ, and draws the powers of the age to come into the
present. It is thus both a historical and an eschatological rite, rooted in
historical events, orientated towards the future fulfilment of God's
Kingdom.

In common understanding, however, sacrifice is confused with
death and with offering of any kind. We speak of death as 'the great
sacrifice', a theme which is brought out powerfully in the hymn, much
loved by the English politician Margaret Thatcher, 'O valiant
hearts':[46]

> O valiant hearts, who to your glory came
> Through dust of conflict and through battle flame;

The hymn goes on to link the deaths of soldiers in war with the death of Christ:

> Long years ago, as earth lay dark and still,
> Rose a loud cry upon a lonely hill,
> While in the frailty of our human clay
> Christ our Redeemer passed the self-same way.
>
> Still stands his Cross from that dread hour to this,
> Like some bright star above the dark abyss;
> Still, through the veil, the Victor's pitying eyes
> Look down to bless our lesser Calvaries.
>
> These were his servants, in his steps they trod,
> Following through death the martyred Son of God;
> Victor he rose; victorious too shall rise
> They who have drunk his cup of sacrifice.

Leaving aside the more or less blasphemous identification of deaths in war with the atoning death of Christ, not to mention the uncritical assumption of the righteousness of the specific conflict with which the hymn is concerned, there is here a fundamental and widespread misunderstanding of sacrifice as equivalent to death. It must be stressed that, in biblical and liturgical theology, death is not the same as sacrifice but is a necessary stage which precedes the sacrificial offering. What is central to the sacrifice is the act of conveyance of the offering, though the liturgical action, to a different level or reality in which it is transformed.

It follows then that the second misunderstanding, which equates sacrifice with *any* offering, is also wrong. Offerings are often dedicated, placed upon the altar, and this act is called an 'offertory'. But it is significant that this term is widely used, in Anglican churches, to describe the collection. Indeed, the high point of the service may be the solemn procession of the money which culminates in the elevation of the alms dish while the congregation stand with serious expressions on their faces: as the dish is raised higher, the heads bow lower! In fact, the point of an offertory is that bread and wine are placed upon the altar to await the transforming activity of God in consecration. The offertory is therefore necessary to the sacrifice but is not to be identified with it. St Thomas Aquinas rightly pointed out that 'every sacrifice is an oblation, but not conversely'.[47] We shall return to the importance of the offertory in examining the liturgy of the Christian Eucharist.

The sacrifice which is celebrated in the Eucharist is thus more than a historical recollection of Christ's death, more than our own offerings of materials, certainly more than 'the offering of ourselves, our souls and bodies, to be a true, holy and lively sacrifice'. Such an offering can only take place in so far as it is a sharing in Christ's own offering. And in this sense, the eucharistic sacrifice is a microcosm of the whole Christian life, which is dying and rising with Christ, a process of life through death, a metamorphosis. 'Transubstantiation' does accurately describe the Christian life: the movement of our substance into God's, the 'taking of manhood into God'. The unity between Christ's offering and our worship is brought out well in one of Wesley's eucharistic hymns:[48]

> Victim divine, thy grace we claim
> While thus thy precious death we show;
> Once offer'd up, a spotless lamb
> In thy great temple here below,
> Thou didst for all mankind atone,
> And standest now before the throne.
>
> Thou standest in the holiest place
> As now for guilty sinners slain;
> Thy blood of sprinkling speaks and prays,
> All prevalent for helpless men.
> Thy blood is still our ransom found
> And spreads salvation all around.
>
> The smoke of thy atonement here,
> Darken'd the sun and rent the veil,
> Made the new way to heaven appear
> And show'd the great Invisible;
> Well pleased in thee, our God looked down
> And called his rebels to a crown.
>
> He still respects thy sacrifice,
> Its savour sweet doth always please.
> The offering smokes through earth and skies,
> Diffusing life and joy and peace;
> To these thy lower courts it comes
> And fills them with divine perfumes.

True Presence

While the early Christians showed no concern about a 'moment' in the liturgy when the bread and wine became the body and blood of Christ, their sense of the reality of his presence in the sacrament was strong and clearly stated. 'This food is called by us Eucharist', wrote Justin Martyr, and he continued:[49]

For we do not receive these things as common bread or common drink: but as Jesus Christ our Saviour having been made flesh by a word of God, had flesh and blood for our salvation, so we have learned that the food made Eucharist by a word of prayer that comes from him, from which our blood and flesh are nourished, by change are the flesh and blood of the incarnate Jesus.

Justin speaks of 'change' and of 'the food made Eucharist by a word of prayer', themes which are soon to reappear in the writings of Origen, who speaks of 'food sanctified by the Word of God and prayer', [50] and of Irenaeus, who speaks of the 'word of invocation'. The theme of the powerful, transforming Word of God is one which appears in numerous patristic writings, and it is closely linked with the invocation of the Holy Spirit. According to Athanasius, the Word descends upon the bread and the cup. [51] John Chrysostom says that the Word transforms the gifts, and will continue to do so until his Coming. [52]

An invocation of the Holy Spirit is present in the eucharistic liturgy as early as Hippolytus, where it is noticeable that the prayer is also for the pouring out of the Spirit upon the people present. 'And we pray thee that thou wouldest grant to all who partake that they may be filled with the Holy Spirit for the confirmation of their faith in truth.' [53] In the Byzantine rite the prayer for the people remained: 'Send down thy Holy Spirit upon us and upon these gifts . . .' Later writing and liturgy came to stress more the transformation of the elements themselves. 'Our Creator', wrote Gregory the Great, '. . . changes the bread and the wine mixed with water . . . into his body and blood . . . by the hallowing of his Spirit'. [54] The role of the Holy Spirit in sanctifying the bread and wine, and in sanctifying the people also, is one that receives great emphasis throughout the Fathers. As a recent study has pointed out: [55]

> The Fathers generally saw the Holy Spirit as well as Christ playing an active role in the eucharistic 'consecration'. No amount of emphasis either on the words of institution or on the words of the 'epiclesis', whatever that word meant to the different Fathers, can obscure the vital role attributed to the Holy Spirit in the eucharistic thought of the Fathers.

At the same time it is important to recognize the close connection between the transforming action of the Spirit upon the bread and wine, and the transformation of the human persons themselves so that they become what they receive. Cyril of Jerusalem speaks of those who receive Christ in Holy Communion as having become concorporal and consanguinary with Christ. [56] Augustine describes the effect of the sacrament as being one of transformation into Christ's body: 'that we might *be* what we *receive*' (*simus quod accipimus*).[57] Similar language is used by Leo the Great: we are changed, he says, into that which we receive (*non enim aliud agit participatio corporis et sanguinis Christi quam ut in id quod sumimus transeamus*).[58] In the East, in common with virtually all the Eastern writers, St John of Damascus describes communion as 'participation in his flesh and in his divinity'.[59] In a passage which Wainwright has described as 'outlandish', Ephraim the Syrian speaks of the relationship of the Holy Spirit with the Eucharist:

> Jesus took into his hands plain bread and blessed, signed and hallowed it in the name of the Father and in the name of the Holy Spirit, and broke it and distributed it piecemeal to his disciples in his good favour. He called the bread his living body, and he filled it with himself and the Spirit. Stretching out his hand, he gave them the bread which his own right hand had hallowed: 'Take and eat, all of you, of this which my word has hallowed ... Take, eat in faith, nothing doubting that this is my body, and whoever eats it in faith eats it in fire and spirit ... Take of it, all of you eat, and in it eat the Holy Spirit; for it is truly my body.[60]

Whatever variations in expression, there is a consensus throughout the Christian writers of the first few centuries that there is a true presence of Christ in the eucharistic action and particularly in the bread and wine hallowed and received. During the controversies of the Reformation period, the reality of that presence needed to be affirmed. It was this which led the Council of Trent to insist that, after the consecration of the bread and wine, the Lord Jesus is contained 'truly, really and substantially' (*vere, realiter ac substantialiter*) under the species of those sensible things, bread and wine.[61] And the Catechism of the Book of Common Prayer equally stressed that the body and blood of Christ were 'verily and indeed taken and received', and English version of *vere et reipsa*. To reinforce the stress on the reality of Christ's presence, one of the homilies stressed that 'in the Supper of the Lord, there is no vain ceremony, no bare sign, no untrue figure of a thing absent', for 'we receive not the figure but the truth, not the shadow only but the body'. Throughout the controversies and the confusion, much of which is, happily, now behind us, the reality of the presence was maintained.[62]

However, while Christ is present in the sacrament, not all receive him, says Augustine, for faith and sincerity are necessary to the worthy reception of his body and blood. St Paul had claimed that those who received the body and blood of the Lord unworthily merely ate and drank damnation, and this is a theme to which Augustine returned in one of his sermons:

> Do so many who either with hypocrisy eat that flesh and drink that blood, or who, after they have eaten and drunk, become apostate: do they dwell in Christ or Christ in them? Yet assuredly there is a certain manner of eating that flesh and of drinking that blood in which whosoever eateth and drinketh it dwelleth in Christ. He then doth not dwell in Christ, and Christ in him, who eateth the flesh and drinketh the blood of Christ in any manner whatever.[63]

In the act of communion, Christians believe, there is a real sharing in the life of God. Holy Communion is the supreme mystical experience, the heart of Christian contemplation, the climax of the life of prayer. It is a common act and yet at the same time deeply, intensely personal. Through this essentially material, physical activity, there is a participation in the being of God, a true union of the divine and human realms. In this act Christ is truly present.

And yet it is mistaken to restrict his presence to the moment of communion or to the sacramental species itself. One of the most striking features of the liturgical renewal which has followed from the revision of the Roman Missal has been the emphasis on the presence of Christ in the gathering together of the people of God, not simply in the act of communion. Christ is present throughout the entire liturgical action, for wherever two or three are gathered together in his name, he is in the midst of them. Christ is present also in the world, and the *Instructio Generalis* of the Roman Missal sees the Eucharist as the culminating point of the action by which God sanctifies the entire world in Christ. Christ's presence in the Eucharist is unique, but it is not the only form of his presence in the sacrament in relation to his presence in the world, in the Church, and in the bodies and souls of men and women made in his likeness.

The doctrine of the omnipresence of God is an important element in Christian belief, and is often acknowledged even in the crudest forms of belief in God's localized presence. 'If God lets it rain today,' said the legendary old lady before the outdoor Corpus Christi procession in Dublin, 'he'll have brought it on himself!' In those words perhaps is summarized the whole paradox of transcendence and immanence, of God beyond the world, and God in the intimacy and materiality of the sacrament. Clearly God is not seen as present in the sacrament in the pagan sense of territorial gods in which the gods were seen as having their own restricted territories. By contrast the God of the Jews is a *Deus mobilis*, a God who is always on the move, the symbols of whose presence are moving pillars of cloud and fire.

There is a sense then in which we can never speak of the absence of God, however much human sin and finitude can obscure the awareness of that presence. There is no part of the universe from which the incarnate Christ has removed his presence. So we can say, with the Psalmist:

Whither shall I go from thy Spirit?
Or whither shall I flee from thy presence?
If I ascend to heaven, thou art there!
If I make my bed in Sheol, thou art there! (Ps. 139.7–8)

We ought therefore to look with suspicion at phrases such as 'bringing Christ into the situation' or 'take Jesus into your heart' which seem to imply that he was previously absent. On the other hand, clearly there are parts of the universe, as of the human heart, from which the conscious recognition, the awareness, the vision of God's presence have been removed, and so we can, in this sense, speak of the eclipse or even of the absence of God.

Again, while God is present everywhere, he is contained nowhere. Thus to speak of God's presence is essentially different from speaking of my presence, or the presence of any person, where to be present within a confined space is necessarily to be absent from all other locations. What then does it mean to speak of the 'real presence' of Christ, or of God? Is there an 'unreal presence'? Of course, applied to persons, the idea of presence does not exclude a kind of semi-absence. People often appear to be only partly present with us – 'I'm not with you' is common as an expression of absentedness, and many people are familiar with paranormal, out-of-the-body experiences, in which presence and absence seem to be somewhat blurred. However, what is crucial about God is that he is not an object and is beyond concepts. We need therefore to avoid models of presence which are only applicable to objects or to finite beings.

In approaching the presence of Christ in the Eucharist, it is vital to begin with the recognition of the variety of forms of his presence. Sydney Carter's song 'Catch the Bird of Heaven' brings out the danger of attempts to capture God within our limited notions. Yet the God who is unknowable in his essential being still manifests himself to men and women, and the Blessed Sacrament is one important manifestation of his presence. But it is not the only manifestation. In the Old Testament, God is held to be present to his people in a variety of ways: in the cloud and the thick darkness; in the events and actions which make up history, including conflicts and trials; in the ritual celebrations by which the saving events of the past are re-enacted; and in the pursuit of justice and mercy. Similarly, in the sacramental manifestation of the presence of the incarnate Christ, we can identify the mystery, the historical reality, the liturgical presence, and the manifestation through justice.

Firstly, we can recognize that Christ's presence in the Eucharist, like the presence of Yahweh on Sinai, is mystical, hidden. The Eucharist is the climax of mystical prayer, it is a transforming mystery, and in it Christ is hidden.

Secondly, we can recognize that Christ is present in the actual gathering together of people. For the group who come to offer and to receive the Body of Christ is, by its baptismal incorporation, already that Body. And so Christ is present wherever two or three are gathered together in his name, in the activities, the struggles, the experiences which we bring in the Offertory. Christ is in the midst of us.

Thirdly, we can recognize that Christ is present in the liturgical re-calling. 'Christ will come again' – not simply at the end of time, but *now*, by the transforming power of the Spirit. Christ is re-called.

Finally, we can recognize that Christ is present in the extension of the Eucharist into the social order, a theme to which we shall shortly return.

Christ's presence in the Eucharist is unique, but it calls for response: for faith in the mystery, for commitment to action, for knowledge of the saving events, for continuity in the extension of that presence into daily life. There is nothing magical about it; it demands co-operation.

Moreover, there is in the Eucharist a straining towards the future coming of Christ in glory. As Wainwright says:[64]

> At every Eucharist, the Church is in fact praying that the parousia may take place at that very moment, and if the Father 'merely' sends his Son in the sacramental mode we have at least a taste of that future which God reserves for himself to give one day.

The sense of being raised to share the life of the future, of the new age, is already present in the Sursum Corda: 'Lift up your hearts' is an invitation to ascend into the heavens, to enter the coming age, to taste the powers of the world to come. To share in the Eucharist at all is 'an eschatological anticipation both of the Advent of the Son of Man and the rapture of the Church'.[65] It is, as Maximus the Confessor often stressed, a prefiguration of heaven, the altar symbolizing the heavenly throne. It is a foretaste of the messianic banquet. Wesley, in his eucharistic hymns, spoke of 'the Sacrament, a Pledge of Heaven', and of the worshippers as those

Who here begin by faith to eat

The supper of the Lamb.[66]

It is thus

> a provisional instance of that glorification of men and nature by
> God which will mark the new heavens and new earth, and ... the
> anticipation of that glorification of God by men and all creation
> which will be the final and complete acknowledgement of his
> universal Kingdom.[67]

Finally, the Eucharist can be seen as the 'extension of the
incarnation', not only in the sense that the incarnate Christ is present
here in many thousands of places, and in his fullness, but also in the
sense that this presence is extended from the altar to the street, as the
incarnational process itself is extended from Galilee and Jerusalem to
the world. The term 'extension of the incarnation' was used by
Charles Gore in relation to the Church itself, which was, he claimed,
'the extension and perpetuation of the incarnation in the world'.[68] But
it had been used earlier about the Blessed Sacrament, as, for example,
by Thomassin and by Jeremy Taylor.[69] Yet, as it is possible – and
common – to profess faith in the incarnation while denying Christ in
the poor and the rejected, so it is possible – and common – to worship
Christ in the Eucharist while failing to see him in the bodies of men
and women. In the message of the Roman Catholic bishops of
England and Wales issued after the National Pastoral Congress in
1980, the bishops stressed the need to 'discern the image of God and
the face of Christ in the world and in people'.[70] This represented an
appalling watering-down of what was actually said by the report from
the Congress groups:

> He dies today in every prisoner of conscience, in every woman who
> cannot feed her children, in all those who suffer in Northern
> Ireland, and in those whose racial origins place them at the margins
> of our society. He rises again in every peasant who wins the right to
> land on which to grow food for those he loves, in every person
> unjustly imprisoned who is set free, in all the unborn children
> whose right to live is protected, in all those who are liberated from
> the glitter of the consumer society, and in every country whose
> people win the struggle for self-determination.[71]

Here there is the specificity, the crudity of a Christology which sees
the presence, the humanity, the dying and rising, of Christ in the
bodies and spirits of his sisters and brothers in the world today. It is
this same sense of the overflowing presence of incarnation and
sacrament which comes through in some of the writing of Mother

Theresa of Calcutta. Thus she speaks of the presence of Christ in the poor:[72]

> 'During the Mass,' I said, 'you saw that the priest touched the body of Christ with great love and tenderness. When you touch the poor today, you too will be touching the body of Christ. Give them the same love and tenderness.' When they returned several hours later, a new sister came up to me, her face shining with joy. 'I have been touching the body of Christ for three hours', she said. I asked her what she had done. 'Just as we arrived, the sister brought in a man covered with maggots. He had been picked up from a drain. I have been taking care of him. I have been touching Christ. I knew it was him.'

Playing with Fire: the Subversive Power of Liturgy
The origins of liturgical worship can be traced to early cultic activity in which drama and sacred art were used to manifest reality. Through the liturgy, the ritual and ceremonial actions of a community, events of the past were re-enacted and *realized*. The word is significant: the liturgy is a *real*izing, a making real, of the work of redemption. Through symbols, and the extension of symbols into sacrament, the events of the past are recaptured, in a sense repeated, and exercise a transforming and liberating effect on the participants. The Greek dramas were liturgies, using ritual props – altar, steps, choirs, and so on – and the dramatic dance survived in the Christian liturgy till the Middle Ages. The idea of liturgy is closely linked to that of drama: it is a celebratory event in which something is expected to happen. The Word of life is liberated and awakened, the still and waiting soul is ignited. Liturgy is dangerous stuff, for it is an opening-up of self and community to the possibility of transformation.

In the liturgical process, one of the most important elements is that of repetition and habit. There is a rhythm in the liturgy which has to be 'lived into' in such a way that the rite becomes part of our consciousness, the framework and context for the divine encounter. Liturgy is not entirely spontaneous; it depends for its power upon a base of habit:

> Chants, scales, tables and repetitions are ways of freeing the attention by making a lower hierarchy of habit purely automatic. An absolutely familiar sequence allows the mind to stand outside for a moment: in suspension, in recollection, in interpretation, or in ecstasy.

The same author suggests that even an element of boredom is a necessary part of the process, for it represents the mid-point between dislocation and the shift to ecstasy: it forms the 'infrastructure of illumination'.[73]

In our present liturgical rites, the eucharistic action is preceded by a series of prayers and hymns, readings and responses, a homily, and the proclamation of the creed. The Eucharist proper is introduced by the sharing of the Sign of Peace, one of the most ancient parts of the liturgy. In the Bible, a kiss was a sign of reconciliation (Gen. 33.4) or of farewell (45.15). In the Christian community the 'holy kiss' was evidently an important feature of the fellowship of love (Rom. 16.16; 1 Cor. 16.20; 2 Cor. 13.12; 1 Thess. 5.26; 1 Pet. 5.14). In the references in 2 Corinthians, 1 Thessalonians, and 1 Peter, the kiss is linked with the theme of peace, though the term 'kiss of peace' is not explicitly present in the New Testament.[74] The first clear reference to the liturgical kiss of peace comes in Justin Martyr who says that, after the baptism, the new Christian receives a kiss before the preparation of the bread and wine.[75] Similarly Hippolytus describes the baptismal liturgy in which the signing is followed by prayers and the 'kiss of peace'.[76] By the early third century, the kiss is associated with peace and harmony, and there is an atmosphere of rejoicing, expressed powerfully by St John Chrysostom:[77]

As soon as they come up from those sacred waters, all present embrace them, greet them, kiss them, congratulate and rejoice with them, because those who before were slaves and prisoners have all at once become free men and sons who are invited to the royal table. For as soon as they come up from the font, they are led to the awesome table which is laden with good things. They taste the body and blood of the Lord.

Later the Peace became clericalized and formalized, and the actual kiss died out, while 'the tendency to kiss everything else but people increased'.[78] In recent years the revival of the Sign of Peace as a necessary prelude to the eucharistic sharing has been of great significance, for it symbolizes the unity of the Body of Christ in harmony.

The Sign of Peace is immediately followed by the Offertory, a greatly neglected yet vital part of the rite. Rediscovered during the Parish Communion movement in the Church of England after the war, the Offertory has virtually disappeared from the recent revisions. The earlier emphasis, which led to the development of the Offertory procession, is now criticized as placing exaggerated attention on the human offering when, in fact, all that men and women can truly offer to God is their thankfulness.[79] However, in order to see the importance of the Offertory we need to relate it both to the incarnation and to the nature of the baptized community of faith on the other. The bread and wine issue from a baptized Christian group. They are, to that extent, not ordinary, but are offered already, before the consecration, within the sacramental world of grace. In his work *Sacrifice: a doctrinal homily*,[80] an almost unknown study, the late Frederick Hastings Smyth discussed the Offertory in some detail, and his analysis is worthy of attention. According to Smyth, the bread and wine at the Offertory are 'substances of Christian redeeming historical activity'.[81] Every Offertory contains in its substance the historical event of Calvary and the events of subsequent Offertories. In an earlier study, Smyth develops this theme:[72]

> As material objects they have not been produced by unaided man; neither do they emerge from an unredeemed social process. They emerge from the social relationships of a Community which lives and moves in a new Incarnational World, a Communion of the Holy Ghost, a world which continues to clothe the Divine Logos in an ordered pattern whose social perfection triumphs over the difficulties which inhere in the disordered human time-process. They are thus material objects embodying structures of human life still on the natural level of this world, but not *of the fallen world*; for they have been rescued from the meshes of Original Sin. They have been perfected thus by Our Lord himself as he enlarges the boundaries of his redeeming action through the growth of his social humanity. The bread and wine at the Offertory set forth structures in history which have been brought out of the fallen world into the first stage of its redemption.

In his 'high' view of the Offertory, Smyth finds no support in the thought of St Thomas Aquinas, for Aquinas knew nothing of the idea that the bread and wine, prior to their consecration, are already substances which participate in the substance of the incarnate Christ. Transubstantiation comes, in Thomist thought, to mean the replacement of bread and wine by the body and blood, rather than the movement of the one into the other. Smyth, however, introduces the term 'ensubstantiation' to describe the process of Offertory. By this term he means that 'substances formed within our time process have been moved under forms of natural objects, portions of bread and wine, fully and perfectly, into the substances of the growing history of the natural and socially redeeming life of our Lord himself within this present world.'[83] Transubstantiation takes the movement to a further stage: it is a true movement of our Lord's ensubstantiated natural Body and Blood into the supernatural Body and Blood of the Resurrection and Ascension. It refers to the true movement of the substances of the Incarnate Lord's natural Body and Blood under the form of the liturgical Offertorial Bread and Wine, emerging within his social Body the Church, into the substances of that same Body and Blood in their ascended state.[84]

The strength and importance of Smyth's re-interpretation of the relationship of Offertory to eucharistic consecration is in his emphasis that there is *movement*. He goes on to argue – in 1953! – that the 'liturgical and incarnational task' of the Church in the present age is to develop this more accurate view of transubstantiation, for only in this way can the liturgy adequately link time and eternity in a way which does justice to an incarnational materialism. The progress of this movement, to God through matter, is what the Christian liturgy is about. It stresses, through its use of material things, the necessary continuity between time and eternity: 'the operation of the Liturgy is one which deals with the *movement* of substances between two levels of material being'.[85] The neglect of the Offertory through the Middle Ages and beyond, so that it simply became a stage-set for the consecration, led to an unbalanced theology of a descending God and a static view of transformation. The idea of the liturgy as bringing about an actual dynamic transformation both of the bread and wine and of the people through the incarnational movement initiated at the Offertory was lost. If the Church today is to abandon otherworldly spirituality and return to a world-redeeming view of its task, the stress on the role of the liturgy in bringing about real change will need to be recovered. Smyth predicted that 'the political watchword of the New Reformation will be the reaffirmation of Transubstantiation',[86] but not in the static Thomist sense. Rather will it be proclaimed as a word of transforming power, pointing to the fulfilment of the incarnation in the redemption of the material world. The liturgy is thus a deeply subversive act, a spiritual force working within the fallen world to undermine it and renew it.

However, throughout Christian worship runs the perpetual danger of a lapse into otherworldliness and false spirituality, as we seek to break the connection between matter and the work of salvation. John Robinson expressed this danger very well:[87]

The Eucharist presupposes production, and all the means of production, distribution and exchange that lie behind every crumb of bread and drop of wine ... This emphasis is important in connection with the Christian doctrine of matter, and is what distinguishes it from pagan religion and from much harvest festival religion. When men are not altogether averse to any connection between matter and religion, they lean to the idea that God can be encountered in 'nature' – that is, in unspoilt nature. 'God made the countryside, man made the town' is a theme that evokes a ready response in all of us. Bread and wine seem to take us further from God than earth and water, not nearer to him; the element of production bars more than it mediates the divine encounter. At our harvest festivals we fill our churches with vegetable marrows to the exclusion of the much more questionable manufactures, which bear the smear of trade and industry. In this way we seek to find a way to God through matter that bypasses the need for redemption.

Yet it is precisely the need for redemption which is stressed in the movement of the liturgy from Offertory to Consecration. The bread of our lives becomes the Body of Christ, the wine of fellowship becomes his Blood. And in the process we are transformed. The Eucharist is the symbol of the unity of Christ's Body, an effective symbol which brings about what it represents. So the entire eucharistic action reaches its climax in Holy Communion. In one of his sermons, St Augustine describes how the eucharistic sharing creates and develops the unity of the body:

> If now you have received aright, you are what you have received: and so the Apostle expounds the Sacrament of the Lord's Table: *We who are many are one bread, one body.* The bread signifies to you how you ought to love unity. It was made out of many grains of wheat, which were originally separated, but were united by application of water, by a kind of rubbing together, and baked with fire. So have you been ground together by the fast and the exorcism, wetted in Baptism, and baked by the fire of Christ and the mystery of the Holy Spirit . . . and you are made bread, which is the Body of Christ: and here is the symbol of unity.[88]

The bread has often been seen as the symbol of human labour and human struggle, placed upon the altar so that it can be sanctified. It is bread 'which earth has given and human hands have made'.[89] Similarly, the wine has been seen as symbolizing human fellowship, mirth, and hilarity. The theme of 'sober drunkenness' is one which recurs in a number of writers. Thus St Ambrose begins one of his hymns:[90]

Laeti bibamus sobriam
Ebrietatem spiritus –

'Let us joyfully drink of the sober drunkenness of the Spirit.' For, he explains:[91]

> Every time you drink, you receive the remission of sins and are inebriated by the Spirit. That is why the apostle says: Do not get drunk with wine but be filled with the Spirit (Eph. 5.18). For he who gets drunk with wine totters and reels; he who gets drunk with the Spirit is rooted in Christ. So it is an excellent drunkenness that produces sobriety of mind.

Commenting on Ambrose's theme, the late Stanley Evans wrote: 'To be a Christian is to become a controlled drunk, purposively intoxicated with the joy of the life which is perpetually created by God himself.'[92]

In Holy Communion, the liturgical action reaches its peak: here human beings share in the life of the social God, the eucharistic God, the God of the common life. Here God becomes as small as a piece of bread, and little people taste the wonder of eternity. In this essentially social act, the mystical quest becomes one with the quest for community and equality among people.

Throughout the Christian liturgy what is perhaps most vital is that the connection with the world is maintained in its intensity and disturbing character. Liturgy is a microcosm of the work which God is doing in the world, and it is there that salvation is being worked out. In Karl Rahner's words, 'the world and its history are the terrible and sublime liturgy'.[93] Liturgy must never become an alternative world to that of social reality, and liturgical spirituality is based upon

> ... the recognition that worship does not create an 'alternative world' to which we can retreat when ordinary life becomes intolerable ... When liturgy becomes a self-absorbed attempt at 'religious behaviour' or when it calls attention to itself as something 'unworldly', it ceases to be worship and becomes an exercise in self-consciousness. Christian worship is inherently worldly. Its primary symbols are drawn from the messiest activities of human life: giving birth and dying, washing and smearing bodies with oil, eating and drinking, unburdening one's heart in the presence of another. All this is the septic stuff of the world's drama – and the stuff of Christian liturgy as well.[94]

In liturgical worship, the impurity of the materials is important, for it 'invites us to see and hear God in the soiled language of humankind. If this offends us, it is only because we usually prefer to keep God at a distance.' But it is this which the message of the incarnate Christ proclaims to be impossible, and it is to this that the Christian liturgy bears witness in its messiness, impurity, and closeness. Indeed 'liturgical spirituality is possible only for people who are willing to let life be messy, language impure, and God dangerously intimate'.[95] The liturgy is of its very essence incomplete. Its completion must, and can only, lie within the world of the streets and the trouble spots. So the Eucharist ends with the order 'Go in peace to love and serve the Lord': ends, that is, in incompleteness, and in the call to continuity with action in the world. But at the same time the liturgical celebration is a foretaste of the Kingdom that is coming, and it is here that its subversive character exists:

> To take part in the Christian liturgy is to take on one's role in a new kingdom: one that 'shall have no end'. It is the political act of all time and is therefore potentially seditious within the secular politics of a specific time and place. Caesar understood the political nature of the liturgy all too well.[96]

The politics of the liturgy calls all secular political systems into question. For it points, in a hopeful and disturbing way, to the liberation of humankind and of the creation.

The Eucharist and Liberation

The Eucharist thus does not merely look back to the past, or create an alternative religious world in the present: it is 'the first fruits of the sanctification of all creation'.[97] The relationship of the sacrament to reality, of liturgy to life, is crucial, and around this relationship has grown up a fundamental division among Christians. On the one hand are those who see the sacramental world as a wholly separate realm, offering solace and spiritual values unconnected with the way this world runs. The purpose of the sacraments is to enable men and women to ascend from the trials and tribulations of this world to the world of the supernatural. On the other are those for whom the sacrament is the foretaste of a world redeemed. But if this is the case, the eucharistic fellowship places demands upon all who take part in it. For, as Hastings Smyth stressed, Christ

> perfects our present imperfections through his all-encompassing Sacrifice, but only upon the condition that, as he returns our accepted offerings to us in our Holy Communion, we shall determine, with the help of his grace there imparted and quite regardless of the cost to those of us who now lead comfortable lives in the outside world, to better the quality of our gifts at each succeeding Mass. For such bread and wine as we can now obtain within our present economic system can be placed by Catholics

upon their Altars only under firm resolution to eleminate within the world those intolerable disorders which, so long as our present economic system is permitted to endure, must unavoidably continue to enter into their preparation. And this resolution must be taken no matter what the immediate consequences within a disordered world environment, no matter what the danger of great dislocations in economic and political systems, no matter that our resolution may lead us, through the savage resistance of an unredeemed world, on and up the slopes of Calvary and to the Cross.[98]

According to Smyth, Christians who celebrate the Eucharist must always ask: where does this bread, this wine, come from? Was the wheat sown and reaped by men and women living free and happy lives? Was the flour ground in mills and carried on trains or ships by workers employed in conditions of maximal social justice? How have the wheat, the flour, and the bread been brought on to the market? How have they been sold? What of the conditions under which the wine was produced? And so on. In asking these and related questions, Smyth was following in the footsteps of many earlier Anglican socialist thinkers for whom the liturgy of the Eucharist was a symbolic celebration of a transformed world order. Thus for Steward Headlam, the controversial Bethnal Green curate of the late nineteenth century, the Eucharist was the 'sacrament of brotherhood', the 'great Emancipator's supper'.[99] It was also the source of Christian joy and hilarity. 'Our worship, our adoration must be Eucharistic: all joy, mirth, beauty are sanctified by it.'[100] The God of the Eucharist was the God of beauty. Yet, Headlam saw, for many there was no beauty in their lives at all, but only crushing poverty. The Eucharist therefore posed demands in the sphere of justice, for the God of beauty was the God of justice also. Headlam drew direct consequences from the eucharistic sharing for the social and political life of humanity. Those who assisted at Holy Communion, he said, must be holy communists.[101] Similar views on the revolutionary demands of the liturgy were expressed later by Conrad Noel[102] and by Jim Wilson in his pamphlets for the Industrial Christian Fellowship.[103]

In recent years the sense of the Eucharist as a foretaste and anticipation of a new world order in which sharing is expressed in material terms has been recoverd by many Christians. While thousands of churches continue to celebrate the liturgy in a way which proclaims and perpetuates its disconnectedness with real life, there is a widespread, and growing, unease with and rejection of such a posture. The Eucharist is not a world apart, a finished, polished product of the divine order, but part of a movement involving struggle. It can therefore only be celebrated in fear and trembling, in penitence and weakness, in the midst of struggle to effect its life in the world. As a letter from the community at Taizé expressed it:[104]

> The Eucharist is there for us who are weak and defenceless. We receive it in a spirit of poverty and repentence of heart. In our journey through the desert towards a church of sharing, the Eucharist gives us courage not to store up the manna, to give up material reserves, and to share not only the bread of life but also the goods of the earth.

How does the Eucharist give us this courage? Is there something in the act of worship and celebration which provides the link between vision and struggle, which enables us to maintain hope in the midst of despair, which provides us with food for our journey?

In one of his essays, the German theologian Jurgen Moltmann writes of the Eucharist as 'the Feast of Freedom'.[105] For Moltmann, a basic ingredient of eucharistic worship is the element of ecstasy, exuberance, celebration. Liturgy should be an act of festivity, of joy, of liberation, an act in which the powers of the age to come are celebrated in anticipation. Through such festivity, we not only stretch and are stretched beyond ourselves, but we begin now to experience something of the freedom and ecstasy of the Kingdom of God. In the early days of the Church, Athanasius had written that 'the resurrected Christ makes of life a continual feast',[106] and it is this sense of feasting, the 'party spirit' of worship, which we need to recover. The liturgy is a celebration of life, of renewed life, of intense, transformed, liberated life, in which, in the words of Hippolytus, the Church dances with Christ her bridegroom.[107] In the eucharistic festival, Christians are nourished by the memory of past deliverance and look forward in joyful hope to future deliverance. 'It is at the same time the sacrament of memory and hope and, in the harmony of both, the expression of presently experienced liberation.'[108]

However, as Headlam saw clearly in the nineteenth century, unless there is an extension of eucharistic life and eucharistic principles into the social and economic order, unless the experience of Holy Communion produces holy communists, there remains a disconnection between sacrament and reality. The sacramental world becomes a world of separateness, a sanctuary into which we retreat from the harshness and injustice of life. Headlam and his colleagues insisted, against the prevailing thought of Catholic Anglicans, that the sacrament, and the incarnation which was its source, hallowed the whole of the material creation. When Headlam's friend John Oakley approached the Anglo-Catholic divine Canon Liddon with the view that the incarnate Christ, sacramentally present in the Eucharist, had thereby sanctified the beauty of the stage, Liddon was horrified. The purpose of eucharistic worship, he stressed, was to 'enable the soul to mount to the Unseen and the Supersensuous'. Friendship with the things of this world, on the other hand, was pagan rather than Christian.[109] In this clash of positions, one sees in fact two different theologies of the Eucharist and its relation to the world and to human society: a theology of withdrawal and spiritualization, against a theology of transformation.

It is the latter view which has recently been restated by Tissa Balasuriya and Monika Hellwig.[110] Balasuriya calls us to examine the social conditions in which the Eucharist is offered. While eucharistic worship is, in many places, 'still a bulwark of social conservatism and not yet a means of human liberation',[111] this situation represents a serious distortion of the inner meaning and reality of the sacrament. It has been domesticated and so has become an alienating experience, reflecting and even reinforcing the inequalities in the world, instead of undermining them:

> There have been serious distortions in its meaning. Whereas it began with the sacrifice of self for the liberation of others, it has for long been a means of enslavement and domestication of believers. The Eucharist has always remained central to Christianity; but it has been adjusted to suit the needs of the dominant groups in the churches. There has been a *social conditioning of the Eucharist*.[112]

Christians today are called to help free the Eucharist from its social captivity so that it can again become the source of divine freedom and of human transformation. It is a call to move from magical and non-historical approaches to the sacrament and return to the historical realism within which alone eucharistic worship makes sense.[113]

In our time there have been many who have felt so painfully the alienating character of worship and the violent split between liturgy and life that they have felt pushed to abandon the celebration of the Eucharist altogether. Thus the South American priest Camillo Torres, on 24 June 1965, ceased to celebrate the Eucharist, and surrendered 'one of the rights I love most dearly – to be able to celebrate the external rite of the church as a priest – in order to create the conditions that make the cult more authentic'.[114] That is a position which demands respect. But it cannot be satisfying to many Christians who wish to hold fast both to the external rite and to the changing of conditions which are anti-eucharistic. They can only remain faithful in their discipleship if their eucharistic celebration leads them to struggle and strive to create a eucharistic world, reflecting the image and character of the eucharistic God.

10

The Crucified God

*God has died! If this does not startle us, what will? The
Church must keep this astonishment alive. The Church
ceases to exist when she loses this astonishment. Theology,
the precise understanding of the gospel, must be seized by
this astonishment more than anyone else.*

Kazah Kitamori[1]

The Divine Pain

Thousands of people were crucified during the sixty-five-year period
between the incorporation of Judaea into the provincial structure of
the Roman Empire and the end of the Jewish War. Virtually all of
them are forgotten. For crucifixion was a shameful death, a cursed
death. Certainly there was a Jewish tradition that prophets were
killed, and that the righteous man was exalted through suffering and
death. But the idea of a crucified saviour, even less a 'crucified
Messiah', would have seemed barbaric and insane to the pious Jewish
mind. Yet it was precisely this claim which the Christian community
held out as its message of salvation: that in the crucifixion of Jesus of
Nazareth, the divine purpose of salvation was accomplished through
the experience of divine pain. God was in the pain, in the suffering, in
the dying of Jesus. And yet the very idea of a crucified God could only
be received with amazement and horror. If that experience of the
cross of Christ is central to the Christian movement, then Christian
theology, Christian reflection on the drama of salvation, can only take
its origin from the experience of amazement and horror. Like
Jeremiah the theologian may well cry out: 'Be appalled, O heavens, at
this, be shocked, be utterly desolate.' (Jer. 2.12)

In the death of Jesus, according to the Christian Church, God
suffered and died. God was in Christ reconciling the world to himself
(2 Cor. 5.19). God suffered pain. Many writers have claimed that it is
only the intense implication of God in the pain of the world which
makes belief in God possible at all. So Frances Young speaks of the
moral necessity of a 'Calvary-centred religious myth':

> It is only because I can see God entering the darkness of human
> suffering and evil in his creation, recognizing it for what it really is,
> meeting it and conquering it, that I can accept a religious view of
> the world. Without the religious dimension, life would be

299

senseless, and endurance of its cruelty pointless; yet without the cross it would be impossible to believe in God.[2]

Faith therefore calls for an experience of atonement, calls for God to deal with evil. Christians hold that in the event of Calvary, God entered the darkness of human pain and changed it, made it glorious and redemptive, made it the instrument of deliverance and transformation. But for this to be so, it is necessary to see God in the pain and the dying. There must have been a Calvary in the heart of God before it could have been planted on that hill outside the city of Jerusalem. In Luther's words, 'the absolute necessity for the sacrifice of the Son is grounded in God himself'.[3] Some Christian thinkers, such as Pascal, have spoken of Jesus being in agony until the end of time: for his suffering cannot cease until human liberation and human salvation has been fulfilled.[4] So while the physical suffering of Jesus on Calvary occurred once and for all and can never be repeated, there is a prolonged sharing by God in the pain of humankind, God remains a suffering God, a passionate God.

It is, however, possible to hold to the suffering of Christ, and to see in that suffering an identity with our own, and yet to make no progress beyond the affirmation of ourselves in our plight. The crucified God must also be seen as the God beyond crucifixion, the God of the new age, the risen Saviour. For without the victory over death, nothing has changed. God has expressed sympathy, solidarity, but that is all. So while Christ can never be, in Edwin Muir's term, the 'uncrucified',[5] he is none the less the Christ who lives beyond crucifixion. It is in this experience of suffering and of death that the Christian faith sees the manifestation of the love and mercy of God. And somehow that love and the mercy are only manifested through the experience of the horror of human sin:

> It seems that in the love of God, in the love which is God, there is something which only sin can let us understand. The paradox is bold; but the Church has made it her own in singing on Holy Saturday *O felix culpa!* Sin kindles divine wrath. But approached, as it were, across his wrath, God's love is shown us anew: and it is as if we enjoy, by his favour, a sudden piercing insight into the eternal secrets of his very heart. This is the incomprehensible mystery of the kenosis, of the God who becomes poor to make us rich, who compels himself to feel bodily the blows we inflict on him in order to pardon the infliction. On the Cross the godhead seems to lay itself waste. God the ultimate judge of all the world interposes himself as a screen against his own anger. Better – the Almighty gives himself up to sinners and they work their will on

him. But had the creature never seen this *Deus patiens*, would he never have understood the limitless self-giving which is the very inner stuff of God's being? So maybe this torrent of fire had to be poured out upon the world that in the floods we should catch some far-off echo of the eternal springs.[6]

Through the event of the crucified God, Christians claim, we can perceive something of the divine self-giving.

In the cross of Christ we begin to experience the yearning of the heart of God (Jer. 31.20), literally the piercing of that heart. Luther translated this line from Jeremiah as *darum bricht mir mein herz*: therefore my heart is broken. God is in pain, and this pain is an aspect of the divine–human relationship. God on the cross means God in pain. Yet through his wounds we have been healed (1 Pet. 2.24). Our God is an 'agonizing God',[7] a crucified God, a suffering God. In the very beginnings of the Christian era, Ignatius of Antioch spoke of the suffering of God. But the crucial step towards understanding the identity of Christ's pain with the pain of God was the formula of the Council of Ephesus of 431 concerning the divine motherhood of Mary. Mary, proclaimed Ephesus, was *Theotokos*, the God-bearer, the Mother of God. She was the mother of the flesh of God. It was this assertion which, after centuries of reflection, led to the theopaschite (literally, 'God-suffering') formula, the claim that God had suffered in the flesh.[8] For, as Gregory of Nazianzen had stressed, 'we needed a God made flesh and put to death in order that we could live again'.[9] Gregory speaks of the blood of God and of the crucified God, a term which was later taken up by Luther who speaks of the *Deus crucifixus*. The essential theological point is that the suffering of Jesus is not something which can be separated from the suffering of God. Rather, in the words of a nineteenth-century writer:[10]

> The whole Deity is in it, in it from eternity, and will to eternity be ... Nay, there is a cross in God before the wood is seen upon Calvary; hid in God's own virtue itself, struggling on heavily in burdened feeling through all the previous ages, struggling as heavily now even in the throne of the worlds.

In reflecting and brooding on the suffering of God on the Christ event, Christians have been led to see the extension of the Passion into the life of the human family. So the poet Wilfred Owen could write of his wartime experience:[11]

> For fourteen hours yesterday I was at work – teaching Christ to lift his cross by numbers, and how to adjust his crown, and not to imagine he thirst until the last halt. I attended his supper to see that

there were no complaints; and inspected his feet that they should be worthy of the nails. I see to it that he is dumb and stands at attention before his accusers. With a piece of silver I buy him every day, and with maps I make him familiar with the topography of Golgotha.

Owen, in his bitterness of soul bordering on despair, saw in the pain of warfare and the suffering it caused, something of the pain of Christ. Shaped and nourished by the same period, the Anglican archbishop William Temple spoke of the suffering of God,[12] while his contemporary G. A. Studdert Kennedy (known throughout Britain as 'Woodbine Willie') 'spoke of God as the greatest sufferer of all'.[13] The German theologian Karl Barth, who, more than any other Christian writer of his day, stressed the transcendence of God, also pointed to the participation of God in suffering:

> It is not at all the case that God has no part in the suffering of Jesus Christ even in his mode of being as the Father ... This fatherly fellow-suffering of God is the mystery, the basis of the humiliation of his Son, the truth of that which takes place historically in his crucifixion.[14]

Barth saw the horror and hopelessness of the human predicament:

> So dark is our situation that God himself must enter and occupy it in order that it may be light. We cannot fully understand the Christian 'God with us' without the greatest astonishment at the glory of the divine grace and the greatest horror at our own plight.[15]

In the cross, therefore, we see the activity of the Trinity. God is in Christ, engaged in the work of atonement and reconciliation. Without this direct involvement of God, human life is without hope and without fulfilment. Such is the enormity of the Christian claim.

The most detailed and most widely read theological study of the suffering of God in Christ to have appeared in recent years is undoubtedly Jurgen Moltmann's *The Crucified God*.[16] Moltmann points out that in the theme of the suffering God we are actually confronted with a view of God which is opposed to the god of conventional theism:

> In the metaphysical concept of God from ancient cosmology and the modern psychological concept of God, the being of the Godhead ... as the zone of the impossibility of death stands in juxtaposition to human being as the zone of the necessity of death. If this concept of God is applied to Christ's death on the cross, the

cross *must* be 'evacuated' of deity, for by definition God cannot suffer and die. He is pure causality. But Christian theology must think of God's being in suffering and dying and finally in the death of Jesus, if it is not to surrender itself and lose its identity. Suffering and dying and similar negations simply cannot be predicated of that which is conceived of as pure causality and the unconditional mover. The God who was the subject of suffering could not be truly God ... With the Christian message of the Cross of Christ, something new and strange has entered the metaphysical world. For this faith must understand the deity of God from the event of the suffering and death of the Son of God, and thus bring about a fundamental change in the orders of being of metaphysical thought ... It must think of the suffering of Christ as the power of God and the death of Christ as God's potentiality.[17]

Christian faith then, according to Moltmann, must be clearly distinguished from radical monotheism. It stands over against the theistic concept of God as the unmoved mover, and instead sees God as supremely revealed in the suffering of the human Christ. Theism thinks of God at the expense of humanity, as an all-powerful, perfect, and infinite being. The human person, by contrast, is weak, imperfect, and finite. Atheism, on the other hand, is, according to Moltmann, simply a reversed form of theism, thinking of man at God's expense. In the crucified Christ he sees a way of understanding, and responding to, God beyond theism and atheism, a way which unites the divine and human, a way in which we begin to see into the heart of suffering and thus into the inner reality of God. Through his self-humiliation in the death of Christ, God creates the conditions for communion with himself. So God is known and loved in and through the pain of the dying Christ.

Moltmann sees his understanding of the crucified God to have important consequences for our response to the presence of God in the sufferings of others. God bears in his heart all the wounds of the human family, and it is through the encounter with pain and suffering that we come to see the meaning of God's presence in the world. The point is brought home forcibly in an account by Elie Wiesel of one of the Nazi atrocities in which two Jewish men and a boy are killed before a gathering:[18]

The SS bury two Jewish men and a boy before the assembled inhabitants of the camp. The men died quickly, but the death struggle of the boy lasted half an hour. 'Where is God? Where is he?' a man behind me asked. As the boy, after a long time, was still in agony on the rope, I heard the man cry again 'Where is God now?' And I heard a voice within me answer, 'Here he is – he is hanging here on this gallows.'

So the victim figure of Christ is seen and identified in the tortured figures and faces of countless victims of human sin and cruelty. Both incarnation and passion are extended into the world of men and women made in God's image, stamped with his capacity for pain, affirmed in their deified humanity by the pain and the victory of the divine sufferer.

'We preach Christ crucified'

The cross, in Christian understanding, is an act within the being of God. God is in Christ, in the work of reconciliation. The whole of the Godhead is present in the experience of Calvary. The New Testament speaks of God delivering up his Son: he gave him up for us all as Abraham gave up his only son (Rom. 8.32; Gen. 22.12). Jesus was put to death for our trespasses as was the suffering servant of Isaiah 53 (Rom. 4.25; Isa. 53.12). Elsewhere Jesus is said to have given up his own life. He gave himself for our sins (Gal. 1.4), gave himself for me (2.20), for us (Eph. 5.2), for the Church (5.25), for the people (Titus 2.14), for everyone (1 Tim. 2.6). Christ died for our sins (1 Cor. 15.3).

It is very likely that the claim of Jesus to be the Christ was taken to involve the abolition of the temple as the place of atonement. As the one who would destroy the temple, this figure was seen as subverting the entire redemptive process of the Jewish religion. Because of this, Paul saw his role to be that of persecutor of the Church. Looking back to the historical Jesus, he saw a man who, in his life and teaching, undermined the capacity of the law to achieve purification and sanctification, to bring men and women into the holy place, the place of communion with God. Later, after his conversion, Paul refused any longer to know Christ according to the flesh. 'From now on, therefore, we regard no one from a human point of view; even though we once regarded Christ from a human point of view, we regard him thus no longer.' (2 Cor. 5.16) On the other hand, he was in no doubt that Christ was known and manifested *in* the flesh (Rom. 8.3). And it was the event of his crucifixion, the event of his dying in the flesh, which was to become the central word in the proclamation of salvation. Paul preached 'the word of the cross' (1 Cor. 1.18), the message of the crucified Messiah, Christ crucified (1.23).

In the writings of St Paul, Christ's death is seen as an offering for humanity. Christ died *for* us. This idea has often, in Christian history, been described in the language of substitution. Yet in the Jewish ritual, the guilt of the offerer of a sacrifice was not transferred to the victim offered (by substitution). It was in fact precisely because the victim was pure and not contaminated by human sin that it was offered at all. In the New Testament writings, Christ is seen as the sinless offering who suffers on our behalf. The Greek words which are used are *huper* (on behalf of, Rom. 5.6; 14.15; 1 Cor. 15.3; 2 Cor. 5.14–15; 1 Thess. 5.10; 1 Tim. 2.6) or *dia* (because of, 1 Cor. 8.1) or *peri* (Acts 20.28). The word *anti*, on which substitutionary views are based, occurs only in Mark 10.45 and Matt. 20.28. In fact, the support for a substitutionary view of atonement as representing the theology of St Paul is very weak. Speaking of the Pauline texts, a careful scholar has written that 'the support which they lend to this theory is much less solid that some scholars have supposed, and . . . in none of them is it stated unambiguously'.[19] However, he goes on to say that there are passages in which the possibility of substitutionary thought cannot be excluded.

The substitutionary view of Christ's atoning work is based on a number of Pauline texts, in particular on Romans 8.3–4, 2 Corinthians 5.21, and Galatians 3.13. In Romans 8.3–4, God is said to have sent his Son in the likeness of sinful flesh and for sin, and so to have condemned sin in the flesh. Thus the just requirement of the law has been fulfilled in us. Christ is thus seen as an offering for sin, seen in fact as dealing with sin as the law required (Lev. 4.3). In 2 Corinthians 5.21 God is said to have 'made him to be sin who knew no sin, so that in him we might become the righteousness of God' (5.21). Galatians 3.13 says that Christ became a curse for us, and it cites the line from Deuteronomy 21.23: 'Cursed be every one who hangs on a tree.' In fact, none of these texts necessarily involves a substitutionary doctrine. The first teaches that Christ was sent in a human form like that of sinful humanity, and in his humanity was made a sin-offering, a sacrifice for sin. St Augustine, commenting on the passage in Corinthians, interprets it in sacrificial terms, while Gregory of Nyssa stresses the transformation of sin into righteousness.[20]

Again, there are certainly ideas of ransom and purchase in connection with Christ's death. 'You were bought with a price' says Paul (1 Cor. 6.20; 7.23). Christ has redeemed us, that is, bought us back (Gal. 3.13; 4.5). However, in none of these sentences is there any reference to the question of to whom the purchase price was paid, and the theme should not be pressed too far in a literal way. The word *lutron*, ransom, is not in fact found in Paul, but only in Mark 10.45/ Matthew 20.28 where Jesus is said to have come to give his life as a ransom for many. *Lutron* occurs nowhere else in the New Testament, though *antilutron* appears in 1 Timothy 2.6. It is from *lutron* that the word *apolutrōsis* is derived, with its original meaning of the price paid for freedom. The verb *lutrousthai*, used with God as its subject, means that God has secured our release by his power. In the New Testament it is often used in the general sense of release or deliverance without any reference to price. Thus God has visited and redeemed his people (Luke 1.68). Christ has secured an eternal redemption (Heb. 9.12). At the end of Luke's Gospel, the disciples speak of their hope that Jesus was the one who was to redeem Israel (Luke 24.21). Again, Jesus is said by Paul to have given himself for us to redeem us (Titus 2.14), and Peter speaks of our having been 'ransomed from our foolish ways' (1 Pet. 1.18). In none of these references is price involved.

In Romans 3.25 Christ is referred to as *hilastērion*, the term used in Hebrews 9.5 and translated there as 'mercy seat'. Some have seen this term to involve propitiation.[21] But again it is not clear that this is the meaning. The late T. W. Manson[22] argued that the point was that Christ was identified with the mercy seat, the place of atonement, and that his cross was the place where God's mercy was supremely shown. The term is one of a number of sacrificial terms used in connection with the death of Christ. Thus his blood is described as the blood of the new covenant (1 Cor. 11.25). It brings justification and salvation (Rom. 5.9). Christ is identified with the paschal lamb of the old covenant, yet he brings a greater and universal deliverance (1 Cor. 5.7). Through the blood of the cross he has reconciled to himself all things and has created a state of peace (Col. 1.20; Eph. 2.17). Through his blood, we enjoy peace with God (Rom. 5.1). The stress in the New Testament letters is not on propitiation. Certainly any idea of celestial bribery is absent.[23] Rather the stress is on the restoration of a right relationship with God, a relationship which involves the transformation of human beings who, set free by the cross of Christ, are to be changed, to become a new creation, and to share his glory.

Thus a central idea in the early Christian understanding of the cross is that of reconciliation. This is not, however, to say that the actual words 'reconciliation' or 'to reconcile' are frequent in New Testament writing. Indeed we have to recognize 'the statistical fact that both noun (reconciliation) and verb (to reconcile) are only sparsely represented in the New Testament literature'.[24] It is certainly wrong to see reconciliation as the only theme in the understanding of salvation. As Lochman has written:[25]

> The doctrine of reconciliation has only a relatively narrow base in the New Testament and in church history. It would be a dubious restriction of soteriology if we were to reduce the message of

salvation to the theme of reconciliation.

The actual terms occur only in Paul (apart from the reference in Matthew 5.24 about the need to be reconciled with one's brother before offering a gift at the altar). According to Paul, we *were* reconciled to God by the death of his Son. Now that we *are* reconciled, we *shall be* saved by his life (Rom. 5.10). In this one verse, past, present, and future tenses are used. Reconciliation was achieved by the historic event of Christ's death. It is also a present experience, a present reality, and from this experience we look forward to a salvation through the life of Christ in us. Reconciliation is thus something which we have received from God through Christ (5.11).

Another key passage for reconciliation language is 2 Corinthians 5.1–21. To be in Christ, Paul says, is to exist within a new creation. God, through Christ has reconciled us to himself, and has also given to us 'the ministry (*diakonia*) of reconciliation' (5.18). God was in Christ reconciling the world to himself, and has given to us the message of reconciliation. Thus, as ambassadors of Christ, Christians urge others to 'be reconciled to God' (5.20). In two magnificent passages in Ephesians and Colossians, the reconciliation is seen in cosmic terms. Those who were far off have been 'brought near in the blood of Christ'. Christ is our peace, has broken down the dividing wall of hostility, created one new humanity, and so reconciled us to God (Eph. 2.13–16). In Colossians, the purpose of Christ is described as being 'to reconcile to himself all things, whether on earth or in heaven, making peace by the blood of his cross'. And it is the death of Christ which is seen as central to this reconciling work, for 'he has now reconciled in his body of flesh by his death' those who were formerly estranged and alienated (Col. 1.19–21).

While the actual terms are not widely used in Paul, the theme of reconciliation is much wider than the use of the words. For reconciliation is close in its meaning to justification, to peace, to that ending of division and hostility which is seen as basic to the achievement of Christ. Central to all these terms is the idea of a change in relationship. In secular usage, the term reconciliation was often used of changes in the social and political area. So the death of Christ is seen as bringing about a real change in human life and human society. But at no point is reconciliation seen as something which is easily achieved. There is no comfortable harmony in the New Testament: reconciliation and atonement are brought about only through suffering and the shedding of blood, through bitter death, through terrible struggle with the principalities and powers of the fallen world. So reconciliation is seen as the culmination of a work of sacrifice. And the theme of Christ's death as sacrificial is located in the symbolism of the Passover, the great act of deliverance which provides the framework for the Christian liturgy of the passion and resurrection.

'To be a Christian, Paul says, is to live at Passover time, to stand in the light of Easter morning, in a new life.'[26] The Christian Passover begins with the sacrifice of the paschal lamb on Calvary. In Paul Christ is also compared to the sacrifice offered on the Day of Atonement (Rom. 3.25), to the sin-offering (8.3) and to the burnt offering (Eph. 5.2). His death is seen as the culmination of the entire sacrificial system, the one perfect sacrifice for the sins of all people. And this sacrifice is not merely an event for which we are grateful; it begins the process of transformation and sanctification of a paschal community:

> Do you not know that a little leaven leavens the whole lump? Cleanse out the old leaven that you may be a new lump, as you really are unleavened. For Christ, our paschal lamb, has been sacrificed. Let us therefore celebrate the festival, not with the old leaven, the leaven of malice and evil, but with the unleavened bread of sincerity and truth. (Cor. 5.6–8)

Similarly Paul speaks in Romans of the consecration of the whole lump through the first portion; 'If the dough offered as first fruits is holy, so is the whole lump; and if the root is holy, so are the branches' (Rom. 11.16). Christ's death thus initiates the process of sanctification. It reverses the Adamic realm of death, so that whereas all people died 'in Adam' so will all come to new life 'in Christ' (1 Cor. 15.22). Christ is the 'first fruits' (15.23). Through his death we have access to God.

In Romans 5, Paul writes that peace is the result of justification, and through the restoration of peace with God, we have also received 'access' to grace. Through this grace we come to share in God's glory (5.1–2). The idea comes again in Ephesians: 'And he came and preached peace to you who were far off and peace to those who were near; for through him we both have access in one Spirit to the Father' (Eph. 2.17). In Christ we 'have boldness and confidence of access' (3.12). The access theme is central in the cultic symbolism of Hebrews in which Christ is seen as the new High Priest:

> Since then we have a great high priest who has passed through the heavens, Jesus, the Son of God, let us hold fast our confession. For we have not a high priest who is unable to sympathize with our weaknesses, but one who in every respect has been tempted as we

are, yet without sin. Let us then with confidence draw near to the throne of grace, that we may receive mercy and find grace to help in time of need. (Heb. 4.14–16)

We have confidence, says the author, to enter the heavenly sanctuary by the blood of Jesus, by a new and living way, that is, through the flesh of Christ (10.19–20). In similar vein, Peter explains that the purpose of Christ's death was to bring us to God (1 Pet. 3.18). To do justice to the central importance of the death of Christ in the New Testament letters would require a more detailed and lengthier treatment. The cross is the heart of all the teaching and preaching. That God was in Christ, at work through the mystery of his death, is basic to the faith of the earliest Christians. But how did Jesus himself view his own death?

Jesus and His Cross

The theme of the dying hero was one with which Roman and Greek society was familiar. There are many accounts and legends of deaths leading to deification. But such themes are entirely absent from the Old Testament. There is no case of the transportation of a dead person to heaven, though there are two cases of living persons, Enoch and Elijah, who were transported. But there is no cultus of dead heroes, and indeed Yahwism forbade any such cultus: 'the glorification or even the superhuman transfiguration of the martyr is completely alien to the Old Testament. It simply does not occur in ancient Israel.'[27] Only in the apocalyptic section of Daniel does martyrdom become an issue in the canonical Old Testament (Dan. 11.33ff). Until the Maccabean period there is no instance of a martyr who dies for Israel. Those who die for God's sake are mourned rather than celebrated, and God is blamed:

Nay, for thy sake we are slain all the day long,
and accounted as sheep for the slaughter.
Rouse thyself! Why sleepest thou, O Lord?
Awake! Do not cast us off for ever! (Ps. 44.22–3)

The Old Testament knows no theology of martyrdom. Only in the Books of Maccabees is there any suggestion that death might be in some sense sacrificial, or that sacrifice and sin-bearing might be united. In 1 Maccabees, Mattathias tells his sons to give their lives for (huper) the covenant, and that in doing so they will receive glory and an everlasting name (1 Macc. 2.50). Eleazar gave his life to save his people (6.44) and prayed that his death may help to cleanse the nation (4 Macc. 6.27–9). He spoke of the blood of the righteous and of their deaths of propitiatory (*hilastērion*, 4 Macc. 17.20–22).

However, it seems highly unlikely that these ideas influenced the understanding of Jesus in regard to his own death and its significance. Nor was the idea of a suffering Messiah a part of the widespread Messianic hope in mainstream Judaism. Only in Isaiah 53 can we see a possible source for such a view of Jesus as a suffering Messiah. Here is described one without form or comeliness, a 'man of sorrows' who is despised and rejected (Isa. 53.2–3). The passage continues:

> Surely he has borne our griefs
> and carried our sorrows;
> yet we esteemed him stricken,
> smitten by God, and afflicted.
> But he was wounded for our transgressions,
> he was bruised for our iniquities;
> upon him was the chastisement that made us whole,
> and with his stripes we are healed.
> All we like sheep have gone astray;
> we have turned every one to his own way;
> and the Lord has laid on him
> the iniquity of us all. (53.4–6)

Isaiah 53 is 'the only Old Testament text which could have prompted the beginning of [the] development' of the theme of a crucified Messiah, though there is no clear evidence from pre-Christian Judaism that it was interpreted in this way.[28] At the same time, it cannot be written off, for the language of the 'surrender' of Jesus, of his representative dying 'for many' and 'for us' would probably not have come into use had it not been for the background of this prophecy.

Did Jesus see his own death in this way? We cannot know for certain. In the Gospel accounts he is accused of Sabbath-breaking, of blasphemy, and of sorcery, all of which carried death penalties by stoning and the hanging of the dead body. However, there is no reference to death in Mark until Chapter 6, and this is to the death of John the Baptist. Perhaps the first suggestion of a reference to Jesus' own death is in the saying about the generation which demands a sign. Mark simply records that no sign will be given (Mark 8.12) but in Matthew there is the addition 'except the sign of Jonah' (16.2), and this is explained in an earlier passage with reference to the presence of the Son of Man for three days in the heart of the earth (12.40). However, the Marcan chapter continues by a very clear reference to the death of the Son of Man.

And he began to teach them that the Son of Man must suffer many things, and be rejected by the elders and the chief priests and the scribes, and be killed, and after three days rise again. And he said this plainly. (8.31–2)

Matthew notes that from this time he began to show his disciples that death was inevitable (16.21). The Son of Man was to be delivered up, killed, and after three days would rise again. But the disciples did not understand what he meant (Mark 9.31–2). The teaching is repeated from then onwards (10.33).

It seems likely that Jesus saw himself as a prophet, and death was a common fate of prophets. Thus he lashes out in fury at the Pharisees:

Woe to you, scribes and Pharisees, hypocrites! for you build the tombs of the prophets and adorn the monuments of the righteous, saying, 'If we had lived in the days of our fathers, we would not have taken part with them in shedding the blood of the prophets.' Thus you witness against yourselves, that you are sons of those who murdered the prophets. Fill up, then, the measure of your fathers. You serpents, you brood of vipers, how are you to escape being sentenced to hell? Therefore I send you prophets and wise men and scribes, some of whom you will kill and crucify, and some you will scourge in your synagogues and persecute from town to town, that upon you may come all the righteous blood shed on earth, from the blood of innocent Abel to the blood of Zechariah the son of Barachiah, whom you murdered between the sanctuary and the altar. Truly, I say to you, all this will come upon this generation.

O Jerusalem, Jerusalem, killing the prophets and stoning those who are sent to you! How often would I have gathered your children together as a hen gathers her brood under her wings, and you could not! Behold, your house is forsaken and desolate. For I tell you, you will not see me again, until you say, 'Blessed is he who comes in the name of the Lord.' (Matt. 23.29–39)

This is an interesting passage, for it not only seems to identify Jesus with the prophetic tradition, but it also relates the sufferings of the earlier prophets and indeed of all righteous persons from Abel onwards to a universal guilt, focused upon the scribes and Pharisees as representative of a rejecting and hard-hearted people. There is a specific reference to crucifixion, and an implicit identification of Jesus himself with God as a mother hen. In the equivalent passage in Luke, the identification of Jesus with the prophetic movement is even clearer, for 'it cannot be that a prophet should perish away from

Jerusalem' (Luke 13.33).

Jesus' sense that death was his fate is linked in Mark with the fulfilment of Old Testament prophecy, an element which is later developed by Matthew with increased use of Old Testament texts. At his trial before Caiaphas, the claim is made that he had threatened to destroy the temple, and while this is interpreted in John as a reference to his body (2.19) it is likely that it was seen from an early stage as an attack on the sacrificial system.

So important are the events of the passion and death of Jesus in the Gospels that they occupy a considerable amount of space. In Mark one-third of the narrative is taken up with the last week of Jesus' life. All the writers are agreed that the death was predicted and predetermined, and that it was a result also of human plotting. In Mark, the path of Jesus to his death is marked by an intense loneliness, as the sheep are scattered and fall away (14.26). Yet he is convinced that through his death salvation will be achieved (10.45). Mark records that at his death the veil of the temple was torn (15.38). Whether this was literal or symbolic, the sacrificial meaning is inescapable: that the death of Jesus has opened the way to the Holy of Holies, an action for which his cleansing of the temple, with its citation of Isaiah 56.7, had prepared the ground. The old sacrificial order has been superseded. In his death Jesus sees both the ending of the old era and the beginning of the new, for his death is seen in relation to the coming of the Son of Man in power and glory (Mark 14.62).

However, had the final charge been one of blasphemy, such as the threat to the temple which might have been seen as both blasphemous and a claim to messianic status, the penalty would have been stoning. It is clear from the accounts that there were political motives also for the trial and sentence of Jesus. The Sanhedrin condemned him but did not execute the sentence although they could have had Jesus stoned, burned, beheaded, or strangled. Instead he was crucified, and Mark 15.26 makes it clear that the charge was one of sedition. This fact has led to considerable speculation about the relationship of Jesus to the Zealot movements and to the Galilean resistance. It is certainly clear that a 'non-political' understanding of the death of Jesus does not do justice to the Gospels. Many, however, have seen the political interpretation of Jesus as an unfortunate misunderstanding of his role and claims. Thus Bultmann:[29]

> What is certain is merely that he was crucified by the Romans, and thus suffered the death of a political criminal. This death can scarcely be understood as an inherent and necessary consequence of his activity; rather it took place because his activity was

misconstrued as a political activity. In that case it would have been
– historically speaking – a meaningless fate.

Such a view has come under heavy fire in recent years. Jesus did not
live in a world in which a simple distinction between religion and
politics was possible. The proclamation of the Kingdom of God in the
context of the Galilean movements was bound to be a deeply political
activity. In Moltmann's words:[30]

> The gospel of Jesus and his public behaviour were political in the
> extreme. He was bound to be understood as both religious and
> political, even if this did not mean that he himself was not
> understood as an object of faith. Consequently, he alienated both
> the anti-Roman Zealots and the anti-Jewish Romans. Both knew
> their business, the use of armed force as divine judgement, as was
> the custom in the world of that time. But Jesus interfered in this
> religious and political business to challenge and disrupt its rules,
> and 'had to be' removed.

The cross was, from one important perspective, a political act. Jesus
was killed by the combined powers of church and state, by the
religious and political establishments, by 'a coalition of the worldlings
and the next-worldlings'.[31] Yet clearly a purely political understanding of his death would be as incomplete as a purely religious one. The
politics of Jesus involved a commitment to the redemptive power of
suffering, to the power of non-violent love as the way of Messiahship.
How much the human Jesus was conscious of his messianic role
remains, and doubtless will remain, unclear. Yet 'if Jesus had no
messianic features at all, the origin of the Christian kerygma would
remain completely inexplicable and mysterious'.[32]

Theologia Crucis

As a historical and political reality, the cross of Christ undermines all
attempts to spiritualize the meaning of salvation. God works salvation
in the midst of the earth, and this salvation cannot be reduced to an
otherworldly or inward experience. As a theological and spiritual
reality, the cross stands over against all earthly political and religious
systems, like a divine question mark. In Moltmann's words, 'the
theology of the cross is a critical and liberating theory of God and
man',[33] A Church identified with the cross as the pivotal point of its
theology must stand over against its surrounding culture and
environment, and see God revealed in weakness and God-forsaken-
ness, in darkness and negation. The theology of the cross is a theology
of contradiction, of protest, of conflict, a theology which refuses an

easy conformity with conventional norms and attitudes. It begins, as crucifixion itself did, in horror and scandal, for this most degrading form of punishment was not even fit to be spoken of among decent people.[34]

So scandalous was the whole idea of death by crucifixion that 'the idea of a "crucified God" to whom veneration and worship were due was regarded in the ancient world as totally inappropriate to God'.[35] One early drawing showed Christ crucified with the head of an ass, so absurd was the notion of a crucified God seen by intelligent people. It was, as Paul said, foolishness (1 Cor. 1.23), yet the early Christians saw it as 'the foolishness of God' (1.25). Through this act of foolishness, they claimed, salvation had come to the world.

'To save' comes from the Hebrew *jasha* (with the noun *Jeshua*, saviour). Its root means to be roomy, broad, its opposite being oppressed, or hemmed in, confined. It was often used of the future gathering in of God's people (Jer. 31.7; 46.27; Zeph. 3.19; Zech. 8.7; Ps. 106.47). And in the New Testament too salvation is seen in terms of a future act. Thus Christ who was offered once for all to bear the sins of many will appear a second time not to deal with sin but to save those who wait for him (Heb. 9.28). Salvation will be revealed in the last time (1 Pet. 1.5). Salvation is seen as something which will happen (1.9), something to which we 'grew up' (2.2). There is progress in salvation for we are 'being saved' (Acts 2.47). Yet the New Testament is clear that there is a sense in which the decisive act of salvation has already happened. By grace we *have been* saved (Eph. 2.8), we *were* saved (Rom. 8.24). And at the centre of the saving process stands the cross.

While there have been a number of ways of interpreting the cross in Christian history, the tradition which has survived and continues to offer the most satisfactory approach to a theology of the cross is that which Gustav Aulen termed the 'classical' view.[36] It was expressed in the early centuries of the Church by Irenaeus: 'The Word of God was made flesh in order that he might destroy death and bring man to life: for we were tied and bound in sin, we were born in sin and live under the dominion of death.'[37] Through the cross Christ has achieved victory and set men and women free from bondage to slavery and all forms of oppression. The cross is therefore to be seen primarily as an act of liberation. It is only through liberation that reconciliation comes. In his critique of 'one-dimensional' views of salvation, the Czech theologian Jan Milic Lochman points to the potential within the classical doctrine.

There is a dimension of solidarity . . . a cosmic and ecumenical dimension in this theory of the atonement, inseparable from its realism ... The classical theory of the atonement deserves to be taken very seriously today not least for its vision of reconciliation as liberation.[38]

The classical view speaks of Christ's conquest, his work of deliverance, through the apparent defeat of the cross. The tree of defeat has become the tree of victory. In the words of the ancient office hymn for Passiontide:

> Fulfilled is all that David told
> In true prophetic song of old.
> 'Amidst the nations, God' saith he,
> 'Hath reigned and triumphed from the tree.'

Yet this victory is only achieved through the experience of dereliction and pain. Thus both a masochistic theology of acquiescence in suffering, and an easy triumphalism, are rejected by the theology of the cross. The good news is a message of victory through pain, victory over death by death. The cross is not tragedy, a tragic event which was then rectified by the experience of Easter morning. Victory is within the cross itself: there death tasted of life and was vanquished. And yet Christ's despoiling of the powers occurred in the context of his own separation from God, of his own identification with the plight of humanity. In his encounter with death, Christ entered into the darkness of the human condition, entered the abyss, and gave to it both light and life.

The sense of victory in and through the bitterness of Calvary is expressed most powerfully in liturgy. In the Solemn Liturgy of the Passion, as celebrated in the Western Church on Good Friday, there is a threefold pattern: the reading of the Passion in the Johannine account; the Exaltation and Veneration of the Cross; and finally the reception of Communion. So there is remembrance, there is worship, and there is union. We recall the cross, we venerate it, and we seek to be identified in heart and in activity with the crucified. In the exaltation of the cross there is the cry 'Behold, the wood of the cross on which was hung the world's salvation!' and afterwards the hymn *Pange lingua* is sung:

> Sing my tongue the glorious battle!
> Sing the ending of the fray!
> Now above the Cross the trophy.
> Sound the loud triumphal lay!
> Tell how Christ the world's Redeemer
> As a victim won the day!

That victory takes place within the being of God. The cross is a rejection of the apathetic God, the God who is incapable of suffering, and an assertion of the passionate God, the God in whose heart there is pain, the crucified God.

That passionate involvement of God in the pain of the world brings about a real transformation of men and women. For, as the New Testament understands it, the death of Christ is more than a once for all event. We are called to enter into it, indeed we have been baptized into that death. In baptism we died and were buried with Christ, united with him in a death like his, our old self crucified, and so set free from sin (Rom. 6.3–6). So Paul can say 'I have been crucified with Christ; it is no longer I who live, but Christ who lives in me' (Gal. 2.20). That is more than the 'imitation of Christ', it is an incorporation into Christ, a Christ-ening, a true sharing of the Christ nature. Paul goes on to speak of carrying the marks of Jesus in his body (6.17), and, elsewhere, of sharing abundantly in his sufferings (2 Cor. 1.5) and even being conformed to him in his death (Phil. 3.10). We carry always in our own bodies the dying of Jesus (2 Cor. 4.10).

The theology of the cross then is a practical theology. 'The theology of the cross can never be a brilliant statement about the brokenness of life: it has to be a broken statement about life's brokenness because it participates in what it seeks to describe.'[39] It is a theology of lived relationship in which we were shaped and renewed by the Calvary experience. As limbs and organs of the crucified, we share in his dereliction and his brokenness, and so share in the work of salvation. The message of the crucified God includes the amazing truth that God allows us a share in his passion and death. Made in his image, we are signed with his cross, healed by his wounds, set free by his strange work of love.

Passionate Discipleship

To be a Christian is to be a follower of the crucified, a cross-bearer, one who is grafted into the organism of the crucified God. Christian discipleship is thus more than admiration of a past event, more even than imitation of that event: it is a real sharing in the passion and death of Christ, a 'participation in the powerlessness of God in the world' as Bonhoeffer expressed it in a memorable phrase. For Bonhoeffer, discipleship means the cross, for 'the disciple is a disciple only in so far as he shares his Lord's sufferings and rejection and crucifixion'. To be a Christian is to be part of a passion-centred community, the Church, 'the people under the cross'.[40]

The cross is therefore a perpetual symbol of God's action in Christ. Throughout Christian history it has been a source of strength, of inspiration, and of healing to men and women. Sebastian Moore, having meditated on the meaning of Christ's cross, came to see it as an attack upon life itself by the forces of death at work in us, and this came to be seen as an entire spirituality for action:

Finally as I lived with this new vision of the crucified, as I prayed it and shared it, I came to see that it contains a whole ascetico-mystical programme. The art of contemplating Jesus crucified is to come to understand, in painful situations, that the cross that I always first experience as life's crucifixion of me is, in reality, my crucifixion of life, in other words the Jesus-cross.[41]

Jesus on the cross represents an identity which we crucify rather than enter. And yet our crucifying is our way of entry. We kill life, and through this act express ourselves to sorrow and are reborn. The cross then is a symbol of our lost and recovered identity. 'We crucify Jesus rather than be him, and thus, through the healing power of sorrow, we become him.'[42] The crucified Jesus is not for imitation. His agony is not chosen as a way of life, and imitation of it would be a kind of spiritual masochism. As Moore stresses:[43]

We do not follow in the footsteps of a sufferer: we find ourselves in the suffering that, understood as our infliction, resolves the evil in our condition. The reason why Jesus is not for imitation is not that he is beyond our scope or understanding but that he is the identity of each of us.

Devotion to the passion as it developed in the Middle Ages in the West was centred on participation more than on imitation. Through the cross we are in Christ, in his wounds, in his pain, baptized into his dying and rising. So St Bernard of Clairvaux developed an intense devotion to the wounds of Christ. The Church, he wrote, dwells in the wounds of Christ and must remain there in perpetual medi-tation.[44] In his meditation on 'the richness of God's mercy in the open wounds of Christ', he writes:[45]

The piercing nail (clavus) has been turned for me into a master key (clavis) to show me the will of the Lord ... His body's open wounds lay bare the secret of his heart, that mighty mystery of love, the tender mercy of our God whereby the Dayspring from on high hath visited us. Never, O kind and gentle Lord, hast though more clearly shown thine inmost heart than through thy wounds.

In Hilda Graef's words, 'the contemplation of the wounds of Christ has led Bernard to his heart, marking the way which Christian spirituality was to follow throughout the next centuries.'[46]

The Cistercian movement as it developed took on an extreme and marginal character.[47] These men were God's fools, marked by the sign of the foolishness of God. William of St Thierry (1085–1148), one of the great Cistercians and a close friend of St Bernard, wrote:[48]

> From him [Christ] a new wisdom has come into the world, a wisdom that transcends all wordly wisdom, and makes it mad, the new wisdom of those who understand and appreciate that what is foolish or weak with God is wiser and stronger than men, the wisdom of those who taste, in the sweet savour of the Spirit, the humility of the Son of God, who was obedient unto death, even death on a cross, that Passion which he bore for our sakes, the derision, the slaps on the face, the spittings, the scourgings, the thorns and the nails.

Shaped and patterned after the folly of the cross, Cistercian houses became centres for the poor, the sick, and the social outcasts, all those in whom were made visible the wounds of the suffering Christ.

Devotion to the passion was equally intense and central in the growth of the Franciscan movement. St Francis was dominated by the vision of Christ crucified, eventually receiving into his own body the marks of Christ's wounds. He urged his followers to keep their hearts and minds fixed upon the footprints of the crucified. St Bonaventure called Francis *insignia sectator crucifixi Iesu*, the outstanding follower of Jesus crucified.[49] In his devotion to the passion, there is a strong sense of the physical suffering of Christ, and of seeing our participation in that suffering as the source of perfect joy. Nowhere is Franciscan spirituality of the cross expressed more powerfully than in the works of St Bonaventure. A person can only make the journey of the soul, Bonaventure insisted, by passing through Christ crucified. 'There is no other path but through the burning love of the Crucified . . .'[50] In *The Tree of Life*, Bonaventure portrays Christ himself as the tree. One third of the book deals with the sufferings of Christ, with meditations on the bloody sweat, the scourging, the piercing, and so on. The true disciple, he says, must seek to carry about continually in soul and flesh the cross of Christ.[51]

In his book *The Mystical Vine*, Bonaventure considers the intense love of the heart of Jesus. But his heart and the heart of the Christian are one heart. That heart of God is the centre of the Church, the school of virtue. Through that pierced heart we are healed:

> Let us be bound with the passion-bonds of our good and loving Jesus, that we may be worthy of sharing his bonds of charity. For it was those bonds of charity that drew him from heaven to earth to

endure the bonds of his passion.[52]

However, there was a negative aspect to much Franciscan devotion in that, in spite of the deep love for the created order in Francis's prayer and praise, there grew up a hostility to the world and the body, and a stress on the interior, purely personal piety to the neglect of any real zeal for justice among peoples.

An equally strong sense of solidarity with, and sanctification through, the cross comes over in the Eastern orthodox tradition. Thus St Theodosius, who established the Studite Rule in the eleventh century, wrote of the sharing in Christ's sufferings:[53]

> Our Lord Jesus Christ became poor and humbled himself, offering himself as an example so that we should humble ourselves in his name. He suffered insults, was spat upon, and beaten, for our salvation; how just it is, then, that we should suffer in order to gain Christ.

The humiliated Christ became a central and very powerful theme in Russian literature.[54] But it was the 'holy fools' who, in their recklessness and extremity of discipleship, sought a total identity with the folly of the crucified.[55] Like St Paul, they sought to complete whatever was lacking in Christ's afflictions (Col. 1.24) and so to share the folly of God (1.25). The fool in Russian spirituality is

> a poor inadequate being deserving of jest and even brutality ... But the memory of the Cross and the Crucified, the memory that *he* was slapped, spat upon and scourged, lives in his heart and compels him for Christ's sake to endure at every moment grace and persecution.[56]

The fool is in a sense the true charismatic figure, the sign of contradiction, the unmasker of illusion, the walking symbol of the crucified God. As Saward has written in his study of folly in the Christian tradition:[57]

> A God who empties himself and becomes a slave, who endures mockery and humiliating death, and yet is raised from the dead in glory, exposes the lie, the real madness, of living only for self: God's ecstasy-in-Incarnation, his leaping down from heaven, demonstrates once and for all that self-preservation leads to death while self-oblation leads to eternal life. The Gospel of 'an incarnate God, a God put to death', disrupts and subverts the worldly mind, shows it up for the madness it is.

One vital aspect of the solidarity of the Christian with the passion of

Christ and with his foolishness is the passionate and compassionate character of spiritual guidance and direction. The priest, the spiritual guide, the pastor, the Christian brother or sister who is privileged to enter into, and share, the progress of a fellow disciple: all of us are frail earthen vessels used by God, we are all 'pigmies in giants' armour'.[58] The ministry of spiritual guidance is very far removed from the professional models of caring which have dominated the social service professions. It calls for a real identification with the crucified in every person, and it lays upon us a burden which can often be terrifying:

> Anyone who has entered into the darkness of another's pain, loss or bewilderment and who has done so without the defences of a detached professionalism will know the feeling of wanting to escape, of wishing they had not become involved. Caring is costly, unsettling, even distasteful at times. The valley of deep shadows in another person's life frightens us too, and we lack the courage and constancy to enter it.[59]

In the New Testament, Jesus is seen as the smitten shepherd (Mark 14.27f), the shepherd who is willing to die for the sheep (John 10), the sacrificial lamb who is the pastor and who guides to springs of life-giving water (Rev. 7.17). Sacrifice and shepherding are closely linked in Christ himself, and, by extension, in the ministries of those who have put on Christ.

Christian pastors and guides are 'wounded healers'. Our wounds are of very great pastoral importance, and it is not too dramatic to claim that 'by *our* wounds *they* are healed'. The Jungian writer James Hillman has pointed out that, in personal ministry to individuals, 'I will be forced to pay attention to my own sufferings and needs if I am to be of service to anyone else.'[60] Pastoral care, according to Henri Nouwen, does not remove pain but deepens it. The wounds are vital to our condition and necessary for our healing and salvation. Pastoral care therefore cannot be concerned simply with the dispensing of comfort: 'It does not allow people to live with illusions of immortality and wholeness. It keeps reminding others that they are mortal and broken, but also that with the recognition of this condition liberation starts.'[61] Pastoral care then must be passionate care, cross-centred care, the care of the wounded for the wounded within the life and love of the wounded Saviour who 'bears in his heart all wounds'.[62] The dialectic of woundedness and healing, of sickness and salvation, is brought out in T. S. Eliot's 'East Coker':[63]

> The wounded surgeon plies the steel
> That questions the distempered part;

Beneath the bleeding hands we feel
The sharp compassion of the healer's art
Resolving the enigma of the fever chart.

Our only health is the disease
If we obey the dying nurse
Whose constant care is not to please
But to remind of our, and Adam's curse,
And that, to be restored, our sickness must grow worse.

The dripping blood our only drink,
The bloody flesh our only food:
In spite of which we like to think
That we are sound, substantial flesh and blood –
Again, in spite of that, we call this Friday good.

In our solidarity, in prayer and pastoral practice, with the stricken
Christ, we are seeking what Kosuke Koyama calls 'a crucified mind':
not a crusading mind, but a mind marked by self-denial, by loving
service, by brokenness and gentle but fierce love.[64] The crusading
mind is rooted in intolerance, and its ultimate end is destruction of its
opposition. The crucified mind is rooted in the love which grows
deeper through pain, and which seeks its end through what may seem
a harsh and dreadful love, but whose aim is the transformation of its
opponents. It is this mind which is expressed so often in the writings
and speeches of the late Martin Luther King, and nowhere more
powerfully than in his letter of May 1963 after the children's march.
He wrote:[65]

We must say to our white brothers all over the South who try to
keep us down: We will match your capacity to inflict suffering with
our capacity to endure suffering. We will meet your physical force
with soul force. We will not hate you. And yet we cannot in all good
conscience obey your evil laws. Do to us what you will. Threaten
our children and we will still love you ... Say that we're too low,
that we're too degraded, yet we will still love you. Bomb our homes
and go by our churches early in the morning and bomb them if you
please, and we will still love you. We will wear you down by our
capacity to suffer. In winning the victory we will not only win our
freedom. We will so appeal to your heart and your conscience that
we will win you in the process.

King wrote out of the background experience of the black church in
North America which had for years been nourished by the devotion to
the cross, a devotion expressed in spirituals and the sacred hymns of

black Christians. 'Were you there when they crucified my Lord?' they asked. While many of these hymns appear to exhibit an escapist attitude, it would be a serious error to see them solely in this way. For they kept hope alive in times of great oppression and trial:

> In Jesus' death black slaves saw themselves, and they unleashed their imagination in describing what they felt and saw ... His death was a symbol of their suffering trials and tribulations in an unfriendly world. They knew the agony of rejection and the pain of hanging from a tree ... Because black slaves knew the significance of the pain and shame of Jesus' death on the cross, they found themselves by his side.[66]

Far from leading towards acquiescence and endurance, the solidarity in and with Christ crucified was nourishment for a Christian community in conflict with oppressive worldly power. In the cross they discovered the power of divine discontent and divine contradiction.

Throughout the centuries Christians have worshipped a crucified God, a suffering God, a God put to death that we might have life. The cross is the heart of Christian knowledge, of Christian experience, of Christian preaching, and of Christian prayer. In its foolishness and scandalous crudity, the divine condescension is revealed: and we are able to rejoice and sing:

> Fulfilled is all that David told
> In true prophetic song of old.
> 'Amidst the nations God', saith he,
> 'Hath reigned and triumphed from the tree.'

11

God of the Abyss

God is nearer to us than our own soul, for he is the ground in which it stands.
Julian of Norwich, *Revelations of Divine Love*

The Divine Ground

The truth that God is incomprehensible and deeply mysterious is central to Christian spiritual theology and to all mystical religion. Gregory of Nyssa used over forty different words to speak of this incomprehensibility.[1] However much we may attempt to speak of his nature, God remains unutterable, unfathomable, the unsearchable depths of reality. And yet, the mystical writers insist, God is *our* depth, the ground of *our* being also. However, so neglected had this truth become in the West that when, in the 1960s, the notion of God as the ground of being was rediscovered, many believed that it was a new idea, demanding a break with traditional modes of thought. 'He who knows about depth knows about God', wrote Paul Tillich. And the recognition of this fact meant that one must 'forget everything traditional', perhaps even the word 'God'. More important than the name was the reality. 'The name of this infinite and inexhaustible ground of history is God. That is what the word means . . .'[2] And the English writer John Robinson wrote in similar vein.[3]

In fact, the theme of God as the ground of the self, the ground of being, the unfathomable depth, was common in the Christian writers of the early centuries. Augustine in particular devoted considerable attention to the need to return to the depths of his own being in order to discover God:

> Being admonished by all this to return to myself, I entered into my own depths, with you as guide; and I was able to do it because you were my helper.[4]

> I return to myself and look closely at myself, who I may be who seek such things . . . Seeking my God in visible and corporeal things and not finding him, seeking his substance in myself, as though it were something such as I am and not finding this either, I perceive that God is something above the soul.[5]

For Augustine, God is both depth and height, both the ground of the soul, and beyond the soul. While God and the soul of the human person are distinct, the knowledge of self and the knowledge of God are closely connected. So Augustine writes: 'I desired to know God and the soul.'[6] Those words were written at the beginning of his life as a Catholic Christian. The more he entered into the heart of orthodox spirituality, the more he recognized the integral unity of self-knowledge and the knowledge of God.

Augustine laid great emphasis on the place of experience in spiritual theology. 'Before experiencing God, you thought you could talk about him; when you begin to experience him, you realized that what you are experiencing you cannot put into words.'[7] The discovery of God at the centre of the human personality is described by Augustine as the return to the heart. By such a return to the heart, the centre of the person, the quest for God begins. For God is nearer to us than we are to ourselves.[8] This truth, repeated by Eckhart, Julian of Norwich, and other spiritual writers, was of fundamental importance to Augustine's whole approach to spiritual theology. God is at the centre of the human person, in the heart. Without a return to the heart, we must remain unfinished creatures:

> Let Truth, the light of my heart, speak to me, not my own darkness! I fell away and my sight was darkened: but from that depth, even from that depth, I loved you. I wandered afar, but I remembered you. I heard your voice behind me, calling me to return, but I could scarcely hear it for the tumult of my unquiet passions. And now behold I return to your fountain, panting and with burning thirst. Let none bar my way: I shall drink of it, and so I shall live. Let me not be my own life: of myself I lived evilly and to myself I was death. In you I live again.[9]

So it was that Augustine discovered God in the depths of his own soul, for 'I was outside. You were within.'[10] And this discovery was a spiritual crisis, a breakthrough, of the most dramatic and ecstatic kind:

> How late I came to love you, O beauty so ancient and so fresh, how late I came to love you! You were within me while I had gone outside to seek you. Unlovely myself, I rushed towards all those lovely things you had made. And always you were with me, I was not with you. All these beauties kept me far from you – although they would not have existed at all unless they had their being in you. You called, you cried, you shattered my deafness. You sparkled, you blazed, you drove away my blindness. You shed your fragrance, and I drew in my breath and I pant for you. I tasted and

now I hunger and thirst. You touched me and now I burn with longing for your peace.[11]

For Augustine, Christ is the centre of all spiritual life and experience. The divine Christ is the home to which we go, the human Christ is the way.[12]

The presence of God in the depths of the human person is even more strongly emphasized in the spiritual literature of the Eastern Church. God is seen here as depth, abyss. The vital spiritual task therefore is to attain purity of heart so that the divine nature and the divine beauty shine forth in all their splendour. In the words of Gregory of Nyssa:[13]

> . . . in so far as you recover the grace of the image deposited in you at the beginning, you possess what you seek within you. Divinity is in fact purity, impassibility, the removal of all evil. If this is what you are within, then God is within.

Later Symeon the New Theologian was to stress the close connection between human experience and the knowledge of God, the experimental character of all genuine theology:

> But if you have not discerned that the eye
> of your mind has been opened, and that it has seen the light,
> if you have not perceived the sweetness of the divinity,
> if you have not been enlightened by the divine Spirit,
> if you have not shed tears without feeling any pain,
> if you have not contemplated that your soul has been cleansed,
> if you have not known that your heart has been purified,
> that it has shone with its luminous reflections,
> if you have not found the Christ within yourself, contrary to all
>   expectations,
> if you have not been struck with stupour on seeing the divine
>   beauty,
> and have not forgotten human nature
> on seeing yourself completely transformed,
> how do you not tremble, tell me, to speak of God?[14]

The language of the abyss, of God as depth, was also used in the Western tradition by such writers as Richard of St Victor in the twelfth century;[15] while in the fourteenth century it was developed and became central in the theology of Meister Eckhart.

It was Eckhart who first used the term 'spark of the soul' in German, but he had inherited the term from the *scintilla animae* of Richard of St Victor. He uses a whole range of words for the divine spark at the heart of every person: it is described as *fünklein*, apex, centre, ground, divine light, ray of divinity, innermost essence, bottomless abyss. For Eckhart, God is both ultimate depth and inaccessible height: 'he dwells in the innermost dimension of the soul and in the highest aspect of the soul'.[16] Following Augustine, he says that 'God is nearer to me than I am to my own self'.[17] 'When the soul enters into her Ground, into the innermost recesses of her being, divine power suddenly pours into her.' 'When I saw into myself, I saw God in me.' 'To gauge the soul, one must gauge her with God, for the Ground of God and the Ground of the soul are one nature.' 'The eye with which I see God is the same as that with which he sees me.'[18]

For Eckhart, the essential inwardness of God is central. There is within the human soul or person something which is so akin to God that there is already a unity. What is important is not to create unity, but rather to awaken the consciousness of that which already is. This divine ground (*grunt*) is the hidden source of all things. By awakening to the realization of that which cannot be known by the intellect, we can come to live out of the unknowable divine ground. Eckhart, in common with the tradition of apophatic mystical theology, is emphatic that God cannot be grasped or known by the mind, and cannot be conceptualized. He is beyond existence. 'Nothing is formally in both a cause and its effect if the cause is a true cause. Now God is the cause of all existence. It follows that existence is not formally present in God.'[19] However, since God's ground and the soul's ground are one, human beings can come to know God through the journey inwards. There the hidden God will be found and embraced:

> One should not accept or esteem God as being outside oneself, but as one's own, and as what is within one; nor should one serve or labour for any recompense, not for God or for his honour or for anything that is outside oneself, but only for that which, one's own being and one's own life, is within one. Some simple people think they will see God as if he were standing there and they here. It is not so. God and I, we are one. I accept God into me in knowing: I go into God in loving.[20]

So he calls upon the Christian soul to leap into the adventure of this inward journey to discover God at the centre of her being: 'Up, noble soul, put on they jumping shoes, understanding and love, and leap the workings of thy powers: leap thine own understanding . . . and spring into the heart of God, into this hiddenness wherein though art hidden from all creatures.'[21]

Following Eckhart, and influenced to an immense degree by his thought, Jan von Ruysbroeck (1293–1381) also saw God as the 'abyss of pure being', inaccessible height and fathomless depth, incomprehensible breadth and eternal length. Ruysbroeck speaks of the 'deep quiet of the Godhead', 'the fathomless Abyss that is the Being of god'. As in Eckhart's thought, God is described as the ground of the soul. Within us all is the divine spark, 'the inward and natural tendency of the soul towards its source'.[22] Like most Christian mystical writers, Ruysbroeck uses the vocabulary of deification. As other writers have done, he compares the relationship of the Christian soul to God with that of iron to fire:

> The iron doth not become fire, nor the fire iron; but each retaineth its substance and its nature. So likewise the spirit of man doth not become God, but is God-formed and knoweth itself breadth and length and height and depth.[23]

Although he was accused of pantheism, he insists that the human person remains 'eternally other than God and distinct from him' and that 'no creature is able to be or to become holy to the point of losing his created nature or to become God'.[24]

Ruysbroeck speaks of the approach to God as one which involves the laying aside of reason, and the emptying of the mind:

> Here our reason must be put aside, like every distinct work; for our powers become simple in love, they are silent and bowed down in the presence of the Father. This revelation of the Father, in fact, raises the soul above reason, to an imageless nakedness. The soul there is simple, pure and spotless, empty of all things, and it is in this state of absolute emptiness that the Father shows his divine brightness. To this brightness neither reason nor sense nor remark nor distinction may serve; all that must remain below; for the measureless brightness blinds the eyes of the reason, and compels them to yield to the incomprehensible light.[25]

Ruysbroeck sees the path of the inward life as involving three stages. In the first, the soul possesses God in fruitive love. Of this stage he writes:[26]

> At times the inward man performs his introspection simply according to the fruitive tendency, above all activity and above all virtues, through a simple inward gazing in the fruition of love. And here he meets God without intermediary. And from out of the Divine Unity there shines into him a simple light: and this light shows him Darkness and Nakedness and Nothingness. In the Darkness he is enwrapped and falls into somewhat which is in no

wise even as one who has lost his way. In the Nakedness he loses the perception and discernment of all things, and is transfigured and penetrated by a simple light. In the Nothingness all his activity fails him; for he is vanquished by the working of God's abysmal love, and in the fruitive inclination of his spirit he vanquishes God and becomes one spirit with him. And in the oneness with the Spirit of God, he enters into a fruitive tasting and possesses the Being of God.

However, the second stage is that in which the soul possesses himself in adhering to God and in the manifesting of active love, and Ruysbroeck considers this stage to be more desirable and more beneficial. In the third stage, the soul possesses her whole life in virtues according to righteousness. So there is a movement from the soul to God, from God to the soul, and from the soul to society and the world. The comtemplative life can never be one of self-indulgent absorption, even of a purely personal absorption in and enjoyment of God. Rather there must be an active expression of the inward union and love in relation to the world.

We find a similar approach to the mystical life in the Dominican writer Johann Tauler (1300–61). Like Eckhart and Ruysbroeck, Tauler sees God as closer to us than we are to ourselves:

> The inward Word is so unutterably near to us inwardly, in the very principle of our being, that not even man himself, not even his own thought, is so high, or is planted so deep within him, as the Eternal Word in man.

The reality of God can be discovered only by the process of interiorizing. The soul must move inwards in stillness and reflective prayer. Through the continued practice of such contemplative inwardness, the abyss which is God opens up to the human soul:

> Whoever has practised beforehand and has purified his nature and spirit to the best of his ability can then pleasantly sink inward; and when nature has done her part, and can do no more, but finds her innermost limits, then appears the divine abyss, sending out its sparks throughout the spirit. With supernatural aid, the transfigured, purified spirit is drawn out of itself, and into its unique, purified and inexpressible intending of God.[27]

Tauler, like the others, speaks of God as the 'ground of the soul' and as the abyss. He speaks also of the abyss of man, but stresses that this is a 'created abyss'. Yet our way to the uncreated is through the created, and the soul moves towards God through the exploration of the abyss of her own being in a process of continuing and ever-deepening inwardness. Tauler calls this process one of 'sinking into the divine abyss', one of his favourite and oft-repeated expressions.

Finally, among the great Christian mystics of the fourteenth century, it is important to consider the English solitary Julian of Norwich (1342–after 1413). Much attention hs been focused on Julian in recent years, not least because of her concern with the motherhood of God (see Chapter 12 for further discussion of this). But Julian is of wider significance, for she represented the recovery of a much richer and more integral approach to human nature than that which prevailed in the Augustinian tradition of her day. She represents the resurgence of a Christian optimism, a spirituality which is not dominated by sin and fallenness, but by grace and glory, a materialistic spirituality which rejoices in the goodness of nature. Nature is all good and fair in itself, says Julian, and grace was sent to save it.[28] Again, like the other three writers, she is emphatic that God is the ground of our souls. Our soul is so deeply grounded in God that we must know God before we are able truly to know our own soul. However we cannot move to the knowledge of God except through the encounter with our own depths:

> God is nearer to us than our own soul, for he is the Ground in which it stands, and he is the means by which substance and sensuality are so held together that they can never separate. Our soul reposes in God its true rest, and stands in God its true strength, and is fundamentally rooted in God its eternal love. So if we want to come to know our soul, and enjoy its fellowship, as it were, it is necessary to seek it in our Lord God in whom it is enclosed.[29]

In the manuscript of Julian which is in the Bibliothèque Nationale in Paris, there is a remarkable passage which develops this theme of the unity of the physical and the spiritual, and their enclosure in God:

> A man walks upright, and the food in his body is shut in, as if in a well-made purse. When the time of his necessity comes, the purse is opened and then shut again, in most seemly fashion. And it is God who does this, as it is shown when he says that he comes down to us in our humblest needs. For he does not despise what he has made, nor does he disdain to serve us in the simplest natural functions of the body, for love of the soul which he created in his likeness. For as the body is clad in the cloth, and the flesh in the skin, and the bones in the flesh, and the heart in the trunk, so are we, soul and body, clad and enclosed in the goodness of God.[30]

After death, Julian says, 'we shall come to God, knowing ourselves clearly, having God wholly ... enfolded in God for ever'.[31] This process of being 'enfolded' in God, a process which reaches its culmination after death, is the work of God the Father and Mother of us all:

> In our Father, God Almighty, we have our being; in our merciful Mother, we are remade and restored. Our fragmented lives are knit together and made perfect man. And by giving ourselves through grace to the Holy Spirit, we are made whole.[32]

Julian regards prayer as an act of yearning which leads to beseeching, and beseeching which leads to beholding. Yearning is the first mark of the awakened soul, the beginning of its movement back to its source, its deep rootedness in the being of God.

It would be possible to examine how God at the centre of the human personality, the divine ground, is treated in other mystical writers. Walter Hilton stresses the need for the Christian to 'enter into himself and to understand his own soul' if he is to know God.[33] St John of the Cross speaks of God as the soul's centre:

> The centre of the soul is God, and when the soul has attained to him according to the whole capacity of its being, and according to the force of its operation and inclination, it will have reached its last and deepest centre in God, which will be when, with all its powers, it understands and loves and enjoys God.[34]

The flame of love, says St John, wounds the human soul in its deepest centre. For St Teresa of Avila also God is the centre of the soul.[35] Indeed, for all the spiritual writers of the mainstream Christian tradition, there is a profound relationship between the depth of God and the depth of the human person, depth calling unto depth. As Thomas Merton expressed it:[36]

> Now I had entered into the everlasting movement of that gravitation which is the very life and spirit of God: God's own gravitation towards the depths of his own infinite nature, his goodness without end. And God, that centre who is everywhere and whose circumference is nowhere, finding me ... And he called out to me from his own immense depths.

So the way of the knowledge of God must go through the way of purity of heart. For the heart, the centre and depth of the human person, is the essential point of discovery of, and encounter with, the reality of God in whose image we are created.

Hence the importance of what the Easter Christian tradition calls the 'prayer of the heart'. In Eastern theology, the heart is the 'inmost self' (Rom. 7.22), the place of the divine encounter. This unified view had broken down in the West by the time of St Bernard who speaks of two kinds of contemplation, one seated in the intellect and issuing in light, and the other seated in the heart and issuing in warmth.[37] Such a division was unknown to early writers who saw the personality as essentially a unity, grounded in God, and saw prayer as the awakening to, and the continual strengthening of, that unity. Thus St Symeon in the eighth century writes of prayer as the unifying of the personality:[38]

> Prayer in which the body does not toil by means of the heart, and the heart by means of the mind, together with the intellect and the intelligence, all gathered together in deep-felt groaning, but there instead prayer is just allowed to float across the heart, such prayer, you should realize, is just a miscarriage, for while you are praying, your mind is drawing you away to some other business that you are going to see to after praying. In such a case, you have not yet managed to pray in a unified manner.

Similarly, St Isaac of Nineveh sees the heart as the controlling centre of the person. The mind can, by meditation on the Scriptures, by fasting and by inner stillness, attain purity, but it is easily defiled again. The heart, however, is 'only purified through great afflictions', but, once purified, it can survive very severe struggles.[39]

The heart is therefore central to the entire work of spiritual theology and to the encounter with the divine abyss. Thus Sahdona's *Book of Perfection*, a mystical work of the ancient Syrian Christians, praises the heart that is lucid and is therefore able to enjoy the divine encounter:[40]

> Blessed are you, O heart that is lucid, the abode of the Divinity; blessed are you, heart that is pure, which beholds the hidden Essence. Happy are you, O flesh and blood, the dwelling place of the Consuming Fire: happy are you, mortal body made out of dust, wherein resides the Fire that sets the worlds alight. It is truly a matter for wonder and astonishment that he, before whom the heavens are not pure, who puts awe into his angels, should take delight and pleasure in a heart of flesh that is filled with love for him, that is open wide to him, that is purified so as to act as his holy dwelling place, joyfully serving and ministering to him in whose presence thousand upon thousand, ten thousand upon ten thousand, fiery angels stand in awe, ministering to his glory. Happy are you, O heart, so small and confined, yet you have caused him,

whom heaven and earth cannot contain, to dwell spiritually in your womb as in a restful abode. Happy that luminous eye of the heart which, in its purity, clearly beholds him, before the sight of whom the seraphs veil their faces . . . Blessed indeed are the pure in heart.

The Mystic Way

The word 'mysticism' comes from the Greek *muō*, to close. It was a verb used particularly of the closing of the eyes, and the terminology of mysticism was first used in connection with the 'mystery religions'. From the notion of closedness, the term came to be associated with ideas of the esoteric and the secret. Happold has pointed to the variety of ways in which the term has come to be used. The word, he says, is used

> with a number of different meanings and carries different connotations to different minds. To some it is simply a type of confused irrational thinking. In the popular mind, it is associated with spiritualism and clairvoyance, with hypnotism, and even with occultism and magic, with obscure psychological states and happenings, some of which are the result of neurasthenia or other morbid pathological conditions. To some, it is bound up with visions and revelations. Others use it as a synonym for otherworldliness or to describe a nebulous outlook upon the world, or a religious observance. Some would limit its use to that rare state of consciousness which is found in the contemplative saints.[41]

Even Happold's own list includes some descriptions which raise their own problems of interpretation, for many would question whether the states of consciousness found in the great contemplatives are as rare as we might think.

However, a generally accepted definition of mysticism is that used at the turn of the century by Rufus Jones: it is 'a type of religion which puts the emphasis on immediate awareness of relation with God, on direct and intimate consciousness of the Divine Presence. It is religion in its most acute, intense and living stage.'[42] More recently, Charles Davis has defined mysticism as

> the coming into explicit consciousness of the primary constitutive element of all genuine religion; namely religious feeling, understood as an immediate spontaneous connatural response to transcendent reality. In the mystic, the awareness of mystery becomes explicit, and this allows it to dominate consciousness, sometimes absorbing it completely.[43]

Mysticism thus understood is present in many religious traditions

and in cultures and sub-cultures which are not specifically theistic.
Behind all forms of mysticism there is the belief that an intimate and
direct relationship with God or with 'transcendent reality' is possible,
and that this constitutes a mode of existence and a mode of knowing
which is different from, and perhaps superior to, normal existence
and knowledge.[44] There are many forms of non-theistic mysticism,
cosmic consciousness, experiences of union, and unifying visions,
many of which were described in William James's classic study *The
Varieties of Religious Experience* in 1902.[45] Characteristic of most
forms of mystical consciousness is a sense of the paradoxical.[46] There
is usually a sense of the union of the person with a wider reality, as in
Wordsworth's poem 'Tintern Abbey':

> And I have felt
> A presence that disturbs me with the joy
> Of elevated thoughts; a sense sublime
> Of something far more deeply interfused,
> Whose dwelling is the light of setting suns,
> And the round ocean and the living air,
> And the blue sky, and in the mind of man,
> A motion and a spirit that impels
> All thinking things, all objects of all thought,
> And rolls through all things.

Many have seen in these words of Wordsworth an example of 'nature
mysticism' but it is clear from his 'Intimations of Immortality' that he
is conscious of a reality beyond the natural world, to which he gives
the name God:

> But trailing clouds of glory do we come
> From God who is our home.

He speaks too of 'God and Nature communing'.

Mystical writers often speak of union with God, using the language
of absorption, of being swallowed up, plunged into the incomprehensible being of God, seeing God in all things and all things in God, and
so on. They use the symbolism of fire and of water, of being melted by
the divine heat or engulfed in the ocean of God's love. These
experiences of union are seen as having a transforming effect, and the
mystics are suspicious of experiences which have no transforming
character, and of people who collect better and better experiences but
remain unchanged. The mystical literature is full of warnings against
the misuse of experiences. In recent years the quest for mystical
experience through the use of psycho-active drugs has reinforced
earlier warnings.

For the Christian, the mystical experience is one of abiding in Christ (John 15.4). Christ lives in the Christian (Phil. 1.21; Gal. 2.20), and he is the source of life and of future glorification. This grounding of the person, and indeed of all creation, in Christ is brought out most forcibly in the Letter to the Colossians. Christ is the image of God and all things were created in him. In him all things hold together, and in him the fullness of God dwelt (1.15–19). The author speaks of 'the glory of this mystery', and the mystery is 'Christ in you, the hope of glory' (1.27). In Christ are hid all the treasures of wisdom and knowledge (2.3). And Christians have died in Christ and been raised:

> If then you have been raised with Christ, seek the things that are above, where Christ is, seated at the right hand of God. Set your minds on things that are above, not on things that are on earth. For you have died, and your life is hid … with Christ in God. When Christ who is our life appears, then you also will appear with him in glory (3.1–4).

The mystical life is thus the ordinary condition of the Christian, the life which is hid with Christ in God. Mystical theology is basic Christian theology, mysticism a fundamental constituent of all Christian experience. This fundamental rootedness of mystical experience in Christian life must not be misunderstood to mean that all Christians are led to extraordinary experiences, but rather that there is not a sharp division to be made between that consciousness which is common to all who have been born again in Christ, and these unusual experiences.

It is important to stress the origin of Christian mysticism in Christian theology. There has been much suspicion of the mystical dimension in Christian faith, some seeing it as an alien intrusion, a distortion of the biblical revelation. Karl Barth discussed mysticism and atheism together![47] But Christian mysticism is not a denial of the truths of redemption and sanctification through the work of God in Christ, but a necessary consequence of those realities. In fact, it is the neglect of mystical theology, particularly in the Western Churches, which has led many to look outside the Christian tradition, as a Korean writer, Jung Young Lee, has pointed out:[48]

> Thus Christianity is allied with technology to reject the non-rational aspects of human life. It suppressed occult phenomena and devalued the emotional aspects of religious life. Mysticism did not thrive in the life of the Western Church. The Western Church considered the exploration of psychic matter as the works of the

devil ... Thus Christianity in the West, and especially Protestantism, failed to meet the needs of the whole man whose nature includes mystic elements, and this failure is responsible for youth turning away from the Church and seeking to satisfy its spiritual needs in Eastern mysticism.

The search for spirituality through the use of chemicals or through the pursuit of westernized versions of eastern non-Christian traditions may also have its origins in the neglect of mystical theology in the western Christian tradition.

In recent years much discussion has centred upon the apparent similarity in phenomenological terms between mysticism and psychosis. Are those whom we label 'mad' actually on a spiritual journey? Do they perhaps see more than we do? It was to this area that R. D. Laing devoted his attention in the late 1960s in his reflections on the spiritual significance of madness.[49] Earlier C. G. Jung had written of the way in which what he termed 'inflation' of the ego, often mistaken for mystical enlightenment, could lead either to megalomania or to ego-annihilation.[50] Such experiences of inflation or expansion were well known in the mystical writings of the east, and the Sufis advised their followers to 'be chary of expansion and beware of it'.[51] From a different context, a student of Zen has written:[52]

An ancient Zen saying has it that to become attached to one's own enlightenment is as much a sickness as to exhibit a maddeningly active ego. Indeed the profounder the enlightenment, the worse the illness. In her case [a young woman disciple], I think it would have taken two or three months for the most obvious symptoms to disappear, two or three years for the less obvious, and seven or eight for the most insidious. Such symptoms are less pronounced on one as gentle as she, but in some they are positively nauseating. Those who practise Zen must guard against them. My own sickness lasted ten years.

Mystical writings, eastern and western, are full of warnings against the quest for ecstasy for its own sake, against the accumulation of better and better experiences, against the attachment to methods and techniques. The association of mysticism with paranormal experiences or with the extremes of asceticism is also rejected by the most respected writers. The Buddha emphasized the 'middle way', St John of the Cross warned against attachment to visions and unusual experiences, while the Sufi tradition stressed the importance of spiritual sobriety. In the *Bhagavad Gita*, ascetical extremes are attacked:[53]

Yoga is not for him who eats too much, nor yet for him who does not eat at all, nor for him who is all too prone to sleep, nor yet for him who always stays awake. Rather Yoga is for him who is moderate in food and recreation, controlled in his deeds and gestures, moderate in sleeping as in waking.

It is possible to enjoy and pursue mystical experiences for their own sake and so to be overpowered by them and perhaps destroyed by them. It is the spiritual *context* of the experience, what one *does* with it, which is so crucial. Viewed purely in terms of the experience, the use of psychedelic drugs, the experience of psychosis, and the mystical experience may reveal striking similarities. What is important is how these experiences are related to life, to loving, to the process of human spritual maturation. Mystical theology then is concerned with reflecting upon the whole life of the spirit, not merely upon the manifestation of certain experiences. The mystical life is then, in Thomas Merton's words, 'the normal way of Christian perfection'.[54] Mystical theology was the theology behind the Nicene Creed, and, as the Eastern Orthodox tradition has always insisted, all Christian theology is mystical.[55]

In Christian reflection on the spiritual way, there has been, from very early times, a tradition of using a threefold classification. This threefold way has its roots in New Testament teaching about repentance, sanctification, and union with God. It appears in the writings of Clement of Alexandria who speaks of the transition from paganism to faith, from faith to knowledge, and from knowledge to love;[56] and in Origen who speaks of purification, learning, and love.[57] In Gregory of Nyssa, there is also a threefold pattern, symbolized by the Night, the Cloud, and the Darkness. The Night stands for the time of purification, the Cloud for that of contemplation, and the deep Darkness for that of pure love of God.[58] And in pseudo-Dionysius, there is a clear description of the Three Ways as the path of Christian progress. There is

> the Active Life through the Way of Purification, whereby men may become true servants of God; the Inner Life, the Way of Illumination, and or real sonship with God; and the Contemplative Life which is the Unitive Way, whereby men may attain to true friendship with God.[59]

In the Western tradition, St Bernard speaks of three kisses: the kiss on the feet, the kiss of the penitent; the kiss on the hands, the kiss of the growing Christian; and the kiss on the mouth, the kiss of intuitive union. It is, however, in Bonaventure's *De Triplici Via*, that we find the first detailed treatment of the Three Ways as applied to the developing life of the ordinary Christian. The Way of Purgation leads to peace, the Way of Illumination to truth, and the Way of Union to love.

In this progress, great emphasis is placed in the mystical writers on the early stages of ascetical discipline and purification, on the necessary process of stripping and the confrontation with sin and self-centredness. This Way of Purgation may take many years and will often be intensely painful, for it involves the encounter with illusion and falsehood in oneself. One's identity seems to be under attack. C. S. Lewis captures something of the experience of stripping in his account of the 'undragoning' of Eustace in *The Voyage of the Dawn Treader*:[60]

> I started scratching myself and my scales began coming off all over the place. And then I scratched a little deeper, and, instead of just scales coming off here and there, my whole skin started peeling off
> ... Well, exactly the same thing happened again. And I thought to myself, oh dear, how many skins have I got to take off? ... The very first tear [the lion] made was so deep that I thought it had gone right into my heart. And when he began pulling the skin off, it hurt worse than anything I've ever felt.

Yet this stripping, this liberation from false identity, must take place before the Way of Illumination, the entry into the darkness of knowledge, can begin. Enough has been written earlier to show how central is this path of 'unknowing' in the Christian mystical tradition.

The end of the mystical life is union with God. Throughout the Christian mystics, the language of divine union is used. Thus Angela da Foligno (1248–1309) wrote: 'I see myself along with God, all pure, all holy, all truth, all righteousness, all secure, all heavenly in him.'[61] Here the human and the divine seem to be intermingled. But distinction is also stressed. Ruysbroeck, while he frequently uses expressions of absorption and unitive love, also stresses that 'even here does the creature feel a distinction and otherness between itself and God in its inward ground'.[62] Ruysbroeck, like many mystics, uses the symbolism of fire to communicate the intense heat of the unitive love of God: 'that measureless love which is God himself dwells in the pure deeps of our spirit like a burning brazier of coal.'[63] St Bernard uses a variety of symbols – water and wine, iron and fire, sun and air:

> Just as a little drop of water mixed with a lot of wine seems entirely to lose its own identity while it takes on the taste of wine and its colour; just as iron, heated and glowing, looks very much like fire,

having divested itself of its original and characteristic appearance; and just as air flooded with the light of the sun is transformed into the same splendour of light also that it appears not so much lifted up as to be light itself: so it will inevitably happen that in saints every human affection will then, in some ineffable manner, melt away from self and be entirely transfused into the will of God.[64]

Some have noted in St Bernard a tendency to see the human personality as being annihiliated and dissolved into God. But the texts do not support this.[65] He certainly compares the deified soul to a drop of water dissolved in wine, and to iron in the fire. The drop of water, he says, *seems* not to exist: *deficere a se tota videtur*. Similarly with regard to the iron in the fire: *igni simillimum fit*, that is, it becomes as like fire as is possible, and yet it is not fire. The air to is illuminated by the sun and penetrated by light *ut non tam illuminatus, quam ipsum lumen esse videtur*. Yet the distinctions between the two realities remain.

Bernard is speaking then not of the abolition of the human identity but of its transformation, of its glorification by being taken up into the being of God. So, speaking of human beings united to God, he says:[66]

their human love will then ineffably be melted out of them, and all poured over, so to speak, into the will of God. It must be so. How otherwise could God be *all in all* if anything of man remained in man. And yet our human substance will remain. We shall still be ourselves, but in another form, another glory, and another power.

In a passage of remarkable similarity to Bernard, Ruysboeck writes:[67]

That measureless love which is God himself dwells in the pure deeps of our spirit, like a burning brazier of coals. And it throws forth brilliant and fiery sparks which stir and enkindle heart and senses, will and desire, and all the powers of the soul, with a fire and love . . . As air is penetrated by the brightness and heat of the sun, and iron is penetrated by fire; so that it works through fire the works of fire, since it burns and shines like the fire . . . yet each of them keeps its own nature – the fire does not become iron, and the iron does not become fire, so likewise is God in the being of the soul . . . The creature never becomes God, nor does God ever become the creature.

Elsewhere Ruysbroeck explains the sense in which his language of union with God is to be understood.

Where I write that we are one with God, by that is to be understood one in love, not in being or in nature. For God's being is uncreated, and our being is created, and God and the creature are immeasurably unlike: and therefore, though they may be united, they cannot become one. If our being were to become nothing, we should know nothing, love nothing, have no blessedness. But our created being is to be regarded as a wild and barren desert where God lives who governs it.[68]

Throughout this life, he says, there is a continual restlessness for God in whom alone human persons can find completion and fulfilment. There is

... an impatient hunger, ever striving for what it lacks, ever swimming against the stream. One cannot leave it, one cannot have it; one cannot lack it, one cannot gain it; one cannot tell it, one cannot conceal it, for it is above reason and understanding ... but if we look deep into ourselves, there we shall feel God's Spirit driving and urging us on in the impatience of love: and if we look high above ourselves, there we shall feel God's Spirit driving us out of ourselves and bringing us to nothing in the essence of God, that is, in the essential love in which we are one with him, the love which we possess deeper and wider than every other thing.[69]

In this passage we see the paradoxical nature of mystical experience. God is the source and ground of human life, the end of our yearning, and yet to seek God is to swim against the stream. We hunger and thirst for the divine, and yet the way is marked by darkness and emptiness. God is both deep within us and high beyond us, intimate and inaccessible. The mystical experience is at the same time so close to human relationships and so far beyond all our conceptions and images.

The paradoxical nature of mysticism is brought out in the use of sexual imagery by so many of the great mystical writers. Much of the language used by the mystics about the experience with the divine is explicitly sexual. Zaehner commented of this fact:[70]

There is no point at all in blinking the fact that the raptures of the theistic mystic are closely akin to the transports of sexual union, the soul playing the part of the female, and God appearing as the male. There is nothing surprising in this, for if man is made in the image of God, then it would be natural that God's love would be reflected in human love, and that the love of man for woman should reflect the love of God for the soul ... To drive home the close parallel between the sexual act and the mystical union with God may seem blasphemous today. Yet the blasphemy is not in the comparison, but in the degrading of the one act of which man is capable that makes him like God both in the intensity of his union with his partner, and in the fact that by this union he is a co-creator with God.

We can see a good illustration of the use of sexual imagery to describe the mystical experience in an account by St Teresa of Avila of a vision which she had. She wrote:[71]

> Our Lord was pleased that I should sometimes see a vision of that kind. Beside me on the left hand appeared an angel in bodily form such as I am not in the habit of seeing except very rarely. Though I often have visions of angels, I do not see them ... In his hands I saw a great golden spear, and at the iron tip there appeared to be a point of fire. This he plunged into my heart several times so that it penetrated to my entrails. When he pulled it out, I felt that he took them with it, and left me utterly consumed by the great love of God. The pain was so severe that it made me utter several moans. The sweetness caused by this intense pain is so extreme that one cannot possibly wish it to cease, nor is one's soul then content with anything but God. This is not a physical but a spiritual pain, though the body has some share in it.

Here the parallel with sexual union is very close: the phallic imagery, the act of penetration, the experience of being 'utterly consumed', the mingling of joy and pain, the moaning, the wish never to lose the experience.

Such sexual imagery is common in the mystical writers. Moreover, it must be stressed that they compare, rather than contrast, the experience of sexual and divine union. The one reflects, and point towards, the other. There is no attempt to diminish the intensity and importance of sexuality as in the Manichean tradition. Nor is there a contrast between erotic love (of the flesh) and agapeic love (of the spirit). The contrast is rather between the movement of love which sinks into the hell of self-absorption, and the movement of love which rises to the state of 'engodding'.[72] God does not seek a purely spiritual love in which the flesh and sexuality play no part: he demands *ahabah*, the same word used in the Song of Songs to describe sexual arousal. The mystical climax, union with God, represents the peak of human sexual longing, it is a union more ecstatic and more wonderful than any human union can be. And it is endless, for as Augustine wrote: 'There we shall be still and see; we shall see and we shall love; we shall love and we shall praise. Behold, what will be in the end, and will not end.'[73]

Growing Downwards

At the heart of all mysticism is the recognition that the human person is an 'unfinished animal', seeking his or her source. In Christian mysticism that quest for fulfilment is seen as a quest for God, in whom we can become what potentially we are. The mystical path is a process of awakening to reality, a recognition of one's own true nature. But this awakening is hindered by many obstacles and dangers, and so many writers emphasize the value of a spiritual guide, a companion or 'soul friend'. Nevertheless, important as spiritual guidance or direction is, the essential work is interior. Eckhart speaks of the joyful recognition of one's inner rootedness in and unity with God: 'In bursting forth I discover that God and I are one.'[74] Many of the mystical writers speak of an inner persistent restlessness until this return to source occurs, or rather begins. 'You have made us for yourself,' Augustine wrote, 'and our hearts are restless until they rest in you.'[75] Augustine often speaks of the 'restless heart'. It ceaselessly desires God, yet at the same time it is a battlefield.[76] There is then a continual warfare within the heart, that heart which remains 'God's Field'.[77] Augustine addresses God as 'God of my heart'[78] and is clear that God's dwelling place is there. Yet he also describes the interior conflict within the depths of the heart, a fleeing from itself: 'my heart fled from my heart'.[79]

The theme of the heart as the centre of the personality, and the place in which God is found, was mentioned earlier. In his account of the spiritual journey, Augustine sees the inward movement, the 'return to the heart' as the essential aspect. 'Being admonished by all this to return to myself, I entered into my own depths with you as guide; and I was able to do this because you were my helper.'[80] Through this inward movement, he came to see with the eyes of the heart, to see the God who was within him. 'For that light was within while I was looking outward.'[81] 'But you, Lord . . . turned me back toward myself . . . that I might see how vile I was, how twisted and unclean and spotted and ulcerous. I saw myself and was horrified, but there was no way to flee from myself.'[82] As a result, the first effect of the inward movement was alienation: 'a mighty storm arose within me'.[83] From the midst of this tumult, he cried to God, and found that he was embraced and welcomed home:

'Return, O transgressor, to your heart' (Isa. 46.8). Return to your heart: Why go from yourselves and perish from yourselves? Why go the ways of loneliness? You go astray by wandering. Return! Where? To the Lord! It is quickly done. First return to your own heart. You have wandered abroad, an exile from yourself. You

know not yourself and yet you ask who made you. Return! Return
to your heart![84]

So God, who made the heart and who dwells there, is recognized and
becomes one with the heart's desire. The experience is one of conflict,
involving the 'shuddering' of the heart, but resulting in healing and
integration.[85]

For return to the heart thus involves the discovery of God the Abyss
in the created abyss of the human person. For the heart, in the
spiritual tradition,

> refers to the deepest psychological ground of one's personality, the
> inner sanctuary where self-awareness goes beyond analytical
> reflection and opens out into metaphysical and theological confron-
> tation with the Abyss of the unknown yet present – one who is
> 'more intimate to us than we are to ourselves'.[86]

This spiritual pilgrimage to the heart, this growing downwards, is
rooted in the truth that human beings are made in God's image. The
aim of all spirituality is the recovery of this image, the restoration of
humanity to its true identity and the progress of humanity to its divine
fulfilment. However, such a movement assumes that the divine image
in human persons has not been totally obliterated, the view held in
much Reformation theology. Calvin, in particular, while he admitted
that 'the divine image was not utterly annihilated and effaced',[87] went
on to insist that 'the natural talents in man have been corrupted by sin;
but of the supernatural ones he has been entirely deprived'.[88] Human
beings are 'despoiled of his divine array', 'a miserable ruin', 'an
immense mass of depravity'.[89] Even to think of humanity is to think
'within the confines of human pollution'. For our whole nature has
been condemned so that 'in our nature there is nothing but
perversity'; 'our whole nature is vitiated that we can do nothing but
sin'.[90] A human being, therefore, is 'a creature in whom the image of
God has been defaced', indeed 'wholly defaced and wiped out by the
sin of Adam'.[91] The doctrine of total depravity could not be put more
clearly than that!

While Christians should be grateful to Calvin and his successors for
their stress on the terrible reality of human sin, the stress on human
fallenness at the expense of the original glory has led to a theological
pessimism which sees sin as almost the final word about the human
condition. Yet to treat the fallen condition, which is strictly
accidental, as if it were basic to the relation of humanity to God, is
'very mistaken'.[92] The teaching of the Greek Fathers is much more
hopeful and stresses human glory more than human sinfulness. The

human person is fundamentally deiform, fundamentally open to God. While sin may, and does, impede spiritual progress, it has not utterly destroyed that image and likeness. As Thomas Merton has written:[93]

> The human soul is still the image of God, and no matter how far it travels from him into the region of unreality, it never becomes so completely unreal that its original destiny can cease to torment it with a need to return to itself in God and become once again real.

The image in fact is indestructible though it can be buried and imprisoned. To quote Merton again:[94]

> The image of God in man is not destroyed by sin, but is utterly disfigured by it. To be exact, the image of God in man becomes self-contradictory when its openness closes in upon itself, when it ceases to be a capacity for love, and becomes simply an appetite for domination and possession; when it ceases to give and seeks only to get.

Thus the path of spirituality involves the cleansing of the mirror so that it once again reflects God. Thus the Eastern writer John the Elder urges:[95]

> Cleanse your mirror, and then without any doubt the triune Light will be manifested to you in it; place the mirror in your heart, and you will realise that your God is indeed alive . . . You are the image of God, O man. Do you wish the image to take on the likeness of its Maker? Then silence all activity of any kind, and carry the yoke of your Lord in your heart, and wonder at his majesty in your mind continuously, until the image becomes resplendent with his glory, and it is transformed into the likeness, and you shall become in God a god who has acquired the likeness of his Maker by means of the union which makes like to himself.

Guidance and direction in the spiritual path must therefore begin from the truth that human beings are made in God's image, made for God, and incomplete and unfinished without him. The path is one of discovery, of awakening to the reality that we are already deiform, and that, through the transforming work of God in Christ, we share a new nature. On the other hand, the obstacles in the path are formidable, and so the journey of the spirit is one which is marked by frequent slides backward, by falls and crises of many kinds. Hence the importance, in the spiritual tradition, of finding an ascetical framework which can enable progress to be made and the obstacles to be identified, seen clearly, and overcome. Ascetical techniques are not a regression from grace to law, nor are they based upon a body/soul dualism of gnostic type. The purpose of asceticism is spiritual freedom. Indeed, 'the only justifiable asceticism is that which liberates man and restores him to authentic realities'.[96] By the use of certain techniques and disciplines, the person can be helped to move towards a more complete simplicity, a condition of wholeness and of interior integration. That is the point of all spiritual discipline.

It is the point too of what is known in the Christian tradition as 'spiritual direction', a term which is often associated with authoritarian and dominating modes of thought. Spiritual direction basically means a way of establishing a person-to-person relationship of guidance in which there is companionship and supportive help given by one to the other on his or her spiritual path. The relationship is an intimate and continuing one. It is not problem-centred, nor is it an alternative to therapy or counselling. It is a friendship of souls, and so the spiritual director or guide has been called a 'soul friend'.[97] The creation and development of such a relationship is of great value in encouraging the journey inwards. For as God is known at the centre of the human personality, so the way to God is illuminated through our fellow human beings who are also made in his image. So we make the journey to our true centre in solidarity with, and guided by, our comrades, our sisters and brothers in Christ.

The Eye of the Storm: Mysticism, Theology, and Politics

The essential rootedness of Christian mysticism in Christian theology has already been stressed. However, it is clear that between the mystical theology of the patristic age and our own understanding of theological work there is a great gulf fixed, and the overcoming of this gulf is one of the most urgent tasks of Christian theologians and pastors today. It has rightly been said of the Fathers:[98]

> Their theology began and ended in mystical prayer. They wrote from what they had seen with the eyes of their spirit, and loved from the depths of their hearts. Their theology flowed from their mysticism, and their mysticism flowed from their theology.

The insistence in particular within the Eastern Orthodox tradition that all theology is mystical theology is marked by the recognition in that tradition of only three theologians – St John the Divine, St Gregory Nazianzen, and St Symeon the New Theologian. All of these were mystics, poets, and visionaries rather than academics or theoreticians: their theology was inseparable from their visionary insight and their intense prayer. However, today the gulf between the mystic and the theologian (in the modern sense of the word) is among the most worrying aspects of the contemporary religious scene:

In fact, the divorce between mystical experience and the theology of the schools stamps much of the contemporary theological scene. In no small way has theology succumbed to its perennial temptation to sunder itself from mystical experience and living faith in favour of an over-emphasized academic theology. Spirituality and piety have also given in to their classic temptation to separate themselves from critical self-interpretation and evaluation. That many contemporary theologians relegate the great Christian saints and mystics to the realm of piety and spirituality, often pejorative terms in academic circles, and that many contemporary charismatics view theology or any hard thinking about the faith with great suspicion says much about the contemporary situation.[99]

The reversal of this split is a matter of the greatest urgency. Theological progress must again come to be recognized as interior spiritual progress, not simply a movement which occurs in the realm of ideas. The work of theology itself needs to be rescued from the intellectual ghettos, and reintegrated with the struggles for justice in the world and for personal and corporate holiness.

In recent years the liberation theologians of Latin America have recalled us to the need for such a unity of theology, social struggle, and spirituality. While liberation theology is often criticized as being 'horizontalist' and lacking in spiritual depth, there has been in fact a strong emphasis from a number of writers and groups on the need for a spirituality of liberation, a spirituality which unites the mystical and prophetic trends in Christian life. One such writer is the Chilean pastor Segundo Galilea who has written of the link between politics and contemplation:[100]

> Authentic Christian contemplation, passing through the desert, transforms contemplatives into prophets and heroes of commitment, and militants into mystics. Christianity achieves the synthesis of the politician and the mystic, the militant and the contemplative, and abolishes the false antithesis between the religious contemplatives and the militantly committed.

But this stress on the unity of mystical and political is not unique to Latin American thought. In the life and theology of Martin Luther King, for example, we see a similar emphasis. In King's active and militant campaign for racial justice there is a continual current of inner spirituality. At the height of his most 'activist' phase, King vowed to set aside one day each week for meditation and fasting, for, he held, 'my failure to reflect will do harm not only to me as a person but to the total movement'.[101] From the same period came the writings of the former Secretary-General of the United Nations, Dag Hammarskjöld, one of the most interesting contemporary mystics. Hammarskjöld held that 'in our era the road to sanctification necessarily passes through action'.[102] In his book *Markings*, which appeared first in Swedish in 1963, he stressed the importance of a mystical dimension to political activity, the dimension of interior silence and stillness. For those concerned with world peace, the inner life of sacrifice and of abiding in the light was vital.[103]

Among those concerned at a more local level with work for justice, there is an expressed need to develop spiritual resources, rejecting the false polarization of spirituality and social action. Thus a recent journal raises the question 'How can activists stay spiritually fit?' and points out that there is a new quest for the unity of contemplation and action. For some years there had developed a false polarity, but now the desire was for unity:

> But today the activism of the 60s and the spiritual emphasis of the 70s seems to be melding into a holistic self-understanding. Christians are beginning to learn that to attempt activism without a spiritual discipline is like trying to make wine without first making grape juice.[104]

More recently still we find a young Anglican priest in the United States claiming that the discovery and nurturing of this fundamental unity of mysticism and politics is one of the most crucial developments, the great 'new thing', which God is doing in our age:

> God is acting in the last years of the twentieth century to bring about the convergence of two impulses that Christians have long thought contradictory: the contemplative impulse to prayer, and the impulse to Christian social and political action. Mysticism and politics, things we had thought incompatible in one human soul or one Christian community, are being revealed in the practice of Christians today as aspects of one another, two sides of the same human coin. What is happening in historical terms is the reversal of the dichotomy of religion and politics.[105]

The mystic and the prophet are necessary to each other, but we need to assert more than that. All Christians are called to a ministry and a spirituality which contains both mystical and prophetic insights and aspects. In our age, we need more than almost anything else to restore the political dimensions of mystical vision and the visionary dimensions of political action.

In fact, the more we look at classical prophecy, the more we see that at its heart was a mystical experience. The old contrast between the prophetic and mystical approaches to God may have some validity in terms of the contrast between the earthiness of the Jewish prophets and the escapist and pietist aspects of some mystical trends, but the contrast between prophet and mystic has been overdrawn. All prophecy has its origins in vision, in insight into the reality of God, in mystical theology. The prophets are often called seers, never hearers.[106] 'The Word of God ... which he *saw*' (Amos 1.1). The prophets were people of intense vision, clear insight and perception, without which there would have been no proclamation. The vision of God and the identification of oppression went together. Out of the sense of divine holiness and justice there came a sense of the viciousness of injustice and sin. Knowledge of God led to a deeper knowledge of human realities. So the prophets spent much time gazing at the ground, seeing how the poor were treated, how the aliens, orphans, and widows fared, and so on. The central element in prophecy is not prediction but rather the seizing on reality in its moment of highest expectation and tension towards the new, and this tension is discovered not in a state of hypnotic elation but rather in the light of everyday experience.[107] Mystical insight takes place in and through the ordinary, the social and political events of cities and nations.

In nurturing a spirituality of the depths, therefore, we need to help expose people more to the suffering of the world, for 'the Christian needs to have more, not less, exposed nerves than others to see the world with honesty enough to grasp its appalling cruelties'.[108] An important part of spiritual direction must be to enable this exposure to occur and to issue in positive, mature action. Central to all spiritual direction must be the growth in discernment, in *diakrisis*, in the ability to see more clearly and with sanctified and sensitized eyes. Yet much spirituality has been concerned to enable and encourage Christians to avert their eyes, to retreat from the world into the piety of the ghetto, and this may well be one of the reasons why the product called 'spirituality' is so easily marketed today in many parts of the United States. In identifying criteria for discriminating between true spirituality and false we need to ask whether a spiritual movement has enabled us to see with greater penetration and insight into the roots of the world's pain, enabled us to respond more dynamically and more effectively to that pain. At the turn of the century, Nicholas Berdyaev made the contrast between the two types of spirituality:[109]

Christian piety all too often has seemed to be the withdrawal from the world and from men, a sort of transcendent egoism, the unwillingness to share the suffering of the world and of man. It was not sufficiently infused with Christian love and mercy. It lacked human warmth. And the world has risen in protest against this form of piety as a refined form of egoism, an indifference to the world's sorrow. Against this protest only a reborn piety can stand. Care for the life of another, material bodily care, is spiritual in essence. Bread for myself is a material question: bread for my neighbour is a spiritual question.

Today the issue of discernment between true and false mysticism, true and false spirituality, is of even greater urgency.

Authentic mysticism involves a penetration into the depths of reality, a penetration beyond the phoney and the superficial. It involves therefore a confrontation with all forms of illusion and pretence both within our own persons and in our society. The mystical way is essentially subversive. It demands the unmasking of illusion, the purification of the self, the rejection of falsehood. The road to God is the road which involves darkness and mystery, a *via negativa* in which all human constructs are relativized, and all inherited assumptions and languages are called into question. 'The *via negativa* has profound political implications. It is a rejection of everything in order to start anew.'[110] In the journey to the abyss, we lose control of ourselves, abandon our obsession with ownership, and enter the 'abysmal waylessness', the ignorance of which no one can truly speak.

Nothing is further from the truth than the notion that the mystic way is one in which reality is bypassed, treated as itself illusory. Where this occurs, the path taken is one which is hostile to Christian perceptions of truth. Rather the mystic way should lead to an awakening to the needs of the world, an ability to see those needs more clearly and respond to them with deeper insight and realism. When the contemplative orientation of the Christian community is lost, then that community becomes vulnerable to the seductions of the political ideologies who seek to use it for their own ends. It is likely to become an opiate. True contemplation, on the other hand, leads to enriched vision out of which action can grow:

> Contemplation is the movement from darkness to light. It is the movement from that place in which the true shape and identity of things are muffled in the obscurity of fear and illusion to that place in which false perceptions and misleading notions are burned away by the light of God's love. It is the movement from the night of loneliness and despair in which we cannot discern the faces of our brothers and sisters to the dawn of recognition and community.[111]

There is thus the closest link between the mystical vision and the prophetic response, between contemplation and action, between the exploration of the Abyss which is God and the conflict with the abyss of sin in the world. What happens within us is of the greatest social and political import, and this recognition is growing today among many sections of the community. As Roszak has written: 'We can now understand that the fate of the soul is the fate of the social order, that if the spirit within us withers, so to will all the world we build about us.'[112]

12

God the Mother

Those who reject their heavenly Mother do thereby reject true wisdom. And this accounts for the self-evident want of wisdom in all human governments and societies, civil and religious ... Another necessary consequence of sinning against and hating wisdom the Mother Spirit in the Godhead is the degradation and oppression of Woman. The lost and fallen world, although numbering in its population one half females, knows only male rulers and governors; male priests and religious teachers; male doctors and physicians; masters males, females slaves.
William Leonard (1853)[1]

Today the Goddess is no longer worshipped. Her shrines are lost in the dust of ages, while her statues line the walls of museums. But the law or power of which she was but the personification is unabated in its strength and lifegiving potency.
Mary Esther Harding[2]

In a study published in 1861, Johann Bachofen claimed that the mother was the original focus of civilization.[3] Since then, considerable research in the fields of anthropology, psychology, myth and ritual, and archaeological excavations, have vastly increased our knowledge of the role played by the female in early cultures and early notions of deity. Some have argued that the world was once inhabited by a matriarchal culture, and that later, perhaps around 5000–6000BC, there occurred a shift towards patriarchy.[4] Certainly the symbol of the nature Goddess is of very great antiquity. The symbol of the cosmos as a 'world egg' occurs in various forms. Yet later, after the emergence of distinct God figures, there is considerable evidence for the prevalence of the female God in many ancient societies.

The Mother Goddess in fact dominates the archaeological records of the ancient world.[5] Every major excavation in Palestine has produced some Goddess figurines.[6] The Ras Shamra texts show the cult of the Great Mother, under the name of Anat, to be established in Canaan at the time of the Hebrew settlement.[7] E. O. James, who studied the Mother Goddess in great detail, claimed that there was in fact *one* Goddess worshipped under many names – Demeter

(Eleusis), Isis (Egypt), Inanna–Ishtar (Sumeria), Astarte (Syria), Tiamat (Babylonia), Athena (Athens). Behind the specific female deities there was the great primal Mother, the source of all reality. In Greek myth, the earth goddes Ge/Gaia gave birth to the universe, while in Egypt the goddess Nut gave birth to the sun. In Sumeria, Gestin, a genderless earth mother, was seen as the source of the heavens, the earth, and all life. It is clear beyond serious dispute that the theme of God as female played a central role in ancient religious life. 'There can be no doubt that in the very earliest ages of human history, the magical force and wonder of the female was no less a marvel than the universe itself.'[8]

The discussion of the early ideas about the sexuality of God is complex and controversial. Some have argued that primitive mentality was bisexual, and that a purely male God would be seen as incomplete. A Roman Catholic missionary, writing some time ago, argued that the failure of much Christian missionary work was due to its inability to recognize this fundamental concept of bisexuality in the view of deity in many cultures.[9] Others have suggested that perhaps the bisexual notion of God was itself a development from an earlier notion of a sexless power.[10] However unfamiliar modern Western Christians may be with feminine concepts of God, many non-Christian traditions, such as Hinduism, have had no difficulty in embracing such a concept.[11] Nor did female deities disappear from Old Testament religion. Before the Exile, Jeremiah complained that women were kneading dough to make cakes for the Queen of Heaven (Jer. 7.18) while, during the Exile in Babylon, Ezekiel saw in a vision women in Jerusalem weeping for Tammuz (Ezek. 8.14). Canaanite religion in fact included a range of gods and goddesses, but principally Asherah and her son Baal. Temples of Asherah and Yahweh were found painted side by side on the walls of Mizpeh and survived until the city was destroyed.[12] Many relics of goddess cults survived down to post-exilic times when Yahwism was purged of these elements which were associated with Canaanite idolatry, though the cult of Asherah did not totally die out even then. It is possible that the Song of Solomon was based on the sacred marriage (hieros gamos) derived from the Asherah/Baal cult. In much popular religion, Yahweh was seen as married to Asherah. But in pure Yahwism, God had no consort, lover, sister, or mother, an astonishing fact when one considers that Yahwistic faith grew up in the very heartland of the religion of the Great Mother.

After the Babylonian exile, official Yahwism was purged of its feminine and 'bodily' elements. The festivals of earth were reinterpreted as festivals of the history of salvation. Feminine elements were rewritten, for goddesses were associated with paganism and idolatry. The female was excluded both from the deity and from full membership in the community of Israel, and Jewish religious life came to be characterized by a 'strictly masculine structure'.[13] Only males were true Israelites. So it has been said that the Old Testament 'stands midway between the worship of women and their total condemnation'.[14] As women were excluded from the official cult, so the condemnation of female sacrality, in the form of witchcraft, more and more led to the view of woman-centred religious life as demonic.

So God came to be seen exclusively in male terms, as Father and not Mother. This exclusive use of symbolism replaced the variety and richness of both the Bible and of earlier Christian history. Yet the theme of God the Mother, and the need to see a feminine dimension of the divine nature never totally disappeared either in the Old Testament or in early Christian spirituality. It will be the purpose of this chapter to examine some of the ways in which, in Jewish and Christian experience, God has been seen in feminine symbols. So dominant has the theme of the Fatherhood of God been in Christian history that it is widely taken to be the *only* symbol of divine relationship, and arguments, for example, about women's ordination, are based upon this. So one theologian can write: 'The Christian priest is to exercise fatherhood and not motherhood to God's family because his office is a participation in God's own relationship to his people, and God is our Father in heaven and not our Mother.'[15] In fact the question is by no means so simple.

Feminine Dimensions of God in the Bible

Human beings, so the Genesis account of creation tells us, were made in the image of God. There are in fact two different accounts in Genesis, the later one of which presents the creation of humanity as male and female as the climax of God's creative work, while the former (Chapters 2–4) tends more to stress the human being as fallen and created from dust. In the later account, however, there is a sense of the build-up of the work of creation until the man is completed in the creation of woman. Woman, according to this account, is not simply moulded from clay but built (Gen. 2.22). In Yahwist theology of creation, as expressed in the P tradition of Genesis woman and man in communion reflect the image of God. There is a high view of womanhood, and in the account of the experience of deliverance in Hosea, Israel calls Yahweh not my master (*baali*) but rather my man (*ishi*, Hos. 2.16). In Genesis too, the woman is created as a helper and partner to the man. Man, that is, humanity, male and female together, is made in the image of God (Gen. 1.26–7, repeated at 5.1–2). Adam is divided into *zakar* (male) and *neqebah* (female), the image being the total person.

This being so, it is difficult to see how one can avoid the conclusion that Yahweh is both male and female. This is certainly not something emphasized in the Bible, but it is in accordance with the ancient view of divinity as bipolar.[16]

Some feminist writers have claimed that the word *Elohim*, one of the key words for God in Genesis, is in fact a Hebrew female noun with a masculine plural ending, and that, while the word is generally treated as a masculine singular word, it may originally have indicated a desire to unite masculine and feminine dimensions of deity, and was later revised to satisfy the Yahwistic purists and exclude the feminine. However, this is unlikely, and it is probably more true to say that Elohim is a masculine singular name, with the ending added to make the final syllable audible.

However, there is no doubt that there was an exclusion of the feminine symbols of divine activity as Judaism developed. Yet such symbols are present in the Old Testament. While it would be wrong to see them as central to the tradition, they do represent an important and under-developed theological resource. Thus in the Psalms, God is pictured as a midwife, one who takes a person out of the womb and keeps her safe on her mother's breasts (Ps. 22.9); as a winged bird under whose wings men take refuge (36.8), and, similarly, as a nesting place for the sparrows with their young ones (84.4). In another psalm, God is compared both to a master and a mistress (123.2). Of particular interest is Psalm 51.1, a plea for mercy and for the compassion of God. The word used for compassion, *rachmim*, is the plural of *rechem*, womb, and thus conveys the notion of God's motherly compassion. This theme of God's compassion occurs also in Exodus 34.6: the Lord is seen here as merciful and gracious, abounding in steadfast love and faithfulness. Again the same word, *rachmim*, is used, suggesting the trembling womb of the mother.

There is maternal symbolism too in Deuteronomy 32. Here God is referred to as 'the Rock that begot you . . . the God who gave you birth' (32.18). 'Begot' is more accurately rendered 'bore', God being seen as having writhed in labour. Earlier in the same chapter, God is compared to an eagle, stirring up her nest, fluttering over her young ones, and bearing them on her pinions (32.11). Maternal symbols occur also in Second Isaiah. In 42.13–14 there is a mingling of masculine and feminine symbolism. First God is seen as a mighty man, a man of war (v. 13), then as a woman, in travail, gasping and panting (v. 14). Later God is described as 'the Lord who made you, who formed you from the womb' (44.2; see also 44.24). The comparison with a mother recurs at 49.15:

Can a woman forget her suckling child,
    that she should have no compassion on the son of her womb?
Even these may forget,
    yet I will not forget you.

Perhaps the most striking passage is in 66.12–13:

Behold, I will extend prosperity to her like a river,
    and the wealth of the nations like an overflowing stream;
and you shall suck, you shall be carried upon her hip,
    and dandled upon her knees.
As one whom his mother comforts,
    so I will comfort you:
    you shall be comforted in Jerusalem.

It has been said of this passage that it is 'the first time in the Old Testament that the witness borne to Yahweh breaks through the reserve which elsewhere it observes so strictly, and associates feminine predications with him.'[17] As we have seen, however, it does not stand alone.

Comparisons with women in labour occur elsewhere. The mystery of the work of God is compared to the mystery of 'how the spirit comes to the bones in the womb of a woman with child' (Eccles. 11.5). In Ecclesiasticus, the Lord and the Law are referred to in parallel, the Law then being compared to a mother and a virgin bride (Ecclus. 15.1), while earlier the love of the Lord is said to surpasss that of mothers (4.10). Virtually nothing of this maternal symbolism survives into the New Testament apart from the oft-cited passage in Matthew 23.37: 'O Jerusalem, Jerusalem . . . How often would I have gathered your children together as a hen gathers her brood under her wings, and you would not!' The comparison of Christ to the mother hen is one which is taken up by spiritual writers from the early Church onwards.

However, the Old Testament and inter-testamental literature does contain some important passages in which Wisdom, closely identified with God, is personified in feminine terms. The feminine character of Wisdom (*hokhma*) is more than grammatical as the passages show. In the Book of Proverbs, Wisdom is seen as a woman who has built her house, mixed wine and set her table, and who invites her disciples to eat and drink with her (9.1–6). Wisdom appears in female form also in the Book of Wisdom where she is seen as the breath of the power of God, an emanation of God's glory, a reflection of the eternal light and image of God's goodness. She makes all things new, God loves only those who live with her, and she orders all things for good (7.25–8.1). Ecclesiasticus also contains a lengthy chapter in praise of Wisdom (24.1–31). In Wisdom 10.15–17 she is virtually identified with God as redeemer and guide. It is correct then to see Wisdom as 'the divine power active in history'.[18] The accounts of Wisdom suggest not so much an attempt to identify female qualities in God as a way of experiencing the divine activity. In the Hellenistic period, Wisdom emerged as a hypostasis of God, and by the first century BC 'functioned virtually as a goddess'.[19]

The theology of Wisdom was developed later by gnostic writers, especially by Valentinus, and also by Eastern Orthodox thinkers who saw Wisdom as the original being of God from which the three Persons of the Trinity arose.[20] However, in the New Testament and mainstream early Christian thought, the tendency increasingly led to the dominance of the Logos over Wisdom. Much of the Wisdom theology was attributed to Christ, and in St John it seems that the Wisdom speeches in Proverbs, Wisdom, and Ecclesiasticus were an important influence.[21] But with the transfer of this tradition to Jesus, the feminine dimension of the symbolism was blocked: 'Although many of the attributes of Sophia were retained in Christology, direct access to the feminine dimension of the divine was effectively barred by the maleness of Jesus.'[22] In the process of the gradual disappearance of the feminine dimension, Philo is of crucial importance in at least three ways. He transferred the figure of Sophia, Wisdom, from earth to heaven, where she came to be addressed as ever virgin, maiden, daughter of God. This transference paved the way for later developments in Mariology, for the next time this kind of language comes to be used, it is of the Virgin Mary. Philo was important also for his hostility to women whom he saw as sensual and carnal, a view which was to dominate Christian thought in the West for hundreds of years. And Philo was important also in that he transformed feminine attributes to masculine ones.[23] So the strands in Scripture which pointed to the motherhood of God and spoke of God in a feminine way became more and more obscured.

The Femininity of God in Christian Spirituality

However, we do find references to God as mother in the patristic period. Clement of Alexandria, Origen, Irenaeus, John Chrysostom, Ambrose, and Augustine all use this image. It is probably true to say that the Greek tradition was more at home with maternal symbolism than the Latin, and the Latin translators of the Acts of Peter suppressed the use of 'mother' as a title for Christ. Clement of

Alexandria is of particular interest. He sees the male/female distinction as belonging only to this world.[24] He speaks of God as his nurse, as well as using the popular image of the mother bird.[25] God, he says, is both Father and Mother:

> And God himself is love; and out of love to us became feminine. In his ineffable essence he is Father; in his compassion to us he became Mother. The Father by loving became feminine; and the great proof of this is he whom he begot of himself; and fruit brought forth by love is love.[26]

In his *Paidagogos*, a study of Christ the Instructor, there is a whole chapter devoted to this theme, in which he speaks of the work of God in suckling. Christ is seen as the milk of God, and God as nourisher of his people. He speaks of the breasts of God and of the milk of the Lord.

In Irenaeus too there is reference to the 'mother's breasts' of Christ, while Justin Martyr speaks of the 'belly of Christ'. Ephraim the Syrian uses maternal symbols in his hymns, while both Maximus the Confessor and Symeon the New Theologian speak of each Christian as giving birth to Christ, an extension of the mother imagery to the Church as a whole. Synesius, Bishop of Ptolemais in the early fifth century, writes: 'You are Father, your are Mother. You are male, and you are female.'[27] John Chrysostom speaks of Christ as sister and mother.[28] He relates the maternal symbolism to the nourishing work of Christ in the Eucharist. Ambrose too speaks of the breasts of God,[29] while Augustine uses a variety of maternal symbols. He draws on 1 Corinthians 1.24 alongside Wisdom 7.12 to speak of 'our Mother, the Wisdom of God'.[30] God, he says, is our Father and our Mother, and he identifies Christ with Wisdom.[31] Christ is the 'Hen of the Gospel'. Augustine makes use of the idea of the bird hovering, and of the mother hen. 'The comparison of the hen to the very Wisdom of God is not without ground.'[32] The symbol of the mother hen is used very widely by the patristic writers.

It is therefore wrong to see the symbolism of divine motherhood as something very marginal to orthodox spirituality, or as something found only in heretical and gnostic writings. It was in fact 'a well-known and centrally orthodox metaphor . . . It permeates exegesis, typology, sermons and liturgy.'[33] However, in recent years attention has been focused more upon the use of the feminine dimension of God in gnostic works. Certainly there are such uses. Thus the early third-century work the *Acts of Peter* addresses God: 'Thou art my Father, thou art my Mother . . .'[34] The *Gospel of Truth* says: 'The Father opens his bosom, but his bosom is the Holy Spirit.'[35] In a recent and well-publicized study, Elaine Pagels has argued that the gnostics used masculine and feminine terms for God and practised the 'principle of equality': 'Gnostic sources continually use sexual symbolism to describe God . . . Yet instead of describing a monistic and masculine God, many of these texts speak of God as a dyad who embraces both masculine and feminine elements.'[36] She goes on, as do many of her disciples, to contrast this egalitarian and proto-feminist tradition within gnosticism with the hierarchical and anti-feminist tradition of mainline orthodoxy. In fact, however, the gnostics are uneasy allies for a feminist cause, and further study of their theology shows how disastrous a dependence on this source would be.

In gnostic theology, the female principle represents the material realm, the realm of the fallen, physical world. Femaleness belongs to the created order, characterized by lust and decay. Transcendence lies with the male, the spiritual, rational principle. Thus the Pseudo-Clementine *Homilies* can say:[39] 'The present world is female, as the mother bringing forth the souls of the children, but the world to come is male, as a father receiving his children.' The terms male and female, as used in gnostic writings, do not stand for actual people but for dualistic principles. Salvation comes, according to some texts, through transcendence of the female principle. Thus the *Gospel of Thomas* tells us that woman can become man and so enter the Kingdom of Heaven.[38] In gnosticism, the destruction of the female principle is necessary in the more dualistic systems, while more moderate ones seem to hold out the possibility for a unification of male and female principles. Either way, femaleness is secondary and inferior. Nothing could be further from the truth than the view, popularized in recent years, that the gnostics were the original Christian feminists. In fact, heresy and feminism are not very good bedfellows at all.[39] As Christ says in the *Gospel of the Egyptians*, 'I have come to destroy the works of the female.'[40]

Central to the use of the feminine symbols for the divine presence and activity is the belief that man and woman together form the image of God. As this belief was eroded, so the use of feminine symbols declined. According to Augustine, man should not cover his head because he is the image of God and reflects God's glory, while woman reflects man's glory. Woman and man together certainly form the image of God, but woman alone does not while man alone does.[41] As the Christian tradition developed, feminine symbols became obscured, but they did not disappear. The themes of the holy city, of vessels, of the tree of life, of the earth, the cave, and the mountain, and particularly the symbolism of the font, bear witness to the dramatic power of the feminine. Erich Neumann has said that 'whenever we encounter the symbol of rebirth, we have to do with a matriarchal transformation mystery, and this is true even when its symbolism or interpretation bears a patriarchal disguise'.[42] The Catholic liturgical and spiritual tradition preserved the feminine and maternal symbolism, but much of it became dissociated from God. Rather the feminine came to represent the relationship of the Church or the individual soul to God, the masculine principle. 'Father religions,' wrote Erikson, 'have mother churches.'[43]

Nevertheless, the use of female symbolism for the Holy Spirit occurs both in gnostic and orthodox writers. The gnostic *Gospel of the Hebrews* speaks of 'my Mother, the Holy Spirit',[44] while the *Gospel of Philip* argues that the Holy Spirit cannot have impregnated Mary because the Spirit is known to be female.[45] In the *Acts of Thomas*, the eucharistic epiclesis has a female aspect, God being addressed as 'Mother of the ineffable mystery'.[46] But the femaleness of the Holy Spirit occurs also in Gregory of Nazianzen, who compares the Spirit to Eve, and in Methodius of Olympus, who calls the Spirit the 'rib of the Logos'.[47] It is, however, in the Syrian Christian tradition that we find the notion of the Holy Spirit as Mother in its strongest form. In the oldest Syriac version of the Bible, the Holy Spirit is referred to as 'she'. Thus John 14.26 is rendered: '*She* shall teach you everything.' Syrian writers see the motherhood of the Spirit in Genesis 1.2, the symbol of the mother bird brooding over the fruit of her womb, and in Luke 1.35, the Spirit's hovering over Mary. The Syrian father Aphrahat speaks of the 'Holy Spirit, his Mother'.[48] At baptism, she opens the heavens, and the baptized Christians are clothed with her nature.[49] In the *Odes of Solomon*, the Holy Spirit is seen as a female dove, while Ode 28 calls the Holy Spirit the Mother of Christ. In Ode 19 we read:[50]

> The Holy Spirit opened her bosom
> And mixed the milk of the two breasts of the Father.
> Then she gave the mixture to the generation without their
>   knowing,
> And those who have received it are in the perfection of the right
>   hand.

In the Syrian *Didascalia Apostolorum*, the description of the work of deaconesses is linked with the femaleness of the Holy Spirit.[51] Later, some of these early Syrian texts were purged in the interests of an increasingly male-dominated orthodoxy.[52]

In other eastern religious traditions, we find trinities of Father, Mother, and Son, while Christianity replaced the Mother by what Ernest Jones called 'an ambiguously nebulous character', the Holy

Spirit.[53] Yet as late as the fourteenth century, we find a fresco in a church near Munich where the three figures of the Trinity are emerging from a common stem with the female Holy Spirit.[54] In much medieval spirituality, God is experienced and described as mother, sister, and nurse, as well as king, knight, lover, and brother. The official view, as expressed by Aquinas, was that, while God was beyond gender categorization, he was more truly father than mother:

Father and mother are loved as principles of our natural origin. Now the father is principle in a more excellent way than the mother, because he is the active principle, while the mother is a passive and material principle. Consequently, strictly speaking, the father is to be loved more.[55]

However, this did not prevent much speculation about the feminine character of the coming age. Some of the disciples of Joachim of Fiore saw the Third Age of the Spirit as involving the recovery of the feminine dimension.[56]

The twelfth century was crucial for the re-emergence of feminine symbols of the divine. While many believe that it was through women that this symbolism was rediscovered, the twelfth-century material shows that it was men who first began to use feminine symbols. This was an age which also saw a feminization of language, and a deepening interiority of devotion. Spiritual literature was filled with images of food and drink, of brimming fountains and springs of blood. It was the period of the Béguines who have been called 'the first women's movement in western history'.[57] It was a period also in which the humanity of Christ came to be emphasized as part of a general shift in spirituality from atonement–resurrection–law–judgement motifs towards an increased stress on creation and incarnation. In this shift of emphasis, the influence of women was very important. It was women who created and developed devotion to the infant Jesus, to his sacred heart and wounds, while women mystics were responsible for the introduction of the feast of Corpus Christi.[58] There was a paradoxical element here, for, after the Gregorian reforms of the mid-eleventh century, the clergy had less contact with women, and there was a marked growth in clericalism. So 'as the priest became more distant, God became more accessible; as the priest was "divinized", God became "human".'[59] In fact, in this period, women, along with priests, were widely viewed as being possessed of spiritual powers. So the Béguine mystic Mechtild of Magdeburg, in one of her visions, sees a friar in purgatory, who cries 'Have women and priests pray for me'.[60]

It was in the twelfth century also that we see the first flowering of the image of Jesus as Mother. It was a devotion originally developed by men such as Bernard of Clairvaux, Aelred of Rievaulx, Guerric of Igny, Isaac of Stella, William of St Thierry, and, in particular, Anselm of Canterbury. 'There is no reason to assert, as some have done, that the theme of the motherhood of God is a "feminine insight".'[61] In fact, the major female theological writer of the twelfth century, Hildegard of Bingen, does not use the symbol at all. Guerric of Igny, on the other hand, uses the symbolism of the divine pregnancy and maternal care to a great extent. God, he says, draws us into his bowels. Christ, he says,

... has breasts lest he should be lacking any one of all duties and titles of loving kindness. He is father in virtue of natural creation ... and also in virtue of the authority with which he instructs. He is mother too in the mildness of his affection and a nurse ...[62]

Guerric speaks also of the Christian community itself as pregnant with the mystery of Christ:

I see by your gift not one but countless faithful souls pregnant with this glorious seed; watch over your word, lest any of it miscarry. And you, happy mothers of so splendid a child, care for yourselves until Christ be formed in you.[63]

Similarly, Aelred of Rievaulx speaks of the 'maternal breasts of Jesus'.[64] 'His naked breasts will feed you with the milk of sweetness to console you.'[65] Mechtild of Hackeborn, who died at the end of the thirteenth century, speaks of both Christ and the Holy Spirit as mothers. Mother images are found also in the Middle English prayers collected by the author of *The Talkyng of the Luv of God* and in the *Ancren Riwle* Christ gives suck to the redeemed by blood from his wounds.[66] Margaret of Oyngt, a Carthusian, uses mother symbolism in her reflections on the work of Christ on the cross:[67]

Ah, who has seen a woman give birth thus!
And when the hour of birth came, they placed
You on the bed of the cross. And it is not astonishing
Your veins ruptured as you gave birth in one single day
To the whole world.

Bernard too uses a wide range of maternal images, especially those of nurturing and suckling. He sees the breasts as symbolic of the pouring out of affection. He sees Christ as nursing his children, and speaks of his fostering wings. Many medieval hymns address Christ as mother. But it is St Anselm of Canterbury who is best remembered for his use of this symbol, and is even proclaimed as 'the originator of the devotion to our Lord, our Mother'.[68]

If it is correct to speak of Anselm as holding a doctrine of 'divine androgyny', it is because medieval Christians saw themselves in a more androgynous way than we do.[69] Some see only absurdities and extravagant word play in Anselm's mother language.[70] But that would be to trivialize and undervalue something which permeates his devotions and is clearly of considerable spiritual importance. Thus in his Prayer to St Paul, Anselm speaks of the maternal aspect of Christ. He speaks both of Paul as his mother in faith, then of Christ as mother both of Paul and of himself:

And you, Jesus, are you not also a mother?
Are you not the mother who, like a hen,
gathers her chickens under her wings?
Truly, Lord, you are a mother;
for both they who are in labour
and they who are brought forth
are accepted by you.
You have died more than they, that they may labour to bear.
It is by your death that they have been born,
for if you had not been in labour,
you could not have borne death;
and if you had not died you would not have brought forth.

So, he concludes, 'So, you, Lord God, are the great mother.'[71] Anslem goes on to describe both Christ and Paul as fathers and mothers:

And you, my soul, dead in yourself,
run under the wings of Jesus your mother,
and lament your griefs under his feathers.
Ask that your wounds may be healed,
and that comforted you might live again.[72]

In his Prayer to St John, Anselm refers to him as reclining on the 'glorious breast of the Most High'.[73] Through his passion, Jesus has given birth to Christians: by dying he begot us.[74] Again, he uses the symbol of the mother hen with her chicks:[75]

Christ my mother, you gather your chickens under your wings; this dead chicken of yours puts himself under those wings. For by your gentleness the badly frightened are comforted, by your sweet smell the despairing are revived, your warmth gives life to the dead, your touch justifies sinners. Mother, now gain your dead son, both by the sign of your cross, and the voice of his confession.

Warm your chicken, give life to your dead man, justify your sinner. Let your terrified one be consoled by you: and in your whole and unceasing grace, let him be refashioned by you. For from you flows consolation for sinners; to you be blessing for ages and ages. Amen.

It is out of this rich patristic and medieval background of devotion to God as mother that Julian of Norwich in the fourteenth century can write a whole cycle of divine maternal activity. Julian is often seen as a kind of theological freak, writing of God the Mother in a total theological and spiritual vacuum. But this is certainly not the case. There is, as we have shown, a continuous occurrence of her central symbol of divine motherhood throughout many writers. As one Julian scholar has commented, 'She could scarcely have escaped its influence'.[76] In Julian's *Revelations of Divine Love*, we find the entire cycle of divine motherhood: the womb, birth, infancy, care, education, washing, healing – all are seen as aspects of God's activity and nature. God is seen as a lover, nurse, teacher, as a point, a light, a flower, and as clothing. A whole range of symbols is used of which the mother symbol is one. God is our Mother, Julian claims, the fount and origin of all motherhood. We owe our being to God who is the essence of motherhood. God is as really our Mother as s/he is our Father.[77]

God is 'our Mother by nature and grace'.[78] Four chapters of the *Revelations* (Chapters 58–61) deal almost exclusively with this theme. Some extracts from Chapter 60 will illustrate how Julian sees this divine motherhood:

> Thus he carries us within himself in love. And he is in labour until the time has fully come for him to suffer the sharpest pangs and most appalling pain possible – and in the end he dies . . .

> The human mother will suckle her child with her own milk, but our beloved Mother Jesus feeds us with himself, and with the most tender courtesy does it by means of the Blessed Sacrament, the precious food of all true life . . . The human mother may put her child tenderly to her breast, but our tender Mother Jesus simply leads us into his blessed breast through his open side . . .

> This fine and lovely word *Mother* is so sweet and so much its own that it cannot properly be used of any but him, and of her who is his own true Mother – and ours.[79]

Thus, says Julian, in Jesus our true Mother has our life been grounded.[80] Julian draws particularly on breast feeding and on table imagery in her portrayal of the divine maternal role. According to her,

God *is* Mother, not simply *like* a mother. It is interesting that there is no reference in Julian's writing to the 'mother hen', which is such a favourite of earlier writers. Julian is more concerned to stress the human mother than the bird. It is also notable that in Julian's descriptions of God, there is nothing which is exclusively male.

Julian's mother symbolism has either been seized upon by devotees of God the Mother and isolated to the detriment of the tradtion, or ignored as a minor oddity. Thus the world authority on the text, Sister Anna Maria Reynolds pays little attention to it, nor does the English translator Clifton Wolters apart from one paragraph.[81] It must therefore be stressed that the mother symbolism is both an important element in Julian's theology and also part of a continuous tradition. Julian is 'not a lonely or peculiar voice. She stands in a long tradition of Christians, men and women, who experience God in a feminine way.'[82] Yet Julian is important because she exhibits the tradition in its strongest and most developed form. As Jennifer Heimmel has written:[83]

> In the *Revelations*, Julian presents her vision of God in the feminine maternal role, not in the isolated fragments of the tradition but in a complete connected cycle of life, from before birth, through after death. Julian's majestic vision proceeds through all the various stages of: enclosure and growth within the womb; the trauma of labour and birth; the suckling of the infant and feeding of the child; the care and education of the older child; the setting of examples and disciplining of the child as it matures; and the continual loving, touching and guiding of the child even to the point of its own death, which becomes in turn a rebirth and return to the original womb ... There is no single previous example which even begins to approach the depth with which Julian has explored the varied potentials of the image of a Christian maternal God.

Julian thus represents the climax of the medieval affective tradition of devotion to God as Mother, a tradition which looks back beyond the constricting influence of Augustine to an earlier tendency, less dominated by fallenness, more optimistic, more human, more holistic in its approach to both God and humanity.

But the tradition recovered and emphasized by Julian was not developed to any great extent within orthodox Christianity. It was centuries later that the feminine dimension of God was re-emphasized by a variety of fringe Protestant groups, notably the Shakers in the late eighteenth century. In the Shaker view, a male redemption was necessarily incomplete. So they looked for a future female redeemer, and they saw in the figure of Ann Lee, born in Manchester in 1736, a female Christ principle. In early Shaker writing, Ann Lee is referred to as Ann the Christ, Ann the Word, and Daughter of Zion. What was central to Shaker theology was the view that there must be a second manifestation of the Christ, this time in female form, and this rediscovery of the feminine dimension in God has rightly been seen as 'the most significant Shaker contribution to American religion'.[84] The Shakers thought of God in four persons: Father, Mother (Wisdom), Son, and Daughter. Similar ideas of God as female appeared in the Mormon movement and in Christian Science.[85] The Mormons saw the human race as children of divine parents, and they expressed their notion of a divine family in their hymns:

> In the heavns, are parents single?
> No! The tho't makes reason stare!
> Truth is reason; truth eternal
> Tells me I've a Mother there.[86]

Earlier the Shaker Hymnal had expressed a similar theme:

> Long ere this fleeting world began,
> Or dust was fashioned into man,
> There power and wisdom we can view.
> Names of the Everlasting Two.
>
> The Father's high eternal throne
> Was never filled by one alone:
> There Wisdom holds the Mother's seat,
> And is the Father's helper meet.[87]

So, while conventional mainstream Christianity proclaimed a masculine God, it was left to the heretical movements, often millenarian, to restate the feminine dimension of God which had previously found its place within orthodox Christian tradition.

In the twentieth century, a number of writers have reopened the question of the feminine in God. The poet W. B. Yeats attacked the orthodox Christian 'masculine Trinity' as 'an abstract Greek absurdity'.[88] Paul Tillich complained of the neglect of the feminine in Christian theology.[89] The Dominican Victor White warned that if religion became dominated by a male, father symbolism, with a consequent stress on law, order, and the super ego, neglecting the mother symbol, with its emphasis on instinct, feeling, and eros, then religion was likely to lead to repression and disintegration, and not to bind together.[90] White certainly showed some sympathy with the idea of divine motherhood, though all his subsequent discussion centres upon the Virgin Mary.[91]

White was deeply concerned with the work of C. G. Jung, and much of his discussion was coloured by Jung's commitment to the feminine in God. Jungian writers today lay great stress on androgyny and on the need to recover the feminine side, and they have been much criticized by feminist writers for appearing to offer a solution while still maintaining patriarchal structures.[92] Writing at the same time as Jung, Thomas Merton was grappling with the idea of the feminine principle in God. In a letter written in 1959 he responded to a friend's inquiry about Wisdom:

> The first thing to be said, of course, is that Hagia Sophia is God himself. God is not only Father but a Mother. He is both at the same time, and it is the 'feminine aspect' or feminine principle in the divinity that is the Hagia Sophia. But, of course, as soon as you say this the whole thing becomes misleading: a division of an 'abstract' divinity into two abstract principles. Nevertheless, to ignore this distinction is to lose touch with the fullness of God.[93]

Merton saw Sophia as standing for the primordial darkness, the centre and meaning of all reality, the principle of being and source of creativity. While there is little in his more theological works to indicate whether or not he pursued this time, he was beginning to move towards a recovery of a strand in Christian experience and reflection which had been all but lost. And he rightly warned that when that dimension has been lost in the Christian Church, we have started to 'lose touch with the fullness of God'.

The Problem of Mariology

To speak of Mariology, the theology and spirituality concerned with the role of the Virgin Mary, as a problem is already to arouse suspicions or preconceptions in some minds. Devout Catholics will protest that, far from presenting a problem, Mariology is a most important and integral part of Christian faith, a gift to the Church, a priceless source of enrichment and of spiritual life. Hostile Protestant readers will be pleased to have the Marian issue presented in problem terms, for that is how they see it: a problem, a deviation, a distortion of the pure Christ-centred faith. In speaking of Mariology as a problem. I have no intention of denying its necessary place in the Church. Indeed, attitudes to Mary are a decisive test of Christological orthodoxy. Mariology does not, in my view, present a problem in the sense that many Protestants would suggest, but it does present a problem in relation to the theme of the feminine dimension in God. For the cult of Mary grew as the use of feminine images for God declined. Much of the Wisdom material in particular was transferred to Mary as were other attributes previously applied to God. So the Mother of God replaced God the Mother. Mary might be highly exalted, but she was not divine: the feminine dimension was now safely removed from the divine realm.

The main outlines of Marian theology are clear by the second century. It has been suggested that a major factor in the development of devotion to Mary was the fact that the Logos Christology tended to make Jesus a remote, heavenly figure. So the more intimate human figure of Mary compensated for the seeming lack of humanity in Christ.[94] There is almost certainly some truth in this, though it was not what the doctrine of the incarnation was meant to uphold. At the same time, the emphasis on Mary grew as a by-product also of christological emphases: so the question of how one saw Mary became a diagnostic test of one's understanding of the nature of Christ. 'This name,' wrote St John of Damascus of the term Theotokos (God-bearer, or Mother of God), 'contains the whole mystery of the Incarnation.'[95] Mary came also to be seen as the embodiment of divine Wisdom, and the passage in Ecclesiasticus 24.9–10 which speaks of the origins of Wisdom came to be the standard reading in the Mass of Our Lady in the Roman rite. In the Eastern Church too Mary was seen as identical with Sophia:

> In her is realized the idea of Divine Wisdom in the creation of the world. She is Divine Wisdom in the created world. In her that Divine Wisdom is justified, and thus the veneration of the Virgin blends with that of Holy Wisdom. In the Virgin there are united Holy Wisdom and the wisdom of the created world, the Holy Spirit and the created hypostases. Her body is completely spiritual and transfigured. She is the justification, the end, the meaning of creation. She is, in this sense, the glory of the world. In her God is already all in all.[96]

Thus the relationship of Mary to Christ is paradoxical. On the one hand, she is seen as the Mother of God, bearer of the incarnate Word. On the other hand, she is the recipient of titles and characteristics previously associated with divinity itself.

Another essential element in the development of Mariology was the link made by the early Fathers between Mary and Eve. Paul saw Eve as the source of sin (1 Tim. 2.9–15), and early Christian writers saw Mary as the new Eve, the woman who reversed the curse. Justin Martyr tells us that Eve brought disobedience and death, while Mary brings obedience.[97] Gnostic writings, such as the Gospel of Philip and the Gospel of Bartholomew, also make the point that Christ was created from a virgin so that he might make good the false step made at the beginning. It is Irenaeus who most explicitly states the doctrine of Mary as the instrument of reversal of the curse of Eve. The human race fell through a virgin, and now is saved by a virgin. The knot of Eve's disobedience is loosed by the obedience of Mary. Already there is the idea of Mary as a co-redemptrix.[98] And this theme of the reversal of Eve's work later entered into popular hymns.

When the salutation
Gabriel had spoken,
Peace was shed upon us,
Eva's bonds were broken.

As Eve, when she her fontal sin reviewed,
Wept for herself and all she should include,
Blest Mary with man's Saviour in embrace
Joyed for herself and for all human race.

So Mary is seen as the mother of a new people, a free people. She comes to be seen as the first fruits of the new creation, the Church. 'Eve, Mary, Church: early theology always saw these three personages as it were through a single transparent image.'[99]

The climax of the Marian debate in the early Church was the ascription to her by the Council of Ephesus in 431 of the title Theotokos: literally God-bearer, but more popularly Mother of God. The Antiochenes would have preferred the title Christotokos, mother of the human Jesus. Theotokos was seen as a decisive victory and a vital christological issue. To deny that Mary was Mother of God was to deny the truth of the incarnation. Yet, as Cyril of Alexandria was anxious to stress, the ascription of the title must not be understood to imply ascription of divine status to Mary. 'We . . . who call her Mother of God have never at all deified any one of those that are numbered among creatures . . . and we know that the Blessed Virgin was woman as we.'[100] What was being asserted was the truth of God's taking of full humanity to himself. So fundamental was this truth to Christian faith that Gregory of Nazianzus could say that 'if one does not acknowledge Mary as Theotokos, he is estranged from God.'[101] The title is therefore seen, particularly by Eastern Orthodox theologians, as the 'ultimate test of christological orthodoxy . . . a key word to the whole of Christology'.[102]

In much of the early Eastern devotion to Mary, a close link is made between Mary and the Eucharist. In both of them, there is an overshadowing of the Holy Spirit. As the Spirit, the power of the Most High, came upon Mary (Luke 1.35), so God overshadows the bread and wine in the epiclesis of the eucharistic rite.[103] As Mary is the meeting place of God and humanity at a specific point in time, so the Eucharist is the meeting place of God and humanity throughout time. As Mary gave birth to the incarnate Word, so the sacraments give birth to Christ in us, we all conceive Christ, a theme which occurs in the writings of St Symeon the New Theologian and is later taken up by Eckhart. However, in medieval Western spirituality, there is no doubt that it was Mary who overshadowed both Father and Son![104] While in the Eastern Church, Marian devotion was located firmly, and to Western eyes at times shockingly, within the framework of Christology and of Eucharist, in the West Mary came increasingly to represent the tenderness and warmth which had been excluded from the transcendent Godhead. Henry Adams put it well in a study of the Middle Ages:[105]

> God could not be Love. God was Justice, Order, Unity, Perfection: He could not be human and imperfect, nor could the Son or the Holy Ghost be other than the Father. The Mother alone was human, imperfect, and could love; she alone was Favour, Duality, Diversity. Under any conceivable form of religion, this duality must find embodiment somewhere, and the Middle Ages logically insisted that, as it could not be in the Trinity, either separately or together, it must be in the Mother.

Nor did the resurgence of the theme of the maternal dimension in God from the twelfth century onwards diminish the devotion to Mary. In popular devotion, the two feminine-directed trends flourished together. Mary, wrote Aelred of Rievaulx, is the one 'who has given us life, who nourishes and raises us. She is our mother, much more than our mother according to the flesh'.[106] More than that, in some forms of Marian devotion, Mary is our mother much more than the Trinity. In one sixteenth-century French statue, a seated Madonna holds in one hand a small world, and in the other a baby. The body of the statue is also a door, and when it is open, it reveals God the Father holding up the crucified Christ, while all the saints look on. The entire drama occurs within the womb of Mary the Great Mother![107]

The way in which Mariology has taken over crucial areas of divine experience is of fundamental importance for understanding the strength of the resistance to it, as well as the strength of its own grip on peoples and communities. For the opponents of Marian devotion have been right to sense that, in spite of protests to the contrary, elements formerly ascribed to God have been absorbed into the cult of Mary. It is highly significant that so orthodox a theologian as Hans Urs von Balthasar, whose influence on the thought of Pope John Paul II is considerable, can even suggest that Mariology is the only guarantee of the humanity of the Church:

> Without Mariology, Christianity threatens imperceptibly to become inhuman. The church becomes functionalistic, soulless, a hectic enterprise without any point of rest, estranged from its true nature by planners. And because, in this masculine world, all that we have is one ideology replacing another, everything becomes polemical, critical, bitter, humourless, and ultimately boring, and people in their masses turn away from such a church.[108]

Von Balthasar may well be right. But what is disturbing in this passage is that Mary seems to be seen as a necessary corrective to the masculinization of God. Mary is needed to make up for deficiencies in God, or perhaps in our theology. For it is 'without *Mariology*', not without a more holistic doctrine of God, that this writer sees the dangers of a masculine, functionalist Church. It is not therefore surprising that feminist critics of the Christian tradition such as Mary Daly, who once hoped for a reform of the Church and a reintegration of feminine insights into its theology, now suggests that Mariology be examined as a possible alternative to Christology. Mary, the Virgin, who conceived without the aid of man, stands for female autonomy, integrity, completeness; her Assumption stands for the reintegration of the divine androgyne. For if Mary can do what God the Father cannot, perhaps she can stand alone.[109]

In orthodox Christian thought, Mary does not stand alone. Yet the exclusion of feminine understandings and symbols from the doctrine of God has meant that, on the one hand, Mary comes to carry much of the weight of deity, while, on the other, she remains firmly in her place, as an inferior being. The masculine God may be inadequate, and will need to be supplemented by devotion to the human mother, but the distance between masculine Creator and feminine creature must be firmly maintained. So it is that those who exalt Mary may at the same time be performing a major disservice to the cause of a more whole theology as well as to that of real women in the world.

We see the ambivalence of a highly developed Marian theology if we look at the place of Mary in the thought of the late C. G. Jung. For Jung, Mariology is important as symbolizing the spiritual feminine. Men, and male-dominated society, need to recover that feminine dimension, but there is no suggestion that this cannot be accomplished without any really fundamental ideological or structural shift. It is rather a question of an inner, symbolic corrective.[110] However, those Christians who welcomed Jung's praise for the decree of the Dogma of the Assumption may have missed the crucial point in this welcome. For Jung, the Assumption of Mary was a pointer to a greater recovery in theology:

> The *Assumptio Mariae* paves the way not only for the divinity of Theotokos (i.e. her ultimate recognition as a goddess) but also the quaternity. At the same time, matter is included in the metaphysical realm together with the corrupting principle of the cosmos, evil.[111]

In other words, Jung sees the logical next step after the Assumption to be the development from Trinity to Quaternity, in which not only the feminine, but also the principle of evil (which he associates with matter, as well as, implicitly, with the feminine), is restored to its place in the Godhead.

There is not the space here for an examination of the background to this notion in Jung. Many writers have pointed to the crucial place played by gnostic ideas in his thought. But, in suggesting that Mariology was a pointer to the need for restoring the feminine dimension to God, he was surely right. For, while Mariology is of crucial importance in defending the Christian doctrine of the incarnation, it becomes a serious distortion when elements of the divine character become, as it were, split off, so that they can only be found in the creature and not in the Creator. As Rosemary Ruether has observed:[112]

> The feminine then can appear in Christian theology only as an expression of the creature, not as an aspect of God. The feminine represents either the original creation, the good material shaped by the hand of God, or the new creature, the eschatological community reborn from the Passion of Christ. As such, the good feminine is a spiritual principle of passive receptivity to the regenerating power of God.

Mariology may thus prevent the pursuit of the vital task of recovering a more whole doctrine of God.

Another related distortion of Mariology has been the idealization of Mary so that she comes to represent, not real womanhood, but some 'pure', spiritual model of femininity, safely removed both from the power of sexuality and the dirt and violence of social life. In much nineteenth-century devotion in popular Catholicism, Mary becomes an asexual being. To her, men and women pray for deliverance from 'impurity'. So, taught by Father Faber, we ask:[113]

> Thou who wert pure as driven snow,
> Make me as thou wert here below.

These, and many other hymns of the period, identify sex with sin, Mary with purity, virginity with the Christian ideal. Mary the Virgin both symbolizes and ratifies an ethic of sexual repression, seen very clearly in the effect of this devotion on the Irish manual workers' view of the world.[114] But as a model, Mary cannot easily be imitated by women, most of whom are not called to virginity and are hardly likely to be virgin mothers, or by men. She becomes an impossible ideal, and, because of the gulf between the ideal and the reality of human life, we often find that the result is to widen the gulf between religious devotion and personal and social activity. Mary then takes her place in the grotto, the shrine, the cultic place to which we flee for a transitory escape from the real world. For men, devotion to Mary can all too easily become an escape from the demands of real women in the world.

If Marian devotion can deteriorate into a false purity, it can equally move in the direction of a weak and passive Mary. Sheila Collins links this with the previous aspect of the cult:[115]

> When the Christian church took over the symbol of the great goddess in the form of Mary, she became deflated, emptied of most of her visionary and transcendent meaning. Gone was her function of unifying the spiritual with the sensual and with the earth, life with death, heaven with earth. Gone was her overarching meaning as the mother of all life. Henceforth she was only to be known as the 'Mother of God'. Mary could only be a mediatrix between humans and the mystery which is God by denying her humanness, her sexuality, her taint of human mortality and limitation. She became the ethereal, saccarine, spiritualized *essence* of womanhood, to which women could aspire only by denying the fullness of their own humanity.

So it is not surprising that, in many statues and pictures, Mary assumes a posture of resignation, with her head tilted, her look melancholy, her entire posture one of female passivity and submission.

Against the background of the corrupt and sentimental Mariology of most of Western Christianity, the words of the late Pope Paul VI in his encyclical *Marialis Cultus* come as something of a surprise:[116]

> The modern woman will note with pleasant surprise that Mary of Nazareth . . . was far from being a timidly submissive woman. On the contrary, she was a woman who did not hesitate to proclaim that God vindicates the humble and oppressed and removes the powerful people of the world from their privileged positions.

In recent Marian writings, it is the Mary of the Magnificat who has been the theme. The present pope returned to this theme in his address at Zapopan at the time of the Puebla Conference of Latin American bishops. There he said:[117]

> From Mary, who in her Magnificat proclaims that salvation has to do with justice, there flows authentic commitment to the rest of humanity, our brothers and sisters, especially for the poorest and the most needy, and to the transformation of society.

This is a striking shift from most Marian devotion of past years. Rosemary Ruether comments that 'for Christian women, who, through a process of painful growth, have at length freed themselves from this repressive ideal, Mary is not exactly someone they want to welcome back as a liberator'.[118] However, she goes on to speak of the revolutionary side of the Marian symbol, and argues for a 'liberation Mariology' as an urgent need of the Church.[119]

If this need is to be met, it will be necessary to purge Mariology of its harmful and repressive aspects. Mary is no substitute for the living God, no compensation for inadequate and one-sided theologies, no escape from sexuality and from the rights and struggles of her sisters. Yet, as the small, poor Galilean woman, who became the God-bearer and sang that most radical of freedom songs, she is a central figure of hope for a Church which seeks to respond to the incarnation. In Ruether's words:[120]

> The church is the ongoing Christ as the liberated poor who continue to serve and liberate others. And also as those who suffer, as those who pay the price for their struggle for liberation. Mary as the personified church, the liberated poor, cannot become model for continued subjugation, but rather of messianic empowerment. She is *alter Christus*. She is the messianic people who continues the liberating action of God in the world. The last becomes first, and the first last. A poor woman of despised race is the head of the church.

The Importance of Feminist Theology

In this chapter, it has been suggested that the loss of the feminine dimension in God has been a serious impoverishment and distortion of Christian understanding. The seriousness of this distortion has been brought home most forcibly in recent years by feminist writers and critics of the masculine-dominated tradition of the churches. Yet even today, and particularly in Britain, the feminist critique is not heard, or is trivialized, by many Christians. Feminist theology is hardly known in church circles. The cost of this deafness and lack of seriousness about so important an issue may be the loss of the bulk of educated women in Britain to organized Christianity.

For centuries, women have been seen in Christian spirituality as 'symbols of dangerous carnality'.[121] Tertullian called women the 'devil's gateway'[122] and the early female martyr Perpetua is said to have imagined herself as a man before she could enter heaven.[123] Early ascetical writers claim that virgins, by their celibacy, assume a male nature, and so transcend their ordinary female, carnal nature. The suppression of the order of deaconesses was largely due to worries about menstruation, while most of the references to women in early Canon Law are concerned with their exclusion from the sanctuary and from contact with priests.[124] Nor can it legitimately be argued that the marginalization and theologically-rooted oppression of women belongs to a later stage in Christian history, against which one can set the egalitarian nature of the early Christian witness. Undoubtedly there were contradictory pressures at work in the early Church, but it does seem clear that 'the Christian marginality of women has its roots in the patriarchal beginnings of the church and in the androcentrism of Christian revelation.'[125]

In Britain the bulk of the women's movement of recent years has grown up outside, and unconnected with, the Christian tradition. Indeed, it is probably true to say that most feminists would regard the Church as an integral part of institutional sexism, a force to be resisted and opposed. Yet from its early days there has been a powerful sense that feminism is much more than a rearrangement of society, and is involved with a profound spiritual process of change. Mary Daly, in her formative work *Beyond God the Father* (1973), sought

> to show that the women's revolution, in so far as it is true to its own essential dynamics, is an ontological spiritual revolution, pointing beyond the idolatries of a sexist society, and sparking creative action in and towards transcendence. The becoming of women implies universal becoming. It has everything to do with the search for ultimate meaning and reality which some would call God.[126]

Daly has removed far from organized Christianity which she and her disciples now regard as irredeemably sexist and patriarchal. However, others who have stayed with the mainstream of the Christian tradition have sought to develop within it a current of feminist theology, and Rosemary Ruether has, in a number of studies, attempted to outline the main concerns of such a movement. 'The uniqueness of feminist theology,' she writes, 'lies not in its use of the criterion of experience, but rather in its use of *women's* experience which has been almost

entirely shut out of theological reflection in the past'.[127] The critical
principle which governs feminist theology is the promotion of the full
humanity of women. Whatever denies, diminishes, or distorts that
full humanity is not redemptive. For Ruether, as for Letty Russell,
feminist theology is necessarily a theology of liberation.[128]

One of the chief concerns of feminist theology has been the use of
inclusive language, that is, language which does not speak merely on
behalf of men. In much Christian language, liturgical and other types,
the masculine form dominates. 'Man' appears on every page: it is
concerned with God's way with man, with man's salvation, with our
sins against our fellow men, and so on. Women are only defined in
their relations with men, included as an invisible component within
'man'. In addition, much Christian language speaks also of God in the
male form. Feminist theology therefore has raised the question of the
character of this God-language. Does it imply that God is in some
sense male and not female, father and not mother? Certainly some
writers have seen it thus, and have used the fact of the maleness of
God as an argument against the ability of women to be representative
of God in the world. Thus C. S. Lewis could claim that only a person
who wore the masculine uniform could represent God to the Church
since the Church was essentially feminine to God.[129] E. L. Mascall
has written that 'religions that lack a firmly male idea of deity lapse
into an immanentism in which the sense of a transcendent Creator is
absent, to say nothing of the corresponding nature and fertility rites,
with the sexual licence which provoked the denunciations of the
Hebrew prophets'.[130]

However, the central issue raised by feminist theology is not about
whether it is legitimate to use masculine images of God, but whether
the exclusive use of such images is adequate. For clearly all images are
images and are not themselves the reality. All language is, as Aquinas
recognized, metaphorical. God is beyond naming, but can be spoken
of metaphorically and analogically, that is, partially.[131] Gregory
Nazianzen ridiculed those who took such language literally and
assumed that God was male.[132] But this has been precisely the effect
of a linguistic form which has in fact excluded female images and
symbols from theological language.

The feminist critique of theological and liturgical language points
also to the disparagement of women in such language. In the liturgy
women are often 'overwhelmed by a linguistic form that excludes
them from visible existence'.[133] Translation of the Bible speak of sons
of God even when the original is clearly inclusive.[134] This linguistic
exclusion of women has had the effect that increasing numbers of
women feel themselves and their experiences to be ignored and to

have no place within Christian worship and spirituality. They have moved either to the fringes of the Christian tradition or away from it altogether as it has become clear that 'women's demands are coming more and more into direct confrontation with Christianity'.[135] The path taken by Mary Daly, a path from reformism through a dramatic exodus to a position distant from Christian theology, is a path which many other women of spirit have taken and continue to take.[136] Others, such as Meinrad Craighead, while remaining within the parameters of Christian orthodoxy, have survived spiritually by supplementing their public worship by a 'secret worship of God the Mother'. It was this secret worship, Craighead says, which, throughout much of her years as a Benedictine nun, was the sure ground of her spirituality, and which led her at length to 'a personal revaluation of patriarchal Christianity'.[137] Contrasted with this, the official liturgical forms of the Church seemed to her profoundly alienating:

> The use of exclusively male language in Christian worship continually reiterates the limited reality of God as a male being, and prevents women from valuing and expressing themselves and their very different spiritual experience. Male-dominated Christian teaching and practice, instead of affirming the Female as an authentic image of God and encouraging women's mature autonomy, has significantly distorted the biblical revelation ... and alienated women from their deepest and truest understanding of God as Mother.[138]

Craighead sees the Tree of Life as the most powerful symbol of female spirituality.

The nurturing of a spiritual tradition which affirms women's experience of God has been one of the most significant developments of recent years. Like so much else in feminist thinking and feeling, it has made little impression on the Church as an institution. Nevertheless, many women have been praying through their experience of God as Mother, seeking to express something of that experience in their writings. Take, for example, two prayers in a small volume *She Prays: Prayers by Women*. The first addresses the Trinity in a female way:

> Thou who art Wisdom and Word,
> Whom once the world adored
> For Mother love and compassion,
> We now call thee 'Father' and 'Lord' –
> Still in the world we shall know thee
> As one whose image we bear.
> Still in the world we seek thee,

Mother beyond compare.

Thou who art Wisdom and Word,
By whom the world was made,
Thou who art Holy Spirit,
Uniting the soul to God;
Wisdom is one with Spirit and Word,
And feminine from the start.
So it is written in Scripture.
So shall it be in my heart.

A second prayer addresses God as the Mother of all people and source of all life:

Mother of all, Giver of Life:
Thou Holy One:
Live in each soul that Divine life
To which we are born.
By that Divine breath
That scattered the most,
Brought form out of chaos,
Caught planets in space;

By that Divine breath,
All of thy daughters
Renew in thy likeness:
That we may create the world anew until
Out of the mist of famine and war arise
Whole nations who know and rejoice to do thy will
Who first conceived an earthly paradise;
The voice and will of the women shall someday call
A world into being with peace and justice for all.[139]

Another prayer addresses the womb of God. Its author, Sally Dyck, a Methodist pastor in Ohio, stressed that the importance of the maternal imagery used here was not to deify motherhood but rather to express some new insights in a religious language which had become jaded and bereft of powerful symbols:

Transforming Womb of God,
Conceive in us.
Create anew life:
    Faith, the confidence to bear
    Hope, continuously expectant
    Love, the true beginning.

Break forth your living waters, O birthing-Spirit;
Streaming grace upon us,
Waters from your belly,
Cleansing us, causing us to be whole,
Giving us this living water,
Overflowing our cup,
Thirsting no more
Longing for your welling pool,
Healing as the juices of crushed aloe.
Breaking waters, life-giving Spirit,
Trusting in your presence through the rushing rapids.

Kind hands upon your full belly;
Expecting the yet unseen,
Anticipating the given moment,
Moving with your birthing rhythms;
Breathing with the pain.
Body suffering, shedding blood.
Dying into life from the dark
Night of the uniting womb.
Signs of new beginnings
Casting forth into light.
Meeting of the Creator and newly born;
A joyful morning! A jubilee!
First-born, your name upon us;
Our name engraved upon your palm.

Hearing our nightly crying –
   the sick, the brokenhearted, the bound,
   the foolish, the weak, the unlovely –
Offering your loving breast, our banquet table,
Warm milk of sustenance
Given freely, freely flowing, flowing in abundance.

Nurturing the Nurturer: our mission
In memory of your body and your blood,
Returning our cup to the thirsty;
Working together, labourers of the Body.
Lovers in our service.
Your whole creation, our field;
Your wisdom, our teacher;
Your inspiration, our vision;
Your presence, our altar

Transforming Womb of God,

Conceive in us.
Create anew life:
    Faith, the confidence to bear
    Hope, continuously expectant
    Love, the true beginning.[140]

There are countless examples of ways in which, while continuing within the Christian stream, women's spirituality has been manifested, and women's experience has been related to the understanding of God. The importance of feminist theology, however, is not simply in its recovery of neglected elements in spirituality, but in its critique of sexist theology, a theology which is rooted in male domination and the devaluing of women as children of God. The theological repurcussions of this critique are only beginning to be felt. As Rosemary Ruether has written:[141]

... the exorcism of the demonic spirit of sexism in the church touches off a revolution which must transform all the relations of alienation and domination – between self and body, between leaders and community, between person and person, between social groups, between church and world, between humanity and nature, finally our model of God in relation to creation – all of which have been modelled on the sexist schizophrenia.

13

God of Justice

The theological foundation of a classless society is the classless Godhead himself as a classless Nuclear Family.
Mar Ostathios[1]

Certainly God is a God of the Jews and of the heathen, but he is not a God of the exalted and the lowly. He is one-sidedly a God of the lowly.
Karl Barth[2]

The relationship between the pursuit of justice and the knowledge of God is basic to Old Testament theology. To know God is to seek justice and to correct oppression. The Law and the Prophets are largely taken up with the issues of justice in society. Worship without a concern for justice is denounced as evil and unacceptable. For the God of Israel is a just God who has made humanity in his image, and has made men and women responsible for the just ordering of the earth. Nowhere does the Old Testament tradition make a separation between the 'social' and the 'spiritual' of the kind to which we have become accustomed in the modern western world. Such a division is in fact quite alien to biblical thought. It has been shown earlier (see Chapter 2) that the spirituality of the Old Testament writers is a justice spirituality, in marked contrast to the false division between issues considered as spiritual and those considered social or political. Union and communion with God cannot be achieved apart from the achievement of earthly justice and *shalom*, peace, and this peace is not compatible with wickedness (Isa. 48.22). On the contrary, the breaking of the covenant with God has consequences which are earthly and material: a broken covenant leads to a broken and devastated earth (Isa. 24).

The divine justice is to be expressed within the context of earthly societies, however faltering and imperfect human efforts to achieve it may be. To dissociate the divine justice from the struggle for justice within the human community is to make nonsense of the biblical record. Thus we find, for example, a profound concern in Palestine after the conquest for the achievement of equality, and 'excavations in Israelite towns bear witness to this equality in standards of living'.[3] Under the monarchy, as the prophet Samuel had warned, inequality increased, and the prophetic writings are filled with condemnations of the oppression of the poor. It is quite impossible to read the prophets and fail to see the way in which, in their thought, the spiritual and the social were united. Equally it is impossible to make any sense of the ministry of Jesus without taking account of the Old Testament background to his teaching, for he came to fulfil the Law and the Prophets. The view, commonly expressed today, that the Church has been traditionally concerned with the condition of the inward soul, and has recently begun to deal with matters of social justice, is utterly incorrect. Orthodox Christianity has never taken such a narrow and purely inward view of religion. We need therefore a 'return to biblical Christianity'[4] if we are to move away from the false spirituality which is gaining popularity, and if we are to recover the centrality of the divine justice.

The biblical faith in the divine justice is rooted in a realistic optimism about the possibilities of human and social change, an optimism which is different from naive idealism (of which it is often accused) and different also from the fatalistic pessimism which is often mistakenly identified with 'the Christian position'. Much of the criticism of Christian concern with social justice has drawn on the insights of the late Reinhold Niebuhr who rightly insisted on the need to take human sinfulness into account in social programmes. However, a naive devotion to Niebuhr has led many to overdraw the contrast between 'moral man and immoral society', thus making a sharp division between personal and social morality. It has also led to an ethical stance which pays more attention to sin than to grace, stressing the social and cosmic dimensions of the fall, yet paying less attention to the social and cosmic effects of the work of redemption. The late Martin Luther King once commented that Niebuhr was 'so involved in diagnosing man's sickness of sin that he overlooked the cure of grace'.[5] A Christian realism does not ignore sin; indeed it is precisely because of its sense that the effects of sin are social and cosmic that it insists on the non-necessity of all imperfect structures, and the need to work towards a society which is more in accord with the divine character. It is motivated not by a theology which seeks to baptize a current social order but by a theology of dissatisfaction with *all* current social orders, a theology of the God-inspired future which draws future vision into present reality.

In fact, far from neglecting sin and the fall, Christians who seek to follow the God of justice have a higher doctrine of sin than do their critics. It is because they see that sin is more than the sum total of personal sins, and that the fall has distorted the whole structure of human society, that they see the need for a theology which is concerned with more than the removal of personal failures and which takes seriously the embodiment of sin in social structures. The notion of 'social sin', though its roots are in Scripture, is unfamiliar to many people. In its simplest form, it recognizes that it is not only individuals but whole societies and their institutions which have been twisted and warped by sin, and that any approach which concentrates purely on personal change will be inadequate. The theme of social sin has become widely used in Catholic circles since the Second Vatican Council.[6] But years earlier, the World Council of Churches at its 1954 Assembly, pointed to its importance:[7]

> The ignorance and wilful wrongdoing of many generations of men has distorted God's work and subjected human life itself to grievous corruption. Every man is born into a social order deeply pervaded by the accumulated results of individual and corporate aggression, deceit and irresponsible self-seeking. Evil, deeply ingrained and powerfully operating in all creation, often quite beyond our understanding or control, bedevils the whole course of earthly history.

Many of those who claim to hold a high view of sin in fact neglect these social dimensions, and so locate sin only in personal misdeeds. As a result, they become uncritical of their societies and incapable of exercising any critical judgement upon them. Worse than this, their sense of the seriousness of sin, in itself defective, is not matched by any sense of the power of grace to overcome the effects of the fall. So it is that many of these Christians who constantly point to the fall seem to regard it as the only Christian doctrine! Their view of sin may even be social and cosmic, but their view of grace is personal and limited.

Much of what passes for Christianity in the western world at the present time is of this personal and limited kind. In our day Christianity is widely seen as a religion of personal pronouns, a purely individual faith; and this understanding is felt to be traditional, though it is in fact of recent origin. The traditional social doctrine of orthodox Christianity has been largely forgotten and replaced by an individualistic theology, the religious equivalent of the political doctrine of free enterprise. This revision of Christian theology is seen in the view of Christianity which appears in the thought of the British politician Margaret Thatcher. Thatcher sees free choice as the basis of ethics.[8] The dignity of the individual is what Christianity is about. And this is closely connected with the individual acquisition of money, for even the Good Samaritan would not have been remembered had he not had money in his pocket.[9] The New Testament, according to Thatcherite theology, is 'preoccupied with the individual', and in fact all biblical principles 'refer back to the individual'.[10] We find here then a version of Christian theology in which all the stress is on the individual, in contrast to the social emphasis of the Church throughout the ages.

It has been rightly said of Margaret Thatcher and her followers that they are 'a long way out of touch with the predominant mood in institutional Christianity in Britain which does not have much time for her'.[11] However, she does represent a view of Christian theology which is widely accepted. It is comfortable and fits well into the western capitalist model of reality. But in recent years it has come under attack from within the Church itself as the values of Thatcherism have come under fire from Christians on issues such as nuclear weapons, the increase in poverty, racism, and so on. Some politicians have advised the Church to 'stick to souls and sin' which is their proper sphere of concern.[12] At times the polemic has become almost lunatic in its expression. So, according to one Tory peer, the Church of England was the 'self-appointed fifth column of the Communist Party'.[13] Yet behind this bizarre upsurge of feeling lies a major theological controversy. The critics of the Church are working from a view of Christianity which sees individuals, in competition with other individuals, as the focal point of the religious question. And this individualism does have its roots in a particular, and characteristically western, view of Christianity. For

... a misconceived individualism has created a climate where other persons and groups are viewed as competitors for resources and as threats to our priesthood. This view has been dominant in much of western culture, but is particularly prevalent in the United States. In many respects this misconceived individualism has its roots in the western Christian tradition.[14]

The individualist interpretation of Christian theology has been bred in us by a long process of development, but it was unlikely to survive in the atmosphere of ecumenical and international Christian thought.[15] In the very early years of the World Council of Churches, the Russian philosopher Nicholas Berdyaev had observed that 'a religion of merely *personal* salvation is an essential contradiction to the good news of the coming of God's Kingdom. That Kingdom means not only a personal but a social and cosmic transformation.'[16] This recognition was not, as is often claimed, the result of some kind of capitulation of Christians to secular influence. It was due rather to a rediscovery of the social nature of traditional, and biblical, Christianity, a rediscovery of the truth that 'God created men for fellowship with himself and with each other' and that 'earthly society should be as close as possible a reflection of that fellowship'.[17]

In recent years the biblical roots of a concern for the divine justice have led many evangelical Christians to question their own past record and its tendency to reduce the historic faith.[18] A century ago the English theologian Henry Scott Holland pointed to the theological basis of Christian concern for justice in society, and rejected the notion that 'to be a social reformer, you must be shadowy in your creed ... To care about drains was supposed to mean that you sat loose to the creed.' On the contrary, Scott Holland insisted, 'the more you believe in the Incarnation, the more you care about drains'.[19] This inseparable link between doctrine and social action was taken for granted by nineteenth-century Anglicans. Similarly, in spite of the common attacks upon them, the followers of the 'social gospel' movement of the early twentieth century insisted that the concern for social justice was rooted in the gospel itself: 'the idea of redeeming the social order will be but one annex to the orthodox conception of the scheme of salvation'.[20] These thinkers saw that Christian theology, as it arose in the Old and New Testaments, was not individualist but social in its emphasis. As Stewart Headlam wrote of the parables of Jesus:[21]

Take the Parables, those words of eternal life. Of what do they tell? Of a heaven beyond the grave? No. Hardly a single word was uttered by Jesus about such a life, or such a heaven; they tell of a Kingdom of heaven to be set up upon earth, of a righteous communistic society in which all were to be fed as surely as the birds, and clothed as beautifully as the lilies, of a real genuine good news for the poor weary workers. The eternal life according to Jesus was to be enjoyed here, not merely hereafter: we are present inheritors and not only future heirs of the Kingdom of Heaven.

Concern for justice in society therefore is rooted in the social teachings of the Bible, both in Old and New Testaments.

It is rooted beyond this in the social nature and character of God. Christian theology does not hold to a simple monotheism, a belief in a solitary being distinct from and above the world, but to a divine community of persons, a divine solidarity. This doctrine of the social God was central to the thought of the great Anglican visionary Conrad Noel who wrote of 'the Blessed Trinity as the basis of a new world order':

Let us then consider the Blessed Trinity as the source of our own personal lives, and of the life of the world. Each one of us is a trinity in unity – body, mind and spirit: the disunity between these is not according to the original intention of the Triune God. The world has in it plenty of variety, but the variety is not always healthy, is often antagonistic and discordant, because it is not a variety in unity, and does not yet express the 'Three in One and One in Three'. It cannot be said of the world as at present constituted that it contains no differences or inequalities, or that within it 'none is afore or after other; none is greater or less than another'. We Look forward to a world of infinite variety in harmony, of living unity, not of dead uniformity; if man is to create so delightful a world he must 'thus think of the Trinity', for it is the will of the Triune God to inspire men to renew the world in such a way as to make it the perfect expression of his own Being.[22]

In these words, written over forty years ago, we see an intimate and dynamic relationship between orthodox dogma and social action. The social being of God is seen as the basis for a quest for human society to be refashioned according to the divine qualities of equality and co-operation. Human fulfilment can only be achieved through the combination of equality and diversity, a society in which all people can give from their diversity and share the riches of the common life. To share the divine image, the image of the Trinity, means that we are committed to work for such a society.

Of course, the relationship between theology and society is not a simple one. While theological ideas influence and shape, for good or ill, attitudes and actions in the social order, the relationship is not only one-way. Ideas and images of God are themselves influenced and affected by the prevailing social order. Thus we find that medieval ideas of God tend to stress order, while Reformation theology is concerned with the question of the divine sovereignty. Theological images do not simply come into being in a pure state or free of political input. It has been suggested that we tend today to hold a 'welfare conception of God', a view which fits into the social and political concepts of social democracy.[23] All theology is influenced by its context, and human beings rarely move straight from the intellectual grasp of certain abstract truths to practical involvement in the struggles for peace and justice. Both context and dogma are important. Without context, dogma is not earthed, not related to any living world, it remains disconnected. But what happens when theology becomes captured by its context, by the prevailing culture? Theology, and the institutional church in which theological reflection takes place, then becomes a resource of the culture, and no longer its critic. Theology becomes the servant of the social order, the God of justice is tamed and put at the service of organized injustice.

This kind of captivity of theology and of the Church is not a new phenomenon, and can certainly be traced back to the time of Constantine when the imperial ideology infiltrated the Church.[24] Since then established churches, armed with theologies which serve the status quo, have been the norm rather than the exception of religious life. The gospel comes to be identified with the values of the prevailing ideology, and its values and notions are often read back into the Scriptures. A crude, and disturbing, recent example of such a pattern is the movement in the United States called the Moral Majority, a right-wing grouping based on Christian fundamentalism. Its leader, Jerry Falwell, explains how the Bible supports competition and the free enterprise system. President Reagan is welcomed as a powerful spiritual and pro-Christian force. Support for capital punishment and for increased arms spending, and opposition to socialism, women's rights, and homosexuality, are all found in the Bible.[25] In the past, biblical fundamentalists supported slavery and racism in a similar way, while close parallels are found in Catholic Europe where the same kind of baptizing of particular social systems has occurred.

Nor can more liberal-minded English Christians dismiss such groups as the Moral Majority as the lunatic expression of American religion. It is true that fundamentalism is far more central to American Christianity than is the case anywhere in Britain, but the same kind of uncritical acceptance of the values of 'the British way of life' as if they were identical with Christianity is common in the Church of England. Nor is this at all surprising in an established church which is so closely identified with the monarchy, the aristocracy, and the ruling class. As a social phenomenon, the Church of England is an integral part of the English class structure, closely linked with that tiny percentage of the population who effectively run society. Take, as a crucial example, the public schools, institutions which continue to see themselves as preserving the framework of Christian society. Only four per cent of the population are educated at such schools. Yet from within this tiny segment of the population come 86 per cent of senior army officers, 81 per cent of the senior judges, 73 per cent of directors of the biggest industrial companies, 60 per cent of permanent secretaries in the Civil Service, and 70 per cent of the bishops of the Church of England. It is therefore unlikely that a church so allied, in its power structure, with the ruling élite should not reflect the values of that élite. Yet if a church, and its theology, is so entangled with the power structure of a particular society, how can it then speak to that society of the God of justice? For the injustice against which a prophetic and critical church might speak, may be integral to the very society which the established church seeks to defend. The idea that a national church should take up a radically different position on a major national issue from that taken by the government is therefore unthinkable, and if such a situation were to arise where this became the norm, a church–state crisis would be inevitable.

Of course, in the history of the Church, there are many examples of church–state crises. There are even more examples of ways in which the Church has sought to avoid them, not least by developing theological positions which support a relationship of peaceful coexistence. One common theological formula by which churches live in peaceful relationship with the prevailing social order is the doctrine of the 'two kingdoms' or 'two cities'. Augustine originally developed the theme of 'two cities', the earthly city based upon the love of self, the heavenly city based upon the love of God.[26] Later the theme of 'two kingdoms' came to play an important part in Lutheranism, and some writers have claimed that this sharp division between the Kingdom of God (spiritual and inward) and the political structures of this world was a major theological factor in the capitulation of the German churches to Hitler.[27] Certainly there were serious theological problems which were central to the church–state crisis of the Nazi period. Although Karl Barth must be recognized and remembered as a key figure in the resistance to Hitler, in important ways Barthian theology played into the hands of the Nazis.[28] Barth himself in 1943 argued that it was essential to carry on theological work *as if nothing had happened* (*als wäre nichts geschehen*).[29] The Church did not exist to serve mankind or the German people but only the Word of God. It was the Word, not the Kingdom, which was the controlling motif of Barthian theology, and this led to a serious, and fatal, neglect of human solidarity. There was a sharp distinction between God and humanity, between Church and world. And so, while the Synod of Barmen in 1934 attacked the theology of the German Christians, it was careful not to attack the ideology or practice of National Socialism. What mattered was purity of doctrine. So issues which affected human beings as such were not considered as worthy of Christian attention. The crucial issue at Barmen was the freedom of the Church and the eligibility of Jews as candidates for the Church's sacraments: the human sufferings of the Jews was not a matter of Christian comment, still less the political ideology of the regime which sanctioned that suffering. A world-renowned theologian like Rudolf Bultmann did not allow himself even a passing reference to state legislation.[30] The Kingdom of God was a kingdom of the spirit: the affairs of earthly political regimes were matters of no real concern to the Church. Later Barth admitted that the Nazi disaster might not have happened had the Church not been so accustomed to remain silent over matters to do with the exercise of earthly power.[31]

The theology of the two kingdoms is by no means dead. Much conventional Christianity works with the notion that there are two realms, the realm of God and the realm of Caesar, and that these two realms are equal and separate. Such a division was hardly in the mind of Jesus when he spoke of rendering to Caesar what belonged to Caesar and to God what belonged to God. Indeed, the whole point was that money (Mammon) was the real rival to God, and that the best thing to do with Caesar's money was to give it back. (The verb *apodidomi* means 'give back' everywhere it is used in the Gospels.) But the text continues to be used as if it meant that the two realms were equal and distinct, and each should keep to his own clearly defined territory. Thus Margaret Thatcher, in a lecture on her understanding of Christianity and politics, could say:[32]

> For the truth of the matter is this: the Bible as well as the traditions of the Church tell us very little directly about political systems or social programmes. The nearest we get is Christ telling his disciples to render unto Caesar that which is Caesar's and to God that which is God's.

And so two thousand years of Christian social thinking are dismissed as if they were a mist across the face of the moon. The theology of the remark seems to be that there is a division of loyalties in which God and Caesar each control their separate territories, the religious and political arenas. The concern of the Church is with the former, with spiritual verities. And in fact the recent comments of Conservative politicians on matters to do with the role of the Church show that this is indeed their view.[33] And in this they are enthusiastically supported by sections of the media who advise the Church to stick to 'religious' issues such as how to fill empty pews.[34]

While simplistic comparisons need to be avoided, the parallels with the German church situation are close. In both periods there was an inability to see the spiritual character of the quest for justice and of the critique of political systems, an inability to see the total claim of God over the limited claim of Caesar. There was a theological failure which contributed to a disastrous political consequence.

God and the Social Order

So God is invoked, and religious institutions are used, to sanctify a particular social order, often one which is marked by, and maintained by, gross injustice, and which seeks to use the Church to give credibility and provide ideological support. We find a classic and terrifying example of such ideological use of theology in the history of Fascism. From the time of Mussolini to the present regimes in Latin America, churches have been welcomed as allies when they help to bolster up a regime. In the majority of cases, it has seemed that the interests of the Fascist state and those of the Christian Church were identical or, at least, similar. It was in the period of Nazism that the underlying conflict became clear, at least for some people, between the theology of the Christian Church and the world-view of Fascism. For many, it is not clear yet.

In Fascist societies, we find a totally repressive government and state machine which presides over the dissolution of all other forms of social and political life, though remaining within the overall framework of capitalism. Historically such Fascist states have often arisen within an officially Christian culture, and have been supported by local established churches and their hierarchies. However, in the case of Nazism, which differed from Italian Fascism in some major ways, the conflict with biblical Christianity was revealed. In fact, Nazism owed much of its religious impetus to pagan religion and specifically to occultism. The spiritual origins of the Nazi movement lay in the Thule Society of Munich, an occult group which saw the Aryan/ Jewish struggle in terms of a cosmic warfare between gods and beasts. It was from this essentially religious notion of a cosmic warfare that the rituals of the Hitler Youth were derived.[35] Of course, the Nazi movement was also a political ideology and arose at a time of economic chaos, but it is a serious error to ignore its basic irrationality and mythological roots.[36] In its myth of a racial deity, it drew on earlier theories of racism, as well as on Darwinism, occult traditions, and theosophy, and today we often find that pagan religious ideas which stress Nordic ancestry and the culture of the fatherland find support within Nazi-type movements.

So it is true to say that 'at the back of Hitler's anti-Semitism there is revealed an actual war of Gods'.[37] Many of Hitler's followers did not see this, for in public he supported Christianity, and so was widely hailed as a defender of Christian civilization against the communist peril. However, in private Hitler held that 'the heaviest blow that ever struck humanity was the coming of Christianity'.[38] The Church was an obstacle to the Nazi ideology, and it was Hitler's aim to destroy it. Similarly, Heinrich Himmler contrasted the weak and gentle ethos of Christianity with the aggressive masculinity of the pagan gods:

> Which of us wandering through the lovely German countryside and coming unawares upon a crucifix does not feel deep in his heart

... a strange but enduring sense of shame? The gods of our ancestors were different. They were men, and carried in their hands a weapon which typified the natural characteristics of our race, namely readiness to get and self-reliance. How different is yonder pale figure on the Cross, whose passivity and emphasized mien of suffering express only humility and self-abnegation, qualities which we, conscious of our heroic blood, utterly deny ... The corruption of our blood, caused by the intrusion of this alien philosophy, must be ended.[39]

Never was the conflict between paganism and the gospel of the crucified God more clearly stated.

Yet it is this essentially pagan view of God and of religion which lies close to the heart of the Fascist vision. The late Sir Oswald Mosley, one of the founders of the Fascist movement in Britain, held that the Fascist philosophy was a fusion of Christian ideas and those of Nietzsche.[40] Certainly the symbol of the superman was an important one.[41] In the religion of European paganism, the Nazi movement saw the idolizing of the aggressive male warrior, while women were valued solely as 'breeders of race and nation'. Christianity, on the other hand, by its stress on such virtues as love, compassion, suffering, and human unity across racial and national barriers, undermined those characteristics which were so prized by the fascist philosophy. The conflict is deeply theological, and it is this which makes fascism unique among modern political philosophies, for it offers a total spiritual world-view which is fundamentally incompatible with that offered by the Christian gospel. 'The Fascist vision is unique precisely because it glorifies those elements in his nature which man must actually transcend if he is to become human and create a humane society.'[42]

The attraction of paganism, with its static hierarchies of gods and its ritual celebration of the social order, has meant that it often happens that a Christian vocabulary and ceremonial are retained to disguise essentially pagan ideas. Much folk religion, in which harvest festivals, remembrances of past wars, and civic celebrations take precedence over Easter and Pentecost, is of this pagan type. Sometimes, as in Nazi Germany, even the vocabulary is changed, and so one found sermons preached in Christian churches from which all specifically Christian references had been removed.[43] Where the vocabulary and outward manifestations of Christianity remain, as under Mussolini, Franco, and Salazar, Fascism has been shown to actually transcend if he is to become human and create a humane attract Catholic Christians, and in Britain in the 1930s Roman Catholics were disproportionately represented in Fascist groups.[44] Anglicans were not immune from the seductions of Nazism, and one

Anglican clergyman saw Hitler as a saviour, describing the Jews as parasitic, a cancer to be eradicated.[45]

In recent years the theological position which helped prepare the soil for Hitler's victory, the doctrine of the two kingdoms, has come under sustained attack from the mainstream of most Christian churches. Since the Second Vatican Council, there has been an assertion of the interaction of spirituality and society, and the unified nature of grace. The document *Gaudium et Spes* in particular stressed the role of Christians in the world as 'artisans of a new humanity'.[46] Pope Paul VI often stressed the inseparable link between evangelism and the transformation of society.[47] Earlier theologies which made a sharp distinction between natural and supernatural, or which saw the Church as the cement of the unchanging order, were abandoned. During the same period, the World Council of Churches was pointing to God at work in social change, even revolutionary change.[48] Ideas of a Church which uncritically supported a given society, or the 'long-standing British Christian assumption that no party political tradition is more Christian than any other',[49] have become increasingly difficult to maintain. No given society can be taken for granted; all systems are under critique. To follow the God of justice involves a willingness to question all our social and political assumptions. At the same time, since certain principles and values are enshrined in the Christian tradition, it is clear that some social systems are likely to be more in accord with these than others are, and that it is nonsense to say that all are equally valid options for Christian support.

However, a theology of the God of justice cannot accept an uncritical relationship between theology and the social order. It is motivated by a divine discontent, a refusal to be satisfied with society as it is. This discontent must be nourished and sustained, for the greatest enemy of the struggle for the divine justice is apathy and weariness. They commit iniquity and are too weary to repent, complained Jeremiah (9.5). The prophetic zeal for justice was always oriented towards the future, always dissatisfied, never prepared to acquiesce in the false realism of those who see the attainment of justice as an impossible demand. Indeed, as Miranda has said, 'whoever is capable of resigning himself to the fact that justice will never be realized is incapable of taking the prophets seriously'.[50] The recovery of the prophetic dimension in Christian witness in recent years has been a major factor in the renewal of the Christian social conscience, for the prophetic attack was directed against all attempts to dissociate religion from justice, and against all attempts to capture and contain God within the structure of a given ritual or social framework.

A commitment to the God of justice, and to the quest for social change which will more adequately reflect that justice, is bound to lead to conflict. Conflict is basic to the prophetic tradition and indeed to the entire Christian tradition of social action. And yet we find that much Christian writing and thought exalts peace and harmony at the expense of justice. The aim of the gospel is said to be the attainment of reconciliation: conflict is to be avoided at all costs. Where conflict arises, it is due to the activity of troublemakers, agitators, subversives. The governing bodies of society, on the other hand, are seen as the upholders of law and order, perhaps even of the divinely ordained order. Certainly harmony is seen to be more in accord with the will of God than is struggle. It is sinful to rock the boat, to cause trouble, to rebel, to organize dissent. Against this tradition stands the figure of Jesus who disrupted peace and order with a message of conflict, bringing not peace but a sword, and upturning the values of his society. Following the leadership of Jesus, his Church needs to stand as a sign of contradiction and of conflict, 'affecting and, as it were, upsetting, through the power of the Gospel, mankind's criteria of judgement, determining values, points of interest, lines of thought, sources of inspiration, and models of life which are in contrast with the Word of God and the plan of salvation'.[51]

Disciples of the God of justice reject the view that to create tension and provoke crisis is incompatible with the gospel. On the contrary, it is false peace which is the real enemy of the gospel. The point was put well by Martin Luther King in his Letter from Birmingham Jail in April 1963:[52]

> Just as Socrates felt that it was necessary to create a tension in the mind so that individuals could rise from the bondage of myths and half-truths to the unfettered realm of creative analysis and objective appraisal, so we must see the need for non-violent gadflies to create the kind of tension in society that will help men rise from the dark depths of prejudice and racism to the majestic heights of understanding and brotherhood.

Through his non-violent direct action, King brought to the surface hidden tensions which were already alive. By bringing these tensions out into the open, he enabled them to be recognized and dealt with. By hiding and obscuring them, the process of change and of healing is set back. There is therefore a call to conflict and struggle which is basic to the Christian commitment to truth and to healing.

Yet the aim of all struggle is the achievement on earth of a society which more adequately reflects the divine character than does our present one. Many Christians, particularly in the Third World, have come to see their struggle as part of a world-wide quest for a socialist order, for a society which will replace the idolatry of wealth and profit by a concern for human equality, sharing, and freedom. The relationship of Christian theology to socialism is a complex one. Since the 1840s there has been a tradition in Britain of 'Christian socialism' though the term has been used to cover a wide range of quite different theological and political tendencies. Roman Catholic social teaching until recent years condemned socialism even of a 'mitigated' kind. Certainly, from the perspective of Pius XI in *Quadragesimo Anno*, no one could be at the same time a sincere Catholic and a true socialist.[53] Since those days, and particularly since 1970, 'the Catholic Church's official position has shifted to the left'.[54] The bishops of the Third World who issued a letter in that year, while they stressed that the Church must never be bound up with any one social and political system, went on to say that, when a system ceased to promote the common good, then the Church must break with it, and be prepared to work with another system. The bishops rejoiced at the emergence of socialism as a system which was less at variance with the Christian moral vision.[55]

For Christians, socialism is linked with the understanding of God as the embodiment of equality and sharing, and with the understanding of human persons as created for co-operation rather than competition. It is therefore correct to say that socialism and capitalism assume two different views of humanity, and perhaps two different theologies. Of course, this does not mean that one can move straight from a theology to a set of political strategies. It does mean that at the heart of the socialist vision as seen by Christians is a spirituality of fellowship and of *koinōnia*, common life. This sense of fellowship antedates later ideas of state ownership. (Many early socialists warned against the extension of state control.[56] Keir Hardie, for example, saw the essence of socialism to be fraternity founded on justice, and he saw the transfer of land and capital to public ownership to be a 'mere incident' in this larger crusade.[57]) Recent socialist thinkers have emphasized the need to recover the visionary and personal dimensions and the need to change consciousness over against the concern with organization and bureaucratic control.[58] Socialist Christians certainly would wish to stress the spiritual roots of socialism in the quest for the divine justice within human society.

Those Christians who, in both the nineteenth and twentieth centuries, have found that their discipleship has led them into the socialist movement and the political struggles of the common people, have derived their inspiration and theological impetus from their understanding of the social character of God as Trinity. However, it has been a frequent criticism of much earlier Christian socialism that it was insufficiently earthed in the world of institutions. One writer has claimed:[59]

> By emphasizing that socialism was a religious matter, concerned with the whole human situation in relation to the divine, it inflated it to a significance which was then too elevated to comprehend actual detail. Its distrust of, and lack of interest in, institutions reflected a disengagement from social reality which could be justified at a theological level; socialism meant the incarnation of the divine in human society, but the centre of interest could then be the divine rather than the human.

Today, particularly under the influence of theologians from Central and South America and in reaction against the values and practice of governments in Britain and the United States, increasing numbers of Christians are finding theological meaning in their involvement in the organized socialist movement and in working for a new economic order in which power and resources are more justly shared. The quest for forms of common ownership and economic and political sharing is a contemporary version of the commitment to *koinōnia* which was so central to the spirituality of Christians in the apostolic age. Like the early Christians and their Jewish forerunners, they recognize that God is known in the pursuit of justice, and that to perpetuate oppression is to refuse to know the Lord (Jer. 9.3–6).

God and the Unity of Races

There is no more urgent issue facing humanity than the struggle against racism and for a non-racial society, and Christians who are involved in anti-racist work naturally seek resources in the Christian tradition. Yet for the authors of the Bible, the notion of race in the modern sense of that word does not exist. It is a 'non-concept': 'the idea of "race" is not one that ancient man had formulated'.[60] Of course, we find tribal antagonisms, religious separatism, and attitudes of superiority based on culture, but nothing comparable to the concept of race. The Roman Empire was in fact a truly multi-racial society. The distinctions were between slaves and free men, or between citizens and non-citizens, rather than between different races. Indeed when the Bible speaks of a race, it is of the human race as distinct from the animal or plant creations. *To genos tōn anthrōpōn* (or, in Latin, *genus humanum*) means the human community. In Hebrew there is no word for what we would today mean by race. In one sense therefore the biblical tradition has nothing to say about race and racism, for it comes out of a non-racial tradition of thought.

Of course, there is a good deal in Scripture about the treatment of strangers and aliens (for example, Deut. 10.19; Lev. 19.34; Exod. 22.21; 23.9). There is a good deal about migration. Indeed one could write the entire history of the Old Testament in terms of migration from the command to migrate in Genesis (1.28) to the revelation in Amos (9.7) that God is he who brought Israel from Egypt, the Philistines from Caphtor, and the Syrians from Kir. The Old Testament is full of stories of migrations: Abraham, Ruth, Ebedmelech, Ittai and the Gittites in Israel, and so on. It is in fact a record of the deliverance by God of a people from one space into a new space, the calling by God of disparate tribes into a new peoplehood.[61] In the New Testament, we find Jesus attacking anti-Samaritan views (Luke 9.54), stressing the value of the Gentile peoples (Matt. 8.10; Luke 17.18) and praising the Samaritan for his neighbourliness (Luke 10.33). The unity of nations and peoples in Christ is a central part of the proclamation of the apostolic evangel (Eph. 2.11–21; Gal. 3.28). This has not prevented people from looking to the Bible for a justification and support for racist positions. The notorious 'curse of Canaan' (Gen. 9) has often been cited as a theological basis for the oppression of black people, wrongly believed to be descended from Canaan.[62] Slavery was defended by appeal to biblical texts.[63] Even today we find fundamentalist groups in the United States and in Britain which misuse parts of the Old Testament to defend their racist viewpoints.

   Black people who see Christianity as having played a major role in the justification of their oppression have a strong historical case to present. One American Christian leader wrote sadly that 'throughout my lifetime, the local white church has been society's most conservative and hypocritical institution in the area of white–negro relations'.[64] Throughout history the Christian churches have condoned and defended racial oppression and done so biblically and theologically. The have promoted the notion of a white God, white angels, white saints, white salvation, contrasted with the blackness of sin, corruption, and ignorance. On the historical evidence and association of Christianity with whiteness is pervasive. Moreover, the association in the western collective psyche of whiteness with goodness and purity, and of blackness with negative ideas is too deep and too widespread to be dismissed as over-reaction. In the few references to blackness in the Bible, the picture is a negative one (for example, Job 3.4–6; Jer. 4.28; Jude 1.13). White, on the other hand, is associated with purity and sanctity (see Rev. 1.14; 20.11; 14.4; 7.14). A scrutiny of Roget's *Thesaurus* reveals that most of the synonyms for black are pejorative. This negative image of blackness occurs throughout western history and literature. 'The devil damn thee black' writes

Shakespeare in *Hamlet*. In *Titus Andronicus*, the villain is black, just as in a recently published children's illustrated Bible, all the characters are white with one exception – Cain! The association of blackness with a lack of personhood is brought out most powerfully and painfully in William Blake's poem about the black boy who yearns for whiteness:

My mother bore me in the southern wild,
And I am black, but O! my soul is white;
White as an angel is the English child,
But I am black, as if bereaved of light . . .
When our souls have learned the heat to bear,
The cloud will vanish; we shall hear his voice,
Saying: 'Come out from the grove, my love, and care,
And round my golden tent like lambs rejoice.'
Thus did my mother say and kissed me;
And thus I say to little English boy.
When I from black and he from white cloud free
And round the tent of God like lambs we joy,
I'll shade him from the heat till he can bear
To lean in joy upon our Father's knee;
And then I'll stand and stroke his silver hair,
And be like him, and he will then love me.

So the black boy seeks and achieves whiteness, the colour of wholeness and of true identity. His soul was, he says, already white. The sense of an interior whiteness of soul or of heart comes over too in the statement made some years ago by the politician Quintin Hogg (Lord Hailsham): 'I would rather be a black man with a white heart, than a white man with a black heart.'[65] White is good and godly, and God himself is white and is to be found within a sacred grove of whiteness. It is hard to escape the conclusion that this association of whiteness with goodness and purity, blackness with evil and sin, is intimately linked with Christian theology. This is not, of course, to say that racism is a peculiarly white, western, Christian phenomenon. However, there is abundant and very disturbing evidence to suggest that often religious belief is highly correlated with prejudice and intolerance. Not only does religion, including the Christian religion, seem to attract the insecure and the prejudiced members of the community, but it also serves to reinforce, and provide support for, their prejudices.[66] Many studies have shown that devout church members often show higher degrees of racial prejudice than do other sections of the community around them. Historically both Christianity and racist ideas are associated with imperialism. In Britain, imperialist ideology did include notions of the superiority and spiritual dominance of the Anglo-Saxon race.[67] It became difficult therefore for colonial and ex-colonial people to dissociate Christian theology from the ideology of their colonial masters, since both religion and imperialist ideology went together.

However, the history of racial intolerance in Christianity did not begin with colonial expansion, and it is impossible to begin to understand, and to seek to correct, the distortion of Christianity by racist ideas without giving attention to the phenomenon of anti-Semitism. While there is no doubt that anti-Semitism has eaten deep into Christian history, many writers in the past have assumed that this represented a marginal deviation, and that the anti-Semitic dimension in Christian history was accidental and peripheral.[68] More recent study has shown that it cannot be so easily dealt with, and is indeed rooted in the New Testament itself and in the earliest traditions of the Church.[69] If this is so, then it seems to follow that

> ... we cannot be comfortably sure that Christian anti-Semitism did not prepare the ground for the racial troubles we have in respect of other communities in this country today. An act of theological penitence, and a conscious and publicly declared reappraisal of the biblical insights, including a disowning of the distorted features of the New Testament, is essential if the churches are to address themselves to their past in the racial situation with cleansed consciences.[70]

For the anti-Semitic strain has not been marginal but central to much Christian theology and proclamation. In Gregory Baum's words:[71]

> The church made the Jewish people a symbol of unredeemed humanity; it painted a picture of the Jews as a blind, stubborn, carnal and perverse people, an image that was fundamental in Hitler's choice of the Jews as a scapegoat. What the encounter of Auschwitz demands of Christian theologians, therefore, is that they submit Christian teaching to a radical ideological critique.

The horrors of Auschwitz did not therefore appear as a freak within a pure Christian world, but they were the terrible conclusion of a long tradition of thought and feeling, of a profound spiritual sickness at the heart of the western Christian tradition.[72]

When we recognize, with sorrow and pain, how deep-rooted is the anti-Semitic dimension in western Christianity, then the history of the German churches' response to Hitler becomes less surprising if more appalling. Unlike other forms of fascism, Nazi ideology was rooted in a biological determinism and a mystique of race. Within this racist ideology, the Jews played a central role as a demonic, conspiratorial presence in world history. So the leading Lutheran bishop Otto Dibelius claimed, in 1928, that Jewry had always played a leading role in all manifestations of disintegration in modern civilization.[73] Other Lutherans took the same view, for Christianity was identified with mystical interpretations of nationality. German Christian anti-Semitism found a powerful nineteenth-century exponent in Adolf Stoecker who has been seen as an early theological forerunner of the Third Reich.[74] From the later years of the nineteenth century to the Hitler period itself, there was no serious attempt to come to terms with anti-Semitism, and there was no authoritative condemnation of it by evangelical Christians.[75] Indeed, several years before Hitler came to power, the Evangelical Church Congress met in 1927 at Königsberg to discuss 'Volk and Fatherland'. The main speech, by Paul Althaus, urged the adoption of a *volk* theology with strong elements of race-soul and nationalist ideas. Richard Gutteridge, after a detailed survey of attitudes to the Jews over a century, comments:[76]

During the whole period, there is no evidence whatever of any authoritative statement being issued by the Evangelical Church calling for the earnest consideration of the Jewish problem from the purely biblical standpoint in the light of the Christian Gospel of mercy and of love. Nor can we discover any official Church warning against the mounting agitation in certain circles to treat the problem as predominantly one of race.

During the Nazi period, the attitude towards Christianity was ambivalent. On the one hand, there was an attempt to maintain that National Socialist ideology was in fact favourable to, and indeed to be identified with, the defence of the Christian values of the west. Julius Kuptsch, in a study published in 1932 by the official Nazi publishing house, claimed that Christianity and National Socialism were the same. 'The National Socialists carry the Swastika on their breasts, and the Cross of Christ within their breasts.'[77] On the other hand, racial mysticism and anti-Semitism was integral to the National Socialist ideology long before 1933. In the words of Eduard Lohse:[78]

This racial doctrine was central to the National Socialist Weltanschaung. The warfare against the Jews cannot therefore be assessed as a radical misdevelopment caused by various sorts of wrong misunderstanding. It was inexorably and conclusively planned from the beginning and was carried through to its fearful conclusion.

The fearful conclusion to which thoughtful Christians must be led is surely that the anti-Semitism of the Nazi movement, and its embodiment in ideology and in genocide, was not something for which the Christian community and Christian theology can claim no responsibility. The purification of Christian theology and Christian practice in the light of the experience of the holocaust is an urgent task.

Of course, anti-Semitism is not the only form that 'Christian racism' has taken. There is a long and continuing history, particularly in the United States of such groups as the Ku Klux Klan who claim to base their racist doctrines on Christian belief and on Scripture. In Britain, it is probably true to say that the organized racist and fascist groups tend to make little use of Christian ideas, partly because biblical fundamentalism is more peripheral to Christianity in Britain than it is in the United States. The British churches, confronted by the presence of a growing black community, have been guilty not so much of conscious religiously-based racism as of incomprehension and apathy. And yet behind much of the racism in British society lie semi-conscious ideas of national character, patriotism, and 'human nature' which are not unconnected with the Christian tradition. Confronted by the presence of the black community, and of people of other faiths, in twentieth-century Britain, the question of the nature of God becomes a highly political one. Is God to be identified with the white race and with the British nation? Are black people to be seen as a threat to the unity of the Christian nation, and therefore a theological threat?

So it is that the racial question in Britain faces us with the question of God in a sharp and painful form. For it calls into question the nature of our 'Christian' society, the nature of our godliness. Since the anti-black polemic began at the end of the 1950s, one of the central themes in the agitation has been that of preserving the British character and the British way of life.[79] Sir Cyril Osborne, who led the campaign in parliament at the end of the 50s and early 60s to control immigration, warned of the destruction of the British race, and predicted that there would be more coloured than white persons in Britain before very long.[80] Later came Enoch Powell and the gradual deterioration in race relations became a dramatic one. Black people came to be seen as intrinsically problematic, a threat to the culture. A number of Anglican bishops in October 1979 accused Margaret Thatcher, the Prime Minister, of fanning racial prejudice and spoke of 'institutionalized racism which some highly placed politicians have made respectable'. Undoubtedly recent years have seen an increase in genteel racism and a widespread acceptance of intolerance and prejudice within large sections of British society. During the same period we have seen the growth of a new sense of rebellion within sections of the black community, nourished by an acute awareness of rejection. The disturbances in British cities in the summer of 1981 were important in that they indicated a refusal by many black people to accept intolerable and worsening conditions, or to maintain the stereotype of black people as helpless victims. To the extent that the riots brought a new sense of confidence to the black community, they can be seen to contain the seeds of new hope.[81] Christians are right to look for, and recognize, the activity of God in these struggles.

The claim, repeated by Lord Scarman, that 'institutional racism does not exist in Britain',[82] is seriously mistaken. What is even more striking is the way in which, in recent years, many people have looked to the natural sciences for a pseudo-biological basis for racism. The homogeneity of the Anglo-Saxon race is stressed in such a way that black persons, immigrant or not, are seen as an 'alien wedge', undermining and weakening that homogeneous society. Ideas of a fixed 'human nature' are often used. Politicians must operate with 'human nature *as it is*' according to Enoch Powell.[83] Thus we find many of the exponents of 'the new racism' strongly denying that they hold views of racial superiority: rather do they stress 'differences', national consciousness, culture, and that these things are fixed and 'natural'. It is not difficult to see here a kind of secular theology, a view of race and nation and of the nature of the human person, which is strongly at variance with Christian theology with its belief in the universal unity of human beings, and the potential of grace to transform and perfect nature. Racism therefore presents a fundamental threat to the Christian doctrine of God and of humanity, offering as it does an alternative view. Yet it cannot be denied that it is a view which can claim some Christian sources.

It is not surprising that, in a climate which offers God as a God of a white Anglo-Saxon culture, many black people should have looked elsewhere for their spiritual nourishment. In the United States, the black church had long been a powerful social and spiritual force, keeping hope alive through periods of deep despair and apparent hopelessness.[84] In Britain, we have seen in recent years the growth of 'black-led churches' such as the New Testament Church of God, the Pilgrim Wesleyan Holiness Church, the Church of God of Prophecy, and so on. Some research has suggested that around 15–18 per cent of Afro-Caribbean people belong to these churches, and that over 60 per cent of West Indian Christians belong to them. By contrast, while many of these churches existed in the Caribbean, over 90 per cent of Christians there belong to the mainstream churches. Moreover, although these churches have existed in Britain since the 1950s, they only began to grow after 1964, and they have grown rapidly in recent years. It is hard therefore to escape the conclusion that the growth of the black churches is a direct result of, and response to, white racism. It has been claimed that the black churches in Britain are 'part of the "suffering church" which establishes itself around the dispossessed and dehumanized members of society'.[85]

However, this is by no means the whole story, and there are two major qualifications which must be made to the view of the black churches as churches of the marginalized. The first is that many, many black Christians are within the mainstream churches in Britain, and there are, for example, many black Anglicans. But their presence – and they are indeed the majority in some districts in terms of actual church practice – is not reflected at all in terms of the power structure. So there is a white church structure ministering to a large black clientele: not at all a healthy situation or one which omens well for the future. The second qualification is that, while the black churches have been drawing substantial numbers, there is another powerful spiritual movement which has been making rapid headway among large sections of black youth in the last few years and which calls for very serious consideration. This is Ras Tafari.

The Rastafarian movement grew out of the slave culture of Jamaica. It takes its name Ras Tafari from the Emperor of Ethiopia, crowned in the 1930s as Haile Selassie I, King of Kings and Lord of Lords. Haile Selassie is recognized by Rasta as the Conquering Lion of Judah, and as a divine figure. The movement has responded to the white God of the Christian tradition by worshipping a black God. The Rastafarian movement thus represents the only major attempt in the twentieth century to develop a spirituality of blackness and a religion for black people. In the culture of Rasta, there is a coming together of elements of black nationalism, apocalyptic redemption themes, and themes of liberation. The fundamental spiritual idea is that of 'dread', the symbol of buried consciousness. Rasta seeks to undermine the slave culture of Babylon, and to confront the denial of racial selfhood, thus recreating a solidarity and spiritual black community. Rasta in its origins is a religion of the oppressed, and though its appearance on a significant scale in Britain is a phenomenon of recent date, some observers twenty years ago were pointing to the likelihood that the spirit of black rebellion in the Kingston slums would be transplanted to Britain. 'The island is littered with the remnants of a fire that is liable to flare up again', wrote one sociologist in 1962, and she went on:[86]

It is when you go into the slum camps of Kingston (and few
outsiders from the comfortable areas of Jamaica ever do) – it is then
that you are directly confronted by colonial history; you are in the
presence of the aftermath of slavery . . . People stop short in anger,
seeing a white face: the symbol of privilege, the mark of Cain.

So today God has been rediscovered in the Rastafarian culture as a
God of the oppressed, a God of black liberation, a God who delivers
from the Babylonian captivity of both white racism and white
churches.

If it is true that British Christianity needs to take seriously the
spiritual force of Rasta within the black community, it is equally true
that it can only be a matter of time before a British equivalent of the
movement of 'black theology' which has grown up in the United
States and elsewhere takes root here. No account of the relationship
between faith in God and the racial experience can be complete
without a consideration of black theology and its contribution to our
understanding.

Black theology starts from two realities: the liberation of black
people, and the redemption wrought in the work of Christ.[87] It rejects
the idea that black people are called by God to be permanent
sufferers.[88] Reconciliation is only possible after repentance by white
people: without this, it is merely a soft option, an evasion of the
demands of justice. The principal exponent of black theology in the
United States is James Cone. Cone has claimed that God is 'against
white people',[89] but it is important to recognize the context of his
claim. For Cone, white is the colour of the oppressor, black the colour
of the oppressed group. The black/white conflict is the framework
within which one must today understand the meaning of redemption:

To say that Christ is black means that black people are God's poor
people whom Christ has come to liberate . . . To say that Christ is
black means that God in his infinite wisdom and mercy not only
takes colour seriously, he takes it upon himself, and discloses his
will to make us whole – new creatures born in the divine blackness
and redeemed through the blood of the Black Christ . . . The
'blackness of Christ' therefore is not simply a statement about skin
colour, but rather the transcendent affirmation that God has not
ever, no not ever, left the oppressed alone in the struggle.[90]

Some black theologians have questioned the assertion that Christ is
black, insisting that Christ is universal,[91] but all of them are united in
insisting that there can be no reconciliation without liberation, no

harmony without justice. To the extent that blackness can symbolize oppression, the black struggle is seen as the context of Christian understanding. Black theology therefore seeks to illuminate the liberation struggle of black people and to relate it to the work of Christ:

> The Christ-event in Twentieth Century America is a black event, that is, an event of liberation taking place in the black community in which black people recognize that it is incumbent upon them to throw off the chains of white oppression by whatever means they regard as suitable.[92]

By contrast, Cone says, white theology is the theology of the Antichrist for it places God's approval on white oppression. But God is not colour-blind. 'He is not colour blind in the black–white struggle, but has made an unqualified identification with black people.'[93]

Statements such as this will shock and offend many white people, but they need to be heard as authentic voices of black Christians. Cone emphasizes that he uses the idea of blackness as a symbol of all forms of oppression. Because of this he argues that Christians need to see

> ... blackness as the most adequate symbol for pointing to the dimensions of divine activity in America. And insofar as this country is seeking to make whiteness the dominating power throughout the world, whiteness is the symbol for the Antichrist. Whiteness symbolizes the activity of deranged men intrigued by their own image of themselves, and thus unable to see that they are what is wrong with the world. Black Theology seeks to analyse the satanic nature of whiteness, and by doing so to prepare all non-whites for revolutionary action.[94]

It is, says Cone, as impossible to think of Christ today as non-black as it would be to think of him as non-Jewish in the first century.[95]

Racism has deeply infected the Church, and both black and white Christians are affected and damaged by it. No encounter with God in the twentieth century can bypass the encounter with the reality of black oppression, or ignore the racial conflict as a central context for our understanding of God's justice in our day.

God of Peace

The notion that God is a God of peace is well integrated into conventional religion. Religion itself is seen as a source of peace. Yet peace can be an empty term unless translated into active work for justice in the world. Certainly its use in the Old Testament shows that it cannot be separated from social justice and the common good. God's gift of peace is seen as the culmination of a state of social harmony, security, agricultural success, the removal of fear, the absence of violence (Lev. 26.3–10). Peace is identified with welfare and with hope (Jer. 29.10–11), with the abandonment of evil (Ps. 34.14). Often it means material success and happiness, often it is linked with salvation and divine justice. Peace has messianic associations, for the Messiah will be Prince of Peace (Isa. 9.6). In fact the world *shalom* is much richer and wider in its meaning than our word 'peace'. The fundamental sense of it is wholeness, for it is derived from the verb *shalem*, to be, or make, complete.[96] Our word is an 'inadequate equivalent' for so positive and holistic a concept.[97]

Peace, in the sense of justice leading to harmony and fullness of life for all, is a central biblical theme, related to the character of God as the God of peace. God is described in the prophetic writings as one who makes a 'covenant of peace' with his people, a covenant which will have major ecological consequences in terms of security and health for the animal creation and for the earth itself (Ezek. 34.25ff). The hope of peace is seen as one which involves the blossoming of the barren regions and the liberation of the created order (Isa. 35). Such peace is not possible as long as there is injustice and wickedness (Isa. 48.22), though there is a false peace which is merely a papering over the cracks, a healing of wounds lightly without that radical healing from which true peace must come (Jer. 6.14). Peace therefore does not come easily; it must be 'sown' (Zech. 8.12). God's people are called therefore to a commitment to positive peacemaking. Jesus speaks of peacemakers as the children of God (Matt. 5.9).

Of course, there is a violent and bloodthirsty side to much Old Testament religion. God is seen as a warrior, one who fights for Israel. But the emphasis is on dependence on God as the Saviour, the source of strength, and not on one's own might. Israel's armies were ordered to be inferior both in numbers (Deut. 20.1–9) and in technology (Josh. 11.6). Unlike the pagan nations, Israel was not to trust in chariots but rather look to Yahweh (Isa. 31.1). On the other hand, militarism is seen as a sign of infidelity which inevitably leads to destruction:

> You have ploughed iniquity,
>   you have reaped injustice,
>   you have eaten the fruit of lies.
> Because you have trusted in your chariots
>   and in the multitude of your warriors,
>   therefore the tumult of war shall arise among your people,

and all your fortresses shall be destroyed . . .
Thus it shall be done to you, O house of Israel,
because of your great wickedness. (Hos. 10.13–15)

The Messiah, according to Zechariah, will cut off the chariots and the battle bows, and will instead command peace to the nations (9.9–10).[98]

While the relationship of Jesus to the violent Zealot movement has been a matter of dispute for years, the New Testament and early Christian data strongly suggest that the rejection of violence and the espousal of a non-violent lifestyle was fundamental to the way of Jesus, and was therefore seen as mandatory for the early Church.[99] Jesus held that those who used the sword would perish by it (Matt. 26.52f) and linked his rejection of violence with the nature of the Kingdom of God (John 18.36). The pacifism of the early Christians is well known and well documented. However, the later history of the Church saw the development of a more permissive position on the legitimacy of war, and the doctrine of the *justum bellum* (just war or just struggle) was developed as a way of establishing criteria by which one could judge whether a particular conflict was or was not justified. The criteria of the just war are actually quite strict. The war must be declared by a legitimate authority; there must be a right intention, that is, an intention to promote peace; the war must be a last resort, after other attempts at resolving conflict have failed; there must be 'proportionality' between the aim of the conflict and the harm which might be done by war; there must be a reasonable chance of success; and there must be moderation. The whole point of the just war criteria is to reduce armed conflict to a minimum. And in fact, by these criteria, many modern conflicts would not be seen as just. For example, the Vietnam War was not declared by a legitimate authority since it was not declared at all, and was carried out by the executive, and not the legislative, branch of the American government. It is doubtful if there was a right intention, it was certainly not a last resort, and the bombings actually increased during peace initiatives. The destruction was not proportional, there was no real likelihood of success, and a marked lack of moderation. In fact, for all its good intentions, the just-war doctrine has throughout history been used by nation-states and the churches associated with them to justify wars in which they were involved. John Pairman Brown put the point cynically but accurately:[100]

> The Churches recognize in practice what their theologians missed in theory: the traditional marks of the just war reduce to a single criterion; a just war is one fought by my side. It might seen as if the

Churches relegated the possibility of unjust wars to theory only. Not at all, there are just as many of them: an unjust war is one fought by the other side ... The Establishment patriot and the revolutionary agree in having a side. The just war theory reduces to the same truism for each ... How could a war fought by my side fail to be just?

So the institutional forms which embody the corporate discipleship of the Prince of Peace have, historically, invariably supported the wars declared and fought by their national governments.

A small minority, consisting of many individuals and some churches, has maintained a consistent pacifist witness, seeing pacifism and the way of non-violent love as a necessary constituent element in the living out of the gospel. However, in the last few decades a belief has arisen among many of the victims of oppressive regimes that violence is a possible, and perhaps the only possible, option for Christians in seeking to end situations of systemic injustice. Many Christians in the Third World have now come to speak of the legitimacy of the 'just revolution', indeed have come to see that revolution as obligatory. The right of insurrection under certain conditions has been recognized by Christian moralists for centuries. Thomas Aquinas held that the operation of unjust laws should be seen as equivalent to acts of violence.[101] Where such violence has become so structured that it constitutes a whole system of total oppression, then the right to overthrow that system and end that injustice becomes a major moral issue. So in recent years the debate over violence and over pacifism has reappeared in a new form, and has led some Christians into strange positions. Many of those who have never been pacifist have suddenly come to proclaim the virtues of non-violence when confronted by the prospect of violence from others.

The debate over revolutionary violence will go on, but there is one factor which has shifted the wider conflict over war and peace on to a new level. This is, of course, the advent of nuclear weapons. As a result of this, many Christians argue that the question of pacifism is now a theoretical one. For, whatever might once have been the case, the possibility of a just war under modern conditions can no longer be seriously envisaged. A nuclear and just war is a contradiction in terms. The emergence of conditions in which the evil produced by warfare might be greater than that prevailing under an unjust situation led Pope Pius XII in 1953 to say that 'if the calamity produced by war is out of all proportion to the damage inflicted by the injury suffered, there can be an obligation to accept the injustice.'[102] But in Pius's time, information on nuclear weapons was not considerable. John

XXIII, ten years later, claimed that war was no longer a fit instrument with which to repair the violation of justice, while the Vatican Council document *Gaudium et Spes* insisted that the use of weapons of massive and indiscriminative destruction far exceeded the bounds of legitimate defence.[103] It went on: 'Any act of war aimed indiscriminately at the destruction of entire cities or of extensive areas along with their populations is a crime against God and man himself. It merits unequivocal and unhesitating condemnation.'[104] This statement rules out completely the use of strategic nuclear weapons. Indeed, it is difficult to say how the use of nuclear weapons at all can be justified in terms of traditional Catholic moral theology. While there remain differences on other questions, there does seem to be a consensus in recent Catholic thinking on the essential immorality and unacceptability of the use of nuclear weapons. And this consensus in Catholic theology has come to be shared by evangelical Christians. Thus Dr Billy Graham now sees the nuclear arms race as moving towards a conflagration of such a scale that Auschwitz would seem like a minor rehearsal.[105] In Britain, the well-respected evangelical leader John Stott has said that nuclear weapons are so indiscriminate that 'it seems clear to me that they are ethically indefensible, and that every Christian, whatever he may think of the possibility of a just use of conventional weapons must be a "nuclear pacifist".'[106]

Certainly there can be no excuse for those who seek to justify the nuclear arms race by treating nuclear war as in any sense winnable, or by seeking to minimize the destructive power of the weaponry. Nations are spending more on national security but are more insecure as a result. Even the United States can now be totally destroyed; it is less secure than it was thirty years ago. Yet policies based upon a refusal to trust the Russians depend upon an absurd level of trust in weapons technology. However, for Christians the ethical issues must be paramount if we seek to follow the God of peace, the God who seeks justice for the poor and the hungry of the world. President Eisenhower once spoke of the effect of the arms race on the poor: 'Every gun that is made, every warship launched, every rocket fired, signifies, in a final sense, a theft from those who hunger and are not fed, from those who are cold and are not clothed.'[107] Similarly, the Second Vatican Council pointed out that 'the arms race is doing great harm to humanity, and is an intolerable wrong to the poor'.[108] Thus we find that governments spend around eight times as much on research into new weapons as they do on solving energy problems, and that, for the cost of one new United States mobile intercontinental missile, 50 million undernourished children could be fed, 65,000 health care centres established, and 340,000 primary schools built.[109]

In Britain, over half of government spending on research is related to defence.[110] By contrast, the amount spent on research into alternative methods of peacemaking, or even alternative approaches to defence itself, is minimal. Thus the Alternative Defence Commission at the University of Bradford has been working on an eighteen-month budget of £26,000. The Ministry of Defence budget for research development for 1981–2 came to £1·67 thousand million – 64,230 times as much![111] We are dealing then with a diversion of resources from that which works towards the common good to that which works destruction and devastation, a truly demonic distortion of priorities and of values.

Sadly, once a distortion on so grand a scale has become built into the life of a nation, it is defended by dishonesty and further distortion. Thus it is well known by experts that Britain is particularly vulnerable in the event of nuclear war:

> Britain is one of the most densely populated countries in the world. It also has one of the highest concentrations of nuclear weapons bases . . . Britain is likely to fare badly under a large nuclear attack with perhaps no more than a few million people surviving the first month.[112]

Yet civil defence preparations and propaganda continue on the false assumption that there will be many survivors.[113] Well-documented accounts of medical effects and of fall-out are ignored or suppressed, and policies are framed against the overwhelming evidence of research.[114]

Many Christians defend the possession and siting of nuclear weapons, and the amounts of money spent on them on the grounds of 'deterrence'. The possession of these weapons, it is argued, is itself a deterrent, a way of preventing war, and has in fact prevented war for over thirty years. In fact, this is both a distortion of language, and a peculiarly European way of looking at the world. A distortion, because it would be wrong to describe the last thirty-five years in Europe as years of peace and freedom. 'Peace and freedom have, in this context, acquired meanings that are only distantly related to the dictionary definition of these words. A byproduct of the cold war has been the corruption of language.'[115] What we have experienced has not been peace but rather cold war. But, secondly, this experience of the absence of military conflicts has been only true of Europe. In the Third World there have been numerous wars in this period of 'deterrence', and there are now over sixteen million refugees as a result of those wars. Deterrence is increasingly a precarious and dangerous path, increasingly thrown into question by proliferation and by the increased likelihood of nuclear accidents.

The morality of deterrence must be questioned by those who follow the God of peace. In 1976 this question was taken up by the Roman Catholic bishops in the United States in their document *To Live in Christ Jesus*. Here they said:[116]

> With respect to nuclear weapons, at least those with massive destructive capacity, the first imperative is to prevent their use. As possessors of a vast nuclear arsenal, we must also be aware that not only is it wrong to attack civilian populations, but it is also wrong to threaten to attack them as part of a strategy of deterrence. We urge the continued development and implementation of policies which seek to bring these weapons more securely under control, progressively reduce their presence in the world, and ultimately remove them entirely.

In 1979, the (on the whole, conservative) Cardinal Krol of Philadelphia testified before the Senate Foreign Relations Committee in favour of ratifying the SALT 2 Treaty. In his testimony he cited the 1976 statement and then continued:[117]

> The moral judgement of this statement is that not only the *use* of strategic nuclear weapons, but also the *declared intent* to use them involved in our deterrence policy is wrong. This explains the Catholic dissatisfaction with nuclear deterrence and the urgency of the Catholic demand that the nuclear arms race be reversed. It is of the utmost importance that negotiations proceed to meaningful and continuing reductions in nuclear stockpiles, and eventually to the phasing out altogether of nuclear deterrence and the threat of mutual-assured destruction. As long as there is hope of this occurring, Catholic moral teaching is willing, while negotiations proceed, to tolerate the possession of nuclear weapons for deterrence as the lesser of two evils. If that hope were to disappear, the moral attitude of the Catholic Church would almost certainly have to shift to one of uncompromising condemnation of both use *and* possession of such weapons.

The meaning of this is clear, and its significance is very great. Deterrence is not acceptable, but may be tolerated so long as there is real evidence of a commitment to negotiation and to disarmament. If such commitment is not apparent, then Catholic Christians must reject the deterrence strategy altogether and seek other approaches. This was made clear also in the delegation of the English Roman Catholic bishops to the Foreign Secretary on 6 December 1982. Here they referred to the Pope's oft-misused statement to the United

Nations Special Session on Disarmament in which he claimed that deterrence was morally acceptable. But the bishops emphasized that 'this rejects the use of nuclear weapons against civilian targets, and regards deterrence as morally tolerable only if it is seen as a stage towards progressive mutual and verifiable disarmament'.[118] Since 1976 in the United States, an increasing number of bishops have come to reject the deterrence approach altogether. These include Bishop Thomas Gumbleton of Detroit and Archbishop Raymond Hunthausen of Seattle.[119]

In Britain too the Christian support for the growing peace movement has been very marked and shows every sign of increasing. As it increases the need to nourish and develop a spirituality of non-violence, a non-violent heart, becomes a matter of urgency. Christians who seek to follow the God of peace are coming to see that their discipleship will lead them into conflict with governments committed to different and contradictory policies. And they will return to the biblical truth that God alone is sovereign. From the books of Esther and Daniel in the Old Testament to the Acts and Revelation in the New, the history of the people of God has been marked by acts of non-cooperation with worldly powers. The peace movement of today stands in a long tradition of godly dissent. The early Christians believed that they should obey God rather than men (Acts 5.29) and saw the unmasking of the unfruitful works of darkness as an essential spiritual task (Eph. 5.11). So those who seek to be peacemakers, children of the God of peace, will find that they are led into acts of holy disobedience. In such activity, they will act from motives of profound love, the love of the Crucified, as they confront powers of concentrated evil. They will be marginalized and rejected, treated as the scum of the earth, ridiculed, written off as mad. Yet as Shelley Douglass, founder of the Ground Zero Centre for Non-Violent Action next to the Trident submarine base in Bangor, Washington, has said: 'We have come over a long time to the belief that our nuclear madness is such that only a different kind of madness can counter it at all. This different kind of madness must be the madness of love, the foolishness of God.'[120]

God of the Poor

All over the world the fate of the poor is an issue of urgency. As the arms race escalates, the condition of the poor of the world deteriorates. Four countries – India, Bangladesh, Pakistan, and Indonesia – contain two-thirds of the world's absolute poor. Yet all over the world, the problem of wealth is linked to the problem of poverty. In eighty-three countries, over three per cent of people own or control eighty per cent of agricultural land. Aid often does not alleviate poverty but perpetuates injustice.[121] And poverty exists also in the affluent west, juxtaposed with great wealth and power. In American cities one sees the polarized scenes in the big cities where ghettos and fashionable down-town districts adjoin. In the United States, as in Britain, poverty has been increasing in the 1980s after earlier periods of decline. In both countries also, in recent years, we have witnessed a growth of punitive and contemptuous attitudes to the poor, and these attitudes have come to be expressed in government policy. To be poor is to be almost criminal.

In Britain, while research on poverty, and documentation of poverty, have been considerable, the *consciousness* of this poverty among many sections of the population has not increased in relation to the available data. It is still widely believed that, since the coming of the welfare state, the class divisions of British society have been largely eroded, whereas in fact 'the myth of serious movement between classes ... is not substantiated by careful research'.[122] Indeed, in recent years, the numbers of poor people, even on government estimates, have increased to an alarming degree. In 1976 the Greater London Council informed the Royal Commission on the Distribution of Income and Wealth that one in four households were living below the official poverty line.[123] In the country as a whole in 1976–7, the bottom 50 per cent received 24·1 per cent of all incomes, while the top 10 per cent received 26·2 per cent. (The 1949 figures were 23·7 and 33·2 per cent respectively.) The earnings of the bottom 10 per cent of adult male manual workers have stood at 68 per cent of all earnings from 1886 to 1980.[124] In fact, research shows that the lowest paid were relatively worse off in 1980 than they were 95 years ago. In 1980, 4·7 million full-time workers, and 2·8 million part-time workers were earning below £75 per week.[125] The New Earnings Survey of 1982 showed that the relative earnings of the lowest paid men was lower than at any time during the 1970s, and was in fact lower than in 1886 when these data were first collected. This is not surprising since the increase of the numbers of those on low pay is one of the aims of the present government.[126]

In fact, since the General Election of 1979 the numbers of poor have grown at a record rate in Britain. Workers claiming Supplementary Benefit have increased by 65 per cent, those dependent on them by 86 per cent, and the numbers of poor children by 90 per cent. This increase did not occur in isolation, but was the culmination of processes begun earlier. The Royal Commission on the Distribution of Income and Wealth showed that, while there was a levelling off of inequalities between 1939 and 1948, there was a reversal of this process during the 50s and 60s. In fact, the continuing high concentration of wealth in Britain is in striking contrast to that in many other countries, and has been less eroded over a century than most people believe.

Those who are concerned with the alleviation of poverty know that in recent years conditions have worsened, not only in terms of an overall increase of people suffering, but also in terms of the hardening of official attitudes as well as those in sections of society which have been less affected. The increase in the numbers of children living at or below the poverty level is particularly alarming: some 25 per cent of the poor in Britain are children. The vast majority of the poor are decent, responsible people, and do not conform to the stereotype of the scrounger or layabout. Many of them suffer from inability to pay the rising cost of fuel. Thus a study in Merseyside in 1977 described 130 families whose fuel supplies had been disconnected through inability to pay. Some of them remained disconnected for a long time, the average being eleven months.[127] Again, the incidence of ill-health is directly related to class and to the persistence or increase of poverty. Infant mortality is twelve times higher than average in the Inner London area, while the suicide and psychiatric hospital admission rates are also higher.[128] Inequalities of health continue to show a definite class basis. Tower Hamlets, the London borough which contains most of the East End, had the highest perinatal mortality rate in Britain at the 1971 Census, while morbidity, mortality, and incidence of bronchial diseases were 60 per cent above the national average. A government study, quickly shelved, showed that the clear divisions in health and health care had increased since 1949 and that class divisions were deeper than was the case thirty years ago.[129] All this information is well known to everyone working in the field, but it makes little impression on those who are out of touch with the growing problems of our poorer districts.

For, while there is no doubt that poverty and inequality have increased markedly in our society, the consciousness of these facts has not increased comparably. Thus in a survey by the EEC in 1977, nearly two-thirds of British people claimed that there was no poverty in Britain, or that they did not know of any. Of those who did recognize some poverty, nearly half said that it was due to laziness, drink, or the personal defects of the poor themselves. In the same year, government data showed that there were over two million people living below the minimum wage level.[130] The tendency to blame poverty on the defects of the poor has, in recent years, been increased by the ideology of the government. The impression left by government policies and the thinking behind them is that not to be rich indicates a serious defect of character, while to be poor is little short of criminal. A real contempt for the poor has developed, and to a great extent has been encouraged to develop.[131] However, it would be wrong to see such contempt as a purely personal set of attitudes which could be changed within the framework of the same system of values. Contempt for the poor is a natural and predictable by-product of Mammon-worship. As Thomas Cullinan has written: 'If we idolize wealth, then we create poverty; if we idolize success, we create the inadequate; if we idolize power, we create powerlessness. And these processes are inevitable.'[132] Inevitable, that is, until the fundamental orientation of the society is tackled. Hence the urgency of seeing how our perspective on poverty and inequality is related to our understanding of God and his relation to human society.

In the Old Testament, the notion of justice was closely linked with the defence of the poor, for the existence of the poor in itself violated the just order 'From the first the term had an inherent bias towards the poor and needy.'[133] In the pages of the Old Testament there are many references to 'the poor': some 245 references under six main terms.[134] God does not forget the poor (Ps. 9.12; 10.12), he pities them (Ps. 97.41; 132.15; Isa. 25.4; Jer. 20.13). The Messiah is particularly seen as one who will satisfy the poor with bread (Ps. 132.15). The existence of poverty is seen as evil (Prov. 15.15), and the aim of the Law is that there should be no poor in the land (Deut. 15.4). The prophets are particularly concerned with the defence of the poor against their attackers, those who 'trample upon the needy and bring the poor of the land to an end', who 'deal deceitfully with false balances' and 'buy the poor for silver and the needy for a pair of sandals' (Amos 8.4–6). The demands of justice are contrasted with the actions of those who 'tear the skin from off my people' (Mic. 3.1–2), and grind the faces of the poor (Isa. 3.15). Jeremiah attacks the rich as a class, and accuses them of injustice and of failing to 'defend the rights of the needy' (Jer. 5.26–8). Similarly, Ezekiel points to the fact that sojourners suffer extortion through the dishonest gain of the princes of Israel (Ezek. 22.6–13). Such attacks as these in the prophetic writings are clearly 'not directed against individuals but against the class as such'.[135] Injustice and riches are closely linked in the thought of the biblical writers. Profit (*besa*) and interest (*neshek*) are condemned (e.g. Exod. 22.24; Lev. 25.36–7; Deut. 23.19; etc.). Indeed 'wealth is *always* condemned as something which does not help the human being to receive the justice of God'.[136]

Biblical teaching then makes the connection between poverty and wealth. It is impossible to deal with poverty in isolation from wealth. The possession of wealth is seen consistently as an impediment to relationship with God. It is impossible therefore to escape the conclusion that, as Karl Barth wrote, God is one-sidedly the God of the lowly.[137] Indeed, as the American evangelical writer Jim Wallis has written:[138]

> That God is on the side of the poor and that the Scriptures are uncompromising in their demand for economic and social justice is much more clear biblically than are most of the issues over which churches have divided. The Scriptures claim that to know God is to do justice and to plead the cause of the oppressed. Yet this central biblical imperative is one of the first to be purged from a church that has conformed and made accommodations to the established order.

It is vital then to recover this close connection which the Bible makes between the defence of the poor and the knowledge of God. The prophetic witness is continued in the life and teaching of Jesus and in the early Church. In Jesus' life and ministry, we see the offer of entry into the Kingdom to those who had been excluded from all earthly privilege: the poor, the sick, the Samaritans, the sinners, the despised and impure. In fact, Jesus becomes himself despised and impure, moving to the margins to share the life of the marginal people. His work of reconciliation depended upon his identification with the poor and the powerless. On the other hand, he condemned as fools those who trusted in wealth (Luke 12.16 21), and insisted that devotion to wealth was not compatible with devotion to God (16.3) and that the disciple must renounce all his or her possessions (14.33). Money is called Mammon (Matt. 6.24; Luke 16.13) as if it were a kind of pseudo-deity.[139]

The earliest Christians took the demands of poverty in discipleship very seriously, and poverty was eradicated within their communities (Acts 2.42–7; 4.32–5). The existing order was overthrown by the poor and despised (1 Cor. 1.28). Their significance is central to the whole meaning of the gospel.

> . . . in the New Testament the poor are related, not to the world and the system of man, but to the Kingdom of God. Only from this perspective can the cruelty and the blindness of man be exposed and judged. The poor possess the secret of the Kingdom, for they are the judgement of the present age . . . the poor exist as a sign of promise. In the New Testament, God acts precisely through those who have nothing to expect from the world, and for whom the structure and life of the world have become enemies. God acts through the outcast, the despised, through those without possibilities, without any future, through those who, in possessing nothing

on earth, bear the promise of a new age in which all people can possess everything equally.[140]

So for the early Christians, the sharing of property and possessions was a profoundly theological activity, 'a principle which is at the very heart of social justice in the early Church'.[141] And this concern with sharing is continued through the works of the early Fathers. St Basil speaks of the 'common and universal sharing of possessions' and condemns obsession with wealth and the accumulation of possessions.[142] For him, care for the poor and needy was a matter which affected a person's eternal salvation:

> You have not been merciful, so you will not be shown mercy; you have not opened your doors, so those of the Kingdom of Heaven will be closed to you; you have not given a piece of bread, so you will be refused eternal life.[143]

St John Chrysostom also warned that we will suffer unless we cease to plunder the poor. He compares the state of humanity before the fall to the life of animals, a life without the later divisions and inequality.[144] The rich are condemned because they do not share, and therefore 'damage the common good'. If they did share, the result would be 'a universal upheaval'.[145] Moreover, Chrysostom says, in the face of the poor, we see the face of Christ himself:

> Your Lord is out there, dying of hunger, and you give yourself up to gluttony. And the terrible thing is not only this, but as you give yourselves up to gluttony, you calmly despise him, and it is very little he asks of you: a piece of bread to assuage his hunger. He is out there, dying of cold, and you dress yourself in silk and turn your gaze away from him, showing him no compassion, but go on your way without mercy. What pardon can such action merit? Then let us not devote our efforts to accumulating wealth at all costs. Let us also consider the way of administering it properly and helping the needy, and let us not exaggerate in the good which remain and cannot be transferred.[146]

St Ambrose says that in giving to the poor, we are simply returning what is theirs by right, for the earth is common property.[147]

Of course, the complex issues of poverty and maldistribution of resources cannot be solved by a few quotations from the early Fathers for whom social conditions were very different. Yet it is important to see that behind the specifics of the life of the early Christians there lay profound beliefs about the nature of God and the character of the created world. The social demands made by the early Christians 'introduced new stimuli to the ancient world which can be described without exaggeration as revolutionary'.[148] It is necessary now for a Church which seeks to know and serve God to try to grapple with the consequences of this revolutionary faith in terms of the present. Today, many Christians in Latin America, viewing the enormity of poverty, are stressing that the call now is not simply one for a generous act to poor persons, but for a radical change in the social order which produces poverty as its by-product.[149] If the Church today is to be the helper of the helpless, it will be led increasingly into the arena of politics.

Certainly, the question of the poor is one which is crucial for the very identity of the Church, for it can be argued that 'a church without the poor is a place he has obviously left'. The poor therefore constitute an 'ecclesiological criterion', one which determines the authenticity of the Church's claim to manifest Christ to the world.[150] It is possible also to see the poor as a criterion of the Church's spirituality. In John Atherton's words:[151]

> In all these ways, the Christian is concerned with what it means to be human because that is what God created, what God became, and . . . what in his Incarnation he is. To be concerned with humanity in the form of the poor is therefore a kind of taking part in God.

Atherton also stresses that it is by the supreme test of caring for the poor that we will all be judged.

Thus the poor are of central significance for understanding our gospel as well as the character of our present society. It is in the poor that we see the dehumanizing and anti-human, and therefore ungodly, forces in our society. The poor are thus revelatory, they reveal to us the divine cry for justice, they are signs of the judgement which the Kingdom brings.[152] There can be no true knowledge of God which does not include care for the poor, and the ability to hear the cry of the poor. But more than this, it is necessary to see God taking the side of the poor and lowly: that is part of the character of God as revealed in the Christian Scriptures, however uncomfortable and unacceptable it may be to worldly and secure churches, and to the corridors of power. Karl Barth's words abide:[153]

> . . . the human righteousness required by God . . . has necessarily the character of a vindication of right in favour of the threatened innocent, the oppressed poor, widows, orphans and aliens. For this reason, the relations and events in the life of his people, God always takes his stand unconditionally and passionately on this side, and on this side alone: against the lofty, and on behalf of the

lowly; against those who already enjoy right and privilege, and on behalf of those who are denied and deprived of it.

God the Liberator

Since the 1960s a theological tendency has swept the western Christian world from Central and South America: it has become known as Liberation Theology. It seeks to recognize and serve God as he is revealed in the process of liberation of captive peoples. Not that the theme of liberation was invented by Christians in Latin America in these years. It is a very old Christian word. However, in its modern political connotations, it began to enter theological vocabulary after the Bandung Conference of 1955, and has been increasingly stressed in Catholic theology since the Second Vatican Council. For that Council, by its stress on the human and social dimensions of grace, and its abandonment of earlier 'two places' theologies, prepared the way for a theological approach which did not divide reality into natural and supernatural, material and spiritual realms, but saw things in a more unified way.[154] Following on Vatican 2 came Paul VI's important encyclical of 1968 *Populorum Progressio*. Then, in 1971, the Synod of Bishops meeting in Rome issued their document *Justice in the World*. They stressed that redemption includes the liberation from all oppressed conditions of human life, and that participation in the transformation of society is a 'constitutive element' in the living of the gospel:

> Action on behalf of justice and participation in the transformation of the world fully appears to us as a constitutive dimension of the preaching of the Gospel, or, in other words, in the Church's mission for the redemption of the human race, and its liberation from every oppressive situation.[155]

Pope Paul VI was particularly emphatic that liberation was a central gospel theme, and this was stressed particularly in his Apostolic Exhortation *Evangelii Nuntiandi* of 8 December 1975. This is so important, as part of the 'official' background to the theology of liberation, that it needs to be quoted at length. Liberation, Paul says, is 'not foreign to evangelism', and he goes on:[156]

> Between evangelization and human advancement – development and liberation – there are in fact profound links. These include links of an anthropological order, because the man who is to be evangelized is not an abstract being, but is subject to social and economic questions. They also include links in the theological order since one cannot dissociate the plan of creation from the plan

of redemption. The latter plan touches the very concrete situation of injustice to be combated, and of justice to be restored. They include links of the eminently evangelical order which is that of charity: how in fact can one proclaim the new commandment without promoting in justice and in peace the true authentic advancement of man? We ourself have taken care to point this out by recalling that it is impossible to accept 'that in evangelization one could or should ignore the importance of the problems so much discussed today concerning justice, liberation, development and peace in the world. This would be to forget the lesson which comes to us from the Gospel concerning love of our neighbour who is suffering and in need.' [Paul VI, Address for the Opening of the Third General Assembly of the Synod of Bishops, 27 September 1974]

The same voices which, during the Synod, touched on this burning theme with zeal, intelligence and courage, have, to our great joy, furnished the enlightening principles for a proper understanding of the importance and profound meaning of liberation, such as it was proclaimed and achieved by Jesus of Nazareth, and such as it is preached by the Church.

A few paragraphs later in the same document, Paul stresses:[157]

The Church links human liberation and salvation in Jesus Christ, but ohe never identifies them because she knows . . . that not every notion of liberation is necessarily consistent and compatible with an evangelical vision of man, of things, and of events; she knows too that in order that God's Kingdom should come, it is not enough to establish liberation and to create well-being and development.

Pope Paul then links together liberation and salvation, justice and evangelism. It was during his pontificate that the major theologial developments in Latin American theology took place.

It is sometimes claimed that Pope John Paul II has rejected the claims of the liberation tradition. Yet he also, speaking in Rome in 1979, brings together liberation and the gospel, insisting on the Church's duty to speak out on behalf of the victims of injustice:

So liberation then is certainly a reality of faith, one of the fundamental biblical themes which are a deep part of Christ's salvific mission, of the work of redemption, of his teaching. This subject has never ceased to constitute the content of the spiritual life of Christians. The conference of the Latin American episco-pate bears witness that the subject returns in a new historical context. Therefore it must be taken up again in the teaching of the

Church, in theology, and in the apostolate. The theology of liberation is often connected too exclusively with Latin America. It must be admitted that one of the great contemporary theologians, Hans Urs von Balthasar, is right when he demands the theology of liberation on a universal scale. Only the contexts are different, but the reality itself of the freedom for which Christ set us free is universal. The task of theology is to find its real significance in the different historical and contemporary contexts.

Christ himself links liberation particularly with the knowledge of the truth. 'You will know the truth, and the truth will make you free.' Truth is important not only for the growth of human knowledge, deepening man's interior life in this way. Truth also has a prophetic significance and power. It constitutes the content of testimony, and it calls for testimony. We find this prophetic power of truth in the teaching of Christ. As a prophet, as a witness to truth, Christ repeatedly opposes non-truth. He does so with great forcefulness and decision, and often he does not hesitate to condemn falsehood. Let us reread the Gospel carefully. We will find in it a good many severe expressions (for example, whitened sepulchres, blind guides, hypocrites) which Christ utters, fully aware of the consequences that are in store for him. So this service of truth, this participation in Christ's prophetic service, is the task of the Church, which tries to carry it out in the various historical contexts. It is necessary to call by their real names injustice, the exploitation of man by man, or the exploitation of man by the state, institutions, mechanisms, or systems and regimes which sometimes operate without sensitivity. It is necessary to call by their real names every social injustice, discrimination, violence, inflicted on men against the body, against the spirit, against the conscience, and against the convictions. Christ teaches us a special sensitivity for man, for the dignity of the human person, for human life, for the human spirit and body.[158]

A fuller examination would wish to place such statements as these in parallel with similar statements from Anglican and other churches, and from the World Council of Churches. Over the years a remarkable consensus has occurred within most sections of world Christianity on the thrust of the gospel towards human liberation. Many Christians today would agree with James Cone's observation nearly fifteen years ago that any theology which is indifferent to the theme of liberation is not Christian theology.[159]

However, it is from Latin America that the movement of theological reflection with which liberation themes have been most associated has come. Liberation Theology has now been discussed in many studies, and this is not the place to attempt another discussion. As a theological tradition, it is desperately concerned with the liberation of theology itself. It sees one of the major problems to be not the 'death of God' but rather the death of the theologians, and it seeks therefore to set theology free from its academic captivity to be at the service of oppressed peoples and deprived groups.[160] It is a theological movement which has emerged from a continent marked by extreme suffering. In El Salvador, which has produced some of the most formative theological thinkers of the school, nearly 7,000 people were assassinated in the first six months of 1980 alone. In a three-year period, a number of priests, including Archbishop Romero, were killed. It is against this background, in which the proclamation of the gospel is a highly dangerous exercise, that Liberation Theology has made its important contribution to the Christian world.

Like most Christians who seek to apply the gospel to the political realm, Latin American theologians are commonly accused of forsaking the gospel for politics. Archbishop Romero, in one of his last homilies, rejected this accusation, insisting that he was seeking rather to be faithful to the demands of the gospel.[161] Equally, these theologians would reject the Marxist interpretation of religion. 'Over against Marx,' wrote Juan Luis Segundo, 'we would affirm that religion can perform the function of unsettling people.'[162] They seek to recover the dynamic and explosive, rather than the analgesic and sedative, qualities in religion. As a theological method, Liberation Theology begins with reflection on the practical situation, and with commitment to the human struggle. Theology follows this preliminary reflection and commitment as a second step.[163]

It is often said that Liberation Theology is not sufficiently 'spiritual'. Again, this is a false accusation, based on ignorance. In the words of Gutierrez, 'an authentic theology is always a spiritual theology'.[164] In the last few years there has in fact been a tremendous upsurge of concern for a 'liberation spirituality'. It has become one of the major themes in Latin American writing. But these writers refuse to separate spirituality from the political struggle and the demands of social justice. Any form of pietism which seeks to compartmentalize areas of Christian life is unacceptable to them. But no one could read the works of the Latin American writers without being profoundly aware of the centrality of biblical reflection and biblical study. Thus, the key study by the Peruvian theologian José Miranda, *Marx and the Bible*, contains 312 pages. Of these, 42 consist of socio-economic analysis, and no less than 270 of biblical exegesis. A similar pattern appears in Miranda's other main work on St John, *Being and the*

Messiah. Here, out of 225 pages, 25 are concerned with socio-economic questions, and 199 to biblical exegesis.[165] These theologians are, in fact, deeply concerned with recovering the wholeness of the faith. While they are accused, by people ignorant of their works, of being revisionists and watering down the faith, Miranda's words of response are worth pondering. He and his colleagues are, he says, 'shameless conservatives':

> ... the one thing the Christian revolutionaries advocate and defend is the adoration of the true God in contrast with the adoration of idols which, for many centuries now, has been inculcated by a theology radically ignorant of the Bible.[166]

Christians who seek to follow the God revealed in the Bible in the context of today's world cannot afford to ignore their words and their courageous witness.

At heart what Liberation Theology offers us is a route towards a renewed understanding of the good news of the Kingdom of God. It is Kingdom theology before it is anything else:

> The most precious contribution of Latin American theology, rooted as it is in an historical practice of liberation, is to allow us a new understanding of the concept of 'the Kingdom of God'. The Kingdom of God is not only a spiritual reality, but a universal revolution of the structures of the old world ... The effort of all the poor to liberate themselves is one of the ways of putting the Kingdom of God into practice in history.[167]

Christians in the West can best learn from their Latin American brothers and sisters by reflecting upon, and involving themselves in, the issues of their own society, including such areas as the persistence of social injustice, the incidence of racism, the nuclear threat, and the increase in poverty, and then using the insights and the methods developed in Latin America to seek an indigenous liberation theology for Britain. The task is long overdue. It is a gospel task for those who seek to follow the God of justice in today's world.

POSTSCRIPT
Towards a Renewed Spirituality: a Manifesto

1 A renewed Christian spirituality will be concerned with the
recovery of the vision of God in the contemporary world. It will
seek to speak of God and of the deep things of the spirit in ways
which are meaningful in the present climate. It will seek, humbly
and carefully, to take account of the insights presented by
Marxism, by depth psychology, and by the secular quest for
enriched consciousness, while seeking also to remain faithful to
the Christian spiritual tradition.

2 It will be a spirituality which is rooted in the experience of God in
the life of the Jewish people. In the study of the Old Testament, it
will bear witness to the revelation of God in the desert to a people
of pilgrimage. It will speak of God's holiness and of God's justice,
and will seek holiness and justice in personal and social life.

3 It will be a spirituality which finds its centre in Jesus Christ, seeing
in him the fullness of the Godhead dwelling bodily. It will seek to
be faithful to his proclamation of the Kingdom of God. It will see
in Jesus both God incarnate and a human comrade, the divine
revealed and the human raised up.

4 It will be a spirituality which looks to the faith of the Apostolic
Church as exhibited in the New Testament: the faith in God who
brings unity to the human race, and who has wrought salvation
and reconciliation through Christ; a God of light and love; a God
whose Spirit brings freedom; a God who nourishes and builds up
the Body of Christ. In the New Testament, as in the Old, it will
seek to deepen knowledge of the living and true God.

5 It will be a spirituality of the desert. From the desert experience it
will cherish and seek to strengthen the contemplative life of the
Church. It will seek both solitude and communion as equally
important aspects of the life of the spirit.

6 It will be a spirituality of cloud and darkness. It will bear witness
to the mystery at the heart of God, and to the mystery at the heart
of the human encounter with the divine. It will seek to lead people
away from a religion of easy answers into the dark night of faith. It
will be a contemplative spirituality.

7 It will be a spirituality of water and of fire, of cleansing and

421

purifying, of renewal and spiritual warmth. In the symbols of the water of baptism and the fire of the Spirit, it will see the call to continual rebirth and the daily challenge of the God whose nature is consuming fire. It will be a charismatic spirituality.

8 It will be a spirituality rooted in the Word made flesh. It will hold to the truth of God incarnate, and will seek to find and serve God in the flesh and blood of God's children. It will rejoice in the divine gifts of matter and of sexuality, seeing in the human the gateway to the divine. It will be a materialistic spirituality.

9 It will be a eucharistic spirituality. At its heart will be the celebration of the Eucharist, the sacrament of Christ's body and blood. It will recognize Christ both in the Eucharist and in those who share his nature. It will seek to manifest the eucharistic life of sharing and equality in the world. It will therefore be a spirituality of the common life, of holy communion.

10 It will be a spirituality of pain, seeing in the passion and death of Jesus the heart of the gospel. It will preach Jesus crucified and will seek to follow the way of the cross.

11 It will learn from the mystical writers to see God as the ground of all reality and of our own beings. It will seek to recover and promote a true Christian mysticism as an integral element in Christian theology. It will seek to discover and promote the ministry of spiritual guidance and deepening of the inner life and to hold together the mystical and political dimensions of the life of faith.

12 It will be a spirituality which will take seriously the experience of God in women's history; the feminine namings of God in Scripture and tradition; and the forgotten or neglected insights of writers who have experienced and described God in a feminine way. It will seek also to listen to, and learn from, the critique of Christian tradition offered by the contemporary women's movement.

13 It will be a spirituality of justice and of peace. It will seek to know and follow God in the pursuit of justice for all people, in the struggle against racism and other forms of domination, in the movement for world peace and for nuclear disarmament, and in the campaign against poverty and inequality. In the struggles for a more human world, a renewed spirituality will come to discern the face of God, the holy and just One, and to share in the peace of God which passes all understanding.

References

CHAPTER 1

1 Cited in Os Guinness, *The Dust of Death* (Inter Varsity Press 1973), p. 318.
2 A. N. Whitehead, *Adventures of Ideas* (Cambridge UP 1933), p. 157.
3 R. H. Tawney, *The Acquisitive Society* (Fontana 1961 edn), p. 18.
4 Speech on 21 June 1924, cited in *International* 5.1 (1979), p. 21.
5 T. S. Eliot, *The Idea of a Christian Society* (Faber 1939).
6 *A Kind of Believing* (General Synod Board of Education 1977).
7 *Sunday Times*, 22 April 1973.
8 NOP 1976. See David Hay, 'The spiritual experiences of the British', *New Society*, 12 April 1979, pp. 72–4.
9 *The Times* and *The Guardian*, 21 September 1978.
10 Gallup Poll, Day One, BBC 1, 10 September 1981.
11 *Social Trends* (Central Statistical Office 1976).
12 *Prospects for the 80s* (Bible Society 1980).
13 *Religion in America 1979–60* (Princeton, Religion Research Center 1979).
14 Op. cit.
15 J. Hitchcock, *Catholicism and Modernity* (Seabury Press 1979) p. 23.
16 Peter L. Halverson and William M. Newman, *Atlas of Religious Change in America 1952–1971* (Glenmary Research Centre, 1978).
17 Jim Wallis, *The Call to Conversion* (Harper & Row, 1982) p. 20.
18 See Peter Steinfels, 'Baptizing Reaganism', *Christianity and Crisis*, 29 March 1982 pp. 80–5; S. M. Miller, 'Reagan, Reaganism and the real world', *New Society*, 15 January 1981, pp. 91–3; Peggy L. Shriver, *The Bible Vote: religion and the New Right* (New York, Pilgrim Press 1981); Erling Jorstad, *The Politics of Moralism: the new Christian Right in American life* (Minneapolis, Augsburg, 1981).
19 Cited in *Christianity and Crisis*, 15 February 1982, p. 29.
20 Important issues and events which have contributed to this growing gulf include nuclear disarmament, poverty policies, racism and nationality, the Falklands War, the miners' strike, and monetarist economics.
21 Enoch Powell, a prominent British politician of the extreme Right, complained that the Queen had become afraid to speak as

a Christian monarch to a Christian nation, and as a British monarch to the British nation. (*The Times*, 21 January 1984.)

22 Examples of this can be seen in the journals *National Catholic Reporter* and *Sojourners*.

23 Nietzsche, *Collected Works*, vol. 10, p. 168.

24 Cited in A. Kee, *The Way of Transcendence: Christian faith without belief in God* (Penguin 1971), p. 127. On Nietzsche see pp. 113–32.

25 Kee, p. 131.

26 T. T. J. Altizer and William Hamilton, *Radical Theology and the Death of God* (Penguin 1968).

27 T. T. J. Altizer, *The Gospel of Christian Atheism* (Collins 1967).

28 Gabriel Vahanian, *The Death of God* (New York, George Braziller 1961).

29 *Christian Century*, 27 September 1978.

30 Altizer, op. cit., pp. 102–31.

31 Cited in Alan Ecclestone, *The Night Sky of the Lord* (Darton, Longman and Todd 1980), p. 210.

32 Martin Buber, *Eclipse of God* (New York, Harper 1957), pp. 65ff.

33 J. Ellul, *Hope in Time of Abandonment* (Seabury 1973), pp. 71ff.

34 SCM Press 1963.

35 See *The Honest to God Debate* (ed. D. L. Edwards, SCM Press 1963).

36 See David Jenkins in ibid, pp. 194ff.

37 *Exploration into God* (SCM Press 1967), pp. 29–59.

38 E. L. Mascall, *The Christian Universe* (Darton, Longman and Todd 1966), pp. 9–10.

39 David Jenkins, *Guide to the Debate about God* (SCM Press 1966), p. 109.

40 Langdon Gilkey, *Naming the Whirlwind: the renewal of God-language* (Indianapolis 1967).

41 *Journal of Theological Studies* (New Series) 7 (1956), p. 340.

42 E. Farley, *The Transcendence of God* (1962), p. 77.

43 Nathan Scott, *The Broken Center* (1966), p. 147.

44 Cf. Charles Glicksberg, *Modern Literature and the Death of God* (The Hague, Martinas Nijhoff 1966), p. 25.

45 Saul Bellow, *Herzog*, cited in *New Theology* 5 (1968), p. 79.

46 See Alasdair MacIntyre and Paul Ricoeur, *The Religious Significance of Atheism* (New York, Columbia UP 1969).

47 Colin E. Gunton, *Becoming and Being* (Oxford UP 1978), p. 1.

48 John Macquarrie, *God Talk: an examination of the language and logic of theology* (Seabury, 1979).

49 John Macquarrie, *God and Secularity*. New Directions in Theology Today vol, 3 (Philadelphia, Westminster Press 1967),

50 Schubert M. Ogden, *The Reality of God* (SCM Press 1967) p.14.
51 Address to the British Association at York, 2 September 1981, cited in *The Times*, 3 September 1981.
52 Thomas Kuhn, *The Structure of Scientific Revolutions* (University of Chicago Press 1967); Michael Polanyi, *Personal Knowledge: towards a post-critical philosophy* (University of Chicago Press 1959).
53 See, for this view, M. B. Foster, *Mystery and Philosophy* (SCM Press 1957).
54 Cf. such titles as J. W. Draper, *The Conflict between Religion and Science* (1874); A. D. White, *A History of the Warfare of Science with Theology in Christendom* (1897); J. Y. Simpson, *Landmarks in the Struggle between Science and Religion* (1925); H. H. Price, *Some Aspects of the Conflict between Science and Religion* (1953).
55 Cf. Pius XII, Allocution to Pontifical Academy of Sciences, November 1951, in *The Tablet*, 1 December 1951; and Sir Edmund Whittaker, *Space and Spirit* (Nelson 1946).
56 Harold K. Schilling, *The New Consciousness in Science and Religion* (SCM Press 1973).
57 Cf. Alasdair MacIntyre (ed.), *Metaphysical Beliefs* (SCM Press 1970 edn).
58 In Basil Mitchell (ed.), *Faith and Logic* (1957), p. 73.
59 Sebastian Moore, *God Is a New Language* (Darton, Longman and Todd 1967).
60 Penguin 1973.
61 Paul Oestreicher (ed.), *The Christian–Marxist Dialogue: an international symposium* (New York, Macmillan 1969), p. 22.
62 Karl Marx and Frederick Engels, *On Religion* (Moscow, FLPH, 1955 edn), pp. 9, 10.
63 Cf. MacIntyre, *Marxism and Christianity* (Penguin 1971).
64 *Collected Works* Vol. 3, pp. 17, 175.
65 Ibid., p. 176.
66 See Helmut Gollwitzer, *The Christian Faith and the Marxist Critique of Religion* (ET, St Andrew's Press 1970).
67 J. L. Segundo, *The Liberation of Theology* (Orbis 1976), p. 59.
68 See Trevor Beeson, *Discretion and Valour: religious conditions in Russia and Eastern Europe* (Fontana 1974); and the journal *Religion in Communist Lands* (Keston College, Keston, Kent).
69 *Questions of Scientific Atheism* Vol. 9 (1970), cited in Michael Bordeaux and Katharine Murray, *Young Christians in Russia* (Lakeland 1976), p. 10.

70 Ibid., pp. 23–4.
70 Milan Prucha, cited in J. M. Lochman, *Encountering Marx* (Philadelphia, Fortress Press 1977), p. 41.
72 George Patterson, 'The spirit of Mao', *Third Way*, 27 January 1977, p. 13.
73 Roger Garaudy, *The Alternative Future: a vision of Christian Marxism* (Penguin 1976). See also Russell B. Norris, *God, Marx and the Future: dialogue with Roger Garaudy* (Fortress Press 1974).
74 MacIntyre, *Marxism and Christianity*, op. cit.
75 *The Real Situation in Russia* (1928), cited in Stanley G. Evans, *The Social Hope of the Christian Church* (Hodder and Stoughton 1965), p. 241.
76 See Michael Langford 'Marx and atheism' in *After Marx* (Jubilee Lent Lectures 1983, ed. K. Leech, Jubilee Group 1984).
77 Alasdair MacIntyre, *Marxism: an interpretation* (SCM Press 1953), pp. 10, 14.
78 Garaudy, cited in Paul Oestreicher (ed.), *The Christian–Marxist Dialogue: an international symposium* (New York, Macmillan 1969), p. 200.
79 Cited in Evans, op. cit., p. 233.
80 See Roy S. Lee, *Freud and Christianity* (Penguin 1967); B. G. Sanders, *Christianity after Freud* (Bles 1949).
81 H. C. Rümke *The Psychology of Unbelief* (Rockliff 1952).
82 Cited in Dorothee Soelle, *The Inward Road* (Darton, Longman and Todd 1979), p. 117.
83 C. G. Jung, *Two Essays in Analytical Psychology* in *Collected Works* Vol. 7 (New York, 1953), p. 203.
84 Cited in Morton T. Kelsey, *Encounter with God* (Hodder and Stoughton 1974), p. 119.
85 Ibid., p. 38.
86 *The Structure and Dynamics of the Psyche* in *Collected Works* Vol. 8 (1969), pp. 228, 336.
87 *Psychology of the Unconscious* (1911), p. 38.
88 *Two Essays in Analytical Psychology* (1926), pp. 72–3.
89 *Essays on Contemporary Events* (1936), p. 7.
90 Raymond Hostie, *Religion and the Psychology of Jung* (Sheed and Ward 1957), p. 117.
91 Eugene C. Bianchi, 'Jungian psychology and religious experience', *Anglican Theological Review* 61.2 (1979), pp. 182–99.
92 Michael Fordham, *The Objective Psyche* (Routledge and Kegan Paul 1958), p. 128.
93 Theodore Roszak, *Unfinished Animal* (Faber 1975), p. 240.

94 R. D. Laing, *The Politics of Experience and the Bird of Paradise* (Penguin 1967), and other works.

95 See R. Gordon Wasson, *Soma: divine mushroom of immortality* (Harcourt, Brace Jovanovich 1971).

96 William James, *The Varieties of Religious Experience* (New York, Mentor 1958 edn), p. 298.

97 Aldous Huxley, *Heaven and Hell* (1956 edn), p. 63.

98 See David E. Smith and Alan J. Rose, *Love Needs Care* (1970).

99 See, from an immense literature, Timothy Leary, Ralph Metzner and Richard Alpert, *The Psychedelic Experience* (1966); Timothy Leary, *The Politics of Ecstasy* (Paladin 1970 edn); Gunther M. Weil, Ralph Metzner and Timothy Leary, *The Psychedelic Reader* (1965).

100 *Politics of Ecstasy*, p. 40.

101 Ibid., p. 212.

102 Ibid., pp. 2, 73.

103 See Allan Y. Cohen, 'Psychedelic drugs and the student: educational strategies', *Journal of College Student Personnel*, March 1969, pp. 96–101.

104 William Sargent, 'The physiology of faith', *New Society*, 17 July 1969, pp. 90–2.

105 Brian Wells, *Psychedelic Drugs: psychological, medical and social issues* (Penguin 1973), p. 189.

106 See, for example, W. N. Pahnke, 'LSD and religious experience' in R. C. DeBold and R. C. Leaf (eds) *LSD, Man and Society* (1969), pp. 60–84.

107 Allan Y. Cohen, *LSD and the search for God* (Church Literature Association 1973).

108 Ibid.

109 Theodore Roszak, *The Making of a Counter-Culture* (Faber 1968), p. 177.

110 Meher Baba, *God in a Pill?* (San Francisco, Sufism Reoriented 1966).

111 Alasdair MacIntyre, 'A society without a metaphysics', *The Listener*, 13 September 1956, pp. 375–6.

112 Ibid., p. 375.

113 Ibid., p. 376.

114 Theodore Roszak, *Unfinished Animal* (Faber 1975), p. 3.

115 Meher Baba, op. cit.

116 I have not been able to trace the source of this quotation.

117 *Peking Review*, cited in *New Society*, 8 March 1979.

118 Vittorio Lanternari, *The Religions of the Oppresed* (New York, Mentor 1965).

119 Norman Cohn, *The Pursuit of the Millennium* (Secker and Warburg 1957).

120 Laing, *The Politics of Experience*, op. cit., pp. 109–10.

121 *Time*, 19 June 1972.

122 G. K. Nelson and Rosemary Clews, *Mobility and Religious Commitment* (Birmingham, Institute for the Study of Worship and Religious Architecture 1971).

123 Report of the National Association of Evangelicals, October 1978.

124 Jeremy Seabrook, *New Society*, 28 February 1980, p. 440.

125 See my *Youthquake* (Sheldon Press 1973).

126 Theodore Roszak, *Unfinished Animal* (Faber 1975), p. 68.

127 Ibid., p. 201.

128 Robert E. Terwilliger in *The Charismatic Christ* (Darton, Longman and Todd 1974), p. 57.

129 See Andrew Greeley, *The Persistence of Religion* (1973).

130 Jacques Ellul, *Hope in Time of Abandonment* (Seabury 1973), p. 78.

131 Roszak, *Unfinished Animal*, op. cit., pp. 31, 20.

132 Victor Frankl, *From Death Camp to Existentialism* (Boston, Beacon Press 1962), p. 109.

133 Irenaeus, *Adv. Haer.*

134 Alan Ecclestone, *The Night Sky of the Lord* (Darton, Longman and Todd 1980), p. 9.

135 1 Apol. 6.1.

136 Rudolf Bultmann, *Jesus and the Word* (ET, Fontana 1958), pp. 113f.

CHAPTER 2

1 Th. C. Vriezen, *The Religion of Ancient Israel* (Lutterworth 1967).

2 R. W. Funk, 'The Wilderness', *Journal of Biblical Literature* 78 (1959), pp. 205–14.

3 H. and H. A. Frankfort, *Before Philosophy* (Penguin 1961), p. 246.

4 Ibid., p. 245.

5 William McNamara, *Desert Call* 16.1 (1981), p. 4.

6 Sir Leonard Woolley, *Abraham* (Faber 1936), p. 251.

7 G. W. Anderson, *The History and Religion of Israel* (Oxford UP, 1966), p. 20.

8 John L. McKenzie SJ, *The Two Edged Sword* (Milwaukee, Bruce 1956), p. 28.

9 Jacob Jocz, *The Spiritual History of Israel* (Eyre and Spottis-

woode 1961), p. 63.

10 Yehezkel Kaufmann, *The Religion of Israel* (ET, Allen and Unwin 1961), p. 223.

11 Ibid., p. 224.

12 Antonio Pérez-Esclarín, *Atheism and Liberation* (SCM Press 1980), p. 80.

13 B. W. Anderson, *The Living World of the Old Testament* (Longmans 1958), p. 6.

14 L. John Topel SJ, *The Way to Peace: liberation through the Bible* (Gill and Macmillan 1980), p. 2.

15 Jean Daniélou SJ, *The Bible and the Liturgy* (Darton, Longman and Todd 1960), p. 87.

16 Jean Daniélou SJ, *Sacramentum Futuri*. Études de Théologie Historique (Paris, Beauchesne 1950), p. 143.

17 *Paschal Homily*, tr. P. Nautin (*Sources Chrétiènnes*, 1951), p. 143.

18 Kaufmann, op. cit., p. 232.

19 Ulrich Mauser, *Christ in the Wilderness* (SM Press 1963), p. 21.

20 Ibid., p. 37.

21 Ibid., pp. 15, 29.

22 See George W. Coats, *Rebellion in the Wilderness: the murmuring motif in the wilderness tradition of the Old Testament* (Nashville, Abingdon Press 1968). But contrast the view of John Pedersen, *Israel: its life and culture* 1–2 (Oxford 1926), pp. 453–70.

23 Alan Ecclestone, *The Night Sky of the Lord* (Darton, Longman and Todd 1980), p. 37.

24 Jean Steinmann, *St John the Baptist and the Desert Tradition* (ET, Longmans 1958), p. 49.

25 N. H. Snaith, *The Distinctive Ideas of the Old Testament* (Epworth 1944), p. 21.

26 J. G. Davies, *Everyday God* (SCM Press 1973).

27 Snaith, op. cit., p. 24.

28 G. von Rad, *Old Testament Theology* Vol. 1 (ET, Edinburgh, Oliver and Boyd 1962), p. 207.

29 Ibid., p. 205.

30 ET, Oxford UP, 1950 edn.

31 Cited in Robert F. Davidson, *Rudolf Otto's Interpretation of Religion* (Princeton UP 1947), p. 78.

32 Kosuke Koyama, *Three Mile An Hour God* (SCM Press 1970), pp. 21–4.

33 Article, 'Holiness' in *Interpreter's Dictionary of the Bible* Vol. 2 (Nashville, Abingdon Press 1962) p. 616.

34 Nathan Söderblöm, article, 'Holiness' in *Hastings Encyclopaedia*

of Religion and Ethics (ed. J. Hastings, T. and T. Clark 1913) vol. 6, p. 731.

35 Helmer Ringgren, *Israelite Religion* (SPCK 1966), p. 74. See also his *The prophetical concept of holiness* (Uppsala, Universitas Arkskrift 12, 1948).

36 N. H. Snaith, *Leviticus and Numbers* (Century Bible, Nelson 1967), p. 78.

37 Th. C. Vriezen, *An Outline of Old Testament Theology* (Newton, Mass., Charles T. Bradford 1970), p. 298.

38 Robert C. Dentan, *The Knowledge of God in Ancient Israel* (New York, Seabury 1968), pp. 38–9.

39 Pedersen, *Israel* 3–4 (1946), p. 266.

40 Snaith, *The Distinctive Ideas* ... op. cit., p. 53.

41 E. W. Heaton, *The Old Testament Prophets* (Penguin 1956 edn), p. 116.

42 Snaith, op. cit., pp. 69–70.

43 José P. Miranda, *Marx and the Bible* (SCM Press 1977), pp. 14ff.

44 Ibid., pp. 48, 51.

45 Heaton, op. cit., p. 106.

46 George Fohrer, *History of Israelite Religion* (ET, SPCK 1973), p. 302.

47 Johannes Hoekendijk, cited in J. H. Yoder, *The Politics of Jesus* (Grand Rapids, Eerdmans 1975 edn), p. 38.

48 Frederick Verinder, 'The Bible and the land question', *Church Reformer*, 5.7 (15 July 1885), p. 152. See also his *My Neighbour's Landmark* (Andrew Melrose 1911).

49 Snaith, op. cit., p. 69.

50 Ibid., p. 92.

51 Cf. Emil Brunner, *Justice and the Social Order* (ET, Lutterworth 1945).

52 Joseph Fletcher, *Situation Ethics* (SCM Press 1966), p. 87.

53 Fohrer, op. cit., p. 281.

54 G. E. Wright, *The Old Testament Against Its Environment* (1954), p. 45.

55 J. Pritchard (ed.), *Ancient Near Eastern Texts relating to the Old Testament* (Princeton 1955 edn), pp. 60ff.

56 I. Engnell, *Studies in Divine Kingship in the Ancient Near East* (Uppsala 1943).

57 See Engnell, ibid., p. 177.

58 Yehezkel Kaufmann, *The Religion of Israel* (ET, Allen and Unwin 1961), p. 224.

59 Pedersen, *Israel* 1–2, p. 104.

60 W. Eichrodt, *Theology of the Old Testament*, Vol. 2 (ET, SCM

Press 1967), p. 48.
61 Von Rad, *Old Testament Theology*, Vol. 2 (1965), pp. 56ff.
62 Eichrodt, op. cit., p. 56.
63 Karl Barth, *Church Dogmatics* 1.1, 2nd edn (ET, Edinburgh, T. and T. Clark 1975), p.198.
64 Wright, op. cit., p. 19.
65 Ibid., p. 22.
66 Robert C. Dentan, *The Knowledge of God in Ancient Israel* (New York, Seabury 1968), p. 235.
67 Alan Ecclestone, *The Night Sky of the Lord* (Darton, Longman and Todd 1980), p. 37.
68 Cf. Lionel Blue, *To Heaven with Scribes and Pharisees* (Darton, Longman and Todd 1975), p. 9.
69 Eichrodt, op. cit. See also D. R. Hillers, *Covenant: the history of a biblical idea* (Baltimore UP 1969).
70 Cf. Murray Lee Newman Jr, *The People of the Covenant* (Carey Kingsgate Press 1962).
71 Ibid., pp. 112–18.
72 Eichrodt, op. cit., vol. 1, p. 292.
73 Cited in Richard Gutteridge, *Open thy Mouth for the Dumb* (Blackwell 1976), p. 283.
74 Ecclestone, op. cit., p.39.
75 Blue, op. cit., p. 10.
76 Ecclestone, op. cit., p. 37.

CHAPTER 3

1 R. H. Fuller, *The Foundations of New Testament Christology* (Lutterworth 1965), p. 15.
2 F. Hahn, *The Titles of Jesus in Christology* (Lutterworth 1969), p. 15.
3 This division is slightly different from that of Rudolf Bultman in *Theology of the New Testament* (ET, SCM Press 1952, Vol. 1, p. 30), where he divides the sayings into those concerned with earthly activity, death and resurrection, and future return.
4 Rudolf Bultmann, *The Gospel of John: a commentary* (ET, Blackwell 1971), p. 107.
5 See F. H. Borsch, *The Christian and Gnostic Son of Man* (1970).
6 Geza Vermes, *Jesus the Jew* (Collins 1973), pp. 160–91. See also his 'The use of *bar nash/bar nasha* in Jewish Aramaic' in Matthew Black, *An Aramaic Approach to the Gospels and Acts* (Oxford, Clarendon Press 1967), pp. 310–28.
7 G. B. Caird, *The Gospel of Luke* (Penguin 1963), p. 94.
8 C. H. Dodd, *The Interpretation of the Fourth Gospel* (Cambridge

UP 1953), p. 249.

9 T. W. Manson, *The Teaching of Jesus* (Cambridge UP 1963 edn), pp. 227–8.

10 T. W. Manson, *The Servant Messiah* (Cambridge UP 1953).

11 See on the whole debate Morna D. Hooker, *Jesus and the Servant* (SPCK 1959); A.J.B. Higgins, *Jesus and the Son of Man* (Lutterworth 1964) and *The Son of Man in the Teaching of Jesus* (Cambridge UP 1980); and many other studies.

12 John A. T. Robinson, 'The one Baptism as a category of New Testament soteriology', *Scottish Journal of Theology* 6.3 (1953), p. 259.

13 *The Return of Christendom* (Allen and Unwin 1922), p. 95.

14 Jim Wallis, *Agenda for Biblical People* (Harper and Row 1972), p. 15.

15 Norman Perrin, *Jesus and the Language of the Kingdom* (SCM Press 1976), p. 16.

16 Henri Berr, preface to A. Lods, *Les prophètes d'Israel* (1936), p. xx.

17 George V. Pixley, *God's Kingdom* (SCM Press 1981), p. 21.

18 Ibid., p. 22.

19 K. L. Schmidt, *Basileia* (Bible Keywords from Kittel, A. and C. Black 1957), pp. 16–17.

20 Cited in Perrin, *Rediscovering the Teaching of Jesus* (SCM Press 1967).

21 For uses of 'kingdom' see Dan. 3.54 LXX; 4.34; Tobit 13.2; Ps. Sol. 5.18; 17.4; Eth. Enoch 84.2; Ass. Moses 10.1; Wis. 6.4; 10.10; Or. Sib. 3.47; 7.66.

22 T. F. Glasson, 'What is apocalyptic?' *New Testament Studies* 27.1 (1980), pp. 98–105; 'Schweitzer's influence – blessing or bane?' *Journal of Theological Studies* 28 (1977), pp. 289–302; *Jesus and the End of the World* (St Andrew Press 1980).

23 *The Kingdom of God and Primitive Christianity* (Black 1968), p. 94.

24 *The Quest of the Historical Jesus* (1954 edn), cited in Glasson, *Jesus and the End of the World*, op. cit., p. 26.

25 *The Kingdom of God in the Teaching of Jesus* (SCM Press 1963), pp. 69, 72.

26 *When Prophecy Failed* (SCM Press 1979), p. 213.

27 G. von Rad, *The Message of the Prophets* (SCM Press 1968), p. 274.

28 Perrin, *Rediscovering the Teaching of Jesus*, op. cit., p. 54.

29 Perrin, *Jesus and the Language of the Kingdom* op. cit., p. 1.

30 G. E. Ladd, *The Presence of the Future* (SPCK 1980), p. 122.

31 *New Testament Theology* Part 1 (SCM Press 1971), p. 35.
32 Ronald Sider, *Evangelism, Salvation and Social Justice* (Nottingham, Shaftesbury Project n.d.), p. 4.
33 G. E. Ladd, *Crucial Questions about the Kingdom of God* (Grand Rapids, Eerdmans 1952), p. 128.
34 Ladd, *The Gospel of the Kingdom* (Eerdmans, 1959), pp. 60–1.
35 Ibid., pp. 63–4.
36 A. M. Hunter, *Interpreting the Parables* (SCM Press 1960), p. 44.
37 Adolf Harnack, *What is Christianity?* (New York, Putnams 1901).
38 *New Testament Theology*, op. cit., p. 101.
39 *The Parables of the Kingdom* (Nisbet 1940).
40 Ladd, *The Presence of the Future*, op. cit., p. 3.
41 Second Report of the Advisory Commission on the Theme of the Second Assembly of the World Council of Churches in *Ecumenical Review* 5.1 (October 1952), p. 76.
42 Jean Héring, *The First Epistle of St Paul to the Corinthians* (Epworth 1962), p. 10.
43 Markus Barth, *The Broken Wall* (Collins 1960), p. 98.
44 Manifesto of the Catholic Crusade 1918 (ed. Reg Groves, Archive One 1970).
45 Karl Rahner, cited in J. B. Metz, *New Theology* No. 5 (New York, Macmillan 1968), p. 137.
46 I. Howard Marshall, *The Gospel of Luke* (Paternoster Press 1978), p. 156.
47 Joachim Jeremias, *The Prayers of Jesus* (SCM Press 1967), pp. 54–7; *New Testament Theology*, op. cit., p. 62.
48 Jean Galot, *La Conscience de Jésus* (Gembloux, Duculot, and Paris, Lethielleux 1971), pp. 90f.
49 A. A. Vogel, *The Next Christian Epoch* (New York, Harper and Row 1966), p. 37.
50 Alan Richardson, *An Introduction to the Theology of the New Testament* (SCM Press 1958), p. 43.
51 Rudolf Bultmann, *Gnosis* (Bible Key Words, Vol. 5 1952), p. 50.
52 Richard Longenecker, *The Christology of Early Jewish Christianity* (SCM Press 1970), pp. 63–4.
53 Ibid., pp. 64ff.
54 Robert Bryan Sloan Jr, *The Favourable Year of the Lord: a study of Jubilary theology in the Gospel of Luke* (Austin, Texas, Schola Press 1977), p. 48.
55 H. Conzelmann, *The Theology of St Luke* (ET, Harper and Row 1961), p. 180.

56 James D. G. Dunn, *Jesus and the Spirit* (SCM Press 1975) and *Christology in the Making* (SCM Press 1980).

57 C. F. D. Moule, *The Origins of Christology* (Cambridge UP 1977), p. 53.

58 Clement, cited Eusebius H. E. 6.14.7; Origen, Comm. on Jn. 10.4–6.

59 J. H. Bernard, *A Critical and Exegetical Commentary on the Gospel according to St John* (1928), cited in C. K. Barrett, *New Testament Essays* (SPCK 1972), p. 30.

60 Barnabas Lindars in *Studies in the Fourth Gospel* (ed. F. L. Cross, Mowbray 1957), p. 26.

61 C. H. Dodd, *The Interpretation of the Fourth Gospel* (Cambridge UP 1953), p. 285.

62 Ernst Kasemann, *The Testament of Jesus* (Philadelphia, Fortress Press 1968), p. 26.

63 Cited in Michael J. Taylor, *A Companion to John* (New York, Alba House 1977), p. 57.

64 On the relationship between John and Qumran see Raymond E. Brown, 'The Qumran Scrolls and John' in Taylor, op. cit., pp. 69–90.

65 Rudolf Bultmann, *The Gospel of John: a commentary* (ET, Blackwell 1971), p. 9.

66 A. E. Harvey, *Jesus on Trial* (SPCK 1976), p.8.

67 See further on this question Francis J. Moloney, *The Johannine Son of Man* (Rome, Las 1978); S. S. Smalley, 'The Johannine Son of Man sayings', *New Testament Studies* 15 (1968–9), pp. 278–81; Barnabas Lindars, 'The Son of Man in the Johannine Christology' in *Christ and Spirit in the New Testament: studies in honour of C. F. D. Moule* (ed. B. Lindars and S. S. Smalley, Cambridge UP 1973).

68 *The Interpretation of the Fourth Gospel*, op. cit., p. 169. See the section on 'The Knowledge of God' (pp. 151–69). See also André Feuillet, 'Man's participation in God's life: a key concept in John' in Taylor, op. cit., pp. 141–51. On the use of *einai en* and *menein en* in John, and on the theme of interiority, see Edward Malatesta SJ, *Interiority and Covenant* (Rome, Biblical Institute Press 1978).

69 See Matthew Vellanickal, *The Divine Sonship of Christians in the Johannine Writings* (Rome, Biblical Institute Press 1977).

CHAPTER 4

1 E. Masure, cited in Henri de Lubac SJ, *Catholicism* (Burns Oates 1962 edn), p. xv.

2 Markus Barth, *The Broken Wall* (Collins 1960), p. 34.
3 L. J. Baggott, *A New Approach to Colossians* (1961), p. 3.
4 Ibid., p.43.
5 Ralph P. Martin, *Colossians: the Church's Lord and the Christian's liberty* (Paternoster 1972), p. x.
6 See Halvar Moxnes, *Theology in Conflict: studies in Paul's understanding of God in Romans* (Supplement to Novum Testamentum vol. 53, Leiden, E. J. Brill 1980), p. 16.
7 Ibid., p. 89.
8 P. Minear, *Images of the Church in the New Testament* (Philadelphia, 1960), p. 211.
9 See Hendrik Berkhof, *Christ and the Powers* (Scotdale, Herald Press 1962) and G. H. C. Macgregor, 'Principalities and powers: the cosmic background to Paul's thought', *New Testament Studies* 1 (1954–5), pp. 17–28.
10 Berkhof, op. cit., 1977 edn, p. 23.
11 Ibid., p. 66. See also Heinrich Schlier, *Principalities and Powers in the New Testament* (Herder 1962).
12 Macgregor, op. cit., p. 23.
13 Markus Barth, 'Jews and Gentiles: the social character of justification in Paul' in *Journal of Ecumenical Studies* 5.2 (1968), pp. 241ff.
14 On Paul's theology see Ralph P. Martin, *Reconciliation: a study of Paul's theology* (Marshalls 1981); and D. E. H. Whiteley, *The Theology of St Paul* (Oxford, Blackwell 1970 edn).
15 See Franz J. Leenhardt, *The Epistle to the Romans* (Lutterworth 1961), p. 50.
16 Cf. E. Kasemann, 'Some thoughts on the theme "the doctrine of reconciliation in the New Testament"' in *The Future of our Religious Past: Essays in Honour of Rudolf Bultmann* (ed. J. M. Robinson, Harper and Row 1971), pp. 49–64.
17 See Ralph P. Martin, 'The theme of reconciliation', *Expository Times*, 91.12 (1980), pp. 364–8.
18 James Denney, *The Death of Christ* (Tyndale Press 1951 edn), p. 85.
19 C. F. D. Moule, *The Sacrifice of Christ* (Hodder and Stoughton 1957), p. 32.
20 Whiteley, op. cit., pp. 130, 255.
21 For a propitiatory interpretation of this verse see Leon Morris, *The Apostolic Preaching of the Cross* (Tyndale Press 1955), p. 170; 'The use of ἱλασκεσθαι in biblical Greek' *Expository Times* 62.8 and 'The meaning of ἱλαστηριον in Romans 3.25' *New Testament Studies* 2.1 (1955), pp. 33–43.

22 Morris, *Expository Times*, op. cit.

23 Moule, op. cit., p. 28.

24 See F. F. Bruce, 'Our God and Saviour: a recurring biblical problem' in *The Saviour God* (ed. S. G. F. Brandon, Manchester UP 1963), pp. 51–65.

25 Karl Barth, *Church Dogmatics* 4, Part 1 (T. and T. Clark 1961), p. ix.

26 Ibid., p. 13.

27 L. S. Thornton, *The Common Life in the Body of Christ* (Dacre 1942), p. 419.

28 See Edward Malatesta, SJ, *Interiority and Covenant* (Rome, Biblical Institute Press 1978).

29 See Matthew Vellanickal, *The Divine Sonship of Christians in the Johannine Writings* (Rome, Biblical Institute Press 1977).

30 *Soliloquia* 1.1.2.

31 1 QS 1.9–11. See E. J. Sutcliffe, 'Hatred at Qumran', *Revue de Qumran* 2 (1960), p. 355, for a different view.

32 Raymond E. Brown, *The Gospel according to John* Vol. 2 (Chapman, Anchor Bible 1978), p. 613.

33 *Ad Scapulam* 1.

34 The nearest we get is Rom. 12.9, Rev. 2.6 and Jude 23.

35 Aelred Graham, OSB, *The Love of God* (Fontana 1964 edn), p. 67.

36 C. K. Barrett, *The Holy Spirit and the Gospel Tradition* (SPCK 1947), p. 39.

37 J. V. Taylor, *The Go Between God* (SCM Press 1973), pp. 86–7.

38 J. E. Fison, *The Blessing of the Holy Spirit* (Darton, Longman and Todd 1965 edn), p. 86.

39 See George Johnston, *The Spirit-Paraclete in the Gospel of John* (Cambridge UP 1970).

40 L. S. Thornton, *The Incarnate Lord* (Longmans 1928), pp. 317, 327.

41 E. L. Mascall, *Christ, the Christian and the Church* (Longmans 1959), p. 78.

42 A. Schweitzer, *The Mysticism of Paul the Apostle* (ET, 1931), p. 125.

43 See on this Michel Bouttier, *Christianity according to St Paul* (SCM Press, Studies in Biblical Theology 1966).

44 Irenaeus, *Adv. Haer.* 4.33.14.

45 Eusebius, *H.E.*, passim.

46 See A. M. Ramsey, *The Gospel and the Catholic Church* (Longmans 1936), p. 35.

47 John A. T. Robinson, *The Body* (SCM Press 1961), p. 9.
48 Ibid., p. 31.
49 Thornton, *The Common Life in the Body of Christ* (Dacre 1942), p. 295.
50 Ibid., p. 148.
51 *Mystici Corporis Christi* (1943), para. 51.
52 L. S. Thornton, *Christ and the Church* (Dacre 1956), p. 17.
53 Robinson, op. cit., p. 80.
54 Markus Barth, *The Broken Wall* (Collins 1960), pp. 62, 98, 102.
55 Thornton, *The Common Life*, op. cit., p. 298.
56 See Bouttier, op. cit., pp. 52–8.
57 See N. A. Dahl, 'Christ, creation and the church' in *The Background of the New Testament and its Eschatology* (ed. W. D. Davies and D. Daube, Cambridge UP 1956), pp. 422–43.
58 See T. F. Glasson, *The Second Advent: the origins of the New Testament* (1945).
59 *Apol.* 52.3; *Dial.* 32.2; 40.4; 49.2; 52.1, 4, etc.
60 *Apol.* 52.3; *Dial.* 14.8; 40.4; 54.1; 69.7; 110.2, etc.
61 Jeremias, *New Testament Theology* Part 1 (SCM Press 1971), p. 95.
62 E. Kasemann, *New Testament Questions for Today* (SCM Press 1969), p. 102.
63 Klaus Koch, *The Rediscovery of Apocalyptic* (1972), p. 33.
64 See D. S. Russell, *The Method and Message of Jewish Apocalyptic* (1964).
65 Mathias Rissi, *Time and History: a study in the Revelation* (Richmond, 1966), p. 134.
66 Alan Richardson, *The Political Christ* (SCM Press 1973), p. 85.
67 See Massey H. Shepherd, *The Paschal Liturgy and the Apocalypse* (Lutterworth 1960).
68 See A. Oepke in Kittel, *Theological Wordbook of the New Testament* vol. 5, pp. 856–69.
69 Mathias Rissi, *The Future of the World: an exegetical study of Revelation 19.11—22.10* (SCM Press, Studies in Biblical Theology, 2nd Series, No. 23, 1972), p. 8.
70 Ibid., p.9.
71 Paul Minear, *I Saw a New Earth* (Washington, 1968), p. 78.
72 Cited in James Bentley, *Between Marx and Christ* (Verso/New Left Books 1982), p. 26.
73 Ibid., p. 27.
74 Barth, *Church Dogmatics* 2, Part 1 (T. and T. Clark 1957), p. 633.
75 Barth, cited in Bentley, op. cit., p. 78.

CHAPTER 5

1 Harvard UP 1971, p. 9.
2 Ibid.
3 John Gray, *Archaeology and the Old Testament World* (1962), p. 19.
4 Roland Walls in *Solitude and Communion* (ed. A. M. Allchin, SLG Press 1977), p. 52.
5 *Against those who put off baptism* (PG 46.421A).
6 Thomas Merton, 'Elias', cited in George Woodcock, *Thomas Merton, Monk and Poet* (Edinburgh, Canongate 1978), p. 77.
7 See William McNamara in *Desert Call* (Spring 1980), pp. 4–11.
8 *Shepherd of Hermas* 50.1.
9 Thomas Merton, *The Wisdom of the Desert* (London, Sheldon Press 1974), p. 1.
10 Barth, *Church Dogmatics* 4, Part 2 (T. and T. Clark 1957), p. 13.
11 Eusebius, *H.E.* 6.9.
12 Phyllis McGinley, *Times Three* (New York, Image Books 1975), pp. 46–7.
13 *H.E.* 1.13.
14 *Raids on the Unspeakable* (Burns Oates 1977), p. 12.
15 Merton, cited in Woodcock, op. cit., p. 77.
16 Benedicta Ward SLG (ed.), *Sayings of the Desert Fathers, The Alphabetical Collection* (Mowbrays 1975), p. 5.
17 Ibid., p. 2.
18 Life of Antony (*PG* 26.844B).
19 Ibid., 860B.
20 Ward, op. cit., p. 7.
21 Ibid., p. 6.
22 Athanasius, Life of Antony, cited in Eileen Mary SLG, *Contemplation and Enclosure* (SLG Press 1971), p. 7.
23 *Praktikos* 5.
24 Ward, op. cit., p. 75.
25 Cassian, Institutes 8.18, 16, 19, cited in Peter F. Anson, *The Call of the Desert: the solitary life in the Christian church* (SPCK 1964), p. 51.
26 *On Prayer* 124–5 (PG 79.1193C). See *The Praktikos, Chapters on Prayer* (tr. J. E. Bamberger OCSO, Cistercian Studies, Series 4, Spencer, Mass., 1972).
27 Ward, op. cit., p. 2.
28 D. J. Chitty (ed.) *The Letters of St Anthony the Great* (SLG Press 1975); Ward, op. cit., p. 115.
29 Ward, op. cit., p. 104.
30 *Longer Rules* 7.

31 *Longer Rules* 3.1 (PG 917A).
32 *Longer Rules* 7.4 (PG 31.933B).
33 Cited in Irénée Hausherr, *The Name of Jesus* (ET, Kalamazoo, Cistercian Publications 1978), p. 314.
34 Ward, op. cit., p. 31.
35 Peter Brown, 'The rise and function of the holy man in late antiquity', *Journal of Roman Studies* 61 (1971), pp. 80–101.
36 Thomas Merton, *The Wisdom of the Desert* (Sheldon Press 1974), p. 3.
37 Benedicta Ward SLG, introduction to *The Lives of the Desert Fathers* (tr. Norman Russell and Benedicta Ward, Mowbrays 1980), p. 13.
38 *Life of Antony* 17 (PG 26.869).
39 See Jean-Claude Guy SJ, 'Educational innovation in the Desert Fathers', *Eastern Churches Review* 6.1 (1974), pp. 44–51.
40 C. G. Jung, *Psychology and Religion West and East* (tr. R. F. C. Hull, 1958), p. 331.
41 Brown, op. cit., p. 81.
42 Cited in Owen Chadwick, *Western Asceticism* (1958), p. 60.
43 Brown, op. cit., p. 97.
44 Gail Marie Priestley, 'Some Jungian parallels to the sayings of the Desert Fathers', *Cistercian Studies* 11.2 (1976), p. 104. See the whole article on pp. 102–23.
45 Russell and Ward, op. cit., pp. 49, 50.
46 On discernment see Morton T. Kelsey, *Discernment* (Paulist 1978).
47 E. A. Wallis Budge, *The Paradise of the Holy Fathers* (1908), p. 76.
48 Ward, op. cit., p. 143.
49 Budge, op. cit., p. 31.
50 Thomas Merton, *Disputed Questions* (Hollis and Carter 1961), p. 85.
51 Ward, op. cit., p. xvi.
52 Ibid., p. 8.
53 PG 65.284C.
54 Kallistos Ware, 'Silence in prayer: the meaning of hesychia' in *Theology and Prayer* (ed. A. M. Allchin, Fellowship of St Alban and St Sergius 1975), pp. 8–28.
55 Cited Ware, op. cit., p. 10.
56 Rufinus, *PL* 21.444C.
57 See John O. Meany and Anthony Ipsaro, 'Depth psychology and the experience of hesychast prayer', University of Notre Dame, MS. 1973.

58 Budge, op. cit., p. 3.
59 *Collatio* 1.4 (PL 49.486).
60 Ward, op. cit., p. 49.
61 Russell and Ward, op. cit., p. 27.
62 *Institutes* 3.2; *Conferences* 3.
63 Ward, op. cit., p. 18.
64 Cited in J. Wellard, *Desert Pilgrimage* (Hutchinson 1970), p. 15.
65 D. J. Chitty, *The Desert a City* (Oxford 1966), p. xvi.
66 Russell and Ward, op. cit., p. 50.
67 E. F. Morrison, *St Basil and his Rule* (Oxford 1912), p. 7.
68 See Charles Marson 'Social teaching of the early fathers', in *Vox Clamantium* (ed. Andrew Reid, A. D. Innes 1894), pp. 198–224.
69 Cassian, cited in Garcia M. Colombas, 'The ancient concept of the monastic life', *Monastic Studies* 2 (1964), p. 67.
70 Eusebius, *Com. on Ps.* 67.7.
71 Thomas Merton, *The Silent Life* (Burns Oates 1957), pp. 11–12.
72 Abbot Bessarion, cited in Merton, *The Wisdom of the Desert* (Sheldon Press 1974), p. 47.
73 *Rule of St Benedict* 7.55; 43.15; 72.8.
74 *Dialogues* 2.36.
75 *Rule* 52.
76 *Rule* 31.
77 *En. in Ps.* 132.6.
78 *St Peter Damien: Selected Writings on the Spiritual Life* (tr. Patricia McNulty, Faber 1959), p. 64.
79 Adolf Harnack, *History of Dogma* (ET, 1905), vol. 5, p. 10.
80 Sermon for Advent 4 (PL 185.22–3).
81 Cited in G. A. Maloney, *Russian Hesychasm: the spirituality of Nils Sorsky* (The Hague, 1973), p. 111.
82 Cited in G. P. Fedotov, *A Treasury of Russian Spirituality* (1950), p. 248.
83 See my essay 'Not survival but prophecy' in *The Social God* (Sheldon Press 1981), pp. 81–7.
84 Cited in George Woodcock, *Thomas Merton, Monk and Poet* (Edinburgh, Canongate 1978), p. 4.
85 Ibid, p. 120.
86 Adrian Hastings, 'Marginality' in *The Faces of God* (Geoffrey Chapman 1975), pp. 18–23.
87 Rosemary Haughton in *Desert Call* 15.1 (1980), p. 5.
88 *Areopagitica*, cited in H. B. Workman, *The Evolution of the Monastic Ideal* (Epworth 1927), p. 337.
89 Cited in Woodcock, op. cit., pp. 41–2.

90 Raymond Panikkar in *Cistercian Studies* 10.2 (1976), p. 76.
91 Jean Steinmann, *St John the Baptist and the Desert Tradition* (Longmans 1958), p. 157.
92 Margot Astrov (ed.), *American Indian Prose and Poetry* (New York, Capricorn Books 1962), p. 300.
93 Cassian, 1st Conference 6–7, cited in Gilbert Shaw, *The Christian Solitary* (SLG Press 1971), p. 2.
94 *Dark Night of the Soul*, 2.17.6
95 Henri J. M. Nouwen, *The Way of the Heart: desert spirituality and contemporary ministry* (Darton, Longman and Todd 1981), p. 26.
96 Cited in Morton T. Kelsey, *Encounter with God* (Hodder and Stoughton 1974), pp. 181–2.
97 Thomas Merton, *Raids on the Unspeakable* (Burns Oates 1977), p. 16.
98 *Cloud of Unknowing*, ch. 25.
99 Shaw, op. cit., p. 7.
100 Ward, op. cit., p. 2.
101 Jean Leclerq OSB, *S. Pierre Damien, ermite et homme d'église* (Rome 1960), p. 49f.
102 William McNamara in *Desert Call* 15.1 (1980), p. 9.
103 Cited in Woodcock, op. cit., p. 153.
104 Daniel Berrigan, *America is Hard to Find* (SPCK 1973), pp. 77–8.
105 'Notes for a philosophy of solitude' in *Disputed Questions* (1961), p. 199.
106 Preface to Jean Leclercq OSB, *Alone with God* (Hodder and Stoughton 1962), p. 12.
107 Jean Daniélou SJ, *The Lord of History* (Longmans 1958), p. 77.
108 Susan Annette Muto, 'Living the desert experience' in *A Practical Guide to Spiritual Reading* (Denville, NJ, Dimension Books 1976), pp. 58–95.
109 Charles Cummings OCSO, *Spirituality and the Desert Experience* (Studies in Formative Spirituality, Denville, NJ, Dimension Books 1978).
110 Cummings, op. cit., p. 21.
111 René Voillaume in *Jesus Caritas* 6 (1961), p. 55.
112 Hubert van Zeller OSB, *Famine of the Spirit* (Burns Oates 1950), p. 8.
113 Michel Siffre, 'Six months alone in a cave', *National Geographic* 147.3 (1975), p. 432.
114 Simone Weil, *Gravity and Grace* (Routledge and Kegan Paul 1963), p. 34.

115 McNamara, op. cit., p. 5.
116 Ibid., p. 7.
117 Thomas Merton, *The Sign of Jonas* (Sheldon Press 1975), pp. 34–5.
118 T. S. Eliot, 'Choruses from the Rock' in *Complete Poems and Plays* (1971), p. 98.
119 Jacques Ellul, *Hope in Time of Abandonment* (Seabury 1973), pp. 262, 264.
120 Cited in Igumen Chariton of Valamo, *The Art of Prayer: an Orthodox anthology* (tr. E. Kadloubovsky and E. M. Palmer, 1966), p. 63.
121 René Voillaume, 'The essential aspects of the message of Père de Foucauld', *Jesus Caritas* 1 (1959), p. 6.
122 James Kennedy, 'The contemplative life in the urban desert', *Fairacres Chronicle* 14.3 (1981), p. 19.
123 Ward, op. cit., p. 75.
124 Alan Ecclestone, *The Night Sky of the Lord* (Darton, Longman and Todd 1980), p. 9.
125 Mother Mary Clare SLG in A. M. Allchin (ed.) *Solitude and Communion* (SLG Press 1977), p. 67.
126 Raphael Vernay OSB, cited Allchin, op. cit., p. 76.

CHAPTER 6

1 Ch. 3.
2 Michael B. Foster, *Mystery and Philosophy* (SCM Press 1957), p. 28.
3 J. P. Miranda, *Communism and the Bible* (SCM Press 1982), p. 5.
4 Andrew Louth, *The Origins of the Christian Mystical Tradition* (Oxford, Clarendon Press 1981), pp. 1–17. My debt to this excellent book will be obvious throughout this chapter.
5 Louth, op. cit., p. 19.
6 *Quis Her.* 264ff.
7 *De Specialibus Legibus* 1.43ff.
8 *De Posteritate Caini* 15.
9 *Enneads* 1.8.13.
10 *Statesman* 273D.
11 Louth, op. cit., p. 43.
12 *Com. on John* 2.28.
13 Louth, op. cit., p. 74.
14 Vladimir Lossky, *In the Image and Likeness of God* (Mowbrays 1975), p. 35.
15 *Stromata* 5.11.

16 *Incomprehensibility of God* 3, cited in Thomas Merton, *Contemplative Prayer* (Darton, Longman and Todd 1973), p. 100.
17 *Gnostic Chapters* 3.88. See Irénée Hausherr, 'Ignorance infinie ou science infinie' in *Hésychasme et prière* (Rome 1966), pp. 238–46.
18 Cited in Owen Chadwick, *Western Asceticism* (1958), p. 160.
19 *Praktikos* 70.
20 *On Prayer* 146.
21 *De octo vitiosis cogit* 9.
22 *Hom.* 28.5.
23 *Hom.* 1.2.
24 *Hom.* 15.38.
25 *Cat. Orat.* 9.
26 Cited in Maurice Wiles, 'Looking into the sun', *Church Quarterly*, January 1969, p. 191.
27 Vladimir Lossky, *Orthodox Theology: an introduction* (New York, St Vladimir's Press 1978), p. 24–5.
28 Lossky, *The Mystical Theology of the Eastern Church* (James Clarke 1957), pp. 26, 39.
29 Kallistos Ware, 'God hidden and revealed: the apophatic way and the essence–energies distinction', *Eastern Churches Review* 7 (1975), p. 127.
30 *Com. on Song of Songs, Hom.* 6.1271.
31 Ibid. (PG 44.893B).
32 See John Meyendorff, *Byzantine Theology* (Mowbrays 1975), p. 12.
33 *Com. on Eccl.*, Sermon 7 (PG 44.73D).
34 *Com. on Song of Songs* 11 (PG 44.1000C).
35 Ibid.
36 See Gabriel Horn, 'Le "miroir", la Nuée, deux manières de voir Dieu d'après S. Grégoire de Nyssé', *Revue d'ascétique et de mystique* 8 (1927), pp. 113–31.
37 *Life of Moses* 2.162–4.
38 PG 44.892–3.
39 *Life of Moses*, op. cit.
40 Ibid. 231–2, 238–9.
41 See Horn, op. cit.
42 PG 44.1000.
43 Andrew Louth, *The Origins of the Christian Mystical Tradition* (Oxford, Clarendon Press 1981), p. 95.
44 *Poemata de seipso* 1 (PG 37.984–5).
45 Ibid 11 (PG 37.1165–6).
46 *Oratio* 40.41 (PG 36.417).

47 *Mystical Theology* 21. On Dionysius see Louth, op. cit., pp. 159–78.

48 *Divine Names* 7 (PG 3.869–72).

49 *Mystical Theology* 1. In the following references I have followed the version of C. E. Rolt (SPCK 1966 edn).

50 Ibid.

51 Ibid 2.

52 Ibid 3.

53 Ibid 5.

54 Vladimir Lossky, *The Mystical Theology of the Eastern Church* (James Clarke 1957), p. 23.

55 William Johnston, *The Inner Eye of Love: mysticism and religion* (Harper and Row 1978), p. 18.

56 See H-C. Puech, 'La ténèbre mystique chez le Pseudo-Denys', *Études Carmélitaines* 23.2 (1938), pp. 33–53.

57 Lossky, op. cit., p. 125.

58 See Louth, op. cit., pp. 181–90.

59 Cited Lossky, op. cit., p. 231.

60 Ibid, p. 39.

61 See George Dragas, *The Meaning of Theology: an essay in Greek Patristics* (Darlington, 1980).

62 *Com. on Psalms* (PG 39.1449B).

63 Cited in Lossky, op. cit., p. 36.

64 *Mystical Theology* 5.

65 See on this Rowan Williams, 'The philosophical structures of Palamism', *Eastern Churches Review* 9.1–2 (1977), pp. 27–44.

66 *Homily on the Presentation of the Holy Virgin in the Temple,* cited Lossky, op. cit., p. 224.

67 Cited in Evelyn Underhill, *Mysticism* (Methuen, University Paperbacks 1960), p. 115.

68 *In Ps.* 99.6.

69 Louth, op. cit., p. 180.

70 *Summa Theologica* 1a.2.3.

71 Ibid., 1a.q.12. art. 1.

72 *De Potentia in Boetium de Trinitate*, cited in Thomas Merton, *The Ascent to Truth* (Harcourt Brace 1951), pp. 100–1.

73 See J. P. H. Clark, 'Walter Hilton and "liberty of spirit"', *Downside Review* 96.322 (1978), pp. 61–78.

74 See J. P. H. Clark, 'The Cloud of Unknowing, Walter Hilton and St John of the Cross: a comparison', *Downside Review* 96.325 (1978), pp. 281–98.

75 J. P. H. Clark, 'The "lightsome darkness": aspects of Walter Hilton's theological background', *Downside Review* 95.319

(1977), pp. 95–109.
76 Scale of Perfection 2.25 (tr. G. Sitwell, Burns Oates, 1953), p. 209.
77 G. Sitwell in *English Spiritual Writers* (ed. C. Davis, Burns Oates, 1961), p. 38.
78 *Scale*, tr. Sitwell, op. cit., p. 207.
79 *Adornment of the Spiritual Marriage* 2.
80 Sermon 11 for Monday in Passion Week in *Spiritual Conferences of John Tauler* (tr. Eric Coledge, St Louis 1961), p. 177.
81 *Cloud* ch. 70, tr. William Johnston, *The Cloud of Unknowing and The Book of Privy Counselling* (Image Books 1973). For the quotations from the *Cloud* I have also used the versions of Justin McCann (Burns Oates 1952 edn) and Clifton Wolters (Penguin 1961 edn).
82 Clark 1977, op. cit., p. 96.
83 Cloud, ch. 3. tr. Johnston.
84 Ch. 6.
85 Ch. 12.
86 Ch. 4.
87 Ibid.
88 Ch. 5.
89 Ch. 45.
90 See Johnston, op. cit., p. 21.
91 *Epistle of Privy Counsel*, ch. 21, tr. Johnston.
92 Ibid., ch. 1.
93 *De doc. ig.* 1.26.
94 Ibid.
95 See Donald R. Duclow, 'Gregory of Nyssa and Nicholas of Cusa: infinity, anthropology, and the via negativa', *Downside Review* 92.307 (1974), pp. 102–8.
96 Cited in Dorothee Soelle, *The Inward Road* (Darton, Longman, and Todd 1979), p. 117.
97 Thomas Merton, *Zen and the Birds of Appetite* (New York, New Directions 1968), p. 81.
98 See Jean Daniélou SJ, *Platonisme et théologie mystique* (Paris 1953).
99 Don Cupitt, *Taking Leave of God* (SCM Press 1980), p. 139.
100 *Living Flame of Love* 4.5–7.
101 Hubert van Zeller OSB, *Famine of the Spirit* p. 8. See above, p. xx.
102 Thomas Kane, 'The Lord of our disillusionment', *Spiritual Life* 23.4 (1977), p. 214.
103 Rowan Williams, *The Wound of Knowledge: Christian spiritu-*

ality from the New Testament to St John of the Cross (Darton, Longman and Todd 1979), p. 177.

104 *Ascent of Mount Carmel* 3.1.
105 1.4.
106 1.13.
107 Thomas Merton, *Zen and the Birds of Appetite*, op. cit., p. 76f.
108 *Ascent* 2.8.
109 2.9.
110 2.3.
111 Ibid.
112 On the uses of the term 'night' in St John of the Cross see Karol Wojtyla (Pope John Paull II), *Faith according to St John of the Cross* (San Francisco, Ignatius Press 1981), pp. 96–109.
113 *Ascent*, stanzas.
114 *Ascent*, prologue 4.
115 Ibid., 2.4.
116 1.2.
117 Williams, op. cit., p. 169.
118 *Dark Night of the Soul* 1.14.
119 Ibid., 2.5.
120 *Living Flame* 1.16.
121 *Contemplative Prayer* (Darton, Longman and Todd 1973), p. 53.
122 *Living Flame* 3.49.
123 E. E. Larkin, 'The dark night of St John of the Cross', *The Way* 14.1 (1974), p. 15.
124 *Dark Night* 1.10.
125 *Living Flame* 3.31, 38.
126 E. W. Trueman Dicken, *The Crucible of Love* (Darton, Longman and Todd 1963), p. 168.
127 Alan W. Jones, *Journey into Christ* (Seabury 1977), p. 15.
128 Ibid., p. 21. See the whole of Chapter 3 on 'Entering the wasteland' (pp. 20–37).
129 Cf. Nicholas Lash, *Theology on Dover Beach* (Darton, Longman and Todd 1979), p. 30.
130 See Karl Barth, *Church Dogmatics*, vol. 2, Part 1 (T. and T. Clark 1961), pp. 310ff.
131 Barth, *Commentary on Romans* (ET, 6th edn, Oxford UP 1933), p. 141.
132 Barth, *The Knowledge of God and the Service of God* (Hodder 1938), p. 28.
133 Paul Tillich, *The Courage to Be* (Yale UP 1952), pp. 185–6.
134 See, for example, John Robinson in *Honest to God* (SCM Press

THOMAS MERTON

FATHER M. LOUIS, O.C.S.O.

Born in Prades, France	Jan. 31, 1915
Entered Gethsemani Abbey	Dec. 10, 1941
Died in Bangkok, Thailand	Dec. 10, 1968

Portrait by Terrell Dickey

1963). See Yves Raguin SJ, *The Depth of God* (Indiana, St Meinrod Abbey Press 1975).

135 T. J. T. Altizer, *Total Presence: the language of Jesus and the language of today* (Seabury 1980).

136 Richard L. Rubenstein, *After Auschwitz: radical theology and contemporary Judaism* (Indianapolis, Bobbs-Merrill 1966), p. 154.

137 Fred Catherwood, *A Better Way* (Inter Varsity Press 1975), pp. 15, 16, 81.

138 I. Trethowan, *Mysticism and Theology* (1975), p. 36.

139 Alan Ecclestone, *The Night Sky of the Lord* (Darton, Longman and Todd 1980), p. 39.

140 *The World to Come* (SCM Press 1982), p. xv.

141 Merton, *Contemplative Prayer* (Darton, Longman and Todd 1973), p. 27f.

142 *The Shaking of the Foundations* (SCM Press 1949), p. 42.

143 *Journals of Søren Kierkegaard* (ed. A. Dru, Oxford UP 1938), p. 1158.

144 See Antonio Pérez-Esclarín, *Atheism and Liberation* (SCM Press 1980).

145 Colin E. Gunton, 'Transcendence, metaphor and the knowability of God', *Journal of Theological Studies* (NS) 31.2 (1980), p. 516.

146 John F. Teahan, 'A dark and empty way: Thomas Merton and the apophatic tradition', *Journal of Religion* 58 (1958), p. 268. See also William H. Shannon, *Thomas Merton's Dark Path* (New York, Farrar, Strauss, Giroux 1981).

147 Merton, *Contemplative Prayer*, op. cit., pp. 96, 97.

148 Merton, *What is Contemplation?* (Templegate 1978 edn), pp. 48, 50, 41.

149 *The Ascent to Truth* (Harcourt, Brace 1951), p. 155.

150 *New Seeds of Contemplation* (New York, New Directions 1961), pp. 134-5.

151 Aldous Huxley, *Grey Eminence* (New York, 1941), p. 97.

152 See Karl Barth's section on 'The hidden God' in *Church Dogmatics*, op. cit., 2 Part 1, pp. 179-204.

153 *Conjectures of a Guilty Bystander* (1966), p. 58.

154 *The Integration of the Personality* (1934) p. 186.

155 H. A. Williams, *Becoming What I Am* (Darton, Longman and Todd 1977), p. 86ff.

156 Sebastian Moore and Kevin Maguire, *The Experience of Prayer* (Darton, Longman and Todd 1969), pp. 84-5.

CHAPTER 7

1 In *Psychology and Religion West and East* (ET, Princeton UP 1969), p. 452.

2 Cited in *Ecumenism and Charismatic Renewal: theological and pastoral orientations* (Ann Arbor, Servant Books 1978), p. 34.

3 Pavel Alexsandrovich Florensky, in *Ultimate Questions* (ed. A. Schmemann, New York, Holt, Rinehart and Winston 1965), p. 141.

4 J. D. G. Dunn, *Jesus and the Spirit* (SCM Press 1975), p. 194.

5 Theodore Roszak, *Where the Wasteland Ends* (Faber 1972), p. 73.

6 R. D. Laing *The Politics of Experience and the Bird of Paradise* (Penguin 1971 edn), p. 118.

7 See *Dogmatic Constitution of the Church*, para. 12.

8 *On the Ministry and Life of Priests,* para. 5.

9 General Audience, 6 June 1973, *Documentation Catholique* 1635 (1 July 1973), p. 601.

10 23 May 1973.

11 *Sacramentary 1973–4*, approved by the National Office for Liturgy for use in the churches in Canada (Canada GCC Publications Service 1973).

12 John Pedersen, *Israel: its life and culture* 1–2 (Oxford 1926), p. 104.

13 See H. H. Rowley, 'The nature of prophecy in the light of recent study', *Harvard Theological Review* 38.1 (1945), pp. 1–38.

14 Cf. H. Gunkel in *The Expositor*, 9th Series 1 (1924), p. 538. On ecstasy see Abraham J. Heschel, *The Prophets* (Jewish Publication Society of America 1962), pp. 324–66.

15 Heschel, op. cit., p. xiii.

16 Ibid., p. 6.

17 Ibid., p. 7.

18 *Splendor paternae gloriae*. For an English translation see *Hymns Ancient and Modern* No. 2.

19 Cited in *Ecumenism and Charismatic Renewal* (Ann Arbor, Servant Books 1978), pp. xii–xiii.

20 *Cursus Theologicus* q.70 disp. 18 art 1.5.

21 General Audience, 9 July 1969, in *The Pope Speaks* 4 (1969), p. 95.

22 Cf. C. K. Barrett, *The Holy Spirit and the Gospel Tradition* (SPCK 1947), p. 39.

23 See C. H. Kraeling, *John the Baptist* (New York 1951), p. 117.

24 J. D. G. Dunn, 'The birth of a metaphor: baptized in the Spirit', *Expository Times* 89.5 (1978), p. 136.

25 Alexander Schmemann, *Of Water and the Spirit* (New York, St Vladimir's Press 1974), p. 39.

26 *De Baptismo* 4.

27 On the drowning of the demons see Bo Reicke, *The Disobedient Spirits and Christian Baptism* (Copenhagen, Ejnar Munksgaard 1946).

28 *De Baptismo* 8.

29 *Ad Autolycum* 1.12.

30 Gospel of Philip 95 in *The Gospel of Philip* (tr. R. McL. Wilson, 1962), pp. 49f.

31 See J. D. C. Fisher, *Christian Initiation: Baptism in the Medieval West* (SPCK 1965) and *Confirmation: then and now* (SPCK 1978).

32 *De Sacr.* 3.2.

33 *Ep.* 74.7. See Fisher, *Confirmation*, op. cit., p. 47.

34 Cited in Leonid Ouspensky, *Theology of the Icon* (New York, St Vladimir's Press 1978), p. 88.

35 Ibid.

36 Ibid., p. 89. On the symbolism of the living water and the fish see Jean Daniélou SJ, *Primitive Christian Symbols* (Burns Oates 1964 edn), pp. 42–57.

37 *De Baptismo* 6.

38 Ibid.

39 Austin P. Milner OP, *The Theology of Confirmation* (Cork, Mercier Press 1971), p. 7.

40 Ibid., p. 104.

41 Mark the Hermit, *On those who think they can be justified by works* 85.

42 Cited in Simon Tugwell OP, *Did you receive the Spirit?* (Darton, Longman and Todd 1972), pp. 53–4.

43 Ibid.

44 Kilian McDonnell, *The Baptism in the Holy Spirit as an ecumenical problem* (Notre Dame, Indiana, Charismatic Renewal Services 1977), pp. 52–3.

45 *Heythrop Journal* (1972), p. 407.

46 *Oratio* 61, cited Ouspensky, op. cit., p. 38.

47 *Leg. All.* 1.84.

48 David Knowles, *What is Mysticism?* (1967), p. 21.

49 *Brochure of the Spiritual Life Institute*, Nada, Arizona, n.d.

50 *Conference* 9.25 (PG 49.801.)

51 Cap. 85 cited in Meyendorff, *Byzantine Theology* (Mowbrays 1974), op. cit., p. 70.

52 Cited in Paul Evdokimov, *L'Esprit Saint dans la tradition*

Orthodoxe (Paris 1969), p. 98.

53 A. M. Allchin, *The Kingdom of Love and Knowledge* (Darton, Longman and Todd 1979), p. 37.

54 C. G. Jung, *Symbols of Transformation* in *Collected Works* Vol. 5 (Routledge 1956) pp. 90–4.

55 Cited in John Meyendorff, *St Gregory Palamas and Orthodox Spirituality* (New York, St Vladimir's Press 1974), p. 55.

56 *Hymns of Divine Love by St Symeon the New Theologian* (tr. G. A. Maloney SJ, Denville NJ, Dimension n.d.), Hymn 25.9–48 (pp. 256–8).

57 Ibid., pp. 9–10.

58 Hymn 2 in ibid., p. 17; Hymn 6, p. 27.

59 Hymn 11, p. 38.

60 Hymn 16, p. 58.

61 Hymn 20, p. 91.

62 Hymn 22, p. 111.

63 Hymn 30, pp. 168–70.

64 James Billington, *The Icon and the Axe* (Knopf 1966), p. 24f.

65 *In Ps.* 36.14.

66 *De diligendo Deo* 10.

67 Ibid.

68 Richard Rolle, *The Fire of Love* (tr. Clifton Wolters, Penguin 1972), Prologue.

69 Ch. 4.

70 Ch. 5.

71 Ch. 11.

72 Ch. 13.

73 Ch. 15.

74 Ibid.

75 Ch. 17.

76 Ch. 22.

77 Ch. 28.

78 Ch. 32.

79 Ch. 40.

80 *Cloud*, ch. 26.

81 Cited in Evelyn Underhill, *The Mystic Way* (J. M. Dent 1913), p. 34.

82 *Seven Steps of the Ladder of Spiritual Love*, ch. 14.

83 *A Treatise of Divine Providence*, ch. 4.

84 *A Treatise of Discretion*, ch. 19.

85 *A Treatise on Prayer*, ch. 75.

86 Ibid., ch. 85.

87 Ibid., ch. 92.

88 *Treatise on Purgatory* ch. 2. See *The Life and Sayings of St Catherine of Genoa* (tr. Paul Garvin, New York, Alba Hoyse 1964), p. 137.

89 Ibid., ch. 3.

90 Ibid., ch. 10; Garvin, op. cit., p. 139.

91 *Hymn of the Universe* (Fontana 1970), p. 21.

92 Ibid., p. 28.

93 Edith Sitwell, *Collected Poems* (Macmillan 1982 edn), pp. 225–6.

94 'Gold Coast Customs', in ibid., p. 253.

95 'Invocation', in ibid., p. 257.

96 Ibid., p. 267.

97 Ibid., p. 378.

98 Ward, op. cit., p. 11.

99 Ibid., p. 88.

100 *Hom.* 28.5.

101 Cited in A. M. Allchin, *The Kingdom of Love and Knowledge* (Darton, Longman and Todd 1979), p. 202.

102 Valentine Zander, *St. Seraphim of Sarov* (tr. A Religious of SSC, Fellowship of St Alban and St Sergius 1968), p. 38.

103 Ibid., pp. 38–9.

104 Eloi Leclerc, *Le Cantique des Créatures ou les Symboles de l'Union* (Paris 1970), p. 86.

105 For this and the following quotations from St John of the Cross I have used the version of *The Collected Works of St John of the Cross* (tr. Kieran Kavanagh and Otilio Rodriguez, Washington, Institute of Carmelite Studies, 1973).

106 Martin Israel, *Smouldering Fire* (Hodder and Stoughton 1978), p. 141.

107 *Divinum Illud Munus*, 9 May 1897, para. 17.

108 Cited in Simon Tugwell, *Did you receive the Spirit?* (Darton, Longman and Todd 1972), p. 36.

109 J. E. Fison, *The Blessing of the Holy Spirit* (publisher untraced), op. cit., p. 11.

110 General Audience, 6 June 1973.

111 Cited in W. J. Hollenweger, *The Pentecostals* (SCM Press 1972), p. 334.

112 *Redemption Hymnal* (1958), No. 219.

113 Kevin and Dorothy Ranaghan, *Catholic Pentecostals* (New Jersey, Paramus 1969), p. 7.

114 T. A. Small *Reflected Glory: the Spirit in Christ and Christians* (Hodder and Stoughton 1975), p. 58.

115 J. D. G. Dunn, *Jesus and the Spirit* (SCM Press 1975), p. 331.

116 In particular Acts 2.1–14; 2.38; 8.4–25; 9.1–19; 10—11; 19.1–7.

117 See W. E. Boardman, *The Higher Christian Life* (1895).

118 Cited Boardman, op. cit., p. 51.

119 R. A. Torrey in Ralph M. Riggs, *The Spirit Himself* (Springfield, Mo, Gospel Publishing House 1949), p. 147.

120 F. D. Bruner, *A Theology of the Holy Spirit: the Pentecostal experience and the New Testament witness* (Hodder and Stoughton 1971), p. 37.

121 Ibid., p. 42.

122 D. W. Basham, *A Handbook on Holy Spirit Baptism* (1969), p. 10.

123 Cited in Bruner, op. cit., p. 75.

124 J. D. G. Dunn, *Baptism in the Holy Spirit* (SCM Press 1970), p. 4.

125 F. A. Sullivan SJ, 'Baptism in the Holy Spirit', *Gregorianum* 55.1 (1974), p. 51.

126 Tugwell, op. cit., p. 47.

127 See Dunn, *Jesus and the Spirit*, op. cit., p. 246.

128 Irenaeus *Adv. Haer.* 5.6.1

129 1 Cor. 12—14; Acts 2.5–11; 10.46; 19.6; Mark 16, and (possibly) 1 Thess. 5.21ff.

130 Sermon 1 on Ps. 32 (in *The Divine Office*, Office of Readings for St Cecilia's Day, 22 November).

131 Stanley H. Frodsham, *With Signs Following* (Springfield, Mo, Gospel Publishing House 1946 edn), pp. 242–3.

132 Acts 2.1–4; 10—11; 19.1–17.

133 Op. cit., p. 192.

134 *Statement on the Theological Basis of the Catholic Charismatic Renewal* in *One in Christ* 10.2 (1974), p. 211.

135 Simon Tugwell OP, 'Is there a "Pentecostal" experience?', *Theological Renewal* 7 (1977), p. 8f.

136 Thomas Ball Barratt, *When the Fire Fell* (Oslo 1927), p. 109.

137 Donald Gee (ed.) Pentecostal World Conference. *Messages Preached at the 5th Triennial Pentecostal World Conference*, Toronto, 1958 (Full Gospel Publishing House 1958), p. 48.

138 Cited in Morton T. Kelsey, *Tongue Speaking: an experiment in spiritual experience* (Hodder and Stoughton 1968), pp. 2, 3.

139 Barratt, op. cit., p. 109.

140 Simon Tugwell, *Did you receive the Spirit?* (Darton, Longman and Todd 1972). p. 63.

141 J. V. L. Casserley, 'The inarticulate element in religious experience', *American Church Quarterly* 3.3 (1963), pp. 169–73).

142 J. D. G. Dunn, *Jesus and the Spirit*, op. cit., pp. 263–4.

CHAPTER 8

1 James MacGibbon (ed.), *Stevie Smith, Selected Poems* (Penguin 1978), p. 242.
2 *English Hymnal* No. 29. Written by H. R. Bramley (1833–1917).
3 *The Humanity and Divinity of Christ* (Cambridge UP 1967), p. 67.
4 Don Cupitt, 'One Jesus, many Christs' in *Christ, Faith and History* (ed. S. W. Sykes and J. P. Clayton, Cambridge UP 1972), p. 142f.
5 Ed. John Hick, SCM Press 1977.
6 See his 'Does Christology rest on a mistake?' in *Christ, Faith and History*, op. cit., pp. 3ff; *Myth of God Incarnate*, op. cit., pp. 4, 7.
7 E. L. Mascall, *Theology and the Gospel of Christ* (SPCK 1977), p. 40.
8 Rowan Williams, *The Wound of Knowledge: Christian Spirituality from the New Testament to St John of the Cross* (Darton, Longman and Todd 1979), p. 49.
9 *English Hymnal* No. 29, op. cit.
10 Cf. H. E. W. Turner, *Jesus the Christ* (Mowbray 1976).
11 Rom. 6; Eph. 1.
12 *Adv. Marcion* 3.8.
13 *Adv. Haer.* 4.7. See Gustav Wingren, *Man and the Incarnation* (Edinburgh 1959).
14 Cited in John Meyendorff, *Christ in Eastern Christian Thought* (New York, St Vladimir's Press 1975), p. 71.
15 *Ep.* 101.
16 *Sermon* 261.7.
17 Jean Galot SJ, *La Personne de Christ* (Gembloux, Duculot 1969), p. 94f.
18 Karl Barth, *Church Dogmatics*, op. cit. Vol. 4, Part 1, p. 7.
19 *De Fide* 4.7.
20 PG 50.441–52.
21 E. L. Mascall in *The Church of God: an Anglo-Russian symposium* (SPCK 1934), p. 13.
22 See J. K. Mozley, 'Christology and Soteriology' in G. K. A. Bell and A. Deissmann (eds), *Mysterium Christi* (Longmans 1930).
23 Jurgen Moltmann, *The Crucified God* (SCM Press 1974) p. 255.
24 Meyendorff, op. cit., p. 11.
25 Thomas Hancock, *The Return of the Father* (1875), p. 49.

26 Maurice Wiles, *The Making of Christian Doctrine* (Cambridge UP 1967), p. 106.

27 Jean Galot SJ, *Vers une nouvelle Christologie* (Gembloux, Duculot 1971), p. 44f.

28 *Introduction à la théologie chrétiènne* (Paris, Seuil 1974), p. 272.

29 *Prosopopeiae*, cited in Vladimir Lossky, *The Mystical Theology of the Eastern Church* (James Clarke 1957), p. 116.

30 *De hominis opificio* 16.

31 Matthew Fox OP (ed.), *Western Spirituality: historical roots, ecumenical routes* (Fides/Claretian 1979), p. 5.

32 Ibid., p. 12.

33 Rowan Williams, *The Wound of Knowledge* (Darton, Longman and Todd 1979), p. 30.

34 *Quis dives salvetur* 18.

35 *Stromata* 7.40.

36 *Exhortation to Martyrdom* 3.

37 Hom. on Numbers 27.

38 E. Jacob, *Theology of the Old Testament* (Hodder 1958), p. 158.

39 Jean Héring, *The First Epistle of St Paul to the Corinthians* (Epworth 1962), pp. 44–5.

40 Barnabas Lindars, *The Gospel of John* (New Century Bible, Oliphants 1972), p. 94.

41 *Adv. Haer.* 5.2.

42 *Hagioritic Tome* (PG 150.1233B).

43 New York, Round Table Press 1940, pp. 108–9.

44 Cited in Lossky, *The Mystical Theology of the Eastern Church*, op. cit., p. 111.

45 *A Hopkins Reader* (ed. John Pick, Image Books 1966), p. 67.

46 F. D. Maurice, *The Prayer Book* (James Clarke 1966 edn), p. 200.

47 Hancock, op. cit., p. 48.

48 S. D. Headlam, *The Service of Humanity and other sermons* (1882), p. 84.

49 Ibid., p. 16.

50 Ibid., p. 20.

51 Ibid., pp. 22–3.

52 *Church Reformer* November 1890, p. 245.

53 See Alf Härdelin, *The Tractarian Understanding of the Eucharist* (Uppsala, University of Uppsala Press 1965), pp. 84–5.

54 *University Sermons* 2.28, p. 28.

55 John Murray 1904, pp. 158–200.

56 Michael Ramsey, *Charles Gore and Anglican Theology* (SPCK 1955), p. 5.

57 Macmillan 1924, pp. 173–86 and 212–26.

58 *The Return of Christendom* (Allen and Unwin 1922), pp. 61–3, 65, 75.

59 Cited by Robert Woodifield in *For Christ and the People* (ed. M. B. Reckitt, SPCK 1968), p. 155.

60 *Thus Spake Zarathustra*, cited in Sam Keen, 'Manifesto for a dionysian theology', *New Theology* 7 (New York, Macmillan 1970), pp. 79–103.

61 Bruno Brinkman, 'The humanity of Christ: Christ and sexuality', *The Way* 15.3 (1975), p. 219.

62 *Or. Catechetica* 32.

63 John Y. Fenton, 'Bodily Theology' in *Theology and Body* (Philadelphia, Westminster Press 1974), p. 133.

64 *En. in. Ps.* 55.6.

65 Ashley Montagu, *Touching: the human significance of the skin* (1972), p. 273.

66 *Hom. on Luke* 14.

67 Paul Verghese, *The Freedom of Man* (Philadelphia, Westminster Press 1972), p. 55.

68 *In Ps.* 109.5.

69 *In Joan Evang.* 23.

70 *City of God* 14–15.

71 Ibid., 14.24–6.

72 See *Summa Theologica* 3.31.8.

73 Ruether in Matthew Fox (ed.), *Western Spirituality: historical roots, ecumenical routes* (Fides/Claretian 1979), p. 148.

74 'About disinterest' in *Meister Eckhart: a modern translation* by Raymond Bernard Blakney (New York, Harper 1941), p. 90.

75 Karl Rahner, *Theological Investigations* 3 (Darton, Longman and Todd 1967), pp. 194–5.

76 Alex Comfort, *Sex in Society* (Penguin 1964), p. 54.

77 *Anglican Theological Review* 57.4 (1975), p. 424.

78 Sebastian Moore and Kevin Maguire, *The Experience of Prayer* (Darton, Longman and Todd 1969), pp. 28, 40.

79 Charles Davis, *Body as Spirit: the nature of religious feeling* (Hodder and Stoughton 1976), p. 52.

80 *Our Blood* (Women's Press 1982), p. 73.

81 New Canadian Library, Toronto 1969, p. 242.

82 William McNamara, *Mystical Passion* (New York, Paulist Press 1977), p. 3.

83 Eric Fromm, *The Art of Loving* (Unwin 1975), p. 77.

84 *Revelations of Divine Love,* ch. 55.

85 Ibid., ch. 56.

86 Fontana 1970. See especially ch. 5, 'The importance of being carnal: notes for a visceral theology' (pp. 141–60).

87 Ibid., p. 142.

88 Ibid., p. 144.

89 Ibid., pp. 149–50.

90 Ibid., p. 160.

91 Jacob, op. cit., p. 160.

92 James B. Nelson, *Embodiment: an approach to sexuality* (SPCK 1979), pp. 247-8.

93 E. L. Mascall, *The Christian Universe* (Darton, Longman and Todd 1966), p. 53.

94 Mascall, *Via Media: an essay in theological synthesis* (Longmans 1957), p. 121. See ch. 4 on 'Deified Creaturehood' (pp. 121–65).

95 Maximus the Confessor to Thalassius 22.

96 John Meyendorff, *St Gregory Palamas and Orthodox Spirituality* (New York, St Vladimir's Press 1974), p. 38.

97 Vladimir Lossky, *The Mystical Theology of the Eastern Church* (James Clarke 1957), p. 39.

98 *Adv. Haer.* 3.10.

99 *In Ps.* 52.6.

100 *Collected Works,* Library of Anglo-Catholic Theology, Oxford, 11 vols (1841–54), vol. 3, pp. 108–9.

101 *Ad Adelph.* 4 (PG 26.1077).

102 *De Incarnatione* 54; C. Arian 8.996.

103 *De Incarnatione* 54.

104 *De Decretis* 2.

105 Urban T. Holmes, *A History of Christian Spirituality: an analytical introduction* (Seabury 1980), p. 34.

106 *Hom.* 44.8, 9 (PG 34).

107 *Ambigu.* 222.

108 Anastasius of Sinai cited in George Florovsky, *Creation and Redemption* (*Collected Works*, Vol. 3, Belmont, Mass. Nordland Publishing Co. 1976), p. 278, n. 113.

109 *Or. Cat.* 25.

110 *Or.* 40.45.

111 Op. cit., p. 75.

112 Hymn 7 in *Hymns of Divine Love by St Symeon the New Theologian* (tr. G. A. Maloney, Denville NJ, Dimension, n.d.), pp. 28–9.

113 Hymn 9, p. 34.

114 Hymn 15, pp. 53–5.

115 Hymn 16, p. 58.

116 Hymn 30, pp. 169–70.

117 *Writings from the Philokalia* (ed. E. Kadloubovsky and G. E. H. Palmer, 1951), p. 126.
118 *Capita Phys. Theol.* 68–9.
119 Ibid., 92–3.
120 Paul Evdokimov, *L'Orthodoxie* (Neuchatel, Delachaux et Nestlé 1959), p. 88. trs. E. L. Mascall, *Nature and Supernature* (Darton, Longman and Todd 1976), pp. 45–6.
121 See Vladimir Soloviev, *Lectures on Godmanhood* (1877–84. ET, Dennis Dobson 1948).
122 S.T. 1.2.2. ad 1.
123 Evdokimov, op. cit., p. 90.
124 Sermon 61.4 (PL 183.1072).
125 See Josef Stierli (ed.), *Heart of the Saviour* (Herder/Nelson 1957).
126 Eloi Leclerc, *Le Cantique des Créatures ou les Symbols de l'Union* (Paris 1970), p. 200.
127 2 Celano 124.165 in *St Francis of Assisi: Writings and Early Biographies* (ed. M. A. Habig, Chicago 1972), pp. 494–5.
128 Holmes, op. cit., p. 85.
129 Thomas Traherne, *Poems, Centuries, and Three Thanksgivings* (ed. Anne Ridler, 1966), p. 177.
130 Hans Urs von Balthasar, *Prayer* (Geoffrey Chapman 1963), p. 191.
131 *Christian Spirituality Today* (ed. A. M. Ramsey, Faith Press 1961), p. 59.

CHAPTER 9

1 John Pairman Brown, *The Liberated Zone* (SCM Press 1970), p. 179.
2 John A. T. Robinson, *On Being the Church in the World* (SCM Press 1974 edn), p. 71.
3 S. C. Gayford, *Sacrifice and Priesthood* (Methuen 1953 edn), p. 38.
4 George Every, *Lamb to the Slaughter* (James Clarke 1957).
5 Louis Bouyer, *Rite and Man* (University of Notre Dame Press 1963), p. 82.
6 Royden K. Yerkes, *Sacrifice in Greek and Roman Religions and Early Judaism* (A. and C. Black 1953), p. 25f.
7 *Myst. Cat.* 5.15.
8 *De Orat.* 27 (PG 11.517).
9 *De Inc.* 16.
10 *De Fide Orth.* 4.13 (PG 94.1152).
11 Geoffrey Wainwright, *Eucharist and Eschatology* (Epworth

1978 edn), p. 34.

12 Joachim Jeremias, *The Eucharistic Words of Jesus* (1955), pp. 38–51.

13 *De Sacr.* 4.4.

14 David Daube, *Wine in the Bible* (London Diocesan Council for Christian Jewish Understanding, 1974), p. 13.

15 See Massey H. Shepherd, *The Paschal Liturgy and the Apocalypse* (Lutterworth 1960).

16 Jeremias, op. cit., pp. 83–4.

17 Letter 96.

18 Hippolytus 4.11.

19 *English Hymnal* No. 310.

20 *Adv. Haer.* 4.17 (PG 7.1023).

21 Ibid., 5.2 (PG 7.1126f).

22 *Didache* 9.4.

23 Ibid., 10.6.

24 Wainwright, op. cit., p. 72.

25 E. Brightman, *Liturgies Eastern and Western* (Oxford 1896), vol. 1, p. 287.

26 Cited Wainwright, p. 72.

27 Jerome *Ep.* 120.2 (PL 22.985f).

28 Narsai, Ho. 21 in R. H. Connolly, *The Liturgical Homilies of Narsai* (Cambridge 1909), p. 60f.

29 M. Ferotin (ed.) *Liber Sacramentum* col. 234.

30 *Cat. Or.* 37 (PG 45.93).

31 PG 72.912 and 73.581.

32 *Epp.* 1.228 (PG 78.325).

33 *De Sacerdotio* 3.4.

34 *Cat* 6.

35 See Charles Harris, 'Liturgical Silence' in *Liturgy and Worship* (ed. W. K. L. Clarke and C. Harris, 1932), pp. 774ff.

36 Basil Minchin, *Covenant and Sacrifice* (Longmans 1958), p. 4.

37 E. O. James, *The Origins of Sacrifice* (John Murray 1933), pp. 256–7.

38 On the idea of sacrifice see F. C. N. Hicks, *The Fulness of Sacrifice* (1930) and the little-known study of Frederick Hastings Smyth, *Sacrifice: a doctrinal homily* (New York, Vantage Press 1953).

39 R. K. Yerkes, *Sacrifice in Greek and Roman Religions and Early Judaism* (A. and C. Black 1953), p. 24.

40 H. M. Luckock, *The Divine Liturgy* (Longmans 1915), p. 51.

41 *Ad Philad.* 4.

42 See A. G. Mortimer, *The Eucharistic Sacrifice* (Longmans

1901) for a thorough survey.
43 *Ep. 17 ad Nest.* 3.
44 *In Heb. Hom.* 17.3 (PG 63.131).
45 Geoffrey Wainwright, *Eucharist and Eschatology* (Epworth 1978 edn), p. 67.
46 *Hymns Ancient and Modern Revised* No. 584.
47 *Summa Theologica* 2.2.85 art. 3 ad 3.
48 *Hymns on the Lord's Supper* No. 116, cited Wainwright, op. cit., p. 178, n. 210.
49 *1 Apol.* 66.2.
50 *In Matt. Hom.* 11.14 (PG 13.948).
51 PG 26.1325; 86.2401.
52 *Hom. de prod. Iudae* 1.6 (PG 49.380).
53 Hippolytus 4.12. See Gregory Dix, OSB, *The Apostolic Tradition of St Hippolytus* (SPCK 1937).
54 Apud Paul the Deacon, *Vita Greg.* 23 (PL 75.53).
55 John H. McKenna, *Eucharist and Holy Spirit: the eucharistic epiclesis in 20th Century theology* (Alcuin Club Collections 57, Mayhew-McCrimmon 1975), p. 70.
56 *Myst. Cat.* 4.1.
57 Sermon 57.7 (PL 38.389).
58 Sermon 63.7 (PL 54.357).
59 *De Fide Orth.* 4.13 (PG 94.1153).
60 Cited in Wainwright, op. cit., p. 191, n. 317.
61 Session 13, *De Eucharistia*, cap. 1.
62 See H. E. Symonds, *The Council of Trent and Anglican Formularies* (1933), p. 43.
63 Sermon 71.17 (PL 38.453).
64 Wainwright, op. cit., p. 67.
65 T. F. Torrance in *Intercommunion* (ed. D. Baillie and J. Marsh, 1952), p. 337.
66 *Hymns on the Lord's Supper* No. 97.
67 Wainwright, op. cit., p. 104.
68 *The Incarnation of the Son of God* (Bampton Lectures 1891), p. 219.
69 Thomassin, *Dogmata Theologica* (Paris 1680–9), chs. 21–2; Jeremy Taylor, *The Worthy Communicant* (1660), in *Works* (ed. Heber), Vol. 15, p. 420.
70 *The Easter People*, p. 156.
71 *Congress Report* (Catholic Truth Society 1980), G. 4–5.
72 Cited in William Johnston, *The Inner Eye of Love*, op. cit., pp. 26–7.
73 David Martin, 'Profane habit and sacred usage', *Theology* 82.686

(1979), pp. 84–5, 86.

74 See Colin Buchanan, *The Kiss of Peace* (Nottingham, Grove Worship Series No. 80, 1982), p. 5.

75 *1 Apol.* 1.65.

76 Hippolytus 21.

77 Baptismal Homily 2.27 in E. J. Yarnold (ed.), *The Awe-Inspiring Rites of Initiation* (St Paul Publications 1972), p. 169.

78 Buchanan, op. cit., p. 12.

79 Cf. G. J. Cuming in *The Eucharist Today* (ed. R. C. D. Jasper, SPCK 1974), p. 41.

80 New York, Vantage Press 1953.

81 Ibid., p. 53.

82 *Discerning the Lord's Body* (Louisville, Kentucky 1946), pp. 84–5.

83 *Sacrifice,* op. cit., p. 47.

84 Ibid., pp. 58–9.

85 Ibid., p. 62.

86 Ibid., p. 87.

87 John A. T. Robinson, *On Being the Church in the World* (SCM Press 1964 edn), pp. 64–5. See the whole section on 'Matter, power and liturgy' (pp. 31–71).

88 Sermon 227, cited in A. G. Hebert, *Liturgy and Society* (Faber 1935), p. 193.

89 Offertory Prayers of the Roman Rite.

90 *Splendor Paternae Gloriae* in *Hymns Ancient and Modern* No. 2.

91 *De Sacr.* 5.3.

92 Stanley G. Evans, *The Social Hope in the Christian Church* (Hodder and Stoughton 1965), p. 250.

93 Karl Rahner, *Theological Investigations* vol. 14, pp. 169–70.

94 Nathan Mitchell, 'The spirituality of Christian worship', *Spirituality Today* 34.1 (1982), pp. 10–11.

95 Ibid., pp. 13, 14.

96 Richard K. Fenn, *Liturgies and Trials: the secularisation of religious language* (Blackwell 1982), p. 29. See the whole of ch. 2 on 'The political dimensions of the liturgy' (pp. 25–44).

97 N. Arseniev, *Russian Piety* (1964), p. 46.

98 *Manhood into God* (New York, Round Table Press 1940), pp. 219–20.

99 *The Socialist's Church* (G. Allen 1907) p. 5; *The Meaning of the Mass* (S. S. Brown, Langham and Co. 1905) p. 20.

100 *The Laws of Eternal Life* (Frederick Verinder 1888), p. 24.

101 Ibid., p. 52.

102 For Noel, see Reg Groves, *Conrad Noel and the Thaxted*

Movement (Merlin Press 1967).
103 See, for example, Jim Wilson's pamphlets *The Meaning of Worship* (n.d.), *Worship and Life* (n.d.), and *The Social Significance of the Liturgy* (1941), all published by the Industrial Christian Fellowship.
104 Letter from Taizé, May 1970.
105 Jurgen Moltmann, *The Open Church* (SCM Press 1978), ch. 5 'The Feast of Freedom' (pp. 64–81).
106 Cited in ibid., p. 72.
107 Cited in Hugo Rahner, *Man at Play* (Burns Oates 1965), p. 86.
108 Moltmann, op. cit., p. 73.
109 John Octavius Johnston (ed.), *The Life and Letters of Henry Parry Liddon* (Longmans 1904), pp. 282, 286.
110 Tissa Balasuriya, *The Eucharist and Human Liberation* (SCM Press 1979); Monika K. Hellwig, *The Eucharist and the Hunger of the World* (New York, Paulist 1976).
111 Balasuriya, op. cit., p. 8.
112 Ibid., p. 2.
113 See J. L. Segundo, *The Sacraments Today* (Maryknoll, Orbis 1974), p. 63.
114 Cited in Gustavo Gutierrez, *A Theology of Liberation* (Maryknoll, Orbis 1973), p. 282, n. 31.

CHAPTER 10

1 *Theology of the Pain of God* (SCM Press 1966), p. 44.
2 Frances Young in *The Myth of God Incarnate* (ed. John Hick, SCM Press 1977), pp. 34–5.
3 Cited in Kitamori, op. cit., p. 45.
4 *The Thought of Blaise Pascal* (Kegan Paul and Trench 1880), p. 231.
5 Edwin Muir, 'The Transfiguration', *Collected Poems* (Faber 1960), p. 200.
6 Louis Bouyer, *Le Mystère Pascal* (tr. D. M. Mackinnon in *Theology*, December 1952), p. 458.
7 F. W. J. von Schelling, 1809, cited in Kitamori, op. cit., p. 26.
8 See John Meyendorff, *Christ in Eastern Christian Thought* (New York, St Vladimir's Press 1975), ch. 4 'God suffered in flesh' (pp. 69–89).
9 Cited Meyendorff, op. cit., p. 71.
10 Horace Bushnell, *The Vicarious Sacrifice* (1866), pp. 35–6.
11 Personal Letter to Osbert Sitwell, 4 July 1918, cited in C. Day Lewis (ed.), *The Collected Poems of Wilfred Owen* (Chatto and Windus 1963), p. 23.

12 *Christus Veritas* (1942).
13 A. M. Ramsey, *From Gore to Temple* (Longmans 1960), p. 58.
14 Karl Barth, *Church Dogmatics*, op. cit., vol. 4, Part 2, p. 357.
15 Ibid., vol. 4, Part 1, p. 13.
16 SCM Press 1974.
17 Ibid., pp. 214–15.
18 Elie Wiesel, 'Night', cited in Dorothee Soelle, *Suffering* (Darton, Longman and Todd 1975), p. 145.
19 D. E. H. Whiteley, *The Theology of St Paul* (Blackwells 1970), p. 130.
20 Augustine, *De peccato originali* 32; Gregory of Nyssa, *Contra Eunom.* 5.
21 See Leon Morris, *The Apostolic Preaching of the Cross* (Tyndale Press 1955), p. 170.
22 *Journal of Theological Studies* 46 (1945), pp. 1–10.
23 Cf. Morris in *Expository Times* 62.8.
24 Ralph P. Martin, 'The theme of reconciliation', *Expository Times* 91.12 (1980), p. 364.
25 Jan Milac Lochman, *Reconciliation and Liberation: challenging a one-dimensional view of salvation* (Philadelphia, Fortress Press 1980).
26 Joachim Jeremias, *The Central Message of the New Testament* (SCM Press 1965), p. 36.
27 Martin Hengel, *The Atonement* (SCM Press 1981), pp. 6–7.
28 Ibid., p. 57.
29 In *The Historical Jesus and the Kerygmatic Christ* (ed. C. E. Braaten and R. A. Harrisville, New York and Nashville, 1964), p. 24.
30 Jurgen Moltmann, *The Crucified God* (SCM Press 1974), p. 24.
31 Conrad Noel, *Manifesto of the Catholic Crusade* (ed. Reg Groves, Archive One 1970).
32 Hengel, op. cit., p. 48.
33 Moltmann, op. cit., p. 25.
34 Cicero, *Pro Rabirico* 5.16.
35 Moltmann, op. cit., p. 33.
36 Gustav Aulén, *Christus Victor: an historical study of the three main types of the idea of the atonement* (SPCK 1970 edn).
37 Cited in Aulen, p. 36.
38 Lochman, op. cit., pp. 87, 90.
39 Douglas John Hall, *Lighten our Darkness: Towards an indigenous theology of the Cross* (Philadelphia, Westminster Press 1976), p. 117.
40 Dietrich Bonhoeffer, *Letters and Papers from Prison, The*

Enlarged Edition (ed. Eberhard Bethge, SCM Press 1971), p. 362; *The Cost of Discipleship* (SCM Press), pp. 71, 85.

41 Sebastian Moore, *The Crucified Is No Stranger* (Darton, Longman and Todd 1977).

42 Ibid., p. 21.

43 Ibid., p. 23.

44 *Cant.* 617.

45 *St Bernard on the Song of Songs* (tr. CSMV), p. 196.

46 Hilda Graef, *The Light of the Rainbow* (Longmans 1959), p. 214.

47 Cf. John Saward, *Perfect Fools* (Oxford UP 1980), p. 81.

48 *The Mirror of Faith* (ed. M.-M. Davy; ET, T. X. Davis, Kalamazoo, 1969).

49 *Legenda Minor* 3.1.

50 *The Soul's Journey*, Prologue 3.

51 See St Bonaventure, *The Soul's Journey into God, The Tree of Life, The Life of St Francis* (tra. Ewert Cousins, Classics of Western Spirituality, SPCK 1978).

52 *The Mystical Vine* (tr. A Friar of SSF, Mowbrays 1955), p. 27.

53 In *A Treasury of Russian Spirituality* (ed. G. P. Fedotov, 1950), p. 20.

54 See Nadejda Gorodetzky, *The Humiliated Christ in Modern Russian Thought* (SPCK 1938).

55 See Saward, op. cit., pp. 25ff.

56 I. Kologrivoff, *Essai sur la sainteté en Russe* (Bruges 1953) cited in Saward, op. cit., p. 25.

57 Saward, ibid., pp. 6–7.

58 Austin Farrer 'Walking Sacraments' in *A Celebration of Faith* (1970), p. 111.

59 A. V. Campbell, *Rediscovering Pastoral Care* (Darton, Longman and Todd 1981), p. 26.

60 James Hillman, *Insearch* (Hodder and Stoughton 1967), p. 18.

61 Henri J. M. Nouwen, *The Wounded Healer* (New York, Doubleday 1972), p. 94.

62 Edith Sitwell, 'Still Falls the Rain' in *Collected Poems* (Macmillan 1979), p. 272.

63 T. S. Eliot, *Four Quartets* (Faber 1959), pp. 29ff.

64 See Kosuke Koyama 'Towards a crucified mind' in *Waterbuffalo Theology* (SCM Press 1974), pp. 209–24.

65 Cited in Stephen B. Oates, *Let the Trumpet Sound: the life of Martin Luther King, Jr.* (Search Press 1982), p. 236.

66 James H. Cone, *The Spirituals and the Blues* (New York, Seabury Press 1972), pp. 52ff.

CHAPTER 11

1 F. Cavallera and Jean Daniélou, introduction to Jean Chrysostome, *Sur l'Incompréhensibilité de Dieu* (Sources Chrétiènnes 1951), p. 19.
2 Paul Tillich, *The Shaking of the Foundations* (1963 edn), p. 64.
3 John A. T. Robinson, *Honest to God* (SCM Press 1963), p. 54.
4 *Confessions* 7.10.
5 *In Ps.* 41.7, 8.
6 *Soliloqies* 1.2, 7.
7 *In Ps.* 99.6.
8 *Conf.* 3.6.
9 Ibid.
10 Ibid., 10.27.
11 Ibid.
12 Sermon 123.3.
13 *Hom. 6 on the Beatitudes* (PG 44.1272).
14 Hym 21 in *Hymns of Divine Love by St Symeon the New Theologian* (tr. G. A. Maloney, Denville, NJ, Dimension, n.d.), pp. 98–9.
15 Cf. Stephen J. Seleman, 'Richard of St-Victor and the mystical life', *Cistercian Studies* 15.3 (1980), pp. 301–10.
16 In Matthew Fox, *Breakthrough* (Doubleday 1980), p. 64.
17 Sermon 69.
18 Sermon 71; Sister Katrei.
19 In *Meister Eckhart, The Essential Sermons, Commentaries, Treatises, and Defenses* (tr. E. Colledge and B. McGinn, Classics of Western Spirituality, SPCK 1981), p. 33.
20 Sermon 6 in ibid., p. 188.
21 *Works* 2.60 in C. de B. Evans, *The Works of Meister Eckhart* (J. M. Watkins, 1924).
22 *The Mirror of Eternal Salvation*, ch. 8.
23 *The Twelve Béguines*, ch. 14.
24 *The Sparkling Stone*, ch. 10; *The Book of Supreme Truth*, ch. 2.
25 In Richard Woods (ed.), *Understanding Mysticism* (Athlone Press 1980), p. 454.
26 John of Ruysbroeck, *The Adornment of the Spiritual Marriage, The Seven Steps, and the Book of Supreme Truth* (tr. C. A. Wynschenk Dom, Dent 1916), p. 150.
27 Second Sermon for the 12th Sunday after Trinity, in Rufus M. Jones, *The Flowering of Mysticism* (New York, Macmillan 1939), p. 102; J. Tauler, *Predigten* (ed. G. Hofmann, Freiburg, Herder Verlag 1961), pp. 196ff.
28 *Revelations of Divine Love*, ch. 63.

29 Ibid., ch. 56.
30 Ibid., ch. 6 (in Paris MS only).
31 Ibid., ch. 43. See *Enfolded in Love: Daily Readings with Julian of Norwich* (Darton, Longman and Todd 1980), p. 24.
32 Ibid., ch. 58 in *Enfolded . . .*, op. cit., p. 35.
33 *Scale of Perfection* 1.42; *The Ladder of Perfection* (tr. L. Sherley-Price, Penguin 1957), p. 48.
34 *Living Flame of Love* 1.2.
35 *Interior Castle*, 1st Mansion, ch. 1.
36 Cited in Monica Furlong, *Merton: a biography* (Collins 1980), p. 79.
37 *On the Song of Songs* 49 (Pl 183.1018).
38 A. Mingana, *Early Christian Mystics* (Woodbrook Studies 7, 1934), p. 58.
39 Cited in S. Brock, 'The prayer of the heart in Syriac tradition', *Sobornost* 4.2 (1982), pp. 135–6.
40 *Book of Perfections* 2.4, 9, 8, cited in Brock, op. cit., pp. 141–2.
41 *Mysticism* (Penguin 1963), p. 36.
42 Rufus M. Jones, *Studies in Mystical Religion* (Macmillan 1909), p. xv.
43 Charles Davis, *Body as Spirit: the nature of religious feeling* (New York, Seabury Press 1976), p. 34.
44 Cf. André Lolande in *Vocabulaire technique et critique de la philosophie* (Paris 1956), col. 664.
45 Longmans 1902.
46 W. T. Stace, *Mysticism and Philosophy* (Philadelphia, Lippincott 1960), p. 68.
47 *Church Dogmatics* I.2 (1936), pp. 318ff.
48 In *Third World Theologies* (ed. Gerald H. Anderson and Thomas F. Stransky, Mission Trends No. 3, Paulist and Eerdmans 1976), p. 31.
49 R. D. Laing, *The Politics of Experience and the Bird of Paradise* (Penguins 1967).
50 C. G. Jung, *Collected Works* Vol. 16 (Routledge 1954), p. 262.
51 Cited in R. C. Zaehner, *Drugs, Mysticism and Make-Believe* (Collins 1972), p. 99.
52 Philip Kapleau, *The Three Pillars of Zen* (Harper Row, 1966), pp. 288–9.
53 *Bhagavad Gita* 6.16–17.
54 Thomas Merton, 'Is mysticism normal?', *Commonweal* 51 (1949–50), cited in J. J. Higgins, *Thomas Merton's Theology of Prayer* (1971), p.22.
55 See Vladimir Lossky, *The Mystical Theology of the Eastern*

Church (James Clarke 1957).
56 *Stromata* 7.
57 *Commentary on the Song of Songs.*
58 See Jean Daniélou SJ. *Platonisme et Théologie Mystique: doctrine spirituelle de S Grégoire de Nysse* (Aubier, Edition Montaigne).
59 *Mystical Theology* (Goldalming, Shrine of Wisdom 1956 edn), pp. 18–19.
60 New York, Macmillan 1952 edn, pp. 88 –9.
61 *L'Esperienza di Dio Amore* (Rome, 1972 edn), p. 161.
62 *Book of Supreme Truth,* ch. 11.
63 *Mirror of Eternal Salvation*, ch. 17.
64 *On the Love of God*, ch. 10 (tr. Terence L. Connolly in T. S. Kepler, *The Fellowship of the Saints* (New York and Nashville 1948), pp. 122–3.
65 See E. Gilson, *The Mystical Theology of St Bernard* (Sheed and Ward 1940), pp. 121ff.
66 *De Diligendo Deo* 10.28 (tr. CSMV, 1961), p. 45.
67 *Book of Supreme Truth*, ch. 8.
68 *Mirror of Eternal Blessedness*, cited in J. Walsh (ed.), *Spirituality Through the Centuries* (Burns Oates n.d.), p. 203.
69 Ruysbroeck, cited Walsh, ibid., p. 207.
70 R. C. Zaehner, *Mysticism Sacred and Profane* (Oxford, Clarendon Press 1957), p. 151f.
71 *Life of St Teresa* (tr. J. M. Cohen, Penguin 1957), p. 210.
72 Charles Williams, *Religion and Love in Dante* (Dacre n.d.), p. 40.
73 *City of God* 22.30.
74 Eckhart, Sermon 28 (tr. Raymond Blackney, *Meister Eckhart*, New York, 1957), p. 232.
75 *Confessions* 1 (tr. F. J. Sheed, Sheed and Ward 1943).
76 *Enar. in Ps.* 99.11 (PL 37.1277).
77 *Conf.* 2.3.
78 *Conf.* 2.3; 6.1.
79 Ibid., 4.7.
80 Ibid., 7.10.
81 Ibid., 7.7.
82 Ibid., 8.6.
83 Ibid., 7.12.
84 *In John. Ev. Tract* 18.10 (PL 35.1541–2).
85 *Conf.* 10.39.
86 Thomas Merton, *Contemplative Prayer* (Darton, Longman and Todd 1973), p. 38.

87 *Inst.* 1.15.4.
88 Ibid., 2.2.12.
89 Ibid., 1.1.2.
90 *Sermon in Eph.* 2.1; Dedication to Catholic Epistles.
91 *Sermon in Job* 2.1f; *Com. on Gen.* 3.22. See T. F. Torrance, *Calvin's Doctrine of Man* (Lutterworth 1949).
92 E. L. Mascall, *Nature and Supernature* (Darton, Longman and Todd 1976), p. 93.
93 *The New Man* (New York, New American Library 1963), p. 69.
94 Introduction to Amédée Hallier, *The Monastic Theology of Aelred of Rievaulx* (Shannon, Irish UP 1969), p. x.
95 Cited in S. Brock, *Sobornost* 4.2 (1982), pp. 138–9.
96 Nicholas Berdyaev, *Spirit and Reality* (Bles 1939), p. 98.
97 On spiritual direction see Kenneth Leech, *Soul Friend* (Sheldon Press 1978); Alan W. Jones, *Exploring Spiritual Direction: an essay in Christian friendship* (Seabury Press 1982); William A. Barry and William J. Connolly, *The Practice of Spiritual Direction* (Seabury Press 1982); and Carolyn Grattan, *Guidelines for Spiritual Direction* (Denville, NJ, Dimension 1980).
98 Harvey Egan SJ, 'The Christian mystics and today's theological horizon', *Listening* 17.3 (1982), p. 204.
99 Ibid., p. 205.
100 Segundo Galilea, 'Liberation as an encounter with politics and contemplation' in *The Mystical and Political Dimensions of Christian Faith* (ed. Claude Geffre and Gustavo Gutierrez, New York, 1974), p. 28; also in Richard Woods (ed.), *Understanding Mysticism* (Athlone Press 1980), p. 536.
101 Stephen B. Oates, *Let the Trumpet Sound: the life of Martin Luther King, Jr* (Search Press 1982), p. 144.
102 *Markings* (Faber 1962), p. 122; retranslated by G. Aulén. See Aulén's *Dag Hammarskjöld's White Book: an analysis of Markings* (SPCK 1970), pp. 99–102.
103 Aulen, op. cit.
104 Jack Woodard in *The Witness* 66.3 (March 1983), p. 4. The whole issue is on the subject of 'Activists and Prayer'.
105 Emmett Jarrett in *Essays Catholic and Radical* (ed. K. Leech and R. Williams, Bowerdean Press 1983), pp. 81–2.
106 J. Lindblom, *Prophecy in Ancient Israel* (1962), p. 121.
107 Thomas Merton, *Raids on the Unspeakble* (1966), p. 159.
108 Rowan Williams, *The Wound of Knowledge: Christian spirituality from the New Testament to St John of the Cross* (Darton, Longman and Todd 1979), p. 78.
109 Cited by Paul Oestreicher in *Christianity Reinterpreted?* (ed.

K. Leech, Jubilee Group 1982), p. 17.

110 Matthew Fox, 'Meister Eckhart and Karl Marx: the mystic as political theologian' in Richard Woods, op. cit., p. 543. See the whole essay, pp. 541–63.

111 John S. Mogabgab, 'The contemplative movement from darkness to light', *Worship* 55.6 (1981), p. 531.

112 *Where the Wasteland Ends* (Faber 1972), p. xxii.

CHAPTER 12

1 William Leonard, *A discourse on the Second Appearing of Christ in and through the Order of the Female* (Harvard, United Society of Believers 1853), pp. 54–5.

2 Mary Esther Harding, *Women's Mysteries, Ancient and Modern: a psychological interpretation of the feminine principle as portrayed in myth, story and dreams* (New York, G. P. Putnam's Sons 1972), p. 241.

3 Johann Bachofen, *Das Mutterrecht* (1861).

4 See Elizabeth Gould Davis, *The First Sex* (New York, G. P. Putnam's Sons 1971).

5 See E. O. James, *Myth and Ritual in the Ancient Near East* (Thames and Hudson 1958), p. 113.

6 Raphael Patai, *The Hebrew Goddess* (New York, Ktav Publishing House 1967), pp. 15–100.

7 James, op. cit., p. 63.

8 Joseph Campbell, *The Masks of God: primitive mythology* (New York, Viking Press 1970), p. 315.

9 Joseph Winthuis, cited in Victor White, *Soul and Psyche* (Collins 1959), pp. 120ff.

10 Alfred Bertholet, *Das Geschlecht der Gottheit* (Tübingen 1934).

11 See John Moffett, 'God as Mother in Hinduism and Christianity', *Cross Currents* 27 (1978), pp. 129–33.

12 E. O. James, *The Cult of the Mother Goddess* (Thames and Hudson 1959), p. 80.

13 Krister Stendahl, *The Bible and the Role of Women* (Philadelphia, Fortress Press 1966), p. 26.

14 Wolfgang Lederer, *The Fear of Women* (New York, Harcourt Brace Jovanovich 1968), p. 159.

15 E. L. Mascall in *Why Not? Priesthood and the Ministry of Women* (ed. M. Bruce and G. E. Duffield, Abingdon, Marcham Manor Press 1972), p. 112.

16 J. Edgar Bruns, *God as Woman, Woman as God* (Paulist Press 1973), p. 36.

17 Claus Westermann, *Isaiah 40–66: a commentary* (Philadelphia,

Westminster Press 1969), p. 420.

18 Helmer Ringgren, *Word and Wisdom: studies in the hypostasiza-tion of divine qualities and functions in the Ancient Near East* (Lund, H. Ohlssons boktr. 1947), p. 115.

19 Joan Chamberlain Engelsman, *The Feminine Dimension of the Divine* (Philadelphia, Westminster Press 1979), p. 74. See the whole of ch. 5 on 'The expression and repression of Sophia' (pp. 74–120).

20 See Sergius Bulgakov, *The Wisdom of God* (Williams and Norgate 1937).

21 Raymond Brown, *The Gospel According to John* (Anchor Bible vol. 29, New York, Doubleday 1966), p. lxi.

22 Engelsman, op. cit., p. 95.

23 See Richard Arthur Baer, *Philo's Use of the Categories Male and Female* (Leiden, Brill 1970).

24 Christ the Educator in *Fathers of the Church* No. 23 (tr. Simon P. Ward, New York, Fathers of the Church Inc. 1954), pp. 11–12.

25 *Clement of Alexandria* tr. G. W. Butterworth (Harvard UP 1953), pp. 201, 319.

26 *Ante-Nicene Fathers* vol. 2, p. 601.

27 *Synesii* (PG 66.1594).

28 *In Matt. Hom.* 76–7 (PG 58.700).

29 *St Ambrose: Seven Exegetical Works* (tr. Michael P. McHugh, Fathers of the Church No. 65, Washington, Catholic University of America Press 1972), pp. 268–9.

30 *Quaestionum Evangeliorum* 2.26 (PL 35.1330).

31 *Enar. in Ps. 26* (PL 36.208–9).

32 *En. in Ps. 90* (PL 37.1160–1). See on this Ritamary Bradley, 'Patristic background of the motherhood similitude in Julian of Norwich', *Christian Scholars' Review* 8.2 (1978), pp. 101–13.

33 Bradley, op. cit., pp. 101–2.

34 *New Testament Apocrypha* vol. 2 (ed. R. McL. Wilson, Philadelphia, Westminster Press 1964), p. 320.

35 *Gospel of Truth* 24. Cf. *Gospel of Philip* 17.

36 Elaine H. Pagels, *The Gnostic Gospels* (New York, Random House 1979), p. 66, 49.

37 *Pseudo-Clementine Homilies* 2. 15.3.

38 *Gospel of Thomas*, log. 114.

39 See Kathleen McVey, 'Gnosticism, feminism and Elaine Pagels', *Theology Today* 37.4 (1981), pp. 498–501.

40 *Gospel of the Egyptians* 9.63.

41 *On the Trinity*, cited in Julia O'Faolain and Lauro Martines, *Not*

in God's Image (Virago 1979), p. 142.

42 Erich Neumann, *The Great Mother: an analysis of the archetype* (New York, Pantheon Books 1955), p. 59.

43 Erik H. Erikson, *Young Man Luther: a study in psychoanalysis and history* (W. W. Norton 1958), p. 263.

44 *Gospel of the Hebrews*, in *New Testament Apocrypha* vol. 1 (ed. E. Hennecke and W. Schmeemelcher, Philadelphia, Westminster Press 1963), p. 164.

45 *Nag Hammadi Library in English* (ed. J. M. Robinson, New York, Harper and Row 1977), p. 134.

46 *New Testament Apocrypha*, vol. 2, p. 471.

47 Joan Schaupp, *Woman: Image of the Holy Spirit* (Denville, NJ, Dimension 1975), p. 88f.

48 *Demonstration* 18.

49 See P. J. Jacob, 'The motherhood of the Holy Spirit', *Journal of Dharma* (Bangalore) 5.2 (1980), pp. 160–74.

50 *Odes of Solomon* 24; 28; 19.1–7.

51 *Didascalia* 9. 2.26 in R. H. Connolly, *Didascalia Apostolorum: the Syriac version translated and accompanied by the Verona Latin fragments* (Oxford, Clarendon Press 1929).

52 See Robert Murray, *Symbols of Church and Kingdom: a study of early Syriac traditions* (Cambridge UP 1975).

53 *Essays in Analytical Psychoanalysis* vol. 2 (Hogarth Press 1951), p. 209.

54 Rosemary Ruether, *Sexism and God-Talk* (Boston, Beacon Press 1983), p. 60.

55 Cited in Mary Daly, *The Church and the Second Sex* (Geoffrey Chapman, 1968), p. 49.

56 On the Joachite movements see Marjorie Reeves, *The Influence of Prophecy in the Later Middle Ages: a study in Joachimism* (Oxford, Clarendon Press 1969) and *Joachim of Fiore and the Prophetic Future* (New York, Harper and Row 1976).

57 Caroline Walker Bynum, *Jesus as Mother: studies in the spirituality of the High Middle Ages* (University of California Press 1982), p. 14.

58 Ibid., p. 18.

59 Ibid., p. 19.

60 Ibid., p. 20.

61 Ibid., p. 140.

62 *2nd Sermon for Peter and Paul*, cited ibid., p. 122.

63 PL 185.1236, cited in Aelred Squire, 'The Cistercians and the Eastern Fathers' in *Theology and Prayer* (ed. A. M. Allchin, Fellowship of St Alban and St Sergius 1975), p. 67.

64 *Speculum Caritatis* 2.19 (PL 195.568).
65 *De Institutione* 26, cited Bynum, op. cit., p. 123.
66 *Ancren Riwle* (ed. M. B. Salu, Burns Oates 1955 edn).
67 A. Duraffour, P. Gardette and P. Durdilly, *Les Oeuvres de Marguerite d'Oingt* (Paris 1965), pp. 33–6.
68 A. Cabassut, 'Une dévotion médiévale peu connue', *Revue d'Ascétique et de Mystique* 25 (1949), p. 238.
69 See Eleanor McLaughlin 'Male and female in Christian tradition' in *Male and Female: Christian approaches to sexuality* (ed. Ruth Tiffany Barnhouse and Urban T. Holmes, New York, Seabury Press 1976), pp. 39–52.
70 Benedicta Ward SLG, *The Prayers and Meditations of St Anselm* (Penguin 1973), p. 11.
71 Ward, op. cit., pp. 153–4.
72 Ibid., p. 155.
73 Ibid., p. 157.
74 Ibid., p. 153.
75 Ibid., pp. 155–6.
76 Ritamary Bradley, 'Patriotic background of the motherhood similitude in Julian of Norwich', *Christian Scholars' Review* 8.2 (1978), p. 102.
77 *Revelations* 59; tr. Clifton Wolters (Penguin 1966), p. 167.
78 Ibid., 60.
79 Ibid.
80 Ibid., 63.
81 Sister Anna Maria Reynolds in *Pre-Reformation English Spirituality* (ed. J. Walsh, 1966).
82 McLaughlin, op. cit., p. 45.
83 Jennifer P. Heimmel, *'God is our Mother': Julian of Norwich and the medieval image of Christian feminine divinity*. PhD Thesis, St John's University, New York, 1980, pp. 64, 81.
84 Susan M. Setta, 'From Ann the Christ to Holy Mother Wisdom: changing goddess imagery in the Shaker tradition', *Anima* 7.1 (Fall Equinox 1980), p. 5.
85 See Mary Baker Eddy, *Science and Health with Key to the Scriptures* (Boston, E. J. Foster Eddy 1894 edn), p. 510.
86 Eliza R. Snow Smith, *Poems: Religious, Historical and Political* (Salt Lake City, Latter Day Saints Printing House 1877), p. 173.
87 *Millennial Praises: Shaker Hymnal* (1813), cited in Edward Deeming Andrews, *The People Called Shakers* (New York, Dover 1963), p. 158.
88 *Collected Poems* (Macmillan 1969), pp. 328–9.

89 *Systematic Theology* vol. 3 (University of Chicago Press 1963), p. 293f.

90 *Soul and Psyche* (Collins and Harvill 1960), op. cit., p. 122f.

91 Ibid., pp. 128–40.

92 See Ann Belford Ulanov, *The Feminine in Jungian Psychology and in Christian Theology* (Evanston, North Western UP 1971); and Naomi R. Goldenberg, 'A feminist critique of Jung', *Signs* (Winter 1976), pp. 443–9.

93 Thomas Merton, letter to V. Hammer, 14 May 1959, cited in Monica Furlong, *Merton* (Collins 1980), p. 231f.

94 E. O. James, *The Cult of the Mother Goddess,* op. cit., p. 208.

95 *De Fide Orth.* 3.12.

96 Sergius Bulgakov, *The Orthodox Church* (Centenary Press 1935), p. 139f.

97 *Dialogue* 100.

98 *Adv. Haer.* 3.22; 5.19.

99 Hugo Rahner, *Mater Ecclesiae* (Einsiedeln, 1944), p. 14.

100 *Fifteen Tomes Against Nestorius* 1.10.

101 *Ep.* 101.

102 George Florovsky in *The Mother of God* (ed. E. L. Mascall, Dacre Press 1959), p. 52.

103 See Sebastian Brock, 'Passover, Annunciation and Eucharist', *Novum Testamentum* 24 (1982), pp. 222ff; and 'Mary and the Eucharist: an oriental perspective', *Sobornost* 1.2 (1979), p. 58f.

104 Sheila D. Collins, *A Different Heaven and Earth* (Valley Forge, Pa, Judson Press 1974), p. 132.

105 Henry Adams, *Mont-Saint Michel and Chartres* (Boston, Houghton Mifflin Co. 1933), p. 250.

106 *Sermon* 20 (PL 195.323).

107 Erich Neuman, *The Great Mother* (New York, Pantheon 1955), pp. 331–2.

108 Hans Urs von Balthasar, *Elucidations* (SPCK 1974), p. 72.

109 See Mary Daly, *Beyond God the Father* (Boston, Beacon Press 1973), pp. 82–92.

110 See C. G. Jung, 'On the Mother Archetype' in *Archetypes of the Collective Unconscious, Collected Works* vol. 9 (1969); and *Symbols of Transformation, Collected Works* vol. 5 (1967).

111 *Collected Works*, vol. 11, p. 171.

112 Ruether, op. cit., p. 139.

113 F. W. Faber, *Hymns* (1861 edn).

114 See Lynn Hollen Lees, *Exiles of Erin: Irish migrants in Victorian London* (Manchester UP 1979), p. 194.

115 Collins, op. cit., p. 172.

116 *Marialis Cultus* (1974) 37.
117 Cited by Rosemary Ruether in *The Witness* 62.10 (1979), p. 15.
118 Ibid., p. 16.
119 See Ruether's article in *The Witness*, op. cit., pp. 15–19, and her *Sexism and God-Talk* (Boston, Beacon Press 1983), pp. 152ff.
120 *The Witness*, op. cit., p. 18.
121 Rosemary Ruether, *New Woman, New Earth* (New York, Seabury Press 1975), p. 71.
122 *De Cultu Feminarum* 1.
123 *The Passion of St Perpetua* (tr. W. H. Shewring, Sheed and Ward 1931).
124 See Clara Maria Henning, 'Canon Law and the battle of the sexes' in *Religion and Sexism* (ed. R. Ruether and E. McLaughlin, Simon and Schuster 1974), pp. 155–9.
125 Elizabeth Schussler Fiorenza in *Cross Currents* 19.3 (1979), p. 306.
126 Daly, op. cit., p. 6.
127 *Sexism and God-Talk*, op. cit., p. 13.
128 See Letty M. Russell, *Human Liberation in a Feminist Perspective* (Philadelphia, Westminster Press 1974).
129 Cited in Janet Morley, 'In God's image?', *New Blackfriars* 63.747 (1982), p. 375.
130 E. L. Mascall, *Whatever Happened to the Human Mind?* (SPCK 1980), p. 150.
131 *Summa Theologica* 1a.1.9; 1a.13.1.
132 5th Oration on the Spirit, in *Christology of the Later Fathers* (ed. E. R. Hardy and C. C. Richardson, Philadelphia, Westminster Press 1954), p. 198.
133 Ruether, *New Woman, New Earth*, op. cit., p. xiii.
134 See Phyllis Trible, *God and the Rhetoric of Sexuality* (Philadelphia, Fortress Press 1978) and Ruth Hoppin, *Games Bible Translators Play* (Chicago, Ecumenical Task Force on Women and Religion, n.d.).
135 Sara Maitland, *A Map of the New Country: women and Christianity* (Routledge and Kegan Paul 1983), p. 16.
136 For Daly's current position see her *Gyn/Ecology: the metaethics of radical feminism* (Boston, Beacon Press 1978).
137 See Meinrad Craighead, 'Immanent Mother' in *The Feminist Mystic* (ed. Mary E. Giles, New York, Crossroad 1982), pp. 72, 76.
138 Ibid., p. 78.
139 For both these prayers see *She Prays: prayers by women* (Alfred Willetts and St Joan's Alliance 1981).
140 This prayer is printed in *One World* (World Council of

Churches) 47 (June 1979), p. 17.
141 Ruether, op. cit., p. 83.

CHAPTER 13

1 In *Thy Kingdom Come: Mission Perspectives* (World Council of Churches 1980), p. 43.
2 *Der Römerbrief* (Bern 1919), p. 366.
3 Roland de Vaux, *Ancient Israel: its life and institutions* (DLT 1961), p. 72.
4 Jim Wallis, *Agenda for Biblical People* (Harper and Row 1976), p. 11f.
5 Cited in Stephen B. Oates, *Let the Trumpet Sound: the life of Martin Luther King, Jr.* (Search Press 1982), p. 39.
6 See on this Gregory Baum, *The Social Imperative* (Paulist Press 1979) and Peter J. Henriot, 'The concept of social sin', *Catholic Mind* 71.1276 (October 1973), pp. 38–53.
7 Report of the Advisory Commission on the Main Theme, in *Christ the Hope of the World* (Geneva, World Council of Churches 1954), p. 9.
8 *The Times*, 10 May 1978.
9 London Weekend TV, 6 January 1980; *The Times*, 12 January 1980.
10 'Spirit of the Nation', Address by Margaret Thatcher at St Lawrence Jewry, 4 March 1981, reprinted in *Third Way*, May 1981, pp. 14–15.
11 Clifford Longley, *The Times*, 7 February 1983.
12 John Stokes MP, cited in the *Church of England Newspaper*, 6 August 1981.
13 Marquess of Salisbury in *Salisbury Review*, Winter 1982, p. 35.
14 Charles L. Kammer, *The Kingdom Revisited* (University Press of America 1981), p. viii. See also Steven Lukes, *Individualism* (Harper and Row 1973).
15 Cf. H. Kraemer in *Ecumenical Review* 1.3 (1949), p. 263.
16 Ibid., 1.1 (1948), p. 15.
17 William Temple, *Religious Experience* (Clarke 1958 edn), p. 211.
18 See, for example, the Chicago Call to Evangelicals 1977.
19 Cited in Martin Jarrett-Kerr, 'Scott Holland: drains and the Incarnation', *The Times*, 5 February 1983.
20 W. Rauschenbusch, *A Theology for the Social Gospel* (New York, Macmillan 1917), p. 131.
21 *The Service of Humanity* (1882) cited in S. G. Evans, *The Social Hope of the Christian Church* (Hodder and Stoughton 1965), p. 168.

22 *Jesus the Heretic* (Religious Book Club 1939), p. 2. See for a similar contemporary treatment Geevarghese Mar Ostathios, *Theology of a Classless Society* (Lutterworth 1979).

23 David Nicholls, 'Images of God and the state: political analogy and religious discourse', *Theological Studies* 42.2 (June 1981), p. 201.

24 See Alistair Kee, *Constantine versus Christ: the triumph of ideology* (SCM Press 1982).

25 Jerry Falwell, *Listen America!* (New York, Doubleday 1980), pp. 13, 166, 10; and *Christianity Today* (September 1981), p. 1099.

26 *City of God* Book 14, ch. 28. See Rosemary Ruether, 'Augustine and Christian political theology', *Interpretation* 29.3 (1975), pp. 252–65.

27 See Richard Higginson, 'The Two Kingdoms and the Orders of Creation in 20th Century Lutheran Ethics', *Modern Churchman*, New Series, 25.2 (1982), pp. 40–3; Heinrich Bornkamm, *Luther's Doctrine of the Two Kingdoms* (Philadelphia 1966).

28 See Richard Gutteridge, *Open Thy Mouth for the Dumb: the German Evangelical Church and the Jews 1879–1950* (Blackwell 1976), p. 278.

29 *Theological Existence Today* (June 1943).

30 Gutteridge, op. cit., p. 126.

31 Ibid., p. 282.

32 Address in St Lawrence Jewry, 30 March 1978; *Baptist Times*, 6 April 1978.

33 See, for example, Rhodes Boyson on Radio 4, 30 January 1983; Julian Critchley, 'Is the church close to heresy?' *Standard*, 10 February 1983; and many other similar pieces.

34 See *Sunday Express*, 8 August 1982.

35 Dusty Sklor, *Gods and Beasts: the Nazis and the Occult* (Harper and Row 1979).

36 See Wilhelm Reich, *The Mass Psychology of Fascism* (3rd edn 1942).

37 Hermann Rauschning, *The Voice of Destruction* (New York, 1940), p. 49.

38 Said at a dinner party on 11 July 1941, cited in *Hitler's Secret Conversations 1941–44* (New York 1953), p. 37.

39 Cited in C. S. Macfarlane, 'Hitler or Christ?', *American Mercury* 48 (September 1939), pp. 1–2.

40 Oswald Mosley, 'The philosophy of fascism', *The Fascist Quarterly* 1.1 (January 1935), p. 39.

41 See E. Bentley, *The Cult of the Superman* (Gloucester, Mass., 1944).

42 Alistair Kee, 'A Christian critique of fascism', *Modern Churchman* 22.2–3 (1979), p. 81.

43 See, for example, the sermon preached at Solingen on Christmas Day 1936 in John S. Conway, *The Nazi Persecution of the Churches 1933–45* (Weidenfeld and Nicholson 1968), pp. 364–5.

44 See Douglas Hyde, 'Catholics and the National Front', *The Month*, April 1978, pp. 111–14.

45 The Revd Evan E. Thomas, *Hitlerism, Communism and the Christian Faith* (Unicorn Press 1935), pp. 37–8.

46 *Gaudium et Spes*, para. 30.

47 See, for example, the Apostolic Exhortation *Evangelii Nuntiandi* (8 December 1975), para. 18.

48 See *The New Delhi Report* (SCM Press 1962), pp. 84–5.

49 Clifford Longley, *The Times*, 16 May 1983.

50 J. P. Miranda, *Marx and the Bible* (SCM Press 1977), p. 168.

51 Paul VI, *Evangelii Nuntiandi*, op. cit., para. 19.

52 Cited in Stephen B. Oates, *Let the Trumpet Sound: the life of Martin Luther King Jr* (Search Press 1982), p. 224.

53 Cited in Gregory Baum, *The Social Imperative* (New York, Paulist Press 1979), p. 83.

54 Baum, ibid., pp. 83–4.

55 'A Letter to the Peoples of the Third World' in *Between Honesty and Hope: documents from and about the church in Latin America* (Maryknoll, Orbis 1970), p. 5.

56 See Eric Heffer, 'Why the state must never take over', *The Times*, 31 December 1979.

57 Kay Carmichael, 'Hearts and minds: the lessons of the Independent Labour Party', *New Society*, 27 September 1979, pp. 64–6.

58 See Sheila Rowbotham *et al.*, *Beyond the Fragments* (Merlin 1979).

59 Terry Eagleton, in *Catholics and the Left* (Sheed and Ward 1966), p. 71.

60 John Austin Baker, 'Racism and the Bible', *Crucible*, October–December 1980, pp. 166–74.

61 See Norman Gottwald, *The Tribes of Yahweh: a sociology of the religion of liberated Israel 1250–1050 BCE* (Maryknoll, Orbis 1979).

62 See T. B. Maston, *The Bible and Race* (Nashville, Broadman Press 1959), pp. 105–17.

63 See H. Shelton Smith, *In His Image But ...: racism in Southern*

religion 1780–1910 (Duke University Press 1972).

64 Benjamin Mays, *Born to Rebel: an autobiography* (New York, Charles Scribner's Sons, 1971), p. 75.

65 Cited in David Bronnert, *Race: a challenge to Christians* (Falcon Press 1973), p. 4.

66 See G. E. W. Scobie, *Psychology and Religion* (Batsford 1975), p. 76; Michael Argyle and Benjamin Beit-Hallahmi, *The Social Psychology of Religion* (Routledge and Kegan Paul, 1975).

67 See Wolfgang Mock, 'The function of "race" in imperialist ideology: the example of Joseph Chamberlain' in *Nationalist and Racialist Movements in Britain and Germany before 1914* (ed. Paul Kennedy and Anthony Nicholls, Macmillan 1981), pp. 190–203.

68 See Gregory Baum, *Is the New Testament Anti-Semitic?* (New York, Paulist Press 1965). Baum changed his view under the influence of Rosemary Ruether. For his later view see his introduction to Ruether's *Faith and Fraticide: the theological roots of Anti-Semitism* (Scabury 1974), pp. 3ff.

69 See Ruether, ibid.

70 John Austin Baker, op. cit., p. 173.

71 Baum in Ruether, op. cit., p. 7.

72 See Aarne Siirala, *Voice of Illness* (Philadelphia, Fortress Press 1964).

73 *Rundbrief*, 3 April 1928 (in the Wiener Library).

74 See Paul le Seur, *Adolf Stoecker, Prophet of the Third Reich* (1936).

75 See Richard Gutteridge, *Open Thy Mouth for the Dumb: the German Evangelical Church and the Jews 1879–1950* (Oxford, Blackwells 1976), p. 268.

76 Ibid., p. 41.

77 Cited in ibid., p. 64.

78 Eduard Lohse, *Israel und die Christenheit* (Gottingen 1960), p. 44.

79 See, for example, Duncan Sandys's speech at the Conservative Party Conference, 20 October 1967.

80 *Daily Telegraph*, 18 October 1967.

81 This is suggested in David Sheppard, *Bias to the Poor* (Hodder and Stoughton 1983), p. 35.

82 *The Brixton Disorders* (Scarman Report, HMSO 1981), 9.1.

83 Speech to Stretford Young Conservatives, reported in *Daily Telegraph*, 22 January 1977.

84 See Timothy L. Smith, 'Slavery and theology: the emergence of black Christian consciousness in 19th Century America', *Church*

History 41.4 (1972), pp. 497–512.

85 Roswith Gerloff, 'Partnership between black and white: a test case for the mission of the British churches', *Theological Renewal* 7 (1977), p. 24.

86 Ruth Glass, 'Ashes of discontent', *The Listener*, 1 February 1962, pp. 207–9.

87 J. H. Cone, *A Black Theology of Liberation* (Philadelphia, Lippincott 1970), pp. 79–80.

88 Ibid., p. 108.

89 Ibid., pp. 59–60.

90 J. H. Cone, *God of the Oppressed* (Seabury Press 1975), pp. 136–7.

91 J. Deotis Roberts, *Liberation and Reconciliation: a Black Theology* (Philadelphia, Westminster Press 1971), pp. 139–40.

92 Cone, *A Black Theology of Liberation*, op. cit., p. 24.

93 Ibid., p. 26.

94 Ibid., p. 29.

95 Cone, *Black Theology and Black Power* (Seabury 1969), p. 69.

96 Francis Brown, S. R. Driver and C. A. Briggs, *Hebrew and English Lexicon of the Old Testament* (Oxford University Press 1907), p. 1022.

97 G. von Rad, *Old Testament Theology* I, p. 130.

98 On the Old Testament as a whole see Millard C. Lind, *Yahweh is a Warrior: the theology of warfare in ancient Israel* (Scottsdale, Pa, 1980); and Vernard Eller, *War and Peace from Genesis to Revelation* (Herald Press 1981).

99 See Martin Hengel, *Victory over Violence* (Philadelphia, Fortress Press 1973); and Jean-Michel Hornus, *It is not lawful for me to fight: early Christian attitudes towards war, violence and the state* (Herald Press 1980).

100 John Pairman Brown, *The Liberated Zone* (SCM Press 1970), pp. 113–14.

101 *S.T.* 2a.2ae.q.96.4.

102 19 October 1953 *AAS* 45 (1953), 748, 749.

103 *Pacem in Terris* 127 (Catholic Truth Society 1963); *Gaudium et Spes* 80.

104 *Gaudium et Spes* 80.

105 *Sojourners*, August 1979, pp. 12–14.

106 Sermon in All Souls, Langham Place, London, 11 November 1979, printed in *Christianity Today*, 8 February and 7 March 1980.

107 President Dwight D. Eisenhower, cited in *Disarmament and World Development* (ed. Richard Jolly, Pergamon 1978), p. 3.

108 *Gaudium et Spes* 81.

109 Ruth Leger Sivard, *World Military and Social Expenditure 1980* (Campaign Against the Arms Trade, 1980).

110 *Hansard* vol. 978.1181–2, col. 749 (1980).

111 Cited by Alan Kreider in *The Year 2000AD* (ed. John Stott, Marshall, Morgan and Scott 1983), p. 43.

112 Peter Goodwin, *Nuclear War: the facts of our survival* (Ash and Grant 1981), p. 114.

113 On civil defence claims see Duncan Campbell, *War Plan UK: the truth about civil defence in Britain* (Burnett Books 1982).

114 On the medical effects see *The Medical Effects of Nuclear War* (British Medical Association 1983).

115 *The Church and the Bomb* (Church Information Office 1982), p. 67.

116 Cited by Cardinal John Krol in *The Nuclear Threat: reading the signs of the times* (Washington, US Catholic Conference Office 1979), p. 10.

117 Ibid.

118 Catholic Information Service, *Briefing* 12.40 (17 December 1982), p. 1.

119 See *National Catholic Reporter*, 12 March 1982; 12 February 1982.

120 *Sojourners* 12.5 (May 1983), p. 24.

121 See Susan George, *How the Other Half Dies* (Penguin 1976).

122 John Atherton, *The Scandal of Poverty* (Mowbrays 1983), p. 59.

123 *Guardian*, 6 November 1976.

124 Atherton, op. cit., p. 50.

125 *Low Pay Review* 4 (June 1981).

126 *New Earnings Survey* (Department of Employment, October 1982); A. B. Atkinson, *Who are the low paid?* (Low Pay Unit 1982).

127 *Cut Off and Cold* (Merseyside Child Poverty Action Group 1977), cited in David Sheppard, *Bias to the Poor* (Hodder and Stoughton 1983), p. 31.

128 See Brian Jarman, 'Medical problems in Inner London', *Journal of the Royal College of General Practitioners* 28 (1978), pp. 598–604; Peter Townsend and Nick Davidson (eds), *Inequalities in Health: the Black Report* (Penguin 1982).

129 *Inequalities in Health* (DHSS 1980).

130 *The Perception of Poverty in Europe* (Commission of the European Communities, 1977).

131 This contempt was expressed most clearly in Sir Keith Joseph's notorious 'remoralization' speech of 1974 (*The Times*, 21

October 1974).

132 Thomas Cullinan OSB, *The Roots of Social Injustice* (Catholic Housing Aid Society 1973), p. 4.

133 A. E. McGrath, 'Justice and justification: semantic and juristic aspects of the Christian doctrine of justification', *Scottish Journal of Theology* 35 (1982), p. 408.

134 See A. George, 'La pauvreté dans l'ancien Testament' in *La Pauvreté evangélique* (Paris, Editions du Cerf 1971), pp. 14–18; N. W. Porteous, 'The care of the poor in the Old Testament' in *Living the Mystery* (Oxford 1967), pp. 143–55.

135 Friedrich Hauck in *Theological Dictionary of the New Testament* (tr. G. W. Bromiley, Eerdmans 1964–70), vol. 6, cited in J. P. Miranda, *Communism in the Bible* (SCM Press 1981), p. 41.

136 Julio de Santa Ana, *Good News to the Poor* (Maryknoll, Orbis 1979), p. 79.

137 Karl Barth, *Der Römerbrief* (Bern 1919), p. 366.

138 Jim Wallis, *Agenda for Biblical People* (Harper and Row 1976), p. 3.

139 Cf. Jacques Ellul, 'L'Argent', in *Etudes Théologiques et Religieuses* 27th Year, No. 4, p. 31.

140 William R. Coats, *God in Public: political theology beyond Niebuhr* (Grand Rapids, Eerdmans 1974), p. 133.

141 Andre Loiselle, 'The Fathers of the Church and social inequalities' in *Attentive to the Cry of the Needy* (Donum Dei Series No. 19, Canadian Religious Conference 1973), pp. 27–40.

142 *Hom.* 12.4 (PG 31.393).

143 PG 31.292.

144 PG 55.517.

145 Ibid., 61.86–7.

146 Ibid., 54.450.

147 PL 14.731–47; 15.1503.

148 Martin Hengel, *Property and Riches in the Early Church* (SCM Press 1975), p. 82.

149 Cf. Gustavo Gutierrez, *Praxis of Liberation and the Christian Faith* (tr. James and Margaret Goff, MS 1974), p. 7.

150 Julio de Santa Ana (ed.), *Towards a Church of the Poor* (Geneva, WCC), p. 15; Benoit Dumas, *The Two Alienated Faces of the One Church*, cited in Ana, p. 100.

151 Atherton, op. cit., p. 29.

152 Cf. David Jenkins, *The Contradiction of Christianity* (SCM Press 1976), p. 49.

153 *Church Dogmatics* 2.1 (Edinburgh, T. and T. Clark 1957), p. 386.

154 Cf. Juan Luis Segundo, *The Liberation of Theology* (Maryknoll, Orbis 1976), p. 141.

155 In J. Gremillion (ed.), *The Gospel of Peace and Justice* (Orbis 1976), p. 154.

156 *Evangelii Nuntiandi* (1975), para. 31.

157 Ibid., para. 35.

158 General Audience, Rome, 21 February 1979.

159 *Black Theology of Liberation* (Philadelphia, Lippincott 1970), p.11.

160 Cf. Segundo, op. cit., p. 26.

161 *Romero: Martyr for Liberation* (Catholic Institute for International Relations 1982), p. 3.

162 Segundo, op. cit., p. 186.

163 Gustavo Gutierrez, *A Theology of Liberation* (Orbis 1973), p. 11.

164 Gutierrez, cited in Frederick Herzog, 'Birth pangs: liberation theology in North America', *Christian Century* 93.41 (15 December 1976), p. 1122.

165 J. P. Miranda, *Marx and the Bible* (Orbis 1974); *Being and the Messiah: the Message of St John* (Orbis 1977). See J. E. Weir, 'The Bible and Marx: a discussion of the hermeneutics of liberation theology', *Scottish Journal of Theology* 35 (1982), pp. 337–50.

166 J. P. Miranda, *Communism in the Bible* (SCM Press 1981), pp. 1, 5.

167 Claude Geffre, Editorial, 'A prophetic theology', *Concilium* 6.10 (1974), pp. 13–14.

Acknowledgements

Acknowledgements are due to the following for permission to quote from the material listed:

Alba House, for excerpts from Paul Garvin, *The Life and Sayings of St Catherine of Genoa*.

Adam and Charles Black, for excerpts from L. S. Thornton, *The Common Life in the Body of Christ*.

Basil Blackwell, for excerpts from Rudolf Bultmann, *The Gospel of John*, 1971; and I. M. Crombie in B. Mitchell (ed.), *Faith and Logic*, 1957.

John Pairman Brown, for excerpts from *The Liberated Zone*, SCM Press, 1970.

Canongate Publishing, for excerpts from George Woodcock, *Thomas Merton, Monk and Poet*.

Jesus Caritas, for an excerpt from René Voillaume, *Jesus Caritas*, vol. 6 (1961); vol. 1 (1959).

Catholic Truth Society, for excerpts from *Evangelii Nuntiandi* (1975) and General Audience (Rome, 1979).

Geoffrey Chapman, for an excerpt from Hans Urs von Balthasar, *Prayer*, by permission of Geoffrey Chapman, a division of Cassell, Ltd.

Cistercian Studies, for excerpts from Gail Marie Priestly, 'Some Jungian Parallels to the Sayings of the Desert Fathers', *Cistercian Studies*, 11: 2 (1976).

University of Chicago Press, for excerpts from Yehezkel Kaufmann, *The Religion of Israel*.

Cistercian Publications Inc., for excerpts from Thomas Merton, *The Climate of Monastic Prayer*, Cistercian Publications Inc., Kalamazoo, Michigan, 1969 for the Trustees of the Merton Legacy Trust.

James Clarke, for excerpts from Vladimir Lossky, *The Mystical Theology of the Eastern Church*, 1957.

T. & T. Clark Ltd, for excerpts from Karl Barth, *The Knowledge of God and the Service of God*; K. Barth in *Church Dogmatics*, vol. 4.

J. M. Cohen (trs.), for an excerpt from *The Life of St Teresa*, published by Penguin Books, 1957.

William Collins, for an excerpt from *Merton: A Biography*, copyright © 1980 by Monica Furlong.

Darton Longman and Todd, for excerpts taken from Sebastian Moore and Kevin McGuire, *The Experience of Prayer*, 1969; Sebastian Moore, *The Crucified Jesus is No Stranger* (USA copyright by permission of Winston Press); Alan Ecclestone, *The Night Sky of the Lord*, 1980 (USA Copyright by permission of Schocken Books); E. L. Mascall, *Nature and Supernature*, 1976; Rowan Williams, *The Wound of Knowledge* (USA copyright by permission of John Knox Press); H. A. Williams, *Becoming What I Am*, 1977 (USA copyright by permission of Fortress Press). All the above published by Darton, Longman and Todd Ltd, and used by permission of the publishers.

Doubleday & Company Inc., for excerpts from William Johnston, *The Cloud of Unknowing*, copyright © 1973 by William Johnston. Reprinted by permission of Doubleday & Company Inc.

Wm B. Eardmans Publishing Co., for excerpts from Frederick D. Bruner, *A Theology of the Holy Spirit* (Hodder, 1971); and from William R. Coats, *God in Public*, 1974.

Epworth Press, for excerpts from Jean Héring, *The First Epistle of St Paul to the Corinthians*; and Geoffrey Wainwright, *Eucharist and Eschatology*.

Faber and Faber, for excerpts from the poems of T. S. Eliot, *Collected Poems, 1909–1962* (USA copyright by permission of Harcourt Brace Jovanovich Inc.); and from A. G. Herbert, *Liturgy and Society*.

Fellowship of St Alban and St Sergius, for excerpts from S. Brock, 'The Prayer of the Heart in Syrian Tradition', *Sobornost*, 4: 21 (1982); and V. Zander, *St Seraphim of Sarov*, 1968.

Fontana Paperbacks, for excerpts from Sam Keen, *To A Dancing God*.

Harper & Row, for an excerpt from William Johnston, *The Inner Eye of Love*, 1978; and Jim Wallis, *Agenda for Biblical People*, 1972.

Harvard University Press, for an excerpt from Michael Evenari, *The Negev*, 1971.

B. Herder Book Co., for an excerpt from Eric Colledge (trs.), *Spiritual Conferences of John Tauler*.

David Higham Associates Limited, for an excerpt from Edith Sitwell, *Collected Poems* (Macmillan, 1982).

Hodder & Stoughton, for an excerpt from Thomas Merton, Preface to Jean Leclerq OSB, *Alone With God*, 1962, used with permission of the Merton Legacy Trust.

Institute of Carmelite Studies, for excerpts from K. Kavanaugh (trs.), *The Living Flame of Love*, 1973; and from *The Collected Works of St John of the Cross*, copyright © 1979 ICS Publications,

2131 Lincoln Rd, NE, Washington DC, 20002.

The Judson Press, for an excerpt from Sheila D. Collins, *A Different Heaven and Earth*, 1974, used with permission of Judson Press.

Lippincott, for excerpts from J. H. Cone, *A Black Theology of Liberation*, 1970.

Listening, for an excerpt from Harvey S. J. Egan, 'The Christian Mystics', *Listening*, 17: 3 (1982).

James MacGibbon, Executor of the Estate of Stevie Smith, for an excerpt from Stevie Smith, *Selected Poems* (Penguin, 1978).

A. R. Mowbray & Co. Ltd, for excerpts from Benedicta Ward, *The Lives of the Desert Fathers*, 1980.

Novello & Co. Ltd, for an excerpt from *Hymns Ancient & Modern*.

Oxford University Press, for an excerpt from R. C. Zaehner, *Mysticism Sacred and Profane*, 1957.

Penguin Books Ltd, for excerpts from Benedicta Ward, *The Prayers and Meditations of St Anselm*, 1973; F. C. Happold, *Mysticism*, 1963; Alistair Kee, *The Way of Transcendence*, 1971; Richard Rolle, *The Fire of Love*, 1972; *Revelations of Divine Love*, 1966, trs. Clifton Wolters. Reprinted by permission of Penguin Books.

Routledge and Kegan Paul, for an excerpt from C. G. Jung, *The Collected Works of C. G. Jung*, vol. 7 (USA copyright by permission of Princeton University Press, © 1966 by PUP, excerpt p. 203).

SCM Press Ltd, for excerpts from J. Jeremias, *New Testament Theology* 1971 (USA Copyright by permssion of Scribners); Jurgen Moltmann, *The Crucified God*, 1974 (USA copyright by permission of Harper & Row); and John A. T. Robinson, *On Being the Church in the World*, 1970.

Search Press, for excerpts from Stephen B. Oates, *Let the Trumpet Sound*, 1982.

Secker & Warburg, for use of the poem 'Simeon Stylites' in Phyllis McGinley, *Times Three* (Image Books, New York, 1975).

Sheed and Ward, for excerpts from G. P. Fedotov (ed.), *A Treasury of Russian Spirituality*.

Revd Elmer J. Smith, for permission to quote from F. H. Smyth, *Manhood into God* (Round Table Press, New York, 1940).

The Society for Promoting Christian Knowledge (SPCK), for excerpts from Peter F. Anson citing Cassian in *The Call of the Desert*, 1964; and *Dionysius the Areopagite: On The Divine Names and the Mystical Theology*, trs. C. E. Rolt, 1966.

Spirituality Today, for an excerpt from Nathan Mitchell, 'The

Spirituality of Christian Worship', *Spirituality Today*, 34: 1 (1982).

Spiritual Life Institute, for an excerpt from the *Brochure of the Spiritual Life Institute*, Nova Nada, Kemptville, Nova Scotia.

United States Catholic Conference, for excerpts from *To Live in Jesus Christ*, a Pastoral Reflection on the Moral Life, copyright © 1976 Publications Office, United States Catholic Conference Office; the testimony of John Cardinal Krol, Archbishop of Philadelphia, to Senate Foreign Relations Committee on Ratification of the Strategic Arms Limitation Treaty (SALT), 6 Sept. 1979.

St Vladimir's Press, for excerpts from John Meyendorff, *St Gregory Palamas and Orthodox Spirituality*, 1974; and J. Meyendorff, *Christ in Eastern Christian Thought*, 1975.

A. P. Watt Ltd, for excerpts from Charles Davis, *Body as Spirit*.

Alfred Willetts & St Joan's Alliance, 1981, for an excerpt from *She Prays: prayers by women*.

Winston Press, for excerpts from *God of the Oppressed* by James H. Cone, copyright © 1975 Winston/Seabury Press. Published by Winston/Seabury Press (formerly published by Seabury Press), 430 Oak Grove, Minneapolis, MN 55403. All rights reserved. Used with permission; *A History of Christian Spirituality* by Urban T. Holmes III, copyright © 1980 by Urban T. Holmes. Used with permission; *Journey into Christ* by Alan W. Jones, copyright © 1977 Winston/Seabury Press. Used with permission; *The Crucified Jesus is No Stranger* by Sebastian Moore, copyright © 1977 Sebastian Moore. Published by Winston/Seabury Press and used with permission.

World Council of Churches, for an excerpt from Sally Dyck, *One World*, no. 47.

Bible quotations in this book are from the Revised Standard Version of the Bible, copyright 1946, 1952, 1957, 1971, 1973 by the Division of Christian Education of the National Council of The Churches of Christ in the USA, and are used by permission.

Despite diligent enquiry some copyright holders have proved impossible to trace and to them the author and publisher extend their most sincere apologies.

Index

Aaron 39, 68, 276
Abba 85, 114, 136–7
Abbot and Costello 23
Abel 311
Abihu 45, 205
Abraham 25–32, 43, 57, 65, 74, 83, 84, 100, 101, 268, 304, 394
abyss 323–49
Acts of the Apostles 101, 112, 114, 122, 203, 209, 229, 233, 271, 355
Acts of Peter 356
Acts of Thomas 358
Adam 57, 210, 308, 342, 352
Adams, H. 368
Addai 273
Advent 286
Aelred of Rievaulx, St 360, 368
Agathon 140
Agrippa II 87
Ahab 48
Ahaziah 205
Ai 28
Alpha 123
altar 295
Althaus, P. 397
Altizer, T. 5, 191
Ambrose, St 203, 210, 240, 270, 292–3, 355–6, 414
Amen 123
America 364, 385, 394, 402, 404; (Central) 393, 416
Amorites 69

Amos 35, 43, 59, 62, 394
anamnesis 270, 278
Anastasius 259
Anat 350
Ancient of Days 123
Ancren Riwle 360
Andrew, St 92
Andrewes, Lancelot 259
Angela de Foligno 337
Anglicanism 211, 227, 280, 296–7, 302, 346, 383, 389, 390, 398, 400, 418
animals 55
Ann the Christ (Word) 364
Anna 106
Anselm, St 360–1
Antioch(ene) 87, 165, 367
antiphon 274
anti-semitism 70, 388, 396–8
Antony, St 132–5, 151, 153, 159
apocalyptic 73, 81, 120, 121
Apollo 140
Apollos 100
apostles 271, 292
Aquilla 100
Aramean 29, 30
Arianism 140, 237, 241
Arintero, J. G. 227
Armenian 273
Arsenius 135, 222
asceticism 132
Asherah 351
Assumption 369, 370
Assyrians 51

Athanasian Creed 247–8
Athanasius, St 133, 136, 140, 174, 237, 259, 269, 282, 296
atheism 6, 14
Athena 253, 351
Athens 101, 351
Atherton, J. 415
atonement Chapters 3, 4 and 10 passim
Atonement, Day of 308
Augustine, St 111, 145, 164, 167, 175, 176, 178, 216, 220, 232, 235, 239, 251–2, 255, 258, 262, 270, 282–4, 292, 305, 323–5, 341–2, 355–7, 363, 386
Aulén, G. 314
Auschwitz 24, 70, 191, 396, 406
Azazel 34

Baal 58, 65, 205, 351
Baal-Berith 68
Babylon 51, 57, 351, 400, 401
Bachofen, J. 350
Balasuriya, T. 297
Balthasar, H. U. von 368, 369, 418
Bandung 416
Bangladesh 409
Bangor (Washington) 409
Baptism 207–13, 230–2, 292
Baptist Church (Russia) 12
Barachiah 311
Barnabas, St 209
Barrett, T. B. 227, 233
Barth, Karl 8, 70, 107, 125–6, 190, 195, 239, 302, 334, 379, 386–7, 413, 415
Baruch 268
Basil, St 133, 135, 143, 144, 146, 166, 259, 414
Bathsheba 48

Baum, G. 396
Beckett, Samuel 7
Beersheba 58
Béguines 359
Bellow, Saul 7
Benedict, St 143–4
Benedictines 375
Benedictus 273
Berdyaev, Nicholas 227, 347–8, 382
Bernard, St 145, 175, 216, 262, 317–18, 331, 336–8, 360
Bernardine, St 253
Bethel 28, 39, 49
Bethnal Green 248, 295
Bhagavad Gita 335, 336
Bible 46, 83, 125, 162–3, 352, 358, 374, 383, 386, 387, 393, 394, 395, 413, 420
Bibliothèque Nationale 329
Black Theology 401, 402
Blake, William 5, 395
Blumhardt, Christoph 125
Body of Christ 96, 97, 98, 117–18, 286, 292, 377
Bonaventure, St 318, 336
Bonhoeffer, Dietrich 316
Bouyer, L. 266
Boyle, Robert 6
Britain 302, 372–3, 382, 385, 389, 393–5, 398–400, 406–7, 409–11, 420
British Association 9
Brown, J. P. 265, 404
Brown, P. 135–7
Bruner, F. D. 233
Buber, Martin 5, 227
Buddha 186, 335
Bukharin 19
Bultmann, R. 26, 80, 91, 312, 386

Caesar 294, 387

Caesarea Philippi 84, 86, 208
Caiaphas 312
Cain 395, 401
Callaghan, M. 254
Calvary 191, 290, 295, 299, 300, 301, 304, 308, 315
Calvin, John 342
Camus, Albert 7, 24
Canaan 28, 58, 69, 350, 351, 394
Canada 201
cannabis 16
canon law 373
Caphtor 394
Cappadocians 175
Carmelites 129, 173, 183
Carroll, R. P. 81
Carter, S. 285
Carthusians 360
Cassian 134, 136, 140, 142, 144, 213, 214
catechism 283
Catherine of Genoa, St 213, 220
Catherine of Siena, St 219
Catherwood, F. 191
Catholicism 195, 199, 201, 294, 358, 365–70, 381, 385, 389, 392, 406, 408, 416
Chalcedon 237, 241–2
Chaldeans 28, 51
Chapman, John 189
Chardin, Teilhard de 221
charismatic 228
Chesterton, G. K. 24
Children of God 23
China 12
chlorpromazine 18
Christian Science 364
church 30, 84, 87, 97, 100–1, 110, 114, 116–17, 118, 120, 125, 199, 204, 227, 271, 273, 287, 291, 296, 300, 304, 313–

16, 318, 367, 372–5, 380, 382, 385–8, 390–2, 396, 404, 413, 415–17
Church of England 4, 289, 382, 385
Church of God of Prophecy 399
Cistercians 318
city of God 120, 125, 175
Clement of Alexandria, St 89, 122, 165, 243f, 258, 336, 355, 356
Clement of Rome, St 209
cloud 162–98, 336
Cloud of Unknowing 151, 175–83
Cohen, A. Y. 18
Cohen, Leonard 210
Cohn, N. 22
Collins, Sheila 371
Colossians, Epistle to 98, 101, 307, 334
Comfort, A. 253
communism 22, 382
Cone, J. 401, 402, 418
Conservative Party 3
Constantine 385
contemplation 149–53, 158, 162–98
Corinthians, Epistles to 96, 104, 114, 122, 289, 305, 314, 356
Corpus Christi 274, 284, 359
covenant 29, 69
Craighead, M. 375, 376
Crombie, I. M. 9
cross 118, 295, 300, 303, 315, 389, 397
Cullinan, T. 412
Cupitt, D. 184, 192, 237
Curtis, G. 264
Cyprian, St 210
Cyril of Alexandria, St 274,

279, 367
Cyril of Jerusalem, St 166, 269, 282

Daly, Mary 369, 373, 375
Daniel 75, 76, 80, 123, 208, 309, 409
Daniélou, J. 153, 159
darkness 162–98
Darwinism 8, 388
David 35, 36, 40, 48, 68, 213, 271, 315, 322
Davis, C. 254, 332
Dead Sea 37
deification 257–62
Demeter 350
desert 27–38, 127–61
Desert Fathers 130–41
Detroit 409
Deuteronomy 32, 43, 53, 54, 267, 305, 353
Diadochus 214
Diadorus of Tarsus 165
Dibelius, O. 397
Dicken, E. W. T. 189
Didache 84, 273
Didymus the Blind 174
Dionysius the Areopagite 170–8, 181–3, 188, 195, 336
disarmament 409
discernment 132, 137
Dodd, C. H. 83, 94
Dominicans 145, 177, 328, 364
Dostoevsky, F. 19
Douglass, S. 409
dualism 91, 92
Dublin 284
Dunn, J. 228
Duquesne 227
Dworkin, A. 254
Dyck, S. 376

Easter 315, 330
Eastern Orthodoxy 163, 166–7, 173–5, 214, 216, 222, 223, 257–62, 265, 274–5, 283, 319, 325, 336, 344, 355, 366–8
Ebedmelech 394
Ecclesiastes 168
Ecclesiasticus 354–5, 366
Ecclestone, A. 25, 70–1, 160, 192
Eckhart, Meister 252, 324–8, 341, 368
Eden 36
Edom 52
EEC 411
Egypt 30–2, 53, 57, 59, 68, 70, 133, 278, 351–2, 394
Eichrodt, W. 68
Eisenhower, D. 406
El Bethel 58
Eleazar 309
Eleusis 351
El Elyon 29, 58
Elijah 35, 38, 48, 129, 205, 309
Elim 128
Eliot, T. S. 2, 157, 320
Elizabeth 112
Ellul, J. 5, 23
Elohim 59, 353
El Olam 58
El Roi 58
El Salvador 419
El Shaddai 29, 57
English 105, 109, 272, 283, 287, 323, 383, 385, 395
Enoch 43, 75–6, 309
Ephesians, Epistles to 97, 98, 101, 122, 307, 308
Ephesus 227
Ephesus, Council of 239, 301, 367
Ephraim the Syrian, St 214,

215, 283, 356
Epiphanius 140
Esau 30
eschatology 120–6
Essenes 81
Esther 409
Eucharist 140, 214–15, 245, 265–98, 315, 356, 362, 367, 368
Europe 22, 105, 385, 389, 407
Eusebius 142
Evagrius 132, 134, 165–7
Evans, S. G. 293
Evdokimov, P. 261
Eve 358, 366, 377
exile 61, 351
Exodus 31–3, 35–6, 57, 68–9, 104, 129, 266, 268, 271, 353
expiation 107, 109
Ezekiel 35, 36, 51, 62, 74, 202, 206, 267, 351, 412
Ezra 268

Faber, F. W. 370
Falwell, J. 385
feminine in God 350–78
Feuerbach, L. 11
Fison, J. E. 227
fire 199–235
flesh 236–64
Florovsky, G. 259
Foucauld, Charles de 158–9
Fox, M. 242
Francis of Assisi, St 224, 262, 263, 318, 319
Franciscans 145, 318, 319
Franco, General 389
Frankl, V. 24
Freud, S. 10, 13–16
Fromm, E. 15, 183

Gabriel 367
Galatians, Epistle to 97, 98, 100, 101, 106, 122, 305
Galilea, S. 345
Galilee 89, 287, 312, 313, 372
Galot, J. 242
Gandhi 152
Ge/Gaia 351
Gee, D. 230
Geller, U. 23
Genesis 57, 352–3, 358, 394
Gentiles 77, 99, 203
Gideon 61
Gilgal 39
Gilkey, L. 6
Gittites 394
Glasson, T. F. 80
Gleason, R. 6
glossolalia 231
gnosticism 86, 91, 94, 243f, 250f, 256f
God, of Abraham 28, 29, 57; the abyss 323–49; Almighty 29, 57, 330; being of 328, 384; the creator 55, 91, 96, 218, 370, 377; of the desert 27–38; the Father 72, 85–6, 89, 93, 94, 108–9, 112–13, 123, 302, 308, 327, 352, 356, 358–9, 362, 364–5, 369; and the future 120–6; holiness of 38–45; of Israel 45, 77, 266, 279; of justice 45–56; kingdom of 78–84; the liberator 416–20; of light and love 107–12, 221; the Mother 350–78; of peace 402–9; people of 115–20; of the poor 409–16; presence of 332; and race 393–402; the Saviour 107; and the social order 387–93; the Spirit 112–15; unity of 327; and unity of humanity

96–103; wisdom of 366
Golgotha 302
Gollwitzer, H. 6
Good Friday 315
Gore, C. 249, 287
gospel 25, 85, 89, 90, 92,
110, 199, 310, 319, 391, 416,
418
gospels 73, 74, 82, 88, 103,
108, 112, 113, 312, 387
grace 90
Graef, H. 317
Graham, B. 46
Greek 97, 100, 113, 288, 305,
309, 332, 351, 355, 364
Greeley, A. 24
Gregory the Great, St 143,
282
Gregory of Nazianzus, St
170, 239, 242, 259, 301, 344,
359, 367, 374
Gregory of Nyssa, St 129,
164, 167–70, 183, 203, 242,
251, 259, 274, 305, 323, 325,
336
Gregory Palamas, St 146,
174, 175, 242, 245, 261
Guerric of Igny 145, 360
Gumbleton, T. 409
Guild of St Matthew 248
Gutierrez, G. 419
Gutteridge, R. 397
Gwatkin, H. M. 241

Habakkuk 42, 51, 108
Haight-Ashbury 17
Haile Selassie 400
Hamilton, W. 5
Hamlet 8, 395
Hammarskjold, D. 346
Hancock, Thomas 241, 247–8
Happold, F. C. 332
Haran 28

Hardie, Keir 392
Harding, Mary Esther 350
Harnack, A. 83
Hastings, A. 147
Headlam, Stewart 247–8,
295–7, 383
Hebrew 40, 53, 57–60, 314,
350, 353, 374, 393
Hebrews, Epistle to 122, 238,
308
Hebron 28, 58
Hegel, F. 11
Heimmel, J. 363
Hellwig, M. 297
Hemmingway, E. 7
Hermas 130, 209
Herod 101
Herzog, F. 6
Heschel, A. 203
Hesse, H. 7
hesychia 138–9
Hildegard of Bingen 360
Hillman, J. 320
Hilton, Walter 176, 177, 181,
330
Himmler, H. 388
Hinduism 250, 351
Hippolytus 33, 209, 210, 272,
282, 289, 296
Hitler 21, 386, 388, 390, 396,
397
Hittites 69
Hogg, Q. 395
holiness 38, 39, 41–5, 56,
227–30
Holmes, U. T. 263
Holy Spirit 99, 101, 112–15,
117, 119, 166, 181, 191–201,
203–5, 207–16, 218, 220,
223–5, 227–31, 233–4, 282–3,
290, 291, 358–60, 366–7, 376
Hopkins, G. M. 246
Horeb 31

Hosanna 273
Hosea 35, 47, 49, 59, 109, 352
Hunter, A. M. 82, 83
Hunthausen, R. 409
Huxley, A. 195
Huxley, T. H. 8, 17

ichthus 210, 211
idolatry 20, 21
Igjugarjuk 149
Ignatius of Antioch 238f, 279, 301
illuminative way 173, 187
Imitation of Christ 263
Inanna-Ishtar 351
incarnation 230, 236–64, 319, 366, 383
India 409
Indonesia 409
Industrial Christian Fellowship 295
Irenaeus, St 242, 245, 258, 272, 282, 314, 355, 356
Isaac 25, 27, 29, 57, 83, 101, 268
Isaac of Stella 360
Isaac the Syrian 174, 223, 246, 262
Isaiah 87, 267–8, 272, 304, 310, 312, 353
Isidore of Pelusium 274
Isis 351
Israel 27, 30–6, 40, 48, 56, 58–9, 68–71, 76, 79–80, 100–1, 104, 112, 202, 266–7, 271, 276, 306, 309, 352, 379, 394, 403, 412
Ittai 394

Jacob 25, 27–30, 39, 57, 67, 83, 101, 213, 266, 268
Jacob, E. 257

Jamaica 400–1
James, E. O. 350
James, Epistle of 109
James, Liturgy of 275
James, William 17, 333
Jehovah's Witnesses 23
Jenkins, D. E. 6
Jeremiah 35, 46, 59, 62, 64–5, 69, 70, 299, 301, 351, 390, 412
Jeremiah, J. 81, 83, 85, 120
Jerome, St 143, 220, 274
Jerusalem 39, 41, 50–2, 60, 69, 97, 106, 176, 287, 300, 311, 312, 351, 354
Jesus Christ 72–95 and passim
Jesus Prayer 146, 159, 258
Jethro 58, 267
Jews 6, 30–1, 37, 39, 43, 52, 65–7, 70, 71, 75, 79, 80, 87, 89, 93, 97, 99–100, 162–3, 167, 205, 268, 276, 278, 284, 299, 303–4, 313, 346, 352, 390, 393, 396, 397, 402
Joachim of Fiore 359
Job 213
Joel 114, 203
Joffe, A. 13
John, Epistles of St 109–11, 122, 205
John, Gospel of St 74, 76, 78, 89, 90–5, 100, 109, 110, 112, 113, 121–4, 208, 312, 315, 355, 358
John the Baptist, St 38, 112, 148, 208, 310
John Chrysostom, St 165, 240, 274–5, 279, 282, 289, 355–6, 414
John Climacus, St 138, 146
John of the Cross, St 150, 170, 173, 183–90, 213, 224,

225, 230, 253, 330, 335
John of Damascus, St 174, 269, 283, 366
John the Dwarf 134
John the Elder 343
John of Gaza 139
Johnston, W. 173
Jonah 73, 209, 310
Jones, A. W. 190, 253
Jones, Ernest 358
Jones, Rufus 332
Joseph 49
Joseph of Panephysis 222
Joshua 32, 40, 41, 202
Judaism 80, 83, 85, 88, 92, 121, 310, 353
Judas 88
Judea 27, 299
Judges, Book of 79
Julian of Norwich 255f, 323, 324, 329, 330, 362, 363
Jung, C. G. 15, 16, 150, 196, 199, 215, 320, 335, 365, 369–70
Justin Martyr, St 25, 120, 281–2, 289, 356, 366
justice 45–56, 368, 379–420

Kaddish 80
Kaufmann, E. 34
Keen., S. 256f
Kenites 58
Kierkegaard, S. 8, 193
King, Martin Luther 321, 322, 345, 380, 391
Kingdom of God 78, 79–84, 99, 113–14, 117, 120, 126, 199, 268–9, 270, 273–4, 279, 287, 294, 296, 313, 382–3, 386, 404, 413, 415, 417, 420
Kir 394
Kitamori, Kazah 299
Knox, J. 237

Koestler, A. 1
koinonia 274, 392–3
Koyama, K. 41, 321
Krol, John Cardinal 408
Kuhn, T. 9
Ku Klux Klan 398
Kuptsch, J. 397

Labour Party 3
Lahamus 57
Lahmu 57
Laing, R. D. 23, 200, 335
Laplace, J. 8
Larsen, A. B. 227
Last Supper 270–1
Latin 266, 355, 393
Latin American 345, 372, 388, 415–20
law 89, 109, 354, 379, 380
Law, William 213
Leach, E. 8
League of the Kingdom of God 249
Leary, Timothy 17, 18
Lee, Ann 364
Lee, Jung Young 334
Leo the Great, St 283
Leonard, William 350
Levites 40, 42, 269
Leviticus 44, 88, 104
Lewis, C. S. 337, 374
liberation theology 238, 416, 419, 420
Liddon, H. P. 297
Lochman, J. M. 306, 307, 314, 315
Lohse, E. 397
London 411
Lord's Prayer 80, 214, 269
Lossky, V. 165, 167, 173–4, 258
Lot 30
Lot (Abba) 222

Louth, A. 172
LSD 17–18
Lucius 135
Luke, Gospel of St 86–8, 101, 208, 306, 311, 358
Luther, Martin 185, 300–1, 386, 397

Macarian Homilies 135, 166, 223
Macarius 214, 259
Maccabees 37, 309
McDonnell, K. 212, 233
McGinley, P. 131
MacIntyre, A. C. 3, 6, 13, 19, 24
McNamara, W. 255
Macquarrie, J. 8
Magnificat 274, 372
Maguire, K. 197
Malachi 52, 208, 278
Mammon 387, 412, 413
Manchester 364
Manicheism 239, 248, 251, 340
Manoah 162
Mao 12, 21, 22
Marah 127f
Maranatha 271, 273
Margaret of Oyngt 360
Martha, St 92
Marxism 3, 10–14, 22, 277, 419
Mary, Blessed Virgin 239, 268, 301, 355, 358, 365–72
Mascall, E. L. 258, 374
Manson, T. W. 76, 91, 306
Mark, Gospel of St 73, 77, 86, 92, 106, 112, 305, 310–12
Massah 34
materialism 242–50
Mattathias 309
Matthew, Gospel of St 86,

88, 105–6, 122, 208, 305, 310–12, 354
Maurice, F. D. 246
Maximus the Confessor, St 175, 258, 286, 356
Mechtild of Hackeborn 360
Mechtild of Magdeburg 359
Medes 51
Melchizedek 28
Merseyside 411
Merton, Thomas 129, 132, 142, 146–7, 148, 186, 188, 193–6, 330, 336, 343, 365
Messiah, 50, 76, 80, 87–90, 113, 208, 267, 268, 299, 304, 310, 403–4, 412, 420
Methodius of Olympus 358
Methodism 3, 230, 376
Meyendorff, J. 240, 258
Micah 48
Middle Ages 38, 216, 274, 288, 291, 317, 368
Midianites 58
Milton 148
Min Ho 21
Miranda, J. P. 47, 390, 419, 420
Mizpah 39, 266, 351
Moberley, R. C. 277, 249
Moltmann, J. 240, 296, 302, 303, 313
monarchy 48
monasticism 141–9
Montagu, A. 251
Moore, S. 197, 253, 317
Moral Majority 385
Mormons 364
Moses 14, 27, 28, 32, 33, 43–5, 57–9, 68, 85, 138, 162, 168–9, 172, 191, 206–7, 266–7, 276
Mosley, Oswald 389
motherhood of God 350–78

Motovilov, N.   223, 224
Moule, C. F. D.   89
Mozarabic rite   274
Muir, Edwin   300
Murray, J. C.   6
Muslims   6
Mussolini   388–9

Naaman   35
Naboth   48
Nadab   45, 205
Nahum   51, 62
Naioth   202
Napoleon   8
Narcissus   131
Narsai   274
Nathan   48
Nathanael   92
Nazareth   87, 88
Nazirite   35
Nazism   20–2, 70, 303, 387–9, 396–8
negative theology   163
Nehemiah   64
Neoplatonism   163, 168
Nestorians   273, 274
Neumann, E.   357
New Testament   56, 70, 72, 78, 80–3, 86, 92, 99, 103, 105–8, 112–16, 118, 120, 122, 200, 208, 231, 233, 240, 255, 270, 271, 276, 289, 304–7, 309, 314, 316, 336, 354–5, 381, 383, 394, 396, 404, 409, 413
New Testament Church of God   399
Nicene Creed   336
Nicholas of Cusa   183
Nicodemus   74
Niebuhr, R.   380
Nietzsche, F.   4, 250, 389
nihilism   19–26

Nil Sorsky, St   146
Nineveh   51
Noel, Conrad   84, 250, 295, 383
Nouwen, H. J. M.   150, 320
Numbers   68, 208
Nut   351

Oakley, J.   297
Obadiah   52
offertory   280, 286, 289–92
Ogden, S.   6, 8
Ohio   376
Old Testament   27, 28, 35, 37–8, 41–3, 45, 47, 52, 56–8, 60–1, 65–6, 68, 70, 72, 83, 93, 101, 107, 112, 113, 121, 162, 201–3, 206, 251, 257, 266, 270, 273, 276, 285, 309–12, 351–4, 379, 383, 394, 402–3, 409, 412
Origen   89, 164, 165, 244, 251, 258, 269, 282, 336, 355
original sin   290
Osborn, C.   398
Ostathios, Mar   379
Otto, Rudolf   41
Owen, Wilfred   301–2

Pachomius   133, 143
Pagels, E.   357
Pakistan   409
Palestine   27, 350, 379
Paran   27
parousia   120, 122, 273
Pascal, B.   7, 33, 300
passion   124, 301, 315, 318, 370
Passover   31, 104, 270, 271, 278, 308
Paul, St   72, 80, 96–7, 99–106, 109, 114, 116, 117, 119, 122, 227, 231, 244, 272, 283,

304, 305, 307, 308, 314, 316, 361, 366
Paul of Thebes 132
peace 50, 289
Pectorius of Autun 210
Pentecost 199, 201, 211, 227, 231
Pentecostalism 203, 206, 212, 227–35
Perpetua, St 373
Perrin, N. 80
Peter, Epistles of 84, 86, 92, 104, 107, 209, 289, 355
Pharisees 88, 311
Philip, Gospel of 210, 358, 366
Philippians, Epistle to 119, 122
Philistines 394
Philo 163, 164, 213, 355
Philokalia 260
Philoxenes 132
Pilgrim Wesleyan Holiness Church 399
Plato 163, 164
Pliny the Younger 272
Plotinus 164
Polanyi, M. 9
Pontus 165
Pope John XXIII 201, 204, 227, 405, 406; John Paul II 368, 408, 417; Leo XIII, 227; Paul VI 201, 205, 227, 371, 390, 416, 417; Pius XI 392; Pius XII 117, 405
Powell, E. 398–9
Priscilla 100
prophecy 89, 379, 380
Proverbs 354, 355
Pseudo-Clementines 357
psychedelic drugs 16–19
Puebla 372
purgative way 226

Qumran 37, 38, 91, 111, 121

Rahner, K. 293
Ramah 202
Ranaghan, K. 227
Ras Shamra 58, 350
Rastafarianism 400–1
Reagan, Ronald 385
Rechabites 35
reconciliation 105, 106
Red Sea 31, 32
Reformation 78, 342, 384
Reynolds, A. M. 363
Revelation 112, 120, 121, 122, 123, 206, 271, 409
Richard of St Victor 325
Richardson, A. 86
Rig Veda 16
Robinson, J. A. T. 6, 265, 291, 323
Roget's Thesaurus 394
Rolle, Richard 176, 216–19
Roman Catholicism 12, 201, 227, 284, 287, 351, 389, 392, 408
Romans 299, 309, 312–13, 393
Romans, Epistle to 99, 100, 106, 107, 109, 114, 231, 305, 306
Romero, Oscar 419
Romuauld, St 145
Roszak, T. 18, 23, 349
ruach 60–3, 201–2
Rubinstein, R. 191
Ruether, R. 252, 370–4, 378
Rumke, H. 15
Russell, L. M. 374
Russia 216, 223, 319, 382, 406
Ruth 394
Ruysbroeck, Jan van 177, 213, 219, 327, 328, 337, 338, 339

Sabbath 40, 53, 73, 310
Sacred Heart 262
sacrifice 266, 276, 278, 281, 290
Sahdona 331
Salem 28, 58
salvation 45, 55, 103–7, 228, 279, 282, 300, 403
Samaria 92
Samuel 48
Sanhedrin 312
Sarah 30
Satan 83, 120, 121
Saul 202
Saward, J. 319
Schilling, H. K. 9
Schleiermacher 194
Schweitzer, A. 80, 116
scribes 88
Seabrook, J. 23
second coming 120, 273, 282
Segundo, J. L. 12, 419
Seraphim of Sarov, St 223
sexuality 250–7
Shechem 28, 68
Shiloh 39
Shur 27
Siffre, M. 156
silence 138–40
Simeon 112
Simeon Stylites 131–2
Sinai 31, 32, 35, 36, 38, 39, 44, 58, 68, 69, 85, 128, 162, 191, 206, 286
Sirocco 128
Sitwell, Edith 221
Smail, T. 228
Smith, Stevie 236
Smith, R. G. 5
Smyth, F. H. 245, 290, 294, 295
Snaith, N. H. 46

socialism 3, 392
solitude 149–53
Soloviev, V. 261
Son of God 84–89
Son of Man 72–77, 80
Song of Songs 340, 351
spiritual direction 136–7, 343–4
spiritual father 133, 136
Stalin, J. 22
Starratt, A. 6
Studite Rule 319
Studdert Kennedy, G. 302
Suenens, Cardinal 203
Sufism 335
Symeon the New Theologian, St 146, 173, 211–16, 260, 325, 331, 334, 356, 368

Tammuz 351
Tauler, J. 177, 328, 329
Taylor, J. 287
Temple, W. 302
Terah 28
Teresa of Avila, St 330, 340
Tertullian 239
Terwilliger, R. 24
Thatcher, M. 279, 381, 382, 387, 398
theism 6, 7
Theodore of Mopsuestia 275, 281
Theophan the Recluse 158
Theophilus of Antioch 10
Theotokos 301
Theresa of Calcutta, Mother 287, 288
Thessalonians, Letters to 119, 122
Thomas à Kempis 263
Thomas Aquinas, St 176, 204, 220, 252, 255, 261, 274,

280, 290, 291, 359, 374, 405
Thomas, K. 3
Thomassin 287
Thornton, L. S. 249
Tillich, P. 190, 191, 193, 323, 364
Times, The 2
Timothy, Epistles to 107
Titus, Epistle to 107
Torres, C. 297
Torrey, R. A. 230
Traherne, Thomas 264
transubstantiation 281, 288, 290, 291
Tresmontant, C. 242
Trinity 180, 199, 241, 302, 355, 359, 364, 368, 370, 375, 383-4, 392
Trotsky, L. 1, 2
Tugwell, S. 212, 231, 233, 234

United Nations 409
United States 346, 347, 382, 385, 393, 394, 398, 401, 406, 408, 410
unitive way 336
Ur 28
Uriah 48
Uzziah 42

Vahanian, G. 5
Valentinians 355
Verghese, P. 252
Verrinder, F. 54
via negativa 348
Vietnam 404
Voillaume, R. 154, 158
Vulgate 268

Wainwright, G. 269, 279, 283, 286
Wales 287

Wallis, J. 413
Weil, S. 156
Weiss, P. 6
Wesley 227, 229, 230, 281, 286
White, V. 364
Whitehead, A. N. 1
Widdrington, P. E. T. 78
Wiesel, E. 303
Wilberforce, R. I. 249
Wilberforce, S. 8, 9
wilderness 27, 33, 34, 35-8, 113
Wiles, M. 237, 241
William of St Thierry 318, 360
Williams, H. 196
Williams, R. 187
Wilson, J. 295
Wisdom 354, 355, 356, 364-6, 375-6
Wolters, C. 363
"Woodbine Willie" 302
Woolley, L. 29
Word of God 62, 64, 90, 92, 95, 110, 118-19, 230ff, 272, 282, 314, 328, 347, 375-6, 391
Wordsworth, W. 203, 333

Yahweh 29-50, 55-61, 63, 65, 66, 68-70, 72, 79, 127-9, 286, 309, 351, 353, 403
Year of Jubilee 53, 54, 55, 88
Year of Release 53, 54
Yeats, W. B. 364
Yerkes, R. 266
yoga 336
Young, Frances 299

Zaehner, R. C. 339
Zapopon 372
Zealots 81, 313

Zechariah 40, 52, 64, 311, 404

Zeller, H. van 155, 184

Zen 186, 335

Zend Avesta 16

Zephaniah 52, 62

Zeus 253

Zion 48, 50

Harper & Row
SAN FRANCISCO
1700 Montgomery St. CA 94111

1817

To the Literary Editor:

We take pleasure in sending you this review copy of

EXPERIENCING GOD: Theology
as Spirituality

by Kenneth Leech
DATE OF PUBLICATION:

July, 1985

PRICE: $17.95

Direct quotation in reviews is limited to 500 words
unless special permission is given.

Please send us two copies of your review.

Please do not release reviews before publication date.

Kenneth Leech is a graduate of King's College, London and Trinity College, Oxford. He trained for the priesthood at St Stephen's House, Oxford and was ordained in 1964. He worked for several years in the East End of London and in Soho among drug addicts, and wrote *A Practical Guide to the Drug Scene* which has been acclaimed as the best book written on the problems of drug dependence. He is also the author of *Youthquake*, a study of the 1950s and 1960s, *Soul Friend*, a study of Christian spirituality, and its successor *True Prayer*. He has written for many journals, and broadcasts frequently on television and radio. From 1971–4 he was chaplain of St Augustine's College, Canterbury, and from 1974–80 he was Rector of St Matthew's, Bethnal Green. He is presently Race Relations Field Officer for the Board for Social Responsibility.